Sta
Fi

Selected excerpts from '...

Chapter 1, Enthusiasm to Attack

"My (Naval Academy) ranking had been weighed down somewhat by those dirty sinks and the occasional wrinkled trouser ..."

Chapter 3, Fundamental Concepts

"(Ayn Rand) was also wrong about her understanding of the nature of collectives. In (Atlas Shrugged), the collective responds to the heroes of the story in an almost childishly gentle way. In reality, however, the collective is far more aggressive ..."

Chapter 5, Prancing Rabbits

"This episode touched me deeply. And caused an uncontrollable gagging reflex ..."

Chapter 6, The Font of Value

"Energy is the foundation of civilization, and liquid fuel the key pillar in that foundation. So, if one wanted to bring that civilization to its knees a good path to follow would be ..."

Chapter 10, Employment Trends

"Many jobs seem like they create original value, but in fact they merely cleverly conceal a regulatory compliance role ..."

Chapter 13, The Idea Factory

"To start a bubble session, treat yourself to some creature comforts ..."

Chapter 15, Entrepreneurial Success

"Your reaction to this destruction of your value? Follow them down into debt ..."

Chapter 18, The Drug War

"(As) a Marine officer in war I sat in the desert ... (and I realized) that President George Herbert Walker Bush was a worm. And that he was only one of the many ... for whom understanding of or respect for the Constitution eludes ..."

Starving the Monkeys: Fight Back Smarter

by Tom Baugh

Published by
Starve Monkey Press, Inc.

www.StarveMonkeyPress.com

Adam,
Enjoy these thoughts.
Together all of us will
defeat these monkeys

Tom

Copyright © 2009 by Tom Baugh
All rights reserved.

Unless otherwise stated, text and diagrams written and copyrighted by Starve Monkey Press or its authors remain the sole property of Starve Monkey Press or its authors, respectively. You may not modify this material or distribute it, in whole or in part, in any form whatsoever, to any other party, without written permission of Starve Monkey Press.

Published in the United States of America.

ISBN: 978-0-9825431-0-8
Library of Congress Control Number: 2009910592

Publisher Information

Starve Monkey Press, Inc.
Roberta, Georgia

See our website for more information about the publisher, including resources for aspiring authors and contact information:

www.StarveMonkeyPress.com

Trademark Notices

Starve Monkey Press, Starving the Monkeys, Caveman Capitalism, Caveman Capitalist and the Banana Hammer logo are the trademarks or registered trademarks of Starve Monkey Press, Inc.
All other trademarks not specifically listed are trademarks or registered trademarks of their respective owners.

Version History

See the website for this book for errata and version history:

www.StarvingTheMonkeys.com/errata

Original Paperback, *An Entrepreneurial Horror*
First Printing, June 2009
Second Printing, July 2009

Small Paperback, *Fight Back Smarter*
First Printing, October 2009

Table of Contents

Foreword vii
Monkey, Defined ix
Acknowledgments x
Chapter 1, Enthusiasm to Attack 1
Chapter 2, Who Should Read This Book 21
Chapter 3, Fundamental Concepts 37
Chapter 4, Caveman Capitalism™ 53
Chapter 5, Prancing Rabbits 76
Chapter 6, The Font of Value 82
Chapter 7, The Shamans 113
Chapter 8, From Force or Fraud 127
Chapter 9, A Tribe Consumed 148
Chapter 10, Employment Trends 180
Chapter 11, Math and Science 209
Chapter 12, Scholarship and Sadi Carnot . . . 225
Chapter 13, The Idea Factory 240
Chapter 14, Organizational Value 277
Chapter 15, Entrepreneurial Success 309
Chapter 16, On International Relations 322
Chapter 17, Waco and Other Texas Wackos . 336
Chapter 18, The Drug War 352
Chapter 19, Gun Control 372
Chapter 20, Smoke Filled Rooms 385
Chapter 21, Cho 391
Epilogue I 402
Epilogue II 403
Epilogue III 411
Index 414

Foreword

This book is a work of political analysis, illuminated with fiction, and is written for entertainment purposes only. Although most of the autobiographical events in this book unfolded exactly as they are described, nothing in this book should be presumed to be any advice for any course of action whatsoever. If you follow what you perceive as advice in this book in your own life, business decisions, and relationships, then don't blame me when things go sour. I warned you.

On the other hand, if you follow what you read in this book and things turn out great, then I'll be happy to take all the credit.

I came up with the idea for this book several years ago when I wanted to examine the results of some of the business decisions I've made over the years. And how, with very little energy applied, these decisions, and their results, might have been twisted. Sad to say, many of these decisions were based on ideas which have no validity in the modern world, but which seemed at the time to have some merit. I thought that these ideas might be cast as a satire to illustrate their foolishness, but could not find the vehicle in which the story would make sense.

The catalyst for this book came when I read "The End of America: Letter of Warning to a Patriot", by Naomi Wolf. From my reading of her book, Ms. Wolf casts her political opinion as a letter to a relative, and yet doesn't warn the reader that it is satirical. Similarly, I realized I could cast my ideas in the form of a self-help book for budding entrepreneurs. The critical link having been made in my mind, it was just a matter of fitting the puzzle pieces together. For this book, I choose to warn the reader up front.

While writing it, I realized that the principles of the collectivists who lay traps for the unwary entrepreneur happen to be the same underlying causes for all of the increasing, deliberate misery which we see around us. The destruction of the individual is at the heart of all our problems as a nation. Yet, there are simple actions which we as individuals can take to defend ourselves from, and ultimately defeat, the collectivists who are destroying everything of value in our civilization. And none of these things involve scribbling on a scrap of posterboard or waiting breathlessly for the next word or marching order of a false prophet of the collective.

I also enjoy asking myself what might happen if some small detail is changed in the world around us. Fans of Harry Turtledove will understand the fun this idea can generate as he twists and manipulates history in perfectly reasonable ways to create surprising results. While he uses history and cultures as his canvas, I choose the world of small business, and the battle for the individual spirit, as mine.

Often, as you watch a thriller you might become engrossed in the subject so much that for a time it seems real, at least until the credits roll. Likewise, portions of this book are written as an entrepreneurial satire, cast as an autobiographical narrative which might be a small business owner speaking to a close friend. It was my intent that the ideas in this book also sound real, as if they were the result of that narrator's own experiences.

The narrator's ideas are his own, I am merely the conduit, while the autobiographical portions are taken from my own life. The events the narrator describes from his life actually happened to me, simplified where necessary to make a better read. Sadly, in the case of my Virginia Tech experience, the events happened exactly as described. Other experiences may have slight changes to improve the narrative, to simplify description, or to conceal classified information. Where possible and appropriate, I provide unclassified public domain references to help make the points. Or at least provide clues to the points.

After reading this, the more literary among you might agree that Edgar Allan Poe is one of my favorite horror writers. Most of his stories begin with relatively benign descriptions which draw the reader into an increasingly disturbing unfolding of the misery and terror which lies at the end. While I can't come close to his classic, ageless work, I have to admit that he is a key inspiration. And yet, a reader today can easily distance himself from Poe's stories. No one lives in ghastly, drafty mansions at the end of a wooded drive anymore. We live in a world of computers and instant communication within clean, bright drywall boxes with identically manicured lawns at the end of a stub of a concrete slab for a driveway. And so, Poe no longer has the raw primal impact which he once did, because it is harder to relate to the setting of the story.

Yet the battleground which we face involves precisely those drywall boxes and manicured lawns. These are the things which have enslaved us as a nation. That and our collective unwillingness to see the truth and to speak it, unless we are careful to use the correct tone and diction. As if we have become a nation of little girls at a tea party.

Instead, this battle requires that we begin to think differently about the world around us, and that requires recognition of the growing horror which is around us. A horror which many of you may feel, but not have the words to describe because the vocabulary required has been stolen from you. Among other purposes of this book, I intend to restore that vocabulary and to illustrate the horror which we face, and its simple, well-meaning origin, so that we won't ever make this mistake again.

The best in the world for handling modern horror in my mind, without question, is Stephen King. He can take you from the average guy to a buried alien mind-controlling spaceship without your questioning why at any point along the journey. He is also one of my favorite modern authors. I chose this model to illustrate how simple foolishness easily mutates into civilization-destroying nightmares. On the other hand, this book doesn't have any alien spaceships, time travel, virulent diseases, pits or pendulums, or for that matter any blatant descriptions of spurting goo. But it is intended to project a sense of lingering ill-ease of the kind which can only exist within your mind. And to do that it must twist the commonplace around you into the horror which it might actually be.

This isn't a feel-good yes-you-can sort of book, but it could be, if you put it down soon enough. Like right now. Because if you don't, by the end of this book you will be wishing I were an Islamic fundamentalist.

Or an atheist. Or anything other than what I am.

Monkey, Defined

In the context of this book, a monkey is defined as a creature who chooses to collectively seize, by unearned means, the property, material or intellectual, temporal or spiritual, of its rightful owner. The means employed may be fiat, guilt, force, theft, fraud, subterfuge, or anything other than a willing and negotiated exchange of value.

In our modern world, each person is given the opportunity to make a conscious choice whether to be monkeys or men. Conspicuously absent from this definition is race, birth, gender, heritage, cultural influences, or any factor other than that singular deliberate decision.

Men choose to live their lives upon their own merit. It is this very spirit of independence of thought and action which makes men the prey of the monkey collective.

As such, monkeys abandon their claim to the rights of men. But monkeys could just as easily choose not to, and become men themselves.

Acknowledgments

I wish to thank all of those readers of the first version who provided feedback for typos and indicated concepts which should have been explained more clearly. These people are brave souls who ventured past the eye-searing cover of the previous version to take the time to find out what was on its pages. Accordingly, they applied the adage that you shouldn't judge a book by its cover. And yet, in our highly marketed modern world, we all have to accept those limitations. For now. Hang onto those crayon-colored books, my friends, especially those numbered and/or autographed copies some of you have. One day they may be worth something as a limited first version. You never know.

I especially thank all those readers who reached out to me and let me know how this material echoes what they have been thinking for years. That was the point, to let you know that you aren't alone, despite how the collectivists on both sides try to keep you enslaved to them. I appreciate each and every one of those emails. Keep them coming.

Not all who encountered this book were fans of the material, however. More than a few suit-monkeys were horrified by what they found here. Good. That's the point. Thanks to those suit-monkeys who let me know how this work threatens their ability to continue stealing from the rest of us. Accordingly, some of those portions have been dialed up a notch in this version. You suit-monkeys keep those closed doors, emails, reviews and blog hate posts coming too, because this edition is certainly not the last word on the topic. Keep feeding me your fears, for those are the raw material for the engine of war we will use to defeat you.

I also thank Jedi Short for thinking of the new cover concept of the cymbal monkey sitting on a pile of change. Audrey, in addition to her proofreading duties, added to this the Constitution, storm clouds and party buttons. Finally, I thank Monica Yother for her great work pulling all these ideas together into that hilarious cover. Monkey looks most disturbed, doesn't he? He should be.

Chapter 1, Enthusiasm to Attack

The first time I hit someone on the shinbone with a pipe it was a surprisingly satisfying experience. The target of my enthusiasm that time was an elitist thug two years older than me and consisting of about 60% more mass. Elitist, in southern Mississippi terms, meant that his father taught at the junior college, and had a swimming pool. Contrasted to having parents with a menial factory job like my mother, or an oilfield job like my father, or a farmer like most.

The pipe was the natural evolutionary result of the hand I had been dealt. I was a smaller-than-most boy in a mostly agricultural area, unlikely to ever be the first round draft choice to pick up a hay bale and toss it onto a trailer. As I was also doomed to be the valedictorian of my class, bullies were a fact of life. I can be best described as stubby. Built like the result of some horrible industrial accident in which my legs were sawed off to unequal lengths and then sewed back on crudely, my upper body had yet to develop. Given the diet of uni-crock cooking fed to me by my mostly senile but well-meaning grandmother, and nominal caretaker, this situation was unlikely to change.

So, having the physique of a scrawny broad-shouldered penguin, I enjoyed the benefit of the necessarily limited options in regard to fight or flight this presented. Flight, ground or aerial, just wasn't going to happen. Fortunately, most bullies didn't like experiencing pain on a repeatable schedule, so this is the lesson I learned quickly. In their fuzzily limited group perception, I became a more or less rabid housecat who was illegal to shoot, and so they moved on to lesser prey.

Not that I was a tough guy by any stretch of the imagination. As a kid I had my nose broken at least once that I can remember, and probably more that I don't, bruised bones, innumerable black eyes, bloody nose, cracked teeth, etc. I was only taken to a doctor for an injury one time, the rest were left to heal as they may. Many times I cried from the rage and frustration of having to deal with this over and over, only feeling the pain hours later. I often left a fight looking worse than my nemesis, but in most cases the lesson only needed one teaching. Afterward I would accept their advances at friendship and many stayed my friends throughout high school.

I soon learned to never fight fair. This absurd notion from a western ethic which never actually existed lost its charm when faced with a stream of unfairly-sized adversaries each in search of education. Hence the pipe and the time and place of my choosing, that being when Shinbone #1 rounded the corner outside the band hall alone. This particular aspiring bully was particularly annoying, since, overall, he was a little bit prissy and was trying to impress some dainty blonde pigtails. Moving in elitist circles, he hadn't yet encountered the options with which others were becoming familiar. I had also taken that day to affirm the idea that I didn't want to keep bleeding anymore.

As he lay there rolling in pain holding his bruised yet disappointingly unbroken shin with both hands, I abandoned my original plan of smashing his braces into his throat with the pipe. Instead, I took mercy and discussed with him my plans should this event have to be repeated, and how he might fit into my world-view. In today's terms I would have told him that he was now "my bitch", but that phrase wasn't yet available. To reinforce this concept, a week later my friends and I filled his prissy truck cab with trash, and he did nothing about it, to my satisfaction.

That experience opened a new world of opportunity to my eyes. Although there would be more bullies, never again throughout graduation would I suffer so much as a scratch from a fight, fighting in the traditional sense having been rendered obsolete. Later, this new approach would strongly influence how I would run my business.

As a child I aspired to be an astronaut. In that day most astronauts were still either Air Force pilots or Naval Aviators. So, I applied to the Air Force Academy and Naval Academy, and won appointments to both. During the application process I first experienced the unfair fight extended to organizations, or "gaming the system", a term I had not yet heard.

All service academies use the "whole man" concept when selecting among applicants, meaning that one could be a literal rocket scientist, but without physical prowess this excellence would be diminished overall. Extracurricular activities, like being first chair trumpet in the band, were nice, but a sport would be better to round out my application. So, I joined the track team, a choice about as ridiculous as you could ever imagine if you've ever seen me in person, but the only choice which didn't need formal tryouts.

Fortunately for me, the track coach didn't like Shinbone #1 anymore than I did, thinking him needing knocking back a bit. Coach also happened to see what I did to Shinbone #1 while walking to his office in the field house. Enjoying the idea of a band geek who didn't mind mixing it up, he chose to just keep walking that day. I was in, even posing for the group team photo for the yearbook, having never attended even a single competition and only two practices.

At the Naval Academy, I encountered only one bully among the ranks, and that one early into the first semester. Most of my classmates had clued into the idea that you didn't get there without having something going on, and generally treated each other with respect and mutual admiration. But, this one guy needed help understanding that you don't screw with someone while wearing a uniform tie. I didn't even have to hit him.

The Naval Academy was a system waiting to be gamed writ large, but I didn't see that at first. Having taught myself chemistry in junior high, I easily tested out of, or validated, that worst plebe-killer course. As a Mississippi tree-monkey I also validated gymnastics and was offered a spot on the varsity team, an opportunity I later regretted not having taken. At the time I was fearful of not making it through, having had only a rural public school education. Meanwhile, many of my peers there were more well-to-do or had fathers, grandfathers or more who I would soon find out were well-known in naval history. I had not yet learned that this distinction counted for less in my success than I thought at the time it would. So, in my ignorance, I turned down the offer of varsity gymnastics.

I didn't even consider joining the equivalent of the band, which didn't interest me that much anyway. My high school attraction to the subject was primarily the chilly bus rides with cuddly clarinettes rather than the music itself. Worse, my female classmates at Annapolis seemed puggish or bullish and had screechy, mannish voices. All of these attributes, selected mostly by their choice rather than by nature, held not the same charm.

As I decided that I couldn't afford the luxury of either varsity sports or the band, a new obstacle arose to reinforce these decisions. I soon discovered that I had a total and surprising incapacity for swimming, a failing which almost caused me to get kicked out during plebe summer. I shouldn't have been surprised at the need for swimming since there was the word "Navy" scrawled all over the place along with pictures of ships and storms and stuff. Mostly wet stuff.

Swimming started out to be even more of a challenge than running, which I was able to stumble through well enough to do even a little better than passing. As a child in rural Mississippi, one learned to swim through two routes. If you were rich enough to have a pool or regularly pay admission at a pool clean enough to see the bottom, that was the easy route. The only option open to me was to dunk myself in any number of swimming holes in the shallow river downstream of the particle-board plant.

Throughout childhood, none of the ginormous cottonmouth water moccasins I had seen had ever heard of the idea that they were more afraid of me than I was of them. On the contrary, these snakes were usually pretty much aggressive. Watching their behavior, I rightfully assumed that they had an appetite for penguins. One kid dropped off the rope swinging above the creek and swam up under the overhang right into a nest of them. When they pulled his body out it looked like he had been wrapped up in quadra-fanged barbed wire. I opted out, reasoning at the time that I would rarely, if ever, need to swim. The Navy had other plans, as I discovered splashing around that summer wondering if one needed to swim in the Air Force. Fortunately for me, the Navy has processes for everything, including teaching stubby midshipmen how to swim. The student just has to decide that he wishes to learn and better himself, and set aside all his preconceived notions. The Navy's ability to teach stems from the realities of shipboard life.

Life aboard a warship is a unique experience which any aspiring entrepreneur needs to experience at least once. All services have preventative maintenance programs and formalized curricula for the various specialties, but nothing approaching the intensity of the Navy. You can walk away from a broken tank or jump out of a broken plane, but if the ship breaks there is another entire set of problems which suddenly faces you. Imagine the embarrassment of having a missile hit you because you forgot to lubricate the surface-to-air missile launcher. Or choosing not to fire that surface-to-air missile because you aren't sure whether you have the authority or responsibility, when in fact you did.

The military maintains curricula which keeps these massive machines of destruction afloat and ready. Along with tanks and planes and radars and refrigerators, ships are maintained using procedures evolved over years of practiced effectiveness forged in the accumulated lessons of war. The American military is often criticized by the left as a model of inefficiency. This claim is more properly placed on the defense contractors who supply it for hire from safety behind a desk. But the military itself has evolved training techniques which are capable of bestowing more knowledge upon its students faster than any other organization on the face of the planet. As my Uncle John, a war veteran Navy Master Chief, once told his newly minted Second Lieutenant nephew, "it is a crime to send untrained men into battle". In my experience, the Navy and the Marine Corps would not once commit this crime, offering able instruction to all who would learn.

And so, I set aside my shame at past failure, and opened my mind, and learned to swim, well enough to at least not be a liability in combat. Later, the Marines would add to that sufficiency by teaching how to form a two-man gunboat floating atop intertwined packs of socks and food, one firing while his counterpart propels. The Marines at the Naval Academy also taught me how to shoot in order to prepare me to be the second half of that deadly combination. Again, I had to set aside my preconceived notions of my skill and ability, tainted by hours spent torturing pine trees with rifle and shotgun as a child.

The Marines took a plinker and turned him into an expert with rifle and pistol. I learned my lessons so well that I would eventually take first place in rifle and pistol marksmanship among my Marine officer class, Fox 88, at Quantico. This honor would later be twisted into an investigation against my loyalty. I would also eventually become qualified as a rifle and pistol coach in both the Navy and the Marine Corps.

I learned to teach not only others, but also myself. Each instructor at the academy was required to prepare a written plan of instruction for each course taught. This lesson plan was then provided to the students in the first session. So, for example, the student would know that on October 17th of that year what topics would be on the agenda for that lesson. The student would also know what homework would be assigned for that day, and when tests would be given. This turned out to be a valuable resource I would mine to give myself a fighting chance to stay afloat.

I attacked my studies, reading through and working two days' assignments while my classmates worked one. I cleaned my room well enough to get a passing inspection, but no better. The rule books didn't allow expulsion for minor infractions such as misplaced socks, but required it for academic or athletic failure.

Most of my superiors were barely shaving, and in terms of intimidation could hold no candle to my father's drunken oilfield rants. But I complied with their instructions and demands, trying my best to wipe the smiles off my face. I failed at suppressing those smiles often enough to be tagged as "The Happy Plebe" by some of my firstclassmen (Naval Academy slang for seniors). These future war heroes and leaders of industry recognized my cheerful approach as meaning no disrespect to them. After all, I was careful to not defy them in any meaningful way. And I genuinely admired them and their ability.

And so, I focused on the issues which mattered most, the combat-related skills, my physical conditioning such as it could be, and the academic instruction. I left the spit-shine and football rah to others while I loaded and readied my primary weapon, my mind. I did try my best at some of these other distractions in the interest of peace with the more unfocused. Inevitably, the pointlessness of those lesser activities resurfaced and relegated them to falling off the to-do list. This assignment of priorities paid off, not just academically at the academy, but later when I applied in war the military history and tactics I had studied.

My first year I racked up two 4.0 semesters in a row. I would add a third my sophomore year. I would also do well enough on the physical courses to earn the Superintendent's Star, reserved for those midshipmen who excel in both academics and athletics. I received some criticism about this, peppered with references to my mis-assignment of priorities and barely clean room, but that was kind of the point, you see.

Others, struggling, would ask me how I did so well in these difficult courses, and I would lay it all out for them. For many, the self-investment to read two assignments instead of one was just too much for them to ask of themselves. A mere paragraph ahead would suffice to start the ball of accomplishment rolling, but even that was a burden they would not bear. I soon learned to turn a deaf ear to their complaints, having tried to help enough of them to help themselves to no avail. Some wanted a magic pill, but all they really ever needed was their own effort. Some of them, haven't having started with my disadvantages, never learned to try harder in the face of adversity. Most of those wound up being weeded out by the rigor of the system. I felt no pity for them as they left.

The real secret was the self-study in advance. This strategy paid dividends as soon as I walked into the second session of each course in each semester. Having read ahead, I knew not only what the subject was, but where my misunderstandings lay, and how the material of today tied into the material of tomorrow. And so, while some of my peers were struggling to stay awake and keep up with the newness, I was listening intently to fill the gaps in what I already knew. And I learned how to find the gaps, and trained my subconscious mind accordingly. Soon, there were fewer and fewer gaps, I having learned to fill them in for myself. And I effectively finished each of my courses halfway through each semester.

My second year, recognizing that staying afloat was no longer an issue, I began to load my semester with more courses, freed from the background responsibilities of a plebe (freshman). I would eventually run out of required courses my senior year and had to add additional hours to my plate. This was the result of the academy having a minimum hour load each semester regardless of your status. I wound up graduating with about twenty more hours than required, and still in the top three percent of my class.

My ranking had been weighed down somewhat by those dirty sinks and the occasional wrinkled trouser. And the delights of having imported The Audrey, who would become First Wife the day after graduation. Thermodynamics would have to wait as she and I fought the cold Annapolis winters. At least they seemed cold from the point of view of a pair of Mississippi snuggle-bugs.

This habit of working ahead soon presented a dilemma. The last month or so of each semester was absolutely slack for me since I had worked through the course work by then. But, the regulations of the academy prevented me from wandering off into town to enjoy my free time. And so, I turned to mischief for the simple entertainment of it.

The best mischief was finding how I could push the regulations to the edge without crashing over the cliff. So, I began figuring out ways to game the system, having nothing better to do with my time. My roommate was not so fortunate, that future Navy Top Gun war hero spent all but a few months restricted to the campus for one infraction or another.

One diversion I amused myself with involved the importation of a functioning CAR-15 assault rifle, the little brother of a fully automatic M-16, to my dorm room. I filed down the firing pin, rendering it nonfunctional and thus meeting the regulations precisely. I then used it for training my plebes in how to field strip the M-16 blindfolded, a skill which they would otherwise never obtain officially as a midshipmen. My possession of this weapon was challenged by upperclassmen or the Navy or Marine officers who would from time to time discover it during inspections. So challenged, I would innocently point to the regulation book at the previously book-marked section and strip the rifle down to show the disabled firing pin.

I, of course, never pointed out to my inquisitors that I had tucked away two undamaged firing pins, hidden in one of those poorly folded socks. And two hundred rounds of ammunition, genuine yet undiscovered contraband, stacked behind the neatly aligned toiletries. These were the only items in the room arranged in military perfection, and should have been obvious in retrospect.

In a crisis, though, such as attack by the Soviets or other bomb-wielding liberal anarchists, I or any of my plebes could have easily restored the weapon within seconds. And in the dark, including loading the magazines from the stripper clips tucked behind the shaving cream. The Marine officers who inspected would smile and nod knowingly, for reasons I would only understand fully later. But the Navy officers would exasperate, a distinction which made a lasting impression on me.

I decided to broaden my horizons. I, my future Top Gun roommate, and a classmate from down the hall, the son of an American hero of Vietnam, formed a company, Zogco, to sell firearms. For an official address we used The Audrey's Boss's law office.

The three of us, The Audrey or The Boss excepted, applied for and received a Federal Firearms License, and were in business. In return for the use of his office for transacting sales and receiving shipments, The Boss was given list pricing on whatever weapons he desired for himself or his lawyer friends. His first choices were a Galil assault rifle we sold to his buddy, and a nice shotgun for The Boss himself.

We took pains to stay within the letter of the BATF regulations and state gun laws. I used the space under my bunk at the academy to store the long boxes of shotguns, assault rifles and bulky ammunition we sold in town. After all, with my virtual imprisonment there most days, and my skill with the assault rifle I maintained there, which was the safest storage location for miles around. As for myself, I upgraded my CAR-15 to a newer A2 model with a forward assist.

We soon discovered that our midshipmen customers were in need of additional service. So, I fastened my press set to my academy desk and reloaded 9mm pistol rounds with half charges of smokeless powder. The elevator shaft above our top floor dormitory provided essential background noise, and cast off, worn out mattresses from the garbage of the academy facilities shop the backstops. The Zogco Pistol Range was opened for business in the walking attic above the top floor. We posted a youngster (sophomore) on guard at the entrance to the attic stairwell in case of surprise inspections. We paid him and our plebe range assistants in concessions of snacks, beverages and Daddy-Fried chicken nuggets bought from a wholesaler in Glen Burnie. Our gun shop business license and tax certificate sufficed to gain us access at that and other wholesalers.

These concessions were also available to late-night study hounds who weren't in the know about the pistol range or the gun business. But even these outer-circle customers, invited unawares by key inner-circlers, provided excellent cover for the additional floor traffic. We made more in fun than in profits, but it was worth it.

I also revived my interest in chemistry. One incident required unofficially evacuating about a hundred midshipmen from our wing after an experiment went awry. That day clouds of chlorine gas boiled out of our room when my electrolytic sodium chlorate cell stirrer stopped stirring during an unexpectedly longish formation outside. Other experiments were more satisfying, various craters in the lacrosse and soccer fields attesting to their success.

Also, our Average White Guy Studies Group was popular for a time, mostly among minorities and women. Some of those women weren't quite so pugish. Those women and the interested minorities were surprised at the hospitality they encountered there when they arrived as spoilers, snacks from the concession larder available to all. In that group, we studied and critiqued various illustrated gentlemen's periodicals, that being our shared cultural heritage. My five-foot rebel flag hung from my closet door as a dignified backdrop to many debates about Southern heritage, federalism, and the true history of the injustice of slavery. The more small-minded of them stuck to their cultural biases, but ate our snacks anyway.

It wasn't all just fun and games, though. One extra-curricular activity which I really sank my teeth into was the naval combat simulator, known as NAVTAG. An acronym for NAVal TActical Gaming, NAVTAG was growing more popular and sophisticated in the early computer age.

Since, after all, the taxpayer was paying me to learn to fight wars, I saw this system as a way to hone my tactical thinking. This simulator would allow students to pit ship on ship or force on force, using the classified capabilities of actual weapon systems, friend and foe. And, so, short of actual battle with real equipment, there was no better way to test the tactics and weapon systems we had been learning in the classroom. A few times a week, midshipmen companies would compete against each other, with the losing teams eliminated along the way, tournament-style.

My third year, Top Gun and I found ourselves under the direction of a senior, a chemistry major, who thought the way we did. As a condition of being on his team, our team captain assigned some additional reading. This reading included "Fleet Tactics", by Captain Wayne P. Hughes, Jr., an excellent scholarly treatment of the role of effective scouting and attack throughout the history of naval warfare.

The chemistry major, known here as Oscar, would eventually become a nuclear submarine officer. He had studied the characteristics of the Soviet ships as well as our own, compared these to the rules of engagement, and had a plan. To implement his plan, we prepared some special transparent overlays to assist with targeting.

We also programmed our handheld calculators as might a vendor add a firmware upgrade to a shipboard computer. Effectively, we had upgraded the less sophisticated, yet more sturdy and heavily armed Soviet ships with modern software and automation. In the weeks before the first match, we tested his plan with simulator time Oscar had scheduled on the side, over and over, looking for weaknesses in the theory. His plan worked.

Horrifyingly well.

In the meantime, we prepared our minds with the background material and doctrine which would ease communication in the heat of contest. Our plebes became experts in Soviet ships, rattling off their specifications to us every morning instead of the usual news or sports articles or menus of the day. We listened intently, looking for holes in the theory. We found none.

On the opening match of that season, Oscar won the coin toss and chose the Red team. His choice gave us the Soviet ships, which we needed for his strategy to work. Had we lost the coin toss the outcome would have been the same. Since the Soviet choice normally proved suicidal in the first round, the opposing team captain would have left us those ships anyway. Smirking, our opponents slunk away to their destruction.

The normal cat-and-mouse of naval warfare requires that you find the enemy's ships before they find yours. Normally, using your radars is counterproductive as your own searching signal is like a flashlight in the night forest. Active radars give your own position away more easily than it assists you in finding your far-off opponent. So you never lead off by turning on that flashlight of your radars. Unless you fear nothing in the forest. And we didn't fear those two American warships out there in the dark.

While reading the narrative to follow, recall the quote from John Paul Jones: "Men mean more than guns in the rating of a ship." This story is best set to music, so:

Internet Research
Find a recording of the "Soviet National Anthem", the slower

and more dramatic the better. YouTube.com is a good source, but don't select "The Internationale" by mistake. *CatoTheElder* has a nice selection without skips.

Play this music in the background on auto loop as you read this story of American midshipmen fighting from within Soviet ships. Play it until I tell you to stop.

As the contest began, our opponents spent the first round of battle preparing their stalk. Following established doctrine, they launched virtual helicopters which would only turns later be capable of providing useful intelligence without giving away their launch point.

But at this point we were already going hot. Top Gun furiously tapped away on the keys with his junior varsity football fingers as I whispered through checklist after checklist. These checklists held preplanned tactical settings for our two Soviet ships, the *Kirov* and the *Sovremenny*.

Oscar collected human intel as we executed the well-rehearsed plan. His mind was looking forward into the next rounds as his well-trained and doctrinally proficient team did the work of the present. The fourth member of our team was a tactically astute youngster who in later years would lead his own team. He kept the materials we would need organized and available, much as a surgical nurse places the scalpel into the hand of the surgeon.

We also issued a warning over our simulated tactical radios, broadcasting on all available channels in English, the international language of the air and sea.

"This is Admiral Oscar of the peaceful Union of the Soviet Socialist Republics Deep Sea Fleet. We, protector of the freedom of the seas for all peoples, have taken it upon ourselves to ensure the safety of all shipping within these waters. By that authority, all peaceful commercial vessels within the range of this broadcast are ordered to identify yourself or else your safety can not be guaranteed."

You see, this game included innocent merchant ships, whose safety must be guaranteed, whether they cooperate in their safety or not. Striking a merchant ship, by intent or accident, would result in severe penalties for the guilty party, including having their terminals deactivated for the remainder of the contest. A boxing match is often decided by points rather than a knockout. But in our war game, striking a merchant ship would leave insufficient margin for victory as the offending boxer's hands would be tied while his opponent pummels him mercilessly.

But this restriction held a gap which Oscar's plan was about to exploit. That warning wasn't necessary, it was just part of the flourish to distract our opponents. They giggled when they heard it, thinking that we imagined, naively, that we could talk the moderator into revealing the merchants.

And this is exactly where we wanted their minds to be.

When our work was completed and the round ended, the sluggish computers of that day ground through the product of that first furious session. During this break, Oscar briefed us on the excited whispers he had heard from our opponents diagonally across the largish computer-fanned room. They had heard our furious key-tapping. And they had discussed in amazed whispers that we could only have been taking the naive and suicidal step of activating tell-tale radars on both of our ships.

We listened further as they were at that moment congratulating themselves on a battle already won. Breaking the silence, Oscar had us walk through the next round's work, which began soon enough. The next turn, our opponents could hardly believe their fortune. Both our ships were embarrassingly revealed. Each weapon system and radar available to us was warmed up and ready for use. Each of our ships was the mother of all UFOs in that dark forest, looking for the prey still hiding in the shadows.

Giggling across the room, the Americans fired their slower weapons which would still take many turns to arrive. We would not see these launches either, the more sophisticated seeker heads in these wonders of technology remaining stealthy until their final search for their victims. But we didn't have to see the launch to identify the enemy. In fact, we didn't have to identify the enemy at all.

Instead, we saw, near the limits of our primitive surface radars, four ghostly hulls, two enemy, two neutral. We didn't care which, and the game director, to punish our impertinence and defiance of the rules, chose to not reveal the location of his two merchant ships, effectively choosing sides against us. His compliance with our demand was immaterial.

As Oscar repeated his broadcast warning, I plotted the positions and current courses of all four mystery ships on my maneuvering boards. And, then the nurse handed the surgeon the first set of deadly transparencies. Top Gun fired the first salvo of our fewer, heavier and faster missiles, allocating them from both ships towards the farthest targets from each as I whispered parameters to him.

In the third turn, our primitive surface sensors had more detailed position and track information available. We stayed on course and speed, not maneuvering against the coming onslaught of slower, more dainty, yet deadly precise and numerous American weapons. They fired their second salvo ahead of our lumbering, naive, un-maneuvering ships. And they marveled at how our team captain, soon to be a graduate of the Naval Academy and a nuclear submarine officer, could be so stupid and helpless. While they rejoiced I plotted the updated information of all four enemy ships, the merchants having by now ignored two warnings, and had thus explicitly chosen sides.

My transparencies and Hewlett Packard calculator emitted data beyond the reach of the actual Soviets at that time. The actual Soviets, of course, on a grand scale had limited themselves from the best of technology by their very suppression of the individual. With this data Top Gun fired the second of our two salvos, this time from our ships toward the nearer. He and the data effectively spread the launch of our limited firepower out in space and in time. And yet, these missiles paths converged on each enemy ship to best effect at a single point in time and space.

But, we still had time to self-destruct or otherwise disable or redirect our missiles in flight. So we issued the warning for a third time, with an addition. "This is your third, and final warning. Any commercial vessels who do not comply will be destroyed."

None answered, all four vessels remained silently hiding in the dark illuminated by our radars. Our gigantically low-tech supersonic missiles closed the distance to each as the subsonic but far more sophisticated American weapons had barely cleared their own horizons.

The fourth turn dawned with all four targets at the centers of wagon wheels of deadly spokes aimed straight at their doomed hubs. This pattern was a refinement of the normal naval missile attack, which is beyond the scope of this book. Each midshipman knew this technique, unfortunately called "fingering the target", so named because the spokes looked like fingers of an outstretched hand.

Fingering is intended to assist in overwhelming an enemy's defenses. Some of the attacking missiles may approach on courses which lie outside the mechanical stops of the defender, depending on the orientation of the target ship. This geometric configuration is normally accomplished by firing the missiles with a degree or two spread for each, leading to a relatively narrow spread, as seen in a hand.

But the deadly enveloping configuration we now saw was not normally considered capable of being performed with this degree of precision and coordination in time and space. Especially from two Soviet ships at long range from even themselves. And by midshipmen using paper and pencil.

For us, however, this long distance between us opened the available spread. By coordinating the launches from both platforms in time and space with our software, these spreads were almost full circles. This particular spread looked more a wagon wheel, rather than the limited span of fingers. Had the merchant vessels complied with our demands, their spokes would have flown frighteningly overhead, splashing harmlessly beyond. But they didn't. No matter. These merchants had already served our purpose of making our foes think they could hide behind them. What happened to them now didn't matter to us at all.

Our opponents had thought we were still foolishly searching for targets, crashing through the forest with lights blazing. But they were shocked on that turn to find that each of their ships was doomed. Not only were our attacks indefensible, had they been prepared for them, they had not yet activated their own defenses as that would have revealed them to us. Their captain reassured them that although their ships would be destroyed, points would win them the game if they could inflict sufficient damage on us. Small comfort to the nineteen-year-old sailor who joined to see the world. Write that in a letter to his mother, "Johnny died serving his country, but we won on points."

By the rules of engagement, we were not yet deactivated. While our American foes attempted to launch one last desperate third salvo at our last known position, Oscar started a recording of the Soviet National Anthem.

You should be listening to its martial swell as you read these words. Oscar played this anthem within the noise levels allowed by the rules. Even this masked our last preparations from foe and game director alike, before our controls would be deactivated as if by EMP from God Himself. Indeed, He would be the only hope left to the now helpless American team, those arrogant capitalists having placed too much faith in the power of their rules. Even now as they prepared to lick their wounds and count their points, they imagined us playing this music to dramatize our impending defeat. Which is what we expected they would imagine. And what we wanted them to imagine.

Behind that musical veil, the tactical nurse, Top Gun and I turned our ships toward the enemies closest to each, and then turned our ships a little more to overcome our previous drift. We increased our speed to flank, and placed all of our systems in autofire mode to engage any incoming missiles. This time, though, we used a different set of prepared transparencies and software to predict the track of the most likely incoming threats. Our little virtual electronic captains inside our little blips of ships then strapped themselves in, took a cup of coffee, and settled back to watch the fireworks.

Our faster missiles found their targets. All four of them. The fifth turn, our enemies had been swept from the seas, ours the only surviving vessels still afloat. Per the rules of the game, our controls had been deactivated, so we could only watch the action from this point on.

The earliest of the shots of our opponents, fired in the second turn, swept harmlessly over our rear quarters, their targeting so far in the past as to be meaningless. We could see their approaching second salvo. But this salvo was fired in the third turn against what was perceived to be an unthinking adversary. An unthinking adversary who was now no longer where he was supposed to be.

This missile wave, in the sixth turn, would also fall harmlessly in the seas behind us, victim to a strategy named "chasing the salvos". This strategy was known in naval warfare since the first gun was mounted under sail long ago, but was considered by some obsolete in the missile age. Only their third salvo posed a threat in the seventh turn. These weapons were fired at where our ships were only recently. But, they were fired under the duress of having underestimated an enemy thought less clever. Their aim, accordingly, was wildly inaccurate.

So, only a fraction of these miracles of technology would present a virtual threat, but our defensive weapons handled them easily. Our ships suffered only minor damage from the destroyed fragments of their last hitting our imaginary steel. Our nineteen-year-old electronic sailors would sleep soundly that night safely in their virtual bunks. That night, their captains or admirals wrote no letters to mothers.

Throughout the final three short turns, we stood at attention behind Oscar watching our forces sail to automated victory against empty seas. In our jet black United States Navy working uniforms blue alpha, we saluted our electronic fleet in Soviet naval fashion. Tip of the fingers to the brow, palms facing forward rather than down in the typical American style, we listened to the Soviet anthem playing in the background.

The game director, a Navy Lieutenant Commander, was disgusted by both our solemn behavior, our music and our barbarian tactics. But, by the rules, he was nonetheless compelled to award us the game, our unscathed ships and sunken opponents handily outweighing the loss of two merchant ships. These destroyed merchants, after all, did nothing to save themselves from our pre-announced wrath.

You may end the music now.

This same approach, with different ships and increasingly complex scenarios, served us well for many rounds in the tournament. And yet, as our defeated opponents discussed their experiences, our techniques began to proliferate. Our classmates and future fellow officers were as equally intelligent as us. They were also equally as capable as us of deriving their own versions from basic principles. They only needed the will to act.

But, though slow to change, the rules eventually caught up to Oscar's tactical leadership. A month or so later, updated rules inflicted immediate and unconditional forfeiture to any who sank a merchant vessel, and heavy penalties for damage inflicted. These rule changes rendered his superior tactics now unusable upon our virtual seas.

At last, in that year, only those who would follow the spirit of the rules as well as their letter would prevail. To follow those rules the commander must be willing to sacrifice their electronic ships and imaginary men to an unrealistic niceness. Do these rules of engagement sound familiar? And what might the inculcation of such rules do, years later, to a deck officer of an American warship as he watches a little boat drift toward him?

In addition to these political lessons, while at the academy I also learned a deep respect for the men in the Navy's nuclear fleet. The driving force behind this program was a combative admiral, Hyman G. Rickover. He retired shortly before I arrived at the Naval Academy, but his reputation still rang loud and clear there.

Not all American military heroes fight the enemy. Some fight internal battles against entrenched interests. Most of these are shuffled aside with damaged reputations and stained fitness reports. But Rickover was one of the very few who won enough of his battles to make a lasting impact on the ethic of the Navy nuclear fleet. And as a result the United States Navy has a record of operating shipboard reactors with *zero* mishaps.

Internet Research
Research Admiral Hyman G. Rickover and his role in the nuclear Navy.

While reading about Admiral Rickover, note particularly his history of simultaneous bastardry and accomplishment. Wikipedia has an excellent article about him. Read every single word of it.

And so, in my four years at the academy, I learned lessons, both formal and informal, that would shape how I would view warfare and business. I would also learn about the rules by which these are fought or played, for the next two decades. Along the way, I managed, for sport, to systematically break every academy regulation, save one, which wasn't also an actual crime. Yet I didn't get caught for any of them. That last I saved unbroken until the end, marrying First Wife the day after graduation.

I also discovered that I was easily airsick, which popped all sorts of astronaut bubbles for me. The *Challenger* disaster shoved space exploration onto the back burner as the forces of niceness decided that heroism was not in our national ethic any more. These events pretty much made it clear to me that there would be no serious space missions for the rest of my lifetime.

And those Marine officers at the academy were so damn impressive. I had come within a few signatures of being qualified as a Navy Surface Warfare Officer on my senior cruise aboard the USS Ticonderoga, a common practice a hundred years ago. Despite this, I took the first Marine ground spot issued to my class, a future pilot a few spaces ahead of me in line being the first Marine.

I also had the honor to meet General Al Gray, the Commandant of the Marine Corps. He showed up at a social to get to know his new crop of academy officers.

Internet Research
Research General Al Gray and his Marine Corps service.

General Gray was a former enlisted man who had meritoriously climbed his way up all the ranks, and had earned his reputation among Marines the old way. He had been recommended for this position to President Reagan by Jim Webb, another Naval Academy graduate, author and hero of the Marine Corps from the Vietnam war. Webb, the then-Secretary of the Navy was, surprisingly, the first Naval Academy graduate to serve as such. He is now a United States Senator from Virginia.

Internet Research
Research Senator Jim Webb, his positions on women in combatand his struggles against the forces of niceness.

Out of Quantico I was assigned duty as an Air Support Control Officer at Cherry Point in North Carolina. Responsible for allocating air assets among various ground missions, this job is performed in the Marine Corps using a map, grease pencil, and clipboards. And a gigantic dose of what is known as situational awareness, or SA.

The Army and Air Force perform this same task using radars and computers and keyboards. But in the Marines, officers in my specialty keep a three dimensional model of the unseen airspace and the units on the ground below in their heads. They also rely on Marine pilots to keep their own mental SA models. And so, we could do that job from a truck, a jeep, a plane, or on foot if need be. The needs of the mission scale the profile of how you execute that task, and we were immune from computer viruses or other sorts of maintenance hassles. Get us a functioning radio and we were in business.

The lack of functioning radios for similar Marines from the west coast and Okinawa would propel me into an unexpected position when Desert Storm kicked off. That and my having gotten arrested almost a year earlier. Over the Memorial Day weekend of 1990 I offended a North Carolina state trooper who stopped me for a routine license check. The situation threatened to spiral out of control when I refused access to the trunk of my black 1977 Mercury Cougar XR-7.

A few years before this same car had been hauling assault rifles around Annapolis. But now that trunk held classified maps of the operating areas for the Navy and Marine Corps aviation for half of the eastern coastal United States. I steadfastly refused a search of my car until the military police from Cherry Point could arrive to take possession of those maps. The state trooper was also suffering from the stress of a nasty divorce and the resulting emasculation. So, he took my refusal as a personal insult. In the resulting fall-out, the state wished to teach me a lesson. The citizens of that state expressed this wish through the person of the county prosecutor.

The custom of the day was that localities and counties which surround military bases see those bases as a source of revenue. In our case, the Marines who inhabited those bases were kind of a nuisance. "Spend your money, and go away," was pretty much the theme. Numerous local merchants would display flags and other patriotic regalia, and then proceed to rip off young Marines left and right. Young Marines knew a lot about killing, but not much at all about contracts and leases and easy financing. And the county government was the enforcer of those rules, which almost universally benefitted the rip-off artists.

The prosecutor in New Bern was accustomed to uppity Marines, and knew exactly how they should be put in their place. His wishes were not opposed by the senior officers in my command. These officers sought peace in public relations more than they cared about the Constitutional principles they had sworn to defend. They also probably agreed that I needed to be put in my place as my academy mischief-making, now more refined and subtle, had followed me to the fleet. With their abeyance, the county assigned me two days' community service for this non-event.

And so, when Saddam Hussein's tanks rolled into Kuwait that fall, the wheels of justice had ground slowly by then. I found out about this invasion as I was hanging lights in the New Bern old folks home, community service being the modern moral equivalent of slavery. Other Marines would be assigned the task of controlling air in that war, that part of the world being in their slice of it. Marines more senior to me in my unit were assigned a deception mission at sea and left within days. I was left behind partly because I just missed the cut, but also because of my unresolved prosecutorial status.

Of the Marines in my specialty who were left, I wasn't the most senior, but I was one of the most qualified and experienced. This isn't saying much as I had only been in the fleet barely a year. Regardless, I was placed in the position of Senior Air Director, and tasked to train the more junior Marines to execute the primary air support control mission as a contingency. Meanwhile, a few more senior Marines remaining in my unit undertook the planning phases.

I took this assignment more seriously than any I had been given. For the next six months my team prepared for a desert war among the pine trees of North Carolina. We cross-trained on other specialties. We practiced air control while simulating evasion. We read Rommel and practiced his small unit tactics and indirect rifle fire techniques against the day our batteries failed and we became a fighting force out of contact with the rest of the Corps.

A quirk of physics made all of this effort worthwhile once the air war started. The other Marines from the west coast and the Pacific, better equipped and more senior, could not find a position from which critical radio links would function. The air support mission would have to initially be performed from the air.

Anticipating an eventual move into an area with good communication, the current ground package would remain intact. Those Marines on the ground would monitor the progress of the air package until they could regain control. So, they couldn't strip that unit to perform this supposed temporary function. And our Marines onboard ships couldn't be stripped off. That reorganization might give away the deception of an amphibious assault, a deception which pulled Saddam's forces away from the Saudi border. It fell to us, the most junior assortment of Marines in our specialty on the planet, to take on this pivotal role. But, with the most recent and intensive training of any of them, we were ready.

And so, a few days after the air war began, I found myself the junior Senior Air Director of the three air support control teams assigned to execute the temporary air support control mission. As I was the junior of the three, I was assigned the night shift, which turned out to be the most busy of them all. I had deliberately chosen a Marine ground billet from the academy to avoid my airsickness. I even had myself medically disqualified from flight to avoid an accidental assignment thus at limited capacity. Despite this, I was solely responsible for the airborne air support control function for the Marine Air Wing each night during Operation Desert Storm. This temporary mission, because of the operational tempo, turned out to span the entire war.

While First Wife watched it all on TV, I rode in the back of a KC-130. Each night I listened to voices in the ether in a communications van where fuel tanks normally ride. My team and I fought a war visualized in three dimensions inside our heads each night, and I forgot about my airsickness until the downhill leg of the flight back to Jubail each morning.

This was Al Gray's war. For a career spanning over forty years he watched, waited, learned. At last, when he became Commandant of the Marine Corps in 1987, he formally revolutionized the heart of the Marines, a process which had been incubating informally since Vietnam. No more would there be the "hey diddle diddle up the middle" suicide attacks, but instead the Marine Corps would become the force of the mind. This approach was known as Maneuver Warfare.

Internet Research
Research Maneuver Warfare.

Unlike the Marines of old who were famed for amphibious assaults, the Marine Corps of that era planned to fly into battle aboard commandeered airliners. Arriving at a remote battlefield these Marines would face Soviets who drove there. The reality of this match-up was reflected in the renaming of our deployed forces: Marine Amphibious Units, Battalions and Forces became Marine Expeditionary Units, Battalions, and Forces, respectively. Most of the equipment we would ever have was already sitting in forward caches, waiting to be unpacked. Accordingly, throughout any of our expeditions we would be outnumbered and facing an enemy who was better equipped and could drive as much equipment and materiel to the front as they chose.

So, we would have to redefine the front.

Children and generals imagine lines on a map, forces as having substance, battalions and regiments and divisions being solid things. In reality, like the atom, these things are mostly empty space between knots of substance. Smash a blacksmith's hammer against an ingot held against an anvil, and work is done. Replace the ingot and the anvil with a vision in smoke, and the hammer will dislocate the shoulder which swings it, or strike its own knee with a crippling blow.

In Al Gray's vision of the Marine Corps, we would defend Norway and portions of Korea and selected points of the Middle East and the western Pacific against the numerically superior Soviets. We would do this, not by presenting a solid wall, but through smoke, haze, vapor and confusion.

To achieve this effect, control of the battlefield would be decentralized far beyond what would be possible to a collective. Instead, we would rely on the innate American individualism which had not yet been bred out of the populace. It was this aggressive decentralization, far beyond what had been considered acceptable in the past, which shocked Al Gray's detractors. And won him the admiration, respect and determination of the rest. Including me.

Our Commandant assigned a list of books which was mandatory to read. Each sergeant and lieutenant and captain and general, regardless of his day to day job, must understand a soldier's load. Or, the mobility of a nation, or how a young Erwin Rommel attacked and overwhelmed numerically superior enemy units in World War I. He must also understand the outdated principles which we would never use again. And why to not use them, lest these suicidal tactics be revived in ignorance and paid for in the blood of young Marines.

Colonels would no longer fight today's war. The war against a larger enemy would be won by hundreds or thousands of sergeants and corporals, whose battlefield it always was. But now these sergeants and corporals would explicitly control it, always mindful of the common intent.

The colonel, now removed from today's action, would plan tomorrow's. The lieutenants and captains served to communicate that intent and remove obstacles in logistics and capacity. These junior officers would take action when fate intervened. They were in a position to redirect the sergeants and corporals onto valuable targets of opportunity. Often, these targets would be revealed in the confusion far faster than the colonel could receive the information, comprehend it, and issue new orders. And those sergeants and corporals and lieutenants and captains had better be up to the task, and not merely automatons or administrative functionaries.

They were up to it. And all of them were capable of shooting a man at five hundred yards while peering through iron sights should the need or opportunity arise, no scope required. From the chow hall cook to the supply sergeant to the aviation mechanic to the pilot to the admin officer or clerk, they were all lethal killing machines serving their larger role. But each was capable of evaporating into handfuls of destruction when needed.

Shoot down the Marine's plane, and he becomes a reconnaissance asset, special operations unit, and light sniper. And not a victim in need of rescue. Sink his amphibious ship and the enemy will have just created hundreds of two-man gunboats from the survivors. Destroy the Marine's logistics, and he will eat the food and drink the water he takes off of the enemy's dead body after spending the night hunting.

Hills and ridges mean nothing beyond their utility as geographic references, channels and points of feigned defense, not worthwhile beyond that for the cost of a single life. The focus of action turns from geography to the enemy itself. No more would this hill or that town become points to be saved at all costs. Instead these features would extract cost, abandoned when they had served their purpose.

I now knew why those Marine officers had smiled at my disabled rifle. They knew better than to believe my feigned compliance with the regulations. Deceive and confuse the enemy, presenting him with an image, weak or strong, which doesn't exist. Give the enemy multiple tempting targets from which to choose, and lay traps for all of them no matter what course of action they decide. Should he divide his forces and try for them all, pick one and reduce it in detail. Gain local superiority in time and place, leaving the now smaller rest for tomorrow, your forces still intact.

Should the enemy attack your battalion with his division, the battalion evaporates into vapor. Leave him advancing toward your phantom of a few fire teams trading worthless ground for valuable time, yet having the thunder of the gods from air and artillery. The remainder of your forces he passed by, effectively transported miles to his rear by his own effort, destroys his logistics. And shoots him in the back as he attacks your ghosts.

His generals and colonels are left defenseless. To save themselves they turn their massive waves back or commit the reserve. In so doing, they attack themselves in the confusion, as not all of their forces will have received the new plan. The price would be Marine friendly-fire incidents as well, but the overall fratricidal losses from these would be surely less than those sustained by directly repelling the greater force. This results in a net increase in the survivability of the nineteen-year-old lance corporal with the rifle, who was the ultimate customer of all of our services.

The enemy's every strength, and the mass of the collective, is turned to the individual Marine's purpose. These Marines act in groups as small as two, three, or four in unspoken concert with all the others. Even the most capable tank must eventually refuel, its protective infantry drained away chasing downed and deadly pilots. In so doing its valuable, irreplaceable crew may fall prey to a few well-aimed rounds from the fire team waiting above that curiously wide stretch of hillside road. The Marine corporal leading that fire team recognized the pattern from his reading and practice, so his fire team's retreat and hides would already be prepared. And then they vanish into the wild while the enemy gives chase to repeat the cycle.

Each such attack and withdrawal draws retribution from rear area forces who rush to the hunt, exhausted from other chases. The chasers leave cover, abandon cohesion, and expose themselves in their haste to other nearby fire teams. Other Marine fire teams are alerted to the hunt by the rifle shots and the wasteful and unproductive answering panic fire. This endless, fluid, mostly one-sided attrition buys the time for the colonels to plot the counterattack against weaknesses discovered and created by the corporals.

The enemy's divisions drown within a sea of disciplined and productive and aggressive minds. But these minds must be prepared years before the battle by Marines sweating and bleeding, learning skills, accumulating data and watching the patterns emerge. By Marines running, stumbling, crawling through practices for which there seems no immediate purpose, no foreseeable payback, and may, in fact, never be applied. But when the time comes, the Marine's mind is ready.

It was this mindset, inculcated by Al Gray, that would have been used against the Soviets in key locations here and there across the globe. But in late 1990 and early 1991, these ideas met a different enemy. For the six months of Desert Shield, the Army's Green Berets would be reinforced and replaced later by the Marines as they arrived in force. Both of these groups blocked a numerically superior force using many of these same approaches in numerous border skirmishes. Then, and throughout Desert Storm, the Marines applied Al Gray's intent.

At national planning levels the Marines were intended to conduct a holding action to tie up Saddam's forces in Kuwait. Instead, this war became a model of violence and confusion and speed not seen since the Blitzkrieg. Meanwhile, the Army implemented maneuver warfare in its own style writ large in Iraq to the west, to equal effect on a vastly larger scale. The principle had been vindicated. During that month of war I experienced the exhilaration of the years of planning and training culminating in victory. And of having the privilege of serving with some of the best men I have ever known.

For that month, our time had come.

And during that month, I narrowly escaped as many as three courts martial. One of these incidents involved my diversion of a preplanned package from a minefield clearing mission. That mission had been armed with napalm, but I diverted it onto active artillery which was busy shooting at fellow Marines on the ground. This attack created imagery on the television coverage injurious to the parallel public relations war.

My behavior was described later:

"The aircraft in question *may have been* (emphasis added) executing a strike on a higher priority target than the artillery battery that 1stLt Baugh identified. Other assets *may have been* (emphasis added) available to attack the artillery battery. ... In his enthusiasm to attack a known target, 1stLt Baugh exceeded his authority in trying (sic) to divert the aircraft."[1]

Uhh, I didn't *try* to divert it, I diverted it. Oscar Two Bravo, Roger Out. And *may have been* wasn't good enough for me at the time. Regardless, actively firing artillery was up at the top of the target priority list, for what are obvious reasons. If these reasons are not obvious, ask someone who has been on the receiving end. But nonetheless, these words indicated the after-action second-guessing of wartime decisions which grow increasingly common today.

Now this kind of analysis percolates down to each trigger squeeze of each nineteen-year-old lance corporal with a rifle. And for that matter, now includes the second-guessing of each decision made by business leaders across the country. This spirit of continuous and arbitrary oversight has now been shifted by the lobbyists of those titans to weigh on your shoulders. And has possibly cost you fines, your businesses, and for many of you, your jobs. And for a few of you, even the lives of those you held dear. Your time will come.

From this perspective, after a few detours in which I accumulated knowledge and experience which would only later prove important, I started my business determined to apply what I knew worked. And it worked better than I had hoped, but the lessons learned were unexpected and the battlefield has changed. The American economy is now that battlefield, and in particular, the role played by each productive individual in it. The change in the landscape of that battlefield is the total revolution of thought in our nation regarding the definition of success. This revolution will soon precipitate a battle which we did not start, but which we must win.

This change, and my understanding of its true nature, causes me to now reorient toward the new opportunities which have presented themselves, buried within impending crises. Our handling of these opportunities will dictate whether we will succeed or fail in our new endeavors. For if we fail, we will not survive. I mean by this not that our system will not survive, but that we will die at the hands of our oppressors. Or, perhaps worse, our spirits will die inside as we accept their chains.

Our time is coming. And we had better be ready for it.

---

[1] "Marine Corps Gazette", July, 1993, page 11.

Chapter 2, Who Should Read This Book

Foremost, this book is written for those individuals who fear that they are losing their essential right to survival as individuals, along with their individual goals, faith, and aspirations. You are correct in this fear, because you *are* losing this right.

This book is written for those individuals who have tried to follow the rules, and who find after they had invested themselves in that path that the rules had been changed beneath them. And who had everything they have ever worked for destroyed as a result.

This book is written for the individuals who feel disenfranchised from success. And who feel that their own efforts to provide for themselves seem to only put them farther away from that goal.

This book is written for the individual who may have a successful business, at least from an outsider's perspective. But who are nonetheless lacking the fulfillment and sense of well-being which should accompany success. Or who had a successful business, only to see it now being destroyed by forces beyond their control.

This book is written for individuals who think agreements should be based on a handshake. But who are disappointed by partners, above, across, and below, who deliberately fail to satisfy the intent of agreements. These individuals feel that paper agreements only exist to refresh the memory of what each signer intends to actually perform, rather than a foundation from which to weasel out of their obligations. Viewed this way, these individuals believe that contracts are really just a reminder for yourself.

This book is written for those individuals who want to improve their personal financial circumstances, but are unsure where to start. And who have begun to feel like much of the advice they receive in the public domain just seems a little too pat to be believed, especially in the tumult of today.

This book is written for individuals who want to rely on themselves. And are weary of being the only player on their team while the bench-warmers around them get all the benefits of their efforts.

This book is written for the individuals who feel that they are at the end of their ropes, and are considering drastic options.

All of these individuals can benefit from the material in this book. Surprisingly, all of these groups of individuals, despite their seemingly disjoint natures, share common characteristics. For them, the material in this book will resonate deeply. As it turns out, most of the problems we face in our world today stem from a single root cause, the suppression of the individual mind. This book will show why this is true, and steps you can take to fix that.

I can also clearly indicate who should *most definitely not* read this book.

This book is not written for the person who feels that only the mass action of a large team is capable of success.

This book is not written for the person who thinks that someone who is self-taught, self-financed, or otherwise self-reliant has somehow cheated the system. And who feel that those self-reliant individualists have somehow deprived the team of value and, as such, generally should not be trusted by anyone.

This book is not written for the person who thinks that the value of a person or company or the quality of his or its output is determined by how many jobs he or it provides.

This book is not written for the person who feels that only the mass action of a large team is capable of success.

This book is not written for the person who values civility above liberty.

This book is not written for the person who thinks the Founding Fathers of The United States of America are to be discredited as being out of touch with our modern societal issues.

This book is not written for the person who feels that dogma or government should rule people's decisions.

This book is not written for the person who wishes to control the lives of his fellow man beyond protecting himself and his loved ones from direct physical or material harm at the hand of others.

This book is not written for the person who wishes to silence opposition to his opinions through the use of force, threat, legal action or the withdrawal of legitimate opportunity.

This book is not written for the person who feels that opportunity should be provided, not on the basis of merit, but through means which seek to correct historical injustices.

If you find yourself in these latter categories, put this book down right now. You will only be unsettled by the pages which follow. Retreat into your cocoon and await further instructions from your masters.

A third category of potential reader is the person who is fulfilled by being at the head of his small enterprise. This person knows that if his company were dismantled tomorrow he could arise anew and rebuild. If this is you, feel free to read on for entertainment purposes only. But, be forewarned, this book may probe you deeply enough for you to discover that you actually are in the first set of potential readers.

I have operated my own business for over a decade now, and in that time I have discovered some fundamental truths which have been helpful to me. I have also enjoyed a level of individual liberty which has been breathtaking in retrospect. I have avoided the vast majority of spirit-crushing debasement which has become the accepted mode of life for a people who have forgotten what liberty actually means. I have come to understand that the principles which make a small business successful are exactly the same principles which define a free man and which create a free nation. It is as if this pattern had been laid down by God Himself long, long ago.

My business is deliberately very small. I have dozens of products and thousands of customers worldwide, yet my employee footprint is absurdly tiny. The more I accepted these fundamental truths, the more success I found with less staff. Before I had learned these fundamental principles, which have been around since the dawn of man, I started my business in the traditional way:

☐ Conceive of a great product or service which can help others succeed.

☐ Plan how to implement the service or design and distribute the product.
☐ Determine which tasks can be delegated to employees and clearly define their responsibilities.
☐ Interview, hire, train and reward employees, including generous benefits packages.
☐ Market the product through channels which have access to the target market, rewarding the actors in that channel for their service.

I had no idea how wrong I was at first. My story of my business life helps illustrate some of the lessons found later in this book. So join me on this short history.

Sales started slow, and then began to accelerate. Before long, my company was the world leader in its little niche. I had employee problems here and there, but chalked these up to normal attrition and personnel issues. I also wasn't making any money. But, I was providing great jobs, my company had growing revenues, and my customers were thriving.

But still, I wasn't making any money. And I was working eighty-hour weeks, stuck in Atlanta traffic twice each day. Sometimes I made payroll by credit card offers despite our booking of large amounts of what turned out to be, in many cases, paper orders with no meat on the bones.

I was also taking on contract jobs through the business. Rather than just simply keeping this money for myself, I was leaving this income in the business. Essentially, I was paying for product development and payroll and 100% health coverage and monthly steak lunches and flex time. I paid all of these benefits to others from what would have otherwise been lucrative contract proceeds to me.

Sitting in traffic one spring morning three miles and forty minutes away from my office, I was listening to the more radical of many radio programs I enjoy. I realized that I was working myself to death to provide great jobs to other people, both inside my company and for my customers. And yet I was following the rules of what should have been the model for business success. But I was working for pay which I would have laughed at should anyone have offered me the job.

A few months after this epiphany a curious thing happened. Our receipts finally began overwhelming the checks we were writing. Suddenly, we were debt-free. I then made the mistake of paying myself more than pocket change, and then reinvesting this money back into the business in the form of loans.

Why was this a mistake?

It turns out that when I was the lowest-paid employee in the business, everyone was happy. But, when I first paid myself a reasonable amount, an employee doing system maintenance on our database discovered this fact. This amount was entirely reasonable given what I would charge a client for my direct services for the amount of time I was working. And it was reasonable given why I had started this company in the first place. Regardless, it was my money to do with what I chose. Even if I chose to pay it to myself.

Knowledge of this payment was then communicated to the entire staff. And soon I had what amounted to a passive-aggressive revolt on my hands.

Snide comments were whispered about my compensation from people who had a better job than they could find anywhere else. Wide-scale theft of office materials. Rudeness to customers. Endless interoffice drama. Absenteeism.

In the midst of a major product development, employees I had trained to do design tasks suddenly forgot how to do the simplest things. Then, just as I leapt in to do much of this work myself, the beneficiary client of this product development chose to renege on promised marketing.

At this point, I considered cancelling that whole project. But foolishly, out of a sense of misplaced honor, I chose to live up to my end of these obligations *despite every single other party ignoring theirs*. I eventually canceled this product line two years later, after six figures of investment plus more than a year of my time. After reflection, I should have paid attention to my gut and dropped the project on the spot.

You have to trust your gut.

This concept has now been popularized by that same radical radio talk show host. This means trusting yourself, despite the societal programming which the world uses to try to extract unearned value from your efforts. Later, I explain in detail why your gut is correct, and how this destructive programming is implemented. As a teaser, one such destructive program attempts to convince you that your gut is wrong.

I also noticed that I apparently wasn't alone. Many of my customers run small businesses themselves, and I began to discover that they were having many of the same issues. In addition, for some reason a small business magazine showed up in my mailbox every so often, and its pages are littered with tales like:

"We are doing so great thanks to the tips in your magazine. Things are going so well that our fifty employees spread rose petals beneath us each morning as we descend from our coach." Bob and Sue Sapmather operate a $4 million San Jose business providing hand-glazed eco-friendly widgets.

Stories such as this are often accompanied by pasted-on smiles which don't hide the fear and panic in the eyes of the owner. Doing a little bit of math reveals why. First of all, the average gross revenues amount to about eighty-thousand dollars for each employee.

This seems OK, unless you live in San Jose. And have to buy the materials for all of those eco-friendly widgets and the hand glazing. The math reveals that while the Sapmather's are providing great jobs to those fifty glaze-caked mouths, they themselves are probably *pouring their own money into the company*. Just as I was.

At least when I had to jump in to salvage that project I had the presence of mind to fire the weakest of the team members. Amos smiled throughout the entire process. Until I pointed out the well-documented nature of the firing process. This documentation included his repeated failure to perform the assigned tasks for which he had been well-trained. And included his failure to perform them in the manner in which he had been instructed. Because of this documented history, Georgia law prohibited granting him unemployment benefits.

When I informed him of these facts his smile vanished.

For you see, most employers, to avoid a disgruntled shooting or other unpleasantness, tend to *layoff*, not *fire*. A layoff means "lack of work" in unemployment law terms, and is often misused to get rid of some useless deformed cog in their organizational wheel. Lack of work means that you ran out of stuff for this person to do. And further, that this lack of work is not his fault, and that you are entirely willing and eager to rehire him if new work materialized.

Listing lack of work as a reason on the unemployment documentation is both ethically and legally unemployment fraud. Especially when the actual reason is that the individual concerned has been a useless wart. Not all warts are useless, though. Some warts have purpose and motivation. If they had Social Security Numbers I probably would have rather hired a few of them over the years. Regardless, these employers are essentially bribing the former employee against violence or other drama by tapping the state's unemployment fund. Yet, these funds are paid into by all the other employers in the state. But, this fraud is so commonly done that employees have come to expect unemployment benefits even if they sit around all day.

It seemed to me that, given his tender age, Amos had been coached on these presumed benefits. This set of circumstances might also lead one to believe that he deliberately malingered in order to get fired in the first place. I think he needed a better coach.

I enjoy the lowest unemployment tax rate in Georgia, by the way. I wonder why? It could be because in all these years I have only had one unemployment payout. My first firing was from the naive perspective that an employer has a right to hire or fire whomever they please. I learned my lessons from that one well. After a time, I stopped even seeing the dispute forms. I suppose my reputation in the Department of Labor precedes me. In any event, there are precious few digits in my unemployment taxes, most of them to the right of the decimal.

Anywho (as my mother used to affect a Southern charm to indicate a change in conversational course).

Oddly, after this particular firing my paper theft problem essentially evaporated. I also found a reason for some of his reduced productivity when his phone started ringing. "Hello?" I answered, sitting at his desk banging away on the project Amos had just been fired from.

"Uhh, is Amos there?" the voice asked.

"Who is this?" I demanded.

"This is Felicia with Monkey Trends magazine, and I need to work through a survey with Amos," she said.

"He no longer works here," I replied. It is risky to simply say that you fired the worthless sack of monkey pus. This could be considered defamatory, even if it is well-documented that he does, indeed, contain a measurable amount of monkey pus, and that his primary life purpose is to contain said pus, as if a sack. I think that this is due to the possibility that monkey pus has value to someone, and thus cannot be truthfully stated as being *worthless*, and so, by extension, the sack must have some measurable value as well. I kept this analysis to myself.

Felicia responded, "That's terrible. He was our contact person in your company to call with surveys. Are you the person who answers surveys for your company, then?" she inquired. "If so, I can list you in the system as the contact for all the other survey companies as well", she offered helpfully.

That conversation went nowhere good from there, as did dozens of similar calls from other affiliated market survey firms over the next month. I had assigned Amos as the support point for a major product of ours, that product aligning nicely with his development responsibilities. Our support policy was to update our online *Frequently Asked Questions* section of our product pages should even a single call come in about an issue.

Over the years I discovered that my own productivity was greatly enhanced by the solitude of an office, yet destroyed absolutely by cubicle life. Accordingly, I had spent a pretty penny to make sure that *everyone* had a private office. Not one employee sat in a cubicle. More on this later, but all those times I passed by his office, seeing him happily interacting on the phone, I thought he had been talking to customers about his product area. And in so doing improving our support data. But in fact, he had been answering meaningless surveys on my time. Beats working, I guess.

The flip side of this was that the product support was being neglected. This I discovered when I answered about forty support calls to his phone over that same month. Most of these calls came in the first week after his departure. Most were dealing with the same three issues, none of which had been updated on the web. After correcting that, support call volume for his product area dropped precipitously, as desired, these customers now finding the answers for themselves on our site.

Customers were now happier, I had more time, repeat sales of that product area improved, and I had more money in the bank. If I had listened to my gut and dropped the fledgling product which precipitated his firing in the first place things would have been far better. But then again, I might not have been sitting at his desk to take those calls, and I might have not learned that lesson.

Getting rid of Amos turned out to provide so many benefits I started looking around the office. And what I saw were the other neo-disgruntled campers wandering around like productivity zombies.

Looking back, I then saw a string of previous employees who, after having been trained in state-of-the-art techniques and technology, would quit for a cubicle job, many times at reduced pay. Almost universally, these people would say things such as "I need to get a real job" or "I appreciate all you taught me, I really learned a lot." I realized that I should have instead simply implemented their work in the time I took to train them. If I had done that rather than counting on them for future return on investment, I would have been much farther ahead. Or, if I simply sold the training materials I created to train them, I would have had an entire product line on its own.

Others, like Amos, refused to implement their knowledge once taught. So the free training, make that *highly paid training*, had come to an end. And then that decision undercut an entire class of employees currently drifting about. My axe grew sharper at the thought. So next on the list was Archie, who had the longest time in the saddle of the then-current staff. Archie was also the first employee I had ever hired who lacked a degree.

My earlier hires all had degrees ranging from B.S. to Ph.D., but were effectively unteachable and chose to not implement designs the way I wanted them implemented. The fact that those episodes were in the Y2K boom era didn't help with their attitude toward instruction. Years later, after having realized what good jobs they had turned away when that bubble had popped, most of these came back asking for work. I declined each such request. In the meantime, my product concepts flourished when implemented my way, despite the pop of that particular bubble.

My rationale for hiring Archie was that he was to be my go-to guy for little tasks which got in my way. In exchange for this service I would not only pay him well, but also teach him the trade of software development. Sort of like an indentured servant, but without the benefits to me, and with all the benefits to him. Benjamin Franklin would have killed for that job when he left home as a tween.

When I hired Archie, he was working at a big box retailer selling TVs, or more accurately, ringing up TV sales. I'm not sure he ever actually *sold* anything. Archie's first job was to cut my grass. This left me time to work on my first book. Each subsequent hire, degreed or otherwise, was intended to further shed me of relatively simple tasks which kept me from writing that book. But, each new hire also introduced his own set of new tasks and needs, drawing me farther from the pen. So, that book never got finished before the underlying product line became obsolete.

Archie always seemed to have special needs. As a child, he suffered terribly from a medical condition which was genuinely tragic, which he survived heroically. I thought that this background would be a positive, he knowing what bad times were, rather than some of the prima donnas who preceded him. I based this concept on my own appreciation for my work as beating hauling a pack around in the snow or in the desert or in a tropical forest. While potentially getting shot at.

Instead, however, his background constantly became a shield for criticism. Any reprimand or correction was met with "no worries, I'm a childhood survivor." The last such reprimand came when I met Archie at the door as he was coming in the door with my postage meter in hand one morning. Questions about his rationale for taking the postage meter home led only to similar survival assurances. At lunch that day he hauled off his stuff and never came back. Two weeks later I dropped him from the rolls, seeing him only once subsequently as I was shopping for a widescreen TV at the same big box retailer. He referred my inquiry to another sales person.

Taking over his work I found numerous opportunities to implement our internal systems the way I had initially taught him. Yet, these opportunities to excel had somehow been ignored in the quest for free postage. As part of his tutelage years before I had written a list of key style issues which I demand all of our software developers use. After ensuring that he understood each of these issues, and the productivity risks which accompany their violation, I began to inspect his work less as I turned to other dramas. Later, I found that pretty much each page of code he had written in the bulk of his time had violations of these rules. Sweeping away the dust of these errors, I managed to fix numerous issues which had plagued our internal systems for years. Again, I was rewarded by a smaller payroll and more efficient operation. And more available postage. And fewer excuses about childhood trauma.

About this time a target of opportunity arose. At my company, we ship a number of products in a variety of little white boxes. Those boxes arrive at our dock in flat, unfolded bundles. Those bundles have to be folded into boxes by somebody, and then packed with our little goodies prior to landing on the shelves as shippable inventory. For a time, we often only packed items in their little white boxes just prior to shipping. This meant that we kept our shippable inventory in bulk in their silvery cocoons in various cartons on the shelf. But, as business grew in those early days it became obvious that we needed to just go ahead and pack them in their little boxes. Sadly, a clever employee could milk this task for days.

One day, however, the fates smiled upon us in the person of Miss Meadow, who we had hired to help with odd jobs around the office. Goth girl by night, and unassuming office help by day, Meadow for a time seemed perfectly normal, all things considered, given her age and suburban cliques. Pleasant on the phone, charming in person, capable of learning just about anything non-technical, and some things that were, her career seemed on a skyrocket pointed straight up. This girl had the genuine potential to run the entire administrative side of our business.

But, as it turned out, Meadow had a tendency to cause ever increasing amounts of drama, which started out slowly enough. At first, I thought her odd behavioral quirks, which became more and more pronounced over time, were simply the result of lady things. But, the bit rate of these personality changes was far too high to admit any such simple explanation.

One evening, First Wife and I were watching an episode of *CSI*. That particular episode featured the typically cranky Sara Sidel, and I noticed that from time to time Meadow would act exactly like that character. I thought nothing of this until the next day. That afternoon, during a discussion with Archie, her hapless ex-beau who brought her into our fold in the first place, she unleashed a barrage of subtle venom at him. This barrage seemed almost straight out of the script of what I had seen the night before, down to the surly looks and bangs hanging down in front of her eyes. The light bulb went on in my head.

Once I became attuned to the concept, and Meadow noticed that I was noticing, more personalities became apparent as she created them to suit her own needs for attention. One personality which she manufactured was that of an eight-year-old autistic girl who was really into origami. Yet another was a thirty-two-year-old man-hating feminist. She then confided in me how all the different sides of her could be summoned on command. I suppose she imagined that this detail would make her the permanent center of attention at the office.

I immediately set to finding ways in which we could make use of her affected disorders. So, to my delight, Meadow's autistic origamist turned out to be a whiz at folding the little white boxes. Conversely, the man-eater was well suited to calling deadbeats. Fortunately, we had managed to convert her little dramas into useful productivity.

This all changed with Archie's departure, which left her deprived of her normal emotional punching bag. Archie had seemed, from all outward appearances, to enjoy the abuse commensurate with his affinity for playing the victim. Lacking her normal outlet, she turned her dramatic sights on me. But that didn't last for very long, she not finding a delighted victim, and so she decided to leave to plow other fields.

Drama aside, Meadow's departure left a genuine gap in functionality. So, First Wife volunteered to take over her collection and Archie's order-processing tasks, having previously served both roles working for others. Family necessities required that we modify our systems to keep First Wife at home tending to the children between calls and processing orders. This arrangement also helps to keep her barefoot, or at least hygienically slippered, as much as possible. So, we poked a hole in our LAN to allow remote access for her. Her remote access also allowed me to work at home, too, which I had done for years and had forgotten how much I enjoyed it.

The survivors at the office imagined that by conscripting First Wife I had already committed my reserve. They then began to incrementally imagine themselves more irreplaceable. Their calculation was made without knowing of the joy which my bloodlust was bringing as our organization grew more lean and efficient. And I had plenty of plans left, each such plan effectively reconstituted the reserve as I continued automating their jobs away. But, they tried their gambits anyway.

A former steakhouse waiter who had sought to learn HTML and marketing decided that he absolutely could not be taught further coding skills without a hefty increase. I asked that he put his demand in writing, and then restored him to his tip-laden tables. I filed his unconditional demand against any unemployment claims he might present.

His departure further encouraged a quality assurance technician, who became more sluggish with each passing day. A documented test against my pre-teen son, by a four-to-one productivity margin, restored him to the unemployment line, devoid of benefits.

Amos' counterpart on the ill-fated project should have learned the lesson better. After firing Amos, I re-assigned Sparta, a degreed engineer who also had the capacity to run the entire company, to implement firmware for quality assurance tests. This had been his assignment before the mondo project.

Despite his experience in this arena, he dawdled with various projects from day to day. He also took all his accrued leave, and one day beyond. Then, one morning Sparta handed me a letter announcing that he was taking a position with a customer of ours. I, knowing the customer and the environment into which he would be hired, laughed until tears came to my eyes. This hid my relief that he had saved me the trouble of documenting his upcoming firing. He stood there, apparently waiting for a counter-offer. None came, and after regaining my composure, I wished him well.

During this period I hired and fired a couple of other Nintendo™-generation Archies, each as disappointing as the last. Archie II, a grocery bag-boy, had genuine potential, as does *everyone*. But, he tended to whine about anything remotely difficult, such as using a power drill to hang blinds in our new office condo. After a couple of months I thought I had finally virtua-slapped the little girl out of him. This transformation apparently pleased his live-in girlfriend's father, who was having justifiable growing concerns of his own. Promisingly, Archie II had recently snapped-in to converting pages of test instruction notes into hand-assembled test boards and writing the corresponding HTML instructions.

So, one evening I decided to give him a performance-based raise, to be awarded the next morning. This was to be accompanied by an increase in responsibilities, including managing the new guy hired to take over his previous work. I discussed the raise with First Wife during a jaunt to the video store, and there we ran into Archie II. He proudly announced that he would be supplementing his income by working evenings at that very store a few doors down from his old grocery job. Within a week, attributable to night-shift video inventories, his performance plummeted, his excuses mounted, and he began to show up for work later and later.

One of Archie II's few hard-and-fast tasks was to arrive early enough to open the public door of the office promptly at 9AM so that incoming deliveries could be dropped off. During that time, a contractor friend of ours was having trouble with a test board in India, and told me that he was shipping the board for me to take a look at. Day after day, no board, but notices of delivery failure popped up on the express service website. On the third day I arose early, and arriving at the office before Archie II, I found an express sticker on the door. This sticker noted the third delivery failure and that the package would be returned to the sender. Fortunately, First Wife was able to call the express service and have the package held at their depot for pickup, avoiding hideous return and reshipment expenses to ourselves and the contractor.

In the meantime, I rooted around Archie II's office, and found two previous stickers from that same episode, as well as others for shipments which had been eventually received. He had tucked these notices out of (my) sight on the top of his supply cabinet. Mistakes, I understand. I make plenty of them myself. But dishonesty, or equivalently, hiding of mistakes, can kill your business dead, especially when your reputation is based on unimpeachable quality. And please, don't think that the stubby penguin hasn't already run across all the tall-guy hiding places. I have steppie-stool technology at my flipper-tips, after all. I own several steppie-stools, tucked away at strategic locations. Taller ladies needn't despair, so go ahead and wear those adorable high heels you found at Wild Pair.

When Archie II finally rolled in around 11:30 that morning, I asked if he still had the video store job. He answered in the affirmative, at which time I told him that was good as he would need it, and let him go in a swirl of Department of Labor paperwork.

In that same era we hired and fired Archie III within a week, he being too concerned with running what I perceived as homeowner insurance scams out of our shipping room. Allegedly, of course. He had helpfully offered to bring me in on his business, which offer I declined as I introduced him to the door. "No, please, after you." Click. His short tenure required far less paperwork.

Archie IV, hired from the same video chain but at a different branch, showed as much potential as Archie II, but with far less up-front slap time. One day, however, he showed up with painted fingernails. Figuring this was the side effect of a lost bet or prank common to young men his age, I ignored it. However, as the days wore on the fingernails became more gaily painted, and his attire more feminine and I thought I detected the slightest hint of makeup and eye shadow. Now, as you will discover from reading this book, I am nothing if not tolerant of others' lifestyles, but I do have a business to run. So, I asked him what was going on, and more importantly, whether this was a permanent transformation which he was undergoing. My intention was that we might make sure that his performance stayed high and our business reputation didn't suffer.

After a bit of evasiveness, Archie IV blurted out that his girlfriend was making him do these things. His revelation thus to me was apparently part of their fun. After I stopped laughing, I assured him that if he wanted to play his femdom games that was OK with me as long as it didn't interfere with his work performance. And, since his work responsibilities never intersected with visitors, I expected him to keep these style choices out of sight of customers and vendors alike.

I also counseled him that his right to whatever lifestyle he chooses didn't extend to making my business guests and other employees uncomfortable. That kind of intrusiveness would limit my economic opportunity, and thus my opportunity to pay his check. He agreed to the reasonableness of these limitations, as well as the right of the other employees to express themselves about his decisions he chose to flaunt before them. I notified the rest of the staff of my tolerance of his lifestyle choices, as well as their rights to express themselves in reasonable ways also. The wardrobe escalation seemed to cease at that point and held more or less constant. No incidents or confrontations arose, and all seemed at peace with things.

Within a couple of weeks, however, Archie IV's performance began to drop measurably. Upon further investigation, I discovered that he was spending an inordinate amount of time on social networking sites. Now, it has been my policy that social networking sites are the modern equivalent of personal phone calls. Just as it is reasonable to take or make a few personal calls per day, similarly it is reasonable to check personal networking sites a few times during the day. But, he had become a networking junkie, and his cell phone was ringing off the hook. Apparently his new softer persona had become a very popular guy.

At this point, I counseled him on his measurably reduced performance, and told him that he was to limit his personal contact time at work to a reasonable level. Within a week he quit, these terms apparently eating into the dominatrix's plans for him.

In retrospect, I have come to wonder whether, given my status as a former Marine from Mississippi, that entire episode was laid specifically in preparation for a workplace discrimination lawsuit. I wonder if I was supposed to say something like "git outta my office you queer"? While imagining this phrase, supply the appropriate stereotypical accent as you find suitable. Be sure to inflect a nasal tonality. Roy Hollis' or Jackie Gleason's are good choices.

Fortunately, if this experience had been a setup, my *laissez-faire* approach sidestepped that one neatly. On the other hand, why doesn't a business owner have a right to express himself, too? We shall see why in later chapters.

Even temp help was problematic. One individual I hired on a temporary basis to help setup our network kept leaving windows open, in the wintertime, as he worked on the weekends. I found out later that he was considered by some as a habitual marijuana user. I shudder now at what might have happened to our business assets if he had been smoking pot in the office and had been caught. I spent a weekend after that pronouncement tearing the office apart looking for hidden stashes. I found none, which then made me begin to doubt the source of that rumor.

I wasn't alone in dealing with employee excess, of course. An express service driver couldn't understand our technology, and about two years after 9-11 he spread a rumor that we were "making bombs" throughout the business complex. I invited the sheriff to come check things out for himself.

I also demanded that the express service fire the driver. They refused, vaguely citing union contracts and muttering something about brown shirts. Between that episode and their propensity to lose many of my shipments, I steered thousands of packages away from that service for years afterward.

All of these little anecdotes contrast with the reason I started my business in the first place. I originally started my business so that *I might better provide for myself and family, and do so in a way which maximized my personal freedom.*

If I wanted to catch up on missed episodes of *CSI*, I would record them or rent the series. I certainly wouldn't have hired and trained a Meat TiVo™ to re-enact the dramatic portions the next day.

If I wanted to manage the day to day activities of others, I would have stayed an officer in the Marine Corps. Alternatively, I would earn an MBA, take a desk job somewhere, and get paid for it.

If I wanted to provide a space for people to potentially hang out and smoke pot I would move to Amsterdam, and get paid for it. If I wanted to listen to accusations about pot and spend my day looking for contraband, I would have joined the DEA.

If I wanted to train people for new jobs I would take a job as a professor and get paid for it. Of course, I write books which do exactly that, but I'm not *paying my students*.

If I wanted to spend hours each day examining the unemployment tax consequences of each hiring and firing decision, I would take a job in an HR department somewhere. And get paid for it. If I wanted to spend hours each day examining the legal consequences of each word out of my mouth, I would be a lawyer. And get paid for it.

I don't need to be rich, either. Why do most people want to be rich? Well, for many, riches are a way to demand the respect of other people. I don't care about that, because what they are getting isn't respect, at least not from people whose respect has any context for me.

The one, and only, reason I want money is to buy freedom. But, aren't we all guaranteed freedom by the Constitution and Declaration of Independence? Yeah, sure they are. Test this theory by flipping off a cop sometime, or even a government clerk, and then claim freedom of expression. Here in the land of freedom. The freedom I'm talking about here is real and far more important than some classroom theory.

There was a time when it was a truism that "people are a firm's most valuable resource." In those times, managing the drama which accompanies managing people was a necessary cost of doing business. Of course, in those days that statement rang true. Back then, employees didn't look behind them and see gigantic safety cushions to soften the blow if they were fired or the company went under.

Now, as did poor misguided Amos, many employees look forward with glee to practically unlimited unemployment benefits. This problem grows worse each year as many clever minds propose extending benefits *even if fired for cause or if the employee quits*. When that day arrives, my carefully documented processes will then have no value. Whatever shall I, and other employers like me, do? Bear the burden? Or figure out ways to do without employees? Hmmmm. Someone should write a book about that dilemma.

In addition, manufactured legal opportunities abound for those employees lucky enough to make a case for discrimination or harassment, both sexual and otherwise. Or demeaning treatment, emotional trauma, wrongful termination, *et cetera*. Add to that worker's compensation claims which convert a minor injury into a winning lottery ticket.

Workers also enjoy holding their employers hostage to work stoppages, whether unionized or not. In the middle years of my company's growth, we often did below-cost work on projects which were intended to increase our visibility. Some of these projects were quoted based on an understanding that the beneficiary, a major indexed company, would reciprocate with some simple marketing which somehow never seemed to materialize. We will discuss that aspect in more detail later, including the risks large companies pose to your financial well-being and what to do about it.

Regardless, these projects required receiving a large amount of material in a few containers. Upon receipt, we would run it through our quality assurance processes and repackage it. Then, we often shipped it back out the same day and the day after, in hundreds or thousands of parcels with worldwide destinations. These all-hands projects, planned months in advance, were one of the key justifications in my mind for having a significant staff.

Almost without fail, however, despite careful coordination and advance notice, absenteeism peaked on these days. This absenteeism often left First Wife and I, with our small children rooting around underfoot, working until late at night repackaging these ourselves. This after many of our staff had spent their day lounging around at home. One of these projects landed on or about my firing bloodlust, stoking it further.

I declined such projects after that particular exercise. And so evaporated much of the justification for a larger staff, who chose to avoid precisely that work which kept their pay flowing during the slower times. I also began to notice acts of outright sabotage which I had previously chalked up to inattention. For example, permanent markers were left in the whiteboard tray just before key vendor or customer design meetings. These produced bared-teeth smiles from the assembled as the boss looked silly to a customer trusting him, or not, with six figures of design work. Six figures which paid the pranksters' salaries.

Solder flux bottles were moved from the lab to underneath the breakroom sink, requiring hours sunk into pointless searches. Staplers were left with only a few staples in them after having been loaded the previous day, and no staples to be found. A swarm of box cutters were nowhere to be found. Pens in the office supply cabinet had colored caps switched around.

Neglect also abounded. Sparta blew up a computer by not using the protective device *we made for sale to others* and for which *he provided product support.*

Key tasks were ignored, despite these being written in the little cardboard logbooks issued to everyone. And required for use as directed by the in-house time management course required of each new employee. As mentioned earlier, style guidelines for software and quality control procedures were ignored.

Until my employment bloodlust, I had applied unlimited reserves of patience and guidance. Why was I so blind for so long? Two reasons.

First, I had been spoiled by my experience at the Naval Academy and in the Marine Corps. There, I had been surrounded by the cream of the American crop. Even the few relative sluggards, by comparison with my employer experience, were hard-charging racehorses.

The worst of the absolute Marine Corps jackasses were still focused on the mission. Most arguments were about how to get the mission done. Even those solely focused on their careers were trying to accomplish at least that much self-advancement. Was it moonbeams and lollipops and slaps on the back all around? Of course not. There were rivalries and pettiness and ongoing feuds and turf wars all the time. But when it came time to focus on the enemy and the mission, almost all of which was laid aside as we stood shoulder to shoulder.

No one gives out medals for fighting the stupid on one's own side. So once the fighting was done, all of that crap popped back to the surface. But at least the boat anchors kept their mouths shut when the time was right. The only real risk was that some of the boat anchors might percolate up into positions of real authority when paper matters more. And some did. But fortunately, at least in my experience, none of these uber-anchors caused any real damage during the shooting war. They at least had the good grace to fade into the background when one got in their face. And if one was slippery enough and subtle enough about how one got in their face at crunch time, not even their court-martial pens held much ink afterward. Of course, one had to pick the right audience for these encounters.

But men had to have the courage to do so. When the time came, enough did. And this was also part of Al Gray's intent as Commandant. He educated everyone enough so that exercising even this courage was invigorating, knowing that it was saving lives on the battlefield. And he educated even the uber-anchors enough to know that they would find few sympathetic to their offended sensibilities.

In the Marine Corps, tasks did not get forgotten, sabotage was unheard of, and people were where they were supposed to be when required. And everyone knew what suck was, in the form of hard physical labor combined with unending motion and constant mental agility. The newest boot-camp graduate had skill and vigor and motivation which would overwhelm vice presidents my company has had. Or for that matter, Vice Presidents this country has had.

Plus, in the context of the Marine Corps, and the Navy at sea, being a slacker could get you and a lot of your friends killed. The major issues came from the bureaucracy, but the Marines and sailors with whom I had day-to-day contact were exceptional people. Not so much for the typical employee.

Second, I had, as have many, been programmed to believe in the innate goodness of people, and I had extended this belief unconditionally to my employees. Perhaps these same persons in the context of what they perceive as a "real company" may have comported themselves better. But the checks they received and cashed were real, and larger than they could expect elsewhere. Their benefits were real, and similarly larger. The flexibility of work hours were real. The explicit definition of responsibilities and tasks were real. Yet their positions in a small company left them acting as if they were in kindergarten. Perhaps this is why many small companies try to grow large enough to give the impression of "realness".

This lesson required over a million dollars of my own money to learn. And I want to teach it to you for the price of this book and a few hours of your time. The lesson I learned is not *knuckle under and grow large to provide many jobs so that your employees will take their assignments seriously*. This is the lesson the monkeys, in their mindless and uncoordinated way, hope to teach.

No, no, no. No.

The lesson I learned instead is *figure out how to avoid that collectivist extortion in the first place so that your company can stay small. This will allow you to care for your family while you and your family enjoy your ticks of the clock.*

We each have so precious few ticks of the clock. And I am done with spending them trying to get someone else to make the barest effort to lift a finger in his own behalf. This lesson applies to our society as a whole, by the way. And it applies to you, whether you own a small business, are an employee, or unemployed. We shall explore the options each of these have in detail later, but each path leads to the same destination. Note for now, however, that your path to individual liberty, and even your ability to survive a civilization-killing crisis, such as that which will be precipitated by rampant world-wide socialism, is paved with the same stones which are trod by small business. If you do not run your own business, employed or not, you must quickly begin thinking in that direction for reasons I will later make clear.

So if you are a small business owner, or will soon become one, you still have a choice to make, but that choice is rapidly fading. Soon you will have no choice at all. You may choose to take the traditional path and grow to avoid the collectivist extortions which plague small businesses. If so, you will eventually be absorbed and spend your days dealing with the excesses which grow on a daily basis with each whim of legislature and executive alike. If you accept this option you will be eaten alive. Eaten as you imagine you are growing rich as measured solely in paper and numbers on a computer screen. You will spend your days chasing numbers which can shrink into meaninglessness by a stroke of a pen. And for many of you, already have.

The other option will soon be the only choice you have. And that is to shrink your business while maintaining the level and quality of service which your worthwhile customers and clients rightfully expect. This approach will insulate you from the excesses while there is still time. I have learned how to do this, and I can teach it to you.

You picked up this book because something resonated inside you when you first heard about it. If you are still reading, that resonance is growing stronger. If you continue to read it through, by the end you may throw this book aside in disgust. And I will try my hardest to get you to do just that. Or, you will be energized to take actions for the pure benefit of yourself and your family, and share this book with others.

And in time, the economy will change as the storm clouds gather. The course has already been set by the monkeys themselves, its progress is as sure and unstoppable as the rising of the sun in the East.

In the process, the monkeys may starve. That is not my problem anymore. And it shouldn't be yours, either. Because in reality, each monkey, each day and each moment, decides to starve himself.

You now stand in front of this decision, possibly for the first time. Think for a moment about which path you wish to take. Monkey or Man?

So, if you are still willing to proceed, I will introduce some preliminary concepts which are essential to the material in this book. Then, we'll talk about where money first came from.

Chapter 3, Fundamental Concepts

Before we launch into the meat of the material in this book, I need to make sure that everyone is reading from the same level. In general, older readers will be better prepared to understand the concepts in this book, but may be stunted in terms of web usage.

On the other hand, younger readers will need some preparatory work, but generally possess superior Internet skills. In particular, those younger readers who suffered through the emasculating public school system, or especially those who have been disenfranchised by it, will need additional background information.

If you are reading this from the perspective of someone who considers himself well-educated, then feel free to skip this chapter, or for that matter the rest of this book.

Throughout this book, if I think a topic is important, I will direct you to self-study, using a banana symbol:

Reading Assignment
The Wealth of Nations
by Adam Smith

This icon may direct you to read a book, or go to a website, or watch a movie or television program, or have you perform some independent study. All these assignments are essential to get the most out of this book. And each time you learn something, and then apply it for your own benefit, you take a banana away from a monkey somewhere.

The example above directs the reader to a particular title. Some of these titles are so old that copyright protection no longer applies and are considered in the public domain. In the case of "The Wealth of Nations" or "The Communist Manifesto", these materials are available for free on a variety of websites.

Ethically, I hate the idea of taking something from someone else for free, particularly his ideas. However, even if you bought these particular books, you would only be funding some other guy who took the material from the public domain and put it on paper. The original authors' heirs will not receive a penny from these purchases. So, if you insist on paper copies of some of this material, pay the publisher for the service of the printing, which is in itself a service of some value. Otherwise, read it for free today on the web. Other titles are relatively new and must be purchased, but "it's an education that pays for itself". By the way, this is a line I copied from a review of one of my other books. The title you are reading now is an even better education.

Instead of indicating a book to read, I will sometimes direct the reader to watch a particular movie or television series. Just as works of written classical literature contain life lessons which are often analyzed in a classroom, motion pictures or television shows are merely the videotaped versions of written literature. Presented in a multi-media format instead of on a piece of paper, these resources can usually provide more information faster than could be obtained by reading.

Some academic elitists look down their nose at watching movies as a form of education. If you share this elitist opinion, remember that Shakespeare is considered worthy of even graduate education. Yet Shakespeare was merely the Oliver Stone or Francis Ford Coppola of his day, and would have filmed his work had the technology been available.

I may also direct the reader to perform a web search for a particular topic. What particular means of search you use is not nearly so important as the fact that you must be capable of doing this to enjoy the material I present. Also, a clever reader will notice that different search engines will sort and display different information to the user, and yet, for the most part, I don't cite any specific sites to read.

Truth is not dependent on the source. By looking at a variety of sources on a topic, you can form your own opinion about how the world actually works. Unlike material presented in a linear fashion in a textbook, life throws random uncorrelated inputs at you on a regular basis. It is your responsibility to develop and use filtering skills for yourself. You may even find that I am completely wrong about some material I present in this book.

You will find that the web is such a valuable resource which, if properly used and in specific applications, can exceed the utility of a library or formal education. I don't argue that it is probably best to get a formal education in some field which interests you. But, even in that field you will find that you still have only scratched the surface of what you need to learn to be effective. The reality of modern life is that you should never stop learning. Knowledge is power, and by educating yourself constantly you give yourself the power to take more and more control over your own destiny.

Ultimately, attaining that power for yourself is the topic of this book. You will have to develop Internet skills for yourself, though. I know several supremely capable people who were entirely bypassed by the Internet. Some of these great people are under the misconception that value is provided by sweat and muscles. Muscles have some value, but, as we shall discuss in detail later, not nearly to the extent which one might romantically envision.

These people continue to suffer without the access to information or opportunities which the web presents, and some refuse to change to their sole detriment. Some feel that the formal system which subjected them to oppression or arrest uses technology to amplify the power of the weak. Because of this impression, they refuse to access this power for themselves, a sadly short-sighted strategy. If you are in any of these categories, read no further in this book until you get a computer and learn how to use it to find out information on the Internet for yourself.

So first, get a computer. Which flavor you choose, Mac or PC or Linux, isn't that important for the material in this book. You may ultimately choose to get several. Computers are super cheap these days, and will provide you with more personal power per dollar than any other appliance you own, including your car. Artistic and creative types will get more utility from a Mac, while Linux favors plinking around with code all day. The PC is more or less the jack of all trades and the middle of the road. Ask some friends for their opinions and then make your own decision. It's good practice.

Next, get to the internet using your favorite internet service provider such as your phone company, your cable company, or a third party internet service specialist. Which one you choose isn't as important as having one. Ask someone for help getting started if you need to. If you have to, get an account at a public library and start using their computers to access the internet to perform the required research.

The first thing you need to do with your internet-enabled PC (used generically to refer to any of the three flavors) is learn how to perform a web search. Use Google, Yahoo, and whatever others your friends might suggest and compare results.

Your first assignment to test your skill here is to look for "The Communist Manifesto", written in 1848.

Internet Research
The Communist Manifesto
by Karl Marx

You will find that several websites talk about it, others give you the entire text, while still others let you purchase a printed copy. Analysis usually isn't as important as the raw information, in this case the text itself. Learn to distinguish between these types of sites, all of which provide value for different purposes.

Go out on the web now, find that manifesto, and read it from start to finish. Every single word of it. You may be surprised at how well it describes elements of our modern world.

The next thing you need to find on the web is an online encyclopedia. I enjoy Wikipedia, found at www.wikipedia.org. This kind of web content is different from a generic search, and lets you browse around through related material. For example, when you performed your web search for "Communist Manifesto", that topic on Wikipedia probably showed as an option. If you went there, you could click on "Karl Marx" and read something about him. Then from there you might click on "Kingdom of Prussia" and read something about that, then click on "bubonic plague" from there, and so on.

The symbol for Wikipedia is a globe consisting of jigsaw puzzle pieces, which I think is a particularly apt choice. Note that many of the articles you find on Wikipedia have the flavor of a school paper. This is not by accident, since Wikipedia can be authored by anyone. You could even add content if you want. Or edit the content of others. So, take everything you read there with a block of salt, and check out the links to the source material or other citations and follow those threads. Sometimes, the material you find will be so different from the encyclopedic condensation that you will wonder if the article author even read his own references.

This suspicion should be nourished, and used to challenge the ideas which you were taught in formal school, which was free from the restrictions of dissent. The web is a remarkably democratizing influence on ideas. This resource is so empowering for the individual against despots of any stripe that I am surprised it hasn't yet been legislated out of existence. Give them time, but in the meantime take advantage of this powerful resource.

As the book proceeds, I will assign other topics of study for the technologically challenged. Some of these involve working through tutorials for doing things like writing web pages. If you have never touched a computer in your life, don't fear, it is much easier than you think once you do it a while. For the oppressed among you, developing these skills will make your enemies tremble.

You are suspended within a web of lies. Each day you are bombarded with information, much of it flawed. Yet, if you weren't handicapped by a public education or having been ejected from same, you would be better prepared to detect and deflect bad information before it causes you harm. Instead, the spiders which inhabit this web crawl up to you and suck out an imperceptible amount of your life's work and energy on a daily basis.

The best way to protect yourself from these lies and their ill effects is to educate yourself. In particular, educate yourself with information which may not seem at first to be particularly applicable to your current situation. This is fine, as I intend to dramatically change your current situation for the better. Humor me.

Your first video assignment may seem a little hokey. Rent and watch:

Video Assignment
The Matrix

This film is often seen as an anthem for conspiracy theorists. As you will learn later in the book, I am not a big believer in conspiracies. That doesn't mean that you aren't suspended in a web of misinformation, though. The allegory of a human battery is pretty apt, as you will see in the remainder of this book.

We will see how the theme of this movie applies to the web of lies within which we are all entangled. You will also see how, in a figurative sense, all of us are batteries in a system which is beginning to rattle apart. We will also see exactly why this is the case, and the inevitable result of the path which we are on. As it turns out, our modern situation was equally inevitable, and should not be the subject of anger, just awareness.

Some of these lies around us are so intricately crafted that they are impossible to unravel without explaining an equally intricate web of truth. This situation, which protects the web of lies like a mother hen, would not be possible without first crippling the intellectual powers of a vast section of our populace. A hundred and fifty years ago decision-makers, meaning people like you and I, were relatively better educated. Back then, political or business arguments which today pass by without question would have never seen the light of day.

Decision-makers of modern times have more raw information at their disposal, but understand the physical and ethical world far less than their analogues in the 1800s. You and I also have to deal with a set of arbitrary constraints which has almost become overwhelming.

Take for example a modern farmer, who operates perhaps one of the most complex industrial systems, on a per-capita basis, of our modern world. And yet, should his combine break, he must typically rely on a mechanic to fix it. If the computer on his combine breaks, he has no choice but to at least go buy another computer for it. If that computer is out of production, he probably has a pile of junk on his hands now.

But he doesn't just have his equipment to worry about. Should farm workers decide to unionize and strike, there is little he can do about that. He can't negotiate a maze of tax laws without hiring an accountant. He must cope with a nest of environmental regulations and workplace safety regulations. These insane regulations were written and enforced by people far-off who seem to forget that they themselves need to eat.

Let a fuel shortage hit during a critical planting, crop maintenance or harvesting window and the entire year is shot. Find an endangered worm on his property and the entire works is in jeopardy. A worker stumbles and gets a boo boo? I don't even want to think about that one. By comparison, a drought or an insect infestation is far less disruptive than any number of self-imposed disasters which might befall him.

What if one day the modern farmer were to decide that his personal quality of life would be dramatically improved if he just grew his own food and sold enough of it to pay for property taxes? Or clothing or a nice meal out from time to time? He would then bypass the entire swath of regulatory burden which weighs him down. And in the process starve thousands. By the way, each of us, in some way or another, is that farmer. We just operate different equipment.

Now contrast our modern farmer to a farmer in the mid 1800s. He was far more of a master of his universe than we give credit. Droughts were mitigated by irrigation ponds, which now require environmental permits to build in some jurisdictions. Insect infestations were fought with biological weapons, such as crows or chickens. These biological weapons also provided meat and eggs for the table. Rabbits gnawing the bark of your young fruit trees? Paint them with blood and offal and problem solved. Energy was provided by mules, horses and oxen, which required removing some productive land to grow their fuel. But even that allocation of fuel was under the control of the farmer, not the EPA or a far-off hurricane.

It was a hard life, no doubt, and burned a man and his wife into old age by their 40s. Had it not been so painfully hard, we would not have seen the urbanization of the late 1800s. The advent of steam automation in the mid-1800s only eased the pain somewhat, but even then the fuel depot was only as far as the wood-lot across the pasture. On the other hand, he was not yet subjected to the soul tearing weight of crushing debt. Debt which was required to pay for the contrivances which would become a necessity for maintaining profitability in the face of ever-increasing productivity. It was that same productivity which also drove urbanization, allowing fewer people to feed more.

But the farmer of that day was also a rock unto himself. Walk up his drive and tell him that he can't use a certain fertilizer, and his response would probably be to answer with a load of buckshot. Shot from a gun he was still allowed to own, of course, because he wasn't yet perceived as an enemy of the state. Or of the collective. You might get a similar response if you told him he must not drain that swamp or plow that hillside.

When he changed his techniques or materials, it was because the change was beneficial to him, not because failure to change would criminalize him. He knew his world in detail, and was immune to lies about his world. The brightest of them absorbed all the information they could find about the best techniques which could improve his life. Some refused to learn, and so when farms began to fail, but not all of them, we heard tales of how tough farm life could be. And yet, others thrived. How could this be? The answer is simple, but hidden from your modern view.

That long-ago farmer was also a master of many subjects, including mathematics, physics, geometry, genetics, and meteorology. Don't believe me? Ask any school child today how many pecks are in bushel, or what a furlong is, and you'll see what I mean. Or what varieties of wild flowers are helpful to ward off various pests, or how many posts and how much wire is needed to enclose a pasture. Read letters from the Civil War era from the common soldier, particularly the Southern soldier, and you will be amazed at how articulate these supposedly primitive people were. Children today, even those of Northern elites, can hardly compose a written sentence.

His understanding of advanced subjects, such as physics, may have been limited by the state of the art of the day. Even so, all then-existing knowledge of subjects such as physics was available to the common man on a more or less global basis.

As proof, consider how Ernest Rutherford started his scientific career on his father's farm in New Zealand. There, he conducted his first experiments regarding turbulence in water as a boy. This farm boy grew into the father of nuclear physics.

Internet Research
Ernest Rutherford biography. Wikipedia has a good starting point from which to branch to other sources.

Today in this country any farm child can enter the educational system and land anywhere. But, it is highly unlikely that he performs his seminal work among the cattle, or even if he does, to receive anything but disdain for that effort.

The same progression we see with the small farmer is true for the industrialist. In the mid-1800s, cottage industries supplied goods and services for their communities surrounded by friends and family. Competitive forces drove the establishment of factories on a grand scale, and these necessarily led to dehumanizing conditions which begat government regulations to deal with the excesses.

These same regulations, in turn, only ensured that the cottage industry could never return. These were replaced forever with unionized shops which can barely feed themselves while pitting capital against labor in a downward spiral to destruction. Had those regulations not rendered the cottage industry obsolete, this situation could have been reversed through market forces alone. Modern regulations require the modern farmer to be an environmental paralegal, which produces not one more kernel of corn. Similarly, the small shop and the small farm, armed with modern technology, would have eventually overtaken the factory or the agriglot in the long haul of time.

The regulations themselves kept the small innovator and hard worker off of the playing field forever. Much of this book deals with that topic, and the cures to those external forces you can apply to your life today. But, these discussions require that you prepare your intellectual soil with background information to help you understand my perspective.

Then, did you read an Ernest Rutherford biography as I asked? If not, go find one now and read it. Then read between the lines of his early life and imagine yourself in his position and what you might have accomplished in that simple unregulated time. If you are currently trying to run your own business today, you will feel a longing for that regulatory simplicity. Just think of what you could achieve with your skills and ability.

So it is my assertion that people of today, in general, are growing increasingly less educated and capable than those of only a few generations past. It is that trend which creates unlimited opportunities for those of us who are willing to learn and excel. But to do so, we have to recognize where we are and from whence we came.

Our modern experience is a consequence of agricultural and industrial productivity of yesterday, not a cause of it. We get to live in nice homes in manicured suburbs because of the productivity of elsewhere and another time. But, this is an unstable situation which must eventually wobble and collapse, and in so doing witness the birth of better things to come. We are seeing these stirrings already in the world around us.

Classical economists assert that market forces produce all value in the world. I agree with this assertion, but we have to recognize that we do not live in the world in which the classical economic models operate. I found this out by surprise after I read "The Wealth of Nations" and then began hiring employees. The market forces work, but now the economic environment has been skewed by regulations and what I call throughout this book the "forces of niceness". As a result, you have to adjust your decision-making somewhat to accommodate these realities.

Consider an analogy. Imagine that you build houses for a living, and all of your plans and techniques assume that you will get lumber dimensioned in eight-foot lengths. Now assume that the regulatory environment changes. Perhaps because of some far-off legislation regarding some beetle somewhere, you can only get lumber in six-foot lengths. Can you still build houses? Of course you can. They will be more expensive, and require that you change your plans, but you can still build houses, odd as they may now appear. In our analogy, the techniques are the market forces, the lumber is the regulatory environment and labor pool upon which you can draw, while your plans are still your plans.

To understand how our modern world perverts classical economics, you have to first understand classical economics itself. The seminal work in that field is a book written in the mid-1700s, entitled "The Wealth of Nations", written by Adam Smith.

Reading Assignment
The Wealth of Nations
by Adam Smith

Sadly, that book has fallen by the wayside in modern education. In fact, if you ask a hundred graduates with a Master of Business Administration degree, woefully few will have ever read this book, if they even know what it is. And yet, it is chock full of goodness.

Most references to that book in formal education are limited to attempts to discredit it. Most of the attempted discrediting references a socialist named John Maynard Keynes (pronounced "Canes") and his book "The General Theory of Employment, Interest and Money". Interesting, isn't it, that modern business and economics curricula teach the socialist discrediting of this book, but not the book itself? More on that later, but you should start feeling swirlings of that healthy suspicion of formal education I discussed earlier.

"The Wealth of Nations" is a huge book, many hundreds of pages long. It is best read as a text instead of online since it is tough to read in a few sittings. Read the first third of it right now, and give yourself assignments to read thirty to forty pages a day until complete. As you read that book, imagine yourself a mid-1800s farmer or proprietor of a cottage industry. In his day, that book was already a hundred years old. But it was written from the perspective of someone who wasn't that far removed from his everyday experience.

While reading it, you have to insulate yourself from the pre-conceived notions of slavery in that era. Assume that for all intents and purposes slavery doesn't even exist, because those thoughts have been used as a tool to cloud economic thought for a century and a half.

When done with that book, you can reward yourself with the knowledge that in this one important respect you are far ahead of most MBAs you will ever meet. It is fun at parties to ask one if they've ever read this book. Do this a few times and you won't be troubled by having to attend very many parties where MBAs are in attendance.

There is a reason that MBAs get uncomfortable when you discuss that book with them. And why so few of them were able to finish it, even if, with a probability approaching zero, it had been assigned during their studies. By the end of *this* book, you will understand why. And then smile at your own understanding of their discomfiture.

Here are some important consequences of your reading of that book, and important topics you should glean from it. Page number references are of little help since different printings will give different page numbers. I'm also going to avoid giving you specific sections as references, as I want you to read the entire thing and not cheat by just reading the portions I reference. That book is, no kidding, the foundation for everything else I will say for the rest of this text, and must be read from cover to cover for fullest understanding.

Imagine yourself a peasant in Smith's time, and free to work for whomever you choose. You want to scratch together a little extra coin, for purposes to be named later, and so you start working out a plan. There are many things you can do to raise extra money, such as ask your boss if you can work an extra hour or day. Or maybe find a broken fence and offer a farmer your services to fix it. Or, let a chicken run around out behind your shack and save money on eggs.

Or you might ask the farmer if you can lease a corner of some scrub land to grow more chickens. To pay the rent you offer to keep his paths clear or deliver a cleaned chicken to his wife every Sunday, saving her the trouble. Regardless, you wind up with a source of meat under your control, saving you the cost. Maybe you'll even give another peasant a chicken in exchange for his helping you clear the farmer's paths. The list goes on but there is a common thread among them which we'll discuss in later chapters.

Contrast this to your modern situation. You can ask your boss to work an extra hour or day, but he won't be willing to allow it, in most cases. Why? Not because he is mean, but because if he says yes, then, by law, he is required to pay you overtime rates for that work. Under those conditions, it is simply cheaper for him to hire someone else for that task.

This regulatory influence means that instead of working more at a job at which you are effective and capable, you have to take on a second job. For this second job you are probably doing something at which you are less capable. Thus, you are less valuable and earn less for your time. So much less that if your value to the second boss falls below the minimum wage, you don't get the job. Everyone loses, and the bottom line is that you don't own your hours. The state owns them, and you only get to sell them, and your boss only gets to buy them, in whatever quantity the state allows.

Mend the broken fence? Forget it. The farmer can't afford to hire you. He is subject to the same wage regulations as your boss. In addition, for that job he would have to report you not only as a wage-earning employee, but also as a laborer qualifying for workmen's compensation. Worse, he can not distinguish you from a scam artist looking for a "slip and fall" lawsuit. Regardless, the sheer volume of paperwork for logging you as an employee and filling out the workmen's compensation insurance rolls makes that broken fence just wait a little longer. And the potential increase in value for everyone vanishes.

Maybe you could help the farmer out by incorporating, and thus take upon yourself the responsibilities of handling taxes and workmen's compensation. Chances are, if you are destitute enough to need to take on that fence job to get that extra coin you aren't in any position to start wading through those waters. At least until you read this book.

Chicken? Manicured subdivision? I think not. Or, in many jurisdictions health regulations prevent housing livestock within an area containing so many persons per acre, and so on. Better take that minimum wage coin to the grocer instead.

Lease land from the farmer? If you think it is a nightmare for him to hire you to fix a fence, imagine the terror of wading through a lease. It will cost him hundreds of dollars, minimum, to even get started with having a lawyer look it over. Add to that his legal risks should you hurt yourself or your chickens get loose and flap a driver into a tree. Now that scrub land isn't looking so bad as it is.

Add to all of these your own issues such as dealing with the health department after that backyard fiasco. Then mix in the tax laws which regulate barter and exchange transactions. Now that welfare check isn't looking like so much of a disgrace.

Hire another peasant to help you clean the scrub land? Congratulations, you just became boss and farmer rolled into one. Get ready for the hassles of both. Workplace safety, environmental regulations, food and drug compliance issues, taxes, insurance, liability and the entire mountain of modern employment just fell upon your starving peasant shoulders. Now stop dreaming and get back to your miserable life from which there is no lawful escape.

Wow. Now let's try some other topics from Smith's book.

In Smith's world, the reason to squirrel away some extra coin is that you then have the chance to become your own boss. As your own boss, you might then manage your own day to the best of your abilities. Our first hypothetical peasant might deal with the farmer to provide mutual benefit, and then perhaps hire another peasant to assist with the requisite labor. Similarly, that second peasant might go into the scrub-clearing business himself. However, in our modern world the hurdle to even start your own business means that most will never try. And the few that do face such a regulatory uphill battle that most fail very quickly.

The only purpose for the state, in Smith's classical model, is to prevent fraud or theft. If peasant number three steals chickens from your leased lot, the magistrate handles that. And the barrister takes care of things should you fail to clear the scrub as you promised. You pay taxes to support the first, and fees to support the second, with the sheriff, also supported by taxes, standing by to enforce the judgements.

But in our modern world, and to a greater degree, the state becomes an instrument of coercion to allow the transfer of ill-gotten gains. Including those ill-gotten gains such as the settlement of a frivolous lawsuit. Or, through the blunt-handed intrusion of paperwork and regulations, the state prevents the free exchange of labor, services and material itself.

Smith writes from the perspective of a subject of the British monarchy. As such, the feudal system had just been overthrown, but much of that system still lingered in his time in the form of land ownership and rents. So, Smith's farmer doesn't necessarily own his land, but instead rents it for long periods, essentially for life, from a lord or the king. This, by the way is the origin of the term "landlord", or lord of the land which you are renting to till. If you are a lord in that day, you can choose to rent to whomever you wish, as long as they are willing to pay. You can also decide not to rent to someone for whatever reason you choose, but you would be foolish to turn down good money.

As far as the farmer is concerned, he may be induced to give up his current lease to another farmer through a suitable cash payment. After this transaction is completed, the second farmer is then free to use the land, but now he must pay rent to the lord or king or be booted off. Note that it is absolutely irrelevant how much the second farmer paid to the first farmer for the right to take up the lease.

In modern terms, imagine if the second farmer paid the first farmer four hundred thousand dollars for the right to lease from the lord for four thousand dollars a year. But, the second farmer's failure to pay the lord the relatively small sum per year invalidates the entire lease. Viewed this way, you don't own your house, you only own the right to pay the lease, which we call property tax, to the county lord. When you sell a house, you are really just selling that lease to another. If you rent, not even your landlord owns the house. He just, in turn, pays his own version of protection money to the king.

That last one should have hit you in the stomach. If it didn't, you're not paying attention and the rest of this book will be of little value to you. You own nothing. The king, meaning in our case the state, and thus *the people*, do. Your right to property is a fiction. Yet right to property is a cornerstone of a free people. You are not free if you cannot own and build from what you have. You are merely a servant in a collectivist state. Governments, and collectivists, love property taxes as you must slave away to pay them even if your efforts put not one scrap of food on your own table.

You may start to see why no one teaches from Adam Smith's book anymore. Radical stuff. Particularly if you want to convince someone to go off to war and fight for a set of freedoms. Freedoms which include your right to property, or right to sell your time and services to others for whatever terms you can agree upon. Freedoms which don't really exist and haven't for a very long time.

Beyond that, though, the economic principles involved are just as valid today as before. You just have to substitute "machine" for "worker" and then Smith's work applies word for word. We'll see how in more detail as we progress.

Once you have absorbed Adam Smith's seminal work, you will then be ready for some philosophy. So go off and read an even larger book:

Reading Assignment
Atlas Shrugged
by Ayn Rand

Ayn Rand was a brilliant lady. She was also a refugee from socialism. About a half-century ago she wrote that book to highlight the dangers of socialism which she saw following her to this country. At the time she wrote that classic work of economic fiction her ideas seemed a little paranoid.

Now her ideas seem prophetic.

Ask a hundred people who have heard of that book, and very few will have been able to finish it. That's a good screening tool right there, by the way. Most who start reading it have to eventually put it aside as it makes them feel kind of bad. Those who finish it tend to like it.

Like it a lot, in fact.

Some of the economic nonsense which we suffer through today was predicted by Ayn in that book. The names of various policies are different, but the policies themselves are eerily similar.

She was wrong about a couple of things, though. First, the book completely ignores children, except for a couple of helpful waifs. Those who might want to take her ideas to heart, and to implement them directly, might run into a problem when they take the needs of their children to heart. Unfortunately, to some degree or another one's children in the modern world are held hostage to your compliance with popular reason. For example, very few cubicle slaves would choose their lifestyle if they didn't have kids to take care of.

After you read this book, though, you might find a solution to this dilemma. It turns out that you can apply Ayn's ideas, even if you have children. And they will probably benefit from the experience.

She was also wrong about her understanding of the nature of collectives. In her eyes, the collective responds to the heroes of the story in an almost childishly gentle way. In reality, however, the collective is far more aggressive about stamping out dissent from individuals. With brutality, if necessary.

Ayn was also a bit naive about the character of the man on the street. Later portions of this book will highlight where my thoughts diverge from hers.

Once those two books are under your belt, you need to read the essential explanation of evolutionary principles:

Reading Assignment
The Selfish Gene
by Richard Dawkins

Warning: Theologians hate that book and its author with a hell-fire burning passion. I have actually been dis-invited from speaking at theological seminaries after recommending that book as part of the preparatory material for the attendees.

Dawkins wrote that book in 1976, and then released an update in 1989. He then released a 30th anniversary edition in 2006. Get the anniversary edition if you can, it has some pretty interesting notes and changes in it.

The central theme of the book is how organisms and ideas evolve over time. Organisms evolve through the use of genes, while ideas, in Dawkin's terminology, evolve through the use of *memes*. Meme is a word which means memory, or idea, genes.

Dawkins also explains that Darwin didn't really explain evolution, he just expounded a theory which could explain some characteristics of animals. Like it or not, evolution is a fact of life. Does that mean that men evolved from monkeys or that God didn't create life? Of course not. Evolution is no better equipped to explain the origin of life than creationism, or even the best of science. No one, to my knowledge, has yet to explain how to create a cellulose molecule from water and carbon using mechanisms which are built of cellulose and self-replicating. Or even how to build up a cellulose molecule from glucose molecules. Much less how to use that cellulose molecule, along with lots of other stuff, to make that mechanism which we call a cell.

And while we're putting requirements on scientists, let's add in the nifty detail of making this hypothetical mechanism run on solar energy. And eat carbon dioxide and water for raw materials. And spit out pure oxygen as a waste product. And look pretty. And smell good. And make more of itself.

Wow. We can't even figure out a really good way of breaking cellulose down into its constituent glucose molecules. At least without using special bacteria, another living thing which we can't make, to help us. If we could crack that nut, we would have an unlimited amount of food and liquid fuel at our disposal.

Yet a cow does exactly this all day long. Using those same bacteria, which evolution equipped it with. And which we found using brains which evolution provided us with. But neither evolution nor creationism explains how that bacteria works, or how the cow came to have some of them along with special organs to host them. Other than, "because."

In my opinion, evolution works because that's what God designed it to do. Evolution explains lots of things, like why stupid results in bad stuff. Or at least why it should. Evolutionary forces are at work around us, and the best examples of evolution involve those memes. Bad ideas should die out. When we promote bad ideas over good ideas, bad things start to happen. Continuing to do this constitutes a worse idea.

Eventually, the bad things will get bad enough that the brains which promote the worse ideas will run out of stuff like food. And then die. Along with a lot of other brains which didn't having anything at all to do with the worse ideas. Other than not getting rid of those other brains first. And that tolerance is just another kind of worse idea all by itself, isn't it?

See how cool evolution is? If you take away that concept from Dawkin's book, you will see how to direct the natural forces which surround you in ways that benefit you, instead of fighting those forces and losing.

You will also be able to spot those bad ideas and the worse ideas. And understand why bad and worse ideas seem to take over for a while. And why the brains which promote those ideas can't last for very long.

The other key take-away from "The Selfish Gene" is the idea of *suckers*, *cheaters* and *grudgers*. To take the time to explain this concept would take another book, but fortunately Dawkins has already written it all down in his. In a nutshell, lots of human behavior can be boiled down into those three, or suitable variations thereof. There have been philosophical arguments over the most valid ways in which those behaviors can interact with each other to form civilizations.

One day, as Dawkins tells it, some guy named Axelrod did some computer simulations about these ideas. He simplified some aspects of the problem, and made other aspects more complicated, and even opened up some of the simulation to other experts. This is so interesting that my son and I spent a couple of months reproducing these results during our homeschool philosophy and computer science courses. By the way, my son was thirteen at the time we studied this. If he had been in public school, the only philosophy he would have experienced is a meaningful discussion of why plants cry.

Axelrod's results were surprising, as are Dawkin's interpretation of these results. But on reflection, you can see how they make sense by looking around at people you know. And once their behavior makes sense to you, you will realize that a lot of people suck.

Here is a very simplified version of these results. Imagine a world of suckers. Because they are all suckers, no one cheats anybody out of anything. Everyone lives happily ever after.

Now insert one cheater. This cheater can cheat suckers all day long. And prosper like crazy. And then reproduce like crazy. At some point, though, the cheaters start bumping up against each other. And then they stop prospering so much. They still prosper way more than suckers, mind you, but not as much as they did before.

And then, the cheaters start maintaining herds of suckers. Why? Because it is much easier to sucker a captive herd than it is to go out and find a new sucker. Especially if you might run across a fellow cheater. It will take time to figure out you are dealing with another cheater, and like the guy says on TV, "I can't do this all day." The cheater also doesn't want to suck his suckers dry, as it would cut down on his goodies. He also doesn't want some other cheater horning in on his suckers.

The suckers and the cheater will reach a kind of equilibrium, and again, everyone lives happily ever after, except the suckers have a lower quality of life than they would without the cheater. But, since they are suckers, they don't mind.

Now introduce the grudger. A grudger acts like a sucker once. But as soon he encounters a cheater, he puts the cheater on his list. And then our grudger beats the hell out of the cheater every time he sees him again.

Suckers are no problem for the grudger, because he never cheats them, and they never cheat him. Absent a cheater, the suckers would also get along fine with a grudger, or any number of them.

But the cheaters mind the grudger quite a bit, as you might imagine. As much as it sucks to waste time with a fellow cheater, running into a grudger can ruin his whole day. All those hell-beatings get in the way of his cheating, after all.

The cheater's response? Turn his herd of suckers against the grudger.

The cheater's herd is composed of suckers, after all, and easily fooled into thinking the grudger is a problem. The cheaters will also learn to team up with the other cheaters and get all their suckers to turn on the grudger, too. "That bastard has to be stamped out, and hard, before he ruins it for all of us," the cheaters agree among themselves. The suckers are happy to oblige with this universal action. Because, after all, say it together, "they are suckers."

So, in a society of suckers and cheaters, a lone grudger has to act like a sucker and just suck it up when he runs across a cheater. Or, he has to get on the cheating train and start running around cheating. Either choice is anathema to his grudger nature, and causes him a great deal of personal anxiety. But, absent a way to wipe all the cheaters out, it is pretty much the only choice which allows him to avoid, say, a stoning.

By the way, a society filled with grudgers would get along fine. As would a mix of grudgers and suckers. It's the cheaters who are the problem, but the suckers are too sucky to figure that out.

With all the grudgers fading into the background acting like suckers or cheaters and getting ulcers from the stress, it is hard for one grudger to recognize another. Just having the conversation might set off all the alarms the cheaters have installed. Even the suckers will sound the alarm for the cheaters, as they have been instructed to do. But if grudgers could team up, in sufficient numbers, they might have a chance to pick off all the cheaters.

Every last one of them.

You will get more of the flavor for the sucker/cheater/grudger concepts from reading Dawkin's book, but you should have the gist of it by now. After you finish reading my book, the one you are reading now, you might want to revisit the dilemma which the hypothetical grudger faces.

And consider a possible solution to his problem.

Dawkins has another book out, "The God Delusion," which is purportedly a scholarly refutation of the existence of God. I don't know for sure, because I haven't read it yet. So, I really can't say anything good or bad about it. I do know that it has theologians in a tizzy. They are so enraged or offended by the latter book that they then, apparently, transfer that rage onto the first.

I've seen this happen for myself. I can have a great conversation with someone about "The Selfish Gene" until I mention the author's name. If they have been briefed in about "The God Delusion" they then shut down, or at least try to quickly change the topic. His stuff is that powerful. One day I'm going to have to read the latter book and see what all the hub-bub is about. In the meantime, I don't think my faith is in any jeopardy from anyone's point of view. I have no doubt that God created the universe. I just question some of the religious notions which people embrace about the details.

It doesn't matter to me whether the universe is five thousand years old or five billion years or whatever. I know enough about science to know that not even the brightest of us can explain most of it. And we are a long, long way from being able to replicate even a slightest fraction of His Creation.

Or for that matter, even harness it for our use. Or to say with confidence that my use of some of it is bad and your use of some of it is good.

The most beautiful description of creation I have ever seen is found in Ben Stein's documentary about the debate surrounding the origin of life:

> **Video Assignment**
> *EXPELLED: No Intelligence Allowed*

To me, Ben's description of how a cell works, and how we know so little about it, is one of the most touching parts of the entire film. We know so little about so many things that it is foolish to allow anyone to do our thinking for us. God gave us individual minds for a reason. This film also explores the depths to which a collective will sink to crush opposing points of view. It shows many examples in which the liberal collective crushes any discussion of creation, or even of intelligent design versus evolution. And yet, the creation folks can get just as snippy. In their collectives, they also tend to cast out any demons who think differently from them.

I think both extremes of behavior are bad, because both camps want to shut down individual thought and replace it with conformance. Some pundits, even the very successful ones, claim that refusing to adopt an extreme point of view makes one a moderate, and then defines moderation as evil.

Am I a moderate? Probably not. When you are done reading this book, assess me in this regard yourself. I think it is OK to take an extreme position on anything you like, provided that you came to that extreme position by your own thought. And so long as you don't try to force those opinions on anyone else. Try convincing them instead. But be warned, if you approach a discussion with a pure heart you may wind up walking away with your own mind changed. Which is why discussion is so often stunted.

We can discuss opinions and ideas all day long, as heatedly as need be. But when those opinions begin to express themselves as coercion of others, through law or custom, then a line has been crossed. And what suffers as a result is individual liberty as one collective or another uses force to suppress, at first, ideas, and then uses force to constrain action.

Just as my faith in God cannot be shaken by anyone, I am not threatened by anyone else having a different opinion. I could have a great conversation with an atheist or a pope or a rabbi or a mullah or a pagan with equal irreverence. The latter probably has cuter outfits for the chicks, though. Some of these guys, on the other hand, will have a hard time having that conversation with me.

If you are the kind who will have a hard time having that conversation, then you are not going to be able to finish this book. Go ahead and put it down now and get back to your orthodoxy. You'll sleep better that way.

Now that you have been exposed to some of the underlying principles of this book, it is time to talk about where money comes from. Or more appropriately, where money came from, and how the monkey ethic evolved from that.

Chapter 4, Caveman Capitalism™

People start their own businesses, or prepare for crises, for a variety of reasons. In all cases, one key reason for these actions is to provide a source of money, or equivalently, resources, under their own control. So, for any degree of success, one needs to be able to answer the following question:

Where does money (or other resources) come from?

Or, with more flourish:

From whence come money (or other resources)?

This is a simple question. Why do some people have more money or other resources than they need, but others barely have any? This is a question which has been about since the dawn of man. The answer has nothing to do with anything you have ever been told. If you had been told the right answer before, you wouldn't need to be reading this book!

One might also ask the related question: *And whither is money traveling?* For if you can be at its destination it will flow to you naturally. As it turns out, money flows to specific places just as water will find its own level by flowing downhill. Or at least until someone builds a money dam upstream of you. Remarkably, preparing for a crisis, manmade or otherwise, is equivalent to operating a small business. And, done correctly, either can provide an unlimited amount of resources by trading with your fellow productive man, while avoiding the monkeys who eat from your plate.

We now travel back in time to that dawn of man and observe from a safe vantage point. Imagine you are Johnny Caveman. Picking berries is OK, but rats and squirrels just feel better on the tummy. If they are cooked, of course. But how do you know *that*? You really don't, but cooking over a fire just seems, well, right.

The reason it seems that way is that all the grubby cavemen and cavebabes who don't cook their rats tend to keel over at a faster rate than those who do. Over time, the cavelings from the cookers' loins outnumber those from the salmonellated, e-coliated, and trichinosated crowd. Not only is there a cultural influence at work here (Mommy Do, Baby See), but also this natural selection starts to weave its way into the genes. And so, cooked meat imbues an unparalleled satisfaction to our modern palettes. Or provides a way for the collective to identify individuals who might be inclined to crack cheaters in the head if said cheaters steal from them.

Perhaps one tribesman, Og, big, burly and strong, isn't stealthy at all while hunting squirrels, but can haul around a lot of those sticks. And then break them up into smaller sticks with that big rock. Meanwhile, Pok, being small, wiry and fast, can catch squirrels like there is no tomorrow. The day that Pok and Og agree that "Pok give Og four squirrel, Og give Pok half-woman-weight wood", commerce is born, at least in Tribe 1.

On the other hand, over the hill at Tribe 2 a different transaction takes place. If "Og.2 take squirrel from Pok.2" is followed closely by "Pok.2 stick squirrel poke in Og.2 squishy place", then all hell breaks loose.

Correspondingly, Tribe 2 will have fewer resources being produced and more fighting. This may, evolutionarily speaking, produce better fighters, but will necessarily result in fewer resources to fight over.

Natural selection and cultural influences tended to make cooking more likely. Similarly, the commerce version of events cause some tribes (Tribe 1) to be more successful than the Og vs. Pok variety (Tribe 2). For one thing, there wind up being more Og.1 and Pok.1 with rocks and pointy sticks than the remaining Og.2 and Pok.2.

One day, this theory of evolution was put to the test when Og.2 and/or Pok.2 wandered upon Tribe 1. Og.2 and Pok.2 may get away with a raid or two. But eventually, Mar (Og.1's son) and Cor (Pok.1's son), both of which are great at hunting deer, decide to go into the combined arms business on behalf of Tribe 1. In exchange for a squirrel or two and some wood, these guys, using a combination of forward defenses and flank raids, wipe out all opposition to the relatively peaceful and commerce-driven Tribe 1. And chicks dig it. Tribe 1 just got bigger.

Big enough, in fact, to put some guys in business hollowing out gourds with which Mar and Cor carry berries and dried squirrel meat to the front. In exchange for some squirrels and wood, of course. And those same gourds work great for soaking acorns in (thanks, squirrels!) once Tan found out that acorn juice makes squirrel and deer skins tough and long-lasting. Vin finds out that if he leaves some berry juice in a gourd after his cavebabe stepped on them while gathering, then what results is a nice juice which chicks also dig. More growth for Tribe 1, as well as another tribal startup.

Hidden within the few paragraphs of that little tale are all the elements of modern society. Free will versus force, collectivism versus individualism, creation versus destruction, fraud and theft and envy, good and evil, virtue and vice. We'll handle the dark sides of these balances in a bit. The commercial side of these concepts is fleshed in much more fully in the classic volume of economics. Be sure to put "The Wealth of Nations" on your reading list to fully comprehend these points. If possible, start giving yourself daily reading assignments out of it right now. Just don't be lulled into thinking, as I did, that when Adam Smith discusses employees that you have to hire employees as we define them today. More on this distinction later, including the idea that most of the best employees either don't work for you at all, or live in a metal box and look a lot like a computer. Or have hydraulic hoses all over them and get paid in diesel and grease.

So back to our tribe. Clearly, Tribe 1 created money in the form of wood, squirrels, gourds, deer meat, leather and wine. Using this currency, other goods and services are available to anyone with the will to acquire these. In the case of each of the tribe members, the requisite will simply involves work, and not violence or theft or fraud. Og goes out into the forest and drags back wood while Pok traps squirrels and so on.

Each individual in our tribe has decided for themselves how they might best add value for themselves. And at each exchange, each individual's quality of life has improved, sometimes by imperceptible amounts. Should an exchange be offered at a deficit to either party, in a fair marketplace each party has the option to decline the exchange.

Consider what might happen if Og were to try to trap squirrels instead of hauling wood. Perhaps his approach might be to knock down a tree with a squirrel nest atop it. Clearly, the squirrel might leap away to safety, or decide that this forest is a little too uncertain and the whole lot moves out entirely. Maybe on average Og might get a squirrel a day or, generously two, that way. In that same amount of time Pok might get eight squirrels, or Og himself might gather an entire woman-weight of wood.

Now let's turn the tables and set out Pok to haul in wood. Whereas Og could drag home a fallen tree knocked down in the storm last month, little Pok might only be able to uproot and drag home saplings or fallen sticks. Maybe on average Pok hauls home a leg-weight (or equivalently, one quarter-woman-weight) of fallen or uprooted fresh wood each day, leaving the larger fallen trees to rot.

Notice also the effects on resource management. Pok's squirrel-hunting approach leaves the nests, and thus future generations of squirrels, undamaged. His approach results in an ongoing maintenance, and possibly growth, of the squirrel population. But Og's more clumsy efforts totally strips the forest of squirrels quickly.

On the wood side of the economy, Og hauls out large falls, with relatively drier wood. This wood is a better fuel, woman-weight for woman-weight, than the rotten sticks or fresh saplings which Pok can get. Og's forest management will leave an entire range of growth available, including protective mulch on the ground.

But Pok's efforts will segregate the forest into very large and very small trees, the medium growth having been aborted while very young. Yet a storm might wipe out the entire large growth, leaving the bulk to rot unused while Pok strips out the remaining saplings. Worse, these saplings now struggle against encroaching weeds without the protective overhead cover of their older generations, or protective mulch preventing erosion. One day, no wood. But by focusing on the resources which each can best manage, the cooperation between Og and Pok produces more resources for both.

Consider one scenario, then, of how Og and Pok might spend two days, one day gathering wood and one day hunting squirrels. On the first day, Og and Pok each spends his time with his favored resource. At the end of that day, Og has one woman-weight of wood, while Pok has eight squirrels:

Day	Action	Og		Pok	
		Wood	Squirrel	Wood	Squirrel
1	Start	0.00	0	0.00	0
	Work	+1.00	0	0.00	+8
	Trade	0.00	0	0.00	0
	Net	**1.00**	**0**	**0.00**	**8**

The next day they switch tasks, and Og manages to get two squirrels, while Pok gets a quarter-woman-weight of wood:

Day	Action	Og		Pok	
		Wood	Squirrel	Wood	Squirrel
2	Start	1.00	0	0.00	8
	Work	0.00	2	0.25	0
	Trade	0.00	0	0.00	0
	Net	**1.00**	**2**	**0.25**	**8**

At this point, Og has one woman-weight of wood and two squirrels, while Pok has a quarter-weight of wood and eight squirrels.

Now let our heroes focus solely on their respective specialties, and then trade for their other resources. At the end of the first day, Og gathers a woman-weight, and Pok gets eight squirrels. They then meet on the hilltop at the lightered post to trade. Og and Pok exchange a half-woman-weight of wood and four squirrels respectively. Each then walks away with a half-woman-weight and four squirrels.

Day	Action	Og		Pok	
		Wood	Squirrel	Wood	Squirrel
1	Start	0.00	0	0.00	0
	Work	+1.00	0	0.00	+8
	Trade	-0.50	+4	+0.50	-4
	Net	**0.50**	**4**	**0.50**	**4**

The next day, the same gather-hunt-trade cycle repeats, and now each has a woman-weight of wood, and eight squirrels:

Day	Action	Og		Pok	
		Wood	Squirrel	Wood	Squirrel
2	Start	0.50	4	0.50	4
	Work	+1.00	0	0.00	+8
	Trade	-0.50	+4	+0.50	-4
	Net	**1.00**	**8**	**1.00**	**8**

Note now that Og still has a woman-weight of wood, but now has eight squirrels instead of only two. Similarly, Pok still has eight squirrels, but now has an entire woman-weight of wood rather than only one quarter-weight. Each man gained significantly *from the trade alone.*

Equality of outcome, meaning that each actor winds up with equal resources, was an accident in this case, and not instrumental to the point. I could have just as well adjusted the numbers to result in unequal outcome, but then I wouldn't have had the opportunity to explain the accident. Enforcing equality of outcome would be called *socialism.*

Had each man just simply decided to meet and share the wealth, then one might decide to be lazy, or otherwise cheat the other. Pok may one day decide to show up with only six squirrels, perhaps, or Og with only a half-woman's weight of wood. Whichever man starts to bring less to the sharing table, the other would soon learn his lesson and bring less also. In a socialist economy, there would be no incentive to provide one's best, since each would expect the other to provide *his* best, regardless. Any scheme to attain equality of outcome will always lead to a progressive downward spiral of resources for all.

But with their free trade model, each man gets more for himself by providing the best he can offer in trade to the other. So, the self-interested trade itself, almost as if by magic, has increased the quality of life of each man, as well as having protected future resources.

☐ *Classical wealth comes from providing value, specifically, a higher quality of life, to other people.*

Each man has worked two days for these resources. Alone, each would spend one day on his favored resource, and then have to spend four days on the other to get to the same condition. By trading their best work, each man has effectively accomplished five days of work in only two:

Outcome With Work Alone

Day	Action	Og		Pok	
		Wood	Squirrel	Wood	Squirrel
1	Work	+1.00	0	0.00	8
2	Work	0.00	2	+0.25	0
3	Work	0.00	2	+0.25	0
4	Work	0.00	2	+0.25	0
5	Work	0.00	2	+0.25	0
	Net	1.00	8	1.00	8

Outcome With Work Plus Trade

Day	Action	Og		Pok	
		Wood	Squirrel	Wood	Squirrel
1	Work	+1.00	0	0.00	8
	Trade	-0.50	+4	+0.50	-4
2	Work	+1.00	0	0.00	8
	Trade	-0.50	+4	+0.50	-4
	Net	**1.00**	**8**	**1.00**	**8**

Recognizing this, each tribesman elects to spend one of those saved days in careful reflection by a babbling brook, considering the wisdom of his past actions, and planning future work.

One thing which occurs to each of them is that to each man the trades he made are positive experiences from his own perspective. Wood is more valuable to Pok than squirrels, while to Og squirrels are the more valuable resource. And so, Pok happily accepts a half-woman-weight of wood, representing a two-day effort, to give up four squirrels, which represents a half-day of work for him. The reverse trade would not appear to be a good deal for Pok. Similarly, Og is happy with the direction of trade, but not its reverse.

Each man has decided for himself which trades to accept and which to decline. These selfish decisions lead to not only greater resources for a given amount of work, but also a feeling of good will and well-deserved self-esteem. And, each is willing to continue to make this trade each day, knowing that each benefits more than they would without trading. To the recipient, each trade improves their condition.

☐ *Consistently providing more value than you are getting paid will lead to endless opportunities.*

Now expand this single pair of trades over the entire population. It then becomes clear that, in a short period of time, goods and services of all kinds will soon become more available to all. And each week, more and more people will be spending time sitting around thinking instead of scrambling for subsistence. Most of this thinking turns in productive directions, each remembering how tough it was to haul in wood and trap squirrels and fish and gather berries each day. And they think about how things are looking pretty good now. But for some, their thoughts begin to wander off the path.

Let's peek in on some of the productive thoughts first, we'll return to the darker side of things later. Sitting by the stream with daddy Pok, Pok Jr., Cor's little brother, thinks about how things are good, but squirrels are just too darn three-dimensional. But rabbits, he notices, don't climb trees.

So one day Pok, Jr. wanders off into the storm fall and comes back with a whole tangle of fresh branches, too small and green to be useable firewood. Toiling away in his off hours from trapping squirrels, Pok Jr. constructs the world's first bunny hutch and begins breeding rabbits. Soon, Pok Jr.'s bunny ranch provides the ability to spend the day gathering shoots and grasses to feed the bunnies. And yet, with less work, Pok Jr. can provide the same amount of meat for trade which would otherwise require setting and checking squirrel traps. Lucky rabbit's foot, indeed.

☐ *An investment in effort or knowledge effectively allows you to store value for later use.*

Before long, Pok's back yard was full of bunny pellets from junior's bunny ranch. Pok grew weary of this, and sent his daughter Pokette out to haul the bunny pellets away and throw them into the adjacent field. Scantily clad in her tail-tasseled squirrel bikini and fuzzy bunny lace-up slippers, she started hauling the pellets into the field by the gourd-load.

This activity soon attracted the attention of Ahks, Og's younger son, who found reason to be tramping through the field each day. This trampling effectively plowed the pellets under, and soon the grasses were growing like crazy. Soon, the Poks spent less time wandering around in search of grasses, and more time tending their rabbit herd. Productivity improved once again.

☐ *Removing a quality of life detractor from yourself or someone else will often present unique opportunities for you which didn't exist before.*

Amidst the grasses grew brambles as well. One day, about a year back, Pokette was hanging out with Beri, Vin's daughter. Beri had come back from gathering those delicious purple fruit when the two of them got into a giggling berry fight, much to the amusement of Ahks and Pok Jr.

A year later Beri had a baby who looked strangely like Pok Jr. While tending this child a now-harried Beri noticed that those green brambles where she had berry-fought Pokette. She realized that those brambles looked like half of the brambles in her favorite gathering patches. Sitting by the stream washing the baby one day the light comes on in her head, and she realizes that there are two phases of bramble fruit. One year, green shoots grow but bear no fruit, while the next year what had been green shoots are now brown but bear fruit. She realizes now that in her ignorance she had been stomping out of the way the next year's brambles to get to this year's fruit. Which explained, of course, why the brambles which do bear fruit look so trampled and the fruit so hard to reach.

Beri decided to act on this knowledge and prepared an experiment. She arranged with Pok Jr. to haul off all the rabbit pellets he can manage to produce. Finding a little field near her father's hut, she spread the pellets out and called a berry fight among the local ladies. On a whim, Beri charged the interested gentlemen a squirrel or rabbit there, an armful of wood or gourds or leather there, and opened for business.

Sure enough, the next year her field was full of green brambles, and the original field outside of Pok's hut had bearing brambles. These latter have been trampled out of the way to get to those grasses which the bunnies so enjoy. She then decided to cultivate a second field, fertilized with another growing mound of rabbit pellets courtesy of Pok Jr. And, to make her harvest the next year easier, she tied the growing green brambles into stands using honeysuckle vines, leaving easy lanes between the stands.

The next year, Beri's stand of brambles and her annual berry fight proceeds made her the richest girl in the tribe. The bramble stands were so easily managed that even little purple-faced Beryl could toddle among them eating the low berries. The child learned to walk among them with hardly a scratch.

As for Pok Jr., he had already taken a fondness for the little Beryl, and decided to move his bunny ranch next to Beri's fields as the two of them built a hut together. "Smart, hot and rich", he thinks to himself as he watches her and the baby. "Plus, she doesn't mind taking crap off of me."

☐ *Watch the natural rhythms of the world, and learn to nudge them in a direction favorable for you and your customers, rather than push against them. And take in, or host, a berry fight every now and then.*

Growing up many years prior to the berry fights, Ahks would watch his father, Og, and Mar, his older brother, working on the larger tree falls while gathering wood each day. From time to time the men would beat on the falls with large rocks to weaken the wood in order to better split or break it. Or, the men might lever the larger logs with medium logs to add stress. Little Ahks would toddle up and attempt to imitate them, as he would beat vainly on the wood with a smallish rock. Mar, barely older than a teen himself, would laugh and say, "your arms are too little, Ahks, as were mine at your age."

Years later, and growing toward his thirteenth year, Ahks, feeling his growing muscles, threw several heavy rocks off an embankment. One larger rock had crashed into the stream bed below, and cracked into several slivers. For days, he carefully stepped past these slivers as he chased minnows and wondered why Pokette didn't seem as annoying as she had last year. Maybe those squirrel tassels she wore were from her father's fluffier squirrels. Lost in those thoughts, the shards caught his eye, and he imagined putting the rock back together as he tried to fit the pieces into a whole.

Out of curiosity Ahks picked up one of the slivers and carried it to the glen where his father and brother were working. As Og pulled back on a branch, Mar was hammering away with a large rock at the bend. Taking a break, Mar stepped aside and Ahks shot into his place. Beating upon the bend with the sharp edge, the fibers began to separate. Og was amused by this as well, and said "Ahks, if your arms were longer that might help. Now get out of the way and let your brother work. Get back to catching those minnows, that weir on the river isn't going to bait itself."

Inspired, Ahks had an idea about how to get a longer arm. If Og and Mar could make their arms longer by using logs, he could make his arms longer, too. He selected a broken branch with a crook at the end, and tied his blade in the crook with some squirrel leather. This was a miserable failure, as he soon discovered as he chopped at a log. The head simply fell off the branch on impact.

Next, Ahks put the blade in the end of the branch, and struck the flat back of the blade with another rock to drive it in. He had seen his brother and father doing exactly this when they wanted to split a log. The branch split halfway, ruining his handle.

This inspired Ahks to first wrap the next branch part way up in squirrel leather, preventing the blade from penetrating too far. This worked as desired, but now the blade was stuck, as was Ahks for a few days. Until he saw his brother retrieve a stuck splitting rock by hammering a branch into the notch, relieving the pressure. Ahks did the same, writ small, by beating a twig into the split between the blade and the leather. The blade didn't fall free, but loosened enough to turn it sideways. Ahks then wrapped the top of the branch above the blade with more leather. And then gave it a try.

This new tool worked. For a few tries anyway, until the blade retreated into the branch. For months, this was his state of the art, until one day Pokette walked by with a gourd of rabbit pellets. As she cast these about, he noticed that for some reason, her hips had grown since last year. No longer did her body drop straight from her shoulders to her legs. No, now she had a dip at her waist, and her hips swelled more fully, her sleek, tanned legs tapering into her little bunny boots.

Each day, Ahks would take the longer path to the glen, waving at Pokette as she cast about the pellets. She pretended not to notice, but turned in ways which he couldn't help noticing. One day, as he walked by her, Mar approached from the other direction.

"Where have you been, and what has been taking you so long each day?" he shouted at his little brother across the field. Ahks said nothing, but continued staring.

Following his gaze, Mar understood. And laughed. "Go take a dip in the cool stream. Then, catch up with Dad and I in the south glen, we've got a lot of branches to haul today," slapping his little brother on the back.

The cool water helped, indeed. All day, though, hauling branches, Ahks alternately thought about Pokette, her hips, and his barely functional tool. The blade was still slipping out, which really just made it a curiosity, rather than something useful. Again, progress was stalled, his thoughts elsewhere.

Until one day, almost a year later, Ahks heard giggling and laughing from the field near Pok's hut. Running, not knowing why, he ran to the edge of the field where Pok Jr. was watching Beri and Pokette throwing berries at each other. As usual, the older Pok Jr. barely noticed him. But after a time Pok Jr. rushed in and grabbed Beri, two years older than Pokette, by the waist. She pretended to fight him, smearing him with berries also. Soon the two of them ran into the forest, Pok Jr. grabbing at her more generous hips and her squirming away, giggling and laughing. As they ran out of sight, Pokette stared at Ahks for a minute, blushed, and fled for her father's hut.

Suddenly, the inspiration hit him. Just as Pok Jr. had grabbed Beri by the waist, so might a properly shaped blade be grabbed by the handle, preventing it from being pushed through the handle by the blow. Seizing his best blade, Ahks soon put a waist into each side of it with a blunt rock, and after a few adjustments, it was finished. He rushed to the glen where his father and brother were harvesting wood. The first blow, and the next and the next proved the idea. Within minutes, with Mar applying leverage, the tool cut through the fibers of the branch, severing it in far less time than would be required without the blade or the handle. And the blade stayed in place throughout.

Soon, Ahks had made larger versions of the tool for his brother and father, and their output doubled. Og, freed of the necessity for his younger son's labor, set him to work instead refining his craft. Ahks soon had stone and wood tools of every variety, from axes, splitters and shavers to hand tools for cutting smaller branches. And even an arm-sized axe which Mar took to war when necessary, as well as stone tips for Cor's lances.

Ahks also began to learn how to select the right kinds of rock for different tools, and could almost "see" the tool head hiding within each rock as he moved it in his hands. Using this knowledge, and his growing experience bordering on geology, he also improved the tools which helped him make implements for others in exchange for their own produce. Soon, rocks which others moved aside or ignored became valuable resources, and trees and falls which had been out of reach of harvest became accessible.

As for Pokette, one day she didn't flee to her father's hut, but instead stood her ground as Ahks approached her, their eyes locked. Some time later, Ahks made Pokette a little stone knife to help her cut food for the baby girl, whom they called Hatchette.

☐ *Invest in tool making[2]. Find those areas of effort which you can automate away, if not avoid entirely. You may fail many times in these efforts, but keep trying, your inspiration for success may come unexpectedly to your subconscious mind.*

Across the valley, Ken and his woman Chi weren't fortunate enough to have a forest with squirrels. Instead, they had only a meadow and a couple of fields of low scrub. But, chubby birds loved to grouse around in the scrub looking for the bugs and beetles which lived there. Each day or two Chi and Ken would find one of these birds and catch it as it was flapping off, barely flying. The eggs, while small, were also delicious, so finding a nest was a nice bonus.

---

[2] We shall discuss many ways in which you can make tools to help your work, even in the modern world. This may require you to acquire new skills. More later.

One day, Chi just fell in love with a particularly chubby little hen and begged Ken to let her keep it as a pet instead of having it as dinner. Ken relented, and soon the little hen was following Chi around as she cleaned up the hut, looking for bugs which would go scampering underfoot. As it turned out, the chubby hen had a little nest under a fallen tree. Soon, there were yellow little chicks waddling around, each nearly as chubby as their mother. Chi and Ken were delighted at this turn of events. Having seen Pok Jr.'s bunny hutches the pair decided to build a hut for the birds off the ground to protect them from snakes and liberals, I mean, weasels.

Chi and Ken were soon aswarm in chubby little birds, who grew fat and lazy with the abundance of bugs in and about the hut and their droppings. To keep them from escaping, Ken would chase after the more athletic birds as dinner. So the bird population soon became chubbier and chubbier. As for the birds' droppings, the couple followed Beri and Pokette's experience and spread them onto a nearby grain outcrop, and were amazed that the next year the amount of grain tripled. It was as if the little birds, which the tribe soon began to call Chi-Kens, were a blessing straight from God Himself.

Before long, Chi and Ken had more eggs than they could eat themselves. They began traveling the valley with gourds of eggs, trading them for wood, squirrel, rabbit, leather, berries, wine and tools. It became obvious very quickly that a negotiated price of four eggs for a rabbit would produce either a frown or a smile depending upon the size of the eggs in question. As a result, Ken decided that he and Chi would eat the smaller eggs, and save the larger eggs for trade as those would bring a higher return in traded goods.

One day, Ken fell sick and was unable to make his bird and egg rounds for a couple of days. As a result, the larger eggs never made it to the trading gourd. These, rolled out of sight by the hens, later hatched and grew into largish, plumper Chi-Kens. After a few months it became apparent that these larger Chi-Kens themselves produced the large eggs in general, and onto the dinner plate fell most of the smaller Chi-Ken eggs.

☐ *Unexpected events, including accidents and tragedies, will often perturb the normal flow of life and create new opportunities if you will pay attention.*

This turn of events gave Ken an idea as he sat by the stream wondering upon his discovery and now seeing that couple of days of sickness as a blessing. As he looked at the babbling water he imagined little Chi-Kens laying little eggs, and big Chi-Kens laying big eggs. Or little eggs making little Chi-Kens, and big eggs making big Chi-Kens, depending on which came first.

He decided to conduct a scientific experiment. He built several little pens and kept the birds hatched from the smaller eggs segregated from those hatched from the larger eggs. After a year or so, he noticed that there wasn't necessarily a one-to-one correlation between egg size and chicken size. But, there did seem to be a strong correlation between egg sizes between generations, and more importantly, a correlation between chicken sizes between generations.

He and Chi decided they would eat the smaller Chi-Kens and eggs, and reserve the larger Chi-Kens and eggs for trade. But, he reasoned, if he traded away the largest eggs and birds, then soon everyone else in the valley would have birds larger than his. Just as he was pondering this issue, a wise old man named Tith walked up to his hut.

In another less tolerant time, a man such as Tith would have been stoned as a witch or medicated as autistic. As a young boy he was known to wander around the fields at day and by night, living on what he found. Tith would study the most minute detail of a single plant for days, tasting, smelling, pinching. He had a little set of rocks which he would use to crush seeds and leaves that he kept in a leather pouch tied to his waist. Often, he would be found outside in storms, watching the skies. It was said by some that God spoke to him during storms.

As a young man Tith became a hero of the tribe when a storm arose. A family took shelter under a tree near a hillside. Noticing this, and during the worst of the storm, Tith ran to them and begged them to seek shelter elsewhere. Frightened, they relented and followed him downhill into a stream bed. Within minutes, lightning struck the tree which they had sheltered underneath. As this story spread through the tribe, he gained his reputation for wisdom and his advice was considered by all, and often paid for by gifts of wood or meat. Soon after that, it was said that he traveled to far away lands, often returning with strange seeds in curious little pouches, only to leave again soon afterward on another adventure.

Tith had a small hut of his own, which never seemed to be wet inside, and a remarkable variety of wonderful plants happened to grow nearby. He would trade portions of these plants at particular times of the year, but some who picked these plants for themselves would fall ill. Others seemed to have demonic possession for a time, or in some cases, fell dead. The tribe soon learned to leave the harvest of these particular plants to Tith himself.

Tith's most remarkable crop, however, was a carefully ordered arrangement of stones which the old man would fuss over in the moonlight. He was often seen walking back and forth, stopping to stare at the stars as they wheeled overhead, making slight adjustments to positions of his rocks on the ground.

Anyone who stopped by Tith's hut would be treated to a sip of the best water anyone had ever tasted, drawn from a spring bubbling between the rocks on a nearby hillside. Whenever anyone suffered an injury and sought his help, Tith could be counted on to show up with a mixture of herbs from his plants to ease their pain. At times he cast these mixtures onto the fire in the hut. Other times he offered the ailing a strange-tasting drink. His presence alone had a calming effect, and his treatments were welcomed with relief. Even those for whom there was no hope benefitted from Tith's treatments as he helped ease their pain during their departure.

That day, Ken was so lost in thought that he didn't see Tith approaching. As Ken thought, Tith stood there watching him, a smile twinkling in the old man's eyes. As was normal for him, the old man said nothing until spoken to. Eventually, Ken turned and, startled, noticed the old man standing behind him.

"Tith, I didn't see you there, you frightened me", Ken gasped.

"It isn't yet time for anyone to be frightened by someone like me," Tith said, smiling, looking over the hillside as if seeing into the future.

"What?" Ken asked. "Never mind," the old man replied, turning back to Ken, "it seems like you've been thinking hard about something."

"I have," Ken admitted, telling the old man about the dilemma he had been pondering. As Ken spoke, Tith nodded knowingly, and began beaming almost like a parent might when his child began to walk.

"You are wise to eat the smaller birds and eggs for yourself, and trade only the larger," Tith acknowledged when Ken had finished. "And, you are correct that if you trade the larger that you will be harming your flock in the long term." He then paused to wait for the question he knew would come.

"Then how can I trade the best and not harm my flock?" Ken asked, knowing Tith's manner.

"How does God make both the wolf and the rabbit fast?" Tith asked, waiting patiently.

"Well, the wolf can easily catch the slow rabbit, leaving only the faster to make little rabbits," Ken answered. "And the wolf?" Tith asked. The light dawned on Ken's face as he suddenly understood, "And the faster wolves will eat better, and be more likely to make faster cubs."

"Then do as God teaches you from His own work," Tith answered. "I leave the best one of ten of my plants for Him in the field. You leave the best one in ten in your nests, trade the best of the remainder, and eat the dross yourself."

Ken was almost embarrassed at the simplicity of the answer. After all, he had nearly arrived there himself with his Chi-Ken and egg experiment. Nonetheless, he resolved to implement Tith's suggestion. So, Ken elected to reserve one in ten of the best birds and eggs, thus saving them for God to work His genetic miracle on their behalf. He and Chi traded the remainder. This plan worked as desired, and soon he and Chi had the reputation for the best birds and eggs in the valley.

Their reputation was so impressive that at the next berry fight festival, Pok Jr. asked Ken to rise and tell the tribe of their success. Tith, having just passed away a week before, was fresh in all their minds. So, Ken decided to honor the old man who had given them all so much wisdom and comfort during his life. After Ken's telling of the technique and its inspiration, more than a few left the festival that summer determined to apply for themselves the method.

And so, one in ten, the plumpest berries remained in the fields for seed, the most prolific rabbits were preserved for breeding. The largest Chi-Kens and the largest eggs, the straightest trees in the forest, were all reserved for God and His protection of man and provision for his needs. Soon the tribe grew in strength and size. And they weathered famines which decimated others, following the method which would become known as "Tithing", in honor of the old man's wisdom.

☐ *Reinvest in yourself and your business by nurturing the best of your work and ideas. Don't let your old habits drag you down into unproductive effort. Eat your less valuable assets (or worst losses) and move on to focus on the better things which appear before you.*

On one of Mar and Cor's campaigns they met a woman whose village had been destroyed by the very barbarians they were chasing. K'ette, as she was known, offered to help them find the barbarians. After that work was done, Mar invited K'ette back to the tribe. She agreed, having formed a respect and admiration for Mar's character and abilities.

After they returned, Og informed his son and new daughter-of-choice that the lightered post at which he and Pok often traded wood and squirrels was becoming more popular among other members of the tribe. The other tribesmen had begun to meet there in the evenings to trade goods among themselves. However, some tribe members who lived farther away were unable to travel there each evening, only arriving once in several days, or, in some cases, weeks apart. Sadly, some of these goods from far away were the most valuable, and it was rare that two distant tribesmen would arrive on the same day. So, even some of the local tribesmen were beginning to wonder whether they should be bringing their goods elsewhere. This would be a bitter blow to Og and Pok, and the other local tribesmen, who would then have to spend their time traveling elsewhere.

"I've seen this problem before," K'ette said, as she was stroking through her hair with a squirrel rib Ahks had mounted to a little stick as a gift to her. "One of the first huts to be raided in our village was the trading hut where people would come to swap items. The owner of the hut kept some of the items traded and stored them in the hut to allow others to trade for them long after the original trader had left."

Og, Mar and Ahks all thought this was a great idea. Soon, the four of them had constructed a new hut for Mar and his wife to operate as a trading hut. This turned out to be a perfect occupation for Mar. Between campaigns Mar had nothing else to do but help his father with the lumber business. And, he always had a collection of items paid to him by the rest of the tribesmen for his defense services. Some of these items Mar had no immediate use for, but others might. So, the trading hut was started with an assortment of the goods Mar had collected, and a selection of Ahks' tools and Og's wood.

Soon, Pok brought squirrels and Pok Jr. brought some bunnies in little cages. Grasses from Pokette, fermented juices from Vin, acorns and leather from Tan. Some of these items K'ette and her husband consumed directly, such as feeding acorns to the squirrels to sustain them, and similarly with the grasses for the bunnies. Some items she and Mar consumed themselves, and the remainder went on the shelves Mar made of split logs. As with the agricultural practice of tithing, they saved the best of each item for trading, while consuming the least or the oldest stock for themselves. The very best she would trade to the farther tribesmen to allow them to carry as much value as possible in smaller packs on their return trips. This practice had the additional bonus of providing the best possible image of them at the tribal frontier.

And so, word soon spread among the tribe about this marvelous hut, which became known as the Mar-K'ette hut. Some tribesmen began to arrive in the morning, this being more convenient for them as they were not yet tired from their work, and could think more clearly about their needs.

Even Ahsee, Tith's apprentice, traded with little pouches of herbs and ointments he felt were less dangerous for the tribesmen to use on their own. Ahsee, who bore a strange likeness to the old man and to whom the wise one left his entire estate before he died, instructed K'ette in their use.

And the tribesmen from far away began to show up more often with larger packs, as they no longer needed to linger to trade. Thus the space normally taken for extra provisions was dedicated to trade goods instead.

At first, Mar and K'ette tried to establish a price for each item in terms of each other item. For example, a woman-weight of wood might be worth so many squirrels, a different number of bunnies, and yet another number of Ahks' tools in a bewildering variety. Similarly, each of Ahks' tools had to be assigned a number of squirrels, bunnies, and fractional woman-weight of wood. These calculations, which had been performed all along by each tribesman before the Mar-K'ette was established, soon became too complex and error-prone to be useful.

So, following the example of her village, K'ette and Mar soon established a measure of units which each item was worth. Two values were assigned to each item, one as the price at which they would pay for an item. Another, higher, price was the number of units of value required to purchase an item from them. The first price K'ette called the *bid*, while the second she called the *ask*. As an example, Og received sixteen units of value for a woman-weight of wood, this being the bid price. But, that same wood could be purchased for twenty-four units, this being their ask price.

Similarly, Pok's squirrels would bring him two units of value, yet someone wishing to purchase a squirrel would have to provide three units. The difference in these values allowed Mar and K'ette to provide for themselves. They might store this value for their later use, whether for trade or for enjoyment. As a result, they could accept from others, and thus provide to others, a wider variety of goods available for trade. This additional amount also helped them cover their risk for loss, such as for storms or the occasional dead bunny or squirrel.

In turn, the tribesmen did not begrudge them their profit. The tribesmen were still able to trade among themselves, as Og and Pok continued to do among themselves. But most found the convenience of the Mar-K'ette, both in time spent trading and the complexity of calculation, well worth the difference in prices there.

In earlier times, after Pok had traded for all the wood he needed, Og might have additional wood remaining. Then Og or his sons would have had to spend hours or days at the lightered post waiting for enough tribesmen to arrive for his wood. Instead, they could now spend this time working, enjoying their families, or resting and reflecting.

As with Og's early trades with Pok, the tribesmen prospered merely from the availability of trade to take their goods at prices they thought reasonable, or to decline trades if not. This concept K'ette called liquidity, evocative of the ease at which the stream passes by rocks in its path.

☐ *Facilitating a higher quality of life by removing obstacles from the paths of other persons is itself a valuable service.*

In the tribe there was a man whose right leg was almost useless. As a child, Tab was bit on the leg by a snake, had suffered a terrible fever, and it was thought that he would die. Tith managed to treat the child and save his life, but the boy's leg was festered terribly. Normally, the tribe would have cut off the leg, almost certainly killing the child in the process. Instead, Tith treated his leg with concoctions which boiled but grew not hot, and fed the child bread which was green with rot. The child recovered, but the leg remained weak; strong enough to stand upon and drag behind him, but too weak to run or carry heavy loads.

Recovered, Tab spent his days by the stream watching and learning. Although he wished that he could play with the other children, he learned instead to use his mind. Tab spent his time making little toys of wood, bone, leather and strings he wove of bits of fur left behind in the forest as the deer wandered through thickets. Some of these toys would leap from hiding, to the delight of boys and shrieks of girls.

Boys and girls alike would trade bits of things with Tab for his little contraptions. Their parents would trade for his bone fishhooks and animal snares, which included a three-pronged device which was perfect for catching snakes. Snakes, as it turned out, were Tab's favorite delicacy, and he also traded dried snake meat and snake skins with the others. Soon, his reputation as an artificer grew far and wide among the tribe, and he was as successful as any, despite his weakened leg.

But still, his leg prevented him from traveling as much as he would like. His latest adventures would find him on bright sunny days sitting in a stream bed sifting through the clay for bright little rocks. Tab had discovered that these rocks were capable of cutting any other rocks, but were difficult to find. On stormy days he chose to remain in his hut working on some contraption or another, leaving him only the overcast days in which to trade with others. So, when he heard of the Mar-K'ette hut, he leapt in his heart at the opportunity.

As a result, one day soon after Tab arrived at the hut with a bundle of items on his back. Mar was delighted to see him and began telling K'ette excitedly about all the things Tab made. The pair quickly agreed to offer his items for sale. That one load alone was worth an entire woman-weight of wood, which of course, Tab was unable to carry back to his hut in one trip.

"K'ette, as you can see I can't carry all this wood, and I really don't have a need for it right now," he explained. Tab, as usual, was unembarrassed by his disability and treated it simply as the fact it was. "I would like for you to keep most of it in your hut for me for a while." Just as the words left his mouth, and she was nodding assent, transfixed by the wonders on the slab in front of her, he had a better idea.

His keen mind now saw a new opportunity. "Actually, what I would rather you do is, instead of keeping my wood, simply keep a record of the number of credits to which I would otherwise be entitled," he explained. "Then, I can come in, or better, send for any item I need at the time and you can remove this amount from my credits."

Before she could answer, he thought of his determination to not burden others with his disability. So, he added, "In exchange for the extra work for you to keep track of this for me, I will surrender one credit each full moon. Agreed?" K'ette thought this was a great idea, and wished that this had been done in her old village.

Soon, the other tribesmen realized the convenience this could offer them, even the strong and well-bodied. Og, for example, might often have a particularly fruitful week gathering wood after a storm. But, he might have needed only so many bunnies or so much fruit each day. Or Ahks might spend weeks making tools from a generous outcropping of rock, but not want to carry a heavy load each day to the Mar-K'ette. Instead, he may have enjoyed a leisurely walk to get a bunny or some berries there.

This *tabulation*, as it became known, allowed the tribesmen to perform work at times best for them. And to purchase at times best for them, rather than being limited by the weather, seasons, or other uncertainties.

Tabulation had another benefit, as well. The tribesmen soon learned that it was more convenient to trade among each other, not with goods themselves, but also by arranging for services paid for by credits. For example, if a man helped repair another's hut, they might agree to pay the first as three credits from the last's account. By so doing, the helper could then choose whatever items he wished from the Mar-K'ette's shelves. This was much more flexible than being constrained by the beneficiary's goods on hand at that moment. All they had to do was to check-in at the hut and ask Mar or K'ette to transfer the appropriate credits from one to the other.

In this fashion, the original trading benefit which Og and Pok first discovered for goods, then refined through market liquidity, became extended to services as well.

Before long, it seemed that everyone wanted to keep their credits with the Mar-K'ette. And so K'ette had numerous little slate rocks for each family in the tribe, with little marks scratched on them representing their credits. Each full moon, as payment for her service in these transactions, she would deduct one credit from each slate by marking across a credit mark. Each credit she removed, by consent of the account owner, thus gave her and Mar more complete ownership of goods which remained on the shelves.

These slates she purchased from Ahks. And the scratches? Made with those special glittery rocks, which she purchased from Tab. How purchased? With scratches on his slate, of course, effectively transferring value from her shelf to him.

☐ *Don't be thwarted by your limitations or disabilities. Instead, focus on what you can do well, and turn these assets, and your solutions to your own limitations, into opportunities for yourself and others.*

One winter a disease swept through the tribe, and many fell ill. One family in particular was hit very hard, killing both the mother and father. Their deaths left the teenage boy, Ploi, and pre-teen girl, Emma, to fend for themselves. But, they had been taught by their parents from a very young age, as were most children in the tribe. Accordingly, they were far more capable of fending for themselves than might otherwise be expected in our modern world.

One morning Ploi saw K'ette carry a dead bunny out of the trading hut and stopped her to ask what had happened. An exhausted K'ette replied, "I found this bunny dead in its cage this morning, and it appears that it had been underfed. Mar and I have been working so hard with keeping track of all the trades and all our inventory. So, with all that work as well as handling the account tablets, I haven't had time to feed them well."

This gave Ploi an idea. He pointed out to K'ette, "If my sister were to tend to the rabbits, many fewer would die, and the rest would be healthy and worth more for the trade. Is this correct?" K'ette nodded assent.

"So, it would be as if my sister were bringing in fresh rabbits and trading them for the dead and unhealthy ones," he continued. "As such, she would be entitled to credits for these trades, right?" K'ette again nodded.

"Similarly, I could help you manage your other inventory. See that wood over there rotting in the weeds?" he said, pointing to a pile which had just simply fallen into neglect because Mar and K'ette had been so busy.

Ploi then stated the costs to her, "That wood is almost worthless now, hardly anyone wants it. If I were working for you, and a trader wanted wood, I could bring the oldest inventory, none of which would be very old. And, then none would go bad, so you would get to keep more credits for yourself." K'ette began to see the many ways in which Ploi might help in and around the trading hut.

"As for now, I propose to work for you today helping you organize your stock, and I will take that old wood for myself in exchange. Tomorrow I will come with my sister and we will help you manage your stock. I will direct her work, as well as do my own. I would like to receive four credits per day for my work. She should receive three credits each day for hers, as she is small. Do you agree to these terms?"

K'ette agreed to try this new arrangement for a moon. Ploi immediately set to work carefully stacking and organizing the wood. He also cut, with one of Ahks' blades, the grass which had grown around the piles and which was trapping moisture. He fed this grass to the bunnies, and brought them fresh water. At the end of the day, he fashioned a sled out of some of the old wood, stacked the remainder atop it, and hauled it away to his hut.

Seeing him arrive, his sister was delighted. "Ploi, where did you get this wood?" she asked as she began to build a fire. "I can't believe that you found this old wood in one place, it should have taken you days to find this much," she wondered. Ploi stacked the wood loosely where the sun and air would dry it over the next several days. As he worked, Ploi told her, "Emma, you are correct, this much old wood would normally take many days to find. But, I worked for only one day for this wood. And, once it has dried, it will serve as kindling for us for months, making it easier for us to start our fires."

Ploi then told Emma of his arrangement with K'ette, and that she would be working each day as he directed. When he told his sister about the credits she would receive for each day of work, she was astonished. "You don't mean it," she shouted. "It would take me a day and a half of hard work in the heat and rain to catch a squirrel or two to trade to bring that much. Instead, I get to tend bunnies in their hutches?"

"And other little tasks I assign during the day," he reminded her.

"But still," she said, "that is much easier than chasing and trapping squirrels! Sometimes I think the wildcats and boars are chasing *me*. I think I am going to love this!"

Mar was similarly impressed with the arrangement when he returned from a trip a week later. By then, the stock in and about the hut was much better organized and well tended. The bunnies and squirrels and Chi-Kens were healthy in their cages, and, most pleasing, K'ette had much more energy at the end of the day. Plus, by then, Ploi had had the idea of delivering goods to the local tribesmen, much as Mar was doing for the distant.

Of all of the tribe, Tab was the most pleased with the delivery service, as this meant that he didn't have to make so many trips to the hut. This convenience for him was especially true as Ploi would often bring his traps and snake skins back to the trading hut on his return trips, to be credited to the crippled man's slate. Other tribesmen soon availed themselves of this service. So, the amount of trade for the hut increased, simply by allowing Mar and K'ette to delegate some of their work to the two orphaned children. These children, in turn, benefitted by being able to work together each day, and much more safely and more profitably than would have been possible without the employment.

☐ *Even the destitute and unfortunate are capable of providing value for themselves. Similarly, each time you are faced with what seems like an insurmountable misfortune, find ways in which you can make even little steps toward self-sufficiency by providing value to others.*

During these years of relative peace Cor had traveled to more distant lands. He had returned from these trips with some large animals. These looked to the tribe like large, antler-less harts, but were very tame and friendly around the tribesmen. Cor was riding one of them as he arrived at his father's hut, the remainder gathered with leather straps around their heads. "My son," Pok exclaimed as he grabbed the young man and hugged him, "where have you been for so long?"

"Away, far away, father," Cor replied. "And I have brought you a gift to help with your work," he said, pointing to the animals. "In the land from which these come they are called 'cheval'," he said. "And I, am going to raise them," the young man stated, sweeping his arm across the valley.

Following his son's gesture, Pok happened to notice a beautiful black-haired girl riding atop one of the smaller cheval. He was fascinated by the unusual color of her skin. On her, it was stunning. "And what do you call this lovely creature?" Pok asked, grinning, "do you propose to raise these as well?"

"Perhaps, father," Cor laughed. "She is Mowneek, and she is my wife, but she does not understand our language very well. Yet."

Hearing her name, she smiled, and Cor went to her to help her dismount. Watching them, Pok thought the gesture an act which seemed more a caress than a necessity. To him, Mowneek seemed nimble enough to mount and dismount anything she pleased, with or without assistance.

Alighting, she swiftly and skillfully led the cheval into the field to graze and to drink at the stream. The cheval followed her happily, even without the straps.

The next morning, Cor, riding one cheval and another in tow, rode to Tab's hut. The men spoke briefly, after which Cor taught Tab to mount the second animal and ride. Given Tab's attention to detail, and his exceptional upper body strength, he was a swift learner. Tab prepared them both a delicious lunch of snake stew, and then the two rode to Mar's trading hut. Mar, hearing the clopping of the chevals, met them at the rise of the trail west of the hut. Og, Ahks and Tan, having been visited by Cor the previous evening, were just arriving as well.

"Cor, my friend," he shouted, "it has been so long!" The two men slapped each other on the back, and then Mar turned to the cheval Cor had been riding. "I had heard of these from Tith, and how they are used, but I have never seen one before. Chevals, aren't they?" Mar asked. Cor nodded in reply.

"Then if I remember Tith's stories well enough, I think I know why you both are here," Mar said, watching Tab dismount.

The six men then sat in the shade of an oak tree in the field as the chevals grazed nearby. First, Cor explained that he was going to start breeding and selling cheval from his land, as well as instructing the tribesmen of their care and use. He warned that his plans would create both opportunity and challenge for the tribe. He then told of the many uses to which the cheval had been employed.

Og, the elder of the six, was the next to speak as Tab unlimbered a leather pouch of materials he brought with him. Tab then began to lay the sticks and other items in front of him. The woodman explained how Cor, the previous evening, had demonstrated the power of the cheval to haul wood falls out of the forest. The chevals were also useful to apply more tension to the boughs as they were being chopped. Og estimated that with a cheval two men might do the work of six or eight. Ahks, who had assisted with the demonstration, agreed. Mar suddenly realized that the wood sledge Og was describing could also be used to haul goods for trade.

While they were discussing this use of the cheval, Tab had built a little model of sticks. He dragged this through the dirt in front of them. "Look how easily this can dig six furrows instead of only one a man might make by himself", he said.

Mar argued, having tried a similar thing himself as a boy, "But what you have made will just bounce around on top of the ground and barely scratch it."

"Not if you weight it with stones," Ahks interjected, remembering laughing at his brother pulling that contraption long ago. "You even tried that yourself, but it was too heavy for you to pull. Not too heavy for that beast over there, though," he added.

All agreed that use of the cheval represented a revolutionary change in how many tasks could be done. It was at this time that Cor stood up to speak. He described in detail the leather straps which were needed for harnesses. He also told them how the sledge and the harrow would require timber portions of the appropriate size, held together with additional leather straps. In addition, the harrow would require stones for weight. Ahks also pointed out that the harrow would be best served with stone blades, rather than wood points. "But who would build these implements?" Mar asked, each man guessing the answer already.

"I will," Tab responded. "I will buy the leather from Tan, all he can supply. The timber I will buy from Og, and stone blades from Ahks. Each of you will supply materials dimensioned according to the instructions I will give. When I have them done, I can trade them to Mar for his credits. I will divide these credits among myself, Tan, Og, and Ahks, in proportion to the materials, their quality, and the work which each supplied. Or, each man can take in trade the harnesses and implements for themselves."

"Won't this be more work than you can handle?" Mar asked, worried about losing Tab's traps and other legacy trade items. Ploi's delivery work had increased Tab's trap-making output measurably, he didn't want to set that back now. "It is possible that each man in the tribe will want one or two cheval each, once they understand how much work can be done with them."

"Not at all. I've recently taken on an apprentice, Tak. He is better suited for leatherwork and large items such as this than for the fine work of trap-making," Tab assured him.

"There is one more thing," Cor interjected. "The cheval is a powerful animal, but needs care also. Each one requires a stone's square of grazing, and a similar amount of grass even through the winter moons. Also, if a cheval becomes sick, it must be treated quickly or it will surely die."

As each man considered this, Cor added, "The kingdom from which I brought the cheval had already solved these problems." *But created other, more fatal problems, some of which grow closer each day*, he didn't say. "I will show Tab how to make a rake implement which can gather the grass behind a cheval. This implement is used much like a harrow, but instead rolls the cut grass for storage. The people are already cutting the grass for trade themselves with Ahks' tools. But, to store the grasses they will have to let it dry first. I will explain these ideas to each man when they come to trade for a cheval."

"The second problem is more severe," Cor warned. "Mowneek knows how to treat these animals for common problems, but she needs the proper herbs and ointments to do so. That Ahsee, Tith's apprentice, is he any good?"

"Almost as good as the old man himself," Mar proclaimed, "and in some ways better. He has saved many and their animals this past year alone." But not all, he thought to himself as he remembered the loss of Ploi and Emma's parents.

"Good," Cor sighed, relieved that Tith had passed along his knowledge so well. "Mowneek and I will go see him tomorrow to help him know what to grow and blend."

By then the sun was setting, and so the men parted ways and agreed to begin the cheval enterprise right away. By the time of that year's berry fight Tab had some implements ready, and two of the pregnant cheval which Cor brought with him had already birthed their foals. At this festival Cor gave the tribe a demonstration of their use. He also explained that while it would take four or five years to build up a sufficient number of them for trade, he had already sent away for more adults. "In the meantime, before my friends return with more, I can help you use my stock on your own work," he assured the crowd.

During the demonstration of the harrow, Pok Jr. put one hand on Beri's face and his other on her hip. He whispered in that mockingly serious tone of his, "Who needs a cheval? If I could get Tab to make a harness like that for you, I bet you could pull a little one-stone harrow yourself." That earned him a elbow to the ribs and an involuntary blushing smile from Beri, who had thought she had heard it all with the bunny pellet humor. Even little Beryl ran around for over a year calling her "Pellet Wife", surely at Pok Jr.'s coaching. The arrival of the cheval would surely only usher in a new era of Pok Jr.'s twisted humor at her expense.

During the next few years more cheval arrived. The harness and implement business grew as fast as Tak could make them. And so did the ability of the tribe to feed itself and survive winters, droughts, and famines. The tribe once again surged in prosperity, their growth and sustenance no longer limited by the energy available from the sum of the tribe's muscles.

And, under Mowneek's tutelage, Ahsee learned which herbs to grow, and how to prepare their mixtures and ointments to best heal injured or sickly cheval. At first, Cor paid Ahsee with credits to plant the herbs in the early years to support his cheval business. But later, as more tribesmen sought him out Ahsee funded the cultivation of these plants from his own work and credits.

Eventually, any disease or injury, man or animal, was referred to Ahsee's hut and lands, or as it became more simply known, the Farm Ahsee.

☐ *A group of individuals, acting in their own self-interest, can accomplish remarkable and revolutionary things. Don't be fooled into thinking that only large, traditional organizations are the sole source of value. Often, in our modern economy, these companies are merely a conduit for payments for value which originates from small sub-contractors, rather than as sources of value themselves.*

In this chapter I've taken a detour off the normal beaten economics path to make the point that economic principles are very simple. So simple, in fact, that it is easy to ramble on for pages with little stories of happy, trusting cavemen who trade fairly among themselves to improve their lives and the lives of those around them. I could keep going with stories about banking, currency, corporations, investments, foreign trade, etc., but the point has been made already. I'll save those for a children's book, perhaps.

If these stories brought a little tear to your eye, longing for that simple life of innate goodness, but knowing that these ideas can't survive in the modern world, then pat yourself on the back. This book is for you.

If you read these passages, and thought about how to wade through these simpletons, cheating them at every turn, then put this book down now. You won't like how it ends.

If you felt angry at having some key points of your world view exposed to the light, then you probably should put this book down also, and just pretend that these ideas don't exist. Or pretend that you can stamp ideas out through force, via stoning, perhaps. On the other hand, these latter types probably gave up reading this book pages ago anyway.

However, if, as you read these passages, you thought to yourself that these stories are simply the happy naive capitalist equivalent of hippie commune utopias, you missed the point. This error is not your fault, it is the fault of the societal programming to which you have been exposed your entire life. The good news is that you can correct this programming defect any time you wish, as we shall soon see.

Chapter 5, Prancing Rabbits

As I mentioned briefly in the last chapter, the stories about our caveman capitalists illustrate simple economic principles which have been deliberately perverted in our modern world. Some might argue that these stories are fundamentally no different than the simplistic socialist models which have always failed throughout history. In a later chapter we will inject modern reality, and show how the collectivist model has been overlaid on top of our honest cavemen to destroy them. But for now, let's compare the caveman theme to socialist utopias.

The key difference between these caveman utopian stories, and the hippie commune variety, is that the stories in this book show how individuals might improve their lives through their *honest self-interest alone*. The almost-magical, yet easily understood action of the free market and individual decisions ensures that *everyone who participates fairly prospers*. And, when honest self-interest is unfettered there is practically no limit to the quality of life, for everyone who participates, which can be obtained over time.

Conversely, the hippie commune requires a suppression of some, or one, individual's interests for the benefit of the group. Without a *constant injection of external value*, the hippie commune *always fails*.

The communities of the caveman capitalist and the enlightened hippie share several key features, though.

Both communities suffer privation. The key difference is that the caveman capitalist tries to solve privation, while the enlightened hippie treats privation as a virtue. The caveman capitalist's status and value to the community is determined by profiting by enriching the lives of others, the more the better. Contrarily, the hippie's status and value to the community is determined by how much a person is willing to coerce others into self-sacrifice.

Both communities are vulnerable to fraud, theft, and other negative human realities. We shall explore in a later chapter how the caveman capitalist learns to handle these issues, and the attendant risks. History has shown us how the hippie commune uses these negative issues as a resource for greater suppression of the individual. More on that in a moment.

To be fair, hippie communes aren't the only societal groups which:

☐ Value personal privation as a virtue.
☐ Take specific actions calculated to increase the amount of privation in the population as a whole, yet disguise these actions as good works.
☐ Proclaim that only through acceptance of the group's values can man be set free or saved from privation, even that privation deliberately created by the group itself.
☐ Deem self-interest so negative as to be destroyed at all costs.
☐ Seek to suppress individualistic thought or action.
☐ Coerce individuals into self-sacrifice, specifically targeting those who display self-interest.
☐ Reward most those persons in the group best capable of recruiting

victims or imposing more of the above.

In fact, some of the hippie communes were established specifically as a revolt against some of these other groups, only to emulate their worst features. If this last analysis hit you in the gut and made you angry at me, without my even revealing these other groups directly, you really need to put this book down now. On the other hand, if you felt that rush which only comes from truth revealed, keep reading.

While writing this book I delayed working on this chapter, not having a concise example of commune living from which to draw victims. Then one day, the fates smiled upon me.

First Wife and I recently moved our business to the boondocks to work on some alternative energy and agribusiness projects. A few weeks after having our satellite DVR installed, I saw a reality-ish program which seemed to epitomize the struggle between unfettered capitalism and socialist utopian visions.

Video Assignment
Watch the *30 Days* episode "Off The Grid" regarding the Dancing Rabbit green commune. You can probably find that episode online somewhere.

In that episode, a hapless couple, convicted of destroying the planet, were frog-marched off to an indoctrination camp, named Dancing Rabbit, there to be reeducated. To reinforce their guilt, they were told that if everyone on Earth had a similar lifestyle, 12.5 planets would be required to support them. If this claim is true, I want to be on the side which has free markets, freedom of speech, and all those other good things. I heard there's a list somewhere. Add in a 600-ship navy and nuclear weapons. So equipped, we could then probably trim the staff back a little to get down to under one planet. Planet saved!

You can read more about Dancing Rabbit at their website. The episode is referenced on their site at:

Internet Research
http://www.dancingrabbit.org/30Days.php

This episode touched me deeply. And caused an uncontrollable gagging reflex (despite the fact that I have no uvula. If uncertain of what this means, look it up).

For example. One "expert" on that show claimed that grocery store vegetable baggies will last a *hundred thousand years*. Clearly, this individual doesn't understand place value, nor has she ever dropped anything in a Mississippi swamp. First Wife pointed out that the pyramids are made of stone. These are fortunate enough to have spent their entire time in an arid, preserving climate, and yet, are falling apart. And they are only a few thousand years old.

The hypocrisy of these groups also touches me. The alpha-choad of the group met the unlucky couple in a really nice chariot, only to immediately announce how self-sufficient their community was by fueling it with biodiesel. Really. Uhh, what cabbage patch disgorged that nice diesel car? I need some of those seeds. Oh, and that road you are driving it on didn't just grade itself and dig those ditches down the side, either, bucko.

Later in the episode they went around begging for biodiesel fuel stock from restaurants. I didn't catch how that would work if everyone lived like them. They also dumpster-dived for supplies. Again, if we all lived like them, there would be no trash to scavenge. For a practical exercise in this strategy, visit a Goodwill™ store in a prosperous area versus one in say, mid-town Detroit. When I tried this, I found a big difference in the quality of items available. Try it for yourself and check me.

During this treasure hunt, the prancing rabbits happened to find a nearly new hair dryer, which is exactly what one of the victims needed. Seek and ye shall find, indeed. Interestingly, this rare find happened to be carefully wrapped in plastic (gasp) against the ravages of the trash. It has been a long time since I thought something worth throwing away deserved being carefully preserved so that communists could find it later. I'm not saying it was planted there, though.

To make a point about self-sufficiency, they trucked in a $20,000 solar power system and mounted it on a post in the evening shade. For one thing, I don't understand where the $20,000 came from, as these people don't believe in free markets. Fortunately, they do believe in using other people's money, until, as Margaret Thatcher said, those other people run out of it. Or decide to stop making it rather than have it taken away (hint, hint).

Next, what did that delivery truck run on? And where did they plant that solar power system seed? Never mind that it was probably made in a third-world country by slave labor struggling all day in a polluting factory.

And why do they have a website in the first place? That kind of has to put them on the grid, sort of by definition, right? Their website says that most of their residents have phones in their own homes, too. Hmmm... I'm beginning to doubt their sincerity, here.

By far, the crowning act of self-sufficiency was to discard the innovation of indoor plumbing. Somehow, it is a sin against the planet to use water, unlike planet-friendly true essentials such as cars, phones and internet service. Maybe the phones are painted green, but the car wasn't. Regardless, the prohibition against water explains the unwashed appearance of Alpha Choad as he was introduced in Scene Two. But, the downstream consequences are oh so much worse than that.

Here are a few data points to, uhh, digest:

☐ Disconnect your toilet and replace it with a bucket. And not in your own mud hut. Oh, no, that would be living too large. No, let's put the bucket in the "Common House".
☐ Provide a stock of sawdust with which to cover the exudate. How big is a sawdust plant, anyway?

☐ Disconnect running water from the in-house so that everyone touches the doorknob with happy hands.
☐ Put all the people in the community together in the "Common House" for meals and rotate cooking duties so that eventually everyone will have the same strands of e-coli and hepatitis. Or HIV. I'm just saying.
☐ Disconnect the shower, too.
☐ Provide as an alternative an outdoor shower that has to be fired with wood. I thought wood was bad and creates greenhouse gases? Just don't fire it around that bucket, please.
☐ Accept the reality, as was stated by one of the chosen, that due to the inconvenience of a half-hour of wood-firing prep time, showers are really only a one-in-five-day thing. This helps smear the happy hands around for a while longer, too.
☐ Once in a while, enlist some poor sap to process the bucket of "Humanure", as they call it. Stir it around in a pit to make sure that any contagions in the pit since forever have fresh food upon which to munch.
☐ Grow your crops in the community poo. Assure yourselves that it is safe for use. Organic farming, anyone?

Who gets bucket duty, anyway? I suppose that, following the history of collectivist action, this particular assignment probably goes to whoever has strayed from the centerline of conformance. Maybe after a few weeks of humanure duty you get to work your way up to cutting shower wood to show your newly re-educated spirit of compliance.

By the way, that show is hosted by Morgan Spurlock. Hey, Morgan, if you wanted to host a really great episode, give me thirty days with those communists. I'm going to need a handful of waivers, and probably a blanket Presidential pardon, since I'll be bringing my 1987 Ford TLB (Tractor-Loader-Backhoe, for the hippies) and some other choice items. My backhoe runs on biodiesel, too. Sadly, rank-and-file communists, unlike their well-to-do leadership, have very little body fat, so make sure plenty are around. Fortunately, they tend to swarm.

According to their website, these guys also have a local currency. They call it *Lettuce*. Cute. Does this mean that they have a barter system in place? If so, are they tracking all barter transactions, and then reporting these earnings to the IRS, as required? I hope so, I would hate for them to get into trouble by not following the same rules which collectivists force upon the rest of us at the point of a gun. The tax dollars taken from us are probably funneled to them to pay for things like solar panels and diesel cars. And tetanus shots.

If Spurlock picks up my episode proposal, I would probably bring along a brass pole, also. Put some of their honeys under a hot shower for a few hours and soap 'em down, two or three at a time. Then, get them some heels, lipstick, eyeshadow and some twirling lessons and they would probably catch right on. I think I will call them the *Dancing Bunnies*. Note to self: bring along some heads of lettuce and tuck some leaves into their eco-friendly garters if they do a good job. On the other hand, all that hepatitis and HIV humanure risk kind of takes the fun out of that.

Now we've come full circle, as it were, back to infectious diseases.

Og and Pok taught our genes to enjoy cooked meat, lest we stray at our peril. Similarly, civilization developed water purification, indoor plumbing and sanitary sewers or septic systems, toilet paper and handi-wipes because *you live longer with them*. Those genes then prospered, along with the memes for these concepts. Even before mankind had these modern facilities, early man at least had enough sense to not look for his food in the pile of humanure. Remarkably, genes which led their meat robot to think that this was a keen place to look for food did not do all that well. That icky feeling you get when watching this episode is there for a really good reason. Go with that feeling.

These fixtures of modern life are not just for kicks or convenience, they are *essential for life itself*. And the monkeys want to take these things away from you because it makes them feel good about themselves, even if it kills you. Or forces you to watch your children die from typhus. Or kills nations off, millions at a time, from plagues and other epidemics resulting from poor hygiene. Remember, they set the ground rules, not me.

I haven't polled each of the affected parties, but I think that somewhere around three billion people live in sanitary conditions marginally better than prancing rabbits. Without enormous amounts of aid, including food and medicines, from other people (meaning you), this number would probably be more like a half-billion. Do these people really want you to live in conditions which would, unchecked, kill off two and a half billion people? My math says that gets us another five planets right there.

Some would say that this is an unscientific assertion, but OK, let's run an experiment. Cut off all aid for ten years, foreign and domestic, and see where the trend lines go.

No, for the street-level collectivist, of whatever stripe, the agenda is much more simple. They don't really want you to live in these conditions. No, this would limit your ability to provide the resources they need you to contribute, whether voluntarily or otherwise. Instead, they want you to feel guilty because you don't live this way. And that makes you more pliable and more easily controlled. And so they get to drain you of value which they have not earned. This *guilt-drain* mechanism is highly lucrative.

But communists aren't the only ones with that agenda. Recall that Richard Dawkins calls ideas memes, to reflect their genetic character. It turns out that modern civilization has numerous strains of a brain infection, a corrosive meme, which has spread quickly. And this brain infection is virulently communicable, creating monkey zombies by the billions.

Part of the guilt-drain mechanism has spun out of control so fast that it threatens to take down civilization itself. After all, if an infection kills the host, then what? Og and Pok, and all their many uncountable generations of forebears, did such a great job of creating prosperity that the infection ran out of control. And long before anyone knew what was going on.

In retrospect, the infection is easy to see, but the scar it creates leaves a blindness to itself which could not have been designed any better if anyone had tried. If we wanted to kill off humanity itself, we now have the blueprint before us. Being part of that humanity, however, I would rather save some of it, even if we have to amputate the diseased portions. The Tith cures, short of amputation, have all been exhausted.

Recall that, long ago, I listened to a radical radio talk show host way back when I first recognized this infection in my own company. That same radical talk show host has recently proven, to his disappointment, I am sure, that the infection is so out of hand that they do, indeed, surround you.

This situation is possible thanks to a feature of this brain infection which Og and Pok could not have possibly understood.

Sadly, there remains only one cure. We'll dance around that cure for a few chapters, and then get back to it.

Before proceeding, let me give a shout out to my boys, Og and Pok. These guys, whatever their real names were, laid the foundation for all the rest of us to live a high quality of life. So high, in fact, that we forget how much it would suck to throw it all away. Fellas, this book is dedicated to you and your friends.

Chapter 6, The Font of Value

Earlier we followed our friends Og, Pok and the tribe about on their economic adventures. Throughout that chapter the same principles kept popping up, but in different forms. These principles are valid today, but often disguised underneath a veil of obstacles designed to suck value out of you and feed it to various classes of monkeys.

The Four Resources

Stripping away these obstacles reveals that value, and thus money or other resources, comes from four resources available to each of us:

- ☐ Stuff
- ☐ Push
- ☐ Time
- ☐ Ideas

Let's examine each of these in detail.

Stuff

Stuff includes all those things available for your use. For Og, given his strength, wood was readily available. For Pok, given his stealth and cunning, squirrels were readily available. To each, their respective stuff was less valuable than the stuff of the other, which meant that by trading stuff they each obtained more valuable other stuff.

Different stuff thus has different value to different individuals, at different places, and at different times. A resource of stuff in one area, such as gravel in a gravel pit, has less value to the owner of the pit than it does to the farmer on his access road.

One great feature about stuff is that you can pile up many kinds of it for later use. This allows you to gather a bunch of it up when easy to do so. And then, you have the flexibility to dribble it out later at times and places of higher value, or in times of shortage. Og, for example, might collect more wood than he could trade in the summertime. By piling it carefully and shielding the top against rain, he could trade it for more goods in the winter than it would bring in the summer. And in so doing, keep others from freezing in the winter cold.

Note that monkeys have taken to calling this practice *hoarding* and cast it as a civil sin, or in many cases, an actual crime. This term appears, for example, when a gas station owner invests in larger tanks to be able to supply more product during a period of shortage. If that gas station owner then attempts to recoup that investment through higher prices during shortages, monkeys call this practice *price gouging. Even though he would be supplying them with something they couldn't otherwise get at any price.*

I lived through such a fuel shortage in Atlanta in late 2008. I think I would have rather paid the higher price to reward the forward-thinking station owner to make that resource available. But instead, I waited all night and most of the day in a gas line. However, Governor Purdue, on paper a Republican conservative who should have known better, chose to bow to the monkey collective. He decreed these market forces illegal, and so the city just simply ran out. Thanks. At least no one overpaid. Pull that trick sometime in a rural area during a harvest season and let's see how well that turns out.

The miracle of the free market is that it efficiently allocates stuff to the right places, especially in time of shortage. In the 2008 Atlanta gas shortage, if prices had been allowed to float as the market demanded, many who didn't need to make that trip to see Grandma might decide not to buy any gasoline at all. Some who would otherwise top off their tank might choose to avoid the higher price by waiting a week or so to see how things turned out. These individual decisions would leave some fuel, albeit at a higher price, available for those who needed to take care of a loved one in a hospital, perhaps. And reward the station owner who invested in larger tanks, causing others to consider doing the same, limiting the effect of future threatened shortages.

The Governor could have taken a different approach. He could have instead seized the crisis as a teachable moment, and addressed the citizens of the State. With their attention, he could have assured them that the shortage was temporary but the higher prices were merely the market allocating the limited supply more efficiently. And that prices would return to normal after the shortage had been resolved. Of course, he would have been lambasted by the press, but he did ask for the job.

In the long term, another benefit would have arisen. Other station owners would watch our enterprising hero charge $8.00 per gallon for a week. Seeing his work lauded, or at least not punished by the Governor, they would formulate plans of their own. Perhaps they would order extra fuel at each approaching storm in the Gulf. Or perhaps they might invest in adding extra tank capacity. Regardless, during the next crisis they would be ready. When that new crisis arrived, so many stations would have extra fuel that the shortage might not materialize at all. But if it did, because more stations would have more reserve, the price they would demand, in their competition with each other, might drop to $7.00, or less.

Fuel suppliers in other states might get in on the act, and arrange to deliver more fuel to neighboring states in a crisis, in exchange for an extra dollar per gallon, perhaps. Assuming that this wasn't prevented by special formulations demanded by each state or the EPA, of course. And assuming that the suppliers were certain that they wouldn't be punished for their assistance.

Individuals would also act. Knowing that the Governor would not pamper them in his rush to exchange destruction for political capital, they would perhaps watch the storms approaching, and fill their tanks or cans beforehand with $4.00 gasoline. And in so doing implement yet another layer of reserve. Or these individuals might look around them and prepare in other ways. Perhaps they might stock a little more of Super Choco-Bites in their pantry to avoid that extra trip to the store when gas might be tight.

Businessmen might prepare plans and infrastructure to enable work-at-home during crises by rerouting business lines to employee's homes, allowing them to stay off the road.

So, when that next disaster arrived, fewer citizens would be at the pump demanding that resource, and so the crisis price might drop to $6.00. Such is the miracle of market forces when each individual is allowed, or even encouraged, to act in his own selfish interest.

This rational approach would have been political suicide, of course. The monkey collective, in its overwhelming number, demands only immediate gratification, and refuses to think about the consequences of its demands. I present as evidence that, to the best of my knowledge, not one state governor, in the midst of a crisis, has ever bothered to explain the benefit of market forces to the citizenry. Instead, each rattles the mailed fist of populist force to threaten those who are in a position to help the most.

The Governor's actions, as does all price-fixing by a collective, ensured that the shortage worsened. Atlantans rushed to the pumps by the thousands, each fearing a complete outage. Since there was no price incentive to stay away or to limit purchases, everyone bought as much as they could. So gas completely disappeared from the scene. And removed any reason for any station to install tanks larger than that required for the normal business flow. This rationale ensured that similar shortages would be as equally bad, or worse, in the future.

Push

Push, or equivalently pull, is the amount of effort you can expend toward a goal. Og, being stronger, was able to easily break off branches of a fall, and thus get more wood than Pok. Pok was more wiry, and was thus enabled to chase or snare squirrels better than Og. Each man then applied his own variety of specialized push to affect his environment, ultimately to obtain more stuff in less time.

Engineers call this quantity *potential energy* when it is waiting to be used, or *kinetic energy* when it is actually in use. More specifically, when you push an object you use potential energy to create force, which causes acceleration of the object in question. As it moves faster, it gains kinetic energy. The potential energy of Og's muscles, provided by the digestion of that squirrel, is applied to a branch to move it until it breaks.

Work is closely related to push. The engineering definition of work is the application of push over a distance. Note that this means that you can push on a brick wall all day long, but if nothing moves, you haven't done any work. This implies that unless you get something done, you haven't worked. You may have expended an enormous amount of energy in the process, though.

Along these lines, a monkey sitting in a cubicle all day is not working. Neither is a monkey scampering around underfoot at the office or in the shop. But both are consuming enormous amounts of resources which have to come from somewhere. And if either of these creatures is getting in your way, they are not only not doing work, they are removing your opportunity to work. This effect could be considered as *negative work*. So, if you spend your day dealing with monkey-based issues, you aren't working either.

Time

We all have some time available to us, although metaphysically this quantity is uncertain. But, assuming your plan isn't to just sit around waiting to die, you typically decide throughout each day how you will spend your time. Time is one of those "use it or lose it" quantities. For about a third of our lives, the best way to use your time is sleeping, providing rest so that you can do a better job of more efficient or well-planned push later. Or, use some of your time thinking, as our heroes often did by the stream.

Ideas

Of all the quantities we have discussed thus far, ideas are by far the most powerful resource at our disposal. I often combine time, ideas, and rest, thinking as I drift back and forth on the edge of sleep.

Others choose to meditate or pray to achieve the same result: a plan of action. Contrast this with those classes of prayer which amount to spiritual welfare ("help me Jesus"), often implemented as spiritual chain letters ("our Internet-based prayer circle will bombard God with so much worship spam He will *have* to act"). Or, equivalently, spiritual barter ("pray for me and I'll pray for you"). More on this topic in a later chapter.

Some, and I do this myself depending on my mood, enjoy a menial task while the mind is free to think. Choose whatever approach works for you.

Pok Jr. didn't like chasing squirrels all day, and so he decided that raising bunnies in hutches was a much more efficient application of his available push. His idea manifested itself in using push to gather some sticks, and then pushed them around until he wove his little bunny hutches and bunny fences. And then pushed some bunnies inside them, and fed them grasses he pushed into their hutches and pasture.

Pok Jr.'s idea and these little bits of push became magnified over time by the availability of bunnies, which provided a given amount of food with less overall work. Or provided a given amount of wood, when trading with Og, with less overall work. The idea itself increased the output, whether either directly consumed or further magnified with trade.

Quality of Life

For the purposes of this text, an individual's ability to obtain a given quality of life is determined by his use of these four resources, stuff, push, time and ideas. And most importantly, by the value he places on each of these. Some may say that they can "live on love", or similar nonsense. Try that when your children are freezing in a winter rainstorm and you'll quickly come to the conclusion that some stuff, like shelter or a nice fire, is probably necessary after all. Og and Pok knew better, which is why they and their tribe spent a lot of their time going after stuff and pushing and thinking to get rid of these privations.

I am continually amazed at the amount of references in popular culture to a successful guy having to give up his opportunities and career ambitions to prove to some chick that he loves her. That sounds like a great plan. Taken to the extreme, the logical conclusion of this ethic would be to give it all up and run off into the forest and rub noses like bunnies. All day, rain or shine, season after season. In reality, of course, if a guy tried that approach, after the first missed meal she would just divorce or otherwise dump him and demand some kind of support payments. And then move on to destroy some new sap's life.

And yet, this sort of foolishness prevails in the collective ethic. But, this foolishness would not see the light of day if women didn't know that there was this gigantic safety net strung underneath them. A net sewn into the backs of all the producers who pay into these systems.

So, for the rest of this work of entertaining fiction and analysis I'm going to lay aside the thought that love alone, or friendships alone, or family alone are sufficient. If this offends you, put this book down and read no further.

Instead, I am going to treat all of those great relationships as being fueled and enabled by the four resources. The measure of the quality of life for individuals, or families, is a combination of these resources (stuff, push, time and ideas) that the individual or family has at its disposal. And, this measure incorporates the relative value that each individual concerned places on each item of these resources.

Here's one example. Imagine you want to spend time with Junior teaching him how to throw a ball. So, you need some stuff (a ball, maybe a glove, and a place to play). You apply some push (you have to chuck the ball back and forth, as well as go back and forth to the place). You also need some time (got to fit it into the schedule), and ideas ("hey, Junior, put down the Nintendo™ and let's go toss the old ball around"). Plus, things like not having eaten in a week can't be getting in the way, either. Nor can things like custody restrictions, nor your being behind bars.

Here's another example. Say you want to teach Junior to learn a work ethic so that he can toss it all away on some empty-headed mammal later. Maybe you want him to help out with painting the house. So, you need stuff (paint, trays, ladders, rollers, tape, edgers), apply push (that house won't paint itself or the paint doesn't just walk to your house of its own volition). You need sufficient time to do the work or to wait for Junior to paint his hand a few times. And you also need ideas about how to smear the paint around or what order to trim versus hitting the walls with the roller.

I think you have the point by now.

A mathematician might thus express quality of life as follows:

$$Q_i = G_i(S, P, t)$$
$$= \left[k_{S,i} S^{r_{S,i}} \times k_{P,i} P^{r_{P,i}} \right] \times k_{t,i} t^{r_{t,i}}$$

For the mathematically inclined out there, this equation states that the quality of life measure Q is expressed as a matrix of individual quality of life elements for any individual I. This measure is determined by the product of a matrix of subjective quality of life factors k_S, k_P and k_t unique to each individual for each resource stuff, push, and time. And, multiply these factors by the respective resources for each individual, raised to the vectors r_S, r_P and r_t power for each individual resource element, as determined by that individual's preferences.

The effect of ideas are deferred until later, and so don't appear in the expression above.

In simple terms, your quality of life is higher if you have more of those resources you care about. But the resources for which you don't care about, you could take them or leave them.

Why even present this in a complicated mathematical form? Because there is a whole body of control system theory which uses similar notation. The idea behind this control theory is that if you can model a system a certain way, then you can control your little piece of it using well-known techniques. To convert that formulation above requires a more or less straightforward linearization, but the ideas apply equally well.

Those who understand higher mathematics (if this isn't you today, please begin moving in that direction), and by extension the control theory which these make available, can understand the depth of what I mean by quality of life. And how complex that measure is, far more complex than we could imagine attempting to completely control. Some idiot somewhere always thinks he can control the economy. Apply enough planning or central control, he believes, and everyone, especially him, could live well. This idea ultimately leads to square pegs being hammered into round holes through the means of secret police and gulags. History has taught us that a centrally planned economy is just unworkable, no matter how pleasant the overseer's smile as the lash is applied.

That equation above shows the mathematician or controls engineer why central planning is unworkable. Even if you could determine all of those quality of life factors for each individual, you would have to constantly measure all the resource flows at each instant in time. You would also have to manipulate control action. Control action is trivial when you are working with a chicken plucker or a space shuttle. It stops being trivial when dealing with something as complex as a worldwide economy with about six billion or so people involved. Which is, by the way, a highly nonlinear system.

To emphasize the complexity of a planned economy, I give this talk sometimes to engineers or scientists. And I use the following title:

What Green Means to Me

or

The Application of Systems of Practically Infinite Matrices of Nonlinear Differential Equations

I usually get a laugh at that. The title alone usually makes the point to anyone who knows anything about control systems.

"But wait", the collectivists shout, "our world is different now. We have computers. Stalin never had a computer. With a big enough computer and the right software, we can control anything of arbitrary complexity!"

Do you really want the guy who wrote your PC operating system to write the software which controls your happiness? He probably doesn't even speak your native language, and could hardly be expected to understand what makes you happy. Or care. Besides, this software would probably run on some Chinese piece of junk. As it were.

I consider myself one of the best in the world at that sort of thing, but I wouldn't seriously consider ever being able to get that kind of software to work. But I would be happy to take billions, or trillions, in grants for you to get me to try. But of course, that's the point, isn't it?

I would seriously doubt the credentials of anyone who thinks they are smart enough to plan the economy of even a small village. Nothing beats the distributed processing power of individuals working toward their own success.

And now the morons of the collective are thinking they know best about how hot or how cold your house should be. When they dick up something even that simple and easily understood, will their arrogance be blamed?

Nope. They will just claim that the collective needs to give them more authority. "A little more authority, or a little more control, or more marketing, or more police, or more money, and we'll have it right," they will claim. And the collective will give it to them. And the cycle will repeat, only with larger destruction.

But, as the mathematician reads this, he can at least begin to see how, theoretically, to use the differences in resources and the various quality of life matrices. And understand how individuals use them in ways to pump value from one resource and individual to another, creating value at each transaction. And that the only practical way to implement this control is to let each individual make these decisions for themselves.

This is distinct from what the elite of the monkey collective does with this knowledge. Their use for these ideas is to warp your individual preferences to convince or coerce you to assign value to resources they control. Admittedly, warping your preferences is a vastly easier way to extract value from you with little or no return effort required on their part.

Sadly, twisting your preferences, otherwise known as *marketing*, might actually damage you in the process. More on this later.

One implication of the mathematical formulation is that each individual must have at least some of the resources stuff, push or time. Lack any one of these, and game over. At least in quality of life terms.

The Fifth Resource

A fifth resource, *energy*, lurks out there also, but is actually a special case of stuff which can convert itself into push. A tank of diesel sitting in a tractor is stuff. But, when that diesel is burned in the engine, it transforms into push. Push which can do things like plow fields or haul wood or run over the family dog.

A solar panel is a bunch of flimsy stuff which can gather up more stuff, namely, a swarm of electron stuff we call electricity. That stuff swirls around inside some stuff which looks like a motor to make some push.

A wind turbine is a bunch of stuff arranged so that a similar squirt of electron stuff swirls around in that motor, and so on.

A nuclear power plant is a bunch of stuff arranged so that some little blobs of almost nothing sticks to some little nuggets of pimply stuff. This disturbs the pimply stuff, and causes it to wobble and break into a couple of smaller nuggets of pimply stuff. This breakup releases energy and some more of those little blobs of almost nothing. And in so doing releases some heat. Heat, in turn, is actually some stuff wiggling around pushing everything. This wiggling wiggles other stuff into leaping around, which we call boiling. This leaping stuff leaps through some turbine-shaped stuff, pushing it to, in turn, push some generator-shaped stuff which squirts out electrons, and so on.

Anywho. For Cor, a cheval was a bunch of stuff which can push him around to where he wants to go or haul Og's wood out of the forest. Before Cor showed up with the chevals, there were only two sources of energy, wood and muscles. I include wives in the latter category, of course. Before the wood began to be used to cook food, saving untold generations the horrors of death by worm or rot or inability to chew, man's own muscles were the only source of energy.

So let's get this straight. Energy is pretty much a good thing. So good, in fact, that even though it is a bunch of stuff (potential energy) waiting to be turned into push (kinetic energy), we are going to treat it as a special resource. So good that it is the foundation of civilization itself.

So good, that the collective seeks at every turn to limit your access to it or your ability to create your own. Or, allows you to only have access to low-quality forms of it. Or, tries to guilt you into giving it up or ration it from you by force. Because that is the best way to control the individual.

Here is why energy is so good. Ideas are nothing on their own, but when ideas have access to energy they have limitless potential. Of the resources available to you, only ideas and energy have the ability to transform the first three, stuff, push and time. Therefore, without energy, ideas can be stopped dead in their tracks. With energy, the possibilities available to the individual are limited only by the amount of the other resources, and the quantity and quality of energy available.

Let's take a side tour for a moment to ask an important question. *How does energy have a quality?* The quality of energy has been explicitly defined by scientists who study and engineers who work with a branch of science known as *thermodynamics*. The exact definition of the quality of energy is beyond the scope of this book. But in a nutshell, energy is of higher quality if it is packaged as some convenient stuff and can push hard. Especially if it is packed real tight, like in a nutshell. Or in an atom.

Solar and wind energy seem almost like free energy. If you believe that, ask the favored solar or wind lobby of the current administration, whichever it might be when you read this, to send you some for free. Slick marketing, but the reality falls short of the promise. Both solar and wind energy are of low quality when compared to liquid fuels. The sun hardly ever shines when you need to push the most, and you can't very easily carry enough solar collectors around to do anything really useful, like plow a field. A similar rationale applies for wind energy.

Batteries are almost as bad. These let you store some of the solar and wind energy, for example, but still have a very low energy density per unit volume or weight. Batteries also can't usually be completely emptied of energy without damage, and are very expensive when compared to the amount of useable life they possess. Some kinds of batteries also wear out very quickly, while a fuel tank usually lasts the life of the machine.

Now liquid fuels, on the other hand, are high-quality energy. Liquid fuels, such as gasoline or diesel, are far better than the options above. Liquids are easy to store, portion, transport to the point of use, and meter through engines into push on command.

Solid fuels are only able to satisfy the demand of specific subsets of the applications to which liquid fuels apply. For example, fixed location power plants use a lot of solid fuels in the form of coal. But these plants have large amounts of specialized handling equipment and well-planned supply systems to process it efficiently. Ships and trains at one time used a lot of solid fuels, but even these installations were ultimately deemed too small to allow efficient handling of this type of energy. Some hobbyists today experiment with wood-fueled automobiles, but usually in anticipation of the lack of availability of liquid fuels over time. They might be right.

Gaseous fuels, such as propane, natural gas or hydrogen, share some of the benefits and limitations of liquid and solid fuels. Like liquid fuels, once you have them at a point of use, they are relatively easy to meter through an engine on command. But, transporting them to the point of use, or storing them once there, is moderately to very difficult. The difficulty of transportation and storage, both requiring compression at high pressures, are two sides of the same coin. After all, transportation of gases is usually just storage on the move.

On a molecular weight basis, the lighter the fuel, the more impractical it is to transport or store. Of all the gaseous fuels man has or will ever devise, hydrogen is the lightest of them all. This will always be true. So, despite popular mythology hyping its utility, hydrogen as the fuel of the future is an idea stillborn if for no other reason than it is hard to store.

No matter what technology might be applied to mitigate the manufacture, storage or transportation of hydrogen, these same means will produce vastly better results with the heavier fuels such as methane, propane, butane, etc., respectively. For example, a new compression or storage technique, properly modified, will more easily compress methane than hydrogen. Or compress propane more easily than both of these, or butane than any of the previous. Every time. The only limitation of application of a particular methodology to propane versus hydrogen will be laws demanded by the monkey collective to force a particular fuel into dubious application.

Hydrogen has two key advantages in its favor, though. The first advantage is that it is a great fuel for operating an electrical fuel cell. The second advantage is that, pound for pound, it produces the highest specific impulse of any other combustible fuel in the universe.

These two advantages make it the fuel of choice for generating electrical power or thrust, respectively, for spacecraft. But neither of these advantages has any meaning in the context of plowing a field, unless you are willing to fund tractors which have the expensive high-strength materials of NASA rockets. And which have to last through thirty years of rough service instead of ten minutes to space. And not blow up underneath the farmer like the Challenger or the Hindenburg.

Admittedly, this last statement was a little bit of hyperbole. The Challenger blew up because it also had oxygen tanks, and the Hindenburg was a whole other set of issues. When your hydrogen tractor or car springs a leak, it will be because of a crack in the tank. This will lead to a jet of compressed gas, which, if ignited, and it will find an ignition source, will be an unquenchable forty- or fifty-foot flare until the tank empties. Hope it isn't pointed at you, because you won't be able to see it. If you can still hear it, it is pointed the other way. If it is pointed at you, you have no ears with which to hear. At least it didn't explode.

On the other hand, when your diesel tank develops a crack, the fuel either drips on the ground, or, if at the top of the tank, does nothing. Hooray for liquids! And since your diesel tank isn't trying to store compressed gas at low temperatures, you could make it out of an old bucket in a pinch.

Like solid fuels, gaseous fuels do have a place in fixed installations. Natural gas, when transported to the point of use through pipelines, has unbeatable convenience. Shipping it through any other means really sucks. Propane and butane, being easy to liquify, are more convenient to transport, and are almost as convenient as natural gas. But, outside these key applications, gaseous fuels won't make it into the hard places which liquid fuels can.

Nuclear fission power for generating electricity is the highest quality energy source man has yet applied, which is precisely why the monkey collective wants to be shed of it. For a given weight of fuel versus energy output, only fusion or anti-matter will produce more energy. Those exotic installations are successively larger and as yet unproven in the case of the former, or absolutely impractical, in the case of the latter. Good old nuclear fission is the king right now. Even hybrid fusion-fission systems would still draw most of their output power from fission.

Like solid and gaseous fuels, nuclear power is best used for fixed installations or distributed over a fixed network. So, it has the potential to supplant liquid fuels, freeing these for liquid fuel applications, and thus augmenting the solid or gaseous infrastructure as well as implicitly augmenting the liquid fuel supply. Each gallon of liquid fuel unburned to create electricity, because of the availability of nuclear power, is one more gallon of fuel in the tank of a tractor somewhere.

Nuclear power also has another advantage. Solid and gaseous fuels, through a couple of key related chemical processes known for about a hundred years, can be converted into high quality liquid fuels. These chemical processes are energy-intensive, and, when driven by the solid or gaseous fuel in question, consume a significant fraction of the starting material. However, if these processes were driven instead by nuclear power, and used the feedstock fuel only as process material, a much higher proportion of the feedstock could be converted into liquids.

Internet Research
Research the Fischer-Tropsch process.

Nuclear power thus allows inconvenient solid or gaseous fuel feedstock to be converted into high quality liquid fuels. This country, as you know, has practically unlimited supplies of natural gas and coal. Locate a nuclear-powered conversion plant near a distribution point in West Virginia or Kentucky or Tennessee, and those railway cars can carry off liquid fuel instead of coal. This would also allow large scale scrubbers at those processing points. Centralized scrubbers can have far higher efficiency at removing pollutants rather than distributing those scrubbers to stack tops at each individual power plant which would otherwise burn that coal. Those scrubbed pollutants, primarily sulfur, would then be available in such high concentration as to be a valuable industrial product all its own.

Locate a similar nuclear-powered conversion plant near a natural gas pipeline head in Louisiana, or stranded gas in Alaska or under the seabed just about anywhere, and that natural gas can be turned into diesel or gasoline. Or propane or butane or whatever other more convenient fuel you wish.

So, now that we know that energy is so important, and that liquid fuels are the most convenient and practical source of energy for general use, what exactly does energy do for us? Plenty. Energy is transformative. This means that it allows you to transform stuff into other stuff, or provide push or decrease the time required for a task. All of these transformations have some relationship to each other. Let's look more closely at some of these transformations.

Energy can increase the amount of good stuff which we have. Adding energy to any process typically increases the yield of that process. For example, we apply energy to manufacture ammonium nitrate fertilizer from air and water. Then we apply that fertilizer to the soil, again using energy to fuel the tractor. As a result, the yield of plant stuff coming out of the soil will tend to increase. The application of energy increased the crop yield.

Energy extends our reach to get additional stuff. For example, if we apply energy to dig better mines, we can reach additional ore deposits. Or drill deeper. Or lift a worker to pick fruit on larger, more robust trees.

Energy allows better conversion of useless stuff. For example, we use energy to haul oil from the Middle East or Alaska, where it has little intrinsic value, to the continental United States, where it is significantly more valuable. Properly applied energy made the same stuff more valuable by moving it from one place to the other. Similarly, that fertilizer plant used energy to compress air and move it through the plant to yield fertilizer. Air and water became valuable plant food.

That sulfur byproduct at the hypothetical nuclear-powered coal liquification plant in West Virginia, or the similarly fantastic methane liquification plant in Louisiana, becomes sulfuric acid. This acid is the most important non-fuel industrial chemical known to man. By the application of energy, what would have been a nuisance pollutant becomes a valuable feedstock. And thus enables all the downstream products and processes which require sulfuric acid. What are these downstream products and processes? Almost any products or processes you care to name.

Internet Research
Research sulfuric acid and its importance to civilization.

We can use energy to move stuff in time as well as in place, producing a similar increase in value. When we refrigerate food, we use energy to transport that hunk of meat from Tuesday when we bought it or killed it, to Friday when we want to eat it. The meat had less value on Tuesday, when we had a lot of it on hand. And more value on Friday, when we would otherwise have had none. Og used energy to stack his summer wood harvest, when it is of low value, protecting it until winter, when it has higher value.

Similarly, when we use energy to can or otherwise preserve food, we transport it in time. That food moves from harvest time, when it is of relatively low value, to lean months of the year, where it is more valuable. Limit the use of energy in any civilization, and you will quickly learn what Og and Pok knew. And what they knew was that your tribe is limited in population by the lean months, not the times of plenty.

When we till the soil, or manufacture a product, we essentially store the value of that energy in the produce or the products, increasing their value at the time of sale.

Energy performs all these miracles of modern life by amplifying human command. You could stab in the ground with a stick, but far better to till with a tractor. You could carve a table-leg with a knife, but far better to use a powered lathe. In so doing, the paltry push of our bodies, however strong, is multiplied many-fold by the application of energy.

Energy also increases the amount of time at our disposal. Tilling that field by hand or carving that table-leg with a knife can be done. But, you can spend more time with Junior teaching him how to throw a ball or paint a room if you properly apply energy to those tasks. Similarly, the workman in a factory is of hardly any value on his own, unless equipped with a welder. Or, in many cases, we equip a worker with a machine which requires little of him other than pushing its button. When we replace the button-pusher with a computer program, we call that *automation*. More later.

Energy is a Cultural Measure

Energy determines the quality of life for a culture as a whole. To reflect this fact, a wise man once defined a mathematical concept known as *Baugh's Theorem*. Collectivists cringe at the thought of someone daring to name something he thought of after himself. Good. Regardless of their assessments, this theorem requires you to identify the total stuff required to produce quality of life for all the people in a culture. Then, multiply that stuff by the energy cost of each element of stuff. Divide the result by the efficiency of delivering each element of stuff to each individual.

The resulting number must be strictly less than or equal to that culture's total available energy:

$$\sum_{i=1}^{P} \left| \frac{KS_i}{\eta_i} \right| \leq E_{Available} \quad \eta_{j,k} << 1!$$

The matrix K in the expression above includes market factors which vary from transaction to transaction. But, the elements of that matrix indicate a minimum objective energy cost for each item or class of stuff, independent of the individual in question.

Note that the expression applies an energy cost to each item or class of stuff used in the culture, rather than the quality of life factors themselves. This restriction is because stuff is the basic unit of quality of life, from which all other factors flow. Push doesn't happen unless you have diesel to fuel the tractor, or food to fuel the muscles. Time comes to an end unless you have food, water and shelter or, if sick, antibiotics or medical care in the form of stuffy doctors and nurses. These doctors and nurses themselves required enormous amount of stuff-based training and support to develop their skill. And ideas alone are of little value unless you can obtain the stuff to implement them.

A more basic reason to only consider the energy cost of stuff rather than quality of life is that quality of life is subjective. We recall that fact from the matrix formulation of quality of life from several pages back. Whether or not a particular item of stuff enhances a particular individual's quality of life is entirely dependent on whether that individual values an item. A diamond has no immediate value to me (I don't think I have ever bought a real one), as it doesn't delight me, nor, as I have no interest in women who would demand one, help me obtain anything I want. For another, a diamond may be worth several months' pay as it serves a practical purpose of attracting a particular type of woman. Each of us assigns a subjective measure to diamonds and all other stuff in our culture. But, for each of us, there is a minimum amount of energy required to obtain that item, and thus the amount of stuff required for exchange to get it.

So, for the rest of this book, we will consider the minimum energy cost of stuff as the driving force underneath a culture's available resources. I say *minimum energy cost*, because inefficiencies among individuals as well as among distributing those items of stuff around will dramatically increase the energy cost above that minimum. Sometimes much more above.

For example, there is a fixed minimum energy cost for delivering a woman-weight of wood to any individual. Og can collect this amount of wood more efficiently than Pok, so, between the two of them that K factor for wood reflects Og's minimum value, rather than Pok's. Each innovation in the culture, such as Ahks' creation of stone tools to ease the wood harvest, reduces these cost factors as innovations create new cost minimums. After the arrival of this innovation Og, using his muscles alone, is less efficient than perhaps Pok with an axe. The entire culture then benefits from that innovation as the same amount of energy is now capable of delivering a larger amount of stuff overall.

The fact that wood is gathered using more or less efficient techniques is one factor that leads to the inequality in the expression with regard to energy. Not all wood production or collection will be using the most energy-efficient harvesting technique available in the culture.

The other factor leading to the inequality of the expression is the efficiency matrix η_i for delivering a given quality of life to each individual. Mathematicians might quibble over the details of how I have formulated this factor. For them, multiplying by its transpose and dividing by its determinant might be more appropriate, but I have expressed it as shown to make the concept more accessible to a public school algebra education.

Regardless, this efficiency matrix is an indicator of how efficiently the culture can distribute and deliver each quality of life element once it has been produced or otherwise obtained.

When Governor Purdue bowed to the collective he decreed that market forces were suspended in Georgia. He also decreed that anyone who dared apply market forces to help solve the problem would be strictly and swiftly punished as, effectively, an enemy of the State of Georgia. When he pronounced all this, he effectively reduced the state-wide cultural efficiency of resource delivery for gasoline.

The mis-allocation which followed his carefully politically calculated dramatic flourish was sufficiently wasteful that more energy resources were required to deliver that quality of life element, gasoline stuff. Gasoline is stuff which individuals use in their myriad ways to transform their world to their benefit and for the benefit of others. Unfortunately, that additional energy wasn't available, and there wasn't enough time to innovate, so quality of life had to plummet to preserve the balance.

In many cases, this reduction in quality of life manifested itself by tens of thousands waiting in gas lines, missing sleep, work, recreation or innovative activities such as thinking. These secondary inefficiencies percolated throughout the economy as businesses were unable to handle support calls such as fixing HVAC systems or process loan applications, etc. Those workers were bottled up waiting at gas stations or taking the morning off catching up on sleep lost the night before.

These inefficiencies then percolated into tertiary inefficiencies as those customers then had to take time from their work to find another HVAC technician or wait for the napping first one, and so on. Simultaneously, the energy cost to deliver quality of life factors increased as that HVAC technician, his circadian rhythms thrown off for a day or so, took longer for each service call. Or, he burned through pipes while attempting to braze them, requiring even more effort to repair instead of handling other calls. In addition, business owners had invested in service trucks or office space which was now sitting idle. Or, they invested paychecks for technicians who are too tired to handle many calls. Or for staff who waited for a tow truck as their sleepy attention waned moments before their traffic accident. All of these effects reduced the amount of resources available for the business owners to hire or retain employees, or attract and retain customers.

The overall economic impact from the most simple collectivist intervention can be dramatic. And particularly in our modern economies in which the delivery systems for quality of life factors are so marginally tuned to begin with. This fine-tuning itself is the result of having to deal with the artificial costs of almost crippling regulation and intervention already.

The waves of increased cost and reduced efficiency of delivery can slop around and ripple in ways which are difficult to predict or measure, but are just as real nonetheless. These waves often lead to further intervention as hundreds of outraged HVAC customers call the Public Service Commission or whatever government entity or overlord strikes their wounded fancy. Once on the line they demand that their sweat or chill be stopped by those evil HVAC companies. Or demand that energy or other utility providers be punished promptly by more stringent oversight and regulation.

Yet the monkey collective never once questions or blames the real culprit, namely, their own selfishly ignorant insistence that the Governor protect them. And protect them he does, from the one innovator capable of protecting them from discomfort, that gas station owner with the temporarily higher price.

Baugh's Theorem, then, could also be restated as describing the *Conservation of Cultural Energy*. In layman terms, if you want individuals in a culture to have a high quality of life, that culture must have access to a certain minimum amount of energy. We may not be able to calculate that amount precisely, but whatever it is, reduce the amount of energy available to that culture below that amount, and you have to either:

☐ Decrease the quality of life for some or all individuals.
☐ Convince or coerce most or all individuals to adjust their quality of life values. As in re-education, or the "smile for the cameras ye thousands as you bang your drums in unison or we'll kill you and your family" kind of propaganda campaigns.
☐ Increase the efficiency of delivering quality of life to most or all of the individuals. This direction is strictly limited. Note that the efficiency of delivery η_i for each individual must be less than 100%, and in most cases far less. As mentioned, government-based delivery systems tend to be far less efficient than market-driven systems. In any event, these factors max out at 100%, so you won't get very far in cutting your energy budget there.
☐ Innovate to reduce the energy cost of gathering or producing a resource. This generally requires some form of automation which displaces whole segments of workers, effectively reducing their quality of life factors. As we shall see in a moment, because of physics, most resources have a minimum energy cost which cannot be innovated away. In many practical cases we are very close to these limits already.
☐ Reduce the population. Lovely. I want to be on the committee who does the selection. You probably do too, but unfortunately, they surround us.
☐ Some combination of the above.

A Strategy for Destroying Civilization

Energy is the foundation of civilization, and liquid fuel the key pillar in that foundation. So, if one wanted to bring that civilization to its knees a good path to follow would be to:

☐ Demonize nuclear power so that it would not be available to supplant more valuable liquid-fueled power plants. Nuclear power would then also never supplant fixed installation coal or natural gas which might otherwise be easily converted into higher quality liquid fuels.
☐ Demonize coal power, requiring rationed consumption of electrical energy. This would also siphon off liquid fuels from ad-hoc application, like fueling tractors for growing food, into heating homes or powering lights instead.
☐ Demonize traditional liquid fuels and discourage their use through punitive taxation or regulation, despite their high quality and utility, *at any price*.
☐ Demand that hydrogen be used as the fuel of choice for transportation and other uses, *knowing that it is supremely impractical, energy-intensive to manufacture and dangerous for the task*.
☐ Market solar and wind power as free energy, knowing that these are unreliable and weak.
☐ Punish innovators by denying their ability to reap the benefits of their

work. Similarly, demand that innovators expend their efforts innovating around pointless arbitrary mandates, rather than creating true forward progress.

Head down this path far enough, and soon you will push a majority of the population back into the world of Og and Pok, with all those tractors hardly more than rusting lawn ornaments. And people starving by the millions domestically, and by the billions world-wide. Add in even a few "oopsies" in government-run allocations on a massive scale, and you could have a real problem on your hands.

Distribution of Stuff and Quality of Life

The stuff required for quality of life, and so to a large extent quality of life itself, is not distributed evenly. But, it is generally distributed fairly, if market forces were left to their own. Forceful intervention of various kinds causes distortion of the allocation of the various resources. But, in a free market these resources are allocated exactly where they belong. And, for absolutely ethical reasons, in a free market, these resources are allocated *where they must be*, for reasons we shall shortly see.

A sample plot of the distribution of the stuff of quality of life is shown below:

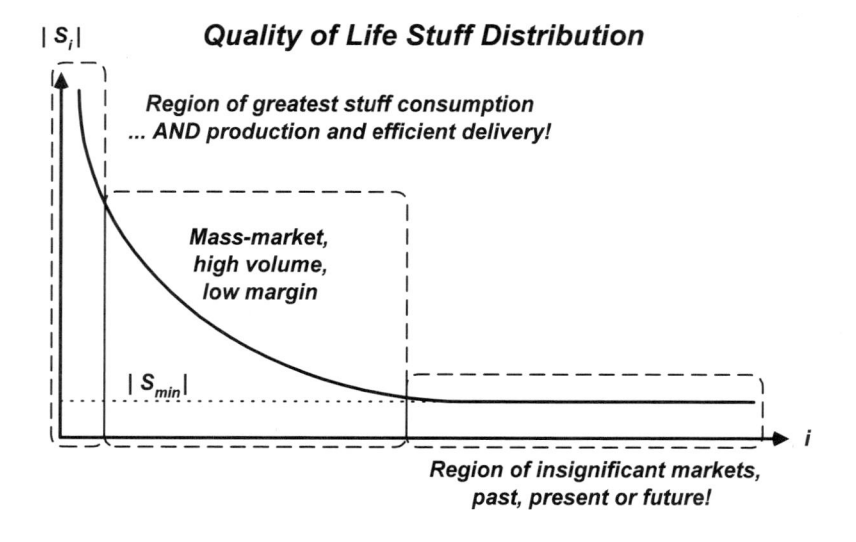

Quality of Life Stuff Distribution

$|S_i|$

Region of greatest stuff consumption ... AND production and efficient delivery!

Mass-market, high volume, low margin

$|S_{min}|$

Region of insignificant markets, past, present or future!

i

It is important to note that this plot is not necessarily geographic, but it could be perceived that way. Instead, view this plot as representative of any random sampling of persons, or the population of a country, or of all mankind. The same analyses apply either way.

As shown in this plot, there are three groups of people among whom the stuff of quality of life is distributed to different extents. The first group are those who enjoy the greatest amount of the stuff of quality of life. This is not to say that these individuals actually have a greater quality of life than others, just that they have the greatest opportunity to have a high quality of life.

Consider wealthy celebrities, for example. Although celebrities are surrounded by seemingly endless pits of wealth, nothing stops them from attempting to destroy their own happiness, such as through drug abuse. For the individuals who make these decisions, their quality of life factors are skewed to place more value on heroin and less on enjoying a spring morning.

But, they have more means with which to procure heroin despite the expense. And, bless their heart, the means to help avoid the consequences of prosecution which would otherwise destroy you or me. Because of this combination, they can enjoy a very high quality of life *on their terms*. We still might imagine we might do a better job with their resources had we them ourselves.

This first group, which has the largest amount of the stuff of quality of life, also includes the evil rich who are so maligned by the masses. But, from the perspective of most of the billions of humanity even the white-collar office worker, such as an engineer or manager, belongs in this group. Again from the perspective of billions who live in relative poverty, an American blue-collar worker such as a welder or a construction equipment operator belongs in this group, too.

As such, this group is often blamed for hoarding the majority of the world's resources for themselves. However, as the note on the figure indicates, these individuals are also able to transform the resources of life into more valuable resources for the use of others. In addition, this group is capable of delivering these improved resources, and thus higher quality of life, to others at high efficiency.

Consider a lowly kilowatt-hour, an essential resource for push which is, for now, taken for granted by most who might be reading this book. We shall see how valuable this ten-cent resource is in a moment, but for now consider its use.

Imagine giving a reasonably functional computer, itself a concentrate of some of the best ideas of humanity, and a kilowatt-hour to an engineer. He might use these resources to design a product or a highway overpass which delivers a higher quality of life to many others for years to come.

Give that same computer and kilowatt-hour to a Zimbabwean farmer, and at best he might use it as a stone to repair a wall or burn a bulb in his hut for a day. This does not mean that the Zimbabwean is stupid or incompetent, just that in his world these items have little consequence as they are completely out of context. For example, his hut may not even have a bulb or wiring to power it. And you thought it was time to label me a racist, didn't you?

Does the engineer consume more than his "fair share" of the world's resources? From the perspective of the typical monkey, you bet! But, does that engineer produce more value more efficiently with those resources than the Zimbabwean farmer? Yep. In fact, the Zimbabwean may receive aid in the form of grain which was grown with that engineer's product or shipped over his bridge. So who should more rightfully be allocated those resources?

The middle group of mankind in the figure includes those who have excess resources beyond mere subsistence. But, these persons may lack access to resources, including ideas or motivation, which would enable them to become significantly productive. Whether or not a particular individual inhabits this group depends on the perspective of the observer. If you spend a non-trivial amount of your income in a big-box discount store, you are probably here. This group is limited to accessing only those resources which are considered, in marketing terms, mass-market, high-volume and low margin.

A large block of humanity trickles down into the subsistence region, populated by the third group. There is a minimum amount of stuff which is required to maintain life, and so by definition no member of humanity has access to resources below this minimum value, at least for very long. Otherwise, they would die of starvation or exposure. As we shall see, collectivist policies and interventions require that these people remain hostage to their circumstances in order to maintain the collectivist's hold on power.

Because their circumstances are so marginal, it is the intent of the collectivist to strip them of their power. The first power which the collectivist seeks to remove is the power of ideas to change those circumstances for themselves. As a result, they will never represent a significant market of return value for the rest of humanity. And so, they will remain a hole into which is poured resources seized from others.

The net effect of this resource distribution from the more prosperous groups to the lower is not that this group improves in their circumstances, but that it increases in size. This increase in size happens both in absolute terms as well as a percentage of population. Some members of the middle group (not to be confused with our notion of *middle class*, although there is significant overlap), frustrated by their being blocked from higher levels, may decide to relax into the resource distribution which guarantees a minimum subsistence. Meanwhile, members of the lower group may increase of their own accord by reproduction or deferred starvation.

Now hand out the collectivist ideal of universal suffrage, unlike that more responsible suffrage envisioned by the founders, and you can easily predict where society will head.

So to what group do monkeys belong? Surprisingly, all of them. We shall see in a moment that monkeys come in all colors, shapes and inhabit a variety of social strata. Many social theorists might imagine, through elitist lenses, that monkeys are concentrated in the lower strata. But, this shortsighted view ignores the fact that children of the successful can turn into absolute brats, while children of the hard-worn can learn lessons which their parents never imagined. Collectivist intervention, however, denies upward mobility to the latter while encouraging the former to plummet as far as they wish.

Similarly, men exist in all these groups as well. In most cases, intervention of the collective seeks to suppress individuality in order to enslave them and push them down in the strata. At the least, this intervention prevents them from moving upward and acquiring additional resources for their own application.

The Value of Work

We will return to the economic philosophy in a moment, but first we need to take time to discuss the notion of *work*. Collectivist ideals, whether originating from the secular or religious realm, imagine that physical work itself has virtue, when in fact man's muscles are of very little consequence. This is not to say that a good sweaty day in the field doesn't release endorphins to improve one's mood. Or improve the form of the lady who sweats as you watch her exertions from the shade. No, I just mean that a diesel tractor might do the actual job better and faster.

Work is the ability to transform stuff into more valuable resources. I mentioned earlier that energy is the means with which stuff is transformed, and so energy powers work. But what exactly is the value of work? Well, within the context of Baugh's Theorem, let's first see how much energy is required to perform a certain amount of work.

In scientific terms, work is measured in Joules. A kilowatt-hour which comes from the wall socket costs, at the time of this writing, about ten cents. If political and environmental rhetoric is to be taken at face value, you will soon pine for this price.

This kilowatt-hour contains three million, six hundred thousand Joules, or 3.6 Mega-Joules (MJ). One might imagine that this is not a lot of energy in our modern terms, it being capable of powering a sixty-watt light bulb for only about sixteen hours. But one would be very, very wrong about what that dime buys.

Imagine that you have a pond which sits six feet below the level of a field which requires irrigation. For kicks, you hand your wife an empty two-liter bottle and tell her to fill it up in the pond and dump it in the field. Ignore for a moment the pleasant undulations which result as she walks back and forth between the pond and the field. Instead, consider only the act of her bending over to fill it and then stretching on her tippy toes to pour it out six feet above.

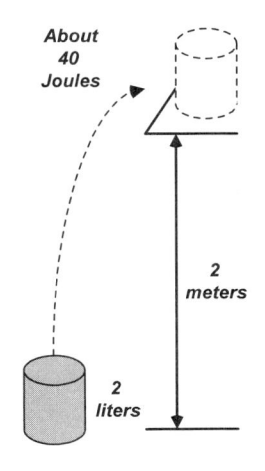

That bottle of water weighs about 2 kilograms, or a little over four pounds. When she is lifting that bottle up a six-foot height she is moving it through a distance of about 2 meters. In scientific terms, assuming you are on Earth around sea-level at the time, she has just performed about 40 Joules of work on the water:

$$2kg \times 9.81 \frac{m}{s^2} \times 2m = 39.24 J$$

Now recall that a kilowatt-hour is 3,600,000 J, or about *ninety thousand times* as large. A completely efficient pump would be able to do this ninety thousand times with that same ten cents of electricity which ran your sixty watt bulb for sixteen hours.

A pump which was only fifty percent efficient would only be able to lift *forty-five thousand* two-liter bottles. But even so, this is far out of proportion to the work required of a person, who would also have to wait for the bottles to fill and empty. For argument's sake, we will assume perfect efficiency, although the same arguments apply equally well with whatever pump of poor efficiency you might care to buy.

A kilowatt-hour can perform the same amount of work whether it takes an hour, a minute or a day. In any of these time periods, ninety thousand bottles are moved uphill. Just for fun, let's assume our pump does this amount of work in an hour. Take any muscle-bound brute you might imagine, and set him at the task in the place of your wife while she takes a break to prepare dinner. There is no chance he can perform this work, which requires lifting just short of 27 bottles per second, with muscle power alone. Even at fifty-percent efficiency he still needs to move more than 13 bottles each second, assuming they were filled and waiting for him to pick up and toss over the dam.

And if he does manage this Herculean feat for an hour, imagine what might happen to you after you offer to pay him a dime for his hour's effort. You at least will get a little head start as he catches his breath.

Yet, a seven-year-old girl might raise little yellow chicks and trade them for a dime. If she trades this dime for electricity, she can get this work done all day long every day so long as she has peeps to pay. These things now retail for about two bucks a peep in small quantities, by the way. Or 1.8 *million* bottles moved uphill per little yellow chick. All she needs is a pump and some hose, and she isn't going to get *that* from Zimbabwe, or from any others in the lower groups, is she?

Electricity, at ten cents per kilowatt-hour, is ridiculously cheap when compared to the work it can perform. To prove my point, I challenge you to get that amount of work done for ten cents using any method you choose. You will rapidly run out of options.

An interesting corollary to this idea is that if you actually need to pump water, there is a certain minimum amount of energy required to get it done. Once you have a perfectly efficient pump, unattainable in reality, you will still need a minimum of one kilowatt-hour to move those ninety-thousand bottles of water up that hill into the irrigation system. Budget any less, and get ready to have less food. Wishing to save the planet, hoping to change physics, or dancing your rabbit isn't going to make any difference.

Gasoline, or diesel for that matter, is also terribly cheap at current prices. 100 mL of either, or a little less than half a cup of these liquid fuels, contains about the same amount of push as a kilowatt-hour of electricity. At $4.00 per gallon, 100 mL of either fuel costs about the same ten cents. So, if gasoline or diesel are less than that per gallon they are *undervalued* compared to electricity, which as we have seen is itself cheap.

Compare either fuel or electricity to minimum wage, and the work capable of being done by minimum wage muscles, and you will see that minimum wage work is worth less than it is paid. Far less. No one in his right mind would hand a minimum wage worker a shovel when there is an option to put skilled operator at the controls of a diesel backhoe. Yet, many job creation programs, or exhortations to work for the good of the soul, are functionally no better than this obviously contrived example.

Notice that I said *skilled operator*. That skilled operator is using his mind to control the machine. The machine amplifies his efforts at his command through the relatively weak and puny apparatus of his body, whatever its form. It is his skill at operating the machine which makes him of value, not the strength of his limbs or his status in a collective. A quadruple amputee operating that backhoe, with a suitable interface to his facial muscles and limb stubs, would beat whatever minimum-wage shoveler you pick. It is the fuel and the machine which make the difference. Put that same amputee at the controls of teleoperated mining equipment, such as in use in Canada today, and there would no longer be any need for heroic coal-miner folk songs.

At ten cents per kilowatt-hour, or $4.00 per gallon, energy is ridiculously cheap compared to the work it enables you to perform. At ten times the price, I would still want it, and will find some way to pay for it. At hundred times the price, it is uncomfortable, but still cheap. Imagine paying that water brute $10.00, or one hundred times the cost of a kilowatt-hour as I write this, to lift your water. Although his hour is now within the economic realm for an hour of labor, he still physically can't compete. The effort required to lift ninety-thousand bottles is just too much.

Not that manual labor is unimportant, far from it. Someone had to assemble that backhoe, and service it, or put the screws in that pump. But unless you want to live in a world in which a shovel is your only option, you had better get in the way of nuts who want to limit access to energy by whatever method. Otherwise, kiss those roads and bridges goodbye, along with all those frozen foods. And start digging and hauling the old way. And learn to ignore the smell of rotting flesh. When it gets to that point the shovel itself is in question, too. Ore had to be hauled, smelted and forged into that shovel's blade. But each of these operations uses carbon (gasp).

As for me, I'm going to figure out how to pay for that ten-dollar kilowatt-hour, or make it myself, no matter how the monkeys choose to starve themselves. You can too.

Ideas are Transformative

Man's most useful tools, and his best weapon against raw nature and privation, are his ideas. His best ideas are those which manipulate his environment in ways which produce a more beneficial arrangement of stuff, which usually leads to an increased quality of life.

However, ideas can be destructive as well as constructive. The destructive forms of ideas are those propounded by monkeys, and which tend to redistribute stuff in ways detrimental to those who worked to accumulate it. Redistribution takes away resources, including stuff and time, from those men best able to transform them into more useful stuff. Redistribution then gives those resources to monkeys who only consume. Because of redistribution, society as a whole suffers. In the short term, however, monkeys prosper from this redistribution, so from their perspective as a loyal constituency of the collective, justice has been done.

Where Money Comes From

We are now prepared to see where all value, and by extension the useless fiat currency known as money, comes from.

All money (meaning more of each resource) is derived from locally increasing the quality of life for someone else. It is that simple.

Value doesn't get created by cheating or scheming or creating a need or a government program. Those things can get you money, but are destructive to the culture as a whole. Schemes remove value from a society, and are the economic equivalent of a tornado. The destruction wrought may create jobs for some, but value was destroyed nonetheless.

No, actual economic value gets created when someone, somewhere is willing to increase your quality of life in exchange for your increasing theirs. A scientist might restate that idea as:

$$\Delta Q > 0$$

Scientists and engineers use the Greek letter Δ, pronounced *delta*, to indicate a change. In the above expression, Q represents the quality of life matrix which we have been discussing, in the context of a particular individual. I now drop the subscript i to indicate that I mean an individual in a culture, as there really is no analog for cultural quality of life.

Quality of life has no context outside the perspective of an individual. A diamond lying on the ground means nothing to a culture unless at least one individual places a value on it. And only then does it have any referential value to another individual who might seek it to trade to the first.

This sounds like that old counter-culture quote: "All values are relative." In economic terms, it is absolutely true. At lunch time that dollar in my pocket isn't worth to me as much as that giga value burger. From the restaurant's perspective, exactly the opposite is true, or else they wouldn't give me that burger for my dollar, they would keep it for themselves.

The same reasoning applies to quality of life. People must have different values for their quality of life. If not, we would all be just fighting over the same stuff. I don't want a diamond. But if I unearthed a bunch of them with my backhoe one day I would certainly start looking around for someone who did want one. The exchange I would subsequently make with them would improve both our lives. Even if I could only find one person whom a diamond would benefit, I would still be able to increase the overall quality of life in the culture by that tiny amount.

If I couldn't find a single individual who placed value on those diamonds, they would just be useless rocks, unless I fooled someone into thinking they were valuable. And then the overall quality of life in the culture would go down, since I would have received valuable money in exchange for ultimately damaging someone else's actual quality of life.

This is an important point. No cultural *more* or value has any intrinsic context unless it benefits at least one individual somewhere. But often in our modern economy, imaginary benefits are substituted for real benefits. If someone tries to convince you to sacrifice some quality of your life, without recompense, then it is because he seeks to transfer that value to himself or others at your expense. To hide this fact the monkey collective will often state this one-sided transfer in other terms, such as "save the planet" or "benefit all mankind" or "reduce your carbon footprint". By allowing your preferences to be manipulated in this way, you are participating willingly in your self-sacrifice.

More importantly, understanding that money (from now on I use *money* to mean the underlying resource value which it is supposed to represent, and not the useless script itself) comes from increasing the quality of life of someone else allows all things to be understood in their proper context. This then is what scientists might call the *Theory of Everything*, at least in sociological terms. Notice that I didn't say in *economic* terms. This idea is more sublime than mere economics, and derives from the way in which God has decided that man should interact with His nature and each other. It also explains the otherwise stupefying ways of the monkey, his destructive nature, and the many gambits which the monkey might employ to eat men alive. This idea also explains the only rational solution which remains to the monkey question, all other efforts having been exhausted.

We saw before that quality of life depends on the amount of stuff (including stored energy), push, time and ideas available to individuals. But quality of life also depends heavily upon the value which each individual chooses to assign to those quantities. From this we can derive several important principles, each of which shows how to increase one's own quality of life in service to one's fellows. Or, as the monkey chooses to do, shows how to seize unearned value from the efforts of their betters. We will first concentrate on the positive side of this idea, which includes increasing the quality of life for others directly, or indirectly by pumping value.

Locally Increase Quality of Life

The first practical way to employ the quality of life formulation of value is, as Og and Pok discovered, to increase the quality of life matrix for others in exchange for quality of life for yourself. I call this concept *increasing Q*, or *adding positive delta Q*. In addition to mere trade of goods, when you help your customers or clients meet their goals through your services, you are doing the same thing by increasing their quality of life.

Conversely, you can increase the quality of life for others by *removing sources of negative delta Q*. When Ploi offered K'ette to have his sister Emma tend to the bunnies in their hutch to prevent their starvation and waste of value, he was proposing to remove a source of negative delta Q. A policeman is theoretically employed to remove local sources of negative delta Q, while I was employed as a Marine to do so on a global scale.

Individuals or organizations are willing to pay for sources of positive delta Q and for removal of sources of negative delta Q. But, experienced individuals often erect trust barriers to prevent themselves from being scammed by monkeys who have gone before or were rumored to be afoot. If you can successfully penetrate this trust barrier, and trade fairly with men, there is practically no limit to the amount of money you can make.

If you find a way to provide me with twenty dollars of value for ten dollars, I am going to be peeling off Hamiltons all day long to you for those Jackson-worths. I will eventually get saturated in getting so much of that twenty-dollar value such that I no longer perceive your service or product as worth my ten dollars. But even so, plenty of others will be lining up behind me to get some of the good stuff, too.

Sadly, we shall see how monkeys have constructed, using tools we have given them, fantastically complex mechanisms to prevent this free exchange of value between men. Monkeys have created these mechanisms so that they might insinuate themselves in the transaction and thus feed from these manufactured teats. And some of these mechanisms, although millennia old, were advocated by Hamilton and Andrew Jackson themselves as a means of increasing the power of the central government. We celebrate some of these mechanisms through their inclusion on the script. Each of these mechanisms are but one of the bars in the prison we ourselves have helped the monkeys erect.

Pump Value

As the tribesmen discovered, not all individuals in a culture will have the time or energy to reach all their potential customers, although in our culture today the Internet and various express services certainly help.

To that end, Mar and K'ette created a means by which stuff could be translated in time and space to where it had more value. Their story illustrates the second means of increasing quality of life, which is to pump value. We pump value when we transport stuff from a quality of life matrix where it has less value, to a quality of life matrix where it has more. There are several ways in which this value pump might be arranged, but in all cases the relative value of stuff, push and time are adjusted to benefit the consumer.

One such value pump might be constructed to transport low value stuff to areas of higher value. We've already seen an example of this form when we discussed transporting oil from Arabia to the continental United States. An entrepreneur who carries a truckload of prepared meals to a disaster area to sell it for twice the retail price is also providing value in a similar way. Left to free market forces, this entrepreneur benefits customers by pumping low value stuff to areas where this stuff has greater relative value.

A related transportation of stuff is across time instead of across space. Og's fifth woman-weight of wood on a given July day is of little value to him, but is of significant value to a customer in November. Similarly, the relatively low value of plentiful gasoline in a station owner's larger tank becomes much more valuable during a crisis or shortage. For the customer to benefit from this value, we would only need to encourage the owner to have it available by allowing him to profit.

A different sort of value pump transforms low value stuff into higher value stuff. A fertilizer plant converts air, water and energy into ammonium nitrate. Similarly, Beri converted Pok Jr.'s low value bunny pellets, which had actually become a source of negative delta Q ($-\Delta Q$) for him, into more valuable berries.

One can also pump value by applying stuff or push to conserve time. A water pump uses ten cents of electricity to lift ninety thousand two-liter bottles into the irrigation system. This pump also allows your wife to avoid serving your dinner late, by freeing her from the task of hauling and lifting all that water. The pump, then, saves you time by letting you get back to your nap quicker instead of wondering where dinner is. Similarly, that diesel backhoe lets you dig a ditch much faster than you or your right-wing extremist chain gang could with shovels.

A related value pump is for someone to apply their relatively low value time in exchange for stuff or push. This value pump, collectivist policies aside, would be available to all monkeys if they would only choose to do so. An employee does exactly this when he exchanges hours of his day for pay.

These three mechanisms encompass the entire spectrum of ways in which money is created. The first is to directly increase the quality of life, or add $+\Delta Q$. The second, removal of sources of $-\Delta Q$, is the counterpart of the first. And the last mechanism to create money, or equivalently, the accumulation of resources, is the pumping of value. In each case, the recipient of the additional value must decide for themselves whether the stuff or push or time which they surrender in exchange for the benefit received is a suitable price. You make this decision when you pay ten cents for a kilowatt-hour of electricity.

Each time you flip a light switch or change the thermostat setting, you effectively ask yourself whether that kilowatt-hour provides sufficient $+\Delta Q$ to make it worth the $-\Delta Q$ you incur by the loss of the dime. If that kilowatt-hour cost ten dollars, you would make exactly the same decision. At a higher price, though, the threshold, of course, will be in a different location. Even at ten dollars per kilowatt-hour, I bet it would still beat hauling water.

These means of obtaining money, and the resulting transactions which, as with Og and Pok, benefit both parties, may be summarized in the following ethic. I believe this ethic is the secret to success in any economy, or survival in any crisis:

☐ *Always provide more positive delta Q than your negative delta Q cost.*

Other means of obtaining money or resources, which we will see shortly, range from the merely benign to the downright destructive. Those means, while they might increase the net worth of specific individuals or groups, only destroy value in a culture overall. And in a crisis, some of those negative means would probably get you killed.

Redistributive Effects

The mechanisms which monkeys of all classes use to redistribute stuff, the foundation of quality of life, takes many forms. But, the effect of monkey redistribution is always to diminish the overall value in a culture. Consider the following diagram which illustrates this effect:

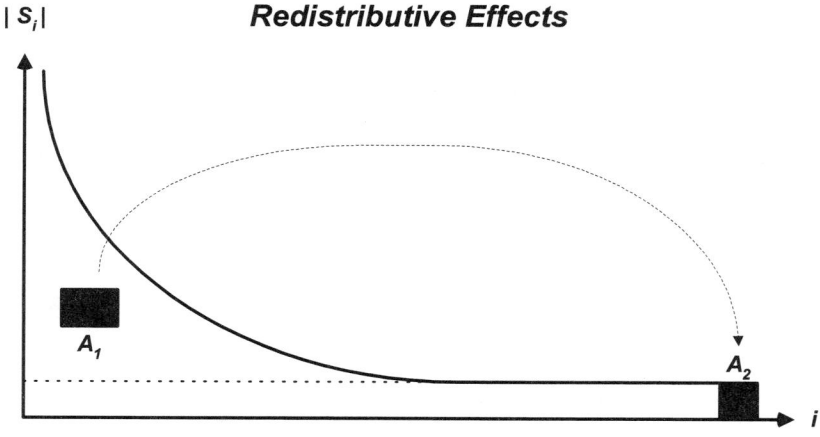

Redistributive Effects

$|S_i|$ vs i

Ex: 1 kWh saved in A_1 leads to a shotglass of gasoline in A_2, or a few briquettes in the brazier.

A popular notion among monkeys is to take resources away from those who have more of them, and then redistribute those resources to those who have little or none. By so doing, the monkeys claim, a sense of fairness or justice will be satisfied. As mentioned before, these redistributed resources typically only add to the number of those who live in subsistence. Even so, these resources are removed from persons who produce value and transferred to persons who only consume them, or who produce value less efficiently than the original holders.

Worse, the relative efficiencies in the two resource regions lead to additional waste, even if the transfer costs such as collection, transportation and distribution are ignored.

Consider that those individuals in the wealthy groups are wealthy precisely because the distribution efficiency is so high for them. Let's call the distribution efficiency for this group η_1. Individuals in the subsistence group tend to be so poor because the distribution efficiency for them, often by their own hand or demand, is low. We will call the distribution efficiency for this group η_2, which must necessarily be less than η_1. We can then define an equation which describes the change in stuff. We will express this change in terms of the energy cost to deliver that stuff. This change results from denying access to this stuff to those in the prosperous group and transferring it instead to the subsistence region:

$$A_2 = \frac{\eta_2}{\eta_1} \times A_1$$

Now, because the subsistence delivery efficiency is low compared to the wealthy delivery efficiency, the amount of stuff which can be delivered has been reduced.

Let's try a concrete example. Assume that the distribution efficiency of a particular item of stuff is 80% for wealthy individuals. Also assume that the distribution efficiency is only 50% for the subsistence group. Then, as shown below, only about two-thirds of the original stuff ever makes it to the poor:

$$A_2 = \frac{0.5}{0.8} \times A_1 = 62.5\% \times A_1$$

The culture has then lost about one-third of the original stuff which could generate quality of life, *even if the remainder isn't pilfered, lost, or diverted by the redistributive agency itself.* Further, as I stated before, the wealthy group can, much like that engineer designing a bridge or the grader operator shaping a road, create value with that stuff. This additional value which the original owner could have imparted would have led to more value and opportunity, while the poor can only consume it.

One might argue that the percentages shown are arbitrary, and skewed to make my point. But consider this. Wealthy people, in a free market, are more capable of getting resources they want without any outside assistance. The poor, by definition, are less capable of getting resources they want on their own. Otherwise, they would have already gotten at least a little more for themselves each day. These facts indicate that the wealthy are more efficient at accumulating wealth, while the poor are less efficient at that same activity.

Notice that I said "in a free market." We do not live in a free market. I shall cover in later chapters exactly how our current economic structure differs wildly from a free market. I shall also show how that difference causes the wrong people to become wealthy, and for the poor to stay poor. This effect, itself, is a redistribution, and as such, is inefficient. More on that topic later.

As our example above shows, the energy cost equivalent of a kilowatt-hour of electricity, if transferred to the social equivalent of Zimbabwe, would necessarily result in fewer resources overall. But when I say Zimbabwe, this could mean wherever in the world or the nation or your state that depressed sector of your economy may be. In Zimbabwe itself, this amount of energy results only in the equivalent of a shotglass of fuel or a few briquettes for the meal.

Regardless, in its original hands the electricity, or other form of energy stuff, is creative. But, in the latter hands after redistribution, this energy stuff is merely subsistive.

Food for Thought

You are now ready to consider a few exercises. There are no right or wrong answers, so I'm not going to give you an answer key. The important thing is that you think about these issues and form your own opinions.

☐ We have often heard the phrase "idle hands are the devil's workshop." Also, some spiritualists promote the concept that loving sleep leads to poverty. Which is better for your success, and ultimately, your well-being:

a) Pointless daily unending struggle pushing against a brick wall, or equivalently, performing piddly tasks simply to keep busy to keep the devil away? Simple tasks done while thinking are not in this category. In fact, given the intent of piddly tasks to make you too tired or busy to think, this type of thoughtful work would pretty much be classified by theologians as apprenticeship in the devil's workshop.

Or,

b) Drowsing about, as Og and Pok might by the stream? And while drowsing, formulate a plan of action to more efficiently apply stuff, push, time or ideas, and then arising to implement those ideas?

☐ Assuming that you answered b) to the above, why might spiritualists seek to cripple your personal resources which could otherwise make you independent of crisis or tragedy? Who benefits from your dependency?

☐ Recall that some interpretations of the Bible indicate that Adam and Eve sinned and condemned us all by eating from the Tree of Knowledge. Accept for argument's sake that ideas are the most powerful resource available to us, as ideas allow us to make more effective use of all the others. Also accept that God created man with a remarkable mind and placed him on a planet with a seemingly endless cache of treasure. If these things are so, then why would God, incomprehensibly, tell man to not use his mind to discover that wealth using the treasure map of math and science which He Himself created?

☐ Imagine that you are Og or Pok, transported into your life and circumstances. Make a list of:

    a) All the *stuff* you have at your disposal.
    b) The various means of *push* you can employ.
    c) The *time* you have available to push your stuff around.

While creating the list above, remove from your mind any limitations whatsoever. These limitations include your need to work at a job somewhere, your background or education, your economic, social, incarceration or probationary status. These include divorce, bankruptcy or other pending or adjudicated legal proceedings or related obligations. It's amazing the variety of snares monkeys have devised, isn't it? Or, for that matter, arbitrary laws which constrain your action.

For example, if you have a chainsaw, but it has been rusting away unused in your garage, include that as stuff. If you have the ability to paint houses, even though you might be an engineer or a teacher, include that on the push list. Also, include time at your current job as time available to you. You are, over and over, deciding to go there each day, after all.

☐ Now limit yourself only by the principle that you will not cheat, actively harm or steal from another person, but instead you will trade with all men fairly as did Og and Pok. What could you then accomplish with your resources? Aggressively include those things which enable you to derive value for yourself while providing improved quality of life to others. Make a list of the top ten most productive of these ideas you could pursue and prioritize the top five based on the amount of value each provides to you. Include in your estimate of value the happiness you receive while implementing and attaining those ideas.

Note that leaving a monkey to wallow in need without giving him anything could be, nonsensically, considered as causing passive harm to him. For example, we have been programmed to be charitable, but choosing to not give to charity is not considered active harm for the purposes of this exercise. So, ignore any bleatings of the monkey that you aren't going out of your way to save him.

☐ What other persons might benefit from these activities? Recall that Og found Pok's squirrels to be more valuable than his wood, and vice versa. How might these other persons return to you stuff, push, time or ideas which would be more valuable to you than what you provided to them? How, at the same time, from their perspective, might you provide more value to them than they returned to you?

☐ Now start adding back limitations based on your personal circumstances. What would you need to change about your life, either immediately or over time, which would enable you to implement the top five ideas on your list? Are there any skills you need which you might learn for yourself, or learn from another? For example, could you offer your services as an apprentice, thus providing value in your service in exchange to the skilled master, to learn a necessary skill?

☐ Now consider the artificial limitations imposed by the society of monkeys, including laws which protect no one from you but merely constrain your freedom. Consider whether these regulatory issues would not be required if men traded fairly and were held accountable for the results, or are simply restrictions which create unnecessary jobs for monkeys. Examples of these limitations, in order, might be drug laws, contractor licensing and tax accounting requirements.

With these limitations in place, how many of the top five ideas have now been placed outside of your reach? Why, and who now benefits from these ideas instead of you? Are there any ways in which you could game the system to achieve these goals while still obeying the letter of the law if not the intent or the spirit? And who defines what is meant by "gaming the system" versus "an effective business model"?

☐ Consider the options you had to improve yourself before these artificial limitations were added. For example, was a potential apprenticeship rendered impractical? Who benefits instead? And why them?

☐ Consider the beneficiaries of your efforts before these artificial limitations were added. Who, other than yourself, now loses the benefits which you might have otherwise provided?

Chapter 7, The Shamans

As we discussed in the previous chapter, the source of all pure wealth, or equivalently, other resources, comes from providing more quality of life to others than you cost them in the process. Og and Pok discovered this miracle long ago, and their tribe lived happily, growing in wealth and number seemingly without end. But this wealth and growth soon became the envy of others who sought to take a shortcut to satisfy their needs. These doomed shortcuts occurred to the envious in several flavors.

The first crack in the foundation of trust in the tribe was outright theft. This theft started almost innocently: a passerby took a stick of wood from a pile here, or picked a handful of berries from the cultivated stands. The root of this theft came from envy for the riches of their productive neighbors, allowing the thieves to justify their actions.

"Og doesn't own the wood, he merely gathered it into this stack here," they reasoned. "Had he not gathered all of it, I wouldn't have to walk so far to get just this one stick, or this other one, too, or maybe these, also, which I need."

"Beri is lucky that this fruit grows so well next to her hut. All the other brambles in the valley are hard to harvest, and grow in a tangle which makes them hard to reach," the others claimed. "She shouldn't hoard all the good fruit for herself."

In the early days of the tribe, before it could even be called such a thing, men the world over simply took what they might from nature and from each other. Only the strongest or the most cunning managed to have any food or other resources, but even they ultimately fell prey to others in an endless cycle of violence. No one could plan beyond the immediate moment at hand. Worse, property ownership was a concept which reached no further than a man's own hand and ceased as soon as what he held was snatched from his grasp.

Some groups of men, like the barbarian tribes, had ceded power to the strongest and most ruthless, hoping to convert fear into referential power for themselves. The barbarian kings ruled by no means other than that it would mean death for any who challenged their rule. Each man in a barbarian tribe hoped to win favor for himself, and thus a larger share of the resources the tribe stole from others. In that hope men would often turn on their neighbors, reporting the slightest lack of loyalty to their king.

Women especially, lacking physical strength which reduced them to mere property in such tribes, often found that they too could hope to curry favor by similar accusations should they be slighted or threatened. The kings, whether the accused was innocent or not, were slaves to their own power. These kings had no choice but to brutally murder each accused usurper to maintain order, and to preserve their own lives. Of course, this system of ruthlessness often meant death for the barbarian kings themselves as factions arose among their barbaric nobility which could depose a ruler by force or subterfuge.

All belonged to the king, and he passed along any excess to the tribesmen as he saw fit. In so doing the king bribed and sustained the tribe to not rise against him in their hunger, or to join in punishing those who defied him. Most of these men ruled with such despotic completeness that even the wild hares and harts were his, only to be hunted with his approval and brought to him when felled.

The barbarian tribes thus lacked any incentive for individuals to excel. Should any try, the fruits of their labor would be easily seized from them by the others, and any resistance would be reported to the king as disloyalty. Even such innocent diversions as studying God's creation, as did Tith, led these kings to fear acts of wizardry which might threaten their hold on the tribe. Therefore, acts of self-sufficiency and strength and knowledge, or even idle entertainment, were often seen as threats of non-compliance bubbling beneath the surface. Not surprisingly, few tried to improve themselves and their means or the knowledge of mankind. Those who did rarely lived long enough to pass along their fleeting and meager wealth and ideas to their children.

And so, the forces of evolution ensured that the barbarian tribes were peopled with the violent, the unprincipled, and the ignorant. And the fearful. Equally unsurprisingly, the barbarian tribes soon devoured the resources upon which they stood. As they consumed these resources like locusts, they sought more elsewhere, finding relative plenty among the neighboring tribes such as those in K'ette's village. Only in these places, where men had, as had Og and Pok, discovered the miracle of trade were there more than subsistence resources. Only where men lived peacefully together were they able to exchange the largess of their work with others, increasing their quality of life to mutual selfish benefit.

A few barbarian kings, seeing the wealth of such places, sought to emulate their productivity after first murdering them and consuming their wealth. A barbarian conqueror, seeing the bounty of Beri's bramble patch for example, might assign a tribesman to manage the patch. In such cases the king might have assigned an expert like Beri herself, had she, or her equivalent, not already been raped and murdered as an example to others.

Whether this task was assigned to a skilled worker such as Beri or an ignorant tribesman, it made no difference. Each fruit plucked from this field must first be sent to the king, with he, and he alone, deciding how much would be returned to the worker as his subsistence. Either tender, lacking incentive to improve or produce, their ration the same regardless, soon fell back to producing only slightly more than that required to avoid the lash or the pyre. Any additional effort purchased only exhaustion.

And the kings, no matter how clever they might be, could not possibly manage or oversee all the details which all the tribesmen individually might easily handle for themselves. Any overseer an enlightened barbarian king might appoint, seeking his own power and prestige and profit, not only lacked the knowledge of prosperity, but disdained it as rude and common.

That prosperous berry patch required much expert and detailed activity, not just the trampling of the bunny pellets. The tying of the younger brambles to form next years trellis, like the tending and care of the bunnies and the training of the cheval, were all required for prosperity. All of these things also required constant attention and self-interest to perform

The Shamans

well. Yet none of these things are of interest to the overseer, who considers only the obedience of his and the king's subjects. Applied at the tip of the lash, these things waned in importance when compared to pleasing the overseer. Further, the overseer deemed the most capable to be the most suitable for harder servitude. So, men in conquered tribes soon learned to hide their ability lest they be taxed the most.

Many tribes overwhelmed by the barbarians had also discovered that miracle our tribe called Tithing. As you recall, with this practice the best of a man's work was carefully preserved so that the following years' flocks and harvests would be more bountiful. Although called by many names by many tribes, the barbarian kings universally saw this practice as the equivalent of secular heresy. Increasing one's holdings, to the king's mind, represented a holdout from his authority, as he demanded only the finest for his kingly tables. And in his ignorance demanded the heads of those who practiced this early genetic engineering.

So over time, under the rule of even the most enlightened barbarian kings, carefully tended brambles, plump fowl, prolific bunnies, husbanded woodlots and resources of every kind devolved back into the wild. And so the barbarians, even the enlightened, were once again compelled to march onward to plunder remote villages and tribes which had not yet fallen.

Some saw the rise of the barbarians as men being swayed by their basest nature. In reality, the barbarian kings could not have ruled had their subjects not seen them as a source of goods easier than their own hand. Lacking confidence in their own ability or ideas, men too easily come under the sway of those who promise to take from others by force. Especially if that promise includes a provision to then hand that largess out to their minions who grasp for it with their own greedy, and often bloody, hands. Even if that largess is paltry in comparison to what these same men might earn for themselves.

And yet, the barbarian kings lived in constant fear that they might themselves be killed by those enslaved by birth and circumstance to serve them. After all, some of those born into slavery might decide that their circumstances might be better in the wild with the king pursuing. Or better, as a benevolent king themselves, having disposed of the former. These ideas usually stemmed from the central idea that man was created in God's image, and thus worthy of being a master of himself and a slave to none. To the king, or the collective which demands the king's largess, these ideas were too dangerous to allow unchecked.

And so, the most successful barbarian kings soon realized that it was essential to cut the bond between a man and God. This division would leave the man with no authority to which to turn but to the king himself. Enter the spiritualist, or shaman, or prophet, or reverend, or saint, or pontiff or any number of names which served the purpose of isolating men from God.

The purpose of a spiritualist was, by inserting himself as a prophet or interpreter of God's vision, to divert man's loyalty and attention away from God. Thus each man's own individual self interest would be diverted toward the spiritualist and, by proxy, the king. This goal of redirected loyalty was achieved by ensuring that the spiritualists' loyalties to the king was paid in wealth and power to the extent that they achieved the cementing of that king's power. The barbarian king thus secured his power by the idea planted in men's minds that he was due his power as if stemming from God Himself. A judo master would have been proud of this spiritual and intellectual redirection of man's attention.

But this was a process best taken slow. At first, the spiritualist might present himself as a wise man who had studied the nature of God more fully than each man might have time to do on his own. Much as a purported mind-reader only needs a few tidbits of information about his mark to make educated guesses which might seem phenomenally insightful (I myself enjoy this game when encountering purported mind-readers or door-to-door evangelists). This technique, known as "cold reading", is fun when done at a party or out on a date. But, if twisted to manipulate the minds of the unwary to redirect power and loyalty, this trick can be a dangerous weapon.

Now, not everyone will fall for this ruse. But the spiritualist only needs a few committed marks to begin to accumulate real power. Witness for example the phenomenal influence wielded by that arch-collectivist, Jim Jones. Merely by resonating with key issues important to the individual, a shaman can easily appear to speak for God. And these issues can be easily detected by forming a model of that individual's quality of life matrix factors.

"God told me in a dream last night that you are suffering," the shaman might say. Most people are, at least in some way. And those more likely to fall under the spiritualist's influence are probably suffering the most.

If the shaman encounters narrowed-eyes at this point, he knows to excuse himself and beat a hasty retreat to the next mark, having only wasted about twenty seconds. Even so, he has gained valuable information about who to deal with later.

But if he sees the faintest glimmer of hope in the eyes, he digs deeper. "In this dream, a loved one, maybe a wife, ... or a child, ... or a parent, ..." he pauses imperceptibly, waiting for recognition. Upon seeing a glimmer of response, or better, outright agreement, he knows which way to turn. If not, "... there was an animal, and it was starving, ..." and so on until he hits paydirt. If not, he can blame himself, such as, "Sometimes God sends me to a neighbor of the afflicted to keep me humble. Which one of your neighbors is suffering? I know God wants you to help them, even if you don't have the means yourself." This last one is pure gold, and can lead to a wealth of information about gender, age, affliction, and so on, which makes a far greater impact when he approaches the neighbor later.

Sometimes, to break the ice, the shaman needs a miracle. This could be any number of science-based tricks, well-known to alchemists and pre-teen boys before the advent of public school. But simpler tricks work as well. During a drought or a famine, our shaman might run around for a while asking the tribesmen to pray for rain or plenty, and eventually rain or plenty will happen. Hardly ever would the shaman ask for the tribesmen to help dig an irrigation channel or work on better means of managing livestock or crops, as this would be counterproductive for their purpose.

But until it does rain or the crops bear fruit, he can start planting the seed that someone is to blame. His best choice for blame is someone who booted him out the door during an earlier visit, "God is telling me that some in His flock are not believing enough."

The shaman waits for recognition, and then continues, "I visited Ungh the other day, and he didn't seem to believe. He thinks that man can solve his own problems. I don't think he really believes in God's power. What do you think?" There is a great chance that the shaman is not the only boot recipient whom Ungh had lost patience with, self-reliant individualist that he is, so this is a great row to plow. If the mark offers another name, that works too. The more the merrier.

With a list of names, now it's time to get a crowd together. So much the better if he has the barbarian king's ear to keep the heat away. Ungh, and the others like him, probably aren't helping the king sleep very well anyway, so this is an easy sell.

And out of this crowd of faithful, our shaman probably has a few who really believe. I mean REALLY believe.

Believe in their souls that they are specially chosen by God for something important. Because they not only WANT to. They NEED to.

Because their miserable, pitiful lives up unto that point have just been a total waste of genetic material. The only thing that has kept some of these righteous from putting an axe to their own head is that it would require some insight and hard work. And it would probably hurt.

But insight and hard work have eluded them, of course, by their own choices. But the lack of these led them to circumstances in their own lives to put them squarely in the shaman's grasp.

The shaman needs at least three willing assistants. At worst, some of the king's own men will be happy to fill this role. The king may send at least one of his own as a failsafe regardless. In any nefarious deed, one might get cold feet, two might discuss it and get cold feet. But, in a sea of at least three collectivists, no one wants to be the one to speak first. We will call these three The Chosen Ones.

So the shaman starts the soft sell. "So many good people are suffering, and God doesn't want us to suffer."

"God just wants us to worship Him, and understand His Glory."

"God told me to teach Ungh and the others. But I have failed Him."

"I prayed heavily about this, and asked for God's forgiveness. He told me, in His Wisdom that He had already sent me angels in the form of men."

"The time is near. The angels were already among us, and I have already met them, but I knew them not."

"The angels have come to deliver God's wrath."

Rattle off enough of this nonsense, and even the dimmest of ruffian bulbs, aspiring for angel-hood, will eventually get the message. If not, he can even volunteer some of these morons one-to-one. "God told me that you are one of His angels, and that, as a test of both our faiths, you would at first be unwilling."

All the shaman has to do now is pick a time. Some astronomical event, like a full moon, or better, a comet or an eclipse, works great. And so, as the appointed time approaches, he begins to rile the faithful.

"The time nears. God has chosen us to display our faith that He will deliver us on (the next full moon, whatever). We must gather together to pray for Ungh at his hut. If our faith is strong enough, he will fall to his knees with us," he requests, reasonably enough. "I have also been instructed that we must build a fire with wood from the seven oaks to represent the seven prophets," he adds, or some similar simple compliance nonsense.

Note, by the way, if it happens to rain or the harvest is bountiful or the herd returns, or whatever, before the appointed hour, the shaman still has a way out. "God wanted to make sure we would all be willing. Once He saw the strength of our faith, He delivered us, but warns us to not be asleep when He knocks again."

And in so doing gets to bank that fervor for the next calamity while taking credit for the deliverance. Eventually, though, the deliverance does not come. And so the plan springs into action. A crowd, glistening with uplifted faces, forms in front of Ungh's hut. At the shaman's urging, they begin to build a bonfire with the seven oaks, or the three calves, or that shrub or this oil, so that God will see their obedience. Ungh comes out to see what the hell is going on.

"Ungh, will you repent and follow God's will?" If Ungh caves, again, the shaman has a victory, since the faithful now have had a demonstration of their imagined power. If so, the lot moves down the list a week or so later to the next victim, all entries cleared in advance by the king. Eventually either the rain returns, or someone on the list fails to repent. Unfortunately for Ungh, it's him.

"Ungh, so many are suffering, and all God wants is for us, all of us, to bow to His will." Ungh is in a no-win situation here, and notices that the king's men, quick to grab him for the slightest disobedience, are strangely absent from this mob. He also lacks a pintle-mounted .50-cal.

The shaman then turns to the crowd, and with a dramatic flourish instructs them, "Fall to your knees and pray that he will repent."

The crowd complies, no one wanting to be seen as siding with Ungh, and in their act of the simplest shared compliance, the die is cast. And established the shaman to all who see this act as their leader.

"Ungh, will you repent and follow God's will?" he repeats. No answer from the stunned and incredulous Ungh. It couldn't have been scripted any better.

"Children, God has told me that from this multitude will rise avenging angels to strike down the disbeliever. Angels, rise and advance!" he shouts, lifting his arms and staff to the heavens.

Now, at least The Chosen Ones, and perhaps the few plants of the king, rise and approach Ungh, prepared stones in hand. Collective action being what it is, and having already demonstrated their willingness to obey by the simple act of falling to pray, one or more of the others will rise, too. Seeing their neighbor rise beside them, and caught up in wanting to be angels, or at the very least of not wanting to be Ungh, others rise and advance. The contagion spreads like wildfire.

The Chosen Ones, closing on the startled Ungh, or better, chasing him as he runs, throw their stones. The rest, not asking why those chosen already had stones in their hands, look around for something to throw. In this act of following the tide they take themselves further down the path of collective obedience. Stones, branches, axes, it doesn't matter. Eventually, they surround the pummeled body, the shaman at the center.

"Children, you have witnessed a miracle." At this point, none dare to speak out to question this nonsense.

"Fall to your knees and join me in prayer." Even if repulsed by what they have just done, everyone complies.

"God, forgive us for not trusting You. Forgive us for taking so long to understand Your will. Forgive us for doubting our king who You sent us to lead us, and who tends to our needs as Your servant." Bingo.

"And forgive Ungh, and let his blood wash away our sins."

"And teach us to trust Your will. And to be swift as Your angels. Amen."

"Children, please rise." They obey.

"And cast the disbeliever upon the fire, that his spirit may rise to God for judgement," he orders, laying the groundwork for associating ritualistic burning and blood sacrifice as necessary conditions for life. The next time, they won't have to bother killing their victim first, they can just tie him, or her, to the fire and light it up. Kind of like upping the spiritual ante.

A mob boss might require a blood crime for membership. Similarly, each man and woman and child present, even if they didn't cast a single stone, share the guilt and shame for what they have done. Or, what they failed to stop.

And now they MUST believe in the righteousness of what they have done. To maintain this internal lie they must convince everyone they meet to believe as well. They must pass this belief onto their children, so strongly that they pass it onto theirs, and so on. Because if they don't, they would come hand-to-face with the blood on their own hands. And being sheep in a collective flock, it was that avoidance of responsibility that led to their rapt attention to the shaman who walked up to them in front of their huts. And it was their longing to belong to the collective that led to their enlistment in the mob that murdered Ungh.

And so the spiritualist contagion gains a permanent foothold. The rain, or whatever precipitating crisis was at hand, no longer matters. If the rain comes, the shaman was right. If not, they move to the next victim until it does. The important thing now is that they believe.

Because now they must. And now the shaman gets to start imposing some rules. Many of these happen to line up nicely with the king's needs, but no one dares point that out.

"Don't kill anybody." Implicit in that one is that it is OK if the shaman or the king tells you to, but don't decide to kill anyone on your own.

"Don't steal stuff." Again, not bad. Pretty much a necessity for civilization.

"Obey the king, because God says to." Neat. That one is worth every dime, goat, perfume, oil and priestess the king will pay the shaman from now on.

"Don't want anything your neighbor has." On the surface, this one was already covered by the stealing thing. But, we can twist this around to keep those individualists in line. Everyone should just be impossibly happy with what circumstances you were born in or assigned to, and not try to improve your station by learning and things like that.

"Don't work on Tuesdays." Everyone has to do something on Tuesdays, but at least this way you get to be guilty of something.

"Come tell me when you do bad stuff and I will ask God to forgive you." Motherlode. Look what the shaman could twist those tiny minds into doing when he got you to rat out your neighbor's cough. Getting that information allowed him to tell said neighbor that God told him about the cough, and thus win the neighbor's compliance. Imagine what can be done with the flood of information this little rule will unleash.

"God hates knowledge." We can't let any of those pesky ideas lead to some embarrassing questions for the shaman or the king. You might even make up some stories about how everyone would be all happy-pants right now if some dumbass smart guy didn't start thinking about stuff long ago. Maybe you could even work in a "hate women" angle while you are at it, if you can show how his primary babe lured him into eating a grape or something.

"The devil makes you do it." This one lets you off the hook for bad stuff from time to time, but only if you show up and tell all. While we are at it, let's claim this devil guy is the one who puts thoughts in our heads to learn stuff, especially that dumbass smart guy and his stupid conniving wench. That one is great as it a) shows you the devil IS real or else you wouldn't be having all those ideas, and b) stop thinking, damn you! Really.

You can also add some great ideas that really do make sense, as these keep the populace alive longer:

"Don't eat dead people."

"Don't have sex with dead people."

"Don't have sex with people who eat dead people."

And a whole bunch of other sex-related rules. Those shamans are horny little one-track-minded bastards, come to think of it. Anyway. Add a few more genuinely beneficial ideas:

"Wash your hands."

"Don't let people with pus make food for you."

Also, mix in some rules to prevent the idiots from doing stuff that people with sense could do just fine:

"Don't have sex with women who charge for sex." She can do your laundry, watch your kids, slap you around for a while, wash your car, bring you burgers, etc., all for money. Or, she can demand diamonds and other shiny stuff all the time, but just not money for doing that one thing. If you do want to have sex with her, make sure she gives it away for free to anyone who wanders by rather than her running it as an entertainment industry.

Otherwise, she might take pains to protect the inventory.

"Only have sex with people with whom you have reached particular contractual arrangements, which must be approved by your local shaman representative, even if such contracts are decades old." There's that sex thing again, but this time contractual arrangements are OK so long as the shamans approve in public rituals.

"Don't smoke that." More later.

"Don't drink that." More later, too.

"Don't eat that pig or catfish or shrimp." The shaman could have easily added "unless you make sure it's cooked thoroughly first." But, that would have required some individual thinking and responsibility, and *that* is a can of worms best left closed.

"Don't judge anybody." Even the idiot who clearly screwed up every opportunity he had been given. Judgement is just more of that pesky thinking, and you might start judging the king or the shaman if you do. Besides, that's their bag.

"Trim the penises of little boys." Hmmm. Maybe that one is only for idiots. Or else it is good as a reminder of what the shaman might do to you if you start using your penis outside of your shaman-approved contracts.

To protect the shaman's interest, he needed a catch-all rule: "Stone anyone who gets out of line." This one pretty much puts the end to that rampant individualism and thought.

With a related: "If you don't make your children or your wife or husband follow these rules, you get stoned."

And the Mother of All Rules: "Give me ten percent of everything you get."

The kings should have seen that one coming. Instantly, despite the fact that the king demands more, the shaman becomes the richest guy in the valley. Sure, the shaman has to hire a few malcontents as priests, perhaps even The Chosen Ones who helped launch this new sensation. He also has to put up some special huts to hold court. But other than these things, the shaman really doesn't have a lot to do with his cash.

The king, on the other hand, is busy building roads to march on, and feeding the masses so they can dig ore and bang out bronze swords. And buying off his allies and foes alike with money he took by force from the productive. The king gets more, but the shaman keeps more of what he gets. Now, the shaman isn't stupid enough to just say it like that. No, the words sound more like: "Give God ten percent of everything you get. He said I can hold it for Him."

As if God doesn't own it all, anyway. But even that isn't good enough. So he adds: "Oh, and make it the best ten percent, too. He doesn't want to think you are holding out on Him."

So much for Tithing, and the genetic miracles that brings. Prosperity gets in the way of all that desperation and the attendant obedience anyway.

Related is: "Give stuff to poor people." Without any judgement calls about whether they deserve it or are just a bum, of course. This one is really neat in that it kind of sidesteps the original selling point for the ten percent.

It also promotes the interest of all those people who listen to the shaman and outnumber you. You don't expect the shaman to be dipping into his till for those waifs, do you? That's *your* problem, not his. Besides, he and his boys are too busy listening to the juicy gossip.

For a while, this one was: "Let the widows and orphans root around in the fields after the harvest so they can pick up what's left and help trample that leftover stuff into mulch." But that sounded too much like work and fair exchange of value. Worse, if the widow has her kids out working they might pick up some skills and a work ethic. Here come those damnable thoughts again! Stop it!

The shamans eventually transformed the way in which men viewed their relationship with God. After a sufficient number of individualists, who saw themselves in direct connection with Him, had been butchered or intimidated into silence, nothing stood in the way of the shamans inserting themselves between God and His creatures. What had previously been an exploration of God's creation became labeled as Occult, or Witchcraft, or Paganism, or Satanism. Or, any number of easily named and capitalized heresies, suitable for burning or stoning.

After a sufficiently long reign of terror, a shaman of sufficient authority need only point at an individualist and name him or her as one of these. And then lean back, smiling righteously upon them, as the swarm attacked in their religious zeal, certain that God smiled upon them as well. Over time, the fear of such retribution silenced dissent or discussion. Celebrations of God's bounty, such as our tribe's annual berry fight, would have served as sufficient evidence for ritualistic execution of the proponents or attendees.

The battle was considered won when the only theological choice available in the landscape of ideas was simple. One side of this simple choice was adherence to and promotion of silly rituals that could only demean the awe of an Infinite Creator. The other side of the choice was atheism or other evil-sounding labels. The third possibility, that of the most simple relationship of man as an individual creation of his God, was stamped out where ever it happened to spring up.

Eventually, some of those shamans became a little too big for their britches. In some cases, some barbarian king had enough of them and decided to whack them and start his own shaman subsidiary. In other cases, the shamans took over the kingdom and went into the barbarian business.

The most successful shaman racket of all time grew larger than a whole bunch of kings. One day, some shamans got together and decided to resolve their differences. To do so, they lumped all of their compliance rituals into one big mash, which might seem a little inconvenient at first. But, this turned out to have a couple of great advantages.

First, the ritual mush became so confusing that the guy on the street had no idea what the hell was going on with God, to put it bluntly. The common man was left with no choice but to either listen to what the regional shamans told him to do, or to think for himself and get stoned.

Second, all those gossip chambers now had the potential for revealing some really good stuff that had real political power. Imagine if some minor functionary in one kingdom blurted out some tidbit that meant some other kingdom was about to get invaded. Then, just like the whole "I had a dream" thing that got it all started, the shamans could use that information as some kind of "God told me this" type of kingdom-vs-kingdom scam for hire. Or, the shamans could get together and decide whether or not to tip off the invadee, and possibly sell that information to the highest bidder. Or, they might just let some jerk king they didn't like get invaded. Or get wiped out while invading someone else. Lots of ways that one could turn out, all of them great for the shaman pocketbook.

On the flip side, this organized shaman glaze had a major flaw. Just as this mondo-shaman thing was getting touched off, the top shamans realized they had a problem. With all those little believer cults out there, each with their own scam going on, someone had to come up with a great common story or else the whole thing could blow apart in no time. All it would take to rattle apart is for one of those lower-level guys to decide that their version of shamanism should predominate.

For a while, things seemed to stagnate. And then, one day a shaman showed up who had been visiting another cult trying to get them into the fold. This other cult was notoriously known as the predominate dick-snippers, they not liking anyone named Richard, and had refused to join up. The snippers, as it turned out, had their own thing going like gang-busters.

The shaman reported that the snippers seemed, in a way, to value individuality, despite their shaman tradition being the one that came up with that whole "knowledge is bad" thing. More oddly, the whole collective of them sometimes acted like an single personality. These qualities allowed the snippers to infiltrate most of the barbarian kingdoms and assist them with handling a lot of the administrative and media needs all around. Unfortunately for them, a few centuries previously their host barbarian king had decided they had grown a little too powerful and decided to disperse them around.

It turned out that this dispersion had happened a couple of times before, too. During one of these previous dispersals there came about a story of a semi-magical radioactive box they used to carry around to neutrate their enemies. Barbarian kings, not liking to be on the receiving end of an ad-hoc neutron bomb, decided enough was enough (I'll write about that one someday, but I'll probably cast it in modern times).

The shaman rep who had gone to visit them, and had been rebuffed, heard a story about some really nice guy, Lam. This Lam had rocked the boat for the snippers by pointing out some stupid stuff that had been going on. As happened to Ungh, the snippers decided to off him, but instead of getting the tribe together, managed to con the barbarian king into subcontracting the work. The snippers did bother to get a crowd together to watch and throw stuff at Lam as he died, though.

As it turned out, this guy Lam had some friends for which he had done some favors, and didn't like the way he had been treated. So, these friends of his had started wandering around, writing stories and letters.

Eventually, most of these guys had died off in obscurity, but not before planting seeds of the stories here and there, mostly where the snippers were wandering around doing their thing.

So, the organized shaman rep thought that, with a little editing, this story could be the one that would help rally the various shaman cults under one flag. But also, as a bonus, this story might discredit the snippers, their biggest competition, in the eyes of their barbarian king hosts. It would also relieve the necessity of the shamans having to off someone periodically, as they were running short on individualists willing to stick their necks out.

After much debate, it was decided that they would cast Lam as a son of God, as all men are. But, unlike the uncooperative Unghs of the world, both God and this guy would be excited about the chance for him to get whacked. Without this mental gymnastics, it would be irrational otherwise for God to just let His boy get strung up without turning everyone involved into roaches.

With the story cast this way, you could get the bonus of a blood sacrifice, but without all the social chaos that results when you get the natives stirred up. Now that the shamans were going to be running things, they couldn't very well have the populace running around with stones and fire, could they? Things like natives with stones and fire sometimes turns out bad for shamans as well as Ungh.

But you still needed the guilt angle, because that was the glue that had kept Ungh's murderers in line. Modern-day abortionists use this strategy also. By performing abortions on young girls, at their request, they have these children's bloody little hands for life. Those hands are best used in the ballot box, even for issues that have nothing to do with abortion but which promote related world-views akin to a religion.

Without guilt, no obedience. It was decided that they would have another rule such that you would be in trouble with God if you didn't get excited about Lam's murder. This rule also included the provision that you had to believe that God was excited about the whole thing, too.

Also, as a bonus, the shamans decided to put in another whole level of indirection. This contractual obligation indicated that you have to talk to the shamans who would then talk to Lam, who would in turn talk to God for you. Or, you could talk to Lam yourself, who would then talk to God, depending on your service area and contract terms. In any case, no one was allowed to talk to God directly anymore. The payoff for the faithful is that by simply buying into this story they would get the good spiritual vibes that had taken a mob an evening's work at Ungh's hut.

It was essential for compliance to make sure that everyone had the same blood on their hands as did those who obediently kneeled and rose and attacked Ungh. To this end, the shaman collective, and subsidiaries, decided that all the faithful would be required to eat little toasted crackers that represented the body of Lam. Further, the faithful would be required to drink various beverages, again depending on the prohibitional status of your subsidiary chapter,[3] that represented his blood. To make this sacrifice OK again, and not seem as bloodthirsty as it is, they decided that after taking a weekend off Lam hopped up like a bunny and wandered away.

This framework was remarkably successful. In arranging this story and the associated rituals, the shaman organizers were able to make sure that little children were sucked into the fold. To grab the kiddies, the shamans associated snacks and goodies with killing off some guy who had just bothered to ask a few questions and tell a few clever little stories about his Father. And hey, everybody wins, since Lam was asking for it, right? By the time these little kids grew up to be adults they wouldn't even stop to think of the horror that they were celebrating. Instead, they would reach for their own stones to hurl at anyone who dared tickle that little part of their mind that revealed the truth.

Also, despite this story having been presented as good news, the shaman organizers managed to throw in one final twist. Recall that the snippers had conned their host king into offing Lam. As a result, the shaman organizers used the history of this manipulation in their favor against the snippers. Over the centuries, each time the snippers got well-established anywhere, the gossip chambers swang into action. In these actions the faithful barbarian kings were coerced, blackmailed, or encouraged to expel the snippers from their lands. Or, encouraged to try to wipe the snippers out entirely, lest the king in question be similarly fooled, and subsequently damned.

This gambit was particularly effective against any snippers who dared to start acting individualistically. Today, modern monkeys would call that "an effective business model" as it ensured that the organized shamans would have a virtual monopoly on theological issues.

Unfortunately, there was another bunch of shamans who had recently sprung up that wasn't buying-in. These guys also had a beef with the snippers. It seems that an old snipper had, at his wife's urging because of her frequent headaches, tapped his maid, Sami, who got pregnant. Then, when wifey got pregnant with her own child, she convinced the old snipper to get rid of the maid and her kid, who had been named Izzy. The old snipper should have told wifey to can it, as it had been her idea, probably so she could lord it over him. Snipper chicks tend to have an endless reserve of drama.

Regardless, the old snipper should have elevated the maid to co-wife status, or at least to subsidiary wife. Instead of manning-up, he took the loser way out and cast Sami and Izzy out into the desert. This strategy of avoiding parallel responsibility eventually became part of the organized shaman canon, and formalized as law in much of the world. So much for the children. Needless to say, Izzy grew up with an axe to grind of his own, said axe launching that other shaman bunch I just mentioned.

---

[3] One of these chapters came up with a famous question-answer joke: Q: "Have you heard the good news?" A: "Lam is toast."

Eventually, the organized shamans wound up going to war with the Izzites several times over many centuries. During these wars the organized shamans tossed the snippers around like bargaining chips. Or, the shamans used the snippers' artisanship, when appropriate for the cause. In time, the Izzites would come up with their own brand of snippers who could serve as whipping boy and charity poster child, or attack robots, as needed.

Throughout all of this nonsense, the shamans, of all varieties, overlooked one simple thing. And this thing was the need for somebody to be doing something to pay for all of this drama, as well as maintain the basics of life. Very few people, on any side, were doing much of anything to secure much of those basic resources or have any ideas, the latter being sufficient grounds for a stoning. Individualism was at an all time low. As a result, the world fell into an age of ignorance and poverty that lasted for about a thousand years. The barbarian kings, and their shaman servants, or masters, depending on your perspective, reigned supreme.

Throughout the early years of that millennia, Og and Pok's tribe was one of those that had not yet fallen to either the barbarians or any of these varieties of spiritualists. Fortunately for them, an accident of geography allowed the tribe to learn of the barbarian danger before more than a handful of scouts had raided their treasure. It was this early warning of danger that gave time, years earlier, for Mar and Cor to lead a counterattack against the forward forces of the most nearby barbarian king.

Fortunately for our tribe, that king was embroiled in battle with other kings. At this point in history, each barbarian tribe had expanded sufficiently to meet and vie for territory at their periphery, having consumed and destroyed all within their own interiors. And so, for now our tribe was spared, these kings having larger battles to fight and lacking the resources to chase our remote tribe through the intervening terrain. And the spiritualists had yet to arrive, either.

During this time, the miracle of selfish trade allowed the tribe to prosper. Meanwhile, evolutionary forces began to destroy the barbarians, but spared those who chose to live peacefully together. Similarly, the tribe had sufficient productive members to ensure that peace and self-interest were the unspoken ethos.

But that was about to change, and this time from within rather than without.

Chapter 8, From Force or Fraud

Not all individuals in a society learn the same lessons. Not all make good decisions, and not all prosper. Just as Og and Pok learned to trade with each other to mutual benefit, some did not. Just as Vin learned to ferment, others did not. Just as Tan discovered how to dip hides in acorn water, some chose to not. The intellect that Tab cultivated into creativity lay fallow in others. On and on, other members of the tribe, too numerous to name, failed to learn these skills at first.

Of these, many subsequently learned by watching and doing, and so became productive and happy, if not wealthy. But those who chose to use their minds and learn soon became well off enough to enjoy their days with their friends and loved ones, or to seek solitude if they chose. But others chose to not learn and instead envied their neighbors, blaming them for their own misfortunes.

Meanwhile, the very peacefulness of their culture made men forget that only a short time previously, the hand that snatched was often shattered by a club from the hand that held the prize. In those days, theft was a practice taken at the risk of the practitioner, and, typically, only the barbarian succeeded at this.

But this new brand of theft was different. This kind took advantage of the peacefulness and sense of fairness of the victim, that very peacefulness that was his strength in trade. And so, the productive victim measured the stolen rabbit or stick of wood against the life of the thief. In this balance the good man viewed this illicit trade against the model of fairness with which he judged his productive fellows, and chose to turn aside from his wrath. The thieves soon delighted in their discovery of this new and so very valuable treasure: the willing compliance of their victims.

Once started, without the natural primitive violent antidote and its attendant risks, the contagion began to spread quickly.

"Pok Jr. was bad to round up all the bunnies and trap them, there are hardly any left in the forest. We deserve to have some of them, too."

"Ahks found all of these great rocks and now they are just left scattered around his hut after he made them into edges. If he had left them in the stream bed we could have chipped them into cutting tools also. But, the rocks he left us are too hard to chip, he took all the easy ones."

"It isn't fair that Tab was born smart and can make all those traps. I remember when we were children he used to sit by himself and scheme about making us buy his toys. Why didn't he just play with us like the rest? Didn't we laugh with him when he tried to run after he got sick? You just can't trust smart people."

"Saved us? Mar didn't save us! He cheated us by pretending to stave off those barbarians. He's lucky we don't stone him for throwing his lot in with them to fool us into giving him and Cor so much of our work. He owes us, they both owe us, and we should take it from his trading hut. He has so much he won't miss it."

"Cor shouldn't keep all the chevals for himself. If I wasn't so busy around here, I could have gone and gotten them, too. He shouldn't get to have all those adventures, find that pretty wife, and then get all the reward from raising the chevals. They pretty much raise themselves, look how tame they are. Even little Mowneek can ride them easily."

The productive tribesmen were unsure of how to handle these opinions and the thefts to which they led. At first, they just tried to ignore the problem and each worked a little harder to make up the losses. Mar was more strident.

"These people are just as bad as the barbarians," Mar erupted one evening as he and K'ette were discussing a recent theft. "I should deal with them the same", he continued.

"No, they aren't as bad as the barbarians," K'ette answered, remembering the devastation that had been wrought on her tribe.

"You are right, they are worse," Mar replied, "at least the barbarians risked their lives and fought like men. These animals are no better than yapping dogs, asserting their needs and right to our work, and then cowering in the shadows when we catch them."

"But at least they don't fight," K'ette added, "yet."

"I wish they would," Mar insisted, "then nothing would hold me back from handling them as barbarians." He continued, "It is as if my own sense of virtue and honor holds me back, and they know this." Mar was right. The thieves, by their softness and lack of violence, avoided the precipitation of retribution. Their softness counted on men like Mar and the others to be unwilling to reciprocate fully for the crimes that were being perpetuated upon them on an increasing basis. One day the productive among them met under the same tree where the cheval enterprise had been started so long ago. Ken, who had been very close to Tith, told them of the ways of other lands that Tith had visited as a young man.

"As Tith told me, there are lands, particularly those of the Izzites, that will sever from the body the hand that steals. Other lands he visited seize from the thief three times as much as he stole," Ken said.

"But, as I recall, he also said that the men who judge guilt and innocence in these issues are often as capable thieves as those whose fate they decide," added Ahsee.

"I have seen these things for myself," interjected Cor. "During my last trip, and after two of my best chevals had been taken, I inquired how we might handle our growing problem," he continued. Cor went on to describe how in many of these lands there was little difference between the despotism of a barbarian tribe and the same autocracy veiled behind a gavel. To the man whose property is seized for the benefit of the clever man who can argue better before authority, the club that punishes defiance is just as real. "At least the barbarians are honest about their oppression," he lamented.

Nonetheless, all agreed that something must be done about the growing problem of theft. A single branch taken in the summer is of little consequence. But, let many tribesmen take a branch whenever they please and before long the original gatherer will freeze in the winter, his efforts stolen away piecemeal while his oppressors live warm in their huts. Recall that it was for this reason in our Old West horse theft was a capital crime.

The tribesmen agreed to form a plan for government, which they would present to the tribe for approval at the next berry festival. Over the next weeks and months they met several times at the tree and formulated a proposal, with the underlying principle of government that the individual tribesman was paramount. A tribesman could only have his liberty or his property removed from him to thrice the extent that he had taken, by force or fraud, the property of another.

In their plan, the government would provide a common means to protect the tribesmen from external attack or internal crime. With this protection it would ensure property rights for each tribesman. The work that Mar and Cor had done previously on an ad-hoc basis to protect the tribe from attack would now be formalized. Training and management of the defense forces and internal security forces would be an explicit responsibility of the new government. Also, the records required to identify which pieces of land were owned by each tribesman would be formally maintained and protected by that government.

The functions of the government would initially be conducted and managed by a manager, not a king. This manager, at least initially, was not considered by the tribe to be their leader, as much as he was actually their servant. He would be empowered only to the extent that his actions served the needs of the tribe.

The actions of the manager would be monitored by a council of tribesmen. The council was to be empowered to enact rules as needed to allow tribesmen to be protected from theft or other threats to their life, liberty or property.

The interests of the tribesmen, regarding both the rules of the council as well as the actions of the manager, were further protected by a chamber of elders. These elders were empowered to monitor, not the tribesmen, but the manager and the council themselves.

The government they envisioned was intended to serve all tribesmen equally. As such, the cost of government would be paid equally by each tribesman; man, woman and child. Tribesmen unable to pay his share could instead perform work for the tribe to maintain common areas, etc.

The details of the arrangement which the tribesmen proposed were too numerous to be considered here. But all of these details were specifically intended to limit the power of the government to be used against the individual. Mar, Cor, Tith and others had seen enough such abuses first-hand during their adventures, and wished to protect their own tribesmen from them. Instead, the government was established specifically to protect the individual against force or fraud, but otherwise to remain a transparent non-entity in their daily lives.

And so, with a few detractors and some haggling about one detail or another, the proposal was presented at the next berry festival. It was soundly approved by the tribe members, most of whom had suffered at the hands of thieves.

Their first experiment into self-government was born. For many years, this arrangement worked as desired. Smiling theft and the occasional fraud ceased to be a problem for the tribe. The thieves and cheats found it easier to work for themselves than to suffer the triple penalty of repaying their victims. And as long as the reason for the establishment of the government remained within the living memory of the governed and a generation or two hence, all remained prosperous and content.

But then, complacency began to sink in. Rather than the governed running the government, the tribesmen selected for the positions of authority too often began to see themselves as existing to be served rather than serve. Other tribesmen, generally the most qualified to oversee the functioning of the government, began to withdraw from service to seek their private fortunes. And in their vacancy they left the operation of government to those hardly qualified to do anything else.

Little by little, then, the tribesmen who participated in the government forgot from whence it came, and they began to realize the enormous power they were capable of wielding. And this power came through the power of taxation, and enforced submission to the will of the government, even when that will stepped beyond the bounds of its genesis.

The catalyst for their destruction came in the form of an elderly widowed woman. Her name is unimportant. We shall call her The Widow. The Widow had lived a life of happiness with her husband and two children. Eventually, the children moved away, and The Widow and Mr. Widow enjoyed their hut and tended the garden together. But one day, Mr. Widow fell ill, and died shortly after. The Widow was understandably grief-stricken. Mr. Widow had handled so many affairs of the household that it was difficult for her to understand how she was to manage for herself.

So the next winter, The Widow showed up at the doorstep of the trading hut which had been built to replace the rotted hulk that had been the Mar-K'ette. But unlike Ploi, who you will recall had encouraged K'ette to hire him and his sister for K'ette's own self-interest, The Widow approached the proprietor with a different proposal. Ploison, who had taken over the trading hut after his father had managed it for years, greeted her as she came in.

"The Widow, I am so sorry to hear of your loss. Mr. Widow and I were glad to see each other whenever he came in. Is there something I can help you with?", Ploison asked.

"Actually, Ploison, there is something you can help me with," she said, clutching her leather pouch in front of her with both hands.

"As you know", she continued, "it is so desperately cold this winter, and Mr. Widow was too ill to gather much this summer. Could you spare some?"

"Sure, we have plenty," Ploison answered as he bent to check his account ledger for her.

"Don't bother checking that rock you keep behind there, we, I mean I, don't have enough anymore to matter. I was hoping you would just give me some for now," she scolded him lightly.

Ploison remembered the story of when his grandparents had died, leaving Ploi and Aunt Emma to fend for themselves. He also remembered the story of how his father, as a young orphaned boy, had approached K'ette with an offer to work for her and Mar. For his whole life, Ploi had been proud of himself for working up from just an errand boy to eventually running the entire trading hut for Mar and K'ette. He worked for them until he had saved enough to purchase the trading hut business from them. Ploison himself had followed in his father's footsteps, at first tending bunnies, then running errands and so on until he now owned the trading hut himself.

Ploison had an idea. "The Widow, I don't have to just give you some wood now, I can offer you something far better."

She brightened, "Oh really? What might that be?"

"Well," he answered, "you are friends with many of the tribeswomen, and so I thought it would be great if you were to work here and help me run things. You could help me manage the accounts and sweep the floor or tidy up here and there. Then I wouldn't be giving you the wood, you would be earning it yourself. Besides, during the day you would be here where it's warm anyway." He thought this was a grand idea, since she tended to do these things all day anyway. Not only would she not be lonely by herself in her hut, but now she could do these things in exchange for a fair amount of goods for the service.

The Widow was speechless. For a moment.

"I can't believe you are doing this to me. And after all the generosity your father and your aunt received from everyone over the years. Now, you are trying to take advantage of me. I knew your grandfather before he died, he would be so ashamed of you right now," she blasted.

"But, this way..." Ploison interjected.

"No, don't try to explain yourself. I know what you are doing. All you merchants are the same, just trying to squeeze everyone for everything you can. And now you are throwing an old widow out into the snow," she shouted as she ran outside, clutching her leather bag.

Indeed, she was friends with many of the tribeswomen. Over the next several days she visited most of them. And to each she told her tale of woe as she sat in their warm huts and drank their broth. By the end of the week at least twenty tribesmen and tribeswomen had expressed their displeasure with Ploison as they met him in the trading hut, or ran into him in the village. At first he tried to explain, but that only seemed to make things worse, so he stopped trying.

Had it gone no further, that would have been bad enough. But, at each opportunity for the next several weeks The Widow collared everyone who would listen.

"I just don't know how I'm going to stay warm this winter," she whimpered.

"That Ploison is such a disappointment. If he had to walk in his father's shoes, or mine, he wouldn't be so greedy," she despaired.

"There should be some way of taking care of us. So few have so much, and we many have so little," she preached.

Little by little, the tribesmen listened to her complaints. Each seemed deaf to the opportunity which Ploison had offered her. Their deafness sprang from their distance from subsistence thanks to men like Og and Pok and all the rest. This distance gave them the luxury of thinking that the miracle of trade, and its riches, was their birthright instead of the fragile thing it really is.

Two of her audience turned out to be on the tribal council. One of these men had been on the council most of his life, having done nothing else for a living. The other of the two had failed at previous attempts to run his own affairs, but turned to government service in desperation.

Both councilmen had worked their way through various low-level but necessary government jobs, road maintenance for one and as a deputy for the other. They rose from these jobs through supervisory positions in various limited tribal government positions as were available, and finally to elected office. Neither harbored any illusions about how successful their lives might be without the benefit of government credits. And so, both were keen to listen to the opportunity they heard in the voice of The Widow.

The Two Councilmen considered The Widow's plight and discussed her situation between them as they walked the dusty roads of the tribe. They gradually came to realize that The Widow was only one of a special class of tribesmen who might serve their purposes well. Other elderly widows throughout the tribe were equally deserving of assistance, as well as elderly couples who were reaching infirmity.

It mattered not that the social *more* of the tribe was that even the elderly, except for the few cases of mental impairment, were capable of providing the essential wisdom of a tribe. This wisdom the elderly traditionally imparted by teaching and tending for the little ones as the intervening generations worked. No, the pair rationalized between them, these elderly citizens needed the dignity of resting after a life hard worked. And, to rest without the chains of familial obligation that had passed the wisdom of Og and Pok and all the rest down to successive generations.

And so, to ease the burden of these The Two Councilmen encouraged the council to exempt the infirm elderly from the burden of taxation. At first the council resisted, but the pair soon found an able ally in the form of a shaman. This particular shaman, Luth, had recently arrived in the valley and represented a sect of the organized shamans mentioned previously.

As a Lamist, the peaceful nature of Luth's beliefs at first seemed hand-in-hand with the peaceful trading values of the tribe. And so, the shaman had easily blended with the tribesmen for weeks, practicing a more advanced form of the "help your neighbor" reconnaissance.

The Lamists had learned that an overtly militant position, as practiced by their forebears, was ultimately a risky proposition once they themselves held power. And so, their softer approach had proven itself over the centuries to stand the test of time. Only the sacrament of the Lam Toast revealed their bloodthirsty origins. Yet, even this was veiled behind soft words, attractive robes, and confusing rituals. The rituals themselves seemed to have no purpose other than veiling an allegory that the novice was careful to never question, and the elect knew to never disturb.

Luth was as skilled at this Lamist tradition as any of his generation.

"Gentlemen, forgive me, but I understand you are troubled about helping your deserving fellows," Luth said to them as the pair approached.

Surprised, the pair didn't reply at first, to some degree taken aback at the presumptuousness of this stranger to intrude upon their delicate matters of state. The shaman was not deterred, he having read the pair and understood their cause more than they could possibly appreciate. After all, his kind had been well trained for this delicate dance.

The Lamists even feigned schisms between the various organized sects for centuries to delude the faithful into believing that they had any real choice among them. This skill they had developed long before this naive little tribe had chosen their form of peaceful self-government. "Well, they would learn, wouldn't they?" Luth thought to himself as he easily fell into the prepared litany.

"I am Luth, a humble servant of God, who was sent here to bring His message to your flock," the shaman said as way of introduction. Luth was careful to invoke a feeling of possession among his marks.

"And what message might that be?" the first councilman asked, warily. His companion was still basking in the idea of "his flock", a concept which had drifted around his mind for years without reaching conscious manifestation until just now.

"A message which you yourselves have been struggling to present, that we should tend to the needs of our brothers," Luth replied. He paused momentarily, as the first councilman's mind reached out to this stranger's understanding of his desires and relaxed his wariness.

Luth smiled to himself as he saw the bait grasped, and continued, "For centuries, our philosophy has been to assist the leaders of men to fulfill their noble purpose. We believe that God's bounty is placed in your hands to be used for His will, and that you are His stewards." And so, deftly, the government which had been started by the early tribesmen, not as their leadership, but as their servant to protect them from force or fraud, revolted silently. At that moment the government cast off its chains and clamped them upon the necks of the governed.

A moment's pause here, Luth thought, but not too long to let the consequences of that responsibility sink in too deeply. And then, diverting, "But so few appreciate the struggles that you face in this noble work of yours. Any man can gather wood, any man can till the fields, any man can manage accounts, any man can study philosophy." He meekly touched his own breast as he said this last, eyes cast down, head bowing slightly as if to his masters. "The fools," he thought to himself, as this act had moved armies under the command of men of far greater intellect than these simpletons.

"But you," as he reached out to them abruptly, touching their arms, "you represent the best of men. You are those who lead and prepare the way and bear all the criticism and none of the regard, as others prosper from your work." The pair nodded at the wisdom of this foolishness.

"And now, you consider the plight of The Widow, who came to you in desperation, you who are her last hope and salvation," he continued.

"The challenge that you face is how to balance the needs of so many, against those who oppose your best nature. You are not alone in this struggle, many kings and emperors before you have faced this very challenge. And yet these men lived to be lifted up as the pride of the people as they overcame the greed of the individual, proving themselves as rightful leaders," he added. And cemented their unspoken and hardly admitted power-lust.

"But this is merely the rantings of a simple philosopher. Who am I to lecture you, forgive me for my presumption," he begged of them.

"No, think nothing of it," the second assured him as he worked the hook farther down his own throat, drifting momentarily out of his reverie.

"If I may, then?" Luth asked of the pair who simply no longer had any choice at this point, reaching into his satchel.

"See these grapes?" Luth asked of them. "These are the bounty of God. But without your protection and blessing, men would fight over them like animals," he theorized.

Luth deliberately neglected to mention that hardly an hour before he had plucked them, uninvited, from the fields of a farmer. A farmer who had struggled against animals to cultivate them, and whose great-grandparents had applied Tithing to guide them into their succulent fullness. This work of generations ripened the fruit into fullness so tempting that those great-grandparents had sided with the other tribesmen to install, as protection against force or fraud, the forebears of the two councilmen. Two councilmen who would soon cast the die to one day take it all away by both force and fraud.

"I could pretend, as many do, that I own these," he said, almost absently as he divided the bunch into three, one small and two large. As he spoke, he handed the two largest of the three divisions to the councilmen, taking care that these two were of equal size to not arouse a division among them. "But I own nothing, I merely hold them until they make their way to the hands that need them the most. I am not in a position to know to whom to give them, but you are. And so, I keep only what I need for my own subsistence, and give the rest to you to do as you will, nourishing yourself or those who need them, as God moves you."

"So many of your flock," refreshing that particular barb again, "pretend that they own the bounty of the valley." At this, he turned, sweeping his arms across the horizons, and then turning back toward the tribal center. Luth began gently walking toward the village as his sheep obediently and subconsciously followed him. They *had* been returning to the village, hadn't they? "But we know that, like the grapes, the tribe and its future is in your hands."

"Your message is important to the tribe," he assured them, they nodding assent. "But busy men such as yourself can't afford to reach each tribesman one-to-one. As it turns out, a number of tribesmen have asked me to speak the word of God to them next Tuesday evening. I would be honored if you would visit and, if so moved, speak to the crowd yourself," he offered. Yet, Luth knew that the sort of man drawn to their position, as if called, would be inexorably drawn to any public gathering.

"We have to check our schedules, of course, but we shall see if we can squeeze that in," the first said, pretending as if his soul was not laid bare.

"Of course," the shaman said, graciously. The sale closed, he left them at the next turn in the road, apologizing for his departure, and nodded his head to each in a formal bow. Each councilman remained silent as they strode into the village, surveying their flock busy at their tasks. "Their needs are so many," one thought silently. "They need me so much," concurred the other to himself.

Barely two dozen tribesmen were at that first Tuesday evening, but that was sufficient. Carefully present were The Widow and a handful of other destitute tribesmen for whom the prosperity available to all had escaped. Also present were The Two Councilmen, as well as a majority of the council. Although these others had been more successful at their private lives, all recognized the value of a collective mass of votes, and so chose to attend. A couple of other councilmen, holdouts who saw their service as temporary rather than ordained, had chosen to stay at their lands to tend to their own work.

Luth mixed easily among the assembled tribesmen, inquiring as to the health of each, and showing interest in the answers. Given that the simple miseries common to most was the font from which his place in society sprang, this interest was hardly feigned as he assured them that God hears their prayers. More than one councilman noted his skill at working the crowd, and reserved judgement as to whether this shaman represented a threat or an asset. This judgement would soon be resolved.

The show began as Luth mounted a low rise before them. The crowd was carefully arranged to look past him at the valley and the hills beyond. The hills were majestic in the waning evening sun, as Luth borrowed God's majesty for himself. The crowd fell silent, each imagining that his earlier inquiries established a personal rapport, each invested in his words.

Luth raised his hands to the heavens, and waited a moment to ensure that he held their attention. "Children of God," he began, holding his arms high, and then bringing his hands to a clasp in front of them. "It warms my soul that God moved you to come here this evening in fellowship," painting his invitations over the past few days with the will of God. And introducing, ever so softly, the power of the collective. And further introducing them to themselves as children, a title he would deftly confer to his spiritual paternity soon by impassioned repetition.

"Children, I am new in this village, and yet you have taken me in as a welcome traveler," Luth said softly. He looked at each one of them in turn, most of whom had done little but whine to him about their troubles. As he paused and lingered his gaze on each, he granted them reward for nothing exchanged but complaints, complaints which were the easily minted currency of his trade.

"God hears your prayers," he assured them, suddenly louder, implicitly associating his arrival with an answer from God.

"He hears all our prayers," pausing. "Sometimes we wonder why we suffer," he pandered to this crowd specifically chosen for their skill at suffering. This aspect of their lives was a selective process which resembled a softer version of that employed by shamans ages past.

"Children, God makes us suffer so that we will listen to Him," he slandered. In truth, however, God had granted each of them the power to fend for themselves, and to think for themselves. But even The Widow, who could have swept the floor for Ploison, but chose not to in her pride and sense of entitlement, felt the stirring of purpose in her soul at that outburst.

"But what is it that God is telling us?" Luth asked, knowing that none would say the only possible rational answer, which is to stop doing that which pains them. Even an animal which is burned once knows to avoid the fire again, but the collective must find someone to blame for their troubles, never looking inward.

"He is telling us," pausing for effect, "to look outside ourselves." Another pause as this twist of reason curved around their rusty minds.

"He is telling us," pausing again, "to stop being selfish." Another pause, some uneasy shufflings.

"He is telling us," yet another pause to establish the rhythm of expectation as he led them down the path, "to consider the pain of our fellow tribesmen." Hope began to bubble up again, he sweeping his arms out to them. He paused again, to allow them to savor the expectation.

"The pain of The Widow as she mourns and is turned away from the doorstep," Luth said rhythmically with careful meter, his right hand sweeping to point at her, palm up. Her heart sprang to life, and tears welled in her eyes. "Yesss!" her mind hissed to herself. The others felt a pang of jealousy at her recognition, mingled with an excitement that they, too, might be special. Luth didn't disappoint them.

"The pain of Ek as he stumbles and is turned away from the doorstep," Luth said rhythmically with equal meter. As he spoke these words his left hand swept to point, palm up, at a man who had suffered a snake bite months ago.

"The pain of Isha as she suffers with child and is turned away from the doorstep," Luth chattered. His right hand now indicated a woman who believed that only she suffered with heavy pregnancy.

To the left, to the right and back again, on and on he singled out those who had been drawn to that hilltop by his words over the weeks prior. Each felt a thrill rise in them as they were noticed for their suffering, and imagined that an unidentified *someone* had done them wrong. What exactly had been done to them, other than a vague and ridiculous claim of having been turned away from some mysterious doorstep, was a mystery best left unsaid. The effect was stronger without the interjection of facts.

Their suffering became a source of reward in the recognition, as if God Himself were speaking to them. They clung to a promise that someone, somewhere, somehow *owed* them. The collective, which had been challenged generations ago by the establishment of that first government to curb soft theft and fraud of shame, began to stir once again.

"Children, it is our sins that cause your pain," he diverted, being careful to not associate *your pain* with *your sin*. Instead, he allowed only a vague collective *our sins* which shifts responsibility from the cricket to include the ant.

"When we reach for that almighty credit, we sin in the eyes of God. When we think instead of pray, we sin in the eyes of God. When we choose works over faith, we sin in the eyes of God," he rhythmically chanted, wiping tears from his eyes. These tears he had learned from long practice to summon as he allowed his voice to waver. And confirmed for them what they had been unable to articulate. And hid the fact that of all of God's creation on this planet, we are the only ones to whom He gave the gift of thinking and the capacity for work. And who He created as miniature creators in our own right, in His image.

"Children, God wants you to prove your love for Him, by prostrating yourself helpless before Him," he whispered. In his blasphemy he equated God to a jealous, petty thing. And yet again, he fed this particular crowd the nectar they so desperately needed to salvage their self-esteem, as they leaned forward to better hear him.

"And by letting Him provide for your needs," he continued, louder, raising his hands and eyes skyward at the reference to God, and downward to the crowd at "your needs", evoking a theological *pinata*.

As the crowd devolved before him, few had minds left to argue, or the will to do so. Had they, one might have said, "But He does, by the gift of your mind and your capacity to work and provide for yourself," but no one spoke. No one ever does, as that would be impolite.

Luth realized that now this crowd was ready for a story to be implanted in them. This would be the first story of many he would tell to lead them where they were already rushing on their own.

"In the beginning, man was at peace. He lived as a creature of nature, drinking the cool water of the stream, taking from the forest only what he needed, fearing no animal."

And yet that man understood no disease which felled or crippled him early, freezing and starving in the winter. That man feared not only animals, but his fellow, violent man the most. Luth declined to say these inconvenient things. Instead, he let them enjoy this pleasant, peaceful fantasy for a moment, smiling wistfully himself.

"But then man sinned against God!" he shouted, suddenly, pausing before answering how.

"Man dared to think!", a softer shout as he clarified for them.

"Man ate from the Tree of Knowledge, which God had forbidden," he whispered, conspiratorially. And yet, he failed to address why God would tease man with a powerful mind, only to tell him not to use it, thus wasting that precious, unique gift. Luth would fill in these details later, but this was enough for now.

"To pay for his sins, man was cast out of the garden, and condemned to bend his back in labor," he said, equating work with punishment. "And some men became greedy, and thought that they owned the forest, and the stream, and the animals," he lamented, pausing slightly.

"They said, THIS IS MINE!" he shouted, feigning his most evil, snarling face and grabbing to his breast in frantic clutching motions, like some insane man-child grabbing at toys.

"And so man turned against man. The farmer and the hunter envied one another's lives, and fought one another, and killed one another," he told them. And sidestepped the economic benefit that the farmer, and the hunter, and the woodman gained by trading their goods with each other, as Og and Pok and the rest had discovered. And that each man had chosen his vocation to most benefit himself.

"Children, God has given us rules to live by. These rules are simple, really," he said, not mentioning the complex and contradictory veils of ritual he would wrap them in.

"'I am your God,' He said. Do not make anything your god above Him, and do not worship it instead of Him," he said, confirming what they already knew. Later, he would introduce the tribal credit as a god worshiped by the successful among them. This introduction would associate success with sin, rather than rejoice in trade as a creation of God discovered by man for his benefit.

"Don't speak of God without reverence, and don't twist His name to your purpose," he instructed. After having done precisely that his entire life.

"Never work on Tuesdays," he continued. And left the taste of work in their minds as a small sin which is tolerated the remainder of the week.

"Honor your father and your mother," he warned. Most did already, but the council was about to change that.

"Do not kill and do not steal," he listed. These two had been at odds with some of the earlier shamans' methods, but their methods had evolved and grown more influential. He would have to dance around these two to justify the legal theft about to arise, and the tribal fratricide in store for those who resisted, but there would be time.

"Do not lie with anyone not your wife," he preached. Soon, he would help the council understand the benefit that social prohibition meant for control of men and women's bodies and thus their minds. Already, many among them were ready to surrender this portion of their liberty in exchange for a promise of subsistence.

"Do not bear false witness," he said, knowing that soon would arise an entire range of vocations devoted to precisely that.

"Do not envy your neighbor for anything," having coached them to do exactly that.

"Children, I am so moved by God's message for us, but the hour grows late," he said, pointing majestically to the colors of the setting sun.

"Before we depart, I want to tell you a story of inspiration. A couple of days ago, I was walking toward the village, when I met a pair of tribesmen. These tribesmen were deep in thought, worried about how they might provide for you", he told them as he watched The Two Councilmen. Predictably, the pair's faces flushed with anticipation.

Knowing that he had them, and that they envied his sway of the crowd, he continued, "The tribesmen I met were two councilmen, and wanted to help a poor widow." At this he gestured to the councilmen as heads were already beginning to turn. The other councilmen present, who had opposed special treatment of any tribesmen, reddened and shifted their weight uncomfortably.

"God moved them to help her in her plight. But, they have been opposed in their efforts," pausing, and then as if to silence the growing rumbles, "not by bad men. But by men who genuinely want to know that they serve the tribe's wishes." The point had been made to the holdouts. These instantly realized that the assembled collective represented more electoral power than a similar number of individuals. Individuals would be difficult to sway so easily and might disagree about specific issues. Individuals who were too likely to be hard at work rather than assembling to wield power.

"We need to pray for each of our leaders," he began, asserting the government as the leaders of them rather than their servants who had been constituted to protect them from force or fraud. "Pray that they might understand God's plan, and help them in their struggles. And we need to pray for our neighbors whose faith is not so strong."

"Children, fall to your knees with me and pray," he instructed them. As they complied with this simple, harmless direction, as had barbarian tribes before them, he knew he held the power to lead them exactly where they demanded to go. After the prayer, which resembled that ancient shaman's prayer, planting seeds of thoughtlessness in their minds, he bid them rise. They now easily obeyed.

"Children, God also moves us to help those who spread His message," he said softly, almost apologetically. "I have been overwhelmed by the generosity of the tribe. It is tradition that at each gathering we give what we can to help reach our neighbors", he said, never specifically identifying himself as the recipient. Or justifying his authority to decide who specifically needed or deserved the help.

At this, three tribesmen moved among them to deposit small gifts, a few sticks of wood, a loaf of bread and a rabbit hide, beside him. Like the ancient Chosen Ones, these men had been prepared, not with stones, but with these items to seed the rain that would follow. A few tribesmen not prepared moved forward to deposit what little items they may have among them. The rest felt the pang of the collective, and would not make a similar mistake the next time.

"Thank you," Luth said to each tribesman as they approached with their gifts. He would formalize this process later to build a chapel and fill it with the larder of their bribes to God for His favor, but for now, this would do.

"Children, not all are in a position to give the things of this Earth," he assured them, "so we give what we can. But all can give gifts of the spirit. Go forth from here, and tell your neighbors of God's plan, and invite them back here with you each Tuesday as we discuss His plan together." And with this, he walked down from the hill, and greeted each among them with gentle clasps and kind words. More than a few, hoping to gain special favor, invited him to their homes for meals, offers he gladly accepted.

A couple of days later, as Luth walked among the people, discussing their needs and woes, the tribal council met. The councilmen who had attended Luth's sermon understood, without a single spoken word, that the tribesmen who had congregated there that evening were a force waiting at their fingertips to be used. And they intended to use that force.

And so, The Two Councilmen proposed that some tribesmen should be exempted from the tax. After only a little debate regarding the details of this proposal rather than its merit, the council agreed that this proposal should become law.

Now, unlike when the government had first been conceived under that oak tree, the government would single out for special treatment groups of citizens, rather than respecting each individual. The government had been formed to protect the rights and the property of each individual, man, woman and child. But now the burden of the cost for this protection would, for the first time, fall unevenly upon the tribesmen. The council agreed that the following would be exempt from taxation:

☐ Widows, of any age, and their children
☐ Orphans, until they reached adulthood
☐ The senile elderly
☐ All children in a family beyond the first three

There were so few of each of these in the tribe that it seemed reasonable to exempt them. This action was communicated to the tribe through the councilmen as they met the tribesmen one-to-one. Most tribesmen could appreciate that they could, through cruel fate, become, or have become, victims in the first three groups. And all might aspire to have more children, landing them in the fourth. Some of the remainder expressed nothing more than curiosity about this minor change in the fundamental form of taxation.

A few individuals, however, protested this action. They argued that while the adults, such as The Widow, in those protected classes of tribesmen were still allowed to vote, their votes now cost them nothing. Or, in the case of large families, less per person. These holdouts were surprised by the reaction they received for these arguments. The councilmen no longer saw these individuals as voices of reason, but instead obstacles to be dealt with somehow. "How could these men not be excited about the brilliance the council had just enacted?" the councilmen wondered to themselves.

The entire ethic of the tribe had changed subtly. The collective, for the first time, had raised its hand against the rights of the individual with the force of law. This assault was first manifested through Luth's congregation, still a small minority of the tribe. But, many more assaults against the individual would follow as the councilmen began to understand the potential voting power of collectives of an almost unlimited variety. The individuals simply fell through the cracks of these groups. And those tribesmen who were part of one group or another began to perceive their own power as deriving from membership, rather than their personal merit.

This action seemed, for a time, to have no measurable effect upon the tribe. The small amount of tax revenue lost by the exemption had very little real effect upon the tax larder from which the tribal manager drew to fund the maintenance of roads or the enforcement of laws. The largest impact seemed to be the psychological effect on the councilmen themselves. Like a drug, the initial gratitude of the recipients gave them a warm feeling of confidence. The natural antidote, the questioning ire of the few tribesmen who opposed them, they simply ignored, as most addicts might. And, like a drug, the high soon began to wear off.

The councilmen received another waft of this drug at the very next Luth sermon, held on the following Tuesday. By then, word had spread from the initial small gathering of the faithful. The Widow brought two of her friends, Ek brought his wife, and Isha her mother. This time, the crowd was about twice the size as the first congregation, and more carried offerings which they presumed were demanded by God. The previous pump-priming the previous week, like a lounge pianist's stuffed tip jar, had done the trick.

Luth repeated portions of the sermons before, especially those concerning sinful work versus righteous faith, to ensure that the newcomers didn't miss out on the basic principles. The central story of this sermon was new, and involved the wrath of God being meted out to disbelievers who were greedy with their possessions. The corresponding instruction, presumably from God, was that men should offer Him one part in ten of their income for maintenance of the shaman. In addition, the faithful were directed to donate additional sums to the needy in their community.

This frightful story of the wrath of God had the desired effect. So, when it came time at the end of the sermon to offer their wares the material was available in volume out of proportion to the relative size of the crowds from the previous week. A small pile accumulated around Luth, who bade the congregation to applaud when each donation came forward, however small. The tribesmen who donated, many of whom had never received any recognition whatsoever in their lives, beamed as if God Himself was applauding. The greatest applause was delivered on behalf of one small boy who dropped a tiny stick onto the pile.

After the donations had come forth, Luth then singled out The Widow, "Children, let me tell you that God has moved within our tribe this past week. Last Tuesday, as we met, The Widow was suffering from her loss. And she still suffers." The Widow perked up at the mention of her name again. "How does Luth know my needs so well?" she wondered to herself, "he truly must be a man of God."

"And yet, because of your prayers, God moved our leaders. Only a few days ago, the tribal council decided to exempt The Widow, and other needy like her, from taxation," he announced, gesturing to the councilmen who were present. Applause erupted, the councilmen inhaling the drug they purchased with credits seized from others. One busty woman, giddy with excitement, hugged each of them with tears streaming from her eyes.

"Children, this is but a small example of the way in which God moves through us. You saw tonight how a small boy can give what he can to help," he said, to more applause.

"And yet, there are neighbors of ours who have not yet seen the plan God has for us," he lamented, shaking his head back and forth as if witnessing a moral tragedy. "Let us now kneel and pray for our leaders to show wisdom. Let us also thank God for the wisdom they have already shown. And, to pray for our neighbors to open their hearts to all who are suffering tonight."

As before, as a simple ritual symbolizing compliance with the collective, the tribesmen fell to their knees as he led them in prayer. As they finished, he gently bade them, "Rise Children, and witness the glory of God's plan." Reaching out a hand to The Widow, he beckoned her forward and helped her up the hill as if she was infirm. The Widow was shaking, tears streaming down her face as she stood beside him, basking in his primal power.

"The Widow, I want you to tell your neighbors how you felt when you heard that the tribal council moved to exempt you from the tribal tax," he urged.

"Well, I, I, I don't know, all I can say is, thank you!" she sputtered to the councilmen as Luth led them in more applause and patted her back. The councilmen soaked in this new hit.

"But, Children, let's be clear about something," he said, turning back to the crowd. "The tribal tax is so small, and the needs of The Widow are so great. While she doesn't have to pay the few bundles of wood or the few rabbits that the tax represents, this really means that she is starting at zero, instead of behind. Exemption from tax can't be burned in the pit, nor feed an empty belly, nor dry the tears of loss, can it?" A faint echo of "no" or "it can't" came from here and there in the crowd.

Turning back to The Widow, he asked, "What is it that you need the most, right now?"

"I, well, I need wood for the fire this winter, and some fur, and food for the table," she said. As she spoke, Luth eyed the pile of goods, and made a quick calculation. "Two should leave plenty," he thought to himself.

"Then God has heard your need, and answered. You two there in the back," he said, motioning to a pair of tribesmen who he had noticed brought nothing with them. The pair had been eyeing the proceedings with a certain amount of suspicion. "Come up here, if you may, and help The Widow take the wood she needs and some fur and food from this pile of gifts. After all, this isn't mine up here, this belongs to God." Their suspicion evaporated, and at the next meeting they would bring with them as much as their neighbors.

After Luth made a big show of loading up The Widow and the two men with as much as they could carry, leaving behind a still-generous offering, he led them in applause. The councilmen present heard all about them whispers of praise for this stranger who had moved them all so skillfully. The lesson of his receiving praise for merely redistributing goods which others had donated was not lost on them.

The next morning, Luth arrived at Ploison's trading hut to deposit the remainder of the goods which he had received the evening before. He spoke to Ploison briefly as the merchant updated his slate, and took his measure as a man who would not be so easily swayed. "No matter," Luth thought to himself, "his kind are always too few to matter."

Once the charity bug took hold in the tribe, the changes in their ethic began to mount. Others, like The Widow, began to see their unusual circumstances not as challenges to be mounted, as had Tab with his infirmity, but instead justification to receive the work of others. One by one, the tribal council began to exclude more and more of the tribe's special cases from taxation. Meanwhile, Luth continued his sermons, which would have seemed strangely like the soft thieves' justifications from generations past.

"Each of us are given our special talents. Some men are best at sowing, some are best at reaping. Some men use their minds, while some work as hard, if not harder, with their bodies. Do you think it pleases God that some men lead lives of ease and comfort while others struggle so hard?"

"It is the workers in the field and in the huts who receive the most favor of God. Their overseers simply reap the bounty which others have provided for them."

"It is more difficult for a wealthy merchant to please God than it is to pass through the eye of a cheval."

"God created his creatures to roam the earth, not to be caged for men's greed."

"When we say that we shall go hither or thither and do this and such, we anger God for our impertinence. None of man's plans matter to God."

"Why should one man collect the rocks of the stream so that others have none? Let him who collects the most rocks distribute them fairly among the others."

"The bounty of the earth is plenty. Let not one man hoard its treasures to the starvation of his fellows. Aren't we all children of God? Should one child hoard the table and elbow his brothers and sisters to the floor?"

"Lam told his flock to sell everything they owned and give it to the poor. Only by doing this were they able to understand God's plan for them."

These sermons resonated deeply with the tribesmen who attended them. A kind of natural selection took hold. Those with whom these messages most deeply touched became the most fervent in their zeal to recruit new tribesmen to attend. But those unmoved or even offended tended to stay away. Accordingly, each new attendee saw the fervor with which the faithful clung to Luth's sermons. Seeing these examples, heavily outnumbered, they wanted to belong, as is the tendency for man. And so the newcomers either absorbed the lessons themselves or began to pretend that they understood lest they stand out as odd. Even if they only pretended to be swayed, their effect on each newcomer was the same, immersion into a unanimous swell of group consciousness which identifies the collective.

Once Luth's congregation reached one in four or five of the tribe, the battle was already lost. At this point, seeing the assembled crowds, the tribal council understood the overwhelming electoral block which they controlled. The weight of this block, more easily reached as a whole, was far out of proportion to any collection of individuals. Yet Luth did not wield the power of this influence directly. But it was certainly in his best interest to see that the council took action which promoted his gospel, without causing any harm to it.

The assembled congregations themselves learned from these sermons a lesson that also resembled a kind of natural selection.

For generations, the tribesmen followed an apprentice-craftsman-master model which had served them well. Young boys would work as apprentices for a master artisan, in order to learn their trades. Often, the masters for whom the apprentices worked were their fathers or uncles or older brothers. Sometimes, however, as in the case of Ploi and Emma, these youngsters worked outside the family. In any case, the apprenticeship period lasted long enough so that the individual could function well without constant supervision. And at that point the tribesman was considered an able craftsmen.

After working for a period of time as a craftsman, which varied from person to person and skill to skill, the individual might decide to follow in the ways of the master. As such, the individual might become a master in his own right. Or, he might switch to another trade or skill. Or, as did Pok Jr., innovate to create an entirely new trade or skill.

In this traditional fashion, the apprentices became masters, and then started their own enterprises, taking on their own apprentices, and so on. Each tribesman knew that hard work and application would eventually see them evolve into masters. Even that term meant self-mastery more so than mastery over others. A tribesman's place in society was not fixed, but based on each individual's own merit, industry and efficiency.

However, the teachings of Luth, cast in the semi-involuntary sacrifice of Lam, began to change the way in which the individual tribesman viewed the traditional meritocracy. Out was the ethic that a trade or skill master was revered for his knowledge and industry, and as a source of potential advancement for others. Luth replaced this ethic with the absurd and blasphemous concept that God abhorred skill and knowledge. Instead, the plan of God taught by the Lamist tradition, is that the skilled "classes" were fixed, as were the worker "classes". As such, the workers banded together under the Lamist tutelage to resent the mastery of their fellows. And, rather than aspiring to join them, saw the skilled masters as one step short of evil, and petty.

This formalized jealousy and envy, despite their ancient prohibitions, served the shamans' agenda. One by one, and in little ways barely perceptible, workers began to resent their employers. By resisting the merit by which the masters had gained their skill, the workers denied themselves those same skills, and thus their own advancement. And so, the workers moved away from apprenticeship, considered one step short of slavery, into a separate class in which the term "worker" attained an almost godlike quality all its own.

Those workers which did learn trades sufficiently to become craftsmen placed subconscious barriers within their own minds which prevented them from mastering the ways of mutually beneficial trade. They turned away from this one skill which underlay all economic endeavor, including their own employment. Trade itself became perceived, not as the mutually beneficial miracle which Og and Pok discovered, but as an evil in which one party triumphed over the other. Free trade became to be seen as a cheat of some kind underlying the transaction.

If cheating must be, reasoned these workers, as they sat listening to their sermons, then they should be the ones who cheat the evil employers and skilled masters. So, the relationships between master and apprentice, now employer and worker, further deteriorated. Workers began to shuffle through their tasks. They began sniping at the employer for cheating them as they refused to give their all, not only to the masters, but more importantly, to themselves. Their struggles, at first imagined at the forked-tongues of the shamans, became real, and deep.

This semi-organized class envy was fostered by a shamanistic ethic which saw knowledge and advancement and effort and skill as disdained by God rather than His true plan for mankind. This envy destroyed the potential of tribesmen throughout the succeeding generations, as their children sat in the sermons hearing the same lessons that had destroyed opportunity for their parents. And so the working class grew. And the employer class shrank. The employer class, seeing the working classes trending toward producing the barest minimums, began to search for ways to design around the necessary detriment of employment. Just as previous generations of their kind had designed around the detriments of the natural world.

Previously, apprentices had applied themselves to their task with vigor. The apparent compensation of an apprentice was low, compared to that of even a craftsman. Yet, the apprentice was being compensated also by being taught a trade or a skill from an expert, the master. To compensate the master for his time and energy spent on teaching an apprentice, that apprentice worked cheap. So, the master was paid for his instruction by cheap labor. In return, the apprentice was paid for his labor by instruction. Both men benefitted by providing that which they had in excess, skill and time, respectively, and receiving the reciprocal, which they lacked, in return.

But the newly evolving shaman-inspired worker class applied themselves with a sense of entitlement at the virtue of their struggle against the greedy. And so, as they disdained the role of the master-employer, they saw no value in the instruction they were being provided, and focused solely on the low wages they received.

Even the craftsman class[4] petered out as the pre-Luth craftsmen

---

[4] I disdain the use of the word "class", as these distinctions are artificial creations in men's minds used by others to enslave and manipulate them in order to extract unearned value from them. In a free society, no man is a permanent member of any class, unless he chooses to be, which is why we must preserve liberty most of all.

became the hated master-employer, and a few disgruntled apprentices moved up to replace them. In the old times, the craftsman served the master by producing quality work as well as assisting in the education of the apprentices. The former labor continued to compensate the master for his previous apprenticeship, while the latter compensated the apprentice by additional instruction on behalf of the master. All of this in exchange for higher wages than an apprentice could, or should, demand.

Eventually, the craftsman simply became seen as either junior drones of the master, with hate and envy to be similarly delegated, or as higher-level workers whose purpose it was to shield the lower workers and advance their causes. This distinction was made purely on the actions exhibited by the craftsmen, who, over time, fell prey to the collectivist pressure to please the greater number of workers rather than the smaller number of employers. This gulf continued to widen as these neo-craftsmen, disdaining the skill and knowledge required to operate all facets of business, again, as evil, failed to move up to supplement the master-employers as in times past.

In a vicious cycle of envy, each Tuesday the shamans fed the workers' righteous indignation. Each Tuesday the shamans whipped these embers of discontent gradually into flames of outrage with soft stories of how God prefers the deliberately weak over the evil, purposeful strong.

There was simply no place in the Lamist tradition for a fair exchange of value between independent minds seeking their own self-interest. In their stories, few references to virtuous employers and workers existed. The few stories of the proper mutually beneficial relationship between employer and worker that did exist were twisted by the Lamists from that intended by the original authors.

"In the afternoon the vintner craftsman returned to the market, and hired another worker, and agreed with him to also pay a twenty-credit. So at the end of the day, as the master vintner saw the work, the craftsman paid the wages, from last to first, as instructed by the master. The first worker, receiving his twenty-credit and comparing it with that received by the newcomer, threw his wage to the ground. He shouted at the craftsman, 'How can you pay this newcomer the same as us, who have toiled in the heat of the day?' And the craftsman said, 'Friend, I do you no wrong, did you not agree with me for a twenty-credit?' The master added, 'Take that which is yours, and go on your way. I will do with my own as I will.' " the Lamist scholar quoted from the hill.

The Lamist's own story was passed down to both them and the Izzites by the snippers. The snipper version told a tale of negotiation of fair exchange between a craftsman who went to a market to hire workers for the master, in the morning, at noon, and in the afternoon. This highly skilled newcomer, who was also paid a twenty-credit, was a free-agent master vintner who had been hired in the afternoon to pinch-reap the best remainder of the harvest before the impending weather destroyed the crop. Given the late hour, his service to gather the choicest fruit, while leaving the desired best one part in ten, was deemed by the craftsman to be worth this pay as well. What little crop the newcomer was able to salvage was worth more than his pay. His work was also worth more than what a lesser skilled worker was capable of, who, in their haste and ignorance, might damage the next year's yield by salvaging the wrong seed.

The original intent of this story was to teach primitive minds the lesson that the workers hired in the morning received exactly the compensation they had agreed to work for. And to not be jealous of the wages received by a newcomer. This story thus taught an important lesson in following through on previously arranged agreements. The further lesson, that some workers are worth more than others due to skill and experience, was lost in the mists of time. That little detail got in the way of all the delightful class envy that the shamans exploit for their power.

Importantly, this story taught that the master, and by his delegation the craftsman, were the sole determinants of who was worth what pay. The master and the craftsman supervisor were not obligated to bow to the pressure of the collective to institute artificial fairness. Nor were they obligated to explain their decisions to anyone. And in return, each worker was free to accept or decline employment under those circumstances. But, once employment was accepted, the worker hired in the morning should not have argued, post-hoc, that his payment was unfair.

But the Lamists, to obscure its mercantile origin, twisted this lesson, and many more, into a story of salvation, and once again glazed work and skill with the stain of unfair punishment. And leaving the distinct impression, not that one should become as skilled as the newcomer-master, who had also spent the morning and afternoons toiling for others, also at higher pay. But, instead, to somehow figure out how to skate in at the last minute and get undeserved benefit.

Story after story, each that had the ring of timeless lessons of virtue and skill, were twisted for the continuing indoctrination by the shamans. In turn, the shamans benefitted from sadness, despair, envy and frustrated accomplishment of the faithful. These faithful, seeking the briber's easy way out, turned back to them in desperation with offerings that God might save them from their self-inflicted sorrow.

Saddest of all, the workers' children, sitting beside them listening to Luth each Tuesday, had no chance. Their little minds were warped as they munched on Lam Toast and sipped their bloody grape juice while they watched their parents give offerings to this demon who had destroyed their futures.

And so, the children lost, over time the gap widened further.[5]

---

[5] I have taken artistic license in compressing generations of social de-evolution into decades or years. This allows me to avoid a pointless series of *begats* which would simply detract from the narrative.

Chapter 9, A Tribe Consumed

As you will recall, our tribe created government for the purpose of protecting the productive from force or fraud. And yet, over time, the best intentions of the electorate was turned against itself, until that same government had become the agent of the thief and the lazy. And these thrived.

At first, charity was formalized, donation required by law, and the largess dispensed when work ethic alone would have been sufficient for relief. And then the work ethic itself was demonized. Individual effort and self-interest were seen as evil. Meanwhile, work of the common man, rather than one of many temporary phases of life, became a virtue in itself, cementing the poorest in their place.

At each step along this path the electorate themselves blazed the trail. The prosperity which had bought them this luxury was seen by most as permanent, and easily squandered on foolishness, rather than the hard-won thing it was.

During this time the tribe experienced a de-evolution of the working classes, a class distinction created in the minds of the workers themselves. It was then that the tribal council took the next step toward enslaving the productive of the tribe.

More of the collective saw their potential as fixed, and limited, rather than viewing their lives as a progression of learning and improvement. Their envy then spilled over into the maintenance of the government which had been established to protect their ability to progress along life's staircase.

"Why should we, the workers who enrich the employer, pay as much in taxes as he? Does he not benefit more from society, and thus should pay a greater share of its expense?" they murmured.

"The trading hut would be nothing without the roads that we all maintain. Should not the trading hut bear most of its cost?" they argued.

"The sheriff who protects the merchant from theft provides him far more protection than I receive. Steal all that I have and you have stolen little. Steal all the merchant has and you would be wealthy. Let the merchant pay more for this protection," they griped.

Hearing these complaints, the tribal council noticed the growing power of the collective, and the shrinking percentage of the wealthy merchants. Understanding this shift in power, the tribal council forced the wealthy merchants to pay more than the previous per-capita tax. This, they reasoned, would provide two benefits at once. First, this action would satisfy the growing disaffection of the collective, to their electoral gain. But it would also provide the council better access to more deeply tap the source of wealth in the tribe. And thus doubly increase their own power.

And so, the tribal council moved to tax the tribe, not on the basis that each tribesman received the same guarantee of protection of their life and property, but instead as a portion of their property. Devaluing their lives as meaningless, property would be taxed one part in forty at the spring equinox, and then again at the autumnal equinox. In so doing, the tribal government would seize five percent of the total property of the tribe. The greatest portion of this was seized when the granaries were fat with the harvest, and the lesser when lean after the winter.

The collective rejoiced at their wisdom, particularly that fall when many carts of goods were taken from the trading hut, while the poor handed out less than they had been taxed before. The shaman's larder, presumed by all to belong to God, and reasoning that it had already passed through the hands of the electorate, and thus already taxed, was exempted from taxation. Of no less influence in this decision was the ability of the shaman to rile the congregation against any councilman who disagreed with this point of view.

The carts hauled from the wealthy, productive individuals were so full that the normal tribal government was unable to carry, store, or account for it all. To handle the additional burden, the council hired additional workers for this harvest, workers who would have been busy with the harvest in the fields. Lacking their normal workmen, the farmers turned to other workmen, at higher wages, to salvage what they may from the fields. And so, the harvest was weaker than it should have been.

These workmen, absent from their normal professions and busy in the fields, produced less in their own shops. And so there were fewer furs, and gourds, and leathers, and axes, and less wine in the cellars. This effect was compensated somewhat by these workmen having been paid in a portion of the harvest to offset their opportunity cost of the additional finished goods they had planned to make. However, as the crops would have been harvested anyway while these artisans worked their crafts, the net effect on the tribe was the loss of finished goods. Accordingly, there was less for the council to confiscate when it came their time.

Lastly, the workers for the council became flush with goods which had not yet been inventoried or stored, and for which there was no time for oversight. Many simply stole portions of what they took from others, seeing this theft as their rightful due for the righteous work of the tribe.

Despite all this wastage, the gain to the government was immediate. That fall this gain became the most wealthy repository of accumulated goods that the tribe had ever known, eclipsing even the shamans. At a stroke, the productive and the merchants grew poorer, the government more powerful. And yet, exempting the poor, like The Widow, from increased taxation did little to improve their personal circumstances.

The shaman, whose larder was never diminished, continued to gain in power relative to the productive individualists. The tribal council, and the tribal manager, never once had to work or think to accumulate that wealth. But now the council controlled a pool of wealth which they had taken by force of the vote, at the will of the electoral collective. And, like the thief, they knew only how to spend, and not to preserve or increase.

That winter was cold, and long. The product of generations of productive individual effort of the tribe sustained them, however. Thanks to those generations, the wastage caused by the taxation that fall was barely noticed. But to a primitive tribe that same wastage would have meant freezing starvation for many.

And yet, more still listened to the shaman's sermons, as he twisted the ebbs and flows of nature into evidence of God's wrath for some imagined infraction. This time, the harsh winter became evidence against the wealthy productive, who still maintained warm fires despite the treasure which had been taken from them. And in the warmth of those fires, the productive thought about their diminished circumstances. Just as Og and Pok and all the rest had thought by the stream as they considered the harshness of their environment.

When spring arrived, only a few tribesmen had fallen prey to the cold, and this number no different than the elderly or sick who might fall during any year. But now, the collective had someone to blame. And that someone was the rich, despite the fact that this year no one had gone without to any extent more than the tribe had in the past.

Luth was there to make sure that blame would be laid exactly where he needed it. Through him, that blame would be laid at the feet of those who didn't need him, or his or Lam's intercession in their personal walks with God.

At the spring equinox, the tribal collectors once again made their rounds. Once again, they carted away the one part in forty. The bulk of their haul came, once again, from the wealthy. The poor, having just survived the winter with little excess, as the poor often do, paid barely anything. This season the collectors' numbers had grown, as the rumors of ill-gained wealth from the inefficiency and hurriedness of the oversight brought more thieves to their ranks. Thieves who, absent this easy opportunity, might have engaged in honest work or learned a skill. Thieves who, believing the teachings of Luth, assured themselves that this larder, coming from the wealthy, was righteously taken from their presumably evil hands.

As had happened with the fall harvest, this season the ranks of the workers who might have sown the crops were instead employed as collectors, honest or otherwise. And so, as had been done at the harvest, the planters employed artisans at higher wages, as the finished goods the artisans might have crafted lay undone. But this time, the planters, having seen their harvests seized from them in the fall, had thought about these consequences over the winter. They realized that any excess which had been seized that spring was the excess remainder which had not been seized in the fall, or consumed or traded in the winter. And so, they planted less, sufficiently less to reach the next spring without too much.

The planters were not the only ones who learned these lessons. As the summer wore on, the wood gatherers chose to gather less of the winter falls and the spring blows. Instead, they left the remainder on the ground to gather in early winter lest it be seized in the coming fall collection. The rabbit and Chi-Ken tenders chose to eat more of their stock rather than breeding them. What would it matter to feed and raise the young birds, only to have them seized? The tanners tanned fewer hides, the fermenters mashed fewer berries, the coopers hollowed fewer gourds, the toolmakers gathered fewer stones.

Not by much, mind you, just a little bit less. At each point of decision as to whether to continue or relax, their minds were shifted just a little bit more in the direction of taking a little less risk[6]. Where the wood gatherer might reach at the end of the day to take that fortieth stick he shrugged it off as the one for the tribal council. As he shrugged, his conscious mind knew that the council would take one fortieth of the first thirty-nine. Yet, this relaxation brought him more joy than that last stick. Across the productive of the tribe, that last little bit of effort went undone.

But still, more was collected that year than the previous. The momentum of growth in the tribe which had gathered over the generations still carried them forward. But now the growth of this year, among the productive, was just a little bit less.

Among the poor and the workers, however, this trend was reversed. Freed from the taxation which had previously been a fixture in their lives, their bias was toward expansion. Especially expansion and growth to consume the excess which the exemption from taxation released, and which Luth's charity provided. And so, as the fall approached, the winter and spring pregnant gave birth to one or two more children than the parents would have previously chosen.

During that summer, the tribal council and the manager met and debated the wastage they had seen the previous fall, and which had been repeated in the spring. Their concern was not that the wastage meant that needless excess had been seized from the wealthy, but that the wastage had kept it from *their* greedy, clutching hands. But the thieves who had taken it were voters, too, and so their needs must be taken into account as well.

A further problem had arisen, also. Some of the wealthy, such as the woodcutters, were wealthy not so much on account of the wood which they maintained in piles to be counted, but which lay on their lands un-gathered. The planters, with fallow fields, were also escaping with some of their property un-seized, as were the toolmaker's stones in the stream, or the vineyards seed stock which had not been harvested. All of these things, in the tribal council and manager's minds, reflecting the minds of the electorate which learned of this crisis from the sermon's of Luth, represented a loss to the tribe.

"But how shall we seize a fortieth of a planter's or a woodcutter's lands? Surely this would be considered as excessive?" they pondered. Each knew that such a plan would be excessive only in that it would leave a patchwork of property ownership, rather than concern over the seizure itself.

"Perhaps we should seize these lands only in the name of the tribe. And then, the planter or the woodcutter should buy them back in the form of goods or credits in the amount of the seizure," a tribal councilman offered, to eager assent of the rest.

"But we must ensure that the poor are exempt," claimed one savvy councilman, as the rest nodded. "We shall exempt each man's own hut and

---

[6] Engineers call this a *bias*.

a twenty-stride garden plot from assessment," he continued. Once again, the poor, consisting of those who had decided to discontinue application of their God-given abilities, would be spared from the taxation aimed at their productive neighbors. As the tribal council had learned, this bowing to the collective electorate would be disguised, not as the theft by force of numbers which it really was, but as charity for the poor.

To implement this proposal, which was announced at that fall's berry festival, the manager would be granted additional funds with which to hire permanent property assessors. The assessors would visit each tribesman and determine which improvements had been made to his property. A value was to be assigned to each property in accordance with what each improvement might bring if it were sold. In addition to the equinox collectors, these assessors represented a permanent increase of the government scope as an employer.

Property improvements were made by the productive tribesmen who built dams and cleared crop lots. And built huts for their livestock, granaries to hold their crops through winter, and lean-tos to protect their tools from the weather. And dug canals to carry irrigation. All of these tribesmen were taxed heavier for their industry to improve the bounty of the earth so that their fellows might eat. Now each tribesman who might improve his land, and thus its productive potential, had to weigh the increase in value which would surely result in greater tax. This greater tax was imposed whether or not the increase in production was realized. Some simply decided to not improve further, and thus the growth of the tribe was incrementally hampered.

That fall, the harvest was still more bountiful than the year before, despite the losses incurred from the reduced planting that spring. And despite the inefficiency of the harvest itself, as many workers were employed as collectors. Yet, this harvest was not so much more bountiful as in years past.

Even more workers solicited the tribal manager for collector work, and so the tribal manager hired additional workers as supervisors, to curtail the theft. Whatever losses in outright theft might have been prevented were simply absorbed by the wages of the supervisors. Or, in the inefficiency of collection as hutches of rabbits were left to starvation or thirst in the heat of the day as the larder was inventoried. In most of these cases, no one thought to feed or water the rabbits as they might had this been their own property.

The tribal council realized that the rate of increase of harvest had slowed. They also saw that the additional supervisors, along with the wastage, had consumed more funds than the year before. And so, the council wished to increase the rate at which the property of the wealthy was taxed, in order to handle the inevitable shortfall. In addition, the woodcutters had increased their harvesting after the fall assessment, and thus were suspected of avoiding the tax. Worse, the woodcutters dared to increase the amount they demanded for their wood, it being more scarce that winter from the reduced collection during the summer. And more of it was soft, as it had laid on the ground through the summer and fall, rather than being carefully stacked and preserved from the weather.

"And God said, 'Give to the tribe that which is the tribe's'," Luth preached from his hill, his own larder safely exempt from assessment and seizure. "See children, these evil rich steal from you thrice as you freeze in the winter," he preached to those who paid a paltry assessment. "Once by cheating the tribe of the tax, again by higher prices, and again by selling you rotted wood."

By the end of the year, the tribal council had decided to change the inventory collection to fall on the full moon of each month, the last moon of the year excepted. This change was to prevent tax avoidance as practiced by the woodcutters, and as suspected of many other merchants. They also needed to cover the projected shortfalls they had estimated after the fall collection. And so the assessment itself would collect one part per gross each assessment, for a total assessment of one in twelve throughout the year. This represented an increase in tax from five percent to a little more than eight percent. But the tribal council reasoned that this increase was needed as the collectors would be employed full-time, rather than twice each year.

The council also moved to simplify the lunar collection, allowing the collectors to focus on property which might otherwise be hidden or missed. To do this, the council decided to modify the real property collection. Recall that this tax was collected on the underlying property itself, such as the land of a planter or a woodsman. As no man could move his land or choose not to have it until after the collection, as the woodmen had done, it was safe to only collect for it once per year. This real property collection would be done during the last full moon, and would be assessed at only one part in twenty. And so, once each full moon, the collectors swarmed the valley, collecting one part per gross of inventory for the first twelve moons. Then they returned to collect one part in twenty for land and improvements on the last full moon of the year.

As the mild winter turned into a mild spring, this new change had an immediate impact on the behavior of the producers. Each of these began to consider ways in which to limit inventory to an as-needed basis.

Previously, some of the woodmen, for example, had traditionally harvested wood from the forest during the summer, to allow the heat of the day to better dry it. This approach preserved its value rather than allowing it to rot on the ground. The woodmen sold their harvest later when it might bring a higher price as the winter approached.

But now, they considered instead how they might harvest only enough to sell during the month, with perhaps a little extra. By doing this, their on-hand inventory was at a minimum during the full moon as the collectors came. Hardly anyone noticed this at first, but eventually this change affected the congregation, who reported it to their shaman.

"See how they steal from you, and anger God, by limiting the wood you can buy," shouted Luth from the mount.

The merchants, such as those operating the trading huts, also sought ways in which to limit their own inventories. They turned away, as the gibbous waxed, those who wished to store their goods in the hut in exchange for credits on their account stones. By this, the temporary influx of inventory was stemmed, creating a significant savings over the year by merely changing when the merchants accepted goods for trade. Those with credits on their accounts were easily able to continue to purchase, and indeed, encouraged to do so by slightly lower prices. But, the poor, who had chosen to live trade to trade by resisting the merchant evils of skill and knowledge, could not buy during these times.

"See how they force their taxation upon you by turning you away from the doorstep, much as they did The Widow, may she rest in peace. It is as if the prophecy is being fulfilled, 'And no one shall buy nor sell unless they bear the mark on their tablet.' Lam weeps at their greed, and what they do to his flock," Luth lamented.

While lamenting, he passed out Lam Toast to the faithful so that his suffering paid for their sins, buying them presumed salvation in return for nothing. "Repent Children, the time of the end is near, for soon His wrath will cleanse them all!" Luth shouted as the faithful munched and sipped. Each considered what great works they had done for the collective, the only souls who mattered to them.

Similarly, the toolmakers ensured that, as the moon waxed, they spent their time collecting rough stones. These rough stones were worth far less as these had no time invested in them. And so, the collectors carried away one part in a gross of rocks they could have easily plucked from the stream or the quarries themselves. But after the collection, work began to transform these into finished tools. However, their hurry to finish before the collection, in many cases subconsciously as their minds sought to solve this artificial problem, caused the quality of the work to suffer almost imperceptibly. And the supply of tools overall dropped.

The tools used by the woodmen, and the other artisans then broke slightly early, or cut slightly less. Should a tool break during the waxing gibbous, the woodman or the artisan might have to wait until as much as two weeks later to obtain a new one. And then at a higher price due to its scarcity as he competed with others for the limited supply. These higher prices each passed along in the cost of their own harvested or finished goods, as they had, to some extent, the taxes all along.

The lesson learned by the toolmaker was that he could manipulate the supply of tools, and thus their prices. With this manipulation he might artificially bring in more value to himself, per tool manufactured, by producing fewer of them. Their overall revenue dropped, however, and as the supply was reduced they had less need for a full staff of apprentices, or even craftsmen. And so the master toolmakers dropped some from their ranks of the employed, choosing at first to shed the lesser-skilled.

"See the evil of these, who create the tools of destroyers, who turn away the workers from their doorstep," Luth wept. As he wept he welcomed the newcomers, bewildered by having no employment despite the seemingly higher cyclical demand for tools and other finished goods, into his fold. The loyalty of these Luth immediately cemented by offering them goods from his larder, knowing that this small investment would pay generous dividends in his reach and influence later. These destitute gratefully accepted these gifts, and took the toast on their tongues as they were applauded by the rest for their symbolic submission to the collective.[7]

Other artisans who could soon followed this trend. Prices for various kinds of finished goods rose slightly, as did the prices for products obtained using these goods, such as wood cut with the axe. Among these products the price increase was hardly noticed. An axe would still exchange with wood at roughly the same proportion, each having increased in value in a similar way. But, goods which could not be shifted around the full moon had no cyclical effect, other than perhaps becoming *less* valuable at the waxing gibbous as they represented an economic hot-potato. No one wanted them on-hand when the tax collectors came.

But still, the rate of taxation was very low compared to what it would soon become, yet the effect began to become more and more noticeable. And, behind the flurry of economic activity, no one noticed that the supply of raw materials, and finished goods, and stored food, began to drop.

We have already seen how the woodmen and the toolmakers manipulated their inventories, with the effect of fewer to sell. Even the hot-potato holders soon dipped their toes as best they might. Planters, to reduce excess seed, sold it as grain rather than saving it for the planting.

The ignorance of the collectors made them unable to distinguish between a good grape and a fair one. This ignorance led the vintners to reduce their stock of the poor grapes to ensure that each gourd of ferment, like the toolmaker's axe, would bring the highest price. Prices rose as opportunity diminished. The workers displaced by the planter and the vintners soon found their way into the open arms of Luth, swelling his ranks, and depleting his larder. He was not concerned at all.

As less land fell into master cultivation, its owners, seeking to avoid taxation on property they chose to not use, sought to sell it. But their fellows, hoping to avoid the land taxation themselves, wished to sell their excess as well. As the rising glut of owners waited for buyers who rarely came, prices for land dropped. But not the underlying assessment for taxation, which would continue to bleed them year by year, as their pastures and orchards and croplands became choked with weeds and saplings.

Some buyers did come, however. As they purchased these lands cheap, their prices gave cause to the assessors to adjust the taxation. And so the seller, who suffered the loss the most, was taxed the highest, while the buyer paid less. Some buyers were individuals who had accumulated enough wealth to purchase their own plot and build a hut, which of course was exempt from land taxation. These created their own little gardens and raised their hens to protect themselves against the uncertainty of work and

---

[7] Cult-watchers call this technique "Love Bombing."

fluctuating prices. By doing this, they unknowingly participated in the de-evolution of specialized productive trade which Og and Pok had begun. But soon, new trades would arise for them.

Tract, a young son of Gage, a tribal councilman, disdained skilled work, but instead sought to make his fortune in other ways. Growing up as the taxes of the tribe had evolved, this artificial world was as natural to him as water is to a fish. Hearing his father and the other councilmen talk as he sat among them, Tract realized that, as the taxation would soon increase, more and more land owners would seek to sell.

Tract realized that the difference in taxation between a productive planter or vintner and a individual exempted owner created a vacuum of economic energy. Accordingly, he encouraged his father and some of the more influential tribesmen (meaning those well-connected within the government) to pool their credits to assist him in buying the most distressed lands. These were easy to find, as the reports of the collectors told him which owners were the most pressed to pay their taxes.

A tradition of the tribe, formalized when the government was first created under the oak tree, was that agreements, and particularly debts, between the tribesmen were to have the force of law. For example, if Og traded with Pok, but lacked the wood with which to trade for the squirrel, Og could become indebted with Pok, allowing the latter to "lean"[8] on the land of the former until the debt was paid. If Og sold the land before the debt was paid, the debt would be paid from the proceeds of the sale before the land was passed, with clear ownership, to the purchaser. Or, if Og chose, he could clear the debt, and thus the lien, at any time by paying Pok in full. This was a reasonable system which benefitted all concerned.

As Tract and Gage were discussing this new venture, they realized that they could employ the same system of liens to allow an entire range of new, less wealthy owners to purchase the hut plots. The access to liens dramatically increased the available market to them, and thus the prices they could charge. And by building the huts for the new owners, rather than the owners building them by hand, he was able to allow them to keep their usual vocations. Or, to avoid developing that skill, depending on your point of view. Either way, the droves could simply move right in.

And so, after each last full moon the land owners who struggled the most could barely pay their assessments. Tract would approach them and offer to take their unproductive lands, at a loss. More than one such landowner, desperate for relief from their losses, agreed to his price.

Tract had long ago realized the benefit of belonging to Luth's congregation, seeing the large numbers of recently displaced workers who gathered there. Tract then, making a big show of modest donations to Luth's larder, employed some of the displaced there to build the huts. "God has answered your prayers," Luth cried, hugging Tract in front of them as

---

[8] Later tribesmen misspelled this as "lien" when it became written law. I shall henceforth use the more common term as it is used today.

he thanked the young man for his donations to his larder. Luth knew that this act of marketing had benefitted them both, and declared, "soon the turned-away shall have homes."

With his new workforce of the faithful, Tract split the lands and built the huts. He split large lots of distressed land into many smaller ones, each qualifying for the land tax exemption. In the process Tract was able to profit many times over on the price he could charge for each lot. He also yielded an additional profit for each hut which his workers built identically, as if by machine.

And soon the younger tribesmen, instead of waiting until they had made their fortunes before taking brides and huts of their own, began buying these hut lots before they would have otherwise. Despite the triple and higher profits available to Tract, the use of the lien allowed the payments to be spread out into many decades into the future.

Few of these naive fully understood the enormous sums which would be paid to Tract's venture over time. Some, unable to bear these costs, defaulted. At each default, Tract merely took the hut and lot back, and sold it anew. A few complained, and some even to Luth. But Tract's generous donations to Luth's larder made sure that only the most glowing praise for the young entrepreneur came from the mount. He reserved that venom to spew at the productive who chose to withhold their bounty from his clutch.

From a tribal perspective, Tract's venture presented many benefits. The creation of a specialized builder vocation made huts in Tract's lots much cheaper than they would have been otherwise. And yet, these new artisans were essentially a captive worker class. Any who tried to leave to create their own enterprises soon realized that without the access to information and funding which Tract possessed, they could only build more expensively, and thus less attractively. Unlike Tract, the individual builder could not purchase a large enough block of land to help the distressed owner very much. Nor could they take advantage of his ability to buy the timber and the thatch for dozens or hundreds of huts at once, and thus command lower prices for these. Many also fell prey to an effect which the taxation, and more importantly its collection, soon caused throughout the tribe.

As each full moon dawned, over a period of a few days each the tribal collectors swarmed the valley. They spent only a few minutes at a poor tribesman's hut, but as many as hours at a merchant's. For the individual workers, these visits were truly more or less friendly conversations as the collector, knowing there was little to take to begin with, assayed their meager belongings. For the merchant, however, these visits became more and more intrusive, with the collector understanding the far greater treasure to be found in the merchants' hands.

Collectors soon learned that the more time they lingered in the merchants' and artisans' huts, the more they might find. On these days, then, the merchants found themselves hosting an unwelcome, and often hostile, guest. Not only did they resent the intrusion, as any free man might, they had to spend the hours with the collectors as they rummaged about. But also, each productive man so disturbed also required a certain cooling-off period after the collector left.

The bubbling resentment before and after, and time lost both directly from the inspection and indirectly from the resentment, cost the merchants valuable time. This loss of time was, in effect, yet another tax on them. The merchants soon found that as many as two days per month of productive effort could be easily destroyed by the collection itself. This tax was far higher than the one part in a gross of the collection.

A typical merchant worked each day of the lunar month, but lost two of these days to the collection process. Then, as much as ten parts per gross of their time was wasted, ten times the actual tax itself. Even if only the few hours of the collection were wasted, a psychological feat available to only the most hardened merchant, then this still represented a loss of as much as twice the actual collection.

So, the resentment of the collection tended to tax most the individual who cared the most about liberty. The more callous merchants, who saw nothing wrong with the intrusiveness of the collection process, saw this as a necessary part of life in a collective. And so were damaged less. This resulted in a separation of the froth of the merchant class, the more collectivist damaged less, the more individualist damaged more. Ever so slightly, the collectivist, weighted less by the intrusion, prospered more, while the individualist prospered less.

Similarly, the poorer workman, if he cared nothing about his liberty, but instead thought that the tax inspection was worth his time and attention, fared no worse than his fellows. But the workman who resented the intrusion, seeing his liberty as supreme, was more harshly treated by the collectors, who reflected his indignation back onto him. In some cases, the collectors goaded the individualist workman into violence. Reacting, he was arrested and punished for his crime of defiance. His crime was punished sternly as those in the government progressively saw themselves as the masters of the tribesmen, rather than their servants.

"Live as a peaceful citizen in the tribe," Luth preached from the mount. The congregated collective nodded in righteous assent. Each of the righteous saw the individual who would react so harshly as more of a threat to them than the state. Each vowed their support of those who stamped out these threats on their behalf.

Then, another separation between the individualist and the collectivist tribesmen began to become apparent. One might view the merchants along a continuum, as is normal for a snapshot of any segment of society at any point in time as their respective fortunes rise and fall. In this light one might find wealthy merchants on one end, and struggling merchants on the other. Some of the wealthy merchants and artisans decided that the best way to manage the intrusion of the collection was to employ the services of an agent. These agents' specific responsibility was to inventory their holdings. And then work with the collector to make the process as smooth as possible, relieving the principal of the process entirely. These agents, who swarmed over the accounts of merchants like insects, soon became known as Account-Ants.

The most wealthy merchants were able to hire these agents with ease, amortizing the additional cost, effectively an additional tax, across their entire enterprise. As this practice allowed them to return their attention to their business, they, like the callous merchant, suffered less from the collection, and prospered more.

The most struggling merchants were unable to afford such a luxury, and had to bear the entire cost of the collection inspection by themselves. The least of these, already teetering on the edge, were unable to tolerate the lost days and simply chose to close their businesses.

In the middle between these two extremes were those who could hire an Account-Ant to assist, but only on a part-time basis. The individualists in this middle group found their days chewed away and prospered less as a result of their inclination to rely on their own efforts and industry. On the other hand, the collectivists in this group, not resenting the additional gaping mouth of the account-ants, prospered more by their employ. And so, the individualist was biased to sink, while the collectivist was biased to rise, or at least not sink as quickly. Either perspective led to a separation in prosperity.

And in the process, the account-ant became an entirely new profession which produced nothing, but merely mitigated the costs of the tax collection. Not a single grain was produced by them, nor a single stick collected, nor a single tool crafted, nor a single gourd hollowed, a hide preserved, or a fruit fermented. They only consumed.

The account-ants knew their bread was buttered not so much by their employers, but by the tax collection process which necessitated them. They found their allegiance swayed toward ever more complicated collection rules and inspections, rules which would fatten their larders as their employers suffered. Indeed, some of these account-ants drifted easily back and forth with employment as collectors themselves. A few were so bold as to advertise their experience as tribal collectors to validate their skills to their merchant and artisan employers.

The account-ants soon learned to attend meetings of the tribal council, and mingle about the congregation of the shamans. At each meeting they urged each group on to levy and demand, respectively, more and more complicated exceptions and special cases to taxation. As pure collectivists, deriving their incomes solely from the actions of the blind, unthinking and self-righteous demands of the electorate, they too contributed to the shamans. In turn, the shamans held them up as good men, thinking only of the needs of the people, and whose concerns should be enacted. Luth and the others needn't have bothered, the congregations were already primed to throw their weight behind any proposal which punished the producer while helping themselves.

In the meantime, the effects of the reduced sowing, and harvests, and intrusion of the collection began to accumulate. As did the removal of previously fertile croplands, pastures and orchards as Tract converted them into hut lots. As the tax base shrank, both for the inventory and the land assessments, the tribal council decided to simply raise the assessments to make up the shortages. Meanwhile, they employed ever more collectors, and more enforcers for the sheriff, and more road workers to build roads out to the complexes of huts, as well as maintain the roads which already existed.

No one in authority seemed to care that the produce of the tribe itself was shrinking, and along with this shrinkage a reduction in the quality of life of each tribesman. All that mattered to the collective, council and shaman alike, was that less was making its way into their hands, and into their constituency. Less for the tribal council meant less power for them, and less for the electorate meant less in the shaman's larder.

Their solution was as simple as it was inspired. "Increase the assessments on the wealthy, while keeping the assessments on the poor low," argued one account-ant to the tribal council. As he spoke these words he imagined the complications which might make him indispensable.

And so the assessment grew, from one, to two, to three parts per gross on the wealthy. The struggling merchants at the bottom gave up their enterprises and sought employ with the wealthy. As the did so they competed for work with their former hires, abandoning their individualist ethic in exchange for the practical expedient of eating. Meanwhile, the account-ants grew ever more indispensable. And the separations between the individualist merchant and the collectivist grew.

"Verily, the poor suffer greatly as it is," countered Luth, seeing his donations decline as fewer merchants employed them, and smaller merchants gave up. Before, five small merchants might employ three workers each, for a total of fifteen. But a larger merchant, for the same work output, might employ only ten, such was the nature of the advantages of scale in the face of the collection[9]. Artisan for artisan, woodcutter for woodcutter, the same per-man output is equivalent regardless of the scale of the enterprise. But only the intrusion of the collection, and the need for the account-ant, tipped the balance in favor of the large. These large might have otherwise suffered from the additional layers of supervision to direct them all.

"Save us from this privation," the poor cried out to all who might listen, as the declining output of the tribe struck them most of all. Their garden lots had not produced nearly the bounty they had expected. Tending these by hand began to seem too much like work, and they couldn't employ the herds of cheval as did the master planter. Og and Pok could have taught them that, but it never occurred to the poor that the master planter had become wealthy by saving them the effort. Or that their previous job was far easier than sweating crops from the ground. Jobs such as tending the chevals for the planters, jobs which they had hated into extinction as the planters sought to reduce their holdings.

"Then shall we increase the assessments on the wealthy even further, and pay the poor from the larder of the tribe?" asked another account-ant?

---

[9] Our tribe had not yet discovered automation, which represents a different economy of scale altogether. More on this later.

"Yes!" shouted the tribal council, who knew this would ensure their hold on the populace.

"Yes!" shouted the account-ants, who knew this would increase their hold on the merchants.

"Yes!" shouted the shamans, who knew this would increase their larders.

"YES!" shouted the poor, their very number and need being their primary value to the tribe.

And so collections on the poor ceased. These collections were replaced by disbursements as the tribal council established huts throughout the valley where the poor might gather to receive their unearned goods. In a mockery of the accounting which Tab had invented, tribal workers, hired for the purpose, checked off each man, woman and child as they arrived to clutch at their reward for existence and for their vote. In return, the poor, relieved of the necessity of work, grew in number. The collectivists, wealthy and poor alike, smiled at each birth, welcoming another of their own.

Meanwhile, the assessments on the wealthy increased to four parts per gross. Not all paid this, however. The most clever among them had hired the best of the account-ants to qualify them for exceptions which had been created for the purpose. Only the individualist merchants, for the most part, paid the full share, they not having hired the account-ants to save them. And so the separation increased in intensity, driving more individualists toward poverty, and more collectivists upwards, their inventories spared.

For the most part, throughout this time the winters remained mild, the springs wet, and the summers long. Despite this declining production the tribe had yet to suffer the payment for its foolishness. Foolishness caused solely by the demand of the collective, whether poor worker or wealthy account-ant or exempted merchant. Or, the least to blame, by the tribal councilman who merely created the laws the electorate demanded.

The next separation of the individualist and the collectivist came about as some of the merchants and artisans, like the woodmen before them, reacted to assessments which seemed to rise without end. These merchants and artisans sought also to divert some of their property away from the hands of the collectors. Before long, the more dishonest of them actively hid their goods from sight, particularly the smaller, more valuable items such as tools. In so doing, the dishonest prospered more, while the honest prospered less.

As this latest separation took hold, the wealthy became more and more what Luth had claimed from the mount that they were, the evil rich who stole from the tribe. He neglected to point out that it was his very flock who had created the conditions to make them this way. After all, this served his purpose, too, as did the actions which were soon to follow.

The tribal revenues continued to decline, when measured against the number of tribesmen, as the productive output of the tribe continued to contract. The council, as they had so often done, concerned themselves not with how to correct the contraction. But instead, they considered how to extract more revenue from what was left, this being the only way to satisfy the electorate who demanded more and more from the council with each passing month.

At the same time, the account-ants were unsatisfied with the work they performed for the merchants for the week around the full moon collection. They wanted to be employed each week of the month rather than fending for themselves the remainder of the time.

And from the mount, Luth, who found himself becoming more and more subject to the whim of the greedy monster he had helped create, reflected the ethic of the faithful. "See how the rich hide their goods from the tribe. They buy and sell, but pretend they are poor while the truly poor starve," he told them. And feigned ignorance of the role that the account-ants, his best benefactors, and his congregation played in this.

The people, in their unsatiable envy, demanded that the tribal council act to stop this theft. Theft which they had enabled by the array of exemptions which they, the tribesmen, had previously demanded.

The merchants themselves participated in the next destruction, as they complained about the tax on property itself. "To satisfy my customers, I must maintain a certain inventory, otherwise I shall have nothing to sell in the lean months. It makes little sense to take more from me month to month. If you must take from me, take from my profits when the transaction is complete," they argued, directly and through their account-ants.

The tribal council considered these points of view, and then decided to reform the tax structure. At first, they considered a tax on each transaction, one part in ten. This would have been far less than the forty-eight parts per gross, or one part in three which would have been accumulated during a year of the inventory tax, they thought. Trade twenty sticks of wood for ten hides, and two sticks of wood and one hide would be surrendered to the tribe. Upon initial consideration, this change seemed fair and reasonable to the council of men who had never lived by their own efforts. And who hardly understood the magic of trade or even math, evidenced by their distance from it.

"But wait, Father," Tract told Gage as the council debated. "I use in my business wood from the woodman, who uses axes from the toolmaker. The toolmaker wraps the heads with leather from the tanner, who purchases acorns gathered by others. These acorns are sent in gourds hollowed out by still others."

Tract continued, "Along this chain, I pay the woodman in grain. Yet my grain has paid for wood which has paid for axes. These axes paid for leather which has paid for acorns. The acorns have paid for gourds to carry them. But trade works in two directions. Accordingly, the gourds are paid for by acorns paid for by leather. This leather is paid for by axes paid for by wood paid for by my grain. If each exchange is taxed at one in ten, I will receive only," he paused to shuffle the numbers in his head, "about one part in three of wood for my grain[10]. This tax would be twice as bad as the current inventory tax."

As the tribal council considered this, he added, "Now, from my perspective I might think that the exchange is only one in ten. But it must necessarily decrease the value of each trade, passing the accumulating costs along each time goods change hands. Worse, increase the chain beyond that and hardly anything else would be left."

Some in the council thought that the heaviness of this tax was perfect, as they imagined it would ensure unlimited earnings to the tribe. Wiser heads prevailed, and the council agreed instead with the proposal of an account-ant who was in attendance.

"Tract is right," began the agent-collector. "It is unwise to tax the entire transaction. Instead, let each tribesman pay the tax on only the profit of the exchange, leaving his costs untaxed. In this way, the cost of the tax will not accumulate so quickly, and he who profits most will be taxed the most." The council rose in applause to the wisdom of this idea, and failed to see the trap it concealed.

Henceforth, in addition to the land tax, which was left unchanged, the tax on inventory was abolished. In its place they instituted a tax on the profits of tribesmen when a trade was effected, one part in ten. Now, a woodmen could hold a stock of wood, and only be taxed when the wood was traded, whether in the summer, the fall or the winter. Similarly, a toolmaker could have as many tools as he wished, but only be taxed when they are traded.

Merchants and artisans of all kinds welcomed this change with relief, not knowing the horror they had just unleashed. The collective rejoiced. No longer would the guilty hide their stock or prevent the poor from trading as the moon grew full. The account-ants smiled knowingly, their futures assured.

Production of all kinds increased dramatically during the first month of the new tax. Wood was gathered and carefully stacked. Tools were laid in for sale at any time. Extra crops were planned as the planters cleared land which had laid fallow for years. Bunny hutches long neglected were repaired and prepared with fresh hay for the increase in stock. As these preparations were made, the full impact of the new tax had yet to materialize. And then the first woodman came to the trading hut bearing his load to trade for other goods.

"One part in ten, the woodman must pay for his profit," the tribal council had decreed.

"One part in ten, the trading hut which received his wood must pay for its profit," the tribal council had decreed.

But what did this mean? One part in ten of what? How exactly did one

---

[10] Each side of each transaction leaves only ninety percent remaining. For the ten sides of this transactional chain, down to the gourds and back, the actual math is $0.9^{10} = 0.349$, or 34.9% remaining after the taxes.

measure profit? No one was sure, not even the tribal council, who had declined to decree the answer, they similarly confused during their debates. But this is what the tribesmen had demanded, to stab at the rich, and so the councilmen complied with the whim of the electorate without reasoning through the consequences.

The account-ants knew the answer, which is that there is no answer, the precise trap they had laid to ensure their continued necessity. The tribal collectors certainly didn't know, these persons selected for their role as fiat thieves. As for Luth, "Give unto the tribe that which is the tribe's," was the best he could muster. The shaman found himself out of his philosophical depth when time for blame and guilt came to an end and solutions were demanded.

When Og and Pok had invented trade for the tribe, not even they had thought precisely about what was meant by profit. All they knew was that each walked away satisfied with the result. Now each tribesman was being asked to quantify that satisfaction, and precisely determine what one part in ten now belonged to the tribal larder.

Recall that Og, by himself, could choose to gather in a single day either a woman-weight of wood or two squirrels. In that same day, Pok could choose to gather either a quarter woman-weight of wood, or eight squirrels.

If they each traded a day's best work with the other, then Og received eight squirrels, when his own efforts would only have netted two. Was his profit then six squirrels?

Similarly, Pok received a woman-weight of wood when his own efforts would have netted only one fourth that. Was his profit three-fourths of a woman-weight?

On the surface, these answers seem fine and reasonable, but there is a hidden destructive implication. Assume now that Pok became lazy, and only trapped four squirrels, spending the rest of the day sleeping. Because there is no better trade available, Og might still be willing to trade his wood for these four. After all, this trade still seems much better than the two squirrels he would have caught on his own. Now, is Og's profit only two squirrels? Did his taxable income go down because Pok, a worker not under his control, chose to spend half the day sleeping? Or does Og get taxed less because he was suckered into a worse, yet still beneficial, deal?

Even this analysis assumes that Og knows precisely how many squirrels he might catch in a day. But if he did, what documentation might he present to the tribal council to prove his increase? And would they believe it? Perhaps the tribal daily standard published by the collectors admits only one squirrel. Then he would be taxed on three squirrels, instead of the two that would be reasonable for him.

What if Og became more skilled at squirrellery, so that he could instead be reasonably expected to catch three of them? Then his actual profit from the four squirrel trade is one squirrel, or five for the eight squirrel trade. The definition of profit, when it comes to a man's own work, doesn't survive the definition which is often applied to trade. And yet, a worker trades his time for pay, the entirety of which is considered income, which implies that a productive individual's time is worth nothing to him. To avoid this dilemma, the collective merely assumes that it owns all our lives. In this assumption the worker which creates original value incurs no cost in doing so, and that we merely work to be taxed for collective benefit.

Another problem arises if Og doesn't gather the wood himself, but instead subcontracts this work out to another. Just as the tribal council imposed this new tax policy, exactly this situation arose with a Brokerog, a descendant of our original woodman hero. Unlike Og, however, Brokerog didn't enjoy labor in the elements. He disavowed his namesake's daily communion with God and celebration of His bounty as decidedly Paganist. This disavowal he learned from Luth as a child. No, Brokerog was far too clever for raw labor.

On the other side of the valley lived the Cog brothers, also descended from that first mercantile woodman, who were following in his footsteps. They were each also rugged individualists. For years, Brokerog had hired his distant cousins to gather wood on his behalf. Using the economics of the original Og and Pok to keep things simple, each day each Cog brought Brokerog a woman-weight of wood, and in exchange Brokerog paid them six squirrels. Brokerog then received on the wood commodity exchange eight squirrels for each woman-weight. So, in exchange for the service of providing wood liquidity, just as the trading hut did for all commodities, the Cog brothers each surrendered two squirrels apiece to Brokerog. Brokerog then spent his time searching out the best prices for his inventory, averaging about eight squirrels apiece, pricing in that commodity remaining relatively historically stable.

Under the new tax structure, the tribal council finds that each of the three Cogs owe tax on six squirrels each. Likewise, the two squirrels which Brokerog profited on each trade with each of the three Cogs are taxable on the six squirrel total. Brokerog's profit is now six squirrels, just the same as each Cog who was working all day. But Brokerog may have done this brokerage in only about an hour, yet he benefits as much as the original worker. Clearly, everyone wants to be Brokerog, and no one wants to be a Cog.

As Brokerog and each Cog are all taxed at the rate of one part in ten, each must pay one-sixth of a squirrel (messy). For Brokerog, this doesn't seem very onerous. He might just have easily negotiated this much difference in the price of the wood in the first place. In fact, he can attempt this anyway by reducing the amount he is willing to pay the three Cogs. Perhaps Brokerog chooses to be generous and split the difference of his tax with them rather than demanding the entire amount to compensate for what he perceives as his loss. In this case, then, Brokerog reduces the amount he is willing to pay each of the Cogs by one-fifth of a squirrel. The Cogs then each pay taxes on 5.8 squirrels, and Brokerog pays taxes on 6.6 squirrels. After taxes, then Brokerog is nearly back to where he would have been pretax, or 5.94 squirrels. He decides the 0.06 squirrels is not too onerous a tax for him and proceeds with his plan, telling the Cogs that the reduction is due mostly to a change in commodity prices.

Alternatively, Brokerog might choose to hire yet another Cog brother to collect more wood. In that case, Brokerog gains 8 squirrels each day, which after tax is now 7.2 squirrels, better than he had before the tax was imposed. Of course, he has to manage the larger amount of wood. If he isn't careful at this he could depress prices by generating an oversupply. As we shall see in a moment, there are ways by which Brokerog can avoid this price depression, as well as taking advantage of it if it happens.

The Cogs are understandably unhappy with this turn of events. But since all the wood brokers are pretty much taking exactly the same approach, they really don't have anywhere else to turn in which they will be treated any better. And, unlike Brokerog, who can hire more workers, they can't create more hours in the day. Nor can they find more strength in their muscles, their stock in trade.[11]

Now, admittedly, some of these pressures exist even absent the new tribal tax structure. However, as we shall see in a moment, the hidden complexity of the tribal tax structure created unique opportunities for collective enterprises. While at the same time this structure punishes or otherwise limits the individualist.

Brokerog, having a limited commodity with which he traded, found his record-keeping relatively simple. But the trading hut, which managed a wide variety of trades of all kinds throughout the day, and at differing rates of exchange, found it difficult to determine what exactly was meant by profit. Did that particular stick of wood come from the trade for six squirrels earlier, or the gourd the day before? Although the system of credits which the hut used helped a little, it didn't eliminate it entirely. Under this new tax structure, the operators of trading huts found it necessary to determine who had credits available. But, also they had to know how many equivalent credits the trading hut gained, or lost, on each trade. Every single one of them.

Just as Ploison was considering this dilemma, in walked an eager account-ant, who offered to help him keep track of this problem each day. In exchange for a reasonable amount of credits, of course. Ploison, until now, had suffered through the tax collection visits alone. He had been determined to not let it force him into hiring a person who he saw as only extracting value, not creating it. But, finally he relented.

Ploison was not alone. All across the tribe account-ants swarmed the merchants and the artisans, offering their services to help mitigate a problem which they, in large part, had helped create. A problem which even now they were helping to worsen. At each merchant they promised their new master-servants that they would bend the ear of the tribal council to exempt, or promote, or punish, in some special way, some aspect of each merchant's or artisan's trade.

---

[11] This is the same problem faced by all original-value workers, traditionally individualists, who ultimately hand most of the value which they create over to essentially brokers, who take little risk.

"Those who hold inventory will be able to exempt from taxation one part in a gross of the portion which has been held for three months or more," offered the tribal council, hoping to increase holdings to ease the winter months.

"Each worker in the wood, stone or leather industries who earns less than six credits per day shall receive a three part in each gross credit toward their net tax," the tribal council generously decreed the next week. They had sought to ease some of the pain of the Cogs and other workers throughout the tribe. Workers who now found their pain increased by having to now keep track of these fractions.

"All contributions to shamans shall be exempt from taxation, provided such amounts are greater than one credit per lunar cycle, but less than two parts in ten of the worker's gross income, averaged on a lunar basis over the entire working year," the council bleated after Luth had his say, both on the mount and in their chambers.

"All planters who sow their fields in alternate wood fuels, including sweet gum, briar wood, pony stripe or pillow wood, but not oak or oak-derived varieties, shall receive three credits toward their tax assessment for each two hundred twenty-stride lots so sown," the tribal council pleaded. They had hoped to increase the tribal stocks of wood, but not at the expense of the favored oak and oak-related products lobby.

On and on, in a never-ending cycle the tribal council was petitioned by account-ants, merchants, the congregation, the workers and artisans to benefit each group in some special way. In so doing, the tribal council itself became overwhelmed, and decided to delegate most of this special work to a tax council. This council was to be overseen by a director appointed by the manager, and confirmed by the tribal council. This tax council would report regularly to a special tax oversight sub-council of the tribal council. But in reality each time a tribal councilman, even one not on the special sub-council, bent their ear the tax council acted as if decrees had been passed.

Councilmen found it easier than ever before to satisfy any who passed through their chambers. Their satisfaction was now purchased at a short walk to the tax council hut nearby. These purchases of favor assured their constituents that their special needs would be handled as vital to the interests of the tribe.

And so, relieved of the necessity of passing each special provision through the vote of the entire council, the tax council merely accelerated the rate of special provisions. The account-ants grew fat, and some learned to petition the tax council directly. Their threats to bring over their too-busy councilman served as sufficient justification for the tax council to leap to the task, knowing that the end would be the same.

The account-ants were merely one of the first professions to benefit from the complexity wrought by the collective to salve the poor and distressed. As each tax council ruling became known, merchants and artisans and brokers found it necessary to not only handle the accounting for these special provisions, but also to hire workers specifically to ensure compliance with the provisions in order to qualify for the benefits.

Tree specialists made their rounds with planters to consult with them on how to qualify for the alternate wood credit. Inventory management specialists assisted with determining and tracking what inventory had aged and how much. This in turn spawned an entire industry dedicated to inventory marking tags and accounting methods. That industry then qualified for special credits after its promoters met with a few influential councilmen, which spawned yet a new specialty in managing the credits.

Workers hoping to qualify for the credits offered them could not afford to hire specialists full-time as the larger merchants and artisans might. Instead, to service their needs special worker-tax kiosk huts sprang up along the tribal population centers. At these huts workers, in exchange for fractions of their meager credits, lined up to get their due. A due which included not only their low-wage credits, but also for any shaman contributions they may have made. Builders who constructed these kiosks, as well as the kiosk workers themselves, applied for special credits enacted to assist kiosk workers who assisted low-wage workers.

As more and more special provisions were applied, tax revenue dropped. Soon, the council increased the assessment to one part in nine, from one part in ten. The change to an inconvenient percentage alone placed an increased burden on the holdouts. In turn, these holdouts began hiring account-ants from school huts created specifically for the purpose of training them. Beside these school huts sprang school huts for inventory managers. And schools for kiosk workers, who began more and more integrating their work with the tribal workers who passed out the tribal contributions to the poor. Even these schools qualified for their own special set of credits, spawning yet another set of specialists employed to track them.

Throughout all of this pseudo-economic activity, tribal employment was at an all-time high. And yet none of these new workers produced a single tangible thing. Not one additional plant sprung from the ground. Even the special wood fuels credits merely displaced another crop which would have been planted. Their efforts harvested not a single stick of wood, nor crafted a single axe nor tanned the smallest hide nor fermented a drop of juice. Even the increased demand for wood and the thatch to build the kiosks and the schools had to have been taken from another tribesman by force. That original tribesman had then lost the opportunity to use it as he might see fit. Although the economic health of the tribe looked fine on paper, it continued to worsen in real terms for those who actually produced.

As the complexity of life increased, and the new psuedo-professions arose, the individualists who resisted participation continued to be pressed downward into poverty. Meanwhile, the collectivists who recognized the trends continued to be elevated, riding the expanding bubble of imagined prosperity. This bubble was inflated by the sheer momentum of the efforts of generations past.

And more and more, cogs aspired to be brokers, rather than improving themselves and their trade. Only the complexity of navigating the tax structure stood in the way of any who might wish to elevate themselves from mere worker to business proprietor. For many, this hurdle alone was enough to keep them in their station, unlike their forefathers, who could become their own businessmen at a thought. The Cog brothers had had enough themselves, and were willing to make the leap.

"But this could not be allowed," Brokerog thought to himself as he sensed the Cog brothers' dissatisfaction. "I am the broker, not they," he consoled himself, fearing the competition which they might wield in a free market. His salvation was coming in the form of a sacrifice, and the fire for that sacrifice was lit in a hut he had just passed on the way from the wood exchange.

Throughout the history of the tribe, and indeed all of mankind, tribesmen had learned through a combination of experience and natural selection to not do foolish things. Pet a viper, and it might kill you. Not eat, and you die. In countless ways, each of the behaviors which had been thought as good were nature's way of teaching men what was good for them and what was bad.

One such bad thing was burning certain vines within their huts. Throughout the forest grew a vine with three leaves, that when touched, or the oil of which landed on your hands, would leave a painful rash which might last for days. This rash, if it became infected, could kill you. Soon after the tribesmen had discovered the use of fire, they learned that burning these vines would release its oils as a vapor. These vapors, if inhaled, would lead to painful breathing and burning eyes, and often death. So, as the tribesmen lived close to God's nature they learned these things and attended to their risks, almost without thinking.

And so, as the woodmen plied their early trade, Og the first among them, it was natural that these vines be pulled from the wood as they harvested it. Otherwise, these vines might make their way into the fires, or burn the hands or shoulders as it was carried. Even so, a certain amount of the vine would make its way on the wood through the various trades, and eventually into the hands of the consumer who would remove it lest it burn. Despite this, from time to time someone would make the mistake of allowing the vine to smoulder on the wood; the results served to refresh the minds of all who might have forgotten.

But now the ethic of the tribe was changing. No longer was a tribesmen responsible for his own life. Instead, men had learned to turn to the tribal council and the shaman for his guidance, and began to neglect their own intellect and ability. More and more men began to rely on others for guidance as to what was good and what was bad. Others who, despite their best intentions, could not possibly manage to make all the decisions or provide the protection needed for all the tribesmen's lives.

And so, a few minutes after Brokerog passed that hut, the owner of the hut lit his fire, not checking beforehand to remove any of the poison vine before doing so. Before long, the poisonous vapors had landed upon the tribesman and his two young children. The owner scooped the children out of the hut as soon as he realized what had happened. Fortunately, no one would die, but he and the children suffered painful rashes to their faces and other exposed skin. These minor injuries in a previous time would have made them simply the brunt of good-natured humor as their appearance for a while reminded themselves and others of the danger.

Not so in the age of the Lamist, however. Luth quickly seized upon this new opportunity as he brought them to the mount with him, "See how the evil rich ply you with poison! Even the little children are the victim of his greed!" The congregation swayed with pity for the children and disdain for the merchant. Others outside the congregation, but within huts near the victims' lot, saw themselves as potential victims as well. Denying their own abilities, they joined the swell. That week the tribal council chamber was thick with tribesmen who had learned to see that ornate hut as the salve for their miseries.

"You must do something about the poison wood of the merchant!" they demanded.

"While you sit here and do nothing, the woodmen grow rich while they kill our children!" they shouted.

"It should be a crime to sell poison to us!" they argued.

"The tribe inspects our taxes, let them also send inspectors to check all the wood!" they shrieked.

The tribal councilmen, as they had been selected to do, reflected the indignation of the populace and enacted a new law. "Henceforth, all wood for sale shall be inspected by agents of the tribal council, working under the direction of the tribal manager." The tribal manager, in turn would delegate this work to a director. That director was appointed by the manager and confirmed by the council, who would employ a staff to assist the director in this task. Work began immediately on a new hut to house the wood inspection directorate, and hired men from the wood industry as well as others less qualified. The cost of these inspectors would be funded by fines they would levy, as well as a special assessment placed on each wood transaction.

Immediately, the wood inspectors fanned out through the tribe. They inspected each and every stick of wood, imposed first warnings and then fines, and collected the special assessments.

"See how they overcharge us now!" the tribesmen howled, as the woodmen and brokers and merchants passed along the additional cost in the only way possible.

Like the tax collection before, the new wood inspection laws led larger merchants to hire specialists. These sprang up for the purpose, to assist them in inspecting their wood before the tribal inspectors might fine them. As before, this new cost of compliance began to separate the productive individualist toward the bottom, while the collectivist moved up. And at the bottom, the smallest merchants who struggled simply left the field, this new requirement exceeding that which they could bear.

Brokerog immediately saw this new development as the opportunity it was. Indeed, only recently had the Cog brothers hoped to form their own brokerage. But the cost of compliance was now seen by them as too risky to endure, as a single poison vine would destroy several days' work in fines.

"Continue selling to me, and I will shield you," Brokerog assured them as he hired a specialist to inspect the wood for them. And as he contracted with other independent woodmen who now sought the same protection.

But this was not enough for Brokerog, who saw further opportunity lurking around the corner. One Tuesday he attended Luth's sermon, and asked to speak, having brought with him a sufficient donation, of course.

"My friends," he began. "I have seen with my own eyes the pain which greed can bring," he lamented, waving his arm toward the children who, fortunately for him, had not yet healed completely. Luth wondered if this broker was in the wrong profession, thinking that he might have become an excellent shaman.

"I have consulted with many wise men," he lied, sweeping his arm back to the gravely nodding Luth beside him, who accepted credit as if this had actually happened. The broker had actually simply presented his plan to the shaman as he had asked to speak, and asked no advice.

"I ask that you join me in demanding that the tribal council approve each merchant, especially brokers like myself, who wishes to trade in wood," he said. His announcement surprised them, surprised that he would ask for laws to be imposed on his vocation. "I know my fellow wood brokers and merchants are as willing as I to be subject to these terms in order to ensure the public safety. I expect they will join me in this request as well," he finished magnificently, to surprised applause.

A few days later, he repeated this show for the tribal council, accompanied by many in the congregation. He also had in attendance some of the larger merchants who were able to spare the time away from their shops. The smaller merchants, busy with other needs they couldn't afford to delegate to hires, were absent, as well as most of the individual woodmen, like the Cog brothers.

The tribal council was moved at this seemingly self-sacrificial act, which surprisingly, had the support of most of the wood industry leaders present. One councilman, worried that the tribe was already spending too much, warned Brokerog and the rest, "We can't expect the tribe to pay the cost of this." Most agreed with this sentiment. He continued, "Instead, I propose that the cost of the approval be born by those of you in this room when you apply for approval, and for your annual renewals."

To the shock of the council, Brokerog said, "This is only reasonable that we should pay. The public interest is too important for petty issues such as who shall bear the cost." After recoiling from their shock, more than one councilman wondered whether this broker was in the wrong business, thinking that he might make an excellent councilman. As the tribal council considered this surprise, Brokerog smiled to himself as they took his bait, yet keeping his countenance wrung with public concern.

The council considered the testimony of those assembled, and decided that indeed Brokerog's proposal was in the interest of the tribe. Henceforth, they decided, a new branch of the wood inspection directorate would be formed, and it would accept applications for what would become known as a license. The application fee for such a license would be one hundred credits, and each annual renewal would cost one hundred credits as well. Licensed woodmen would be required to attend special courses to instruct them as to the proper inspection procedures required for wood which they gathered.

To protect the interest of the individual worker, all employees of a licensed wood merchant would be covered under the same license as the proprietor. To protect the individual tribesman who might wish to still gather his own wood, and thus maintain public support for the measure, gathering for personal use would not require a license. But, as soon as even a stick of wood were offered for sale or trade, the license would be required.

Brokerog couldn't have been more happy. The next month, as the law became enforced, he approached the Cog brothers and asked for their license before he could accept their wood. He knew that they had not applied for one, and fortunately for him, they had been too busy with their work to know his role in its enaction. "We cannot afford this license, it will cost us a hundred credits each. We would have to work for weeks to pay this," they cried.

"Don't worry, my friends. The law allows that if you work for a licensed broker, then you are covered as well," he assured them. "Come to work for me, and I shall save you the cost. You can continue as you have as my employees, and pocket the difference for yourselves" he offered, casting avoidance of this artificial requirement as a benefit to them. He finished with, "Of course, as I have to bear the expense of the license as well as the tax and other regulations, I will have to reduce what I pay you to five squirrels each."

Reluctantly, they agreed, and abandoned any hope of operating their own wood business. All across the tribe, smaller independent wood shops and individual woodmen abandoned their business ambitions. Their former owners were absorbed as employees for the larger brokerages and merchants able to amortize the costs of the licensing. The collective grew larger and more powerful still as the displaced blamed not the industry which had demanded the licenses for exactly for this purpose. Instead, the displaced blamed only the tribal council who had merely followed the wishes of both the industry and the public alike.

From then on, individuals might gather their wood for their own fires. But no one, no matter how effective or how capable, or what ideas they might have for improvements in the gathering, would be able to sell a single stick of it without the license. And the wood fuel industry, continuing to aggregate their power in larger and larger organizations, petitioned for larger and larger licensing fees to ensure they would never face competition from below.

Brokerog, who had nearly been caught at the treachery he wrought on the Cog brothers, learned to never again directly promote his agenda before the tribal council. Instead, he, and others of the larger brokerages, hired specialists for the task, who marketed his industry's agenda both to the public and to the tribal council. Never again would his hands be seen at the controls he operated. Throughout the valley, other industries took notice, and the larger of them banded together to choke away their smaller, individualist competition.

"Stone tools can kill! Only licensed artisans should make them!"
"Bad ferment can blind! License and inspect the fermenters!"
"Don't live in a deathtrap! We must license the hut builders!"

On and on, in each industry, in the feigned interest of the public, and at their demand, smaller shops fell prey to regulations promoted by the larger, and the fees these regulations required. The separation of the tribe into richer and poorer grew wider, the poor demanding this separation which limited their futures alongside the rich who saw opportunity in obstacles. And the tribal council grew more powerful, and saw their purpose less and less to protect the individual, and more and more to promote the collective.

But even this was not enough. The crowning glory of the wood influence specialists was to whip up a public frenzy against the smaller operators. These smaller operators, it was claimed, sold inferior grades of wood which smoked too much. And this smoke was imagined to leave clouds of ash and soot throughout the valley.

"We should force these evil fuel giants to stop polluting our air!" his specialists shouted at the congregation and in the tribal chambers.

"Stop picking on us," Brokerog shouted back at them, moving credits from his accounts to theirs, their service loyally fulfilled. Eventually, the tribal council was swayed by this charade, and the outcry which leapt at them from the public. "You have polluted the air in the valley for the last time," the council warned him. "Henceforth," they demanded gravely, "you, Brokerog, and all your industry, shall sell only approved grades of wood." Brokerog said nothing as he sat in the hearing, feigning incredulity at the result he had paid so preciously to win.

"We shall increase the staff of the wood inspection branch. This branch shall not only approve the licensing and inspect for vines, but also shall now ensure that wood is dried for a period of not less than six months before sale," the councilmen dictated to their scribes.

"Each seven weights of pine shall contain one weight of hickory," they decreed, basing their proportions on reports of studies paid for by the industry. Yet these studies had been presented to them as independent, noble research by the influence specialists. "And each five weights of oak shall contain one of ash", they further arbitrated. "No other blends shall be allowed between the third and the ninth full moon of the year. At all other times only pure oak shall be allowed. In no case shall three parts per gross of sweet gum be permitted."

The public rejoiced that the evil wood giants had now been put in their place. "In my place, indeed, " thought Brokerog to himself. His enterprise gobbled up the smaller businesses around him which had finally been put under by pointless regulations that ensured only the larger collectives could afford to comply.

Once his position was assured, walled in safely by regulations which prevented competition by the small, Brokerog could now manipulate the normally good effects of a free market. These effects, such as labor and wages, or supply and demand, now helped him drive moderately-sized businesses under, and thus allow him to absorb their assets and employees and customers.

In a truly free market, labor, wages, ideas, commodities, finished goods, skills, and all the countless elements of economic value all flow, and like water, seeks its own level. These elements flow to where they can be more efficiently used. In the process the free market rewards those who produce the most value, and punishes those who produce the least. But the market of the tribe, with the walls of regulation placed where they can benefit the collective the most, represented channels or culverts or dams placed to divert the economic flow in unnatural ways.

To the individual participant in the economy these things were looming and unseen, like a mouse running about his business and unable to grasp the larger drainage channels around him. Yet because of these unseen channels, this flow could either be permanently diverted away from him, killing him from thirst, if he sat atop a culvert. Or drown him in it, if he sat in the drainage channel itself.

Neither was good, and he cursed not the artificial walls of the drainage. No, he cursed the flow itself, or lack of it. As he cursed he knew instinctively that this flow should simply be falling on him from time to time like the rains with which he was familiar in the forest. The drought or deluge seemed unfair to him. And yet the mechanism of this unfairness was precisely what he had demanded.

One such natural economic flow is the rising of prices should a commodity be scarce, or the falling of prices should a commodity be in abundance. In a free market, no one person or organization can manipulate these prices very much by artificially withholding or increasing production. Should he try this, his neighbor or his customer will punish him for doing so.

If an artisan withholds production to increase prices, his neighbor might decide to produce instead to benefit by selling what is now scarce. Supply increases, and prices return to normal. The toolmakers and the others in the tribe had been able to do this, and get away with it, to avoid the inventory tax. The tax itself represented an artificial channel which made each artisan want to do exactly the same thing. And so none of them suffered from competition. The free market had been thwarted by the tax.

On the other hand, an artisan may increase his production to drive prices down, for whatever reason. But the marketplace will reward him less and less for this as only so many of his trinkets may be in demand. This will punish his competition as well, but unless the artisan is willing to burn through his own cash reserves he will soon stop this foolishness. Unless he has other reasons which make this loss a worthwhile investment.

Another natural economic flow is the allocation of labor to where it might best be rewarded. Pay too little, and a merchant or artisan loses labor to those who will pay better. Pay too much, and the merchant or artisan is flooded with labor which is not economically efficient. Similarly, should a worker demand too much for his time when compared to his skill, he is soon unemployed. But demand too little and he suffers a hidden cost, but is employed as much as he likes.

Even this flow of labor and wages, in a free market, represents an opportunity for workers to improve themselves. Want higher wages? Learn new skills and become more valuable. Want to learn new skills? Be willing to work for less in an unfamiliar field. But these rules only work if the market is truly free. If it is constrained by regulations which prevent the free flow of labor, then either the worker, or the employer, or both, suffer from the dam which is built in the path of this flow.

Brokerog understood all these forces, and the opportunity which their constriction had placed in his hands. Woodmen could only ply their trade in his regulated industry by either working for him or one of his competitors. And so, he began his latest conquest by lowering the wages of his workers, who were constrained by law from simply starting their own wood businesses and competing directly with him. Of course, many grumbled, and some left to seek employ with others in the wood industry and fanned out across the valley, carrying with them news of Brokerog's reduced wages.

During this time, Brokerog, of course, kept the prices of his commodity constant. Due to his size, the loss of a few workers and their production was nothing compared to the incremental price and wage difference on the large production which remained. And so he began to accumulate a reserve of excess wages which otherwise would have been paid out. The displaced workers included spies placed among them as they arrived at the other wood enterprises. These workers caused a ripple of wage reductions throughout the industry, as now the labor was in oversupply.

Fearing a popping bubble in wood industry wages, some workers chose to leave the industry altogether and went to work in other trades, never to return. For a time, all the traders and brokers in the wood industry profited from the depressed wages. The largest profited most of all as they were the best able to amortize the cost of regulatory compliance among their workers and inventory. The smaller enterprises did well, but not nearly so much as their larger competition.

No one but Brokerog realized what he knew, which was that the wage deflation was artificial. Each of his competition believed that this situation represented a permanent change in the industry. All along, though, with fewer workers, the wood production dropped slightly, and began to eat into the tribal reserves.

Some in the industry believed that this wage reduction was a largess which was being laid at their lap selectively and exclusively. And so they either squandered the wage difference or they invested in more production, such as buying additional chevals or axes with which to gather more effectively. Brokerog, however, held on to his wage reserve, all the while telling his specialists to place rumors that he was similarly expanding his capability.

After a suitable time, Brokerog suddenly announced a wage increase, and demanded increased production from all his staff. All throughout the valley word quickly spread that Brokerog was hiring at higher wages. This rumor spread quickest among the smaller enterprises whom he had seeded with employees feigning resignation from him before taking their new positions. These same seeded employees remained on the private payroll of Brokerog, and had told him of the investments made by their new hosts. They now drummed up dissatisfaction there and, inflating the expectations of new wages, led their workers away to his door.

Arriving there, the wage victims found that Brokerog's wages were higher, but not so much higher as they had been led to believe. The spies simply shrugged, leaving Brokerog blameless. But, the wage victims had also fallen prey to the simple compliance gambit of throwing down their working tools at the feet of their unsuspecting former employers. As they had mimicked the spies who led them in this, they found it difficult to return to their old jobs, so many signed on with Brokerog nonetheless.

Brokerog immediately increased production as much as possible. He also cut his supply to the commodity market, storing now the excess wood production. This cut ate into his wage reserve, and then some, as he traded wages for wood which would soon be scarce. His competition found themselves supplying the commodity market for a time all by themselves, and quickly depleted their stocks of wood. Lacking a full staff of labor, they faced a choice: run dry and only trickle out production, or hire more staff.

Some chose the former strategy, choosing to remain small, and rushed to keep up with the demand with their current staff, although prices on the market had not yet time to react. Eating at them, however, was the regulatory compliance cost, which now was amortized over less production. And recently purchased chevals and tools sat idle.

Some chose the latter strategy. Dipping into their reserves of various goods they rushed to hire whomever they could. But now they hired at wages artificially high as they reacted to the wage phantoms which Brokerog had planted. Some of the new hires, new to the industry and thus unskilled, were a drain on production and consumed much of the expertise of the remaining staff to train them. Recently purchased chevals and tools, in the hands of novices, were destroyed, legs broken, blades cracked. Efficiency suffered, and their wage and price differential threatened to exhaust them if the commodity price did not catch up soon.

But the commodity price only caught up slightly, rising only so much as Brokerog would allow by throttling availability of his production reserves. But not so much that his competition could truly benefit from the increase. Industry watchers saw Brokerog's competition struggling to meet demand, and stockpiles depleting everywhere they looked. Except at Brokerog's yard, where he sold only enough as needed to slow the drain on his wage reserves and keep prices slightly higher each day, falsely indicating a trend.

Brokerog piled stride after stride of wood at his yard, a seemingly suicidal act made possible only by the sheer size of his enterprise. He also, through the medium of his staff account-ants, began to apply for the maximum in the long-forgotten tax credit on this sizeable, and growing, and aging inventory of surplus wood. And so some of his lost sales during this time were returned to him in the form of tax credits. His sheer volume made that meager credit now a sizeable amount worth pursuing.

The merchants, in turn, raised their own prices accordingly. Watching the prices rise slightly day by day, and in anticipation of having to replace their stocks with even higher prices later, the merchants increased the prices to their customers even more. The tribesmen began to notice what seemed like a worsening wood market.

Meanwhile, Brokerog's spies continued to whisper. At the overworked shops they whispered, "Brokerog doesn't work his men so hard. I heard they had a position open up lately, I think I will apply for it next week." To beat the spy to the job, two or three scampered away to take the position, which indeed, Brokerog had waiting for all, but at the reasonable wage.

At the shops filled with novices they whispered, "Brokerog doesn't have so many unskilled men, so it is much safer working there. I heard they had a position open up lately, I think I will apply for it next week." To beat the spy to the job, two or three of the skilled scampered away to take the position, which indeed, Brokerog had waiting for all, but at the reasonable wage.

And so, the overworked were drained of labor, and their situation worsened. The shops laden with novices were drained of skill, and their situation worsened. And production at each began to suffer as the rising prices spurred them on. The seemingly endless price increases, even in the face of reduced consumption, were too good to resist.

By this time, as winter approached, the tribesmen began to truly take notice of the dwindling supply of wood. Some, fearing depletion, began to gather wood on their own, still legal under tribal law, so long as they didn't sell it. Others began to cut back on consumption. Either way, sales dipped slightly, enough to frighten Brokerog's competition, who still had no idea of what was going on. In a normal market, the reduced sales would have lowered prices, but Brokerog was able to continue throttling releases of his reserves to make them trickle higher nonetheless. Nothing seemed to make sense to anyone, and fear began to spread.

And then, Brokerog rose to speak to them. "My friends," he announced from the mount and from the tribal chambers, "we are but one tribe. Cold winter approaches, and we are indeed our brother's keeper. To ensure that none suffers, I am releasing my reserve of wood for sale, and at three parts in four of its normal price. I pray that my companions in the industry will follow me in this act of tribal pride, and that the merchants will pass these savings on to you."

His competition was stunned, having expected a price increase to save them. Brokerog merely traded otherwise worthless excesses of wood for vital reserves of credits, and more importantly, time. Time for his competition to falter. The overworked were at the limit of their ability, their stocks depleted, and now they would receive far less for their work than before. The underskilled were at the limit of their ability, their stocks similarly depleted, and would also receive far less for their work than before. Increasing production would not help, as neither could afford to produce more which would bring them less.

Many of each simply closed, their belongings placed at auctions which Brokerog attended. Some sold their enterprises to Brokerog outright, he being the only purchaser in the valley which could legally enter their business and had the credits to do so. Other than the very largest, the survivors were too damaged to do much but put the pieces back together. Yet Brokerog's power, and that of his larger competitors, grew only stronger.

Over the winter, Brokerog gradually brought prices back to their former levels, earning him more return now on his larger reserve of wood. As his profits mounted, he silently thanked the collective which had placed the tools of manipulation in his hands. Without the regulations which channeled the flow of labor into his hands, and prevented smaller operators from entering the industry to challenge him, he remained free to exercise these gambits whenever he thought a competitor weak enough to take.

"And the workers?" he asked himself in a moment of reflection of those who had voted for him to have this power, "merely tools in my hands." Free trade disappeared at every turn, stoned into oblivion by the collective masses with their ignorance and pettiness. The stonesmen were egged on by shamans and industry giants with agendas to promote. And free trade itself was blamed for each privation.

"Have you seen the price of wood lately? Free trade shouldn't be so free." Yet their own demands removed the independent woodmen who could have competed the price down.

"Why can't I ever get a great stone axe when I need one? We should regulate the tool makers more so that they will do better work." Not realizing that the smaller tool maker could have competed the quality up.

"Workers are treated like mice in a trap. How come free trade works for the wealthy, but not for us?" Not realizing that their own demands prevented them from starting their own enterprises and securing their own liberty.

"You just can't earn a living wage these days, those big brokers (or merchants or artisans or traders) won't pay fairly. Free trade? Hah. More like free labor. For them!" Not realizing that their own demands kept the individual or small traders from staying in business. And thus able to innovate or excel to keep the larger businesses from forming labor monopolies.

"They don't make ferment like they used to. All of the good fermenters sold out to the larger ones. Shame on them!" And on the masses for driving them out of business.

"My hut is leaking, and Tract won't do anything about it. We should get him under control." But they already were under control, and, in a collective, submission to that control trumps customer service.

Free trade was nowhere to be found. But it received all the blame, ensuring that it could never arise again. And throughout this downward spiral, the tribe subjected itself to increasing regulations which dictated who could hire whom, under what conditions, and for what payment. And regulations which dictated under what conditions materials could be obtained and provided to others. Regulations soon infected the fabric of every aspect of tribal life. Freedom itself disappeared from the valley.

Ploison, now an old man, watched this destruction of his beloved tribe, destruction which had been wrought in a surprisingly short time and for the best of intentions. And he understood now the responsibility which lay squarely on his shoulders. "This is all my fault," he thought to himself, the guilt weighing heavily upon his aged heart.

"Perhaps I shouldn't have turned The Widow away after she refused my offer of employment to improve her own situation," he lamented. "Instead, I should have put my arm lovingly around her frail shoulders, and led her through the back of my hut, where she could select whatever she wanted from my inventory yard."

In his mind's eye, he saw his younger self doing just this, leading her around his yard as the warm sun beamed down upon them. He saw her happy face as she walked with him and picked out this, and that, her body capable of performing the work he had offered, if her mind had only willed it so.

He also saw his own face, at peace, knowing that he was saving his tribe from certain destruction. He saw himself saving it from otherwise becoming a mockery of the tribe which his father and his aunt, in their self-salvation as little orphans, helped to build and make wealthy. All the while, knowing that by his generosity he would only encourage her to return again and again, to him and others, and bringing more just like her. But his tribe would be safe.

And then, when her little arms were full, fuller than she was willing to make them in his employ, he saw himself kicking her into the ravine behind. As The Widow fell, her greedy clutching hands were unwilling to release the unearned treasure, even for a moment to save herself. Instead, this stolen treasure added its weight to the momentum of her plunge, more crisply snapping her neck upon the rocks below, his beloved tribe now safe.

Chapter 10, Employment Trends

Our delightfully gentle caveman examples help illustrate a key concept about how employment evolves over time. Consider the thoroughly unscientific chart below:[12]

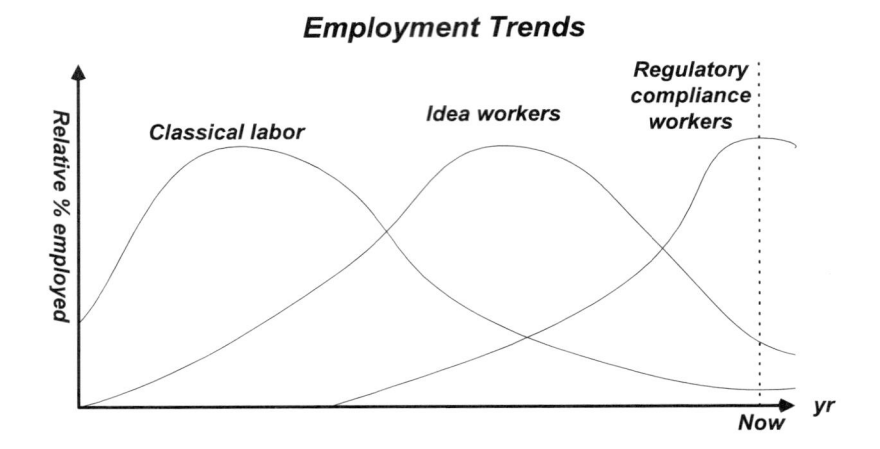

Employment Trends

(Chart: Relative % employed vs. yr. Three overlapping curves labeled "Classical labor" (peaking on the left), "Idea workers" (peaking in the middle), and "Regulatory compliance workers" (peaking on the right, at "Now").)

As time began, to the left of the chart, most people worked for themselves, gathering stuff as needed using their own ideas and energy. Then, somewhere along the way, still to the left of the chart, some people began working for others, trading in the classical sense.

Then, as the chart, and recorded history, begins on the left side of the chart above, some portion of people are working for others to some extent or another. Og and Pok could reasonably be considered as working for each other. From Og's perspective, Pok supplies squirrels as an independent contractor paid in wood, while Pok has a similar perspective about Og. Those who don't work for others in some sense are still in the hunter-gatherer subsistence mode.

For a good chunk of human history, more and more people became involved in trade. Unfortunately, in too many cases, that trade was forced at the tip of a lash, as was prevalent across most of Africa and Asia throughout most of historical time, including now. When despots run out of ideas, they rarely turn to free trade as the solution. But instead they imagine themselves more capable of managing the affairs of their subjects than reality proves. And so, the lack of free trade inevitably turns to harsher and harsher methods to get results. Results which never come.

In the rare cases in which free trade was allowed, such as the early days of our tribe, the self-interest of some workers cause them to make the leap to creating value through ideas. At first slowly, and then more rapidly,

---

[12] Source: My fevered imagination.

ideas become used to reduce the amount of raw labor required by magnifying its effects. For example, the idea of harnessing animal power allows a field to be plowed far faster than a man could do with his own muscles alone. His muscles are still being used, but used to control a large meat tractor pulling a plow rather than by pulling the plow itself.

Evolutionary forces then kick into play. Individuals who use animals to plow do better than those who do all the plowing themselves. Similarly, tribes in which plowing by animal is considered a better thing than whipping people into pulling plows do a lot better, too. Even the shamans and their fear-based sacrifices from time to time don't make much of a difference compared to the vast difference caused by the effective use of energy.

Now, just because everyone in the tribe starts using plow animals does not make them idea workers. No, instead that one idea worker caused a radical change to the structure of the entire tribal economy. And then perhaps faded into the background as just another classical laborer, although perhaps empowered with a better tool.

And so, the growth of the idea worker, as a measurable portion of the workers overall, is very slow, but begins accelerating over time. Once at least one idea worker begins to be able to earn a living predominately through his ideas, the entire tribe begins to benefit in astonishing ways. Imagine if each month one idea worker in a tribe came up with an idea which was the equivalent of harnessing animals for agriculture. A single year of this sort of progress would take decades to propagate throughout the tribe, while a decade of this level of ideas would take generations.

Some tribes are more successful at encouraging idea workers, while other tribes are downright hostile to ideas and idea workers. The former, even if they steal the ideas, will tend to grow over time out of proportion to the quality of the labor component of their society. Provided of course, they at least do no harm to the idea workers themselves and provide them with at least subsistence. The latter sort of tribes, those which, say, stone idea workers to death, will tend to do more poorly.

The treatment of idea workers will correlate directly with how much the culture benefits from them. The more prosperous the idea workers become, the more incentivized they are to improve things for everyone. But, imagine, if you will, that a large country suddenly decided that it wanted to rid itself of lots and lots of smarty-pants. Embarking on a campaign of terror, rooting out anyone who was perhaps more productive or more thoughtful than his fellows, the country would probably kill off a lot of its future progress. Likely, however, would be that some of the good guys would survive and flee to somewhere else and start anew. Perhaps, say, on a few lightly inhabited islands just to the east. Or maybe on a few peninsulas in that general direction.

The gene pool which departed, even if they had to live in primitive conditions for hundreds of years, would still manage to make a good show of things. Their former barbarian home, on the other hand, would appear to an objective observer frozen in time.

Future historians might then wonder why the original country, which managed to invent so many wonderful things centuries or more ahead of everyone else, suddenly seemed to just stop dead still. Or maybe even move backwards a little bit as some great piece of technology somehow didn't make it on some despot's to-do list, he being more attentive to carving figures out of stone with his available whip-labor.

Now, even if the departed lived in primitive stone age conditions, the underlying gene pool would still be bubbling just beneath the surface. All of those generations that should have been thinking up stuff might have been too busy digging around for food. But eventually, some spark, such as newcomers showing up with some fancy stuff, might get everything rolling around in people's heads again. Suddenly, this culture would become imitative, and then innovative.

Unless they became distracted by some nonsense such as taking time out to try to erase their generations-old tormenters from the face of the earth. Don't forget, the same gene patterns which caused them to run in the first place would have also led them to see their old kinfolks as an implicit threat, and want to remove them as a potential threat ever again. Should this ever happen, about the only thing that would be able to stop them, machine guns trumping sticks, would be if some collective somewhere thought it would be keen to just let these little conflicts bubble around for a while (more about this later). Punitive war aside, this experimental culture would probably be able to generate a pretty high quality of life for themselves, and for a lot of other people, too.

So the advent of idea workers, and a culture's response to them, plays a large role in how a culture evolves and advances over time. The most important fundamental idea which enables all the rest of them is free trade. Thank you, Og and Pok. Og wanted to do a great job gathering wood so that he could demand the largest number of squirrels for his wood. Conversely, Pok wanted to catch the best squirrels in the best condition so that he could trade them for the largest amount of wood. Scrimping by either man would have simply scrimped themselves.

Now, earlier I said that just because someone uses an idea it doesn't make them an idea worker. On the other hand, just because someone runs a meat tractor all day it doesn't mean that they aren't, either. The distinction is slight, but important, and it makes the difference between whether, under free trade, someone has chosen to be a man, or chosen to be a monkey. Without free trade, monkey is, eventually, the only choice available, unless you take the advice later in this book. Og and Pok, the freest of traders in history, performed at peak performance because it benefitted them the most to do so. The hapless Cog brothers, once they had been absorbed by Brokerog's manipulation of regulations, had little incentive to excel beyond simply escaping being fired.

If free trade is possible, then each man gets to decide, each day, or each hour, or each moment, whether they are just stumbling along behind the plow, or instead, doing important work which eventually will be traded to someone else for something good. If the work matters enough for him to do well, then, poof, he just became an idea worker. The essential ingredient which even makes this thought possible is whether he will benefit from the better work. Under the lash, no man performs at his best, at least for very long, because there is no motivation to do so once the work has been done well enough to escape it. In our modern world, there are many kinds of lashes, it is just that we've gotten good at hiding them. And have been taught to be very bad at noticing them.

The more idea workers in a culture, the higher the quality of life will be. As we saw in an earlier chapter, ideas empower the transformation of resources in ways which can best satisfy our desires for high quality of life. And with free trade, those resources get best allocated to those who can best employ them. Og is the best at collecting wood, so free trade allows him to do that work to most efficiently collect it. Pok is the best at collecting squirrels, and so free trade assigns that task to him, since he is able to best extract value for himself from this task.

Free trade is an essential precondition for a large number of idea workers. As the lack of free trade restricts the benefit derived from ideas, then ideas will become more scarce. Even this fleeing of ideas from restricted trade is itself a triumph of the free trade in ideas and personal motivation in the face of oppression. And so, over time, as free trade flourished for a shining moment in our history, idea workers also flourished, as did the quality of life for much of humanity.

Just as night follows day, however, a third major class of workers follows the advent of idea workers. This third class is known as regulatory compliance workers. These workers, both inside and outside the government, exist solely to cause, or mitigate, the negative quality of life which results from thwarting or obeying, respectively, various government regulations.

In all fairness, regulatory compliance workers have been around for a long time. From the time that the first barbarian king sought to punish threats to his reign, or even simple disobedience, this class of workers existed. From the time that shamans sought to stone those who threatened to expose their con game, this class of workers existed.

As I use the term here, though, I intend that this class refers to those compliance workers who are employed specifically because the regulatory environment expanded to consume the available excess resources. When the tribe changed taxation from a flat per-citizen model to an inventory-based model, regulatory compliance workers, in the form of assessors and accountants, on both sides of the gavel, arose.

This class of workers, unlike the overseer or the snitch or the shaman's stonesmen, spring into being, generally some time after the implementation of a new idea, because of three key reasons. First, the idea worker, like that unknown hero who thought of plow animals, creates such revolutionary beneficial changes in the economic landscape that it takes some time for this idea to completely saturate the culture. So, the regulatory reaction to this idea may take a while to reach a critical mass to be enacted.

Second, the new idea, once it gains momentum, creates an excess of resources which causes unexpected growth in other sectors of the economy. For example, as the use of plow animals began to produce excess food, for a time food suddenly seems easy to obtain. For many generations afterward significant portions of a population became displaced from growing or herding, thinking all the while that the bounty will never come to an end. Until the day arrives that the excess has finally been absorbed, the population continues to grow until famine or other privation once again rears its head. This process takes a while, however, which contributes to the lagging effect between idea worker and regulatory compliance worker.

Third, the lag between the introduction of the idea and the eventual consumption of its bounty leads to an entire wedge of economic activity which may or may not reflect good sense. During this period, the excess resources can tempt the populace to demand restrictions on previously great ideas, restrictions which would seem suicidal in the face of privation. For example, when wood was plentiful the tribe had the luxury of thinking of silly restrictions on the collection and sale of wood. Similarly, while energy is cheap we have the luxury of thinking of ways to legislate limitations on energy.

Times are good in the heyday of a previous new idea worker's grand thought, or in the middle of an overlapping series of great ideas, which is more often the case. During these good times a collective thinks of ways to use that largess to implement some sort of social justice or other nonsense. Why? Because they can afford to. Or at least think they can afford it.

And when the day arrives that they realize that they can't afford some arbitrary restriction? Well, the collective being what it is, they never think of undoing some previous regulation, but instead imagine that new ones will do the trick. Usually, these new regulations just create more problems. Problems such as limiting idea workers.

Brokerog could never have amassed such disproportionate power without regulations which protected him from competition. As the regulations prevented free trade by barring entry to smaller outfits, or by forcing such heavy compliance costs that such operations could never reach a critical mass, Brokerog was unassailable. No amount of great ideas about better ways of collecting or distributing wood, or of better wood grades or blends, would have made any difference in his power. He would not waste resources on implementing these ideas, as his power was assured without them. Yet others couldn't get a toe hold to implement them and compete him out of business.

Over time, as regulations grow, which they always do until a culture collapses, the proportion of idea workers begin to shrink, while regulatory workers grow, seemingly almost without bound. As shown in the chart, we are now at a time when regulatory compliance workers vastly outnumber the number of idea workers or classical labor, combined.

Don't believe me? Look around at your own organization. Count how many people are involved in creating the original value for your organization, and then count how many people exist to fill some regulatory compliance position. If you work in a government institution, then no one there creates original value, as we shall see in a moment. If you work for an attorney or an accountant or a human resources services firm or department, no one around you creates original value.

Many jobs seem like they create original value, but in fact they merely cleverly conceal a regulatory compliance role. Consider a purchasing agent for a company. Someone has to buy stuff, right? But, in our modern world, stuff has to be bought *in exactly the right way* or someone gets in trouble, usually with the tax law or safety regulations. Or soon with environmental regulations. Purchase this thing or that incorrectly as a capital item or as inventory or as materials or as supplies and the tax man will get you. Buy the wrong thing, or assemble it incorrectly and it is the lawsuit you will fear from the customer more than the lack of quality. Even your manager, who probably spends a lot of time attending and implementing training about sensitivity and other nonsense is spending more time on that kind of stuff and less on actually inspiring you to greatness.

Turning a screw? Great! But how much of how you turn that screw is determined by regulations or contractual obligations which are in turn determined by a regulation somewhere?

Entrepreneur? I don't have to tell you how much of your day is consumed with regulatory compliance, either explicitly or implicitly. If you start analyzing the details of even your own organization you will find a shocking amount of the total amount of manpower is devoted to regulatory compliance which produces not a single positive step forward. And all your compliance efforts can ever do is to prevent backward steps of varying magnitude.

In the lexicon of the chapter regarding quality of life, the original value workers, ideas or labor, create positive delta Q. On the other hand, all that regulatory compliance workers can do is remove artificial sources of negative delta Q. Things are so out of whack today because we are still coasting on the great ideas of past generations. Even our great ideas of today can trace their roots back to ideas more than a hundred years old which are still splashing around and have not yet saturated our world.

Any Internet-based thingy you can think of is still just Alexander's bell ringing or Morse coding. Only the scale of the communication has changed.

Computers? A long time ago someone had to plot a whole bunch of artillery curves, and someone else had figure out what happens to plutonium when you squeeze it into a really hot liquid because it is hard to poke around in the real thing. Yet a lot of what we use computers for is idle entertainment which also doesn't produce anything other than fun. And that's OK, because fun is a lot of fun. But most of the rest of what we use these computers for today is almost completely consumed with complying with and enforcing regulations. Regulations which sprang into being because complying with them was impossible before the advent of the computer. In that case the regulations were only a step or two behind the idea.

Oil-based economy? Poking a pipe in the ground produced resources which were so cheap, and remain so to this day, compared to most of the other options. So cheap that we imagine we have the luxury of denying ourselves some of the best benefits of it. And in so doing create regulations which shield the existing players from competition from you and me.

Nuclear power? This great idea has been stunted through misinformation and the attention-deficit disorder drug which is government monopoly. So stunted that there may not be enough time for it to realize its full potential before its support structure collapses. Now, I think my biggest fear would be that companies of today, staffed as they are by regulation and collective niceness rather than by merit, would try to build a new plant.

Before you think I'm anti-nuke, consider the following thought experiment. The next time you see "Made in China" on some shoddy piece of worn-out crap, or try to navigate through some website or call center or virus-riddled operating system or customer support experience which might as well say "Made in India", pause for a moment. Then, imagine instead that the hardware and software and operating procedures in your next-door plutonium breeder reactor came from those places, too, and you will see what I mean.

In comparison with this mental image, Three Mile Island will appear to be the marvel of engineering safety which it really is. All done by a bunch of guys with slide rules and trucks of concrete and welders and three-ring binders, back when such things mattered.

At some point, though, the cost of compliance becomes too high, and idea workers too dis-incentivized, and classical labor too displaced. At that point, all of those occupations must collapse under the weight of too few people doing anything of useful value. This situation is shown on the right side of the chart. After this collapse is subsistence once again.

Now, to someone looking from the inside out, all of this regulatory compliance will seem to be a good thing. Jobs are created that way, right? Sure, but these are the wrong jobs. Recall that the basis of all economic goodness derives from improving the quality of life of others. We do this through the medium of supplying them with the stuff, push and time which they need to then satisfy their quality of life factors. You can't just push quality of life onto someone else, they first have to value the stuff or push or time which leads to it.

Now, it is true that you have improved the quality of life for someone when you stop beating them with a brick. But, you haven't moved them forward in a real sense, primarily because they would be farther ahead all by themselves if you hadn't beat on them in the first place. The lack of injuries which would have been incurred during the pre-mitigation interval is proof of that.

Similarly, jobs which mitigate the effects of regulation don't provide value to individuals beyond the abeyance of bricking. And, since the regulatory compliance consumes resources which would otherwise go somewhere to provide real improvement for someone else, the overall quality of life in society must suffer. For each regulatory compliance a few individuals benefit, at the expense of resources which would have otherwise trickled to those who could have used them most efficiently.

Thought of this way, regulatory compliance is just a more diffuse version of the mob boss demanding protection money. The guy you give the protection money to could very well be the enforcer if you don't, or at least knows the enforcer. Most of our modern society exists to decouple the brick beater from the enforcer by such a wide gap that you can't perceive them as being at all connected to each other. The collective has so finely tuned their interactions to trap you in this web that it makes you almost feel foolish to even think in these terms.

The complexity and the insanity of regulatory compliance benefits the collective. This benefit accrues especially to the electorate who demands the regulations in the first place. The truth of this can be revealed by reverting back to the simple tribal model and considering what happens when animal power gets applied to food production. We can then compare that primitive example to a more modern example and see how regulations become more palatable.

Before animal power, food was tough to get by hand, and so the population is limited by the available scarcity. Under these circumstances, any idiot who wanted to proscribe what tools one might use to get the job done, perhaps by regulating the kind of wood used in your plow stick, would probably become fertilizer themselves.

As soon as the idea worker produces the innovation of plow animals, and this innovation begins to be adopted, food becomes more plentiful, and so is removed, for a time, as a source of stress. The population naturally increases, but this increase is so gradual that it takes a while for equilibrium to be established at that higher level. With the stress removed, some become relieved from the tedium of agriculture, which is a nice way of saying their jobs just went poof. All of these excess people milling around, including the additional ones coming on line each year as the babies start popping, need something to do. They either turn to abject poverty as a way out, or start making plows and harnesses, or turn to mischief.

As the population increases, the food consumption goes up, and so some can go back into the business of agriculture, there now being additional market for their services. But unfortunately some of the ones who turned to mischief managed to successfully grind an axe against their former competition. These get the government to pass regulations about things like how grain is to be stored or what the working hours might be, or how wide the harness straps have to be. Then, the mischievous go to work enforcing those regulations.

Note that those regulations were only possible during the period between the adoption of the innovation and the new higher equilibrium level of the population. Had those regulations been introduced at the higher equilibrium, they would have been passed off as absurd, or even dangerous, and poof, more fertilizer. But, because they were enacted during the period of plenty, they seem reasonable even when people start starving again at that higher level.

By passing regulations in the period of plenty, the collective benefits in several ways. First, some of the displaced now have something to do with their time by gaining employ as regulatory compliance workers. This group includes those who have to be involved with manufacturing the new wider harnesses or green plows, as well as the king's men who root around for violations. And the solicitors who plead the case. And the jailer.

Next, as there is no stress for that resource at the time the regulations were enacted, fewer prospective regulatory compliance workers wind up as fertilizer.

Most importantly for cementing power for the collective, the existing farmers benefit as the regulations create a barrier to entry. But now that they have surmounted this barrier, the existing farmers find themselves in a semi-monopolistic position. *Even though these are precisely the people who would have complained the loudest about the regulations if they had been enacted at either the lower or the higher equilibrium.*

Importantly, the additional cost of compliance removes resources from the population, even though some benefit through the creation of meaningless jobs. The enactment of regulations during plenty consumes resources which are better used elsewhere. Yet, this pointless consumption is just as wasteful during plenty as it would be at either equilibrium point. A similar argument could be made about charity, which is donated by individuals in plenty rather than the culture as a whole. But those same resources are just as wasted, and even counterproductive, as they are removed from the hands of those who would have made more efficient use of them via free trade.

To illustrate these points, consider the figure below, which plots supply and demand, on a per-capita basis, for a particular resource influenced by an innovation:

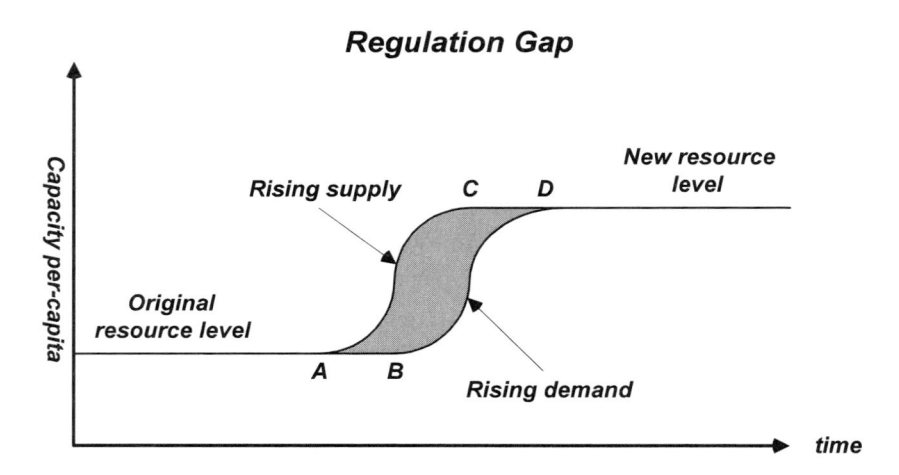

Regulation Gap

This simplified drawing illustrates the lag between the innovation, at point A, and the new demand equilibrium established at point D. Between these times, perhaps as babies are being manufactured, supply will rise unchallenged, other than the normal forces of price regulation. Either increase nonetheless chases suppliers out of the industry. As the innovation is adopted, supply begins rising quickly at first, and then slows down, and stabilizes at point C.

Demand for this newly abundant resource also takes a while to respond. Babies, for example, take a while to come on line and start consuming. But, eventually, at point C, whether through new little toothies, or through the government beginning to store the excess production in strategic reserves, demand also takes a while to start picking up. At first demand increases slowly, and then faster, finally tapering off at point D.

In the period between these two curves, excess capacity lulls the collective into believing that the good times will not end, at least from the point of view of that particular resource. It is during this period that the collective finds it easy to add regulatory pressure in order to achieve the noble purpose of creating what are actually pointless jobs.

Regulating harness widths is an absurd proposition, but many regulations in our modern world are hardly less absurd. Texas, for example, gets offended if you measure liquids without a license. No, not alcohol. I mean water in a graduated cylinder, like in a chemistry lab.

Let's consider a more familiar example now from our modern experience. Prior to the invention of programmable computing, many businesses managed their accounts by hand. Some used punch-card technology, which was itself a relatively new innovation at the time. If you ran a store, you may have wanted to maintain credits for your customers, allowing them to buy now and pay later. To implement this, you might keep punch-cards or other paper tablets for their accounts which told you who owed you how much, and what transactions they had made recently. As well as help you calculate how many credits to charge them each month for maintaining their accounts.

The establishment of store credit had an immediate benefit for the consumers in that they could buy without having to round up the right amount of cash to make a purchase. The benefits were even greater for large purchases, which might make the cash-holder susceptible to robbery, or even the store itself more susceptible to robbery at the end of a busy shopping day. Rob a store which maintains store credit, however, and all you get is a bunch of useless paper cards. Later, when the detailed bill arrived, the customer, via the medium of a check, simply instructed their bank to transfer money to the store's account, again, more or less secure from theft.

So, the store credit added quality of life for the customer in the form of reduced need for cash. In turn, the customer added quality of life to the owner of the store in the form of a small monthly account maintenance charge, interest on aged amounts, and reduced risk of theft. Everyone wins. This model works great at any scale. Small general stores might maintain accounts for a few key approved customers in a hand-written ledger locked in a safe, while larger urban stores with many branches might use the punch-card method. While there is an economy of scale involved for the larger store, this scale difference isn't so large as to make a big difference. Mom and Pop Feed and Biscuit, who did this for themselves, wasn't at any significant risk from Super Big Co, who had specialized employees tucked away in a back room somewhere. Each business filled their own niche nicely.

Enter the innovation of the computer. This machine started as just a big ticket item suitable for government work or large government contractors only. But it moved out into the corporate time share arena in the early 1960s, thanks to Ross Perot. Now, the work of tabulation comes easy to Medium Size Co., who can afford to buy computer time, while Mom and Pop still have to do this work by hand. After a slow startup time, Medium Size Co. can add incremental amounts of this innovation as it deemed profitable. So now the growing chain can creep farther into the hinterland, adding its value as it opens new stores, and in many cases displaces hand-run stores it encounters.

As so often happens with free trade, new businesses spring up to meet new opportunities. Although Mom and Pop still can't afford computer time, a generic credit company can. Enter the credit card, which now allows Mom and Pop, and others like them large and small, to enjoy the benefits of a store card without needing the size of a store card store. Or to deal with any of the requisite bookkeeping. All in exchange for some relatively low fees. Again, everyone wins, including some operators who had never bothered to extend credit in the first place.

Over time, then, the data processing ability quickly proliferated, got cheaper, and launched entirely new professions. These included designing, manufacturing, selling and servicing computers, as well as writing the software, and allocating and selling time to run it. Computers became cheaper and smaller, technology started improving their capabilities, and they became available to smaller and smaller operations, who hired more and more people to operate them. All the while the consumer continued to benefit as these systems enabled more efficient designs, stocking of inventory, fast and accurate checkouts through barcode scans, and on and on.

This revolution has yet to burn out, with most people on the planet benefitting in at least some small way. The beneficiaries include remote tribes who wouldn't know a computer from a rock. But even these manage to get a package of aid thanks to computers running the engine control systems in the truck which dropped the bag in their village.

Thank Ross sometime if you get a chance, even though the collective on the right called him a crackpot when he was in a position to unscrew things by getting elected President.

Interestingly, just as the computer was launching the revolution in account management, the complexity of the tax code really began to take off. If you can imagine a world without computers, try to imagine that same world with today's tax code. Or workplace regulations, including payroll taxes, insurance, worker's compensation, sales taxes and unemployment taxes. No one in their right mind would even consider forcing a small business of the 1960s into complying with today's tax regulations without the aid of a computer. The calculations are just too mind-numbing to even consider.

But, as the computer was making accounting easier, the collective moved to fill that void itself first. Almost as if by deliberate action, as computational power moved down into a segment of industry, that segment became subject to additional complex regulation and taxation. Even the credit card industry became heavily regulated as they were expanding to provide a valuable service. It is as if the collective came to view the excess resource as its own to be consumed as it saw fit.

And during this time, regulators, tax accountants, consultants, risk mitigation specialists, and, yes, even computer programmers specialized for writing tax and employment-related software, became fully employed. And not one of these specialists produced a single iota of original value beyond mitigating the risk of lack of compliance.

And the Mom and Pop? Well, they were unable to amortize the cost of compliance, and so they faded away. The rural countryside of America is dotted with rotting hulks of little stores which all vanished about twenty to thirty years ago. Their departure cemented the hold on the marketplace of the larger stores as Medium Size Co. became Super Big Co.

These larger companies, without pressure to excel in customer service from those who might rise from below to challenge them, turned to clever ploys. Including cheaply outsourced work to supply their networks of stores which grew more consolidated by the year, and stocked with cheap crap that you have to buy again, and again, and again.

When idea workers work on ideas, what kind of ideas are they? Well, that depends on whether the thinker is a man or a monkey. Yes, sadly, even monkeys think. But when a monkey thinks, the monkey imagines ways to extract value which they haven't earned through the power of the collective. The low-rung monkeys think in simple ways, such as in wailing about their needs. This wailing from them grates on the ears of men, but is the sweet nectar of power for uber-monkeys. These latter include the shaman or the regulator or the commercial collectivist. Each of these provide for their flocks by using their combined electoral power to implement further barriers for the productive.

These barriers in turn act like winepresses, extracting the most value from the productive to feed the collective. I shall return to the thoughts of monkeys, both great and small, as idea workers, in a while. For now, though, let's primarily consider the thoughts of men.

When men think, what thoughts do they have? In general, those thoughts tend toward increasing the amount of automation. Or, equivalently, reducing the amount of push or energy or time required to create or transform a given quantity of stuff.

Automation doesn't have to imply what first comes to our modern minds, that of whirring machinery or bleeping computers. All that is necessary is that some act of a person, man or monkey, becomes performed for them. Usually automation requires three costs. First, an up-front design cost (normally called non-recurring engineering, or NRE). Next, a per-installation setup cost. And finally, an ongoing utility cost, usually in the form of energy or service fees. Here are some examples.

☐ The plow animal innovation amplified the control of plowing, rather than plowing consuming the work energy of the operator. The design cost of this innovation included all the stampedes and tramplings and plows attached to animal heads or legs. Or failed attempts to get a walrus to use a shovel before the traditional yoke-and-plow method emerged.

The plow animal per-installation cost involves the breeding, raising and training of a particular animal, as well as making or purchasing the yoke, harnesses and plow. The utility cost includes all of those costs associated with the ongoing use of the animal, including feed, water, grooming and veterinary care. Add to these the costs for ongoing use of the equipment, such as oiling the harnesses and sharpening the plow. And, of course, the cost for the time required for the operator to guide the animal during the actual work.

☐ Bunny hutches automated the trapping of prey animals, allowing much more meat to be available with far less immediate effort or risk. A little bit of ongoing work, most of which could be expected to succeed, replaced pulses of trapping effort, not all of which would be successful. The design cost in this case was relatively small. This cost consisted mostly of figuring out what kinds of cages worked best, as well as what to feed the animals to prevent them from starving, dehydrating, or otherwise falling into ill health.

The per-installation cost of bunny hutches requires the proprietor to build or procure a hutch for each bunny, as well as spare bunnies from the table for breeding so that the little bunnies themselves can be obtained. The ongoing cost for this innovation includes upkeep to the hutches, the feeding and watering of the bunnies, grooming to remove parasites and veterinary care. And ultimately, the slaughtering and preparation of the bunny for the pot.

This last example introduced a new category of cost, which is the cost of an installed plant. In this case an individual bunny hutch, which is used over time to generate finished bunny units, is considered an installed plant. The cost of the hutch, including all the lifetime maintenance, is amortized over the number of bunny units that plant produces during its useful life.

So in this case, compared to the animal plow, the hutches and the breeders are included in installation costs. But the hutch maintenance should be amortized over the product units. For an animal plow, then, the product units are plowed rows, and thus the ongoing costs are amortized over a certain number of plowed rows. You could even imagine a measure of the number of plowed rows to be expected from the use of a particular amount of hay and water. Or, the number of meat units to be expected from the use of a particular hutch plant.

In either example, the maintenance costs, as provided by a licensed vendor of these services, might deviate from a desired norm. Or, the productivity might be too high or too low from a statistical point of view. In either case, in our modern regulatory environment, it would be time for the operator to justify these variations. Based on their answers, the operator might be rewarded with tax credits for production being too low. Or, he might suffer additional tax, such as those which might be demanded on profits for such a windfall. Or fined or even imprisoned if the operator simply failed to keep the required records, even if the operation itself was perfectly legitimate.

These details, by the way, seem absurdly superfluous, except that is the way that the collective has decided one must think lest one incur the wrath of the taxman. Imagine trying to force a tribal bunny hutcher or farmer to keep track of all of their separate costs in such a fashion. Fertilizer time. Yet, because we have computers, we accept this kind of nonsense each day of our lives, and the additional drain it imposes on our productive potential.

☐ Selling of unused computer bandwidth at night in the middle of the twentieth century automated the work of rooms of clerks sifting through receipts and running punch-card machines by hand, or filling out ledgers by hand. This one gets a little more complicated, so hang on. The design cost seems cheap. After all, some salesman working for IBM just had an idea. How much does an idea cost to just think of it? But there was more to it than that, much more.

I will summarize what happened in a moment, but to fully understand the framework in which modern innovation takes place, you should really read the following book:

Reading Assignment
The Innovator's Dilemma
by Clayton M. Christensen

That book doesn't specifically address the example presented here. But, it does provide some interesting insight into how the collective discounts innovation when it first appears. And then how the collective later jumps in to seize the fruits of that innovation once it has proved successful.

So back to Ross Perot, our idea guy I mentioned above (I hear he went to a good school). Perot, whose day job was selling big computers for IBM, realized that a lot of these big computers he had been selling had a lot of extra bandwidth which wasn't being used. His employer, whose only interest was selling big computers, enjoyed a semi-monopolistic position in the market due to government contracts and the economies of scale the collective had legislated for those who hire more of the collective. Accordingly, his employer would rather see these smaller firms simply cough up the cash for a big computer of their own.

After a while Perot left to start his own company, and he knew where all the big computers were. He also knew, from unsuccessful sales calls to sell them big computers, where all the mid-sized companies were which could benefit from his idea. OK, so there are some design costs right there, the jumping from the big company salary and commissions into the entrepreneurial fire, and the absorption of all the attendant risk.

Next, this salesman, who was successful at selling the big computers, called on several dozen potential customers and made his pitch, *all of whom turned him down*. Now keep in mind that in that day a sales call wasn't an email or a phone call. No, a sales call meant scheduling time in front of a decision-maker and personally making a pitch face-to-face.

Depending on what source you choose, Perot succeeded on his 77th or 78th try. Each of the previous unsuccessful pitches, including all the travel and lodging, were design costs, too. Each invariably led the salesman to refine his technique, just as the plow innovator and the hutch maker refined their techniques after either animal bolted.

After this first sale, Ross the salesman then had to deliver. He hired some programming experts, which were desperately few and far between in that time, and also very highly skilled. These he set to the task of writing software which would run at night on an unused computer somewhere. By the way, he also had to convince each machine's owner to let him do this, and at a price which would be reasonable. More sales calls for that, too.

That entrepreneur had to bear the cost of the programming. He also decided how the data would be loaded and then retrieved each night, as well as how payments for the time would be made to the machines' owners. He had to handle thousands of process design details to do something which had never been done before in history, but which we now take for granted as absolutely primitive stuff. All of which he had to handle before he was able to charge the first cent.

Once the design was completed, he had to then pay for his installation costs. These included managing the account of a willing machine owner, who was, in effect, renting him the bunny hutch which he would raise his data bunnies in. He also needed meat robots to move the data back and forth. Many times this work was done physically in the form of boxes of cards and receipts. He also needed someone to punch all that stuff in, and collect the data. And at night, the only time the computers were idle.

Plus, he had to hire and train these people, as well as selling individual customers on his service. And he needed software written peculiar to each customer's needs. All of this had to be done, once again, before he could charge a single penny for his service.

Finally, his on-going costs were simply paying the machines' owners for the time, handling the cards and receipts, and watching the data whir. And billing, and hoping that his customers would actually pay, which meant even more sales calls to hand-hold customers who might be getting dodgy.

The result? The rapid expansion of data automation, credit, technology and all the other benefits we enjoy in the world around us. As well as the ability for the collective to crush us with taxes and regulations. And crush us with all the other artificial constraints which would prevent such an idea, simple in concept but almost daunting in execution, to flourish today.

But at least the DEA gets to monitor how much iodine we buy for our boo-boos, or how much watered-down cold medicine we buy for our sniffles.

Perot was one of the lucky few who actually managed to profit handsomely from an innovation he was instrumental in implementing. Historically, the innovator rarely benefitted directly from the automation he created. No one even knows the name of whoever it was who hitched the first animal to a plow, or built the first bunny hutch or chicken coop. And yet each man, woman and child on the face of the earth today benefits from those simple ideas.

Imagine that if each meal you ate was imposed a royalty of a thousandth of a cent, payable to the animal plow innovator. You hardly even notice the sum of this royalty over the period of your entire life, yet you certainly owe this person that fraction of a dollar for all the meals you will eat. Yet, paid by all the people alive today, almost all of whom benefit somehow from this innovation, that agricultural innovator's estate would increase by approximately two hundred thousand (pre-hyperinflation) dollars per day. Throw in a modest interest rate on the savings and clearly this innovator would be the richest person in the world today by far. And would deserve to be.

Similarly, it is impossible to measure all the wealth and progress of mankind, and the corresponding quality of life for all of us, which was unleashed by Ross Perot's simple idea. An idea which dynamited the logjam that had been IBM's stranglehold on the computing business. IBM itself benefitted from this idea, as marginal customers who had resisted buying big machines could then justify the purchase by selling unused time. IBM also benefitted as the rising demand for smaller machines, demand created by Perot's business model, met the cost of making mid-sized computers. Two decades later that megalithic marvel of the collective would totally mismanage the PC revolution, which once again relied on innovators who were ridiculed by the establishment.

Perot's billions were cheap when compared to what his idea did for the rest of us. And yet the collective assesses the wealth of innovators as merely spoils for their plunder, completely disregarding the disproportionate wealth, and quality of life, which they spawn in others.

The reason we don't know the name of the plow-maker or the bunny-hutcher or the chicken-tender is that for most of human history ideas were merely public plunder. Ideas were usually used for the enrichment of a secular or spiritual tyrant for whom the innovator was merely a slave. It was only the advent of individual rights, particularly property rights to include an individual's ideas, in the period known as the Enlightenment that it became possible for an innovator to be at least known for his achievements, if not richly rewarded. The miracle of government as envisioned by the Founding Fathers to protect us specifically from the tyranny of the collective, added fuel to that intellectual fire.

Even so, even in this country the innovator of a truly revolutionary idea has hardly been richly rewarded. History is full of examples of innovators who died penniless, only to have their ideas enrich others, and usually, devotees to the collective. Tesla died broke, and only enjoyed a fraction of the wealth which should have accrued to him. Yet Edison, the master collectivist, and Westinghouse received all the wealth and acclaim as if those inventions were solely theirs. After Tesla's departure, Edison went so far as to try to block Tesla's demonstration of AC power by enraging the public with an AC electric chair. He also used other blocking tactics to prevent Tesla from using his light bulbs in the demonstration.

When Edison said, "Genius is one per cent inspiration, ninety-nine per cent perspiration," he didn't mean *his* perspiration. And by devaluing inspiration, he intended that the poor sap who he convinced that his idea was worthless would wander off empty-handed. Or come to work for him in desperation so that Edison might take credit for his ideas as the innovator slaved away in his early cubicle.

Time and again, innovators are crushed by the collective as the life is squeezed out of them. In Tesla's case, he agreed to give up ownership as he believed that Westinghouse was struggling, trading one cheater for another. The pattern continues today. Kane Kramer, whose patents underlay the iPod, was recently in court with Apple, not to sue them, but to help them defend themselves in a patent dispute with another company. Kramer's position? Not to collect from Apple, but that his then-expired patents pre-dated the other litigant's patents. This man should own a significant chunk of Apple, in my opinion, but instead, due to the expiration clauses of intellectual property law, he merely gets hired as a consultant to keep up impressions.

File for a patent now, and a Chinese factory will be punching out pirated versions of your products before the certificate is on your wall. Even if you manage to beat them to market, soon some slick-talking TV huckster will be selling cheap low-quality knockoffs which will drive your product under. Because the collective wills it so.

Elisha Gray invented a better telephone, but Bell beat him to the patent office. Later Bell models would use features which Gray, not Bell, had invented. Later evidence would be presented which alleged that patent examiners allowed Bell inspection of Gray's earlier provisional patent filings, presented before Bell's historic filing. And that the examiners had taken bribes to allow these inspections. Antonio Meucci might also have had a word to say about those developments.

Eli Whitney, who filed for one of the first patents in the United States for his cotton gin, was embroiled in disputes against infringers for so long that his patents expired anyway. All profits he made from his invention were consumed by unsuccessful litigation. The collective, even back then, had little sympathy for his claims as he, in their estimation, simply demanded too much return for his ideas. As they lay in wait for the inexpensive fabrics which would soon reach their clutching fingers.

John Kay, who invented the flying shuttle, had to flee for his life from displaced weavers who were angry at his innovation which eventually clothed us all. He died in Paris in poverty. James Hargreaves, the inventor of the spinning jenny, as well as the concept of a factory, had his house burned to the ground by an angry mob.

Thomas Highs had almost every invention he ever made stolen by Sir Richard Arkwright, who amassed a tremendous fortune by patenting Highs' inventions as his own. Highs was simply too poor to afford the costs of either patenting or challenging Arkwright.

More important than product designs are process innovations, which aren't even patent-able except in extremely unusual circumstances. Google didn't invent web search, or search-based advertising, and were more or less late to the table. And yet, they now have the reputation as having innovated better than others. The original inventor of web-search or search advertising is long forgotten, but Google, a darling of the collective, is now the benefactor of collectivist causes. Interestingly, I first heard about Google from a diehard communist, whose recommendation of them as advertisers for my business I thought a bit strange at the time. Looking back, I now see the connection.

First Wife imagines a day in which some poor sap somewhere makes the mistake of finding a cure for AIDS. Should this individual make the mistake of wanting to commercialize it so that he could be rewarded for his hard work and risk, the collective will fall upon him like a pack of rabid wolves. Each day the cure isn't handed over the monkeys will blame him for additional deaths and curse him as a murderer. She believes that the collective will rejoice if it becomes known that he and all his heirs were killed, thus releasing the cure into the public domain. I agree with her dark assessment of most of humanity.

The great thing about stealing ideas from innovators, or convincing them to sell cheap or give up the rights entirely, is that monkeys get to avoid all those icky design costs. The collective benefits from this theft or fraud or outright naivete, as those design costs are not then built into the cost of the product or service. Each monkey then gets his pellet cheaper this way. It is not surprising that the collective often turns a deaf ear to the complaints of innovators as their wealth is stolen away.

To illustrate this concept, and for instructional purposes only, in the next few years someone I know will patent, or attempt to patent, an innovation which has remarkable implications for the production of energy. The downstream effects of this innovation would place energy in the hands of individuals, and take it away from the hands of the collective.

Yet, the collective simply cannot allow these effects, and to thwart this paradigm shift, will spring into action. The innovation itself must be seen as crackpot science, despite the fact that it could be replicated in any garage or basement. Usually, any discovery related to energy is usually attacked as attempting to replicate some sort of perpetual motion machine. As Sadi Carnot pointed out, a perpetual motion machine, however weak, would eventually generate enough engineering work to dislodge the universe.

My friend's innovation is not in the category of perpetual motion machines. No, entropy is alive and well, and sadly, too well. Instead, this innovation merely reduces the price of something which is expensive, and currently, too expensive to use, and is expensive precisely because of the cost of the energy which is required to make it. No perpetual motion here, just economic reality.

In this case, though, the discrediting must be done to conceal the fact that this innovation sits squarely in a hole of silence. Imagine that you wanted to keep a secret, but were so focused on secrecy that you created a black hole of discussion, meaning, every path to that secret dropped off a cliff. That is what I mean by a "hole of silence." This innovation is in such a hole. And the monkeys want it to stay that way.

Normally, scholarship requires that an innovator or a scholar research and reveal the foundation of his research, the prior work which has been done by others. But what if all the prior work is in a hole of silence? What if every single path of basic study, including the reaction of some well-known substances to basic physical phenomena, is completely and blatantly missing from the literature, although information around it in every direction abounds? For that particular field, each innovator might as well be Sadi Carnot, using his mind alone to deduce that innovation, and begin to tease it out of hiding.

Curiously, each research topic my friend has been able to find leading toward this innovation ends abruptly once it reaches the edge of the hole. Some researchers even died at this brink. Others have been arrested, some on drug charges, some on immigration violations, and others on pointless little things which brings their research to a grinding halt as their careers were destroyed. There isn't even any research which shows why this innovation would be impractical. Nothing so brash as complaints of perpetual motion, nor even the gentle analysis which says it is too expensive, or even impractical. No claims that anyone has tried it and rejected it for even the most well-meaning reason.

It just simply isn't there. Yet, the paths leading to it are well-trod and meaningful, and trod by people with credibility in the field. My friend has shown me this information and all of these dead-ends, and I must admit, the evidence is compelling. Which means that something really, really interesting is at the center of that hole.

When that patent is attempted it is my friend's intention to slip it into the system with no fanfare whatsoever. Since no one knows who my friend is but me, good luck trying to predict when this patent application will be submitted, or from what quarter it will come. At first, there will be procedural issues with the patent. I will be watching this, so I can document these for you. Then, there will be delays as the prior art is researched. There will be none, as it sits in a hole of silence.

If my friend is clever enough to avoid fanfare, then the patent might actually get approved, assuming that no one is watching closely enough. Whether it slips through might test the existence of "watchers." In a later chapter I completely discount the possibility of "smoke-filled rooms" of conspirators, and chalk up all the nonsense of our world to blind monkey ambition. I see no reason to deviate from this assessment for the patent office. But I could be wrong.

Regardless, by silently slipping this innovation through the patent process, the discredit phase which faces scholars will have been neatly sidestepped. This same work, if submitted for publication in a scholarly journal, would be silently shouted down as the reviewers pass. For them, the hole itself is sufficient to consider it unworthy. "Who of our fellows have considered this worthy before?", they would have asked. And then answer themselves, "Why, none," as justification for their disdain. By avoiding publication and review, the reviewers lose the opportunity to reject it.

Once the patent is issued, though, the real fun will begin. Because this patent will threaten the underpinnings of the energy industry, control and rationing of which is vital to the monkey on the street and in the ballot box, the patent itself must be rendered impotent. There are several time-honored ways to do this.

First, industry could simply ignore the patent and just begin using it. With sufficiently shallow pockets such an innovator would never be able to find justice in court, and could spend their entire lives and fortunes fighting a fight they will never win. The collective knows this.

Should the innovator graze too close to justice in court, the collective will take the second time-honored path to avoid his patent. Simply declare it as invalid. Although a hole of silence currently exists around this idea, as soon as the collective deems it necessary, out will come the reams of dusty binders. These binders will be full of prior art which had been hidden from view the day before. And on them ink still wet. A third dodge would be to simply locate the plants for this work overseas, and merely ship the product to our shores. The patent covers the means of production only, and who's to say how the product itself was made?

Another would be to declare the means, or the product of it, or both, as illegal and thus remove it from the hands of the individuals who might use it to free themselves from the collective. Armed with this innovation and its product, the individual would no longer need the collective and its web of dependency. Instead, the individual with this means at his disposal would instead sell the collective the energy they need.

The fifth way to defeat this innovation would be to declare the downstream mechanisms which use this product as unsafe, and thus unsuited to trust to mere individuals. Something which is perfectly safe and harmless today will become an outrage to not be tolerated. Perhaps even the shamans, theological and environmental, will assist with this outrage as they claim the product and its mechanisms lure their children into godlessness.

In any of a myriad of ways, the same collective which demands we limit our use of energy would thwart my friend as he opens the door to a practically unlimited resource. Because that energy, while not free, and, at current prices not yet cost-effective, would become a threat to the collective which seeks to throttle the individual at all costs. This innovation will have reduced the cost of energy from astronomical to merely high.

One day, when the costs of energy rise to meet the demand of the collective to limit it, this resource is one which would remain within the reach of the individual in his garage or basement. Or more likely, his workshop out back. Without this resource, the individual would have to bow and curtsey and stay in his cubicle cage to receive his ration. But with it, the individual would be empowered to live his life, and enrich it, and profit from selling energy to the collective which seeks to enslave him. And this empowerment, in either sense, cannot be tolerated.

So the mechanisms, and the product, and the innovation, and my friend, must all be destroyed. Or, my friend may just decide, like John Galt and his motor, to only trade the product of this innovation with those who share his outlook and philosophy. And withhold it for now, bringing it to light only when the monkeys have all withered away. I have advised him to consider this option myself, as it is the noble course for now.

Of course, this book is a work of fiction, isn't it? So, there may not actually be a friend or an innovation or a patent. We'll see.

But you don't need to have a startlingly important innovation to have your more modest ideas stolen or regulated away. The bottom line is that it is highly unlikely that you will ever become wealthy as an inventor. I am not at all advocating that you beat your head against that wall. As I have recommended to my friend, innovations, especially the world-changing innovations, should be held out of the monkeys' reach.

Until there are no monkeys to reach for them. Or to be fed by them. Instead, the sort of innovation which I think is essential for each man are those small innovations which improve one's life. Automating away small tasks, and particularly those which would otherwise require the assistance of monkeys, is often rewarding in and of itself.

As an entrepreneur, you will face numerous situations in which you must make the decision to innovate or to hire. To be enabled to make better decisions in this regard, you must be informed as to the merits of the process of automation itself.

Consider the diagram below:

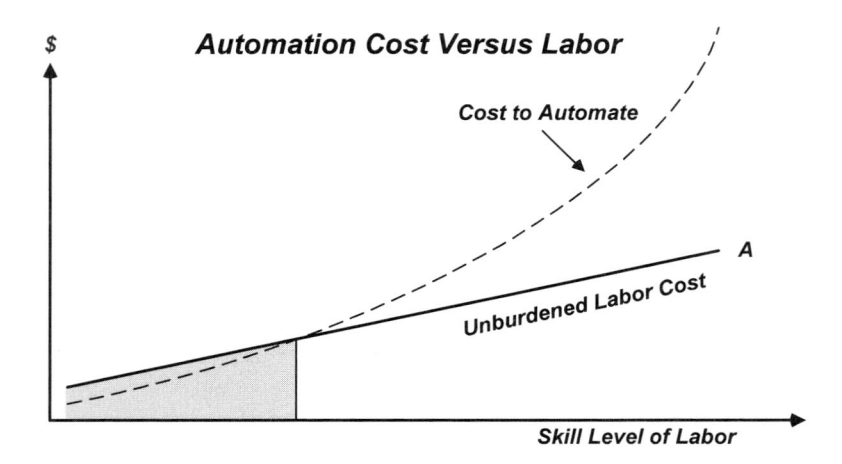

Automation Cost Versus Labor

Cost to Automate

Unburdened Labor Cost — A

Skill Level of Labor

In this diagram, the cost of labor is plotted for what might be called an unburdened laborer. For the purposes of this discussion, an unburdened laborer simply provides work for an employer, without regard to any payroll taxes, workplace regulations, union inefficiencies or other laborer costs. This would be the Og and Pok laborer.

As the skill level of any given task increases, so, in general, does the cost of that labor. Someone shoveling in the dirt can probably demand less than a skilled craftsman, for example. The increasing cost of labor versus the requisite skill level is plotted as curve A. The exact shape of this line is unimportant, all that matters for this discussion is that the labor cost increases as the skill level increases. For most purposes, this is a reasonable assumption.

Also plotted on the diagram is the cost to automate a given unit of labor. Shoveling dirt may require less cost to automate than a skilled potter. For the former, fire up a boiler full of steam, release that into some pistons and scoop up a bucket of dirt. An operator of such a machine may move as much material in a few minutes, or even a single scoop, as would have taken an hour of back-breaking labor before. It wouldn't take very long to amortize the automation cost over the thousands of shovel-fulls that machine can move in a day.

A skilled activity such as making pottery, on the other hand, is a little harder. In the case of skilled work, each of the individual activities can be considered as sub-skills which could then be automated. The mechanics of blending the clays and sand and water, for example, could be easily automated, while the selection of the materials to blend require insight.

On the other hand, effectively managing the loading and temperature control of a kiln to account for material variations might require a little more insight. And yet, once a specific temperature profile was decided upon by a master craftsman, even a rudimentary form of process control might maintain the temperature along a desired profile.

The shaded area in the previous diagram shows all of those tasks for which automation is cost-effective. The dirt shoveling, or the tedious work of blending the clay, or of maintaining the kiln temperature have effectively been outsourced to automation. Viewed differently, the automation serves as a burly, yet low-skilled employee. Before long, very little dirt would be shoveled by hand and very little clay would be blended by hand. The shovel laborer's job has disappeared entirely, while in its place has appeared a shovel operator's job, which requires higher skill, which overlaps to a small extent the skill required of the shoveler.

In the case of the craftsman, automating the blending of the clays has removed a tedious step from the work of the craftsman without replacing the craftsman himself. He is merely more productive, and can produce more pots per month by having water power, perhaps, do the labor of mixing his clay for him. He may have even employed apprentices for this work, but the advent of water power made this assignment obsolete. He and his apprentices can now focus their energy on those portions of the process which require higher skill. He may find, however, that he needs fewer apprentices.

Note that in either case automation is only indicated as a direct result of free trade. If slave labor is plentiful, automation is rarely indicated to tyrants. They merely beat the slaves harder. "Shovel more!" or "Paddle faster!" might be the result. Only the concepts of profit, or equivalently, leisure, they both being aspects of quality of life, enable the insight to determine what parts of the work can be automated. Only profit makes it worthwhile to then invest in the effort to do so.

When Pok, Jr., saw that his life might be made easier by automating the trapping of animals, he decided to build his bunny hutches. If he knew that he would be compelled to hand over all his bunnies to someone else, he would have probably decided to just spend his day in the woods chasing squirrels.

The process of automation, as we have seen for innovation in general, tends to lead to an excess in production. Each day, more dirt is moved, and more clay is blended than before the automation of these tasks. This increase in productivity soon renders all previous means of this work obsolete. No one exclusively shoveling dirt by hand will survive economically once machines begin moving it. Similarly, no potter who continues blending his clays in a bucket with a stick will be able to keep up with the productivity, and lower cost, of the potter who employs the water wheel.

Eventually, this automation will spread throughout the economy, and the jobs of spademan or paddleman disappear forever. Any spade work which is required on a job will usually only be done by the shovel operator as he alights from his machine to handle some small patch, or, more likely, by his operator apprentice. Similarly, some boutique potters might still blend some clays by hand, but only for special purposes rather than bulk production.

To fill these losses, other jobs, fewer in number, arise to fill their place. We've already mentioned the shovel operator. But also there will be shovel designers, shovel manufacturers, shovel salesmen, shovel instructors and shovel repairmen.

Similarly, the blending of the clay will require water wheel designers. And water wheel manufacturers, water wheel salesmen, water wheel installers and water wheel repairmen. In addition, the water wheels and the steam shovels need special materials, and craftsmen will spring up to supply these materials. New industries will arise around the special needs of these machines, such as businesses to provide lubricants.

All of these jobs benefit society by taking the entire level of quality of life up irreversibly across the entire culture. The availability of off-the-shelf items such as water wheels and steam engines, higher grades of iron or steel stock, or pressure fittings, bearings and lubricants, will lower the automation cost for other jobs further than the original curve:

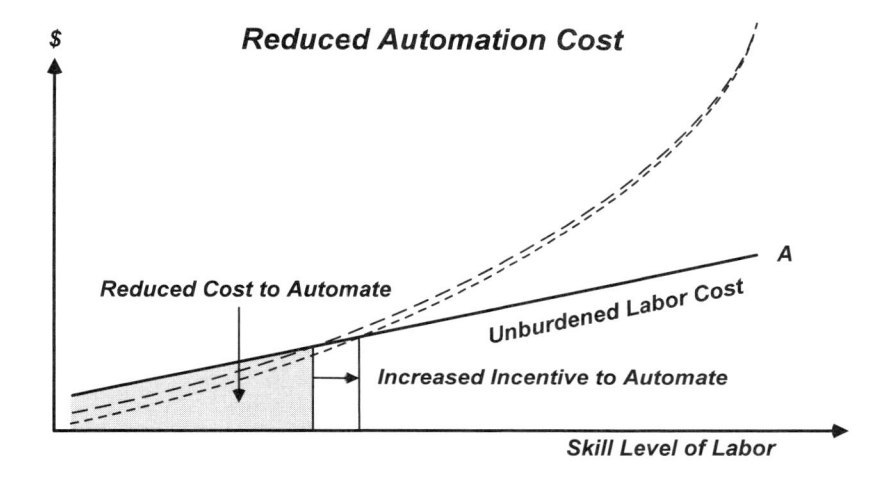

Reduced Automation Cost

Chart showing $ vs Skill Level of Labor, with curves for Unburdened Labor Cost (line A) and automation cost curves, indicating "Reduced Cost to Automate" and "Increased Incentive to Automate" regions.

Note that only a slight reduction in automation cost, made possible by the availability of the necessary components, can cause a dramatic increase in the lower skill levels which can now be automated. For example, the control system which regulates the steam engine can now, with only a slight modification, be used to regulate the temperature of the kiln based on a profile which the master potter selected.

Before the steam engine, there was little incentive to regulate the kiln temperature. To do so would have required the development of control systems which simply weren't cost-effective for the limited application of kiln temperature. A set of witness cones at the back of the kiln would have served well enough. However, now that a control system was in place in other industries, modifying that control system for the new application was made just cheap enough that the cost was worth it.

In turn, the control system for the kiln then could make its way into other industries which need to regulate high temperatures, such as forging and foundries or the manufacture of lime and cement. In reality, this transition probably went the other way, but the specific industries are irrelevant for the point of the discussion.

In any event, now all of those industries could enjoy consistent product quality, and be immune to the damage and loss which an inattentive fireman might cause. With this risk removed, the kilns and the forges and the cement mills could get larger.

The increased productivity could allow all of the means of automation to become cheaper. So, the cost of automation curve could drop even farther, and consume more skill areas. At some point though, the cost of automation will stabilize with the unburdened labor cost. The reason for this stabilization is that the higher skill levels remain expensive to automate, as shown by the old and new automation cost curves meeting near the top of the scale. Some skills will just simply remain out of reach, unless the system is disturbed in a revolutionary way.

Throughout all of this, new industries and skills were created as manual work and tedium was chipped away. The requisite level of thought and insight increased as the digger put down his shovel and became a shovel operator. The apprentice no longer needed to manage the kiln might learn to install firebox control systems. The shovel job lost in one village might be replaced by a foundry job in another. But at least his displacement was made easier by better roads and water he carried in cheaper pots for the journey.

And yet, in this unburdened ideal world, the scale of the kiln or the foundry did little to squash the productive individual. Perhaps it might seem so, as what chance might an individual have to start a pottery business overnight? The cost of building a kiln alone might be prohibitive.

True, the individual would rarely be able to penetrate existing businesses, unless the proprietors of these businesses forgot their customers. The threat of competition kept the large in check from the upstart which might revolutionize the entire industry with a new innovation or automation which displaces *them*.

Even a large factory and its attendant economy of scale was no guarantee against that kind of risk, as a new innovation could obsolete the entire works, and often did.

Enter the regulation, specifically the regulation of work itself. I write elsewhere about regulations which prevent competition, and these regulations have a similar effect as the regulation of work. For now, though, I focus on those regulations which proscribe how work is done or the relationship between the worker and the employer.

Regulation of work, universally lauded as protection for the worker, tends to make that work more expensive. Minimum wage affects the cost of labor in addition to its inflationary effect, as do safety regulations and the threat of lawsuits or harassment cases. Some of these regulations are arguably a good thing, but the net effect, wise or ill-advised, is to increase the cost of labor.

The effect of regulations on the feasibility of automation is significant:

Regulatory Cost

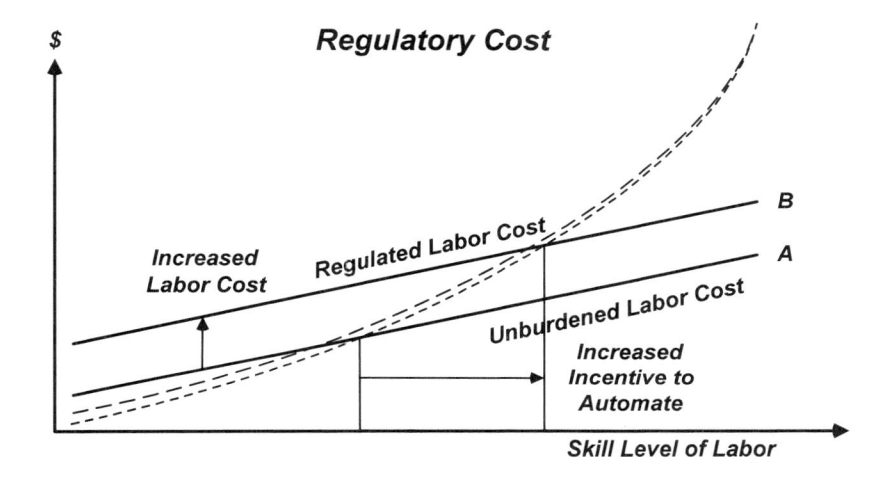

Figure: A graph with "$" on the vertical axis and "Skill Level of Labor" on the horizontal axis. Two parallel solid lines slope upward: the lower line labeled A ("Unburdened Labor Cost") and the upper line labeled B ("Regulated Labor Cost"). A vertical arrow between them indicates "Increased Labor Cost." A dashed exponential curve rises steeply, crossing both lines. A horizontal arrow below shows "Increased Incentive to Automate."

In the diagram above, the cost of labor rises from line A to line B, across the entire spectrum of skill. That human resources department or the legal retainer or the OSHA posters and inspections must be amortized across all skills in the economy. Note how the increase in labor costs across the entire spectrum of skills causes the incentive to automate to increase dramatically. The previous equilibrium of automation and labor is jolted, and more skills fall to the machine.

This jolting of the equilibrium causes new technologies to emerge, just as our hypothetical kiln control was first enabled by the steam engine, and then spread horizontally across other industries.

A new equilibrium will emerge to the right as these new innovative technologies make automation easier. During this time, however, existing skills are irreversibly lost, and lost in the areas most intended to be served by the regulation of work. The worker who was splashing away from the automation lapping at his heels called upon the government to help, and was drowned in the deluge of automation which resulted.

A critic might point at these diagrams and claim that I have manipulated the slopes and the lines and the assumptions to suit my narrative. However, in my defense I challenge you to make a drawing of your own, with curves and slopes and any reasonable assumptions, then perform your own analysis. You will find that the result is the same. Regulation of work consumes skills and occupations which were safe before.

The workers so displaced now demand more and more regulation.

"Pay us while we look for work!" they shout.

"Forbid the employer to fire us unless we misbehave," they agitate.

The result, increased regulatory cost. Each worker paid while not working must be paid by the employed. Each worker protected from the pink slip represents a cost of risk which must be mitigated.

These costs are reflected in a new equilibrium:

Additional Regulatory Cost

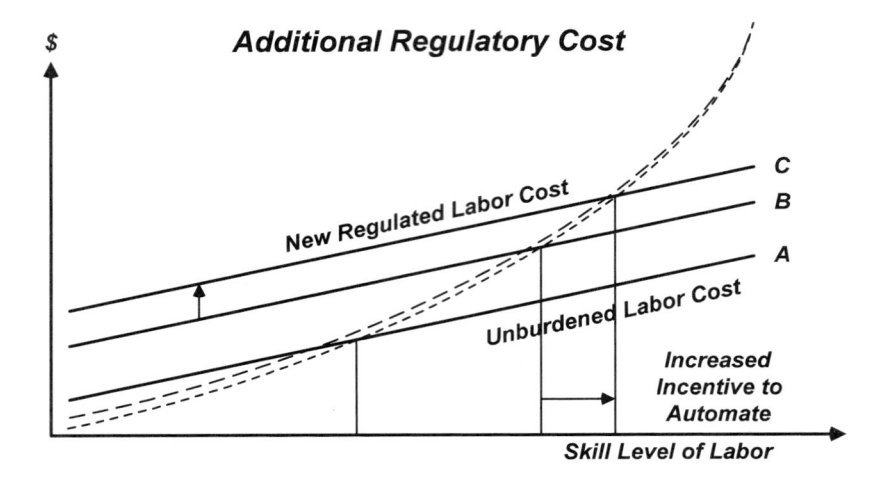

[Graph showing dollar cost vs. Skill Level of Labor, with lines labeled C, B, A, "New Regulated Labor Cost", "Unburdened Labor Cost", and an "Increased Incentive to Automate" region]

The increased labor cost is reflected as line C. As before, the incentive to automate now swallows more of the skills in the economy, skills which had been safe from the machine before.

Not all of those displaced by automation improve themselves and take on the positions of enabling the automation. Some of the displaced, especially those to whom the necessity of learning new skills seems too much like work, simply move into the regulatory compliance jobs which are created. Create a regulation to require a certain boot, and automation creeps closer to displace the man who wears it.

In the process, some of those who lose their jobs become boot inspectors, and ensure that the compliance cost remains high as they grind their axes against their former bosses.

Each time a new workplace regulation is demanded, or an existing one increased in scope or cost, the cycle repeats. The appetite of the collective is insatiable.

In a closed economy, perhaps that within a nation with sealed borders, the effect is to reduce employment, and the average quality of life. In an open economy with open borders, the effect will be to displace jobs overseas to where the labor costs are not so high.

Eventually, even with open borders, the entire global economy can be imagined closed. In a closed economy, the effect of automation is dramatic, as shown in the following diagram:

Effect of Automation

$|S_i|$ — Increased quality of life ↑

Pushed toward subsistence ↓

$|S_{min}|$

Fewer low-skill positions

Fewer supervisory positions

Increased popular demand for more regulation

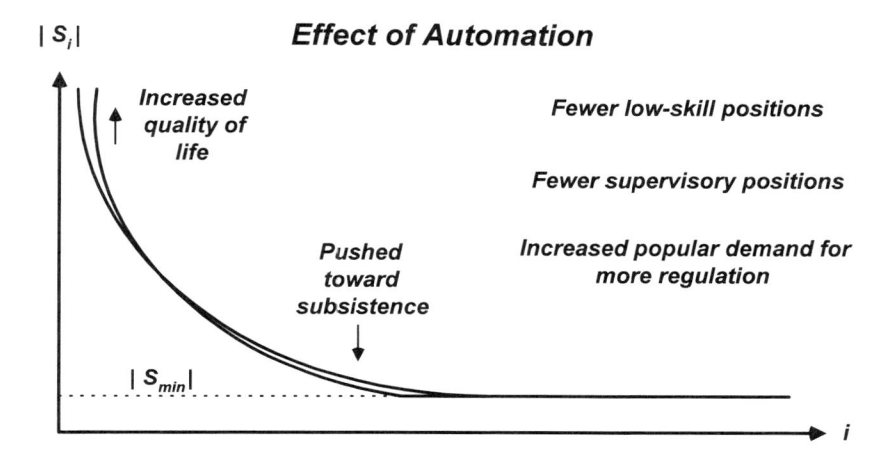

i

The increased regulations result in an aggressive automating away of low-skill positions. The lack of these positions gives fewer opportunities to those with ambition. Worse, the lack of low-skill positions means that fewer supervisory positions are required, leaving less room for the ambitious to advance. And, as popular demand increases for more protective regulation, the conditions worsen, and more and more workers are pushed toward subsistence.

At the other end of the spectrum, the wealthy and skilled whose work is in less danger from automation enjoy more and more of its benefits, at least in proportion to those in subsistence. This tilting of the scale then causes more resentment and division of society, and more demands for punitive regulation and redistribution. This cycle continues in a downward spiral until the stuff curve, shown above, begins to approach an "L" shape. At this point, only the few have excess stuff, but the vast majority have only subsistence, and some not even that.

I leave it to a clever reader to study his history and decide what happens then. Hint: think confiscation and gulags and slave labor. Now wind that history up into the modern day with advanced technology at the disposal of the collective.

Regardless of the cultural implications, the effect of automation determines how you, as an entrepreneur, decide to approach the products and services which you have chosen to provide. Like the skilled potter, chances are that your product or service is the end result of a number of sub-skills, which can be separated from each other to one degree or another.

The temptation you will face is to hire employees to handle each of these sub-skills for you. To illustrate the risks which you face with each decision you make, I will use the example of the potter. Feel free to substitute your widget or service as you see fit.

The potter selects materials, blends them, and then shapes the material into greenware. After a short drying period, he fires the greenware into a bisque, and then glazes the bisque with a glaze he had also selected and mixed beforehand. The last firing then turns the pottery into the final form of his design. For this work, as for the bisque, he must load the kiln. After loading it he must then fire it to the correct temperature profile, using wood he had preselected also for its particular properties, to ensure the quality of his work. After this firing he must inspect the work and then offer it for sale. Throughout, he must handle the myriad of issues which arise with any business, including marketing, taxes, bad debts, inventory, payment of invoices, payroll, and employee drama.

Many of you who are already running your business see yourself precisely in the potter's shoes. Clearly, the potter might decide that he should hire employees to handle some of these tasks for him. In the classical model, that would be the right choice to make, as these employees then act as a form of automation themselves, skilled meat robots who handle the material as he has directed them. Over time, some of these might become craftsmen themselves and be able to take a larger role in the operation of the business.

In our modern regulatory environment, you don't have the luxury of that fantasy. No matter how useful an employee might seem today, the call of the monkey or increasing regulation will eventually convert his productivity into a liability. Historically, regulations never go backward in any meaningful way, at least not from the perspective of the entrepreneur. Regulations only temporarily recede, if ever, to lure more investment into creating jobs.

Once the job has been created, the regulatory holes close in to trap that investment from escape. The job is the payoff for the electorate who demands the regulation.

As an entrepreneur, then, your creativity must be turned to the task of providing your product and service while avoiding the negatives which accompany employment. The only solution to this dilemma is to automate long before a simple cost-benefit calculation would justify this.

"But if you automate before it is cost-effective, then isn't the entrepreneur losing money?" one might legitimately ask.

"No," is the simple answer.

We will answer this question in more detail in a later chapter. But understanding this answer first requires an understanding of basic principles, of the creative process, and an understanding of entrepreneurial thought itself.

And for those of you preparing for a crisis, imagine an economy without a regulatory environment at all, in which your merit alone is sufficient to provide for yourself and family.

Chapter 11, Math and Science

Part of your self-study must include math and science, and to a far deeper level than you would otherwise think necessary. There is a very simple reason why you must master these fields. I will get to that simple reason in a moment. If you aren't yet a master of mathematics, you will have a very hard time understanding why it is so important. Most of us my age were taught math in a very sterile environment, with no explanation at all why we were graphing lines or finding the roots of an equation using the quadratic formula. Worse, if you are a younger reader, there is a good chance that you have been exposed to a hideous atrocity known as "guess and check".

When I found out that my son had been exposed in public school to this method of finding roots of an equation I nearly lost my mind. After closer examination of the curricula, it became clear that the unionized teaching staff had very little actual knowledge of math. And so, they were busy poisoning the little minds under their care instead of teaching them. So, as poorly as math was taught during my day, the establishment has managed to find newer lows today.

The basic crime of poor math education is a gateway act which leads to the more serious offense of failing to teach science to any useful degree. Math is the language of science, and unless you can understand math you have no hope of understanding the world around you, or even your own body, in a meaningful way. In this condition of ignorance, you then become the prey of any who wish to frighten or coerce you into submission. Just as a primitive witch doctor might withhold from you the true nature and predictability of natural phenomena such as comets or eclipses, and reserve the power of fear for himself.

There are some constants afoot today in that math and science are denigrated as subjects for the geeky kids. We have all been fed this lie. You yourself may have bought into this lie, perhaps from peer pressure from the cool kids. Or, because of abusive or humiliating treatment from ignorant teachers hoping to mask their own insufficiencies. Or even just the mistaken assumption that these subjects are hard and hardly worth knowing. If so, you have severely crippled yourself. Fortunately, you can fix this defect in your armor, but it will require some work.

I said before that you will have a hard time understanding math or science unless you know why you are asked to learn a particular skill or algorithm. This is one of those chicken-and-egg problems which plague the system. Only by the hiring of teachers who genuinely know why particular techniques are of use would it be possible to correct this. For example, I might tell you that you need to understand calculus because it will help you determine the moment of inertia for any object you might encounter. Or, I might tell you that you need to understand differential equations because it will help you understand thermodynamics and rates of chemical reactions. Regardless, I really haven't told you anything at all, have I?

Once you understand physics and thermodynamics and rates of chemical reactions, only then can you look back and understand integrals and partial derivatives. But by then you will have already brain-dumped that material, provided you were taught it in the first place. I know you will, I did exactly that myself.

We have a sort of secret society thing going on here. Those already in the know with these subjects know exactly what I am trying to say, yet those not in the know have no idea about anything I said in the previous paragraph. Without understanding where you are going, it is hard to understand why you are being asked to follow a particular path. Without having arrived there, you can't even see the path, but looking back, you see it clearly.

I encountered exactly this problem when I was teaching my son economics and chemistry in the seventh grade, and calculus, physics and genetics in the eighth. I learned that pre-teens and early teenagers possess the biological ability to learn these subjects, but only if properly prepared. But first, I had to overcome the trauma inflicted by the autocratic enforcement of the "guess and check" method. That brainwashing technique used in public school would rate right up there with any sort of psychological child abuse which you care to name.

Why do I claim that autocratically enforced poor teaching is abusive? Because it cripples our children's minds before they have a chance to learn to question their abusers. Perhaps you were abused in this fashion and decided to rebel against this abuse by deciding these subjects were of no consequence to you. Instead, you should consider that these subjects can become powerful weapons in your arsenal which allow you to capture quality of life for yourself.

So how did I overcome this chicken-and-egg problem? By presenting problems, which must be of interest to my student, that can only be solved by using the techniques at hand. This, however, requires that the material be tailored to each students' interests, a practical impossibility in our industrialized schools, yet uniquely available to small private schools or homeschoolers.

Here is an example. Perhaps your child is interested in martial arts. The typical way that martial arts are taught is to memorize a series of moves which define that particular style. The instruction is then limited by the style being taught, as well as the flavor which the individual instructor might impart, and might require years of dedicated work to learn. These moves and styles are the product of, in some cases, centuries of evolution to determine a set of actions against a particular adversary or weapon. However, underlying all of these styles and moves are the basic physical and biological principles common to all of them. If you understand the physics and biology, you can cut through an enormous amount of spiritual mumbo-jumbo and get down to the essentials quickly.

And so, you might present to your budding Jackie Chan a problem formulated as follows: Little Johnny is facing a larger adversary throwing a punch at shoulder level. Model the attacker's arm as a linkage attached to a rotating mass. Using experimental data obtained at a gym regarding the relative strengths of typical muscle groups in the upper body, make reasonable estimates as to the moment arms and torques available in this system. Model Johnny's parry as a force vector applied to the wrist of the adversary and determine, for a given force, accounting for Johnny's own relative strengths, whether Johnny should parry with an adduction or an abduction. I am reminded of that Loony Toons Foghorn Leghorn episode, Little Boy Boo.

Video Assignment
Loony Toons Foghorn Leghorn episode, "Little Boy Boo"

In addition to ordering the episode in a collection from your favorite movies-by-mail vendor, you may also be able to find this episode on the web somewhere. In this story, a little myopic chicken is playing baseball with Foghorn Leghorn. The chick is pitching to Foghorn. After doing some math, the little chicken proceeds to pitch the ball through the bat and a few trees behind. He then follows this victory with a paper airplane which downs Leghorn's plane in aerial combat.

Of course, the denigration of math and science shines through clearly in this episode, particularly when Foghorn Leghorn states that "Never mind, Einstein, knowing the answer wouldn't do me no good anyway." Clearly, in the Little Johnny fighting example, hitting the attacker with a chair is a more practical use of science than calculating his response, which Johnny wouldn't have time to work through. Pulling out a calculator and pencil to scribble through the equations isn't the point.

The point is to frame math and science in a form of interest to the student, allowing their natural curiosity to engage. Physics is then motivated by framing the problem as one of a general class of problems capable of being solved by understanding torques and moments of inertia. Then the need for math is motivated by it being required to understand how to calculate the physics.

The most interesting side effect of the martial arts physics example is that many of the moves seen on the tube or on film will then be understood as calculated. These moves are calculated not to be effective for self-defense, but to just look good. Similarly, many of the martial arts moves taught in classes are only useful as sport, akin to dancing. Regardless, a black-belt will no doubt be more prepared in a fight against a rube whose only weapons are his muscles.

Yet few black belts are capable of withstanding a blow to the head with a non-theatrical chair. Even they, however, will attempt to employ, if only ignorantly, the same physical principles to redirect the blow of the chair safely away. The martial artist's response will be dictated not by recalling the "avoid chair" moves taught to them in dance class.

Instead, their response will be dictated by their subconscious understanding of physics which has been framed in a philosophical context, the only language available when these moves were discovered long ago. But now we have the language of math. More importantly, Little Johnny might then wonder, since the cool fighting moves are fake, whether other lies might be lurking behind the images. And then he will begin to employ his knowledge of math and science to detect these lies. He will begin to think for himself.

Or maybe the student is interested in cars. Math and science will help him understand the lies behind a commercial which shows the latest twenty-horsepower electric roadster darting around those mountain passes on the way to the babe's cabin. Or why an electric vehicle, using any technology available today, won't be economically practical for most Americans. And that the only way to get Americans to adopt them is to commit to a significant lifestyle change in which the family car loses its place as a ubiquitous general purpose conveyance. In that mode of thought the car must become instead a pampered altar to the gods of the day, requiring inordinate sacrifices of time and care.

The monkey collective won't like this sort of independent thought at all. No wonder they try to convince Little Johnny that he can't learn all that scary math and science.

Here is another example of how framing the sciences helps motivate the underlying math. Imagine your particular student is an environmental buff, and wants to explore alternate energy. One approach to alternate energy includes biofuels such as biodiesel, popularized as a way of running diesel cars with fuel made from waste vegetable oils.

Internet Research
Any recipe for biodiesel, one of the best is available from the Collaborative Biodiesel tutorial at their very helpful website www.biodieselcommunity.org/howitsmade/

With any of these recipes, they are just that, a recipe. In a few cases the biodiesel enthusiasts try to explain some of the chemistry behind the processes, but many gaps are left simply because someone who is capable of understanding the underlying chemistry already understands it. More chicken-and-egg.

This isn't to imply that these recipes are of no value. The ancient alchemist could produce formulae which resulted in various kinds of valuable gunpowder or unctions without understanding or explaining the why behind these recipes. Today, the biodiesel community is more or less at that same primitive level.

But, by following the recipes online, you can still get some reasonably decent results. I know, we've done it in homeschool, and then used these results to motivate further research and deeper study. Such as what third-degree burns look like on Daddy's hand and how to treat them.

Now, by using these online recipes as a starting point, one might motivate their student, or themselves, to learn more about the underlying organic chemistry. And in particular, why some oils produce better fuels than others. Armed with that chemical knowledge, the bottle of biodiesel becomes much more understandable as a blend of hydrocarbons, much like an odd sort of crude oil.

Like crude oil, the quality of this fuel can vary widely in quality depending on the source. Unlike diesel derived from crude, the physical properties of biodiesel can include a tendency to cloud or freeze at low temperatures, or have trouble igniting under certain conditions. These properties are handled from a recipe perspective by being selective about the source, but an understanding of chemistry reveals more beneath the surface.

One would never pour raw crude directly into a fuel tank without refining into its various valuable fractions. Similarly, this biocrude should be more appropriately seen as a manufactured resource from which might be fractionally distilled more useful constituents. And, like some of the less valuable fractions obtained from crude, the leftover portions can be converted up or down the family of hydrocarbons through such means as cracking or reforming.

Yet none of these ideas or techniques are intellectually accessible until you decide to learn the underlying science. Without the underlying science one might discard perfectly useful hydrocarbons just to fit the recipe. But knowledge of these things might enable you to obtain fuel when none is available at any price.

So as a motivating factor to a student, one might explain that by understanding the chemistry, physics and mathematics behind first inorganic, and then organic chemistry, one might effectively use waste oils which most biodiesel enthusiasts shun. And thus access a source of energy and harness it for one's own purpose. Or, how you might substitute wood ash, suitably converted to KOH, for the lye used in the process. Or, how ethanol or even propanol might be substituted for the methanol, and the effect that each substitution might have on the output product or the operation of the process itself.

At the end of that educational process of discovery one has unlocked the secrets of biodiesel for oneself. And then, one might even understand what an unforgivable crime has been perpetrated on the American economy by the fact that the youngest refinery in our inventory is about thirty years old. In the process, the student will have learned about many things which impinge on that recipe, and motivate its genesis. And he will begin to understand all the stupid around him, much of which flows out the end of the cable behind the TV.

Both inorganic and organic chemistry allow us to convert the world around us into a form we find more suitable. Exploring the practical aspects of that conversion you might encounter the use of modern computer-based process control. And then you might begin to wonder about the capabilities which new refineries might have versus simply patching up old ones. Such as the application of technology which would allow flexible use of a variety of source material to produce any desired output blend with the clicking of a few keys.

This self-study might lead to other topics as well. You might drift off the biodiesel path and into other alternative fuels such as corn-based ethanol. And then learn about the challenges behind cellulosic ethanol or the vastly superior pyrolysis technologies. On this path one might discover for oneself the insanity behind our current energy policies and our demonic persecution of carbon.

Once you understand the chemistry and physics, you would wonder why we would choose, as a national policy, to turn food into a small quantity of fuel. Instead of turning a much larger base of non-food materials into vastly more fuel of far greater quality. But I can't even begin to explain all the things which Little Johnny, or you, will learn about the world by doing this one simple thing. You have to walk down that path yourself, and then you will know exactly what I mean. And when you hear stories about biodiesel public school buses with frozen tanks you will laugh at the irony, just like I did.

Because all of those little minds on the bus, had they been taught the underlying science, would know exactly what the problem was. And what simple changes to the infrastructure would fix it. And why you don't have to rely on the opinion of an expert at a government-funded lab for the answer. But again, the monkey collective, which depends economically on enslaving their future votes to keep the welfare and bailouts flowing, cannot allow that kind of thinking. Knowledge empowers those little minds too much, and makes them ask too many embarrassing questions. Of both sides.

Being kept ignorant can only lead to your being more pliable to coercion and fear. Ignorance causes people to perceive the monsters of today as being more frightening and complex than they really are. Which might arguably be the end goal of the witch doctors of our time, who wish for you to bow at their altar and ply them with offerings to keep you safe from shadows. I said before that there is a very simple reason why you must master math and the sciences, and here it is.

Math is the language of God, and the various sciences are the books in His bible. I am sure that I offended the theologian and the atheist scientist both with that statement. This feat is understandably difficult, as each imagines themselves as occupying the only pure end of spectrum which is in reality a circular path nearly touching. I attempt to reconcile these views in a later chapter regarding the commingling of our modern atheistic religions. But, for now I will show you the path to mathematical and scientific enlightenment.

Your best ally in your self-education will come from an unlikely quarter: the homeschool community. The same resources which are used to teach children math and physics can be used by you, regardless of your situation, to give yourself power. This power will assist you in your entrepreneurial goals, as well as enhance your quality of life. These resources are valuable to you regardless of your field of endeavor, your race, your personal history, or your current state of incarceration.

Math is the cornerstone which you must first master. Most courses available to homeschoolers have been Biblically watered down beyond the point of usefulness. I have found that the best possible curriculum is produced by a publisher named Saxon. Its founder, John Saxon himself was a former World War II Air Force officer and math instructor. And his own struggle against the forces of niceness is in itself an excellent case-study.

> **Internet Research**
> Research the history of John Saxon. The best concise description I've found is at a popular homeschool resource: http://www.home-school.com/Articles/SaxonEditorial.html

The entire curriculum you will need to master is:

> **Tutorial Materials**
> The following courses, all by John Saxon:
> *Saxon Math 54*
> *Saxon Math 65*
> *Saxon Math 76*
> *Saxon Math 87*
> *Saxon Algebra I*
> *Saxon Algebra II*
> *Saxon Advanced Math*
> *Saxon Math Calculus*

In these titles, *54, 65, 76,* and *87* refer to the grade levels for which this material is appropriate. For example, most fifth graders or advanced fourth graders will find the 54 course to be useful. I recommend you approach these courses in the order shown.

Unless you are confident in your math skills and choose to skip a level or two, you will gain a lot by practicing the material even in the early courses. You might find that a Saxon fifth grader has the equivalent knowledge of a high school student in our times! Remember that in Saxon's time high school children learned calculus routinely. In any event, unless you have a degree in engineering or the sciences you may want to review them all. Even degreed working professionals in these fields will find the reviews in the last two courses helpful. I know I did.

Each of these courses is available in kits, which means that you get the textbook, a set of exams, and a solutions guide for all chapter exercises and exams. Each chapter is an easily digestible chunk of information which is suitable for an hour's work each day. With about 100 to 120 chapters, and roughly one exam for each four lessons, you will complete each course in about six months working diligently one lesson per day. And you can do this by yourself, even in your prison cell.

One word of warning. Because Saxon uses the military style of education, which means relentless drilling of the basics, you might be tempted to skip past problems which look familiar. Don't. The Saxon technique, borrowed from military instruction, is specifically designed to present you problems from different perspectives, and distributed over time. This approach ensures that you haven't just completed the problems, but truly incorporated the material into your subconscious toolbox. The capstone Saxon course is his physics course.

Tutorial Materials
Saxon Physics
by John Saxon

Like the math courses, this course is available as a kit with solved problems, and presented using the same baby steps as his math courses, meaning, with relentless drilling. Once you complete all the material in this course, including taking the exams, you will have a better understanding of physics than most college graduates, despite this course's placement in the realm of high school physics. The distinction between traditional high school physics and college physics is the use of calculus in the latter.

However, in most school systems high school physics has been watered down to barely more than the "heat the balloon and it expands" kind of elementary school fluff. Because of this what had been taught in high schools has been pushed into college, with the college-level calculus-based material often falling off the other end.

As a traditional high school physics course, this material introduces some calculus. But, you can start working the physics course at any time after completing the algebra courses. Your understanding of physics will be better if you wait to finish physics until at least starting the calculus course.

Beyond physics, there are many other math-based courses which you will need to take in order to better understand the world around you and how you can bend it to your purpose. Chemistry is the most important of those courses. Taught in high school, chemistry has also been aggressively watered down to the point of uselessness. Presumably, this is an attempt to prevent high school graduates from entering the drug war on the wrong side or pulling off an Oklahoma City.

Once you start teaching yourself or your child chemistry, if you tell anyone about it they will come to one of two conclusions: a) you are making bombs, or b) you are running a meth lab. So, although you will be doing neither for reasons I will explain in a later chapter, you will want to keep quiet about your studies to avoid the modern equivalent of a Salem witch hunt. Once you get some chemistry behind you, you will really enjoy a fictional account of what the collective fears from you:

Video Assignment
AMC Series "Breaking Bad", Season 1

One thing I like about the first season of this series is that it points out the power which knowledge provides. Although the hero of the story is often too sick with cancer to do little more than vomit, he uses his knowledge of chemistry to solve a variety of seedy problems. I also appreciate the depicted hypocrisy of a DEA agent hosting a weed party. More on that later.

Another theme running throughout that series reflects the paranoia which chemistry invokes in our society. Many of the chemicals which are useful and necessary in our modern world have become listed by the drug enforcement officials, and so these must be tightly controlled. Ironically, when Walt, the central character, needs these materials he simply steals them. This makes the interesting point that compounded charges are of little consequence when he would already be serving multiple life sentences for the original offense. Again, we will address this topic further in another chapter.

For a starter course which is suitable for novice and expert alike, I recommend a charming little book by a clever professor at a remote Virginia campus (thankfully for him, not Virginia Tech, since I respect him deeply):

Reading Assignment
Caveman Chemistry
by Kevin M. Dunn

If you have seen The History Channel's "Acids" episode of the *Modern Marvels* series, you will have seen Professor Dunn demonstrating the power of acids in a couple of lab shots. His book is a series of twenty-eight chapters which give the history of chemistry from fire to plastics. He includes a practical exercise at the end of each chapter accessible by anyone.

Unlike the public school fluff, these exercises have some meat to them, like making paper by extracting cellulose fibers from wood, or making bleach from salt. Unlike web-based recipes, he explains the underlying chemistry behind each of these experiments. Sadly, these experiments at one time were the kind that were within the reach of any high school student. The downside of "Caveman Chemistry" for most folks is that Kevin narrates his book as the four alchemical elements: air, water, fire and earth. This choice makes perfect sense in the context of the book. But, as with Saxon's gremlins and fairies, Kevin's choices will ultimately make him and his book targets for the forces of niceness. Probably by framing him for drug possession. Or by something equally absurd, such as campaigning for revoking his tenure at this little college in the middle of Bibleland.

Out of all the subjects which you have to master, chemistry will be the toughest because of our society's superstitions. While in junior high, I taught myself chemistry from a high school text book from the sixties. By the time I entered high school myself in the early eighties, the material in the seventies book had already been significantly watered down. I looked at a modern chemistry textbook recently, and it was hardly better than a fourth grade science book of my day. As of this writing, I know of no useful self-study chemistry courses at the level of Saxon. I guess we'll have to wait until Kevin writes one after he gets fired.

Or, you could root around at estate sales or used book stores and find an older high school or college chemistry text. But without the solved problems in the hard-to-find teacher's editions you will find it hard to give yourself the feedback necessary to correct your mistakes. If you should happen to find a teacher's edition of a chemistry text from the sixties, guard it like the alchemical gold which it is. Failing that, you can supplement your chemistry text with a solved problems guide, the most popular of which is available from Schaum's in the form of their outline series. I know it seems awkward, but I think the apostrophe "s" is part of their name:

Tutorial Materials
Any sixties or earlier high school chemistry text, and the chemistry volume of the *Schaum's Outline Series*.

The Schaum's outlines are intended as supplemental solved problems for a student in just about any speciality. These are usually applied after a knucklehead missed every problem in his homework, and the professor is too busy to monitor the detailed practice required to get knucklehead up to passing. In your case, use the Schaum's outline as a source of solved problems to practice the material you read in your text. Just cover up the solution below the problem and treat each problem as a mini exam. If you get stuck, the solved problem will fill in the gaps nicely for you. You may have to flip around a little to correlate the solved problems with the material in the text as there is no standard straight line from topic to topic.

The next area of mathematics you need so that you can understand many of the sciences involves how random events have real effects. This discipline is known as *probability*. A lot of what is involved in probability is similar to conventional wisdom involving coin, dice and card games, but there is so much more underneath the surface. Casino gambling is hardly relevant to either running a small business or surviving a crisis. But, in either of those scenarios the knowledge of this field is helpful.

Tutorial Materials
Any probability text and a probability volume of the *Schaum's Outline Series*.

Related to probability is the field of *statistics*, which analyzes trends and patterns to be able to predict likely future outcomes or look for potential improvements. Sadly, much of modern statistics comes into play by looking for potential improvements in ways to tax you further, but beyond that, the techniques are important to know.

Tutorial Materials
Any statistics text and a statistics volume of the *Schaum's Outline Series*.

Often, these previous two disciplines are presented together as a single *probability and statistics* block.

Another course you should prepare for yourself is differential equations. Differential equations, singular, is the name of a branch of mathematics which is used to describe systems which can vary in more than one way over time. These skills are useful in modeling thermodynamic systems or economic systems.

Oddly, the more you learn about the physical world and the economic world, the more you will find that they are similar. Whether you wish to know how a bad idea spreads through a population like a virulent disease, or how fission proceeds in a nuclear bomb, or how detonation proceeds, or doesn't, through a mass of pelletized material when blasting a quarry, the processes are remarkably similar. Differential equations are a powerful tool for understanding the vast majority of natural processes, once you understand the underlying physics, chemistry and calculus. Fortunately, there is no way to water this material down into uselessness.

Tutorial Materials
Any differential equations text and a differential equations volume of the *Schaum's Outline Series*.

If you are starting to feel intimidated, don't be. I will explain later why this feeling has been implanted in you to keep you away from knowledge. In the meantime, forge ahead.

I could continue recommending mathematical courses ad infinitum, but I will stop at one more course, which is *linear algebra*. Linear algebra, sometimes called *matrix algebra*, is a powerful set of techniques which is useful for simultaneously solving equations. When you have spent six months grinding through the Saxon physics book, you will from time to time find yourself wishing there was a better way to solve the equations which result. There is, and linear algebra is the name of that way. As with differential equations, there is no watered down version.

Tutorial Materials
Any linear algebra text, and a linear algebra volume of the *Schaum's Outline Series*.

Rumor has it that a lot of our advanced control theory was developed by the Soviets and their crop of defected German scientists during the Cold War. Most of their way of looking at control systems was through linear algebra rather than pure differential equations as was the predominant Western technique. They did this because they lacked access to the computing technology which we take for granted. Adopt these techniques for yourself, and then apply modern computing. The result is something really powerful in your hands. What is that something? Well, that is up to you, of course.

The third science course you will need after physics and chemistry is biology. As with physics and chemistry, this field is so wide that you will never learn it all, but you need to understand physics and chemistry before tackling this one. For the purposes of our discussion here, a good text on elementary biology and physiology is important, and you should be able to find plenty of references for those topics. Unlike physics and chemistry, which require you to be able to solve problems, biology and physiology are encyclopedic topics which requires you to understand concepts but not necessarily apply them.

While you are at it, carve up some roadkill and see what an intricate and miraculous creation is the body of even the simplest animal. Attempt to draw what you find and notice most of all how what you see defies even the best artist. How can you see something so complex, and be able to describe it, yet not draw it in a way which even comes close to reproducing it with any fidelity?

Be careful to not let anyone see you doing this exercise or else that will kick off its own kind of witch hunt in our world of modern superstition. Carving up a pig in a classroom is science, doing the same thing with a possum you found on the road is just sick.

Tutorial Materials
Any biology and physiology texts you find of interest to you.

By the way, differential equations and calculus can be used to describe how medications are absorbed into the body. This is the domain of pharmacology, which means that the pharmacist and the anesthesiologist must understand aspects of the human body which can never be seen, but only observed indirectly through the body's response to their inputs. Contrast this set of skills with those of the surgeon who applies practiced hands to remove or correct anatomical abnormalities. The pharmacologist's and anesthesiologist's scalpels are their knowledge of differential equations and chemistry.

One of the earliest gaseous modern anaesthetic substances is nitrous oxide, also known as laughing gas. This substance can easily be made from materials which are disturbing to modern society. But, care must be taken in filtering out undesirable byproducts and to ensure that the reaction temperature is not too high or else the whole setup will explode. Notice that producing nitrous oxide requires melting a mass of the essential feedstock. Find a website which describes how nitrous oxide may be prepared, and then apply your new knowledge of chemistry to understand how the requisite materials might be obtained.

Internet Research
Research the history and preparation of nitrous oxide. DO NOT ATTEMPT TO MAKE!

Also notice how useful this substance is in industry, and the curious dilemma which regulatory bodies find themselves in while attempting to regulate it. More about this problem later in the book, and how it affects your efforts to run any legitimate business.

The downside of nitrous oxide is that the patient never actually loses consciousness, merely their sensitivity to pain and their fear. This leaves the patient capable of responding to commands and inquiries, which makes it supremely useful for the dentist who lacks the services of an anesthesiologist. To be of use to the surgeon, an anesthetic must put the patient out cold. Enter diethyl ether, first used as a surgical anesthetic by Dr. Long in Jefferson, Georgia, in 1842.

Internet Research
Research the history and preparation of diethyl ether. DO NOT ATTEMPT TO MAKE!

Again, apply your new knowledge of chemistry to analyze the production of diethyl ether. Note that there is an easy way to synthesize this anesthetic using two simple materials found in almost any home. Again, don't try actually making any, as it is explosive, subject to explosive peroxide formation and will make you vomit. It is this set of properties which made it gradually lose favor for surgical use versus halogenated ethers such as halothane, or 2-bromo-2-chloro-1,1,1-triflouro-ethane. If you seriously applied yourself to learning organic chemistry as I suggested, that last name will make perfect sense to you.

Internet Research
Research the history and preparation of halothane. DO NOT ATTEMPT TO MAKE!

One of the interesting side effects of becoming conversant in a number of fields is that you are able to better comprehend the world around you. For example, if you have educated yourself as I have recommended, and researched the three substances I have indicated, you will find yourself better prepared to undergo surgery, for example. When coming out from under the effects of anesthesia, you will understand why the hospital staff treats you the way they do, and be better able to cooperate and assist in your own care.

In a similar way, understanding the details of the material I recommend that you learn will come to your aid in less obvious ways throughout your experience as an entrepreneur. The veil will be lifted from the mysteries of surgery, allowing you to see the anesthesiologist as a star of the show rather than a mere backup singer. Similarly, knowing more about fields other than yours will allow you to not be deluded by those around you as to their true significance. It is impossible for me to predict in exactly what ways these benefits will accrue to your specific circumstances. But, from my knowledge of the world and its workings, I know that these benefits will arise at times when you least expect. Knowledge works in mysterious ways.

We live in the electronic age, and as such you need to understand electricity and electronics much as the farmer of old needed to understand the weather and the seasons. We already discussed some of the computer skills you need, but you also need some background information about how power gets to that computer and something about the inside of the box itself. Knowing how homes and commercial buildings are wired is important to gain a perspective into a trade which requires licensing in most jurisdictions to do work for hire. But, this work can easily be done for yourself in your own home or office. In your physics course, you will have been introduced to the basics of electronic circuits, but before then you could start learning about electrical wiring. I recommend two books:

> **Reading Assignment**
> *Practical Electrical Wiring*
> by Richter and Hartwell

> **Reading Assignment**
> *Wiring a House*
> by Rex Cauldwell

The first book has an enormous amount of detail and background theory, and so can perform as a self-study reading course. Assign yourself a couple or three chapters a week. Be sure to follow through the example calculations yourself on paper. The second book is a heavily illustrated guide to actual wiring installations. Reading this book has been said to be like watching a master electrician in action.

After you have finished your physics course, you will then be ready to tackle some introductory electrical engineering. In this course, find a college-level electrical engineering textbook and back it up with the Schaum's outline. Then, just as you did with chemistry, read the text then find related exercises in the Schaum's outline. Your goal is to find out how to analyze circuits which involve resistors, capacitors, inductors, diodes and transistors. This knowledge, combined with your electrician's knowledge, will enable you to crack open your HVAC system and understand just about everything going on inside. As well as to strip old appliances for parts if you feel so inclined should the need arise.

> **Tutorial Materials**
> Any college electrical engineering or electrical circuits textbook and a related volume of the *Schaum's Outline Series*.

Everyone reading this book can also benefit by learning at least a little about using computers. I mention throughout this book that it is important for individuals to think of themselves as businesses rather than as employees. The sole negative to this perspective, and a negative which has been deliberately designed to keep you dependent, is that businesses have to handle a layer of taxes which is potentially overwhelming. To overcome this obstacle, you must learn how to use a computer well enough to manipulate the data to handle your taxes on your own. Computers are essential for this work. It doesn't matter whether you drive a truck or weld for a living, you must be able to navigate those tax forms to enjoy independence and control of your own destiny. Otherwise you will be forced to accept the role of a cubicle or cab slave.

After learning something about electrical engineering or circuits, and then computers, some of you will be prepared to learn about a field of computing known as *embedded systems*. One day, there are going to be a lot of those fancy tractors and combines sitting around with weeds growing through them because the on-board computers are shot. The guy who knows how to duct tape an old PC to the chassis and then get that tractor running again is going to be worth the tractor's weight in wives.

Clearly, you might have a lot to learn, depending on your starting point. But, this plan of study is designed to empower you with the tools and skills necessary to most effectively implement the ideas in this book, regardless of how roughly society may have handled you so far. This is a lot of work, but anything worthwhile requires work. Your personal empowerment is no exception. All you really have to do is commit yourself to setting time aside each day and study and work while others play and rest. You can do this, you just have to convince yourself that your quality of life is worth the investment. Or, if you would rather catch this week's super big game, then put this book down, click on the tube, or now panel, I suppose, and don't ever complain to anyone about your situation.

If you want to experience the freedom of action and thought which this book represents, but the task before you seems almost overwhelming, then try this approach. Use this book as a checklist, and get the first Saxon course which seems appropriate for your level of education. Then, assign yourself a lesson each day, and two each on Saturday and Sunday, including exams interspersed as lessons per Saxon's guidance at the front of the book. Full time inmates may choose more lessons per day. For the unincarcerated, this will provide nine lessons per week, allowing you to finish the 120 lessons and 30 exams in approximately four months. In a semester's time, then, you will have completed a year's work in a course, spending less time per day on the subject than you would have in a classroom plus typical homework.

Write these assignments down in advance each month on a calendar, and don't allow yourself to skip a single day. If you skip a day, make those assignments up the next day and don't allow your schedule to slip. By the time you finish that first course, you will have developed a habit of learning and work which will make the later Saxon courses fun, and the non-Saxon courses possible. You will also gain the self-confidence which comes from teaching yourself anything you wish to learn. You might also find that improving yourself becomes more important to you than the super big game.

You may require many years to finish all the self-study I have prescribed in this book thus far. But at that point you will be at par with an engineering sophomore in many areas, and far ahead of that level in others. This information will also help you begin to see how to apply the Adam Smith economic model in our era despite the regulatory obstacles imposed on us all by the forces of nice. In a later chapter, I recommend how to build on this foundation to even better effect.

As you improve your knowledge of the physical world around you, a pattern will begin to present itself. In some plains of knowledge, you will stumble across a chasm which can only exist by design. A conspicuous gap in knowledge arose before, and ignited a chain of events which shapes our modern world today.

Until the 1930s, science was unique in its democratic character, open to all. However, as the world began to understand the path science was taking, prominent physicists began to disappear from publications in an effort to keep the Nazis and the Soviets from unlocking the power of the atom. But the effort to keep the secrets itself gave the secrets away. Stalin's own scientists knew that a bomb was possible when the Western scientists stopped talking about the possibility.

Similarly, today we can identify key gaps which lie astride some of the most important issues of our day. One day we'll get together over a coffee and discuss some of these gaps in knowledge. But one gap in particular to consider is the behavior of the element Protactinium. Protactinium is really only good for one thing. What that one thing is I'll leave you to find for yourself. But, it has a peculiar property which makes it supremely annoying to study, and also supremely useful as a stone in the path for that one thing. Interestingly, the world's supply of protactinium is entirely manmade, using processes which the naive assume are proliferation-resistant.

And, for all intents and purposes, the entire body of knowledge about this substance consists of only a few pages. Yet the key to its use is conspicuously missing in those pages, an omission obvious to those with enough knowledge to notice. I mentioned the idea of a "hole of silence" earlier when talking about my friend's innovation. Similarly, this property is sitting right smack in another one of those holes. One day I might write another fiction book about that one all by itself. Only that book will have plots and characters and stuff. Lots of interesting stuff. Stuff which does interesting things.

Just as Al Gray sought to turn the power of our opponents against themselves, intelligent application of that one annoying property is the key to its use. And knowledge of this key strips away the treasury-crippling expense which is otherwise presumed to protect us all. That one thing, that one annoying property, and the relative behavior of its 232nd, 233rd and 234th isotopes, single neutrons apart, represent a chasm of knowledge. This chasm exists to maintain belief in a lie, which, if revealed, would permanently alter the relationship between science, the individual, and the collective. This little detail has lain hidden within God's texts for millennia, waiting to be decoded. Or should I say re-decoded?

And that last paragraph, when read within the bowels of certain labs, or within the sealed chambers of certain shamans, made those readers' blood run cold with fear. Fear that others might understand what I just said. But of course, much of this book *is* just fiction. Isn't it?

Chapter 12, Scholarship and Sadi Carnot

In the previous chapter, I discussed some subjects which I think are important for you to learn to succeed as an entrepreneur. In the next chapter, we are going to discuss how to think. But first, I want to talk for a moment about the merit of thought itself.

For any of you who have been formally educated, even a little, you will understand the academic concept of scholarship. The popular concept of scholarship is that it is money someone gives you to go to school. Do a web search for "scholarship", and you will be bombarded with endless references to this concept. However, if you look up the definition of the word scholarship, you will find something like:

Scholarship - noun. Learning; knowledge acquired by study; the academic attainments of a scholar.

I found that definition at *dictionary.com*. OK, let's try digging into that a little more. You can imagine, perhaps, that the word *scholar* should be worth defining now, since that kind of person attains scholarship. So, again according to *dictionary.com*:

Scholar - noun. A learned or erudite person, esp. one who has profound knowledge of a particular subject.

OK, that still isn't entirely satisfying. Let's try a different approach and try *dictionary.com* for the word *scholarly*:

Scholarly - adjective. having the qualities of a scholar.

This is no help at all! Try this just for fun, and you will go round and round in circles, and never actually learn anything. Other than that a *bleek* is someone who has *bleeky* qualities and whose work can be defined as *bleeksmanship*. What are *bleeky* qualities? Those which are representative of a *bleek*, of course. Somewhere out there, though, is the definition which I will just paraphrase below:

Scholarship is the production of a work of knowledge which references original or repackaged work by others. Correctly done, the author of said work carefully cites all sources, to further repackage said knowledge. Accordingly said work contains the minimum amount of original content necessary to get it published.

By this definition, the first page of this chapter is scholarly. I looked up some definitions, showed you where I found them, and didn't tell you a single bit of anything. The only original content was making fun of the whole process, and that *funnin' wit you* was the only thing which made that page worth publishing. This has deep, deep implications. I will get back to these implications in a moment.

But first, I want to explore a word I have been using throughout this book so far, starting in the first chapter. And that word is *subconscious*. Here are a couple of definitions, found at dictionary.com:

subconscious - adjective. Existing or operating in the mind beneath or beyond consciousness.

subconscious - noun. The totality of mental processes of which the individual is not aware; unreportable mental activities.

It turns out that the word subconscious grates on practitioners in the field of messing with your head, or presuming to understand your motivations. These practitioners prefer to use the word *unconscious*. Here is what they mean when they use that word:

unconscious - adjective. Not perceived at the level of awareness; occurring below the level of conscious thought.

unconscious - adjective. Not consciously realized, planned, or done; without conscious volition or intent.

Or better,

(the) unconscious - noun. In psychoanalysis, the part of the mind containing psychic (mental, not woo woo) material that is only rarely accessible to awareness but that has a pronounced influence on behavior

Again, all of these definitions were found at dictionary.com. I've suitably modified them to make them more readable, as you may have guessed from that last one. Psycho professionals disdain the use of the word *subconscious*, and use instead the word *unconscious*. But calling this part of your mind "unconscious" makes it sound as if it got hit by a truck and is just lying there on the road. My subconscious mind takes offense at that description. Or, perhaps the word "unconscious" makes it seem as if that part of your mind is sleeping it off after a night of binge drinking. Again, this image isn't soothing.

Regardless of what connotation you assign to the word "unconscious", the common usage of this word doesn't imply an active role of purpose. "Subconscious", which implies a foundation for the "conscious", seems to just fit better. Yet even Freud, the lord of the psychos, didn't use the word "unconscious". Take a moment to read the Wikipedia article on this word for yourself (but remember, with Wikipedia first doubt everything you read there):

Internet Research
Wikipedia article for subconscious.

The dripping, slobbering disrespect for the unwashed is evident in even that short summary, isn't it? The elites in the psycho profession use a different word for a concept than that which comes natural to most people. This is an example of how elites in a body of knowledge try to identify each other, and exclude those who don't understand the secret words or phrases which they share among them.

If you were at a tea party with a room full of psycho professionals, they would immediately recognize you as a rube if you used the word "subconscious". Unless you were making fun of it at the time. Your failure to bow to the use of their word would identify you to them as an outsider just as clearly as if you had a flashing light on your head. Because to the elites in any field, membership is more important than the ideas of that field themselves. Your use of what they define as the correct word is more meaningful than the concept it represents.

But words *do* have meaning, do they not? Of course they do. But why in the world would someone, or a group of someones, attempt to twist the meaning of a word? Way back, when psycho professionals were first getting organized, the word "unconscious" popped into someone's head for use in this context. Now, until then, Freud had been using the word *preconscious*, which is probably far more appropriate than either "subconscious" or "unconscious". The word "unconscious", with our common meaning of disability, had been used for almost two hundred years before Freud started his work.

So why twist a word, "unconscious", which already had an established meaning, instead of using Freud's more meaningful "preconscious"? Or at least use the almost as meaningful, yet untainted word "subconscious"? Simply to confuse and identify those who lie outside the shadow of the ivory tower. If you want to identify a poser, a great way to do this is to come up with a term or a phrase which is easily misunderstood or misinterpreted. Unless someone has been immersed in a collective long enough, their status as an outsider will be evident.

You can easily feel this happening, at least your subconscious mind can, when you hear a white guy saying the word "Gangster" in a particular context, instead of slurring it like "Gangsta". Or if you see a perky blonde say "Gangsta" on the TV as she is reporting some story. Maybe she even bobs her head around as she does it. It just sounds, and feels, odd. Cringingly odd, sometimes. Psycho professionals feel exactly the same thing when someone uses the word "subconscious" when the elites demand the word "unconscious".

Some authors kiss up to them by using the word "unconscious". But just as Blondie seems needy and weak when she says "Gangsta", so do those authors seem needy and weak to the professionals. And the professionals get to sip in that neediness and disdain that author who is so desperately trying to fit in. So, just for fun I have deliberately used "subconscious". Deliberately to make the psycho professionals feel that cringing feeling. Or else to help them reach a state of pompous superiority, only to now kick that stool out from under their pompous asses.

And yet all those pompous asses presume to know what motivates a

Cho. Or a Klebold. Or just about any frightened kid in school just before they prescribe medication. Or a returning war veteran. You psychotics don't know crap. You didn't even know what I was doing to you until just now, and why I was doing it. And don't pretend that you did. So put down those pens or keyboards where you were just about to chuckle about this book to all your elitist buddies. And the next time you think you understand how to analyze a Cho, or a Klebold, or some school kid and his feelings, remember that an outsider just bitch-slapped you. And you didn't even see it coming.

For all you psycho professionals out there, I knew your word and what you think about it. I just chose not to use it to lure you in. Of course you will never admit this, but you know it happened. That lingering little bit of doubt in your head is enough for now. We'll build on that foundation later.

I chose to pick on the psycho professionals, but almost every aspect of our modern lives contains professions which maintain their hold by excluding you. Professions which don't grow another ear of corn, or weave the cloth which keeps a child warm, or heal a damaged organ. Professions which only consume, and lobby for their protection and suppression of individual thought and achievement. Professions which try to convert their dangerous ideas into public policy instead of simply allowing individuals to make their own decisions about their own lives.

So if you run across some group of pompous jackasses in any field, just do what I have done. Find some detail which they use to exclude others, and misuse it on purpose. And then watch them pounce like a bunch of Trekkies. This is a great way of identifying monkeys just about anywhere as they flock to the collective.

Throughout this book I also take liberties with where to put commas and periods with respect to quotations. Along with mangling grammar and traditional sentence structure. English teachers have been squirming for hundreds of pages now. Good. They will emerge from this character-building experience better people for it.

Now let's return to those deep implications of original content I mentioned earlier. Every now and then, when you buy a product of some kind, you will see on it "Assembled in the USA". Huh. OK. What it doesn't say is "Assembled in the USA of cheap, crappy Chinese parts."

"Assembled in the USA" is intended to make you believe that somehow Americans were employed in the building of this thing, or that it is somehow better done than if the Chinese put it together. Of course, the quality of the thing is determined more by whether the steel in those parts is more steelish or more snappish. Or whether the rubber o-ring will not deform under normal use. Or whether the hoses won't crack and burst open after a year.

It doesn't matter who puts all of those crappy parts together into the whole. Chinese hands can aim that air wrench just as well as American hands, except that the latter may be more inclined to put in all the bolts which are required. On the other hand, perhaps the Chinese guy gets shot if he doesn't put them all in. Who's to say?

Further, dig a little deeper into the assembly plant and you will find entire sub-assemblies, such as engines or transmissions, showing up in crates to be bolted onto the thing. All of those sub-assemblies are built overseas, but as long as you bolt them in place here, that's good enough. Quality prevails! Eventually, this will devolve into the entire thing showing up except for some sticker, which, when stuck on by American hands will give us a swell of national pride.

Regardless, you can't build a high-quality item out of shoddy parts, which are in turn made from sub-par material, such as brittle steel or rubber which starts cracking apart when fall turns into winter. It just can't be done. But it sounds good to call it "Assembled in the USA." We even have laws and trading agreements which make this worthwhile to do, even though no one who sees this is fooled.

Modern scholarship is like that. We often hear one work being described as "scholarly", and another work being denounced as "unscholarly" or "stream of consciousness writing". In these cases, what the critic means is that only by heavily referencing the work of others are you capable of writing anything of value. And that the value of what you write is in direct proportion to the amount of content you provide, or reference, which came from others. The implication, of course, is that your original thoughts are of little value. So stop relying on those nasty original thoughts, they say. What better way for the collective to stifle individualism than to deride your thoughts as inherently wrong and dangerous?

Scholarship had a noble original purpose, however. And within the context of that noble origin, it remains worthy. This noble purpose has two worthwhile implications, which also remain valid. But these implications have been twisted over time to prevent original thought. The original noble purpose of scholarship was to teach students that they did not have to take the word of their teacher for granted. Wow. Imagine trying that concept out in a public school or university today.

Scholarship was intended to teach students to go out into the world, and find out for themselves whether what they had been taught was meaningful. Go read what others say, and see whether they agree with me or you or not. See whether the intuition you have matches what others have thought or discovered for themselves of God's creation. And then ask yourself whether you believe them or whether you think they are wrong. Not just gobble their ideas up as if the mystical "someone else said" has final merit. *Scholarship was intended to avoid having to take on faith what anyone told you.*

Often, a student would find something out there in the world from someone else which made sense in the context of the original source, but didn't match what the student had discovered for himself. The student might wander off and think about the disconnect and find that his understanding of the subject was wrong, and thus learn more, and more deeply, than if he had just sat in a class. The knowledge would then be drilled into his subconscious mind, and he would *understand*. Which is better than knowledge by far, which can be misunderstood, or misremembered.

The teacher was merely a guide on this path, and knew where the potholes were. But rather than steer the student clear of the potholes as a mother might, he allowed the student to hit them anyway because falling into these potholes was the best way to learn. And more importantly, learn how to learn, and what the feeling of learning felt like, so that it could be repeated even without the teacher in later life.

Many times, the student would find that, although his original experiment or observation was in error, the error itself led to a new discovery. In 1934 Enrico Fermi was far from a student at this time in his life, but had not yet ossified beyond the understanding of how to think. While trying to reproduce a neutron experiment, he noticed that his lab in Italy had dramatically different results than other labs in other places had obtained. He believed that his colleagues in other places were competent, and yet his own work was sound, too.

Fermi eventually realized, through a series of careful experiments, and original thought about the implications of the results he saw, that the lab tables themselves changed how neutrons behaved in the experiments. His tables were marble, and yet throughout the rest of the world similar lab tables were predominantly wood. The neutrons streaming through his tables weren't slowed by light elements, which are abundant in wood, but scarce in marble. Because his experiments didn't match the others, he discovered the moderating property of hydrogen and carbon, which led to the development of the nuclear reactor.

Other times, the student might find that the original source was entirely wrong, and that information uncovered by the student through his own investigation was right. This gap, between the accepted norm and the new data which the student had found, is where progress takes root and grows. The classic example of this idea was that, long ago, some men believed that flies came from rotting meat. Francesco Redi, an Italian physician, decided to test this idea by sealing some meat in a jar, as well as covering a jar with gauze or leaving a jar open. He discovered that flies didn't come from meat, but, instead, flies came from maggots which came from flies. Had he, and others, not questioned the accepted norm, but instead merely repeated what others had said or written, we would still believe that flies came from rotting meat.

Hardly anyone knows the name Sadi Carnot. Engineers know him, or more likely recognize his name, but only a few know his work well enough to have a conversation with you about it. But his work, done in the early 1800s, comes into play each time you turn on a light or ride around in your car or enjoy the cool air in your house in the summertime.

Internet Research

Research Nicolas Leonard Sadi Carnot. Wikipedia has a great article about him and his work.

The striking thing about his 1824 book, "Reflections on the Motive Power of Fire", was that it was so insightful, and yet relied almost entirely on his thinking about how heat can create a pushing force. And how much push a given amount of heat might create. In his mind alone, he created the entire science of thermodynamics, and wrote down these ideas so compellingly correct that they stand today. Others have added to his work, but never challenged it.

Sadi was the master of the thought experiment. With thought alone, he presented simple examples of steam engines. And showed, correctly, how heat engines might be best designed, and that the efficiency of a heat engine was limited by the temperatures employed to operate it. He also created the concept of a heat pump, such as the one which cools your home or office. He also showed that a nuclear reaction would be the ultimate in powering a steam engine to generate power. And yet, it would be more than a hundred years before this idea would even have words to express it. Read that year again. 1824. Such is the power of the mind alone.

Most impressively, Sadi showed how, using a steam engine, that a perpetual motion engine of *any kind* was impossible. And, if such a thing could be invented, it could be used to dislodge the universe from its mountings. Heavy stuff. And yet so simple and easy to comprehend that it should be taught in every high school physics class, yet almost never is. Pity, as it would bring the lie to the quest for wind and solar power, and focus us instead on nuclear. And yet, perhaps that is the reason that his work is avoided today although it is the foundation upon which all modern energy use is laid. And yet, had Sadi been forced to exercise modern scholarship, and only repeat what he had learned from others, he would have never published those original ideas which benefit us all so much today.

This is the scholarship which the critic intends when he says, "Don't think for yourself, only consider those things which others tell you." And only rely on the thoughts of others for where you find truth. The classical scholarship, on the other hand, set students out to discover for themselves, true or false, what they may about the body of knowledge of God's creation. This is why a Ph.D. is called a "Doctorate of Philosophy." And not, instead, a "Doctorate of Regurgitated Hash." At one time, a Ph.D. meant that the holder was an original thinker who could determine for himself whether new information he encountered was meaningful or not. This made the holder valuable as an idea worker, who was able to challenge the ideas of others. But, at the same time, this idea worker was able to accept challenge to his own ideas, changing his mind when reason prevailed.

Over time, however, the academic orthodoxy, as do all collectives, grew weary of being challenged by upstarts. Gradually, monkeys began to percolate into the culture. As this happened, the old-hands, the true philosophers, accepted their students' ignorance as merely the normal steps on the path to enlightenment. Just as previous teachers had accepted the short-term ignorance of their students before them.

But this crop was different. Not only did they not learn to think for themselves, they began to stifle the generations which followed. And so, rather than philosophical guides, the teachers evolved into the shamans of academia, choking off new discovery until the blatant truth stared them in the face. Only then would they accept the new theories, but then as their own, pretending that the original discoverer had been flawed in some meaningful way.

The threat to the orthodoxy was original thought. Armed with authority out of proportion to their knowledge, the orthodoxy began a careful campaign to stamp out original thought wherever it might be found. Instead, ideas were only accepted to the extent that they sprang from those of its members who had been carefully screened and approved. To accomplish this choking off of original thought the orthodoxy had to subvert two time-honored implications of scholarship: publication and peer review.

Publication was intended originally to allow original thinkers to share their ideas and to learn from the work of others. Eventually, as knowledge grew more rapidly each day, scientific journals of all kinds began to be overwhelmed with submissions. And so, to limit the flow, standards became adopted to ensure that the submissions which became published were only of the highest quality.

To accomplish this quality assurance function, each author had to distinguish between what material he submitted was derived from others, and what portions of his work were original. If an author merely repackaged the work of others, it was rejected as of little merit. So, authors were required to reveal their sources, and to refuse to do so was, rightly, seen as an intellectual offense, almost criminal.

Armed with papers filled with references, the publishers handed these papers to experts in the fields, intellectual peers of the author in the author's field, for review. This peer review process allowed the publisher to focus on the logistics of the publication process. Meanwhile, the peer experts checked the references, determined what references of prior work the author may have missed, and judged the work on its original content. At first, the reviewers' task was not to judge the merit of the work, that was the task of the readership. Instead, the reviewers were only to determine the originality.

Publication and peer review promised an open, free-trade exchange of ideas. From the mid-nineteenth to the mid-twentieth centuries, this refereed journaling launched the progress we see in the modern world today. If an idea was sound, it would be lauded by the readership and the author advanced in esteem. But if an idea could be proven to be wrong, the readership would counter with their own papers to show their results. The first author might then retract his work, or offer additional experimental evidence or theoretical discussion. Although in print, this discussion could continue for years or decades, much as friends might brainstorm in a room over lunch. New knowledge leaked from the seams of this process at every turn. And so, by the back and forth which is normal to the creative process, the truth of God's creation would gradually be teased from behind the curtain. The quest itself was the reward, and often, being hailed as the discoverer was sufficient to bring consultancy to the discoverer's doorstep.

But then, as monkeys began to percolate through academia, original work began to be judged by the reviewers more and more on what the handful of reviewers perceived as its merit. Often this judgement was determined by how much the content threatened the work of the reviewer. Papers were stifled by the opinion of the few, rather than being open for all to see. And although reviewers, officially, were to be selected at random from the scientific community, cliques began to form as publishers sought the advice from the same pool of reviewers.

With cliques come politics, and the suppression of the individual over the collective. A sort of "favorably review my work and I'll favorably review yours" economy developed. The orthodox mutually resented the intrusion of those who might upset their own work, and referred for publication instead the work of other orthodox who were more likely to support the reviewer's own findings. Papers which were not littered with references to the work of others were considered less worthy. Toss in a lot of references, particularly to the work of the pool of likely reviewers, and your paper sails through with less turbulence or critique. Except for, perhaps, suggestions to reference more of the work of this reviewer or that.

Had Sadi Carnot tried to publish his work in that environment, we would have never heard of him. With too much original content, and too few references to his contemporaries, it could have hardly been worthy of publication. How many Sadi Carnots are being turned away today, their ideas stifled at the outset? True individualists with original thought were gradually and progressively shunned, and work considered too controversial was softly banned. Scientists began to work more and more, not in garages or attics above the lecture halls, but in well-funded government labs. And as their work habits changed, the orthodoxy naturally evolved to support the source of their funding. Research from academia, and their government-funded labs, became considered more "correct", while the same paper, submitted from outside the establishment, would be viewed in a harsher light, or rejected entirely.

And then the size of the lab began to matter. Surely, small schools were incapable of producing merit, only the larger with their larger staffs and more expensive equipment and better funding could generate worthy ideas.

Small businesses, which had at one time been the acorns from which large enterprises grew, had to be stifled from the start. Consider the example of the Small Business Innovation Research program, more commonly known as the SBIR. Long ago, the SBIR was started to help keep small businesses in the research game, a goal which could easily have been obtained at zero cost by simply dropping the regulations which kept them out. Instead, a new program was created to fund small businesses by issuing research grants for specific topics.

Even so, topics considered too controversial were not available for grants. Further, such grants could only be issued for topics which could be immediately commercialized. Fermi's neutron research, for example, would have been rejected on both grounds. His research would have failed the first test as it could not have even been anticipated. SBIR solicitations lack requirements such as "develop, in five milestones, using marble tables procured from domestic sources, an entirely new neutron theory which could not possibly have been anticipated."

Fermi's neutron research would have been rejected by the second restriction as well. Decades passed between his 1934 research and the first commercial nuclear power reactor in Calder Hall, in England, which didn't begin operation until 1956. No small business research proposal would have been accepted with a twenty-two-year commercialization window. On the other hand, universities and large contractors were under no such restrictions. For them, funding of basic research was of merit in and of itself. After all, these organizations provided many jobs. And so the orthodoxy further ossified, those researchers outside those protective wings being left to wither away.

Over time, the program evolved further away from the individual. Before Al Gore, the term "small business" allowed SBIRs to be awarded to firms as large as 500, hardly small. But as Vice President, Al Gore insisted that the term "small business" would now include educational institutions, regardless of size. Educational institutions would now compete head-to-head for research dollars with entrepreneurs. As these dollars were to be doled out to those whom independent reviewers, selected from the orthodoxy, determined to be best capable of completing the research, guess who wins?

Even without this windfall, large companies frequently spent a significant fraction of the available SBIR dollars. How? Merely by creating small companies to receive the grants, seeding them with their own staff to flesh out the resumes, and then subcontracting the mother company to do the bulk of the work. While I was an engineer at McDonnell Douglas, many of my contemporaries performed work funneled through small businesses created for this purpose. I myself worked on small business projects while in the employ of that aerospace giant. Crumbs tossed here and there to small sub-sub-contractors, these selected predominantly for their smallishness and loyalty to the sow, satisfied the requirements of these programs.

As the ossification of the scholarly orthodox continues, great ideas, or even bad ones which will spark merely good ideas later are stifled. Want to destroy your career in physics? Dare to challenge their god Einstein and his theories regarding the speed of light. Consider the following question:

Spaceship A leaves Earth traveling toward Jupiter at $0.8c$ (eighty-percent of the speed of light). Meanwhile, Spaceship B leaves Jupiter toward Earth, also at $0.8c$. Are they not closing upon each other at $1.6c$ (sixty percent faster than the speed of light)? From the perspective of Spaceship A, is not Spaceship B screaming in at greater than the speed of light?

Pose this question to the orthodox and enjoy the answer. After they get over the rage of being asked such foolishness, or simply try to drown you out as a fool, they might actually try to explain things. Watch their eyes as they do this. You might think they are just playing a tape, rather than understanding. Now modify your question further:

Once these spaceships pass each other, narrowly, are they not now departing from each other at 1.6c, greater than the speed of light?

And now, after you have endured the torrent:

Assume that Spaceship A launches a probe toward Spaceship B. This probe first decelerates to cancel the 0.8c of Spaceship A to float motionlessly with respect to Earth. And then, the probe accelerates to match the 0.8c of Spaceship B, has it not changed its velocity by greater than the speed of light?

At some point, you will hear the word *relativity*, which claims that there is a mythical space-time continuum, which no one has proved, that is the universal fabric which regulates the speed of light. You will usually hear this idea cast around if you ask what happens if some pre-teen boys on either spaceship are fooling around with flashlights, before or after the craft pass in the night. Time to invoke classical physics, which they say that their god has overturned, destroyed in his petty, jealous rage:

And what if the Earth, and the Sun, and our spaceships and all we know in the universe is sitting on the back of a giant turtle (classical physicists love turtles) with a grid painted on its back, said turtle zipping along at 0.8c in some unknown direction.

Their eyes roll. "Now, the probe's speed is relative to what?," you demand, "the spaceships, the Earth or the turtle? And how would you know?" And you will get something about the turtle itself getting bigger. At 0.8c. Anything to avoid challenging the word of their god. To a physicist, asking these questions means the ultimate death, stoning by peer review. The orthodoxy has provided answers to these which must be accepted on faith, and recited faithfully if challenged. The experiment, and discovery of an earth-shattering principle, may come from an obscure corner.

Similar things have happened. The next energy breakthrough may, literally, be in your neighbor's garage. Sprinkled around the planet, a few diehard hobbyists, known as fusioneers, play with miniature fusion reactors in their garages and basements. Following in the footsteps of Philo Farnsworth, the inventor of the television, they make reactors, known as Farnsworth Fusors. These little miracles of nuclear science are built from mixing bowls and HVAC pumps, and generate little glowing balls of purple plasma in near-vacuum. That plasma is powered by nothing more than the normal power outlet and some stuff they ripped out of some old TVs or microwave ovens. But in that plasma these guys smash deuterium atoms together in a purple haze and watch the fun. And twiddle with their equations and calculators. And think.

Meanwhile, gigantic labs build fantastically expensive contraptions to, uh, smash deuterium atoms together in a purple haze and watch the fun. And twiddle with their equations and supercomputers. And think about their next funding proposal.

The fusor was the last research Farnsworth ever did. This guy, who invented the television, and hid in a corner of ITT to try to protect his work from piracy, was crushed out of existence under the wheels of tax law. How close was he to unlocking the power of fusion? We will never know. And rest assured that should one of these fusioneers come close, the collective will have no choice but to squash them out, having made fools of their trillions of dollars and millions of jobs. Perhaps they will just simply have their purple plasma balls labeled as environmental hazards. Or just brand them as nuclear terrorists and lock them away.

A more well-known example springs to mind. In 1989 two researchers, Martin Fleischmann, in England, and Stanley Pons, in Utah, collaborating on an experiment, reported having measured tabletop fusion at near-room temperature in a liquid apparatus they had been fooling around with. This discovery turned into a media circus, and soon led to a discrediting of the pair and the entire concept.

"Room-temperature fusion on an apparatus which sits on a lab bench? Impossible! Cast them out!" the orthodox shouted from their lairs atop fantastically expensive government-funded labs.

Lost in all of this furor was what Fleischmann and Pons actually said. They hadn't claimed that they had unleashed a source of free power for everyone forever, as the media reported and the orthodoxy fanned. All they really claimed was that they had observed an unexpected phenomenon. Instead, their simple statement was twisted into hype, and that hype was then used to destroy them and their credibility, and cast them as crackpots. So intense was this hype that a few others who had actually reproduced their limited results later withdrew their claims to avoid controversy.

And lost in all of this was the idea that perhaps the pair had stumbled upon a marble table effect which had escaped all the fantastically expensive wooden tables used elsewhere. All that mattered is that their observation challenged the orthodoxy of the collective, and had to be extinguished.

So what are the answers to the speed-of-light question? Or cold fusion? I don't know. But I would like to see an experiment to find out. Because if not, we are keeping ourselves from the stars. To hell with finding out how the universe started. The answer doesn't really matter much at this point. I want to find out what we can *do* with it.

"But we have experimented," they shout in zealous unison.

Oh yeah, there was that star peeking out from behind the Sun thing. About a hundred years ago some guy took some fuzzy pictures of stars which should have been concealed behind the Sun during a solar eclipse. If Einstein was right about this whole speed-of-light and gravity thing, then the Sun should have bent the light from these stars as it passed by. Lo and behold, the fuzzies on the photo seemed to show exactly that. To great acclaim. Never mind that similar experiments repeated by other researchers didn't match that one. Or that the Sun, surrounded by gas, acts like a lens and can bend light from that alone.

Try this experiment sometime. Grab a magnifying glass, or a telescope, or binoculars or a rifle scope. Tape a little paper dot right in the center of the magnifying glass or the front glass of the telescope, or whatever. Right in the center might be some fuzzy, but guess what. You can see stuff behind the dot. Just like you can behind the sun, ever so slightly, during an eclipse, as we look through the largest lens in our solar system, the moon acting like that paper dot in the center. Only now, instead of the stars appearing in the circle of the moon, their light is dragged out from behind the sun to appear near the edge beyond the circle.

"But the measurements were different than a lensing effect!" they shout as they look about for stones with which to welcome their latest infidel. How do you know? Those fuzzy pictures were awfully fuzzy. And how do we know that a solar flare hadn't been erupting at that time to distort the lens, the flare acting like a lens within a lens? Or perhaps the Sun's gravity acts on light in some marble-table way which we don't yet understand, but happens to appear as if it supports their god. At least close enough to allow the elect to avoid looking too closely.

Of course, we can repeat the experiment. And someone did, and was shouted down when the results conflicted. Surely, with our technology today we can do much better experiments. But to even suggest such a thing would challenge the orthodoxy. So the suggestion itself must be shouted down.

"We also have as proof experimental data from orbiting atomic clocks" they shout. Again, atomic clocks in space are in an entirely different environment than those on Earth. Plus, they are whipping around the Earth, accelerating laterally at every moment. How do we know that this strange environment, like Fermi's marble lab tables, aren't having an effect which we can't see on our wood tables on Earth? A wood table, no matter how ornately decorated and at whatever cost, would still not have revealed the effect which Fermi found.

We're not even willing to ask the question, so deep is our faith in the godlike Einstein. And so we may be missing a principle of nature as profound as that Fermi discovered. And so useful.

The orthodoxy has good reason to be threatened. Imagine the revolution of thought which would accompany such a discovery. Assume for a moment that it is discovered that Einstein was wrong, and objects can go faster than the speed of light, and without trickery such as wormholes or so on. Just assume that simple push, push, push is enough. Or pull, pull, pull on a gravity string. However the mechanism, suppose that simple faster-than-light is shown to be fine and dandy, just like we can go faster than the speed of sound. Don't forget that exceeding that barrier was also thought to be impractical not too long ago.

At once, every science classroom in the world would be wrong. Each teacher or professor, who shouted down such questions from their students for decades would be wrong. Each man on the street who didn't believe or understand what he had been told on TV his entire life is vindicated. Each scientific journal, or author, or lab director or peer reviewer who stifled crackpots would be wrong, each oppression against free thought shown as what it is. And their god lying broken at their feet, revealed to simply be an idol made by men. Trillions of dollars diverted, worldwide and wrongly, into programs which were flawed at their core. Because of a faith.

There is a powerful incentive for this to never be discovered. At one time, the discovery that the world is not the center of the universe helped to topple the stranglehold of the Catholic Church on humanity's mind. In defensive response the Church subjected the proponents of this radical idea to torture and humiliation. Similarly, discovery of the possibility for classical faster-than-light motion would be the most important example in human history to date of how the group would have been so terribly wrong, and acted in unspoken concert to stifle dissent.

How many careers and lives would have been destroyed in this century-old farce? For nothing more than unwillingness to tolerate free thought and free expression.

But someone may yet discover that this is possible. If so, there remains a way for the collective to save itself the embarrassment:

☐ The discovery must be announced by a heavily funded lab which justifies the money spent on such labs, and the vast pyramids of jobs which support these things. No outsider will be allowed to announce such a profound and simple thing.

☐ The discovery, in the age of political correctness, must be credited to a woman, or a minority, or anyone who speaks with an accent other than an American white male. Nor can the discoverer be anyone in the traditional scientific ethic, such as a secular Jew of any nationality, as was Fermi. Indian or Chinese ethnicity would be best.

☐ The discovery must not directly challenge their god, but will instead be wrapped in an esoteric theory which is said to *complement*, rather than *contradict*, their god.

☐ The discovery will be explained in terms which justify the labeling of previous detractors as crackpots, as well as explaining away the arguments that schoolchildren had made against it as naive and simplistic.

You probably think I'm a racist or sexist for claiming what I have about how the discovery process is rationed out for political purposes. Consider that, although our entire space program was based on the work of Nazi scientists, it is only after about a half-century that we are able to finally just come out and say this. Hitler put us on the moon. And saved us from the New Deal. Does that make me a neo-Nazi? Nope. Just a student of history and of the nature of the collective.

Still not convinced about how credit will be politically allocated after a major, paradigm-shifting discovery? Consider this:

Recently, in March of 2009, in the same city in which the cold fusion hype began twenty years before, the American Chemical Society held a symposium on new energy technologies. One speaker presented results from experiments, performed by researchers working for a lab funded by the U.S. Navy. This experiment substantially recreated the cold-fusion results, but using techniques which were more sophisticated than those of Fleischmann and Pons, of course. The discoverer credited? Analytical chemist Pamela Mosier-Boss.

Reviewers of this Navy experiment agree that neutrons are being produced, which are indicative of nuclear reactions, which include fusion. But, some reviewers hedged that although neutrons were observed, they might instead be caused by "new, unknown nuclear processes."[13] Really? Like Fermi's marble table, for example? Or processes which Fleischmann and Pons merely said might be interesting enough for someone else to take a look at?

And, as reported, what is some of the preliminary work which Pamela based her work on? Not Fleischmann and Pons, of course. No, those guys are just crackpots, everyone knows that. Instead, work by scientists in places such as the Bhabha Atomic Research Centre, in India.

Similarly, a discovery such as faster-than-light travel, should it ever be made, must never be allowed to vindicate the tens of millions of schoolchildren who have asked these simple questions. After all, the vindication of schoolchildren and their wonder about the world would undermine the entire fabric of belief which the collective demands. Children, their minds not yet fully programmed, tend to ask impertinent questions which threaten to reveal truth. Only later do these children learn bias and shut down their minds to earn acceptance by the group. And then join the group in silencing the next crop of children.

The discovery itself, in whatever field, is unimportant. Options include faster-than-light, simple fusion energy, the dangers of greenness. Or how a single environmental mandate has been silently destroying almost anything electronic which you have purchased since about mid-summer 2006. Or how the USDA is spending millions right now to poison you.

Just about anything which slips in under the expensive orthodoxy will do, such as an understanding of how niceness destroys individualism and liberty. Not just the concept itself, such as faster-than-light, but the entire social principle of doubting yourself, relying instead upon experts, would itself be called into doubt.

Once again, men might choose thought as their counsel, rather than the collective. The monkeys have spent generations trying to stomp out that nasty thinking habit. Too late to turn back now.

Or so they think.

---

[13] Steven Krivit, editor of the *New Energy Times*.

Chapter 13, The Idea Factory

In our industrialized culture, in which education is used primarily as a means of thought and behavior control, very few learn how to think. Most of our day is consumed with stumbling around from task to task, hardly thinking about anything other than how we are going to get it all done. So how do we learn to think? The first step is easy.

Stop. Stop participating in the endless compliance rituals which you are expected to perform each day.

Reading Assignment
Influence, The Psychology of Persuasion
by Robert B. Cialdini

That book, written with a heavy sales and marketing perspective, also has an excellent description of the utility of simple triggers in encouraging compliance. We are all surrounded by more information than we can possibly absorb. Even if you stripped away all the technology and blinking lights and flashing screens there would be too much information, too much detail, in the world around us to comprehend. If we focused on all this detail, we would all become autistic, swimming around in just understanding the details rather than getting anything done. Like eating.

Over the ages our minds evolved ways to handle all this detail and developed certain shortcuts, as described in the book referenced above. As Dr. Cialdini notes, compliance professionals take advantage of our reliance on these shortcuts to slip past our defenses. The most important of all of these shortcuts is to do what we see others doing. If suddenly everyone in a room jumps up and runs out, the typical person would be inclined to jump up and run out also. If everyone else around you starts eating, the typical person would start eating, too. If everyone else started spitting food out, you wouldn't be as likely to start shoveling it in.

I remember hearing about this idea in military psychology classes at the Naval Academy. Classical American success on the battlefield derives from a high level of training, combined with a generous dose of small-unit leadership and leading by example. I contrast this with the eras of collective battlefield strategies, such as those employed by the Union in the Civil War, or World War I, selected battles in World War II, or the meat grinder operations of Korea and Vietnam, in which individual initiative was deliberately suppressed in favor of mass compliance. Not surprisingly, all of those examples cited led to disproportionately higher casualties.

Historically, Americans hardly ever had the best weapons. Although our modern military relies heavily on clever weapons, individual initiative and leadership is ultimately far superior, and not to be counted out just yet. Leading by example is simply a compliance technique which gives the crowd someone to watch in action, which then spurs them to act similarly.

One day, I had a chance to put these ideas to the test. While waiting around in the lobby of Rickover Hall I noticed that there was a sumptuous buffet set up outside a smallish auditorium. This buffet was defended by a sign on a stand clearly identifying this auditorium for a group of

Washington VIPs due to arrive in about a half-hour. Midshipmen are notorious for eating just about everything in sight, but all present were keeping a respectable distance, no one getting closer than about ten feet.

After sizing things up I wandered away from the group I was in, and approached the buffet from a different angle. Walking briskly to the buffet, and confidently grabbing a plate and tongs, I announced, "good, it's here," and proceeded to help myself. Within moments, all uncertainty disappeared and the midshipmen gathered there attacked the goodies. Within a few minutes, it was mostly gone. Toward the end of the experiment, the horrified host for the event, who was setting up his projector in the auditorium, came running out and shooed us away like so many flies. But, it was far too late by then. Serves him right for not posting a guard.

Only later, decades later, did I realize that it is only easy to get a mass of people to do things which resemble monkey behavior. Running out of a room, or gobbling down a pile of food, or stoning the infidels are the easy ones. Try leading a crowd into designing something useful or working more efficiently, as opposed to simply working pointlessly harder. Or performing some highly individualist function. Any of these will help you appreciate the power the collective has to motivate its adherents versus the individualist.

Even the presumably noble act of risking life and limb in storming the enemy requires a pre-existing belief in the righteousness, or at least rightfulness, of the goal. This is why the enemy must be demonized before the campaign begins, or else too many of the lance corporals might wind up asking themselves whether this is a good thing to do. As we will discuss later, this also has implications for your personal liberty. Should the day arise in which a constitutional crisis develops on our own shores, many rest assured that the soldiers will know better than to suspend your civil rights. This fantasy is dangerous and downright foolish.

Should that day arise, each and every soldier or law enforcement professional will be convinced, to their core, that your demand for constitutionality is precisely what makes you a bad American. We've already seen that preparation being started as I write this. Don't expect some corporal or sergeant or lieutenant or captain or major or colonel or general to say, "hold on fellas, let's think about this." If you think this will happen in sufficient numbers to make a difference to your personal situation, then you are out of your mind. These professionals work for the collective, not you.

The techniques by which they are prepared to destroy you is the same as that which prepares you to destroy yourself. Their mechanism is the suspension of your independent thought. To test this statement, try a few simple exercises, and notice how powerful the pull is on your mind, even when you *know* what is going on. Then imagine how much more powerful this pull is on someone who isn't self-aware, and is the product of a public school education.

Here are some simple ones:

☐ Don't check email for two days.
☐ When the phone rings, do something different than what you normally do. If you normally rush to answer it, let it go to voicemail. Or, if you normally let it go to voicemail, answer the call.
☐ Take a different route to work.
☐ Watch a totally different television program than you normally do.
☐ Listen to something your boss/spouse/customer said, and jump on filling that need like a wild mongoose.
☐ Watch a dozen or so reports by John Stossel. Choose any from since about 1990. During his early career he was a die-hard collectivist. He is feeling much better now.

OK, those shouldn't be that hard, and really don't affect anyone else all that much, at least not in a negative way. Time for more of a challenge:

☐ When a stranger greets you, perhaps as a cashier in a store, look them in the eye, but say not one thing, keeping your expression blank.
☐ Look a stranger in the eye, with a curious detached expression, as one might examine a new species, until they look away.
☐ Watch every single episode of Penn and Teller's "B.S." series. If you get angry or upset during any of them, ask yourself why. And then prove them wrong. If you can.
☐ If contacted by a telemarketer, tell them you need their credit card number. If they ask why, keep repeating the question until they hang up.
☐ If contacted by a telemarketer, engage them in a conversation as if you are a therapist hired to solve their personal issues until they hang up.
☐ Telemarketers make this too easy. Pretend you work for the CIA and ask them, in your best fighter pilot voice, for their access code. When they don't know what you mean, tell them "The lock for today is Purple. What is your access code?" As they stammer and ask questions, ignore them and repeat the demand in a cool level voice. After a few such demands, ask them their name and how they got this number. No matter what they say, pretend to badly cover the mouthpiece and say "Brisbane, this is Badger Six, we have a Level Three violation on my line. Trace and lock." Wait a few moments and then ask, "got it?" Pause again, and say "got it now?, uhhh, roger, execute Tango Bravo Nine." Then hang up.
☐ Sell a telemarketer on getting a copy of this book so that they can improve their own lives and not have to work as a telemarketer.

Since those were with strangers, and really didn't harm anyone, other than perhaps their feelings, they still shouldn't have been that hard. But, by now you will probably be feeling some tugs of guilt that you aren't fitting into your role in society. This is a good thing.

Now for some harder ones; these require you to risk conspicuousness in front of people you know. The fact that they make you feel supremely uncomfortable in your conspicuousness is exactly the point:

☐ When prompted to recite the Pledge of Allegiance in a crowd, omit the word "indivisible." Don't rush right through it, but instead pause the requisite amount of time, as in "under God, ..., with liberty and justice for all." Do this until someone notices the gap, and then defend yourself against charges of being a secessionist and blatant racist. Ignore the racism charge, and then engage them in a discussion of what is bad about secessionism.

☐ Expand the previous exercise by emphasizing the word "ALL" at the end. If you are a white male, and anyone hears you, ignore their horrified expression, and then ask yourself why they would be shocked. Then apply your knowledge of individualism versus the collective and answer this question for yourself. Again, defend yourself against charges of racism, which should be patently absurd given your emphasis. Any other category of reader making this emphasis will simply be accepted as making a progressive social statement

☐ If you are a white person, imagine a minority making a similar emphasis. Ask yourself whether you feel included or excluded in the word. Analyze whether you feel a pang of guilt when they do, and what purpose this feeling which has been implanted in you serves for the collective. Ask yourself why you have been made to feel like even this exercise is divisive, instead of inclusive.

☐ If you are a minority making this emphasis around white people, ask yourself if their positive reaction to your doing this is genuine. Or, are they instead pandering to what they think you, and the collective, want to hear, instead of seeing you as a person with a mind of your own? If this discussion starts, engage them as to how much they think "all" means you instead of them.

☐ When you see a news story about a killing or a paternal child abduction or some other similar tragedy, try to think about a reasonable possible motivation the accused has. Attempt to project yourself into their own state of mind. And then decide how, and why, you would make different decisions to cause a different outcome.

☐ When you see one of the news stories I mentioned above, imagine instead that the accused did nothing of the sort. Instead, imagine that the story is merely a cover for some meaningless lack of compliance which was the actual offense.

☐ Imagine you are a fiction writer. Ask yourself, in some horrific dystopian alternate universe, how traffic billboards or Amber alerts or cell-phone tracking could be used to help round up the politically indiscreet. What plot line could you weave around this?

☐ In church, as the collective, I mean congregation, is led to kneel in prayer, pause just a fraction of a moment before complying. Note the wave of unease which percolates around you.

☐ Don't bow your head for a group prayer. Notice how the guy in the front talking starts looking at you as he makes sure everyone is being good little boys and girls, his own head unbowed. I believe God will forgive you for this experiment, He hears your heart no matter what position your body is in. He might even be proud of you for getting in more direct touch with Him.

☐ Put nothing in the collection plate. Feel the wave of unease become a tsunami.
☐ Sitting in a parking lot, open your windows and crank some music anachronistic for your station in life.
☐ Tell a charity collector that you think charity is evil, but offer yard-work to their destitute in question as a way of helping them pay their bills.
☐ Defend someone's reputation to your closest friends as they gossip about that person.
☐ Ask a door-to-door evangelist about their position on blood sacrifice of innocents.
☐ If you live in a nice subdivision, leave your trash can outside for a week straight.
☐ Also in a nice subdivision, get someone you know to leave the worst beater of a car, or mud-coated monster truck, in your driveway for a few days.
☐ Nice subdivisions, like telemarketers, make this too easy. Get a couple of relatives or friends, man and woman, to hang out in your front yard on a weekend on a couple of lawn chairs and play cards all day. Both in cutoff jeans with lots of stringies, both in flip flops, he in a dirty white wife-beater, she in a halter-top and curlers and lots of hot makeup. Have them drink beer from a well-stocked cooler and whoop with laughter from time to time, but ignore passerby. Go about your normal activities as if you haven't even noticed anything unusual.
☐ For a week, when you get your mail from the box, leave the box door hanging open.
☐ Pretend you are an intelligence analyst for a day. Analyze each news story you hear with scepticism, and try to detect the back story of compliance with an agenda to destroy individualism and promote collectivism.
☐ Pick a non-perishable food item you enjoy, and then buy a year's supply of this. Put nothing else in your cart, and offer no explanations. This is best done if the item selected is generally regarded as bad for you.
☐ Walk right past a Girl Scout table without even engaging in conversation, eye contact, or polite exchange of pleasantries.
☐ If approached by a homeless person, tell him to "get a job." Yes, we've all heard the song. How dare you defy it? You are supposed to want to prove that you are better than that.
☐ Wear a Husqvarna® or Stihl® shirt to an environmental rally. Better, see if you can get a stack of promotional materials from either, or both, to hand out there. If challenged about your insensitivity, patiently and softly explain that both of these are made by eco-friendly countries in the European Union, and notice how resistance melts.
☐ Attend an educators' conference and introduce yourself as a principal of a homeschool.
☐ Ignore someone's pet.
☐ If some idiot with an impossibly large dog on a leash lets it threaten you as the animal pulls them, typically her, toward you, ignore the person.

Instead, lean into the dog and growl and bark menacingly at it. Form a clear image in your mind, spurting blood included,[14] of turning the dog inside out. Play back this image in your mind rapidly over and over while growl-barking and staring through its eyes into its soul. If you do this right, with sufficient belief in your mind that this is actually happening, it will sense your intentions and back away. It might even whimper. Notice how the person will not apologize for their dog menacing you. Instead, watch them become hostile that you frightened their "puppy", or more nauseatingly, their "baby." In reality, you will have just scared the crap out of them because they had expected to feel instead a surge of power from their baby inflicting fear in you.

Be prepared to raise bail money if you try that last one, which shows where you, or your small children or pregnant women who may be with you at the time, rank against dogs in the eyes of the collective. Even that radical radio talk show host who inspired me years ago has this particular fetish against the rights of persons versus animals.

If you can complete all of these, pat yourself on the back. I estimate that 99.9% of people can't. You probably can't even imagine yourself doing these exercises without feeling a deep sense of unease merely at the reading. But on reflection, not one of these indicates you are a bad person, but you are made to feel as if you are, simply to get you to comply. Such is the depth of your programming.

Don't just read these exercises, actually do them[15]. Doing is much harder than simply understanding the intellectual content. If you can't do them, then put this book down now and read no further. At this point you should be able to recognize the compliance patterns, and begin to invent more exercises of your own. But be prepared to lose most of the friends you have worked so hard to impress. If you follow that path, you will suffer this loss for nothing more than empowering your own sense of individual worth.

The next step in learning how to think is to understand how great ideas flow from fuzziness. Although a lot of the advice I give to my clients has been applicable to the world of engineering or product design, these ideas apply to entrepreneurs of all kinds. As a disclaimer, I can only really describe to you how my mind works. I am sure licensed professionals of all sorts will disagree with just about everything I am about to tell you.

To have great ideas, in addition to understanding how the creative process itself works, you must have two sets of knowledge, education and experience. In all fairness, for years I had only subconsciously understood the necessity of balancing each of these. I first began to be aware of the explicit distinction between these two sets of knowledge after hearing a

---

[14] OK, I lied in the foreword. My bad. Technically, though, I didn't describe it, I merely mentioned it. Hey, this is a work of fiction anyway, so cut me some slack.

[15] Remember, this book is just for fun. Don't actually do anything I suggest, but if you do, remember, I warned you. Don't blame me for the consequences of what the monkeys will do when they tear into you.

lecture by Dr. Paul Dobransky, M.D. Although Dr. Paul specializes in the psychology of relationships and self-esteem, this one idea applies nicely to learning how to think, also.

By the way, if you feel self-conscious about just about anything, I highly recommend you get some of Dr. Paul's materials. His MindOS™ ideas are really eye-opening, and help build a vocabulary about mental concepts which most of us understand intuitively at some level. From my perspective, his ideas are helpful in teaching you how to deprogram yourself from a lot of negativity which has been implanted in you by the collective to make you easier to control. I feel that the purpose of this programming is to allow monkeys to extract unearned value from you.

As Dr. Paul describes, education is about book-learning, while experience is about learning while doing. In one of his lectures he mentions that activities such as watching movies or reading books, even this one, are a form of a shortcut to experience. His reasoning is that you can borrow someone else's experience, in a limited and highly filtered sense, from these activities. But, there is no substitute for actual hands-on experience for most useful skills. To be able to make the best of both of these kinds of knowledge, it is essential that they be in balance.

Someone who has a lot of book knowledge but no practical experience seems off-balance. Similarly, someone with a lot of practical experience but no reference to what others have discovered before seems almost naively helpless. Either extreme is bad, which is why I have encouraged you to teach yourself, if you have to, certain foundation subjects. I now encourage you to get out and live a lot of different experiences, and read a lot of books like mine where people relate their own real-life mistakes and experiences.

If you sit behind a desk all day, find some way to get out and operate a backhoe for a while. If you run a backhoe all day, find some way to teach yourself something like HTML. Get on the web and learn about how plutonium-238 is made and what it is good for. Get a night job for a while in a restaurant. Buy a junker of a used car, repair it, and sell it. See if you can go on a ride-along with an HVAC repairman for a day. Paint a couple of rooms in your house floor to ceiling, even the trim. Take an adult education class and learn about welding, or political science. Take your kids on a tour of a factory or a farm. Push your boundaries, and talk to everyone you run across during this time. More importantly, ask questions and really listen to the answers.

I challenge you to drive down a road and truly have an appreciation for how that nice grassy slope down to the storm drain got there. Or for what it took for that billboard to wind up perched on top of that post, or how that steak got to the meat market. Or what nonsense a used-car salesman or real estate agent has to deal with. Or why electricity comes spurting out of your wall. When you can fully appreciate these things, then you'll be ready to proceed.

Throughout this chapter I am going to speak about your conscious mind and your subconscious mind as independent portions of your self which work together to solve problems. These problem-solving skills also interact to get you through the day safely and put a smile on your face. Professionals in the field will probably give you different definitions for what these two parts are, but to be clear for this discussion I will define them now.

When I say conscious mind, I mean that part of you which is reading this right now. This mind is logical and process-oriented. It makes plans such as "I am going to go somewhere to get something that I need." The skills exercised by your conscious mind, sometimes called your "left brain", involve objective thinking such as algebraic manipulation or factual understanding. This mind is trained predominantly by education.

On the other hand, when I say subconscious mind, I mean that part of you which has been jolted by some of what you have read. The subconscious mind is best at connecting the dots of a problem, or of understanding an underlying theme, or of recognizing threats, even if those threats are only to your world-view. It doesn't make detailed plans, but instead makes you feel as if you need to go get something. The skills exercised by your subconscious mind, sometimes called your "right brain", involve subjective thinking such as pattern recognition or understanding the whole of something. This mind is trained predominantly by experience. Compared to your conscious mind, your subconscious mind is much, much faster at recognizing an unfolding situation, as well as having the ability to connect seemingly unrelated details and reach a conclusion.

Note that in this definition of the subconscious mind I do not mean the autonomic functions of regulating heartbeat or breathing. The subconscious mind may send signals to those functions to serve its purposes, but the functions themselves are merely an organic/chemical mechanism of your body. The subconscious mind as I intend here sits above and controls those functions.

Nor does the subconscious mind in this model simply serve as a storehouse for forgotten memories or traumatic experiences, although it could, if you let it. An upstairs room in your house might collect the stuff which seemed too good to throw away, but not important enough to use. Similarly, the subconscious mind could collect the cruff of your experiences if you let it. Or, just like that junk room, you could clean it up, sweep out the cobwebs, and put it to good use. But then you might discover that it is your favorite room in the house. Much of this chapter will deal with what you might then use that room for.

As with many things in life, satisfaction comes from placing things in the proper balance. Men are accused of using predominately their conscious minds, and shutting off their subconscious, or, thinking instead of feeling. This may be true to some extent, and it is important to balance both by accessing the vast reservoir of energy which your subconscious can provide you. Women, if they have managed to get this far in the book without throwing it against the wall, are now rejoicing.

Hold on, ladies. The flip side of this balancing act is that women, who rely heavily on their subconscious minds, should also be open to becoming more logical and objective, instead of crying at every commercial of fly-caked starving children which comes your way. For every step of "getting in touch with your feelings" that you expect a man to make, be just as willing to get "out of touch with your feelings" yourself. Viewed this way, it is probably best just to let him be himself. Better yet, ladies, keep trying to change him, because I know you can't resist making the effort, but just accept it as a good thing when he doesn't. You wouldn't like him very much anymore if he did, anyway.

The plot now thickens. Fans of Dr. Paul will note that I am about to blend two of his axes together. For purposes of understanding self-esteem, he is correct to keep them separate, but for my purposes here it makes sense to combine them. Both models work, but for different purposes.

Popular culture would lead you to believe that left-brain conscious stuff is more male, while right-brain subconscious stuff is more female. If you view the conscious/subconscious split from the perspective of a woman, this may be true. In this case, a feminist assigns all of the conscious stuff to guys, and blames them, and conscious thinking, for the evils of the world. Why? Because this assertion absolves them from any responsibility for problems. But, given an objective analysis vis-a-vis our nation, of course, our problems can be shown to stem more from feeling than from thinking. Or, at least from manipulating feelings in others to incite them to act in destructive ways. And yet feeling, we are led to believe, stems more from the subconscious rather than the conscious. An outside observer might then reason that our world has too little male influence, rather than too much.

While I agree with the above analysis, I think that the way that these different portions of the mind interact to solve problems is different from a simple male-female assignment. I think it is more fair to say that the subconscious mind is more primitive, yet unimaginably powerful, while the conscious mind is more modern, but more limited in processing power. Men have a male subconscious and a male conscious mind, while women have a female subconscious and a female conscious mind. I think that the male and female subconscious minds are similar in function, but different in purpose. On the other hand, I think that the conscious minds of either gender are probably more similar in operation than either are to their respective subconscious minds.

We will return to some of the philosophical implications of these distinctions in a moment, but for now I want to return to the topic of creativity. The interaction between these two minds, the subconscious and conscious, of either gender, determines how effective we are at solving problems, or creating new ideas or simply enjoying our lives. When I asked you to do some of those exercises above, I was asking you to probe the relationship between your conscious and subconscious mind. The more difficult you found the exercises, the more you have allowed others to program that relationship for you. And in so doing you have made yourself more vulnerable to exploitation, and less creative, and ultimately, less fulfilled.

Now, the next thing to understand is that all creative processes, such as figuring out how to automate or create something, is more of an art than a science. For example, we know what electrical parts do what, or how software works, or how a backhoe works, and so on. This stuff you learn in school. All that math and science which you must learn is merely a tool, but you must know how that tool operates.

Equally important, then, is reflection. You must take time to think about a problem, and that thinking must be done correctly. Creative types will understand immediately what I mean when I talk about what I call "brain bubbles." I will describe these in more detail in a moment, but understand that your brain bubbles, or your creative flow, must be jealously guarded.

Also note that you cannot be creative on a 9 to 5 schedule. Creativity happens when it is ready, not when you wish for it to happen. There is a reason for this which I will describe shortly. Importantly, your motivation must be more important than just mere money. I am certainly not opposed to making money, but you must understand that the creative side of yourself is absolutely cash-illiterate. Your creativity comes up with neat ideas for the sheer joy of creation and creation of value, of pulling up wonderful things from the primitive elements, air, water, earth and fire.

Of course, if your creativity *is* motivated by pure profit motive, then some of the ideas you come up with are likely to be destructive. This is a distinct concept from the joy which comes from creating value. If you see only the dollar signs when you think, then try to focus for a while on the concepts of stuff, push, time, energy and quality of life which I mentioned a few chapters back. Mix in the concept of free trade and soon your motives will become purified. Only then will you truly profit, as opposed to imagining how to extract unearned value. Your subconscious mind will help you in whatever value system you trained it, so take the time to think about the positive values in life.

So, what is a "brain bubble"? Philosophically, they are the fertile soil from which ideas spring. Some call this "flow". No matter what you call this state, it is an alteration of your consciousness, a taking of your conscious mind out of gear so that ideas can bubble around. To start a bubble session, treat yourself to some creature comforts. Dr. Paul would call this "mothering yourself." The idea here is that you want your subconscious mind to shut down operation of its default survival mode. In survival mode, the caveman in you tries to take care of you by making sure that basic survival needs, such as food, water, air and shelter, are met.

If you've ever wondered why the stereotypical computer geek, as seen on TV, is always surrounded by a pile of snacks, this is it. Others drink a beer or two, some put on a favorite shirt or jacket. Chicks enjoy sipping a glass of wine or slipping into a warm bubble bath (and I enjoy watching them, but that takes me back into caveman mode somehow). A crackling fire or soothing music works for others. Some smoke cigarettes, cigars, or pot. My personal favorite method is to take a nap. The common theme of all of these methods is that it is something which tells your subconscious mind that you are safe. Otherwise, for example, why would you be napping? Thus, your subconscious mind knows it is OK to get to work on problem-solving about your automation task or drain-field problem or financial dilemma or whatever.

Next, while you are in this semi-hypnotic relaxed state, think positive thoughts about your problem. These thoughts have to be in a form which is conducive to a solution. Here are some examples which are not good:

☐ "I want to solve world hunger." Too broad, and arguably, it is solved already just by not worrying about it. Also, just a want.
☐ "I want to make ten thousand widgets without hiring any monkeys." Again, a want, but also includes an artificial constraint. Not hiring monkeys is a noble purpose, but may actually get in the way of reaching your goals.

Why are wants bad? Well, they are distinct from needs, for one thing. You can argue that a want is already satisfied, since you are already wanting that thing. Mission accomplished. Consider the following, which is a recent favorite of mine:

☐ "I want to referee a bearskin tickle fight between Sarah Palin and Michele Bachmann." But, I already have that want. "No more to be done," says Mr. Subconscious, who then goes back to caveman mode to consider the possibilities, including possible misspellings. Bastard.

"Need" is hardly any better, and grates on the rational part of your subconscious, which must be pretty strong already if you are still reading this book. Plus, if you have read "Atlas Shrugged" as I suggested, and enjoyed it, you will be irritated by this word at a deep level.

Negativity also sucks:

☐ "If I don't close this sale I will lose my house." Oops, survival mode just kicked back in. Grab another beer or reach for the lighter and try again.

So, I have found that it is better to state the problem in positive tones:

☐ "Before the end of the summer I will make a widget which saves me the trouble of hiring a monkey to do that job."

Notice how much stronger that is. "I will". And by a specific time, otherwise, "I will" sounds a lot like "I want" if you give it long enough. And this time getting rid of the monkey removes the negativity, since you can now focus on the savings. You have made the monkey removal portion mean something good for you.

You can also leave it a little open-ended to let your subconscious mind fill in the blanks:

☐ "To reach at least one hundred thousand qualified customers who will benefit most from using it, I am going to market my widget by ..." Notice the specific goal, and what you need to do, which is to market it. The open-endedness, if used consistently, establishes a pattern which signals your subconscious mind that it is time for it to now carry the load.

Also note that you get rid of all the negative strategies, such as selling it to little old ladies who don't need one. Instead you are focusing on providing value. This helps your subconscious mind design your next widget as value-based, rather than as trickery-based.

Remember at this stage you are not trying to struggle out an answer. Unless you are truly fortunate, or your problem is insanely simple, a solution simply will not pop out the first time. Instead, you are just letting the problem statement simmer a while. You need to stay in state for a while, refreshing your problem statement from time to time. It is not necessary, or desirable, to chant the problem statement like a mantra. This is like the boss looking over your shoulder asking "Are you done yet? Are you done yet? Are you done yet?" Not good. Instead, enjoy drifting around a little. You might even wander around the house, or out into the yard and look at the trees or some bugs.

The neighbors will think you just became autistic. You may ignore or say stupid things to people around you. I sometimes poke First Wife like a plushy just to see how things move around. Or make up little songs. Cats are great for this stage, their purring seems to be just the right amount of sooth. Maybe that's why evil geniuses on movies always have one around. It could also explain why I, in general, don't like dogs, which are only marginally more useful than some people I've met.

You could, theoretically, maintain one of these states for days. It is at these times that brilliant people are rumored to go out into the cold without a coat, or eat and not remember having done so. I myself have eaten meals and then asked First Wife when dinner will be ready.

On the other hand, a momentary interruption can pop a brain bubble, which is a shame since it takes an hour or two to get one rolling. Usually, questions are all it takes. For example, "Hey, do you have that report ready?" You have to then re-engage the conscious mind, play back the sounds you just heard, or ask for a repeat, and then process the question, and then come up with an answer. All of this pulls you out of the flow state.

With practice, you will learn which portions of your mind does which kind of work. Then, you can selectively inflate a brain bubble in one portion, while the rest does stuff which seems semi-normal in their limited range of action. This kind of sounds like a "high functioning autistic."

When I was doing range shooting in the Marine Corps, I dropped into a state which was almost machine-like. Without thinking, the process is the same for each round:

Body alignment, firm grip with the rifle lying in the frame you have become. Breathe in then halfway out and pause, sight alignment, and squeeeeeezzzzzzz the trigger until the hammerfall surprises you. Then feel the gentle press of the stock as it kicks your shoulder while the bullet leaves the barrel at over twice the speed of sound.

The thought of missing or my score or anything else just didn't matter beyond that one round in the chamber, which I visualized in slow motion drilling a hole right through the target. The entire sequence slowed down in time. I think this was because my subconscious mind shut down other functions, and what was left was essentially over-clocked, so everything important seemed slower and easier to control.

I could see a target come up in slow motion and moments after it came to rest my round was on the way. My mind intersected the motion of the target with my trigger squeeze. The squeeze itself seemed to take a perceptible amount of time but which became a single smooth pull after thousands of rounds. The Marine coaches taught me to remember the last sight picture just before the rifle bucked, and almost without fail I could nail it exactly. "Six inches at six o'clock" I would say to the scorekeeper/spotter behind or beside.

The spotter beside you, just as skilled as you are, saw your entire body in proper alignment relative to the target. He watched your hands and rifle out of his peripheral vision while his eyes saw through the target. "Firm grip, not too hard" or "focus on the front sight tip" he might coach, over and over, to a novice. Until the novice heard these words in his own head, incorporated them into his subconscious programming, and became an expert.

On humid North Carolina mornings, as the bullet left the barrel, the spotter, particularly if using a scope, could see its vapor trail cross the five hundred yards from you through the target. And, from experience he knew also where it had penetrated by extrapolating the part of the vapor trail he could see before it disappeared into the vanilla background surrounding the blackness at the center. All this was calculated in his head before the bang from the muzzle had time to get through the slight delays he had learned to install in his own subconscious mind. These carefully programmed delays prevented a flinch which would cause him to miss the show. In the heat of a desert, the mirage wavers slightly as the wake of the bullet further roils the already roiling air. The effect is the same.

Others watching from the side, or down in the target butts, could see the little puffs of dirt in the berm behind the target. These observers could come to the same conclusion as to the accuracy of the hit. Even this provided valuable experience to know what the misses looked like, and where the shooter might be if the target was you. When the target came back up marked accordingly, it wasn't a big deal. It simply "was", for all of us. For the combat shooting courses, the process and principles were the same. But for those courses the ranges were closer, your body was moving and the clock rate was faster.

Recall that in the Marine Corps in that day air control was performed with grease pencils, maps, clipboards and voices on the radio. No radars, no data-links, no computers and not even very good radios. Each detail had to be juggled in your head using a technique known as "situational awareness." In my air control specialty class at Twenty-Nine Palms, I finished second out of nine highly intelligent and, on demand, supremely calm Marine officers. Number one, who was number one by a wide margin, now occupies the highest rank in this specialty in the Pacific. And he is just as deadly with a rifle.

I was jokingly referred to as "Iceman" by one of the instructors, spoofing the obvious "Top Gun" reference. This particular instructor probably tagged at least one student in each class with this name to make a point. I seriously doubt that I was much more "iceish" than the rest. The instructors would deliberately stress the students by changing everything, including introducing quirks which were physically impossible. Planes at one side of a bombing range were suddenly fifty miles away, to mimic the delays in reporting times and genuine confusion which pilots experience when getting shot at. You couldn't take everything they said to you at face value. You had to insert reasonable fuzziness to make everything make sense.

Under stress, my subconscious mind would take over and drop my voice into an almost monotonic calm which sails through the radio undistorted. Time expanded, and I could "see" the picture which the instructors were painting inside my head. These experts were skilled at using those brushes to teach fresh second lieutenants how to think and imagine what they were hearing in their crackling headsets. Garbled voices in your ear can be untangled from the static and pops you learn to ignore until the meaning in those voices comes through as if the speaker was sitting beside you. Today I can still pull all of the parts of a favorite song on a supermarket speaker out and enjoy them while the people around me jabber and the refrigerator fans whirr.

Two years of training later, in Desert Storm, while in state I could see a three-dimensional map with fuzzy probability clouds around every plane or flight group under our control. In my mind they flew inside tinted rectangular cylinders curving through the sky representing routes to be taken. Ground units were blocks of symbology which could be zoomed at will into little pictures of tanks and artillery. When picking ordinance I could run through all the possible combinations of this stuff hitting those things like little movies in fast-forward. I had experienced all of these combinations in the field during training and saw a lot of that stuff at a place which didn't officially exist.

Here, the physics mattered. Without the probability clouds learned by experience at Twenty-Nine Palms, the confusion would have been overwhelming. And so, seeing which little vector in my head could get there first and at the least risk of getting shot down, the Iraqi artillery took the napalm. This was the fastest way to get it turned off as I watched the curved cone coming out of it and smacking down on Marines in the field. Just after my Tactical Air Director relayed my order I imagined the little vector turning toward the artillery. In my mind the other little vectors turned and grew to get out of the way. Or to get into position to watch the drop and report the results.

Under physical stress the same things happen. At Quantico and Parris Island and Pendleton they shot live machine guns overhead while you crawled around in muck and barbed wire. As long as you didn't stand up, or jump up and down, it was probably safe, but still interesting to experience. The bullets from the machine guns almost seemed like individual things which could be heard snicking overhead. At any distance from the gun their muzzle blasts were now only pahs afterward, the pahs and the moving snick echoing through the trees or off the hills. Hear enough snicks and pahs, and you can learn where the machine gun is. As long as you don't think about one of those snicks hitting you. Which is less likely if you pay attention to the snicks and pahs. Or if you pay attention to the little dirt puffs (which, up close, don't look anything at all like what you see shooting up from the ground in movies). Recognize these, then slow down time and do something about it.

Later, at Virginia Tech, while I was out on bail, some dork let his big dog charge at the heavily pregnant First Wife. That imaginary doggie-eye thing worked. Dork, offended by our lack of fear and intimidation of his "baby", then handed the dog by its collar to his girlie. To prove his mettle to her, he threw down against this guy two-thirds his size who had simply moved to protect his wife and child from his inconsideration.

Time slowed to a crawl, my breathing seemed to slow and get deeper. In slow motion I handed First Wife my axe-handle walking stick for her last line of defense. For a moment I stood there watching the size and tempo of his pace and the swing of his arms as he oozed toward me. He then threw his leash (had it been on the dog, where it belonged, none of this would have happened), his only weapon, to the side as his display of macho to her. Seeing this, I began moving before it drifted to the ground, no longer needing to keep my distance, and cleared to engage.

As I closed the gap, head forward, vectoring slightly to the left of where he was headed, I could see where both of my feet would land relative to his at that last step. I saw where his right wrist would be at that moment, how much torque would be needed. I saw which bones would break first when he hit the ground, how the ligaments would tear in the followup if he was smart and gave in. And how far I would have to step to the side to put my knee through his throat if he was stupid. And whether he had any idea about this sequence which was about to play out while his girlie screamed at him to stop in slow motion. I saw her head twirling, hair defying gravity as she struggled against the jello dog which now just wanted to get back home. When dork reached the same conclusion and stopped advancing, I stopped also. Apparently the doggie-eye thing works sometimes on people, too.

Depending on what service you want it to provide, you can train your subconscious mind to help you in any number of ways. It will summon just about any part of your brain that you need for what you value. Understanding your own personal quality of life value matrix really comes in handy here. It would be more fair to say, however, that you aren't really training it. I think the subconscious mind is much too independent for that. It has to be, since it pretty much took care of ancient versions of you when those prototypes didn't know jack about anything. Instead, you are just informing it what services would be great for both of these layers of you. Assuming that it agrees that you do know a few things and it hasn't had to snatch you away from too much stupidity.

If your subconscious mind has confidence that, indeed, you do know enough to be trusted, then it will play ball. It will then use whatever parts of your brain it chooses to assign to the task at hand. If it doesn't have confidence in you, you are going to have to do a lot of things the hard way, thinking about each of them on the fly. You experience this in operation each time you drive a car. Or run off at the mouth with the same stories at the Christmas party each year.

For some reason, for me, writing books or doing other specific creative activity uses the same part which says "don't keep tweaking the nibbly bits on that soft thing sitting over there." And yet, I can run a tractor just fine during these times, provided there aren't some nibbly bits bobbing by. This is why I try to avoid working in an office as much as possible. Office life around soft things with nibbly bits means that I have to keep from getting in state too deeply to lose that part, which keeps me from operating at peak efficiency.

On the other hand, if I need to think about how to build a char pile to amend the soil, I pretty much can't be driving the tractor then. It takes some experimentation to find out what works best for you for whatever creative work you want to do. However, getting into the flow state isn't always easy. If your primitive needs aren't being satisfied, or some other obstacle arises for your attention, you won't be able to make that brain bubble. Unresolved issues in your life which threaten to later intervene during the bubble will keep it from forming. So, you find yourself having to deal with some meaningless thing now even if it doesn't need attention yet. I will discuss more of this in a moment.

Once your subconscious mind has been armed with all of the education and experience you need, and primed with the problem statement, it is time to let it do its work. If you have never worked this way before it is hard to tell whether anything is getting done at all. You may need several primings while in state to let things get started. At this point you may be able to drop out of state and back into the real world. Or, you may need to stay there a bit longer while your subconscious mind continues communicating with you about the problem. Later, when the subconscious mind needs to deliver the answer it might tell you to get back in state. Or, if it faces an obstacle which it needs your help with, it might need you to get back in state, or it might simply watch as you fill in some missing detail.

While in a flow state, a back and forth communication between your subconscious and conscious mind occurs, with the subconscious mostly driving the show. Perhaps you, in sort of a semi-dream, imagine all the pieces of a transmission coming apart. And then reassembling, with the part in trouble predominating. Or, you feel compelled to get up and read something, or go somewhere, or do something. To an outside observer, this can seem like insanity:

"How can Bob sit there and read / shoot hoops / watch the game / play pool / take me to dinner / waste time on the internet / etc. when we are about to lose the house?" your spouse might wonder. Over time, she will learn better, but if not, consider trading up.

Maybe that arc of the ball, or the movement of a player, or a wall hanging at that restaurant, or a news article you read about a customer of a stock you are following contains a vital detail which your subconscious mind needs to complete its task. Or to work on an unrelated problem which you haven't even articulated yet, or recognized as a threat.

Others may at this point hope to use some of your "wasted time" to do something useful:

"While you are just sitting there, why don't you take out the trash?"

"Can you put down the cue and come change this light bulb?"

When this happens, and interrupts, or threatens to interrupt, a crucial data- or experience-gathering mission your subconscious mind has sent you on, you will know. How? It will tell you. Clearly, I speak as if the subconscious mind is a separate entity, just for convenience of discussion. Of course, it is still you.

So how can you tell when the subconscious mind has a need which has been unaddressed, or has a solution to a problem, or has recognized a threat which you haven't yet?

Simple. It puts a message in the mailbox which God created for this purpose. So what is this mailbox?

Your emotions. This makes sense from an evolutionary point of view. If a primitive version of you were out picking berries and enjoying the day, you felt good. If you saw a flash of stripes in the bushes, your subconscious mind would recognize this as a tiger. And then give you a burst of fear to get your attention long before your mind could decide this was a bad thing. Otherwise, you might stand there and wonder whether the little kitty was endangered.

The same thing happens today when you see a snake, perhaps. Or flashing blue lights on the highway. Notice how many people stomp the brakes, including you or I, when we see blue flashing lights, even if the police car is in no way likely to pull you over. Perhaps it is on the other side of a divided highway, and has already pulled someone else over, for example. Yet, that emotional reaction, prompted by at least a little twinge of fear, is your subconscious mind telling you that there is a situation ahead which can only have negative consequences for you.

Now immediately afterward, especially if we weren't speeding in the first place, we might tell ourselves that we did this because we were good citizens. We might rationalize that we wanted to slow down so as not to endanger the officer. Or, that we were slowing down because we knew that all the other idiots would hit their brakes, just as the idiots behind us are thinking about us. Even these justifications validate the subconscious decision to apply the brakes, whether to avoid a ticket, getting tasered, striking the officer or rear-ending the car in front. Regardless, that little flash of "oh-crap" jumps in to jolt you awake, even if your foot has already done the work on the pedal.

When you are sitting on the couch zoning out, and wifey asks you to take out the trash since you are "just sitting there," you feel some aggravation if your subconscious mind has you working on something. Or, you might feel a sense of cooperation if your subconscious isn't too busy to interrupt.

On the other hand, if you have learned from experience that taking out the trash is just the first step in a long series of dramas about to unfold, then you might feel aggravation in either case. Even so, just as the first aggravation was merely your subconscious trying to keep you on track to help it solve a problem, the second aggravation was warning you of approaching drama danger. The first kind feels like a reward frustrated, more like a mild anger, while the second feels like the flashing blue lights, more of a trapped animal. Learn to distinguish between these subtle emotions, and you will become much more skilled at interpreting the messages your subconscious is placing in your mailbox.

Women might delight at hearing this directed at their men, as it sounds a lot like that "getting in touch with your emotions" crap which they enjoy babbling about as a way of running you down. But this isn't the boobly-hoobly drama kind of getting in touch, far from it. This is the kind of getting in touch which a barbarian king might use. If the porridge your scantily-clad servant girl brings you in the morning doesn't smell right, that little jolt your emotions give you when you lift the spoon probably means something.

It is important to note that articulation of the subconscious message lags behind the subconscious understanding of a situation. You jolt when you see the flashing blue lights, and only later rationalize your reaction. Similarly your subconscious will alert you to a problem, or a solution it has found for you, long before you will be able to articulate what exactly is going on. In some cases, you have to reinflate a brain bubble to find out the details. In other cases, you have to do some things which suddenly feel good to do and find that an obstacle you had before suddenly vanished and now it all seems clear.

This is where the distinction between the male subconscious and the female subconscious comes in. Seeing the tiger, the primitive male subconscious will be more likely to grab a weapon and go into fight mode. But the primitive female subconscious will be more likely to grab the kids and get away. Why the distinction? Well, fighting entails a certain amount of risk of injury which isn't present when running away. But, running away also risks being chased and pounced from behind. However, for the little children to survive it is more important that the mother survive too, as well as surviving injury. A male can suffer an injury, and as long as it doesn't become septic, probably make it through OK. At least if he wins, he has some tiger meat to munch on for a while until he heals up.

Even better, of course, is if they team up. The female grabs the kids and runs, while the male fights off, or at least intimidates, the threat. In this case, even if the male gets eaten, the female and the kids suffer zero injury. At least this time. And, if the male is injured, his females can nurse him back to health for the next time. If he doesn't suffer a scratch but comes home dragging a tiger carcass, then turn on the Barry White music, as it is time for this proven-effective team to make some more kids.

This does not mean that a male won't decide to run, and a female won't decide to fight. No, what I mean by the above analysis is that the male is more biased to fight, and the female is more biased to run with the kids. This is also why the males were more likely to go on hunting parties, while the females were more likely to gather stuff around home while the kids toddled around her. Every now and then some pencil-necked anthropologist pipes up that some tribe or another did it the other way around, but you can count the number of these who thrived through to today on, well, no hands. And if society is working that way now it is only because we are running on the momentum of progress which resulted from the most recent cast-off of a thousand-plus-year reign of stupidity.

Right now, deep inside you, the reader, males and females both, are charmed by the tiger story, even if only for a briefest instant. If you are offended by this sexist claim, it is only after your self-damaged subconscious has awkwardly tried to overlay offense onto what it wants to naturally enjoy. If offended, it is only because you have damaged what comes naturally to you by accepting programming shoved at you by the collective. They have provided the temptation, or the stick if you choose to not conform, but you have made the choice.

Either the male or the female subconscious can be trained to perform any task. But, like the extra room upstairs, different architecture leads to different efficient use. Imagine that in House A the extra room has an attached bath, while in House B the extra room has a really big closet. Same square footage in either case, but different finish.

House A is better equipped to provide a mother-in-law suite, while House B is better for housing your collection of fan trinkets. You could, for example, put a slops bucket in the closet of the spare room in House B and just keep the window open. And, you could stack stuff on the sink or on the back of the toilet in House A. Either can be pressed into either service, but each is more efficient at specific usage.

Similarly, the female subconscious is more adept at nurturing small children, while the male subconscious is more adept at teaching skills required by adults. You can see this if you think of the normal classical reaction to a stubbed toe: Mommy runs to kiss the boo-boo, while Dad says "well, that's what you get for stupid. Don't do that again."

Which one is best? Both are. The kid needs the boo-boo smooched to know that he is loved and will have any injury seen to, but he also needs to learn what things are stupid so as to not repeat them. The first is best for his short-term well-being, the latter is best for the long-term. Both are important. And each behavior is best suited for the respective genders and comes naturally to each.

If, however, the parents listen to the collective and role-swap, it just seems weird. If Dad kisses the boo-boo and Mom says stop it, at a gut level we know that this is stilted. The kid, responding to countless generations of successful parenting programmed into his genetic makeup, thinks they have both lost their minds. And so turns elsewhere for guidance about life's issues, just as the collective needs him to do in order to suit him for their purpose, and not his.

Even worse, if the collective has decreed that neither parent chide him for being stupid, he never learns about stupid and keeps doing things which get him smooched. Both parents are kissing boo-boos, but Mom's psychological architecture is better suited for this use. Dad, squelched from his normal role, either stays silent or awkwardly tries to smooch the boo-boo. But, since Mom is much better equipped to nurture, she gets all the boo-boo business. Dad soon becomes seen, by kid and Mom alike, as a superfluous wart who just brings stuff home. If Mom also has a job, then why do they need him at all?

Add this up over a few generations, and you have a real problem on your hands. Needy kids become needy adults, and vote for more and more of the stuff which made them needy in the first place, because now it is too late to tell them "don't be an idiot." Because they don't know any better, they raise their own kids this way, and so on. At some point, those needlings outnumber the rest of us, and some of them get positions of real power. Ouch. Whatever shall we do? Someone clever should write a book about how to resolve this problem.

For the primitive, Dad's "don't be an idiot", combined with whatever bitch slap he thought appropriate for the occasion, served a purpose. Enough of these chidings, combined with the knowledge of what skills and response worked and what didn't, children learned to grab the kids and run, or fight, as appropriate, and to do so effectively. What you wind up with is a bunch of independent family units. To someone who wants to steal or otherwise take value they haven't earned, this could be a bad thing.

To the subconscious mind of a primitive me, a thief looks just like a furless, upright tiger. Either prompts me to turn to the girls and say "Ladies, get the kids in. And dust off that Barry White album, I'll be there in a minute." And then turn down the dial on that perception clock. The only distinction in these situations is whether or not you decide to eat the carcass.

To a cheater, this situation is intolerable. A cheater may prevail a time or two, but eventually they encounter someone more skilled, or just simply make a fatal mistake. Self-reliant individualists, on the other hand, have no need for the conflict which leads to very many fights, and thus are exposed to hardly any more risk than is encountered from the random tiger. Even the tigers learn to keep their distance, so all is well. Individualism weeds out cheaters through natural selection.

Sure, some cheaters may arise who are particularly skilled at stealing or fighting, and might even band together to make raiding parties. But, absent any external preventative authority, eventually the individualists will get enough of this nonsense, get together, and track them all down. Then go home and bust out the Barry White.

Notice I said "absent any external preventative authority." This part is key. A clever cheater, to be successful, has to deal with all those highly tuned subconscious minds out there, and avoid hitting their tripwires. A clever cheater has to not look so threatening as to be detected, by either gender, as an upright furless tiger. The resulting fight from the males, or flight by the females, defeats his purpose.

Of the two responses, the male's fight is the greater threat. He can still raid the crops if the female runs, of course. Better if he can steal from her basket, though, or get her to give him the basket willingly, but this would trigger a fight with the male.

The optimum plan would be to come up with some way to get the males to behave as if they were females. Then everyone would give him, and his offspring, stuff for free. This will take time to evolve in them, however, so he has to take baby steps. His approach must be gentle, and non-threatening. This allows him to slip below the male radar. As a cheater, he has no willingness to trade value for value. He thus has no appeal which will work with the male, and so he must subvert the female against her male. To appeal to the female nurturer, he must either appear weak or damaged, or claim to represent those who are.

He must appeal to the female's nurturing spirit without triggering a threat-of-mating response in the male. A soft, weak and genderless appearance, perhaps combined with a proclaimed vow of chasteness and virtue, if not outright chastity, helps a lot with hitting that tripwire. These vows don't have to be real, by the way, they just have to sound real.

Now it is time to trigger the female's subconscious. Avoiding the flight response, he triggers her boo-boo smooching, and convinces her to give a little of her excess to the weak. He reinforces her behavior by praising her compliance. He avoids mention of the male subconscious responses at this point. Over time, he encourages the female compliance with a combination of boo-boos and praise. At just below the level at which the male might notice, he then has to modify his approach to the female slightly.

He builds on the female compliance by not only praising her, but also by presenting her female subconscious programming as one of virtue, and implies that the male subconscious is one of violence and vice. This starts the split between the genders which the cheater requires to implement his plan. Thousands of generations of family raising have taught the females to be social creatures, a skill necessary for keeping a hut full of kids from beating each other senseless. So, he provides opportunities for as many females as possible to gather to celebrate their charitable virtues as a group. They then reinforce each other's behavior, at first. Some males will accompany their females to keep them safe, while others will stay at the hut with other stuff to do. The few males who attend pass off the congregating as a harmless outlet for her, but still see no real threat.

Outside a moderating influence, females are notoriously competitive and wily. For the cheater, this is a good thing as, congregating together, they then begin to compete as to who is the best at charity. Left unchecked, the males might soon put a stop to this nonsense as it is beginning to have a noticeable impact on their inventory. The cheater knows he can do nothing about males from what he might call the zeroth generation. But he, and his offspring, have time on their side. The cheater becomes cheaters, and begin to band together to mold the culture in their favor. The male individualists are usually too busy watching for tigers to notice the threat which grows behind them.

The next generation, however, is easier. The females, still not recognizing the danger, then learn from the collective to teach their children the distinction between female virtue and male violence and vice. The girls delight in a congregation which exclusively celebrates their nature. The boys, who might become men who would oppose these changes in their culture, at first learn to accept this stain upon their natures to please Mommy, and then accept, or reject, this philosophy as men.

Those young men who reject this philosophy, and embrace their maleness, are of no consequence, as there is always another generation. The sons of those who accept this philosophy have little chance to reject it later, their own fathers proponents themselves. Soon, there are sufficient females entrenched in the philosophy. These are joined by sufficient males who are either entrenched or merely compliant. Together, they begin to insist, by force of law, that charity, particularly value taken from others, become the rule of the day. The collective begins to win as maleness itself, the only possible check on this philosophy, is increasingly defined as evil and unlawful.

Throughout this process it is necessary to keep the individualist males off guard. So, all authority in the congregation is to remain in the hands of entrenched males, at least at first, to avoid the appearance of a female's collective which has run out of control. The cheater might even toss in a few platitudes about male authority. By choosing for this purpose males who emulate and proclaim the soft chasteness of the original cheater, the mating tripwire is still avoided. Much later, once control is complete, these positions of authority can be handed over to women who have proved their compliance by blatantly denouncing maleness.

The very softness of this approach allows the subconscious programming of both the males and the females to be turned to the purpose of the collective. Each step is so incrementally nice and non-threatening that violent response seems so unreasonable. Over time, violence becomes prohibited for any purpose, no matter how justified, as does maleness itself, the only quarter from which effective resistance, against this cleverly soft tiger, might come.

If you are deeply offended by this discussion, as I have said many times before, put down this book now and read no further. If, however, you were disturbed by the exercises at the start of this chapter, but feel at least a tingle of pleasure, even guilty pleasure, at what you have read, there is hope for you, no matter how much you were disturbed. Each of those exercises was meant to challenge the female subconscious, and to illustrate the depth to which modern society has suppressed maleness.

But you can change the programming you have accepted from others. As you sip your beer or your wine, or reach for the lighter, or go on your walk, ask your subconscious mind one of the following questions, as appropriate.

If a woman, ask, "How can I express my female power of nurturing, soothing, and encouragement to best benefit my family, without having my power manipulated to harm my family by feeling pity for each fly-bitten sack of crap who crosses my path?" Or a theme to that effect as best for you, as you slip beneath the warm bubbles.

If a man, ask, "How can I restore my male power of command, authority, skill and knowledge to best protect and provide for my family, and avoid my power being diluted by the collective?"

Try doing that each day for a week. At the end of that week, you will find that your outlook on life will probably have improved significantly. As such, you will also find it much easier to get in the creative flow state, as your subconscious mind will be under less stress trying to compensate for a world-view for which it is ill-suited.

Over time, you will find yourself avoiding activities which you once scheduled around. People who you merely tolerated before will become more detestable or more likeable. You will perceive them differently to the extent that they had previously attempted to force the values of the collective on you. Or alternatively, to the extent that they had resisted your attempts at projecting collective values on them, respectively.

You will find yourself having interests which you hadn't noticed before, but which seem more satisfying, somehow. Your spouse will find you more attractive, and vice-versa. If not, consider trading up, as life is too short to spend around someone who is constantly trying to mold you into someone you are not. Your children will have more respect for you, although they may not admit it.

All of these things will snowball into a better self-image, which places you closer to that internal creature-comfort state which helps you inflate your brain bubbles. So armed, you can then get to some serious work to start solving life's problems for yourself. To do so, you have to learn the next level of communicating with your subconscious.

To present this topic, I first want to give an example about how to solve a problem which shows how the conscious and subconscious minds interact. I will use the example of a physics problem first. But, I also substitute small engine repair or crop failure at each step to show how this coordinated problem-solving approach is general to a large class of problems in many areas of endeavor.

When first presented with a problem, before the conscious mind has a chance to digest the information, the subconscious mind begins analyzing the details. It will immediately give you some feedback about whether you have the tools necessary to get the job done.

Perhaps when the teacher describes a physics problem, or the engine fails to start, or you see a plant or two not doing well here or there, you feel a sense of confidence. Or, you might feel ill-ease, depending on whether you know how to solve the problem. Or have the resources necessary, or have sufficient confidence in your own abilities to solve problems in general. If you lack fertilizer, for example, but haven't yet consciously decided what kind or confirmed this lack with your stock of supplies, you might feel an urge to go to town.

At this point, you haven't solved the problem, but you get a sense of whether or not you can. If your self-confidence is lacking, this can fool you into thinking you lack the resources to solve it, when in fact you do. If you look around at a lot of life's issues, and constantly feel under fire, then perhaps it is a self-esteem thing which can be fixed separately. The best way to fix self-confidence problems, in my opinion, is to tackle head-on things you think are beyond you and commit to learning from the effort and forget for a moment about the outcome. Over time, this will train your subconscious to distinguish from the things you truly can't do, and those which are just hard or unfamiliar. Having done this a few times, you will probably see a dramatic improvement in your overall self-confidence, which will make it easier for you to get in state and stay there, and so on. The benefits multiply almost endlessly.

OK, so back to our hypothetical problem. At this point, the subconscious mind has recognized the general nature of the problem, and, if familiar with the overall format, has delivered to the conscious mind some idea about how to proceed. At this point the conscious mind can either draw a diagram of the problem, or visualize an exploded diagram of the affected areas of the engine, or imagine a set of possible crop-related issues. Effectively, the conscious mind confirms, "yes, this is the problem I wish to solve." If the conscious mind does not recognize that as the problem to be solved, it should really reconsider, as a well-trained subconscious mind usually deserves to be listened to.

Armed with that mandate, the subconscious springs back into action. The subconscious mind of a physics student will recall various formulae which may be relevant to the problem, while the engine repairman may be presented with a recollection of a repair procedure. The farmer might recall a chain of differential diagnoses to enable him to check for various symptoms in his plants and the conditions of the soil.

The conscious mind then takes over again. The physics student writes down the equations which he has recalled, and manipulates these equations to an end result, and then substitutes the values given to attain an answer. The repairman might start taking parts of the engine off as he drills down to what he thinks might be the problem. Or the farmer looks for insects or checks the pH of the soil, etc., to confirm the diagnosis.

But perhaps the equations don't seem to fit the problem, or the repair procedure isn't yielding fruit, or the diagnoses aren't matching. This will be signaled by a small, but growing, feeling of "oops". It is then time to ask the subconscious to try to come up with something else. The best way to try again is to repeat the problem statement, or symptoms of the engine or of the crops, looking for details missed before that might have led the subconscious mind astray. At some point, the answer is found to the problem. The subconscious will then concur with an "ah-ha!" moment, rewarding the individual with a warm feeling of accomplishment.

Notice that nowhere in this process can a problem be solved by collective action. Somewhere, somehow, an individual must rely upon the interaction of his conscious and subconscious minds to analyze the problem, formulate a possible solution, work toward the solution, and recognize completion. Different individuals may solve different sub-problems, but even so, each individual must perform the same basic procedure to get to an answer to his own specific problem. Problem-solving is an intensely individual activity which no group will ever perform. The group can only get in the way, or get out of the way, to varying degrees. How much the group gets in the way will affect the efficiency with which individuals can do their work.

A key point is that creative minds cannot be jump-started. Organizations cannot dictate that "you will solve this problem now." Organizations may be able to dictate "you will turn this wrench now," but that is an entirely different proposition. If the organization is directing that the wrong bolt is to be turned, chances are the organization will never figure this out. It takes the insight of an individual to correct error, which is a subset of the overall concept of problem-solving. The more authoritarian the organization, the better it is at coercing physical performance, or attendance, or parroted opinions. But the worse it is at solving problems.

Of course even physical labor coercion has a limit. Once the worker begins to feel that he is little better than slave labor, his performance will necessarily decline to the point where he merely avoids the lash. But why, if organizations can dictate manual work, can they not dictate intellectual work? An example from the world of manufacturing is helpful here.

Imagine that you are making a car, which is just a collection of a large number of individual components. Each of these must be assembled in a more or less defined order. You can't put the wheels on a car until the axle is in place, for example. Now, you may be able to place the engine and the axles into place with or without the transmission in place. But, depending on the design, one of these options will be the best for the car in question. Get the operations out of order, and you will just have to take parts back off and put them back on again the right way.

Now let's say that the assembly line runs out of transmissions. No matter how many other parts of the car you have available, without the transmission, you don't have a car. You have a bunch of parts which almost looks like a car. Continuing to work beyond the point at which the transmission needs to be installed is pointless. You may provide jobs putting stuff on and taking it back off over and over, but you aren't making any cars this way.

In fact, even starting to build a car without a supply of transmissions is more or less pointless. You can only get so many in the pipeline like that before your assembly line is jammed. In some cases, keeping a part of a car half-assembled can even be damaging. Exposed parts may start corroding or freeze up without lubrication, or mechanical members which can support unusual stresses during the few hours of assembly begin to deform during days of partial assembly.

Many times, a partially assembled item has to simply be taken back apart, inspected, and put back together. And, your data systems probably can't handle the inventory hiccup of parts neither in inventory, nor represented by a finished unit. You would have been better off to not start at all if a key component is missing.

The subconscious mind of a productive, problem-solving individualist is not inclined to such foolishness. If you try to force it to do silly things like that, it is simply going to go on strike, and wander off to do something else. If you insist, it will punish you with negative emotions.

When examining a problem for you, the subconscious mind sees holes in your knowledge, experience or resources long before your conscious mind does. At first, this shortfall gets reported to you as a feeling of ill-ease, possibly resembling a lack of self-confidence. If you are in touch with your subconscious, you will learn to look around and examine all the features of the problem, and the resources you have with which to deal with this problem.

A dentist sometimes can't tell, just by a visual inspection, which tooth is causing you pain. In these cases, she might touch each facet of each tooth with a probe. If this doesn't help, she may switch to a cold stick, or a warm stick until you let her know where the problem is. Similarly, as you mentally touch each feature and resource related to the problem, you will be able to distinguish which areas produce no response. As well as those which cause you emotional discomfort. By doing this inspection, you will identify possible shortcomings which your subconscious has already recognized as standing in the way of success.

Sometimes you aren't able to find all the touchy spots by yourself. Your subconscious mind may be trying to protect you by telling you to stay away from that particular problem, particularly if the problem is in an area completely new to you. In that case, you may not have enough experience in the subject area to even know where to start probing. Or, your subconscious mind might not allow you to probe the sensitive area at all. This situation is much like the patient who shies away from the dentist holding the ice stick. When that patient is saying "oh no you don't, stay away from me with that thing!", he does so knowing that when the right spot is hit it will hurt *a lot*.

In this case, if your own mental inventory bears no fruit, tell someone familiar with the problem domain about the problem. She doesn't even have to have a solution for you, all she needs to do is ask you questions about the problem or your resources. In effect, this helps you by probing areas which your subconscious might shy away from. You will know she are getting close to the raw tooth when you get aggravated with a particular reasonable suggestion with an angry, "NO, that's not it!"

If you can't find the bottleneck this way, you may have a genuine self-confidence issue. In that case, try doing simpler tasks, or working on subsets of the problem which you can perform. This approach builds confidence in your abilities and removes parts from the problem until you can see the gap. For example, if you have an engine problem which you can't figure out and are afraid to solve, and you can't mentally inventory your shortfall, you might take a part off the engine. Perhaps then you will realize you are missing the wrench which your neighbor borrowed, or part of the engine you uncovered just looks wrong.

If you don't go through the process of looking for the weakness in your knowledge, skills or other resources, your subconscious will stay on strike until you find the problem. It will remind you of its status by making you aggravated each time you even think about the problem. In your mind, the problem will linger out there like a tilted picture frame in a museum which is three inches out of reach. Knowing you can't solve it, your motivation to start remains low. Others may complain that you are avoiding the problem, which is true.

If your mental inventory didn't work, and your third-party inventory didn't work, and your self-confidence exercise didn't work, then you need to set the problem aside for a while. At this point, you should have a feeling of wanting to do something seemingly unrelated. Perhaps you feel an urge to watch TV, or grab a book you haven't read in a while, or browse the internet, or go shopping. This is usually your subconscious trying to direct you to identify that resource you need. Follow this feeling, like water flowing downhill.

At some point, the shortfall will occur to you, and then you can work on removing the obstacle. Once you do find the obstacle, the resolution of it will depend on its nature. If the obstacle is skill-based, you might want to practice on a harmless prototype. Maybe try using that tool in a new way on some scrap wood. If the obstacle is knowledge-based, then perhaps you bone up on some area of knowledge around your shortfall. If the obstacle is the lack of some material or tools, go get some.

The key is to listen to what your subconscious mind tells you. Otherwise, problem-solving will be a constant, uphill struggle as you try to bully it into performance. Eventually, it will win and terrorize you into not trying to solve problems any more, as you will have proved yourself to it as insufficient to the task. After all, no one wants to work for some idiot who just harasses them with their problems but is unwilling to listen to the solutions.

I mentioned before that you have to get into the flow state to be able to communicate esoteric problems to your subconscious. Interestingly, when your subconscious comes up with a possible solution, *if the conditions are right, it will put you into a flow state by itself.* Whether or not you are able to accept this flow state depends on your willingness to listen to the signals, or if your creature comforts are currently being satisfied. When this solution bubble hits you, it will feel exciting if the conditions are right for flow. But, you may feel an unreasonable aggravation with some facet of the outside world if there is an obstacle or conflict blocking the flow state.

Everyone is familiar with examples of the former, and usually invoke images of the mad-scientist rushing around without pants. This concept stems from a story about Archimedes, who, while slipping into a public bath, discovered a way to measure the volume of an irregular object by measuring how much water it displaced. He is reported to have shouted "Eureka!", Greek for "I have found it!" and ran home naked. It is for this reason that I encourage ladies to do their thinking in a bubble bath.

The latter is less familiar, but probably more common. Intellectual types have a reputation for lacking social skills. This is probably an unfair assessment, as intellectual people, under normal circumstances, are no less deficient in this area than anyone else. However, if you happen to cross the path of one of them during one of those solution bubble moments, whatever brought you to their desk is just getting in the way of their flow state. They know how precious these are. If they don't let the solution flow at that moment it could be lost forever. So, they react with what little conscious mind is in gear at the moment to chase you away.

Sometimes, creative people will seem downright schizophrenic or dissociative[16]. One day you talk to some artist and they are as nice as you could imagine. The next day, or even next minute you talk to them and they won't give you the time of day, chasing you off as they are trying to not let the bubble escape. I suspect that quite a many creative children and adults are mis-diagnosed by professionals who benefit from having lots of patients, and thus funding. Besides, the collective certainly benefits by labeling the productive and creative as dysfunctional, and thus ensuring they are easily corralled, doesn't it?

Over time, I have learned to be a little nicer about the chase-offs myself. My family is used to my demands for solace, or a raised hand, or a shaking head as some brilliance comes to me. If they don't respond the first time, I insist more strongly. A decade or so earlier, First Wife would recoil in astonishment when I would shoo her away from kissing the top of my head as I wrote. This act pops bubbles as surely as an ice pick in a balloon. Now she just accepts the nibbly-bitting.

Some creative types aren't so blatant as me. The best diesel engine expert I know has about a dozen little five-minute stories he can repeat as he thinks of something. When you ask him about some problem, you can see him go into the zone as he pops one of these stories into playback mode. To keep you from interjecting with questions which would take him out of flow, he then patters out this story as he thinks. An objective observer might conclude that you are having a conversation with him, if somewhat stilted or socially awkward, but no, he is just trying to get you to keep your mouth shut while he thinks. Once he has an answer he stops talking wherever he was at in the story and grabs a wrench.

Be warned: if you want to improve your problem-solving and creative skills, you will begin to behave this way when you are in the zone. The only way to avoid it is to avoid creativity. It is that simple. This does not mean that creative people are stunted. If they wanted to, they could spend all day pretending to care about your knick-knack collection just like all of your other friends pretend to care. Instead of investing precious mental energy into lying to you, they are just honest with you about it as they go about

---

[16] Dissociative identity disorder, DID, is distinct from schizophrenia. Both of them are characterized by some kind of social dysfunction.

solving problems which are more important than your feelings.

You may depend on a creative person, perhaps as their child or their spouse or their parent or their sibling or their boss or employee or investor. If you do, then you need to decide what is more important: your feelings or your future prosperity. Pick one, or they will pick one for you. Even better, figure out how to help them make you successful, instead of spending time, like the monkey collective does, in how to suppress them and extract value from them.

Otherwise, some of them might decide to turn their creative energy into solving *that* problem. Because they can, if they choose to. And unless you decide to become creative yourself, then you won't be able to stop them. But then again, by making that choice you no longer represent a problem to them, do you? Actually, you might still be a problem to be solved, depending on how you express your creative energy, as we shall see in a few pages.

How a creative person responds to a threat to their solution bubble depends on the threat. Recall that a certain level of creature comfort is required for a bubble to form or stay intact. If the office is too noisy, then a "Will you people shut the hell up?" might come wafting over the cubicle walls as coworkers gab about some reality show. Too cold? "Why the hell is it so cold in here?" Or "Why the hell is it so hot in here?" Guess what problem causes "Which jackass took my turkey sub from the fridge?" or "Why am I the only person in this f***** building who can replace the freaking water cooler jug?"

This is why the monkey collective invented human resource departments. By identifying the socially-don't-give-a-crap, it was also able to identify the most productive members of an organization. If you think your organization runs like a well-oiled machine, you have never had a chance to compare it to those populated by the jerks who smoked and drank and cussed. Jerks who, for inspiration, slapped the secretaries on their size twelve rocket booster butts as they put us on the Moon or invented atomic bombs.

Now the sanctity of that butt, disappointingly slimmer, is more important than getting anything done. And so we now have only a slight glaze of productivity. As with my office nibbly issue, the productive can only afford to let little tiny bubbles form so that the rest of their mental capacity can be devoted to avoiding the HR department. And so now space shuttles blow up or cost about a billion times more than they were promised to.

Other issues which can get in the way of creativity fall more into the obstacle variety rather than creature comforts. Here is a partial list of things which can deflate or prevent brain bubbles:

☐ Unrealistic schedules. Creativity happens when it happens. Instead of counting on invention happening to a time-clock, managers should instead look for obstacles to remove.
☐ Intercoms and open-call paging. "Bob, call your wife" keeps the receptionist from having to get up and deliver a message to Bob. Keeping her nails done is a small price to pay for destroying the productivity of every

thinker in the building.
- ☐ Cubicles. Now every running mouth in the building gets in the way, too. The more pointless the conversation, the better.
- ☐ Speakerphones. For when the mouths in the building aren't enough.
- ☐ Poorly prioritized or missing requirements. Let's make sure that the subconscious has only half the puzzle before you demand it start working.
- ☐ Ties, polyester pants, and sport coats/suits. You may be able to pick out the non-conformists from the boss this way, but nothing beats killing the creature comfort zone faster than having to wear clothes which you can't stand. No one can get anything done, but at least they look snappy while not doing it.
- ☐ Sensitivity training. For when you snapped at all those monkeys.
- ☐ Traffic or threat thereof. Sitting in traffic in the morning just reminds you that you can't start thinking until the chain is properly in place in the appointed cage. At the end of the day, worrying about beating traffic trumps getting that last brain bubble of the day going. Sitting in traffic is also great for dehydrating the creative types, forcing them to water up before getting started after arriving at the office.
- ☐ Lack of sufficient equipment, tools or other materials. This is equivalent to planning for subconscious strikes.
- ☐ Gatekeepers of all kinds. Need some paper or a special office item or a rarely used template or form or a special meter or wrench or hydraulic fitting? The aggravation of having to deal with a monkey whose job is specifically to get in the way is sure to keep those bubbles at bay.

Another kind of gatekeeper is the sort who tries to save the company money by turning the thermostat up in the summer, and down in the winter. So. You spend millions of dollars on highly creative people, and then gamble your entire company's future on what they create for you. Then, to save a few bucks, remove one of the vital creature-comforts which is required for them to enter the flow state. Great idea, bozo.

Enter the smart meter. Imagine the fun when the Department of Energy gets to control the temperature of every building in the country. If we aren't productive as a nation now, wait until that little gem hits the street. But at least someone's cousin gets to make a bundle importing the meters from China, and some jobs get created to install all these things to destroy what is left of creativity nationwide.

First Wife once worked as a title examiner at the headquarters for a nationally recognized title insurance company. Title examiners are the people who make sure you actually own your house, which they determine by creating charts of what could be fantastically complicated chains of title down through the ages. One of the senior executives had a fetish which would only allow the examiners to have one pen on their desk. This guy would skulk around removing extra pens from examiner's desks as they worked. When her pen ran out, she would have to turn it in to get another, like the warden counting spoons to keep anyone from getting shived.

Let's set aside, for a moment, the aggravation of some guy plinking around your desk scarfing up all your pens. Or the frustration of having a pen run out in the middle of something, forcing you to get up and stand in line to trade it in with all the other examiners. Let's say that for whatever reason, as you were walking from file cabinet to your desk, or coming in from having made a trip to a courthouse, you discover your pen is missing. Now, not only don't you have a pen, you don't have one to trade in. So now, you either have to steal one from somewhere or engage in a form of black market. To get a freaking pen. This company was more interested in saving a few bucks on pens than on inspecting your title. Never mind the destruction of all those brain bubbles. At least they had an excuse for billing you for more time while the examiners dealt with all that nonsense.

Most organizations seem specifically designed to prohibit creativity. They seem this way because they are specifically designed to prohibit creativity. Don't believe me? Then what is the business model of a defense contractor who gets to bill for cost plus profit? It sure as hell isn't to get anything finished. Ever. In our modern world, almost every organization you can name exists, not to get anything done, but to create jobs. If they get anything done at all, it is only the bare minimum required to keep you writing checks.

Producers aren't the only creatures who can use their subconscious creatively. As it turns out, monkeys have this ability also. And how do they use this creativity? To get in your way. Recall that earlier I said that, as a productive individualist, you have to be motivated by more than just the money. By focusing on providing value rather than making money, your subconscious gets tuned in the appropriate direction. However, if your focus is, instead, on simply making money, your subconscious will find ways to do so that is easier than just providing value, and getting easier every day. And in so doing, you would join the collective. And you probably would not like this book very much right now.

In fact, your focus on creating value rather than making money identifies you clearly as a productive individual, instead of one of the team. All those guys out on the golf courses aren't wandering around with a solution in their head. No, that would just look odd. Instead, they are in a different kind of flow state, a shmooze state. A cheese bubble, if you will. They are being just as creative as you, it is just that their creativity revolves around the deal. What the deal is, usually doesn't matter at all. Most of these guys get paid on some kind of commission or bonus structure which is hardly ever based on actual economic effect.

A good friend of mine with about thirty years of experience in the microcontroller world, who has worked on more projects than anyone I know, once said that a manager gave him the secret of how managers view engineers. Instead of engineers, of course, you can substitute any creative field you like. The secret? Simple. As the manager put it, "You guys are just too honest. You are focused on facts and solutions. And that is why you will never get ahead."

Wow. The engineer is focused on the design. The diesel engine guy is focused on compression and power. The artist is focused on the mood, the writer the script, the grader operator the slope, the welder the bead and so on. And the monkey with the coat and tie or the golf shoes or the sauna towel? Suit monkey is focused on how to cheat every single one of them out of each dime he can. Otherwise, who needs *him*?

While the driver of the pulp wood truck is keeping the wheels between the lines, somewhere on a golf course some guy is trying to convince his boss that he can make more money with pulp derivatives than with the pulp itself. Or some lawyer is working up an environmental lawsuit or a harassment or wrongful termination case which will put them out of business no matter how much valuable pulp they actually provide. Or increase their operating costs to the point that it is cheaper done overseas. Those pleasingly plump and irresistibly whackable butts became more valuable as risks to be mitigated, for a fee, than as inspiration.

Providing value is too much like work. Theft or fraud is a hell of a lot easier. And, if the fraud is legal, so much the better.

I had a mortgage with Countrywide, who was recently bought by Bank of America. A few months ago, they sent out a nastygram telling me I had to show them proof of insurance or they would jack my payment through the roof to cover it. Now, when our house closed, we sent them proof of insurance. Nothing had changed. But, to be safe, we sent it again. All was fine.

For about two months. Then, as we received our first statement addressed as Bank of America, we received a similar notice. Why? Presumably, hoping that if enough people miss the notice, they get to start charging outrageous fees. As it turned out, they didn't even give you time to miss the notice. When First Wife called them a few days later to discuss, an expensive "lender-based policy" had already been added, even though the notice stated that we had over a month to chase this down.

Their excuse? Our coverage had changed with our original insurer, a change which Bank of America claimed was a cancellation. Imagine all the thousands of customers whose coverage changes for any of hundreds of reasons, who then had to fight with them to get those charges removed. If any of them missed this, or didn't have time to fight, worrying about keeping their jobs, for example, think of all the money they get to collect. For absolutely nothing in return.

We have several credit card accounts, some with Chase. A few years back, they offered some credit card deals with great interest rates. One particular offer was for 3.99%. For life. Hell, yeah, sign me up.

Now, years later, having not missed a single payment in all that time, Chase decided to unilaterally add some fees to the account, start adding high interest rates on those fees, and dramatically increase the minimum payments. When First Wife called to complain, some guy who can barely speak the language offered to cancel these fees. For a fee of course, and only if we switched the money over to a higher interest rate. We refused, because a deal is a deal and they came to us with the original offer. Of course, all along, if we had faltered they could have hit us with a high rate. But we didn't falter, and now they wanted out of their little trap.

So we sent them a nastygram of our own, demanding that they live up to their obligations under the agreement. We got this answer back pretending to be legalese, but written in the same broken language as the customer service guy. A month or so later, we noticed on the news crawler that the New York Attorney General spanked them for this. A few weeks after that, Chase refunded the fees, but didn't refund the interest which had accumulated on them, nor restored the minimum payments to the previous level. Interestingly, although we had three of these offers on three separate accounts, two were hit with this fee, one was not. Which two were? Mine and a corporation of ours. Which one wasn't? First Wife's, who had applied for credit many times before, having listed "paralegal" as a former profession. Huh. I wonder why she didn't get her account hit with this new fee? Could it be that they screened cardholders to determine which ones were less likely, or able, to fight this unjustified fee?

We applied for a commercial mortgage with BB&T, who had impressed us with an Objectivist handout stating their corporate philosophy. #1 on the list is that employees are to be based in reality. Cool, maybe we can do business. So, we filled out all the paperwork and sent it in, First Wife and I personally owning a nice office condo free and clear. A few days later some chick called back and apparently didn't know the difference between an S corporation and C corporation. I came to this conclusion when she tried to weigh down our application with our C corp debt, but didn't include our corporate income. Pick one or the other, lady. And what happened to that whole reality policy?

Now, if BB&T doesn't want to make commercial mortgages right now, fine, just say so. I don't blame them, I probably wouldn't want to right now, either. But instead, their approach seems to be to monkey the numbers to justify their position. If so, what are they doing with our checking account, I wonder? I also wonder whether that Objectivist handout is just intended to sucker in the producers.

DirectTV offers a special deal for a year or so, but to get the special deal you have to go through hoops online and via email to apply for the rebate. If at any point you get hung up, or forget in the first place, or at any point along this journey, you don't get the discount which convinced you to sign up in the first place. I'm sure they aren't the only ones who do this.

I love Apple's commercials where they just point out the stuff that people think Microsoft does. They are hilarious. And then I read about what Apple did with Kramer's iPod ideas, and how they "liberated" Xerox's user interface ideas for the first Macintosh.

As I understand the history, these ideas would later be liberated by Microsoft to create Windows when Gates' disk operating system (DOS) had almost run dry by then. Contrary to popular belief, I don't think Gates wrote the first DOS. So where did it come from, this software which made an industry giant? In accordance with the classical pattern, Gates merely purchased it from Seattle Computer Products, whose owner lacked Mommy's business contacts at IBM.

Gates' actual contribution to the art? As far as I have been able to find, all he did from a technical perspective was to copy a flavor of the then well-known BASIC programming language to an early version of a personal computer. BASIC is a language which, although disdained by experts in the field then and now, was hailed as a way to make programming available to the masses. Underlying many of the Microsoft family of products, this easy programming language did open doors to many. But some of those doors flow into your computer by making Microsoft applications customizable by anyone who knows how to use BASIC. And through those BASIC doors pass most of the viruses and hacks and worms which infect computers worldwide today and destroy your credit as identity thieves steal your credibility. His reward for manipulating contacts and markets, but, in my opinion, demonstrating poor judgement for his actual innovations? The richest man in the world, while the actual inventors from decades past are hardly known.

Elsewhere, and more recently, some chick took over Hewlett Packard to great acclaim about shattering the glass ceiling, and damn near destroyed them by cheapening everything they make. In the space of about three years HP printers went from the quality must-have item to as useless as any other crap on the shelf. And then she gets lauded as some kind of financial wizard. And sought by Presidential candidates for her unique economic perspective, and considered a shoe-in for VP.

GM offered financing through GMAC to get rich on the interest. When that scheme started tanking they changed GMAC to a bank so that you and I have to pay for their little trap not working right.

You can't just buy something, anything, and then the next year get replacement parts for it, because the models have changed. Or different retailers are given different model numbers for similar products, just to force you to go back to the original store.

I recently bought a thermostat which said clearly on the packaging that it was compatible with heat pumps. But inside the package, the manual said that it was not designed for heat pumps. Some percentage of people will be too busy to take it back. Under these circumstances the thermostat really doesn't even have to work, does it?

McDonnell Douglas hired me as a Naval Academy grad and a Marine combat veteran, not to use my experience to help them design better warfighting products, as I had naively imagined. Instead, apparently, my role was to rub the stink of credibility onto, as I described them to their management, their weak and worse than useless product concepts.

All throughout the defense and other government contractor and financial industries there are great people sprinkled around trying to get things done. Of these few, most of them just haven't gotten fed up yet. The few who are fed up would normally leave to start their own businesses. Fortunately for the collective, this is a bad time to try going out on your own. So, the collective can keep milking these folks for a while, getting just enough done to keep getting more contracts to keep all those hordes employed. And we're about to add even more industries, such as green, to that pile.

And outside of those industries, the rest of the service industry feels like they don't have to compete with any upstarts either, so their good ones stay trapped, too. So what is the only rational response? Stop trying. Just collect your check like all the monkeys who surround you until you can leave to do your own thing. But they know this is hard for you, so they count on you to try anyway. That is what you do. And so, you continue to feed them, day after day.

Somewhere some suit monkeys drift off to nappy time, or take a sip, or reach for a lighter, or dip into the bubbles, and think up all this crap. Not, "how can we provide value?". But instead, "how can we think up some gotcha which hopefully no one will notice, but if they do we don't get spanked too hard, and enough won't notice so it works out as a net profit?" This isn't new, either:

Video Assignment
Flash of Genius

In this feel-good movie intended to keep you from giving up hope, knowing you have none, the hero eventually prevails over the auto industry, which ripped off his idea for the intermittent windshield wiper. Today, they would just simply have the parts made in China and then point that-a-way while shrugging. You get the point. It's called an *Effective Business Model*. And no one can compete with them because the entry cost is too high. And the good ones feel trapped because there is too much risk to leave right now.

Throughout all of this nonsense which you face each day, you aren't supposed to listen to your subconscious mind. All of those feelings which are telling you that so many things are wrong are to be suppressed, or else you aren't a nice person. Your subconscious screams at you each day to wake up, but you, instead, put it to sleep.

"Don't get angry, you are being unreasonable."

"Don't be afraid, that's just paranoid."

And even, "Don't be happy about the good stuff which happens to you by your own merit."

All of this programming is to suppress that wonderful subconscious mind God put inside you, and make you doubt what it tells you. If you won't assist them in this, then they diagnose and medicate you, or convict and incarcerate you. The goal of the monkey collective, the oh-so-nice, is to destroy your own ability to provide for yourself. Accordingly, crippled by the chain you place on your own mind, or the drugs you let them pump through your veins, you will be dependent and willing to live your life as a slave to provide for them.

It's not limited to the business world, not by any stretch of the imagination. Soon after 9-11, the FBI sent some Egyptian snitch of theirs my way to ask me to get him a letter of appointment as my product representative in Egypt. I refused, and called the FBI just to keep them off my back later. They demanded that I give him the letter, but strangely, were unwilling to put this demand in writing. How about chasing the real bad guys, jackasses? Oh, I forgot, that might actually get you shot at.

A bunch of guys in the boondocks of Pakistan ordered some remote control boards which could, oddly, really be nice for Improvised Explosive Devices (IEDs). I called the CIA to check on them. Similar story as for the Egyptian, which is "Go ahead and ship them, but don't ask us to put it in writing". While calling me a "great American." Choads.

Some poor sucker in South Carolina got arrested in a flurry of news over shipping capacitors overseas. I'm guessing that great American didn't ask someone to put it in writing. And *capacitors*? Really? You can buy run-of-the-mill capacitors in Radio Shack any day of the week. Or special order those special capacitors from just about anywhere. Or pluck them off the board inside a TV. Besides, who in the US makes capacitors anymore? Almost all of them are made in China. If I were a terrorist, I would just buy direct and cut out the middle man. More cash left over for Jihad.

Speaking of Jihad, what Islamic suit-monkey thought that it would be a great idea to blow up his most motivated soldiers? It sounds like the military version of what the collective does to producers. Apparently monkey cleverness is multicultural. Japan tried that too, it didn't turn out too well. If those guys start thinking like individualists it would be something to watch. Throw in some free trade motivation and they might start wondering which side is which. Reach your own conclusions.

NSA wondered about some backdoors in Chinese phone equipment. They followed this with, "Would you be willing to make a trip to Shanghai?" Nothing official, of course. Hell no, and what the hell do *you people* get paid for?

A weather balloon allegedly came down on my land a while back. It allegedly has a bag and a tag which allegedly says to ship it back to save NOAA some bucks. I'm so wary of twisty crap now that should this have actually happened there would have to be a gotcha. In that case I would wonder if it allegedly has an ounce of Columbian hid in it somewhere. Probably safer just to burn the damn thing and call it a day. Or chuck it into a dumpster.

I actually felt sorry for Obama with his inauguration and the bobbling of the oath of office, which sounded a hell of a lot like a "tee hee hee" setup typical of the Bush clan.

Or for Hillary and the reset button. That's what you hire monkeys for, isn't it, so you don't have to personally check every detail? Does anyone in the State Department speak Russian? Or know someone that does? I do. He told me about Google. And taught me how to say *"ya oochoo Rooskie"*. That's about as far as it got before I found out he was using my intellectual property to win favor with his other clients.

And when the monkeys' twisty manipulations, corporate or government, get exposed? Sue the messenger and try to silence them. Knowing that in court the messenger, likely to be an individualist, is more at risk from the jury of twelve collectivists chosen at random, than the offender. And the collectivists have ensured that the offenders have deeper pockets than the messenger. This in a country which lies about freedom of speech, merely to encourage you to expose yourself.

Even, or perhaps especially, police get in on the action, too. I just heard of this particular variation recently. Cop pulls guy over, and positions subject facing the dashboard camera, cop between subject and camera. With hands hidden, ostensibly to read license, cop needlessly pokes guy with finger over and over until subject reacts. Cop's small motion invisible, any reasonable reaction by subject looks like, on camera, unprovoked assault on a police officer.

This tactic suits the collective especially nicely. The collectivist sheep does nothing, but the individualist, especially the young male individualist, lacking experience, reacts subconsciously. And harmlessly. He may not even remember afterward being poked. But that's all it takes. Maybe the taser comes out. Maybe the subject dies from a weapon which, if it was in the hands of an individualist instead of an enforcer for the collective, would have already been sued out of existence.

Only the actual hard case, like say, a real terrorist or other serial killer, would know better and just stand there impassively and will themselves into inaction. You might want to go ahead and train your subconscious mind accordingly. One day, when they've had enough of your uppityness, it may be you facing the camera.

Each day, while you are feeding them, some monkey, who has the capacity for productive creativity, instead dreams up this crap. Including countless ways to use your own creativity and productivity to identify you, isolate you, use you, and, ultimately, destroy you. And they just won't stop.

But, if you can develop this connection between your conscious and your subconscious mind for yourself, you will be better able to avoid or deflect the ways in which monkeys seek to use and destroy you.

Armed with this skill, you will seem to the simple to be a psychic. But you aren't psychic, you are merely listening to the picture which your subconscious mind is forming from all the little bits of data that you are too busy to comprehend. Unable to understand this, the simple will fear you, and try to destroy you in their fear as they imagine you peering into their souls and finding them lacking.

The foolish will see you as heartless, or as an oppressor to be kept at arm's length or fought. But, you will be none of these, you simply will be able to see the cliffs which they blindly rush toward. The clever and manipulative will see you as a threat, as you see through the veils of deceit they wave in front of you, and fear that you will reveal them to their prey.

All of these make you into something to be feared and hated. This is the price of understanding your subconscious mind, and the power it can place in your hands.

But your life will become your own to live. And that alone is well worth the price.

Chapter 14, Organizational Value

In past chapters we discussed value as increasing the quality of life for those with which you choose to trade. We've also seen how the creative process works. I've discussed ways in which you can increase the efficiency of your own creativity, and the attendant risks thereof. In this chapter I want to tie those concepts together, and in a meaningful way which is most relevant to a prospective entrepreneur.

I start by discussing a concept I like to call *organizational value*, and first within the context of an existing enterprise. All people decide each day, like Og and Pok, to trade with others. Accordingly, as you sit in your cubicle you are making a decision to trade your time and energy and thoughts that day for whatever accrues to you as pay, or some fraction of benefits.

All of the issues which arise in your day at work can either be resources provided to you for your use, or obstacles or additional costs placed in your path. In turn, you either provide stuff, push, time or ideas to others within your own organization. Or a monkey might provide obstacles for someone else by withholding these resources, or inefficiently consuming them.

You then decide, from moment to moment, whether to participate in that system of trading. The fiction of employment leads people to believe that their status is somehow permanent, when it is anything but. The boss decides each day whether it is more worthwhile to replace you; most days the answer is, "no, it's not." Each day you decide whether it is more worthwhile to quit and find another job; most days the answer is also, "no, it's not." If your subconscious mind is feeling bad about going to work each day, it is probably trying to tell you, "yes, it is."

Most enterprises today are so large that very few workers directly impact the customer. The outside salesman may meet the customer to discuss his needs. The inside salesman may take an order. Somewhere in the shipping department a box gets a label slapped onto it and an invoice is generated more or less automatically. Other than these few connections to the customer, almost all activity in any enterprise is purely internal. Just like cells work in unison to make a body function, so do all of these little traders swirl around in a soup of trades back and forth all day long. Hopefully, enough value slops over the edges to get customers to continue paying for this swirl.

It is little surprise that most employees see themselves as somehow entitled to participate in this swirl, and so take actions each day consistent with that perception. It is hard to accept the truth of this point of view. Until the day that you start your own business and see all of this going on right in front of your face as your wallet gets lighter and lighter.

Each individual in a large enterprise, absent collective nonsense, is individually responsible for how well that organization does. Each individual executes this responsibility by conscious decisions at each moment as to whether to provide value or consume it. In other words, whether to add quality of life (by adding $+\Delta Q$), or decrease quality of life (by preventing $+\Delta Q$, or adding $-\Delta Q$) for someone else. These transactions usually are contained within that organization, but sometimes for customers outside of it. The sum total of all of these transactions determines how much residual $+\Delta Q$ remains to slop over the edge and splash onto customers. Technically, as I defined this previously, we are really talking about the push, stuff, time and ideas which get filtered through each individual's quality of life factors to result in net $+\Delta Q$. But, ΔQ, positive or negative, is much more simple to express, and, in a culture in which individuals express similar values, this approximation is close enough. An example of how this breaks down is if you run across someone who genuinely enjoys being hit with a brick.

The collective nonsense, which we previously chose to ignore, is universally an internal source of $-\Delta Q$, as monkeys don't have to add value in order to consume $+\Delta Q$. They get it by fiat. As such, via the monkeys, collective issues, like a giant sponge, can only consume $+\Delta Q$, leaving less to slop onto customers. The fact that you create lots of jobs is absolutely irrelevant.

Since as an entrepreneur you will be handling a wide swath of business activities yourself, let's see how these roles are achieved, ideally, in larger enterprises.

The board of directors, or senior executives, exist to set direction for effort and to mandate allocation of resources. By so doing, their task is to recognize potential sources of $+\Delta Q$. A related executive task is to prevent inefficient wastage of $+\Delta Q$ by placing resources where they are most needed to accomplish the organization's goals. Their job is better done to the extent to which they limit sources of $-\Delta Q$, but they do not, by their executive efforts, directly create any $+\Delta Q$.

So, who does create $+\Delta Q$? High-value idea workers. The exact role of these people, and the ideas with which they trade, depends on the type of organization in question. Their ideas also depend on the focus which each of these persons place on the long-term benefit of the customer, consistent with the goals of the organization. I provide some examples from selected industries below.

Retail Sales

In a retail organization, the corporate buyers, those who find, qualify and order goods, use their ideas to determine what products will be useful to customers. These buyers are high-value idea workers. So are the sales people who meet customers, determine their needs and help decide which items are best suited for those needs.

However, some buyers are looking for only those goods which are good enough to sell. These goods might break in the customers' hands weeks or months after purchase, necessitating constant maintenance or replacement. In this case, those buyers are idea workers, but not of high value. This sort of ethic would be characteristic of a retail company run by, and staffed with, monkeys.

Similarly, monkey salesmen, rather than trying to match their customers' needs to products which fulfill those needs, instead try to convince a customer that an inferior or irrelevant product is best for them.

This organization benefits from the monkey's ideas, but at the cost of their customers' long-term benefit.

This approach has become so entrenched in all of our business dealings that even the word "sales" has become tainted with visions of leisure suits, big hair, gimmicks and slogans. And cheesy TV hucksters with Jersey accents and little headsets selling paper towels for twenty-five dollars, doubling your order to your delight. True salesmanship is not this way at all. But this field has become so perverted that these images bias kids with decent intentions away from it, and instead attract the monkey collective who genuinely sees this approach as noble and worthwhile.

The sales cheese, as with many defective portions of our hijacked culture, is not the cause of the monkey collective. Instead, the cheese is a consequence of the monkey collective itself. There are just too many of them to make the cheating unprofitable. In a culture of thinking producers, this kind of salesman would never be able to find work. But, with almost four hundred million people to wade through, even reaching a small fraction of a percent of those is enough to sell millions. Matching needs to genuine features is just too much hard work.

The monkey sales organization knows how to find a constant stream of customers, and may even outperform other companies who are genuinely customer-focused. The monkey sales company provides a perceived $+\Delta Q$, but with a long-term $-\Delta Q$ hidden inside. This would be like a tribesman selling wood to customers, who find out later that what they thought was wood is actually just a cardboard picture of wood.

"Tonga, my man, how's the family?" the salesman might begin as the customer calls to complain about the cardboard delivered to his hut. "Whoa, whoa whoa. Now, Tonga, that was some primo product which we delivered the other day. That photo was printed on only the highest quality fiber substrate you can get. I don't know where you've been getting your fuel, but I can tell you that what we sent you matches exactly the photo you saw in our product brochure. Even better, our substrate is twenty percent thicker than our closest competitor's substrate. That's like getting extra wood for free. And I know you, Tonga, you want only the finest fuel for your family. Am I right or am I right? Hey look, I don't know how long we're going to be able to stay in business giving away free stuff. I'm not supposed to tell you this, but I heard the big boys in the corner office talking about how we might have to stop. So, before they figure it out, how many more units do you want to order today? I can get them there on, say, Thursday."

We shall see in a moment the role which marketing can play to enable this approach.

Engineering

In an engineering organization, the designers who create the product concepts and bring them into being are the high value idea workers. However, if those same engineers are the ones who enable the production of low-quality goods which last just long enough to cross the warranty gap, then those engineers are behaving like monkeys. An engineer's traditional job was to use his skills and knowledge to create the most value, or $+\Delta Q$, at the least cost for a given amount of value.

Physics demands that things which you want to do require a certain amount of energy and mechanical strength in the components which do them. An ice-maker in a high-end refrigerator contains both a freezer to chill the ice, and a heater to dislodge the ice from the little buckets before dumping the moon cubes into a bigger bucket. This device needs to operate in an extreme temperature environment and handle obstruction by frost. Typically made from plastic, the materials used in these devices need to be tougher than a picnic fork. And yet, for cost savings, you might find that the material used in your icemaker is about as strong as a picnic fork which has been left in the freezer for a year. Left unplugged in a carton unused at room temperature, that icemaker may not degrade at all until the cold comes on.

Over time, materials degrade. How fast they approach failure depends on the exact materials, the operating conditions, and the configuration into which they have been designed. Using experience, an understanding of customer usage patterns and knowledge of the materials, a materials engineer can almost precisely tune the failure point of an item to fall outside the warranty period.

Now, hardly ever would management come to an engineer with a directive to "make it fail in thirteen months after sale. Assume it sits in a carton unused for six months on average before it is sold." People who go into engineering, as mentioned before, are usually so crippled by having to deal with those nasty facts all day that this would rarely motivate success. But, there are measurable cultural biases which allow such a directive to succeed in some cases, depending on the cultural background of the individual. Again, I could be accused of being a racist with this statement, although it would be more fair to say I am a culturalist. I dare anyone who would so label me to fund me to conduct a study of this phenomenon, and let's see how the facts turn out.

Instead, the way this works is that the management comes to engineering with a pre-defined product idea, as determined by focus groups who asked for a set of features. This same focus group also gave feedback as to how long a warranty period they would like, and how much they would be willing to pay for those features.

"Bob, we need to design this widget, and it has to last at least twelve months. Any less, and the customers will be unhappy. It also can't cost any more than X dollars. I want you to design a least-cost solution to get us there."

Bob then goes off and looks up materials and their specifications and cost. He also consults with some outside sales people from materials companies to find out what new innovations they might have at their disposal. This step is often overlooked, but is key for any technology development.

This is one way in which effective salesmen benefit society in a way which is often totally overlooked. Bob might tell an outside salesman about a new requirement for material which operates at zero degrees Fahrenheit. And, that this material has to take X amount of strain and shear and other forces, and needs to last at least a year while doing so. Hearing this, a well-informed outside salesman will offer suggestions about which of his products might best suit that need. This is a great shortcut for Bob. Ask three such outside salesmen, and Bob will be presented with the best each has to offer, they wanting to put their best feet forward. Bob will then be enabled to pick the right material for the job. Otherwise, he could spend weeks looking through datasheets and still not get the best match.

A salesman like that is worth his weight in gold, and soon becomes seen as an integral part of the *customer's* organization. I have met many such salesmen over the years. And about ten times as many monkeys who wear the same clothes. Often, these monkeys slipped in to replace the good ones, the latter having become too expensive due to all the commissions. Commissions they earned from all the sales they have closed with all the successful customers they have enabled. Provided their customers aren't monkeys.

I have found that when a favored vendor does this, the best strategy is to immediately open the door to other vendors. Underlying the departure of that effective salesman, who has participated in your success, is a raft of other issues which you will never get to see, but which has displaced your best interest. If possible, take your business where that guy went, ignoring all inducements which the first vendor might now be promising.

Good engineers will quickly realize which salesmen are the honest ones. If Vendor A has Material Z which is not quite as good as Material Y from Vendor B, then the engineer, in general, will know this. No amount of persuasion or nice lunches will change the facts of the material. But, if Salesman A is just up-front about Material Z, and Material Y is selected for *this* project, you can bet that both Salesman A and Salesman B will get the call on the next project.

On the other hand, Monkey Salesman A might just throw a lot of slick marketing on Bob's desk, and hype it beyond what the data shows. Given this demonstration of uselessness, the engineer is less likely to waste his time calling that guy again. Particularly if Bob spent a week blowing up brain bubbles around Material Z, or at least until his subconscious mind finally aggravated him into throwing that crap out after leading him to review the datasheet again. Regardless, Bob finds himself back at square one.

In the process, Monkey Salesman A will have taught Bob's carefully tuned subconscious mind to be hyper-cynical about him, and possibly, salesmen in general. If Bob generalizes the cynicism, he may then subconsciously, and routinely, torture all or most salesmen during meetings. Why? Just so his subconscious mind can look for those tell-tale signs reminiscent of past fraud.

One day Bob might do this in front of his boss, who doesn't understand the template which is at play to help him succeed. If the boss has a fondness for bananas, Monkey Salesman A now sees an opening with his fellow species.

"Wow, Boss, Bob there sure is looking out for you guys," Monkey Salesman A says to Monkey Boss as he walks with Boss out to his Lexus.

"Yeah, well, you know how those geeks are," Boss replies. They both chuckle to themselves, knowing that this stereotype allows each to take advantage of the source of their revenue. A bond begins to form between them.

"Hey, I just remembered. I've got a reservation at Monkey Pines next Thursday, and one of my guys just called this morning and dropped out. Our company has already paid for the holes, so we might as well use it. Want to come?" lies Monkey Salesman A, knowing he had arranged this in advance. Suppliers at Vendor A see memberships at the nicest golf-courses and reservations at the best hotels and restaurants for the managers as key investments. Along with insulated cups and promotional pens for the engineers, these memberships are a heck of a lot cheaper than investing in better materials. It's all about volume, baby.

"Wow! Monkey Pines? I've been wanting to play that course for years! Sure, I'll be there!"

As Thursday arrives, Bob has been progressively more difficult to manage, continuing to resist using Material Z. Obviously aggravated by the boss insisting that he take another look at it, Bob can't articulate exactly what is going on. But, Monkey Boss doesn't understand the creative process. Accordingly, he fails to realize that the aggravation is simply Bob's subconscious mind trying to tell him to avoid this material, long before Bob is able to articulate why it is a problem.

Pushing Bob to accept Material Z, Monkey Boss is unknowingly denying Bob the opportunity to get in touch with this conflict, or even see the right data to help make his reasoning clear. A downward spiral starts as Bob resists Material Z, but can't say why. Monkey Boss sees this as unreasonable, and pressures Bob. Bob resists harder as his subconscious is screaming at him.

By the time Boss hits the links with Monkey Salesman A, he is just about ready to blow a fuse. The soothing golf course helps.

"I understand, Boss, I understand. I deal with guys like that all day long," Monkey Salesman A consoles as the Boss swings. "Nice shot, when the pros play this course they like to hit that same tree to get it to bounce away from the rough like that. At some point, though, you have to ask yourself what is in the best interest of your company. Now, I know Material Z isn't perfect, nothing is. But it has passed the flavor test from the Monkey Plastic Council, and so you know they just don't hand that out."

Of course, the Monkey Plastic Council is an industry group created specifically by industry giants such as Vendor A to standardize materials to keep Bob from starting up his own boutique materials company. Monkey Salesman A lets that little explanation slide.

"All I'm saying is that Material Z is two-thirds the cost of Material Y, and is just as good in the criteria which matters. They charge a little more for Material Y because it beats out Material Z in a couple of criteria which don't matter for your project. Now, if you were building space probes I would say pay the extra cash for that. You know those trekkies, they all think they are building space probes. Nice guys, but they just don't have a mind for business," Monkey Salesman A says as he deliberately shanks the next tee-off. "Now see, you got me talking business and look what I did."

At the end of the day, as they check their scorecards, Monkey Salesman A hands Monkey Boss some brochures and says, "Hey, I brought you something that I think may help. These reports from the Monkey Plastic Council show some results of industry studies about how long people use their appliances before getting a new one. See this line here? It shows that most people get rid of their refrigerators after about two years." Taking the brochure, Monkey Boss follows through on the simple compliance strategy.

"And notice this curve. This shows that, over time, people are getting rid of their refrigerators sooner each year. You could spend the extra money for Material Y and put a space probe icemaker on it which might last for twenty years. But eighteen of those years are going to be on the trash heap. Why spend the extra money? You would just be taking money out of your company, and, ultimately, charging your customers more for something they are just going to throw away anyway."

Friday morning, Monkey Boss calls Bob into his office. Bob is understandably wary.

"Bob, I've been thinking," Monkey Boss begins. "You are right about how long Material Z will last in our icemaker," he says as Bob is suddenly caught off guard, having expected the latest in the series of one-sided arguments. Monkey Boss then asks, "Do you think a design change can make Material Z last about two years in that application?"

"Well, let me see, I suppose it might, unless..." Bob begins. Asked an objective question like that, Bob begins accessing what he can recall about the various materials, the calculations of wall thickness, the temperatures, etc. Essentially, he is trying to work a final exam in a materials class in about seven seconds. The outside world just sees this as hedging. Bob's subconscious mind starts sensing danger.

"Good, good, I wanted to get your opinion on that," interrupts Monkey Boss. "But to make it last that long we would have to increase the material thickness by about fifty percent," Bob interjects, having interpolated some natural logarithms in his head to make that estimate.

"Whatever. Anyway, write that up in a proposal and get it to me before lunch," Monkey Boss replies. "And easy on that engineering stuff, I need to show this to the product director over lunch. I don't want to put him to sleep."

Bob toddles off, and by lunch the proposal is in Monkey Boss's hands, complete with an analysis of how thick the walls would have to be to use Material Z versus Material Y. Monkey Boss grabs the folder on the way to his lunch with the director.

"I see," hums the director as he flips through the proposal. "But you know, uh, it looks like we could save twenty cents per unit if we use the Y design, and use this Material Z in it." Monkey Boss nods agreement as the director announces, "Let's do this. I'll authorize funding on this just as soon as I get back to my office."

Elated, after lunch Monkey Boss tracks down Bob at the water cooler. "Always wandering around, I see," Monkey Boss thinks to himself. "He must drink about a gallon a day."

"Hey Bob, I've got some great news!" Monkey Boss says, slapping Bob on the shoulder and popping his bubble. Bob looks confused for a moment as he slips back into conscious mind mode. "What a dork," Monkey Boss thinks silently.

"Look, I just had lunch with the director, and he's approved your design. We've got to get started on this right away," he tells the now conscious Bob, who is astonished to have been heard through. Or so he thinks. "Just one little change, though. Let's go with your Y design and put that Material Z plastic in it."

Stop the tape. At this point, what should Bob do?

☐ Go along silently and design the icemaker as directed by management.
☐ Document his position, then design the icemaker as directed by management.
☐ Stand his ground until he is replaced by someone who will design the icemaker as directed by management.
☐ Quit and get a job elsewhere.
☐ Quit and start his own business.

None of these are attractive options, but are decisions faced by creative people in a wide range of fields, not just engineering. Let's explore each of these.

Go Along Silently

By caving to arbitrary attempts to manipulate physics, Bob will be, in effect, signing on to something which he knows will fail. This will begin to irritate Bob's subconscious mind, which will begin to trust him less and less, and so Bob will be come less and less creative. This becomes highly destructive to Bob's self-esteem, and will eventually adopt the attitude of "I just work here."

From the point of view of monkey management, they have scored a victory all the way around. The icemaker gets designed the way that they want it, and Bob has learned his place. As an added bonus, if the icemaker fails prematurely, Bob is to blame. Any outside consultant could alight, look at the design, turn to Bob and say:

"Bob, you should have known that this would have never worked. Even your own calculations showed that the material thickness should have been thicker. What were you thinking? At best, you saved the company twenty cents per icemaker, but look how much you cost them in product returns and lost customer confidence. That's the problem with you guys, you have no head for business. I'm recommending your termination."

Document His Position, Then Go Along

The only difference between this one and the previous option is that Bob once again states his case. Perhaps we imagine that he should write a memo to cover himself. The response of management?

"Bob, why is it that guys like you are never team players? You know, if you geeks had played some sports every now and then you might have learned to work well with others."

As far as the particulars of his position, monkey management always gets to fall back on:

"Bob, you said that you *think* the icemaker *might* fail in fifteen months. But, you can't actually *prove* that it *will* fail in fifteen months, can you?"

This sounds a lot like:

"You *think* that the solid rocket booster o-rings *might* fail if we launch the shuttle in cold weather. But you can't *prove* that the o-rings *will* fail below X degrees, can you?"

Monkey management is also wary that if enough emails and memos exist, and something does go wrong, then it looks bad for them. From their perspective, it seems unfair that each action and decision of theirs is archived for later hindsight review. "People are imperfect creatures," they lament, "Look closely at the daily activities of anyone and you can find enough mistakes to paint an unfair picture of that person."

"Why doesn't Bob just shut up and do his job?" they wonder.

The reaction of Bob's subconscious mind will be to recognize management itself as first a source of humor, and eventually, a threat to his ability to provide for himself. He will respond to humor about dorky bosses, or put up little cartoons. This, in turn, flags him, subconsciously, to management as a trouble-maker. Bob's peers, who may be monkeys themselves, misinterpret Bob's justified reaction to his specific situation as a judgment against management in general, and so even the good managers suffer an undeserved loss of respect.

Ultimately, if Bob exercises this option enough times, he will eventually be fired, using techniques similar to those about to be explained for the next option. You might model this situation as a candle representing Bob's employability at that company. Each time he protests to monkey management about shortchanging quality, he burns a little bit of that candle. Each time he puts his protests in writing, monkey management cuts some off the bottom of the candle.

Eventually, the candle is gone. The question is really, then, whether Bob is ready when it is exhausted.

Stand His Ground and Be Replaced

Bob could just say no. Sounds so easy, doesn't it? We're all taught from an early age that a man should just stand his ground. This from people who have probably never tried it in the real world, and by people who would go ballistic if you tried it with them. It could just be that the platitude to "stand your ground" is a mechanism evolved by the collective to recognize the individualists, and thus single them out for later processing and disposal.

All of the bad stuff in the previous option now accelerates. The first time Bob stands his ground he may just be assigned to another team or department. Shuffling problem employees like Bob around is the time-honored way for large organizations to avoid self-examination. At some point, though, Bob will have been shuffled around all the hands. The last hand at the table has to now find the ultimate solution to the Bob question.

Fortunately, Monkey Salesman A, or some similar figure, is there to help. This approach has to be done just as soon as it is determined that Bob is going to stand his ground. The sooner he can be replaced, the less likely that Bob's subconscious mind will have figured out the shortcoming in Material Z. Otherwise, Bob might then have time to better document the hazards of using this material.

"You know, Boss, I know Bob is a great guy, and he has lots of experience. But technology changes, and sometimes these older guys just don't understand the newer materials which are available now," offers Monkey Salesman A.

"I know, but new kids coming out of college are hardly any better," laments Monkey Boss.

"You are right, most of them aren't, if they haven't been specifically trained in using these materials. But, did you know that the Monkey Plastic Council has been endowing a university in Bangalore to work specifically with these new materials? These kids are just about the best in the world with understanding them," he offers.

"Hmmm, that does sound good. But, I don't know, we've got so much invested in Bob, I don't know if I have time to train his replacement," wonders Monkey Boss aloud.

"That's the great thing about these kids, you don't have to train them. We've had them working in design shops already, they are essentially already experienced in the workplace environment. I think they will blow you away," Monkey Salesman A reassures him.

"Oh, I just remembered, I brought some resumes with me that I had intended to drop off this afternoon with Freezeco. I don't think they will mind if you get a first peek at these kids," he lies conspiratorially with a wink.

As Monkey Boss flips through the resumes he sees pictures of eager little faces who stand in stark contrast to the lost thoughtfulness which Bob often skulks around with. As Monkey Boss is lost in his meat catalog, Salesman A reminds him, "And plus, with the H-1B visa, these kids aren't as likely to get in the way. Bob can just run off and get a job somewhere else, but these kids go back to India if you fire them."

Nudging his contemplative customer, he adds, only half-jokingly, "Cheap, captive and agreeable labor. Probably just about the closest to slaves you are ever going to get in this country. With these kids slugging away getting it done, which leaves more time for you at Monkey Pines!"

Sold. And instead of these kids showing up in chains at a New England slave market, to be sold by auctioneers with elitist brogues, they alight from a 747. Reaching our shores, they are eager to serve. Many will integrate and become great additions to our economy and culture. But some arrive ready to infect our culture with a racist and classist ethic of such deep intensity that it would make a KKK Grand Imperial Wizard or a Black Panther blush with shame.

So then, what exactly is the method of Bob's termination? Simple. While the HR department is processing Wabu's H-1B visa, Monkey Boss documents every thing he does. Look closely at the daily habits of anyone, and you will find much to criticize.

"Bob is often not at his desk, and makes numerous visits to the water cooler and restroom each day. I have counseled him about this behavior, but his reaction to this was barely concealed agitation."

"When given assignments, Bob generally accepts them with grace. But, when supervising him, he seems aggravated at the intrusion. Also, Bob occasionally snaps at coworkers. When challenged about this behavior, he insists that their conversations are 'pointless and annoying.' He has asked about being assigned a private office, but I don't think that it is in the best interest of the company to reward his behavior in this fashion. I directed him to simply focus on his own work for a while before we could even consider such a request."

"Bob's performance on the icemaker project remains at a standstill. He insists that the materials which were selected, from a list of materials he himself recommended, are somehow inadequate. But, he continues to fail to show, using accepted engineering principles, any specific or provable inadequacy."

"Today I counseled him on the icemaker project, and suggested that instead of writing so many memos, he should simply start implementing the design which he had proposed before. I think he is writing so many memos to cover the fact that he is unsure about how to proceed."

"Wabu arrived today. I assigned him to the cubicle next to Bob, and introduced the two. Bob seemed aggravated and out of sorts. This state-of-mind worsened as he, Wabu and I had a design meeting this afternoon. Wabu seemed eager to get started, while Bob merely pummeled him with questions which I thought seemed unfair."

"The relationship between Bob and Wabu seems even more strained. While the rest of the staff has welcomed Wabu, Bob seems resentful at the intrusion on what he clearly sees as 'his' design."

"Today I formally transferred control of the icemaker design to Wabu. I told Bob that he was to perform the role of 'senior consultant' to help Wabu understand the background of the icemaker project."

"Today Monkey Salesman A visited and sat in on a design meeting. The interaction between Wabu and Monkey Salesman A was animated and productive. However, Bob seemed sullen and withdrawn, only offering input when specifically asked, and then after uncomfortable pauses and with as few words as possible. For example, when asked a question about the shear strength of the ice scraper, he sat there for a long moment and said nothing. When prompted again, he said, sullenly, 'I'm thinking.' I am not sure how much value he is providing to this project any more."

"I have become concerned that Bob is becoming emotionally unstable. I referred him to HR counseling for his attitude. At this announcement he exploded and incredulously asked 'What the f***?' I immediately contacted the division head and discussed the problem with her. She agreed that this sort of language was unprofessional and not to be tolerated. She then called some of the floor employees around Bob's cubicle and most agreed that he did seem 'odd'."

"Today I met with the HR Director and asked that we terminate Bob's employment. The director agreed and told me that security would escort Bob out as soon as he returned from lunch. An HR representative was sent this morning to put Bob's personal effects in a carton. While doing so, she found several photos of Bob when he was in the military, along with a sportsmen's magazine which contained numerous advertisements for guns and knives. The HR Director then referred this information to the County Sheriff's office for file."

And when Bob applies for another job? The prospective employer will call and ask for a verification of employment. The response? "Bob was employed here from this date to that date." Click. And into the trash can goes Bob's application. For no one has value unless someone else says you do. Everyone knows that.

Take Another Job

At some point in any of the above processes, Bob may eventually have had enough of this nonsense to encourage him to quit and take another job elsewhere. Assuming that the job market isn't flooded with so many H-1B slaves that he can find a job at all.

But then what? Just more of the same. It doesn't matter where Bob, the thinker, turns, all potential employers are playing versions of the same game, and at different levels of intensity. The critical mass required of any company today, at least of any which is likely to be of a size to be able to make an icemaker, imposes the same restrictions on thought and innovation.

And besides, if one company made a refrigerator which lasted more than two years, then what? Too few people would buy it, because it would cost twenty-percent more, and that is suicidal in the monkey-based market. Besides, look at all the jobs being created to replace all those broken refrigerators. Jobs in China, of course, but who's counting?

Start His Own Business

We'll talk about this option in the next chapter. Don't think, by the way, that any of these options would turn out differently if Bob had a better manager. As long as there is one monkey in the chain, he can render impotent, and eliminate, any thinkers below him. Bob's manager would then face the same dilemma as Bob, only to cave or be replaced, and then the dilemma would fall back to Bob as before.

As I mentioned earlier, these issues aren't confined to a specific industry. They are instead universal to all of our modern collectives.

Construction

In a construction crew, the workers who shape the land are the high value idea workers, as are the architects and civil engineers who plan their work. As we drive down a modern highway, we are blissfully unaware of the intellect which was required to give us a smooth ride which we take for granted. And which brings us our food.

Each cubic foot of earth and clay and gravel and aggregate and asphalt and concrete had to be planned and placed and shaped and smoothed by a thinker. A modern road contains layers which few of us ever even know are there, each of which serves its intended purpose. The orchestrated effort of all of this is to do one simple thing.

Remove water. You see, we don't drive on a road. We drive on a road which doesn't have water in it, or underneath it. Without the influence of water, we could drive on a hard-packed dirt road which would last decades with very little maintenance, other than perhaps scraping off the washboard which would form with heavy, high-speed use. Some unimproved roads in desert areas, assuming the right soil type, need hardly any work at all. Let the rain fall on that road, and run one vehicle over it, and it turns into a goopy mess. This goopy mess then dries into something which is less like a road than it was before. Shockingly few cycles of this are required to render that road undriveable.

All of those layers in the road, and the ditches and the embankments, and the drainage ditches and the slope of the road itself, all of this exists just to get rid of the water. For some roads, even the asphalt on top serves merely to keep the water off of the stack of stuff underneath. That thin layer of asphalt merely sheds the water to the side before it has time to soak in and ruin the real road underneath.

And all of that gets shaped by a mind. The individual who sits in the excavator is an artist. The dirt and gravel are his paints, the hydraulic arm and bucket his brush, and the face of the earth itself is his canvas. And it takes years of experience to develop that artistic skill. Doubt me? Try it.

Don't be fooled by the very short time he spends in school just learning how to safely operate the equipment. That is only the start. And don't be fooled by the hordes of people standing around watching him work. Those workers are paid by the virtue of the collective, whether by regulation or by union, in order to provide more jobs.

This creative individual has seen many different variations in the hundreds or thousands of miles he has shaped. And so, as he sits in the cab of his excavator, or front-end loader, or backhoe or dump truck, when something isn't just right, he knows it.

Maybe the foundation he is shaping for this bridge feels different. Or the material being used isn't the right grade. Or the slopes are all wrong. Like Bob, then, this individual, let's call him Jim, faces a dilemma. It is easier for Jim to just be quiet, and dig away, but not for his foreman or supervisor, who has to sign off on the work. Or for the civil engineer who has to do the same. Either way, Jim faces the team player insult should he step out of line:

"Why is it that guys like you are never team players? You know, if guys like you, who think you know more than you do, had gone to college then you might have learned to work well with others."

Shut up and fall into line? That's the easy choice, unless you have a conscience.

Document and then fall into line? Unlike Bob, Jim doesn't work with paper and email every day, so that one is just awkward. It is this lack of access to documentation which causes idea workers among the tradesmen to turn instead to unions to protect them. But even that collective dilutes his ability and passes out the largess of his work to the monkeys around him.

Stand his ground and get fired? There are plenty of day-worker slaves waiting to take Jim's place. Which explains why the collective isn't all that keen on getting rid of the slave classes, no matter what hubbub they might say to the contrary. Again, the union steps in, pretending to protect the worker as it systematically destroys his job.

Quit and work elsewhere? What's the point? Like Bob's company, the entire industry, by regulation and collectivized union fiat, is more or less uniform.

Quit and start his own business? Maybe, assuming Jim can afford the equipment and hire all that union and regulator staff to stand around and watch him work. He might be able to subcontract himself to the big boys, but then he's right back where he started, isn't he? In the worst irony of all, the union blocks his participation as his own man, effectively enslaving every union member who might aspire to independence.

This doesn't have to be just road construction, either. Thinkers in any industry face exactly this same dilemma all the time. And like the refrigerator industry, each industry which has reached the point where power is consolidated in the collective reaps the same benefits. A failing icemaker allows more refrigerators, replacement parts and maintenance to be sold, in turn providing jobs. Similarly, a road which fails prematurely or a bridge which develops cracks simply creates more work for the big boys to bid on, and jobs for the stand-arounds and slaves to do.

Tax Preparation

In a tax preparation firm, no one is a high value idea worker, no matter how skilled, or helpful or aggressive at finding deductions. All this firm can do for anyone is block the bricks which are being thrown at their customers by artificial sources created for the benefit of the monkey collective.

Machining

In a machine shop, the workers who take the metal and cut, shape and weld it into the proper form are high value idea workers. Like Bob, the engineer, or Jim, the excavator operator, each thinker in this industry faces the same dilemmas, with the additional tradesman restrictions caused by the unionization of the workforce nationwide. And the same regulated high cost of entry if they wanted to start their own businesses.

Restaurants

At a restaurant, the buyer who purchases the materials are high value idea workers. Along with the cooks who prepare the food, the waitresses who entertain and comfort the diners and the guys who clean up the dishes and wash them. Each of these contributes to the experience being purchased by the diner. Fortunately, restaurants are such necessarily compact units of functionality, dotted here and there throughout the landscape, that it is tougher for the collective to sink their teeth in. Right?

Sort of. Unfortunately, the same workplace regulations which all employers face, and the raft of additional regulations specific to the food industry, mean that small Mom-and-Pop restaurants are rare. These small operations can generally only thrive in out-of-the-way places which the chains choose to ignore. There are independent restaurants in thickly populated areas, of course. But almost without exception the regulatory costs are reflected in these independents typically being pricey boutiques, rather than the traditional Sunday afternoon "Grandma's Place" kind of thing.

Accordingly, it is impractical, but not impossible, to start your own business in the food industry. As many a budding chef with great ideas has found to his dismay.

Dentistry

In a dental office, the hygienist who cleans your teeth and screens for more serious problems, as well as the dentist who repairs these problems, are high value idea workers. It may appear at first that these workers merely remove sources of $-\Delta Q$. But keep in mind that these negative issues, such as gingivitis or decay, are features of nature, rather than an act of the monkey collective to extract unearned value. Similarly, the restaurant worker removes the $-\Delta Q$ of hunger, while the tailor removes the $-\Delta Q$ of lacking clothes. In all cases, dentist, chef, or tailor, the customer leaves their shops in better circumstances than nature allowed them before.

On the other hand, what if the dentists hired thugs to break the teeth of potential clients, thus necessitating repair? Then these dentists would join the ranks of the lawyers, the accountants, and the monkey electorate.

Law

In a law firm, no one is a high value idea worker. As with the tax preparation firm, no one inside can create a single thing, and only serve to mitigate harm, suppressing $-\Delta Q$, to their clients, or inflict harm, increasing $-\Delta Q$, on someone else's clients. The harm being inflicted is purely artificial, and usually stems from someone demanding some value to which they are not entitled.

The influence of lawyers, the highest evolved form of the collective, on our society is far out of proportion to their knowledge of how to create value, which is minimal at best. Monkeys demand that their politicians, out of proportion to their representation, be lawyers in droves. We listen to the media pundits, most of whom are lawyers, especially in conservative circles.

Worst of all, we demand that judges, both those in robes and those who sit in regulatory positions in commissions and special panels of all kinds, be lawyers. Judges in robes, as envisioned by the founders, were intended to sit in judgement, not of the individual, but of the collective which seeks to impose its will upon the individual. So long as the law was being applied impartially to individuals, the judge was to be silent. The judges were to act only when the law was twisted to single out men, or when the law itself was in violation of the rights of the individual.

Now, we empower judges to destroy the individual, as well as extend the law when it is insufficient to oppress by itself. And we hire lawyers for this purpose, who are the most skilled among us at twisting reality to suit their purpose in the moment, to be judges to rule us. Instead of protecting us from men like them. It is from this perverted ethic that we empower commissions and panels to seek ways to extend the law even further against the individual. And the monkeys staff these bodies with lawyers as well.

Those who know the least of any of us of how to create value we place in the position to most control those of us who do. Why? Because the mass of the monkey collective demands it. While we were learning how to create, lawyers were learning how to destroy on the behalf of their clients. Who better then, the collective reasons, to employ in positions of power to steal from us en-masse? Don't blame the lawyers. If they are locusts, it is only because the collective releases them upon our crops to eat on their behalf.

I could go on and on, singling out each industry for abuse, and waxing poetic about the virtues of the thinker. I could continue praising the classic American worker, contrasting this individual to the perversion of this theme which has soaked into our national fabric today. The point is, though, that in whatever industry, the high-value idea workers are those who genuinely create value. All the rest just move stuff out of the way to one extent or another, while the worst ones actively get in the way of the idea workers. Briefly, then, here are some examples of support roles which exist just to mitigate $-\Delta Q$, some of which I've touched on already.

Administrative and Clerical

Management exists solely to remove obstacles, or $-\Delta Q$, from the path of idea workers. Once the executive level has set direction, assigned priorities and allocated resources, it is the role of management to exercise those policies as effectively as possible. Managers can only be idea workers to the extent that they creatively recognize obstacles and remove them. Some managers treat the idea workers in their charge as if they are cogs in the machine, when instead the idea workers are the machine itself. This misunderstanding can only place more obstacles in their path, and thus weaken the organization's ability to provide value to their customers.

Human resource departments, like tax accountants and lawyers, are regulatory compliance workers who exist solely to mitigate $-\Delta Q$. But, in their zeal, the workers in these departments often create additional $-\Delta Q$. In their role, HR professionals often come to see themselves as advocates for the oppressed, a corporate version of social workers. Once this flip in attitude occurs, there is practically no limit to the damage which they can inflict upon even the most sensitive and tolerant organizations. For without oppressors and victims, from where would they get their pay?

Clerical and other assistance worker positions were once formed to assist managers and executives and idea workers with the tedium of paperwork, as well as to provide creature comfort to assist the subconscious mind. Modern computer automation has more or less replaced their original core functions.

"Mindy, please (get me/put back/tuck this in) the Abraham file," a function which is now performed by webservers and database engines.

"Steve, draw up this plat and let's see if the lines close," a function which is now performed by drafting software.

"Jane, get Evans on the phone," a function which is now performed by email or contact lists connected to speed-dial.

"Sue, turn this sketch into a flyer, get a copy out to the team, and let's see how it looks," a function which is now performed by collaborative software.

"Jan, call the staff and get them together for a meeting on Tuesday afternoon so we can check on their progress," a function which is now performed by task management software.

"Ye hundreds in this room, perform these simple calculations over and over. By doing this, let's see if the hydrodynamics of plutonium implosion can destroy a city or end a war," a function which is now performed by numerical analysis software.

Other ways in which clerical staff helped the idea workers are now considered taboo. This change was demanded, we are taught, by the clerical staff itself, or their well-meaning advocates, even as their other functions above were becoming obsolete.

"Sally, bring some coffee in for the meeting please." This function is now considered demeaning despite how it assists the idea workers to reach their flow state, this creature comfort now satisfied.

"Felicia, (take/pickup) my dry-cleaning, please," so that the idea worker could stay in flow longer, and thus create more value to pay Felicia's check.

"Bob, get over to my house and cut the grass, please. While you are there, wash my Infiniti if you would," are all functions which enabled the idea worker to stay in flow longer. In addition, this maintenance task, when completed, presented a successful image to those who relied on her the most. Including her family as well the clients she would entertain that evening.

In many cases, the sight of an attractive and subtly sensual young woman attending to their creature comforts sent the further creature comfort message of "All is well in our tribe. Enjoy and prosper." And in so doing both comforted the idea workers and motivated them to excel to impress. Even females in power, executives, management and idea workers alike, secretly enjoy a sweet, pretty, intelligent girl serving them, if for no other reason than the feeling of status it gives them. "Now earn that status and think," the message subtly implies to both genders. And the sweet thing was successful only to the extent which she used her mind to foster this productivity. In her work she traded her talent to those who would most recognize her value, punishing the ungrateful and rude by her departure.

Personal services such as these have now been defined as abusive, and akin to employment rape, presumed advocates of these poor workers shrilly claim. Even imagining such service is considered demeaning and programmed into us as unacceptable. And so, the clerical and assistant functions which cannot be automated away have been regulated away. This leaves only a shell of their former utility, as we then put speaker-phones and intercoms and harassment suits into their hands instead. Thus, creativity suffers twice.

Software and Information Technology

Along the way, information technology (IT) positions evolved as the worthwhile functions of clerical and assistant positions became automated. After all, someone needed to write that software to analyze all those punch-cards. The first software workers were true idea workers, and generated enormous amounts of $+\Delta Q$ in their own right.

Most of the software professionals, at first, wrote the software which enabled the purpose of the organization, such as the database software which replaced filing. In so doing, for a brief period of time they were true idea workers, creating $+\Delta Q$ in the form of new machinery which the other workers would operate. Only this time, the machinery was the software which enabled other idea workers, rather than presses and drills and conveyer belts. At some point, this first generation work would be complete, the database and numerical analysis and project management machines now humming away in service.

But then, a schism developed as regulatory compliance grew to fill the void which computer automation created. Some software workers began to work on the systems which managed the growing complexity of taxes, or managed the employee records to track harassment risks. This class of software workers became no better than the tax accountants or the lawyers, who only exist to mitigate sources of $-\Delta Q$. With the regulatory landscape always changing and encroaching, the employment of this kind is seemingly without bound.

Over time, the software machinery turned its output to grinding out compliance products. Each organization turned its efforts to building virtual factories, with blinking lights and whirring tape drives, which did nothing but obey. It would be just as absurd if a car-maker built an entire manufacturing plant to create shiny new automobiles which reached a lobby where a loading dock should be. There, the cars are smashed into shiny new bits by regulators who operated presses built by the further slavery of others for this purpose of destruction. And yet, because most of us never see the compliance machinery of computers and software, we don't see the absurdity of it. Nonetheless, the collective benefits, as only the large, who pay their ransom in the form of jobs, can afford its cost.

As these electronic compliance factories grew in size and complexity, the pointlessness of it all began to infect the minds of the software professionals themselves. Over the years, the quality of work began to drop as the tools seemed easier and easier to use. Memory expanded, computers became faster, software trickery such as ever-changing operating systems and development tools made keeping up with these advancements seem more important than correctness.

"Computer problems" entered the lexicon as an excuse, when no one would think to say, "well, Bill just dicked it up again." Excuses and lack of situational awareness would have been considered fatal to software written for the companies' strategic use. Yet these same excuses seemed reasonable when applied to a product which would be smashed as soon as it was finished.

Armed with this excuse, the software professionals, many of whom created the computer problems in the first place by their growing laxity, began to be seen as functionaries who fed the machine rather than its skillful trainers. So the skillful artisans, overpaid in the eyes of the collective, were weeded out as the field was opened to more and more industrialization of the software industry. Importation of those whose parents were slogging around in rice paddies or polluted rivers, but now ordained as essential skilled workers because of the expense of hiring experts, didn't help.

The strategic software, growing only as new efficiencies could be imagined to rest on the old, advanced only slowly. For decades, new databases, merely larger or more feature-rich versions of the previous ones which were working fine the day before, were marketed as the salvation of all. Only rarely did a true innovation arise which enabled the idea workers in the field; most innovations were just hype intended to scare executives into expensive overhauls. Without a sufficiently large stick, however, many wouldn't have paid these ransoms.

The stick was compatibility, a manipulation which signaled the entry of the suited monkey into the world of software. No one would think to coerce a leather artisan to throw out his old tools every few years, only to replace them with a set containing punches and mallets with heads at different angles. It might take him months or years of awkward adjustment to regain his former skill. Yet, just as he was comfortable with using them a few years later, we might demand he throw them out again to buy another differently awkward set.

And yet, exactly this same kind of nonsense infected the world of software. The result? Continued buggy software as the developers struggled to keep up with the ever-changing operating systems and development tools. These developers were hardly able to prevent new bugs from creeping in as they molded the old to fit the new. Never mind fixing any of the old bugs, or implementing new strategic features. They didn't mind much, though, this meant job security. Or so they thought.

At least Bob had a chance to convince his manager to not use Material Z. He could at least point at figures on a data sheet and make his case. The executives who increasingly relied on software, though, had no chance. Without any objective way to argue against this new feature or that new paradigm, the executive was easy prey to rabid salesmen. And glowing literature which extolled the virtues of new operating systems or object-oriented design or client-server architectures.

It wasn't that these new things were necessarily bad. In the hands of a skilled artisan, an object-oriented design methodology could produce exceptional results. But in the hands of a monkey this same paradigm could easily destroy your relationship with each and every customer. A scalpel in the hands of a skilled surgeon could save your life. But this same tool, handed to a monkey, might shred every piece of furniture in your house. Some of these new tools were the equivalent of taking the scalpel away from the monkey, and handing him a laser. Now he could destroy at a distance.

Each new must-have feature, some necessitated by regulatory compliance, some by the fear of the competition armed with better tools, came with the ransom of compatibility. This ransom was readily paid by executives and managers who lacked the time to learn enough to protect themselves as they struggled to keep up with new ways to be sued out of existence.

Our ancient leather artisan might need a new tool from time to time, as old ones broke or new needs arose. A thicker harness for an ox might need a new punch for a larger rivet, for example. In that time, the artisan might make the new tool himself, perhaps by modifying an old one. Worst case, he would visit the local blacksmith and commission a new head to his specifications, including to fit a handle shape he found useful.

Early software was like that; the artisan made what he needed at the time, or sought the assistance of a specialist to help him. But the complexity of the software itself placed much of it out of reach of the individual artisan, much as if the leather tools were mysteries to be used, but never understood. In that world, a new punch must be bought from a tools vendor, who could decide to only provide that tool with a handle curved to the right, perhaps. Then, our artisan would be faced with a choice. He might purchase the new tool and use it awkwardly. Or he could purchase an entire set of tools, each with right-curved handles, and hope to one day use them all skillfully again.

Sometimes the choice itself was denied. Should the artisan break a tool (lose the disks after a computer died) or hire a new apprentice, then the new set could only be purchased with handles curved to the right. Eventually, this combination of factors would compel even the most ardent artisan to give up and refit his entire shop with the newly curving tools. Only to have the cycle repeat when the tool vendor chose to start making tools curving to the left.

Free trade would have solved this. Such nonsense can only happen when free trade is suppressed, because at some point a tool vendor in a neighboring village would decide to take over the entire market simply by not being unreasonable. And free trade would make sure that he stayed that way, lest he risk his own supplanting by another.

But, as we have seen over and over, the modern economy is not one of free trade, however much the collectivists might claim that it is, blaming free trade for the flaws which they demanded. Only a decade or so ago, it was still possible for an innovator to introduce a startling new approach which threatened the growing software establishment. The few success stories we heard back then were predominantly those who were gobbled up by the larger players.

Today, to those who might wish to start supplying software tools and operating systems to ease the pain across the industry the barriers to entry are already too high to surmount. And now the gulf is too wide, so wide that the larger players hardly notice the fray anymore, their position secure amidst a foam of version and compatibility changes.

To serve this market, so many features and window-dressings must be provided that no individual or small group of individuals can undertake the task. Should they succeed on technical merit alone, their product could not be priced sufficiently low to overcome the fear of compatibility from the masses. These masses, often stung by compatibility in the past, have learned to fear that such innovative teams might have missed some detail harmful to them, should some unexpected incompatibility arise later.

Should even this fear be overcome, the team would spend its time in its own compatibility race as it sought to implement new must-have features hyped by the originals. Eventually, they would exhaust themselves in this chase. Or, should they staff large enough to reach the market faster, they would find themselves subject to the same spiraling costs of compliance which larger staffs bring. Then, should they reach the pinnacle, they would find themselves, to preserve their own market, immersed in the same compatibility tricks which they sought to erase.

Throughout it all, the software Bob was at even more of a loss. Now, given the changing environment of software, even the rawest novice could claim proficiency with a newly hyped tool. The hapless manager, not understanding how or why Bob might disagree, could only see merit to hiring the groundling who lacked Bob's depth. Cheaper labor and new software became the rule, as the costs of the new mounted ever higher and with progressively less satisfying results. In the face of these influences, the software Bobs continue to fade away. The cost? More and more defective products festooned with glittering lights and sexy curves.

To co-op anyone who might stand in their way, the software giants now bestow upon the lowly servant self-defined certifications of expertise. As certified professionals, these workers hawk their proficiency with managing the raft of bugs which litter their chosen master's software and operating systems, rather than provide original value to those who write their checks. They are ticks on the software dog, and present themselves as ordained high priests of the art. They merely serve to operate the machine, installing software or replacing computers, shadows of their former selves who once were the loyal aides of their employer rather than their vendor.

Today, technology maintenance workers merely try to keep up, paid off in jobs which spring from the insanity that requires them. Their day is consumed with mitigating the losses from potentially enormous $-\Delta Q$s which spring from the constant compatibility war. Each employee who suffers the indignity of a failing computer must call on these workers to relieve his pain. And yet most of this pain is caused primarily by hackers who exploit vulnerabilities exposed by the version froth which the lack of free trade encourages.

Rather than be outraged, the large relish this pain. As with workplace regulations, or harassment suits, or tax complexity or environmental restrictions, the pain of software reliability is just another way of ensuring that critical mass keeps them safe from you. As you struggle with all of these issues, you, as an entrepreneur, find yourself with precious little time left in your day to compete with them.

Manufacturing

Discussing manufacturing staff within the context of ΔQ chews on the rawest of nerves. Manufacturing employees, typically of the unionized variety, imagine that they are creating $+\Delta Q$.

"For without us," they argue, "who would assemble that widget?"

Well, perhaps that robot which you just made more attractive when you went on strike.

When the manufacturing worker was an artisan, crafting a belt or a satchel out of a piece of leather, the mind was the key. Each leather was an individual thing, with a shape and a grain and imperfections to be handled and pulled and turned around and around, until the artisan's subconscious saw the satchel flap hiding in it. No two pieces of work were the same, even if the pattern was identical, and the most proficient artisan would pull a thing of beauty out of a leather which a novice would only ruin.

The road worker has the same claim on the mind. That hill or valley is different, even if only slightly, from all those he has encountered before. The weather is more or less convenient for work, the soil has more or less moisture, clay, sand or organic debris. The aggregate varies from load to load as it was pulled from different settled layers at the mixing heap at the quarry. Even the architectural plans, despite their mind-numbing uniformity, has different curves and approaches to best match the interchange which the civil engineer's subconscious mind saw peeking out of that hill.

The truck driver? Just for fun, I once took a portion of the commercial driver's license test. This was the simplest portion, the part which covered air brakes. I was humiliated within a few questions. I challenge anyone who doubts the truck driver to go down to the DMV and try the same. As he drives, he keeps the rest of us safe as we whizz around him. Rain, snow, blinding sun on the horizon, his mind must always be alert. His subconscious mind tracks the cars in the rear view mirrors, accounting for each one, so that the driver feels you drift into his blind spot before he registers your presence.

Even the unionized supervisor at the plant has a more mindful job as he deals with the absenteeism and the frayed nerves and the work schedules. But the assembler who places that component on that location, over and over, provides the best value when he chooses to *not* innovate. Or when he decides to watch for the missing bolts or the misaligned components or the improperly assembled component as it comes from the packaging. Or to put the component into position without hurting anyone. Clearly, these uses of the mind do not add $+\Delta Q$, but instead prevent the infliction of $-\Delta Q$. Quality is latent in the machines or the design or the materials or the procedures or the sub-assemblies he is given. He can only detract from them by his inattention. Nor can he do a thing to correct a defective design in any meaningful way.

Yet, the collective believes that all $+\Delta Q$ derives from these workers' efforts. But without the machines and the design and the processes or the materials, the worker would be no more effective than a monkey beating on a coconut with a rock.

Recently an automotive union made a show about "giving back" some time off or some other triviality, and expected to be slapped on the back. Well, of course, that was a good thing, but it hardly goes far enough. This move was merely the dialing back a little of some enormous $-\Delta Q$ from years before. They are just throwing slightly smaller bricks now. The manufacturing industry, however, is possibly the most easily automated industry of all.

Automation requires a few prerequisites:

☐ Constrained work environment. The inside environment of a manufacturing floor can be planned and counted on to be invariant. You can bolt a machine in place, and it will stay there, making it easier to deliver a component to a precise location for the machine to work with. One machine can then easily feed another, also located at a precise position. Contrast this environment with bricklaying, where the path from the pallet to the location on the wall varies with the worksite or the weather.

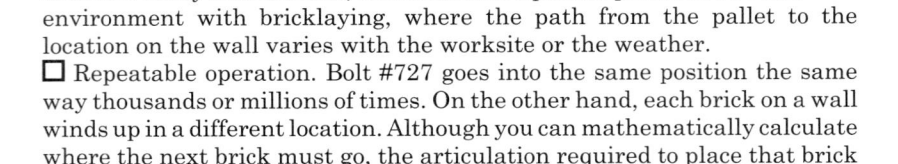

☐ Repeatable operation. Bolt #727 goes into the same position the same way thousands or millions of times. On the other hand, each brick on a wall winds up in a different location. Although you can mathematically calculate where the next brick must go, the articulation required to place that brick becomes tricky. Also, sometimes you need to cut bricks to fit.

☐ Access to sufficient power. Those big chunky conductors going into the wall of the plant help a lot. A construction site, on the other hand, may not even have power anywhere near it yet.

☐ Well-defined material. All of the material which flows into a manufacturing plant is usually tightly specified, and rejected if not. All those bolts are the same, all the struts are the same, all the tires are identical. Each of these materials can be inspected by automated vision or x-ray systems if needed. Or, if a tire, for example, put on a hub and inflated, and then pinged for soundness. The bricklayer, on the other hand, must inspect, to some degree, each brick he handles for faults or other defects, and each brick or defect is unique enough to fool most vision systems.

So the job of the assembly worker is to mitigate -ΔQ. But if while doing so he wields the power of the collective to inflict even more -ΔQ, he merely incentivizes his employer to automate away jobs such as his more and more. And, since his job is easily automated, the level of automation continues to rise each year. The cost? Fewer opportunities for productive individuals who wish to absorb themselves in the work and enjoy the process of creation.

Gatekeeper or Facilitator?

In all of these examples, the true creative individualist sees his role in the organization as a facilitator of creativity. In contrast, the collectivist chooses to perform as a gatekeeper, limiting access to resources required to unleash creativity in others.

The same executive who rations pens could instead lean back and watch. Watch the flow of creativity, and watch for any obstacles which defeat it. And then move to remove those obstacles using his greater authority and resources. Unless his goal is to extract unearned value from his clients by increasing billable hours.

The same salesman who twists the needs of his customers to suit his product regardless of its suitability could instead lean back and listen to his customers. Then flow these customers' true needs back into his own organization to improve future products. By so doing, both the salesman and the vendor become recognized as true partners in their customers' success. Unless the vendor's strategy is to extract unearned value by manipulating his customer's decisions to his short-term gain and their long-term peril.

The same manager who sees the creative need of his staff as threats to his authority could instead lean back and watch. Just like the executive, he could watch the flow of creativity in his own staff. Over time, he might learn to recognize its outward signs not as awkwardness or hostility, but instead clues to him that it is time to shield them from disturbance. And then stoke those creative fires with the simple comforts required to keep them burning hot. Unless his strategy is to promote his status in the company through manipulation, regardless of the long-term health of his company and its image with his customers.

The same laborer who feels the need to unionize could instead lean back and watch. Watch the more skilled masters of his art and learn from them. Learn to become skilled and creative himself so that he earns promotion and greater compensation for his skill. Or create a reputation for himself so that he could attain rewarding work anywhere individualism is cherished. Unless his goal is to abandon his own merit, choosing instead to coerce unearned value from his employer by mass action.

The same administrative assistant who interrupts the creative flow of the entire staff by use of the intercom or dramatic interludes could instead lean back and watch. Watch the creative process and foster it by simple acts such as taking messages and delivering them gently while the creative think. Or tend to the needs of the staff by bringing them water or pens or any other item they may need for their work which may be blocking their subconscious work. And in so doing promote herself by her increased value. Unless her goal is to extract unearned value by feigning offense at harmlessness. Or to entertain herself with drama created for drama's sake.

The same software developer who slakes his desire to learn the latest tool or new methodology could instead lean back and think. Think about whether his company is better served by building on and improving what works now, rather than forcing the upheaval of chasing some unproved trend or unsubstantiated promise. And if that upheaval is required, doing so in a way that is best understood by those other idea workers around him who don't share his zeal for the unfamiliar. Unless his goal is to fortify his own position as a guru, and thus extract unearned value by insisting on the fantastically complex.

The same information technology specialist who delights in torturing the users of his systems could instead lean back and watch. Watch how their efforts produce the value which pays his check, and commit to simplifying and enhancing their work as an unfelt force of nature beneath them. Unless his goal is to extract unearned value by acting instead as a whirlwind of upheaval which leaves destruction and turmoil in his wake.

Gatekeeper or facilitator? Collectivist or individualist? Monkey or man? Industry by industry, job by job, day by day and minute by minute, each member of each organization gets to make this choice. Too often the choice is to twist and manipulate and demand rather than facilitate.

The same gatekeeper functions which exist in large organizations must instead, in small organizations, emanate as facilitation instead. To do otherwise is universally recognized as suicidal for a small business. We've heard our entire lives that entrepreneurs must behave differently from the big company worker. But, even with that behavioral change, or, more precisely, attitudinal shift, entrepreneurs fail more often than they succeed. Usually, the blame for this consistent failure is placed on either too little entrepreneurial spirit, or paradoxically, too much of it. Both cannot exist at the same time, and either explanation averts attention from the true question.

Hardly ever does anyone ask "why is this attitudinal change deemed necessary for the small, but is hardly ever demanded of the large?" If you turn the entrepreneurial light back on the large organizations, much of what I have been saying in this book becomes revealed within their walls.

Why is it that large organizations don't require the customer focus demanded of the small? Why is it that large organizations can afford the wastefulness which would be suicidal in the small? On and on, the comparisons mount. Despite this evidence, we accept the success of the large as reasonable while we simultaneously accept the failure of the small. And even though the small have taken precisely those actions and attitudes universally recognized as required for their success.

Again and again, large organizations prosper despite inefficiency or a lack of quality, while the small flounder despite a focus on the needs of their customer. Know how to make a better air conditioner which provides more comfort with less energy consumption and fewer repairs? It matters not one bit. Before you can sell that first unit you have to comply with a barrier of regulation which probably keeps you from even getting your hands on the refrigerant which you need to make this possible. Or determines how you must structure your manufacturing or your distribution or your support or installation. Or who and how many you must hire, and what economic relationship you must accept between them and you.

All of this keeps the existing players who provide increasingly more shoddy units safe from your ideas and individual effort. Meanwhile, they get to stick labels on their units which proclaim higher efficiency as their customers swelter and suffer through repair after repair. These things are possible because the large organization gives the monkey a safe cave in which to hide. Otherwise, the monkey would have to transform himself, or starve, his de-evolution evident in the open air in which the entrepreneur must work.

To protect his hiding place, then, the monkey, whether in a suit or coveralls, demands protection from his foolishness. This demand he communicates to his lawmakers, his lawyers and his shop stewards, who weave fantastically intricate concealment around him. Concealment which the entrepreneur, his only natural predator, cannot afford, but, outnumbered, must obey and not ferret him out.

Marketing

The protections which large organizations (commercial, government or spiritual) enjoy allows the collective to wield another weapon in its war against the individual. And resulted in the evolution of an entire industry unique to the collective. To introduce this specialty, I am going to exercise some scholarship to define it, and then pick that apart.

According to *dictionary.com*, marketing is defined as:

Marketing - noun. the total of activities involved in the transfer of goods from the producer or seller to the consumer or buyer, including advertising, shipping, storing, and selling.

OK, that definition is a little misleading. Find someone who presents themselves as a marketing professional, and they wouldn't dare admit to something so common as shipping or storing anything. That's too much like useful work. And selling is for the salesman. And advertising, which is a little closer than the rest, is too narrow. Their job instead, is much more important than just advertising. No, a marketing professional paints a picture of his product in your mind.

When you buy a stick of gum, the guy who rings up your purchase is a salesman, from the point of view of a marketer. Imagine that you walk into that same store, with no intention of buying the gum. If the salesman walks up to you and says, "Hey fella, how about buying a stick of gum?" he is still selling. But when he says, "Mmmm, that is some good, good gum. It's all juicy, and tastes just like fruit. Delicious." Then, he is marketing. Or reinforcing marketing you have encountered before.

In fact, it is previous marketing which made it possible for an association to pop in your mind just as you read that. You can see the image of what that pack of gum looks like in your mind, as well as how it tastes. You experience these phantom sensations only because of a barrage of marketing which you have experienced in the past. And you rejected all other options of some delicious gum because of marketing.

Here are some more examples:
"Mmmm, this gum is so big. And red. Tasty". You know exactly what gum that is, even though bigness and redness really has nothing at all to do with enjoying gumness. And, truth be told, it is no bigger than the alternatives.

"Hubba hubba, I want to blow some bubbles." Even though this one is generally bigger, the bigness isn't the trigger, it is the hubbaness.

"Bubbles are great, but I want some yummy yummy yum with them, too." This is a little farther apart in brainspace, but eventually you get there.

Marketing isn't the same as selling, although all effective salesmen do a little of it all the time. But selling is more focused on the mechanics of leading the buyer through the decision process from contact to a close. After this, other sales functionaries then work through the transaction and the logistics and invoicing necessary to exchange the value.

Marketing makes you aware of a need and a product or service which fills that need. Sometimes the need is legitimate, sometimes it is an illusion. Sometimes the product or service is worthwhile, sometimes it is worse than useless. All of these exist in a spectrum of need and utility, in all possible combinations. And in each case it is a hijacking of your subconscious mind to make these associations for you.

Marketing is equally powerful for good or ill, and depends on the values of the one wielding its power. In the hands of an individualist who wants to bring the best value to his customers, so that he might exchange it for more value for himself, its message is positive and truthful. In the hands of the collective, who merely wish to extract as much unearned value from every sucker they can find, it is misleading and destructive.

Sometimes marketing can have unexpected blowback on the company in question. Who doesn't get a feeling of creepy ill-ease as they pass by a Burger King? I used to enjoy going there, but now I don't want to be associated with that freakish chess-piece. I know they are trying to be edgy and hip, but still. And what idiot thought up that Sponge-Bob rap?

That could have been cleverly done, but crossed too many genres. For the kid angle, they could have had a family walking out of a Burger King with square pants after eating there. Or, for the late-nighter, the commercial could have advertised a large sandwich with the same theme. For late-night adults, this commercial could have featured the girls shaking burgers on their butts as the rapper sang, "I like big buns, and I cannot lie..." With no kids around, that would have been funny and cute, in a way.

But mixing the two is just, uh, odd, to be delicate. And this assessment from a guy writing a book which is designed to offend almost everyone who reads it. If a little girl wants to grow up to be a pole-dancer, she needs to make that decision when she is old enough to understand the consequences. But not because Daddy took her to Burger King. And Daddy doesn't want to look as if he is helping her make this career choice. "But Daddy, I don't WANT to pole dance," little Sally whimpers as he brings the tray to the table. "Shut up and eat your burger, honey, your public is waiting. And this time, if the tears streak your makeup I'll make you go see the bad man again. So smile."

That commercial made the beauty-pageant Moms look half-sane. And it will be a long time before I will go there even alone because I don't want to look like I'm there for the show. I also don't want to look like I'm hoping to watch the little girls practice what they saw on TV as they wait in line. This from a guy who sees hitting a strip club as a legitimate and essential way to enjoy the local culture, as essential as hearing some local bands or trying the ethnic dish. Even I have limits.

Most marketing isn't as ham-handed. Some of it is so subtle as to almost escape attention, which almost seems contradictory. Not so, once you appreciate that the best marketing speaks to your subconscious mind while simultaneously trying to avoid triggering your conscious mind. A long time ago, Wal-Mart, founded in Bentonville, Arkansas, was a regional chain which appealed to a western cowboy ethic. In that day, their logo was a saloon font which made you think everyone in there should be wearing a Wild West sheriff's badge. For their region, this was a great thing.

But as the chain grew, that font probably stifled their image, or at least threatened to. As a consequence of growth, they moved into regions of the country where western-ness seemed about as silly and out of place as a Texan trying to run a business or run for President without Daddy's oil money. As proof of this, recall what happens to Texans who run for President based solely on their own entrepreneurial resources or their own ideas of government. Any idea which doesn't originate from the Galveston-Houston-Dallas-Fort Worth corridor is dead on arrival. Even non-Texans shun these native outsiders as not sufficiently Texan.

Had Wal-Mart not changed their logo, they would have faced an unending uphill struggle with non-Western housewives. Each of these ladies might imagine that every towel in the place had patterns woven with little boy fantasies of "Cowboys and Injuns". Or hung on racks which looked like horns on a Cadillac. Tacky. So, in 1981 the logo changed to the blocky sans-serif which we recognize today. Deftly, they decoupled their image from their previous ethic. All was fine for a decade.

Then, Wal-Mart added a generic star in 1992 as the candidacy of Clinton resonated with younger voters or other budding or established domestic communists. All of these were unhappy with the elitist presidency of Bush, and instead were looking for an elitist all their own, hopefully with fresh new Stalinist ideas. Sadly for them, they would have to wait almost a decade for another collectivist Texan to help them in their Stalinist quest and lay the foundation for a dyed-in-the-wool Marxist to arise.

The 1992 Wal-Mart star might be interpreted as a tip-of-the hat not only to these domestic communists, but also the Chinese who were beginning to make everything in the place. And the older generations would be pleased as well, associating that star with that seen on every tank and truck they had ridden into battle. Clever. That marketing ploy managed to sweep them all in, from both sides of the collectivist spectrum.

But today, the Chinese are threatening to directly sell their own brands in this country. As I write this, rumors abound that GM is about to import Chinese-branded cars, presumably sporting a Red Chinese star. Other brands and products will likely follow soon. For the millions who shop Wal-Mart, lacking any real options, the association with that red star might be uncomfortably close. I wonder whether this reasoning had any influence on the 2008 change of the logo to include a sun-burst instead of the classic star. A change which hit the streets a year or so ahead of even rumors about Chinese-branded products hitting the shores?

But just dropping the star or changing its shape wouldn't be enough. Your subconscious mind would still be too likely to plug it in, just as you see your child's face as you talk to her on the phone. To prevent your subconscious from even visualizing the old star, the font had to change, as well as the color. Even the new sunburst shape was moved to the side, effectively decoupling the old star completely in your mind by erasing the previous image entirely.

Sounds paranoid? OK. About as paranoid as thinking I can force an older person to think of the color "yellow" just by having him read the words "juicy" and "fruit" in the proper context. Or make a kid think of a goofy yellow sponge just by singing "Ohhhhhhhh..." in the right intonation.

There is no nuance too subtle to escape the attention of an effective marketer, or as sometimes used, propagandist. Even the impression of paranoia is designed to program your subconscious mind to "just be reasonable" instead of suspicious at the intrusion and manipulation.

Essentially, the marketer is trying to shortcut not only the necessity of thinking for yourself, but also your willingness to do so.

Marketing is a necessary thing in the modern world. It is a consequence of free trade, but is too often used to thwart free trade. It is impossible to imagine a circumstance in which one ancient woodman didn't tell his customers that his wood was better or safer or more woodish than some other woodman's wood. And then to begin lying about these things.

It is a lot easier to lead people to believe that your product is better than another one than it is to actually make it a better product. Making a better product is a lot more expensive than making a better marketing campaign. So, it doesn't take a rocket scientist to figure out, on average, where the dollars will go. And if that doesn't work, it is a lot easier and cheaper to weave a marketing web to convince the masses to regulate that better product out of existence. Or, to automatically assume that your product is superior in some subjective way. As a last resort, factual details can be presented in such a way as to distort reality.

Legitimate marketing is not like this. Legitimate marketing genuinely informs potential customers about the features of your product or service, and the benefits they can expect to receive when using it. Legitimate marketers might undertake their task either passively or actively, or more likely, use both in succession to help you become aware of their product. A passive marketer can perform research to understand the true needs of their potential customers. Or, how those customers respond to product or service prototypes to discover potential flaws or shortcomings in the design.

Once a product or service concept is fully understood through this research, the legitimate firm might then design a product or service to fill that need. Then, they would employ active marketing to inform their potential customers about the product or service and how it might benefit them. And, by the way, where they can buy it.

This legitimate process is what a productive value-based individualist might employ or demand for his company. In quality of life terms, a legitimate marketer looks for unsatisfied gaps in a customer's quality of life matrix. He then figures out ways to fill those needs by supplying stuff, push, time or energy which meets those needs. Sometimes, the customer has a potential gap in their quality of life matrix, but doesn't understand that the need even exists. In that case, the legitimate marketer might find the gap during the research, design the product, and then educate potential customers first about the gap, and then how the product meets the need.

For example, it might be discovered that joint pain is reduced in workers who stand on their feet all day by providing a certain kind of arch support. Perhaps research is conducted specifically to find out what support works best for these workers, or this research simply pops out of some unrelated work by someone else. Shoe Company A might then decide to use this information to make a brand of shoe specifically directed at this kind of worker, and then use active marketing showing some before and after dramatizations. Perfectly legitimate. The customers have a -ΔQ factor in their life, sore joints, and Shoe Company A has created a product which resolves this -ΔQ factor.

On the other hand, illegitimate marketing uses deceit or ungrounded fear to make you inclined to buy their product or service. In this case, the passive marketing stage takes customer feedback not to resolve shortcomings, but instead to devise a marketing strategy to bypass any negatives in the offering. The active phase of illegitimate marketing then doesn't educate the customer, but instead weaves a web of "spin" around him.

This web of spin can take several forms. First, the quality of life factors themselves can be manipulated to view the marketer's offering more attractively, or to view the competitor's offerings more negatively. This can be either a good thing or a bad thing, depending on whether this factor adjustment is done based on facts or nonsense.

Another form of spin is to artificially inflate a product or service's features. This type of marketing is universally illegitimate. A computer chip maker might hype their product as using little power, and then claim that this feature alone is important. Clearly, this approach is intended to make you not look too closely at the raft of shortcomings which chip might have for most users.

A related form of spin is to artificially downplay a negative feature about an offering. This, too is universally illegitimate. For example, a promotion might claim "our saw only rarely decapitates," or more likely, "our saw cures headaches."

Suppose in our standing worker example that, before the miracle shoe, most workers instead took a painkiller tablet each day to head off their pain. That pill may be only pennies a day, while the shoe may be seen as a little too much to pay. Shoe Vendor A might then cite a study which shows that "joint pain, if ignored, can lead to disabling injury later in life." OK, that sounds legitimate, right? Maybe, but not if they also fail to present the next paragraph from that same study which says, "Fortunately, simple exercises can be performed which have been clinically shown to permanently prevent either pain or later injury."

Now let's assume that a workplace health service starts which offers to teach these exercises to employees at various companies. To the shoe company, this is a threat which cannot be tolerated. It might embark on the following marketing campaigns:

"No study has been performed which says that treating workplace joint pain with painkillers is effective at avoiding future injury. Buy ShoeWedge!"

"Exercise can help with workplace joint pain, but only if administered by appropriately trained personnel with the proper equipment. Beware of practitioners who claim they can treat your pain on site. Buy ShoeWedge!"

"Workplace joint injury, caused by ill-fitting or improper shoes, threatens your ability to work. Ask your shop steward to demand that your employer provide you with the proper safety equipment."

"Workplace joint injury, caused by ill-fitting or improper shoes, threatens our national competitiveness. Write your Congressman and demand that your health be protected."

And through cutouts, "Some painkillers can adversely affect those with allergic reactions. Demand that Congress limit access to sharing medications in our schools and at our jobs."

And, more silently, the vendor sends lobbyists to Washington to ensure that when such workplace regulation is enacted, these regulations happen to fit nicely within the boundaries of Shoe Company A's ShoeWedge patents. And promote regulations which seek to block the availability of legitimate painkillers. And impose licensing and other restrictions on practitioners who may have a legitimate claim of success.

Illegitimate marketing cannot stand the test of truth. And so, left to its own, free trade would eventually weed out those customers most susceptible to deception. For example, headless saw users rarely ever are repeat customers, headaches or no. Or for that matter, workers who stand on their feet all day will figure out what works best for them, shoe, pill or exercise, and spread it around. Those who ignore great advice will then be less productive and less capable, and eventually learn or give way to others who will.

To survive, then, illegitimate marketers rely on ignorance and coercion to help them in their work. And to that end, marketers focus more and more, not on the expert in a field who might give them trouble, but instead upon the masses of those who are not as well informed about their offerings.

Increasingly, just as it is cheaper to spin than it is to produce a great product, it is even more easy to advocate regulations which favor a particular product or service. Without regulations to the contrary, free trade would eventually discover spin and weed it out. With regulations in place, however, free trade is forbidden to ferret out the spin. Even the attempt is deemed criminal.

Monkeys invented and support shamans, lawmakers, regulators, lawyers, accountants and all the other regulatory and regulatory compliance workers. As if these weren't bad enough to extract value from the individual, now even the relatively benign deceit of the marketer has been turned to the monkey's purpose. The regulatory marketers serve the collective, and ultimately the will of each monkey, as he whips the collective into more and more regulation and restriction of the individual.

It is in this environment that the modern entrepreneur finds himself struggling to succeed against increasingly larger odds.

Chapter 15, Entrepreneurial Success

Once you make the decision to leave the comfortable prison of your cubicle or union shop to strike out on your own, you take upon yourself the challenges which have been specifically designed to break your spirit. Suitably broken, it is your purpose then to return to your cage. Once there, your place is to serve the monkey collective, to feed them, to provide for them, to sacrifice yourself for their noble purpose. Gone are the days in which you could happily trade your efforts and skills to others, enriching yourself by providing the stuff of quality of life.

The obstacles are too high now. You now have been reduced to the level of a bare animal, yoked to their gleaming plows. The exercises from a few chapters back should have shown you your jailers. And how many of them there are.

They surround us. And yet, if you were to listen to conservatives, you would hear that there is plenty of opportunity for excellence. Then, they hold themselves up as examples of success, but fail to mention that there are precious few opportunities to be a television pundit, or talk show host, or former Speaker of the House. Or best-selling author.

The people who promote entrepreneurship, in the classical rags to riches model, could be seen as merely naive and misguided. Provided, of course, you didn't examine their sponsors very closely, or examine their own views of ways in which their side seeks to control your lives. We will look into a few of these things shortly, but they hope that by struggling, you will eventually feed their own enterprises with the ideas which they need to continue. Both sides of the political spectrum set traps for your productivity and energy, and use your own energy to feed themselves.

At least the progressives are honest about their intentions to enslave you. If they were the only problem we might at least have a fighting chance. But the country club collectives set more obscure traps. They then try to hijack your loyalty to them as "fellow businessmen." Each of their pet issues assists their large collectives, while crippling your entrepreneurial business.

As I give these examples, try to spot which collective benefits at your expense. Hint: sometimes both sides benefit as you lose.

Want to paint houses better than the next guy? The collective imports slave labor to underprice you as you struggle with their regulations.

Thousands reading this know how to solve the problem of nuclear waste by converting it into safe and useful things. But these thousands will never have the chance to break through the walls of regulation to try.

Energy is all around us, but your ideas will be crushed under building codes and safety and environmental laws if you try to flesh them out.

Some are particularly skilled at teaching children but they are resisted by unions on the left and shamans on the right. The liability insurance alone for opening a private school would dash your hopes to provide this service. And in many jurisdictions, you can teach your own children in homeschool, but can't teach the children of others. Even if their parents beg you to do this for them.

Farming, the most fundamental of all the trades, is increasingly overwhelmed with regulations and compliance as their operators try to feed us. The choking out of the family farm paves the way for collective farming, operations whose shares are held by the power brokers.

We hail bio-fuels as our salvation, as we fine and arrest the hobbyist who tries it, calling him a tax evader. These things are only useful to the extent which they provide revenue and jobs, we are taught.

Energy, in particular, is a key area in which the productive mind is stifled. We saw earlier that energy is the foundation of civilization. It is no wonder, then, that energy has the most stifling influences of all of them.

Let's take a simple example and see where the obstacles lie. Over a kilowatt of energy strikes each square meter of the surface of the earth when the sun is at its zenith. While we argue over how best to fund the Chinese for solar cells which might capture twenty percent of this, we ignore Sadi Carnot. His writings tell us that even simple solar thermal installations might capture as much as twenty-five percent of the incident energy. But even a fraction of that would be better than the zero of it we collect today.

For example, a low efficiency thermal collector would trap some of this energy. Simple thermal collectors do not require specialized manufacturing as do solar panels. So, these would be accessible to everyone with a garage where they might work and have the urge to try. Entirely new industries might arise to supply the components. But the hobbyists who would develop these industries are prevented from using the ammonia or ethanol which would be required as working fluids. After all, these materials might supply a drug lab or evade a tax.

Plus, in many jurisdictions the skylines are choked with subdivisions which don't allow you to put a collector of any kind on your roof. Yes, each resident agreed to these restrictions, but practically speaking, they had no choice. Good luck finding a home in most suburban areas which isn't part of a subdivision.

But why can't we find homes which aren't in subdivisions? Well, because individual homes will normally be built by independent general contractors. The large tract builders, with economies of scale enforced by regulations and licensing, are much more effective at scooping up land and plunking down cookie-cutter homes. And even the independent general contractor often finds himself only able to build on specific lots within these subdivisions. He just can't compete with the large builders when it comes to snapping up the available land.

So our low-efficiency thermal collectors are stillborn. And yet, there could be other possible benefits to these. Sadi also tells us that these same thermal power installations, boosted with burning of garbage or wood, would increase their output out of proportion to the heat added. But to do so would be to challenge the planet, we are told. And produce things like icky smoke, which chokes the suited monkeys in their traffic jams, but feeds our plants as the rain washes the smoke from the sky.

This is but one simple example taken from one area of interest. The collective knows no bounds in constructing limitations on your ability to excel, regardless of your specialty. Each day the productive individual considers questions like these, and knows the answers as his subconscious mind excites him to try. But the conscious, rational mind knows that success will be blocked from him at every turn.

So the solution?

Simply give up and accept your place in the service of the collective?

Nope. There is a way out, regardless of your expertise and position in life. And it is simple.

Redefine success.

Appreciate success as control of your life. Enjoy the ticks of the day with those you love the most. Enjoy exploring God's nature and appreciating its beauty.

Start your own business doing whatever it is which improves the quality of life for others, and which they are willing to pay you for. Trade your effort for theirs and you both win. Don't see yourself as a specific business, but instead commit yourself to destroying the monkeys economically by doing whatever they get paid for, only better, faster, cheaper, and with less drama. But don't hire a single soul.

Enjoy denying the monkeys the fruit of your effort. Provide for your needs, and as much more as you wish, but not enough more so that you become sucked in again to their web.

Develop that Depression Era mentality, not to survive collapse or to fight a war against your productive kinsmen, but instead as a weapon to deprive the collective. They surround us. But they need us. But we don't need them. For anything.

Get in touch with the basics of life. Understand the crafts of centuries past. Then apply your knowledge to improve them. Don't abandon the tractor, but instead learn better how to maintain and fuel it. Don't abandon the microchip, but instead learn better how to employ it to pump water.

Grow your own food and raise your own chickens. But not as your grandparents did. Instead, use the technology we now have to ease this task as you enjoy the leisure. And as the monkeys slowly starve without you.

Enlist your subconscious mind to help you answer the question, "What do I *need*?" And not "What do I *crave*?" Because your cravings help them imprison you.

Get your subconscious mind to help you find out what you can do to provide value to your fellow producers so that you might meet your needs through service to these few others. And then excel at that work.

Equally important, collaborate with your subconscious mind on ways to automate away your need for help. If you have to, fire products or services or customers, starting with the most difficult first, to avoid having to hire an employee to handle that work. The high-value tasks which are left are generally the most easy to automate. You may have to learn new skills to do this, but embrace that effort as a joy in itself.

Recall the diagram below, which relates the cost of automation to the cost of labor.

Additional Regulatory Cost

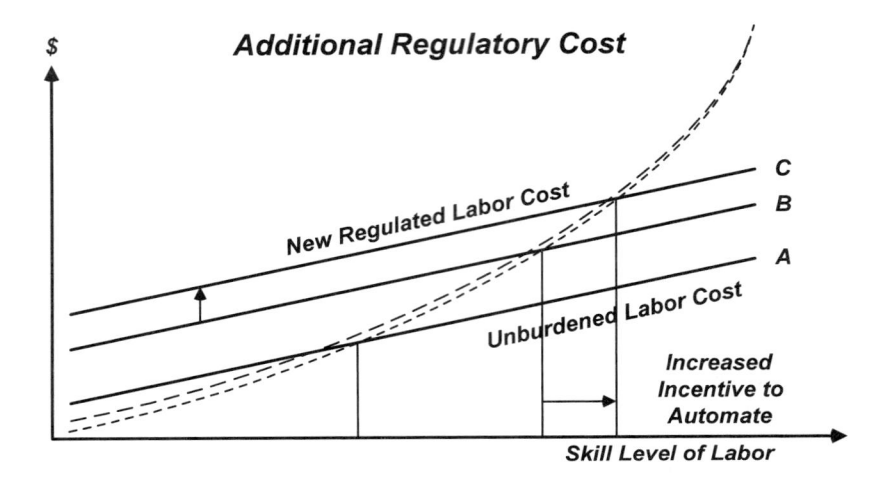

(Figure: graph with axes "$" vs "Skill Level of Labor", showing curves labeled "New Regulated Labor Cost" and "Unburdened Labor Cost", lines A, B, C, and "Increased Incentive to Automate")

As we discussed before, each regulation which comes along forces a purely economic decision whether to automate a task or continue doing it by hand through labor. I also started an example of a potter, and all the tasks which face even this simple vocation, long ago rendered obsolete for other than artistic purposes.

Recall in our discussion that each new regulation increases the cost of labor sufficiently so that additional jobs or skills fall victim to the chopping block. Further, industries or enterprises, large or small, which *don't* automate these tasks soon find themselves as obsolete as the potter is now. It doesn't matter what your level of skill, you can't produce pots by hand cheaply enough without the machine to sell them in quantity.

Some entrepreneurs then take another approach, and that is to advertise their offerings as specialized boutique items. "Hand-crafted pottery!" they might claim. In a shrinking economy, or an imploding economy if this book is taken to heart, boutique dies first. In any event, China has a lot of hands who could be crafting.

Just after presenting that diagram the last time, I asserted that, for an entrepreneur, it makes sense to automate a task away long before a simple cost calculation would justify doing so. How can this be? How can you automate before it makes economic sense to do so?

Two reasons. First, having read this book thus far, you know that costs of employment will continue to rise. As workplaces become more and more adult day care centers, you will be subjected to endlessly increasing regulations and restrictions which increase the cost of employment. These costs never go backwards in any meaningful way.

So, by automating a marginal task now, you have an undeniable edge over your competition, large and small. When a new regulation wanders by which forces the rest of them to scramble to catch up, you will be smiling and thinking about the next task or skill you are automating away. I laugh each time I find myself in this situation.

The second reason to automate before it makes economic sense to do so also relates to the adult day care nature of modern employment. Unless your ambition is to run a day care, chances are you didn't go into business to run one. Especially not for adults. In fact, you probably wanted to start your own business to escape someone else's vision of you as needing day care. Now that you understand the creative process, you can appreciate how employee drama itself creates another category of cost, as shown in the diagram below:

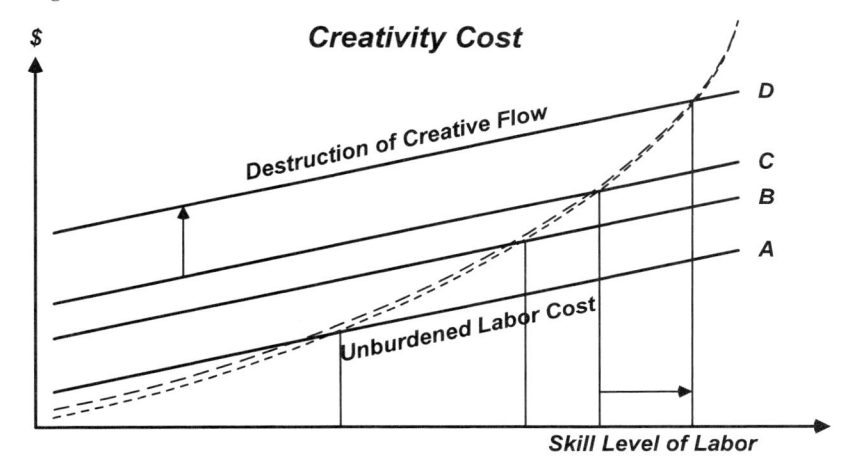

Creativity Cost

Destruction of Creative Flow

D
C
B
A

Unburdened Labor Cost

Skill Level of Labor

The real cost of employee drama, when considered in light of its ability to destroy your creative flow, represents an increase in the cost of labor. The $-\Delta Q$ which this person inflicts, or threatens to inflict, decreases your creativity and your ability to think. The first time a key employee misses a deadline or an important appointment or fails to show for a critical push, you will fully appreciate what I mean. You will appreciate it more when you consider what creativity you lost as you had to fill in to get the work done which you had hired them for. You will appreciate it even more when you hear a sob story about their dog getting loose and you imagine them flinging your cash to the wind as they look for their flea bag.

You may be tempted to hire another monkey to take that one's place, or worse, hire a second so that one can always back up the other. When both are off chasing their drama at the same time you will watch an opportunity vanish in front of you. Or you will scramble even harder to preserve an unexpected opportunity. When this happens, just remember that I told you so. Worst of all, the creativity which they destroyed, while you scrambled to deal with their absenteeism or their demands or the regulations which force your hand, is the seed of your future. While you are busy handling issues which you thought were already planned away, you are prevented from planning your next opportunity.

Rather than reacting to today, lean back and think. Think about how to get rid of that next task which is almost at the edge. Learn how to automate that task or buy a machine to do it, even if you have to take some old bag of bolts and get it running yourself. Come to think about it, that last is probably the best, since you will learn something in the process of fixing it. Or introduce you to new services or products which you can provide. Or decrease your cost of automation across the entire spectrum of work, making it easier to automate all other tasks which face you.

Automation isn't just mechanical, either. Learn how to use spreadsheets and databases and HTML and Javascript or Python, and find out how to get all these things to work together. Commercials on TV make fun of entrepreneurs who try to do these things for themselves. Of course they do, they are trying to sell you Indian bugs so that you can spend your day becoming an expert with their flaky product instead of becoming an expert yourself. Once you start understanding how to manage your data, such as purchasing and invoicing and inventory, and the tools to do so, you will understand the inefficiencies in your business. And then be empowered to fix them yourself instead of hoping they won't take you under.

Or, decide whether that task can be done differently, or in a different order, or eliminated entirely. Does the task stem from a specific problem customer, or a product line which generates endless support costs? Then kill it off and focus your energy somewhere else. If your customer isn't willing to pay the cost which is required to provide that product or service, why should you subsidize it?

By constantly automating and chopping out inessential tasks, tomorrow will be free for you to repeat the process. Eventually, this outlook will create a snowball which makes you more efficient, and your costs lower, your best customers happier and your profitability larger. Or you can let your employees snowball you.

An entrepreneur's task, in our modern world, is now primarily to destroy jobs wherever we can. This is the single most effective way which you can become more efficient in whatever product or service you are hoping to provide. But to do this, you have to learn, and you have to think. No longer can you just struggle and hope that hard work is enough.

I can teach you how to think, but I can't tell you what to think. I can tell you where to go to learn what you need to know, but I can't tell you what you need to do once you know these things. You have to answer these questions for yourself. That is the essence of free trade, that you know best of all what is best for you. Anything else which anyone might tell you about what to do is necessarily worse than listening to your own judgement.

I would like to tell you that you can become completely self-sufficient, but I would be lying to you. The collective ensures that self-sufficiency is out of your reach. Property tax must be paid, or they will seize everything you own. Health insurance is a moral necessity for caring for your family, and this is held deliberately expensive to thwart the individual and force him into a herd. Clothing, medicines, dental care all require cash.

So living in the woods as a hermit is not an option. Nor should it be, you have a right to enjoy the things in life which satisfy you. And your subconscious mind demands some of these comforts so that it can work at peak efficiency to help you succeed. To pay for these things you need cash, and for this you have to play the game. But learn the rules so that you can play it well.

Incorporate so that you can flow your pay through your company. Mend a fence? Have the check written to your company so that you can extract the value through your expenses before the tax man reaches out his hand. Those precious few dollars which make it to you as pay entitle you for assistance as a pauper. Earned income credit will dramatically increase your pay, as your tax bill shrinks. Wear the garb of a monkey and screech as you, your boss, pay you as little as possible, then clutch at all the bananas and coconuts to which a monkey is entitled.

Apply for each dollar of every grant and handout you can find. Need a fence? See if an agricultural grant applies. Dedicate yourself to ferreting out these resources, which were meant as a chain around your neck as you struggled to pay for them. Wrap this chain around the neck of the collective instead and pull with all your might.

The details change from year to year. A deduction which is fine this year will be closed the next as a new one takes its place. These deductions will always exist, as they are intended to serve the needs of this segment or that. Your task is to find them when they change. Filter your health insurance through your company while it is allowed, and then follow the deduction when it isn't. Build fences when the elites clutch at grants for fences, build ponds when the elites fund theirs. The monkey collective will always leave holes for itself as it tries to choke you out of hiding and back into your cage. Train your subconscious mind to find their warrens and then dig your own holes to match theirs.

And always follow the law and document everything you do.

Recognize that the majority of the cost of entrepreneurship comes in the form of those you hire. Each of the workers described in the previous chapter imposed various amounts of transactional $-\Delta Q$ on their organizations. Only the high-value idea workers add $+\Delta Q$. As a productive entrepreneur, this guy is you. All the rest merely mitigate $-\Delta Q$, or impose their own $-\Delta Q$ as they dramatize your life.

The fewer employees you have, the fewer opportunities they have to inflict $-\Delta Q$ on you, and to drain your wallet and your energy. Ask your subconscious mind to help you figure out ways to achieve your goals yourself. And where you can't, contract and trade with others like you so that both of you avoid employees.

Without employees, you can pay yourself and taxes once a quarter and still satisfy the tax man. With an employee, you have to pay taxes each time you pay them. The mere fact of adding the employee adds administrative burden to your life which adds unnecessary $-\Delta Q$. If starting out, aggressively seek ways to avoid that first helper, no matter how much it seems like this should help. This is the most carefully hidden trap of all, and you must avoid it at all costs. You will soon find that a network of corporations, each run by your productive trading partners, sidesteps this trap entirely.

You have to stop seeing your employees as dependents who need your care. This compliance technique traps you into making the wrong short term decisions, instead of the long term decisions you need to be making. Most of the impending legislation which will contribute to a collapse is based on penalizing employers under a false promise of helping the employees.

The single most important thing you can do to avoid the snares of the monkey collective is to get rid of every single employee you have. All of them. Those who you need to help you, help them become incorporated themselves and hire them back as contractors. Then both of you benefit by deducting your legitimate business expenses, which are not deductible in many cases as an employee. The effectiveness of this strategy is based on the same monkey suit which Congressmen and their lobbyists use for their own protection. Like them, you want to appear to be a suit-monkey in your professional life, and a pauper welfare-monkey in your personal life.

You will also need equipment. Welders, power tools, tractors and construction equipment of all kinds will soon be on your list. Avoid buying any of these new, except items like chainsaws, where their nature soon destroys them in careless hands. Learn about hydraulics and diesel engines, as these are the most efficient movers we have. Pneumatic and gasoline engines are more common, and best at some applications, but lack the concentration of effort of the former. Learn to repair anything you need, and soon you will have a skill worthy of serving others in exchange for what they have and can do. Attend auctions for your materials, and scour the salvage yards. Use the Internet, while it still exists, to find deals and avoid scams by learning from the experiences of others. Enjoy the simple satisfaction of providing for yourself, and you will avoid much of the need for cash which would otherwise trap you in servitude.

Ditch your employee mindset, and develop instead an entrepreneurial mind. If you are unemployed, use this opportunity to restructure your life so that you think and act like a business instead of an employee. From this mindset, see those who you work for as clients instead of bosses. The distinction is important. We help our clients become successful so that we get more work from them. But too many see their bosses as merely sources of checks. The idea of a job has been created by monkeys to trap us.

Another advantage of being your own corporation is that you can tap into more than one stream of revenue. This works out better for everyone. Your clients can use your services on demand, which makes them more likely to come to you rather than take on the responsibility to hire someone. And you get to spread your risk of employment out by not depending on only one source of work. A network of producers structured this way is much more like the tribal economy discussed earlier in this book, with all the advantages to the spirit and the pocketbook which come from being in a society of free men trading freely with each other.

Another key advantage of adopting the client-contractor mentality is that this is exactly the economic spirit which will be required to pull us out of a collapse, if such a thing happens. Employees will be concerned about their health benefits and paychecks and where they can spend or deposit their money. Contractors and clients will already have the right attitude, just without all the tax forms anymore.

As we provide the monkeys with less and less, they will clutch more and more at what remains. As they fall deeper in debt, they will print more and more money, which will inflate to be less and less, and dissolve any savings you might have. Your reaction to this destruction of your value? Follow them down into debt. A famous financial pundit advises people to pay off their debt and to accumulate cash instead. At his age, he should know better. Anyone who lived through the seventies or eighties knows the true value of a fixed-interest loan in times of even normal inflation.

And what we are about to experience can best be described as hyperinflation. At no point in our nation's history have we had so much public debt, and so many feeding at the trough, and so few filling the trough. And so many regulations to bind them as they try. Even the nightmare of the seventies looks tame in comparison; as I have said before, I would love to have that simple regulatory environment. Any nation in history which has been in this situation has first turned to printing money faster, rather than casting off the chains on the productive. When that happens, hyperinflation is sure to follow.

Properly prepared, hyperinflation is your friend. And by proper preparation, I don't mean gold. Gold is a fool's game, and relies on others to be willing to accept that gold in trade. Gold only matters if the institutions which accept it themselves stay intact. When it comes down to millions or more of starving monkeys, I only want to hear about things I can use.

Gold is only meaningful if civilization stays intact, and then only as a hedge against inflation. In that world, anything of value will do. I choose to use as this hedge property and tools and machines which I can use to get things done and to get the things which I want. If the dollar deflates by one half, gold is twice as valuable in terms of dollars, but so is the tractor or the welder. The only factor which would skew this is whether more used tractors or welders hit the market, but in that case not many people are going to be taking gold in trade either.

An old snipper banking lesson passed down by the tribe goes as follows: "Owe the bank a thousand dollars and it owns you. Owe the bank a million dollars and you own the bank." Now what if ten thousand of us, or a hundred thousand, or a million, each owed the banks a million dollars? I think you see my point. The monkey collective has taken this to heart, as the entire economy is turned upside down to find ways to bail them out of collective foolishness. And yet, only one or two of them would have simply been swept to the street.

Find as many sources of credit as you can, and be prepared to tap them all for things which you need. Low-interest fixed rates are the best, followed by medium-interest fixed rates, followed by low-interest adjustable rates, then medium-interest adjustable rates.

Have a fixed-rate mortgage on your house? Don't take the Financial Fool's advice and pay it down. (Don't take my advice, either. Remember that this book is just for entertainment purposes only.) If things hit the fan in the worst way, then you want to be snuggled into the nest of monkeys when the collective waves its hand and absolves them all. Otherwise, you will be the sucker who sank all his cash.

Financial Fool also advises everyone to cut up their credit cards, as if they are the tool of the devil. This financial shaman couldn't be giving a single worse piece of advice than that. The only time I have been in serious financial trouble was when I aggressively paid down my mortgage and had few credit cards, and those at low rates. When the contracts dried up as they sometimes do, that emergency cash gets drained pretty fast. Especially when you have to start traveling to work or look for work.

Better is to have the credit cards, and with large available balances. There is no practical difference between accumulating debt on a credit card for six months versus draining a six-month supply of cash. Any reasonable interest rate isn't going to accumulate enough in six months to make any difference whatsoever. And if you get stuck for longer than that, being able to keep charging makes a nice buffer at any interest rate.

Is a credit card company making you a low-interest rate short-term offer? Take it, if for no reason than to buoy your credit rating when you pay it off and encourage them to make another offer later. When you get stuck by economic circumstances, you will know sooner than the credit card company and can usually pop one of those babies into your bank at a rate lower than your purchase rate. Drop your credit card accounts and you will have a tough time getting more when you need them.

Financial Fool advocates an employee mindset, and as such, he identifies himself as part of the collective. From time to time, he tries to enforce this mindset by having his suckers call in and announce how they have destroyed their flexibility by paying off all their debt. He fails to ask them what opportunities they had missed by being afraid to follow up on these for their single-minded purpose of debt reduction. Oh, and to solidify the scam he casts it all in shamanistic terms. Somehow, I think God is OK with you buying stuff on credit.

Financial Fool does, however, make an excellent point about credit, particularly unsecured credit such as credit cards. For some reason, it seems perfectly valid for the collective to think that it can shirk its obligations. When it does, the collectivist monkey expects a credit card company to take a fraction of what they owe for frivolous purchases of knick-knacks. If this truly is the case, then why not, if you get in trouble, offer them a fraction of what you owe for money you took to buy a country place or a tractor? Somehow, the collective thinks this practice evil, but looks with sympathy on the wastrel.

I'm certainly not advocating stiffing anyone, and don't borrow any money which you don't intend to put to good use and repay. But, if it hits the fan, I would much rather be sitting on stuff which I need and can use, and a bill for unsecured credit which I can't pay. This situation is far superior to being caught unprepared, and needy and useless.

This is where hyperinflation comes to the rescue. Remember that fixed-interest rate? Give hyperinflation long enough to run wild, and you will be able to pay off hundreds of thousands of dollars for fixed-interest paper debt in exchange for a chicken. Have the same hundreds of thousands of dollars in the bank, under identical circumstances, and it will be able to buy, drum roll, a chicken. Which transaction would you rather make? I personally would rather be letting hyperinflation eat away the money of the monkey suits who caused this mess, rather than having it eat mine. Even better if during the interim I can use the stuff I bought with the monkeys' money.

But what about that variable-interest rate? This is where the see-monkey do-monkey comes into play. Even at high purchase rates, true hyperinflation will strip it out. The monkey collective, itself trapped at variable rates, won't allow the government to allow the rates to rise very much, lest they themselves be liable. By fitting into that monkey-shaped slot, your debt gets inflated away along with theirs. Almost worst case, the government will back the debt with paper money which inflates away anyway. Worst case, the government nationalizes the debt, and you get to hide yours in with all the monkey faces.

The only catch is a rare set of circumstances which could hurt, in which the economy collapses, but the monkeys resist printing money. Ohhh, that hurts when I laugh. If such an astronomically-unlikely alignment occurred, then you would be facing a large debt with no means of paying it back. But you would still be sitting on that useful stuff and so you might at least be able to feed yourself for a while. And as long as you prioritized which debts you would defend and which you would let go, there is still a great chance of hanging onto your house. Even if your credit rating gets holes shot all in it. Don't fear, though, the monkey collective will simply see you as one of their own and swing into action to protect the millions of themselves by hitting the "ON" switch on the printing presses. It's just that you won't be behind the machine feeding it value anymore.

With this mindset, you will tap credit whenever you need in order to obtain those things which you and your subconscious mind have determined are necessary to secure your new definition of success. Your credit rating, rather than a yoke of approval, becomes instead a tool which you use to implement that success. Freed from that mental chain forged in your mind by the monkeys, you will find yourself no more willing to follow your credit rating over the cliff than you would a runaway tractor. A credit rating is just a tool, nothing more. Abandon it if it threatens your success.

As you look around in your life, you will see other arbitrary measures like the credit rating. These are there to be abandoned when they no longer have utility to you, but are used by the collective to judge and shame you if you abandon them.

Married? Consider divorce if the tax advantages or entitlement advantages merit it. Your relationship with your beloved need not change at all, but now you can impoverish her and put her and the kids on welfare as you charge them exorbitant rent. Maybe you can get a big black cape and top hat and wear it as you collect. Perhaps you can even play a little game where she negotiates with you for an extension. "Bwaaa haaa haa," you can chortle as you make your demands and she quivers before you. Spices up the weekends.

Why not? Some members of Congress maintain or have maintained primary or side families this way. And we've trained entire generations of the poor to act like this, so why not you? Plus, her new-found poverty will make her look even more monkey-like and thus qualify her for whatever goodies the monkeys might legislate for themselves. Maybe the kids will get free scholarships this way, too. But in all cases, scrupulously obey the law, and fraud no one. We aren't criminals or cheats, by definition. Merely use what they have created to feed themselves to feed yourself instead.

Nice car? Don't need one. The only people who these impress are the monkey suits who are trying to scam something out of you. The producers you will find and trade with see through the car behind the wheel. If you already have one, and enjoy it, fine, keep it. Financial Fool advises unconditionally turning it in for a clunker, and, oddly, this is the one circumstance in which he advises you going into debt if you have to in order to pay it off. Curious. I wonder if he is in the used-car business on the side, as a trade-down is almost always a losing proposition, as is any trade-in.

Nice house? Smaller houses need fewer furnishings, and less maintenance. To a point, they consume fewer utilities, also. And make you less attractive when the monkeys come to pillage. Clothes for the kids? Shop the charity stores, particularly in areas which used to be well-to-do. Hurry, though, these stores are going down fast if this book gets popular.

Find a way so that you don't need stuff, and if you do need it, find a way to stretch your cash. Before long, that cubicle will seem like it was a part of another life as you get more and more independent of the collective.

Some of you will be rubbing your greedy little hands, thinking that if you hang back, you will be able to scoop up some of the best goodies for yourselves by staying plugged in. "The monkeys will have to get their pellets from somewhere," the reasoning goes, "so they will be willing to pay me more for them."

If you are thinking this way, have you been reading this book at all? Do you really think the monkeys are going to let you profit from what they will classify as hoarding? Look what happens in any disaster to those who plan ahead to profit from the shortages, and you will see what I mean.

More sinister, all collectives, in their pangs of collapse, universally turn to slave labor to meet their needs. And, universally, they all enslave, and thus cripple, those most capable of saving them from their plight. Does this mean that there will be concentration-camps where workers, particularly the productive, get herded to work as slaves for the monkeys?

Not necessarily. Thanks to us, they don't need anything that crude. While writing this section I happened upon a story about a "killing chip" which some Texan, uhh, I mean Saudi, hoped to patent in Germany. This device is a little injectable pod which contains a GPS receiver and a cyanide capsule. The intent was to inject these in freed terrorists or the politically unreliable so that if they get out of hand or start causing trouble, then poof, the capsule could release its poison into the victim.

Don't worry, though. This device is eco-friendly as it presumably uses an ultra-low-power chip. Extends battery life a lot. By the way, as of this writing, the patent was denied by the Germans because there was "no assurance that the information in the chip could be protected, notwithstanding health risks." You don't say. At least the patent was denied. Thankfully, there won't be that pesky intellectual property idea slowing this thing down any. Technically, when the Chinese start making this thing by the, say, six billion, they won't even get any challenges in court on those grounds. Sweet. If for no other reason than this, by the way, you really need to learn something about physics.

Now imagine yourself trying to scarf up the last of the goodies as the last producer in action on the planet. As your bankroll mounts, perhaps even slightly faster than hyperinflation chews it away, you are going to become more and more skylined to the monkeys as they look for someone to blame. Guess who gets the first killer chip implant to make sure you stay in your cage? Or, at least, who gets the blame for the hyperinflation?

Monkeys won't be the only ones who notice you, though, as you grasp for the evasive profit that we have chosen not to make. Concentration-camps or killer chips aside, you don't want to be the last producer standing. You don't even want to be recently on the list to take off to this virtual Galt's Gulch I'm talking about. When that day arrives we will be waiting the few weeks or months for the billions of monkeys to starve. And you want to be safely tucked away wearing your monkey suit as you trade with your productive fellows. You really want those guys to already know who you are.

But not all of you can escape. Some of you are trapped by circumstance, but not always trapped as much as you have been taught to think that you are. Even from within your cubicle cage, with its neutral-colored cloth-covered walls, you can still fight them. Fight them by fading into the background. Spout their nonsense and attend their meetings, while you read this book and recommend it to your fellows. Denounce me and these words, spreading these words to others, while you take them to heart and plan your escape. Deny them the fruit of your mind, and keep that for yourself and family and the future which will soon be yours.

Not consumed with chasing the pellet, we have time to watch and see who is still making pellets while the monkeys fight each other for the last of them. To us, that guy looks a lot like a monkey. And we can tell the difference between the man who is trapped and the traitor who provides for them. Understand these words, and you will pass the tests when you come to us. Or when we come for those of them who are left.

And when The Widow bounces off the rocks at the bottom of that ravine, her lolling head is going to come to rest on the broken spines of these traitors who tried to sell us out, just before we took it all apart.

And relax, this *is* just fiction, isn't it?

Chapter 16, On International Relations

For an individualist to fully appreciate the way of the monkey, it is important to understand international relations. Most businesses today, even small businesses, are global. And so, at some point you, your business or service may very well run into international issues. Plus, the international issues we face, and how we handle them as a nation, are a reflection of the values of the collectives which we have nurtured over the decades.

Unfortunately, the monkey collective weaves its webs of intrigue internationally, as well as around those of us here. In international affairs, the collective works through a variety of agencies. If you ship anything overseas, or receive anything from overseas, you will probably bump up against some of these officials. Keep in mind, however, that organizations such as the Department of State, or Department of Commerce, or even the CIA, were created to protect the interests of Americans. However, you as an entrepreneur will quickly find that these organizations merely exist to impose another layer of collective nonsense which you must struggle to overcome.

This will come home to you on a personal basis when one of these calls, or worse, shows up at your office to introduce themselves to you. And to help you, of course. The only time the NSA, CIA, or the FBI have been in my office, the low-level representatives of each have been refreshingly unattractive, unlike selected members of their management. I think that ugliness is a good thing. I would hope that the state department would follow suit and make sure that all of our diplomats and ambassadors were as ugly as Franklin. Then they might have a chance of being worth a damn.

I have this lingering uneasiness about good-looking people in key decision-making or international contact roles. Sure, it makes a nice image at parties, but the idea of Biff and Muffy Pinkypants representing our national image fills me with dread. I would much rather our ambassadors be shot-up former Marines who are missing parts, including things which are obvious as you reach for a crepe. This staffing decision would say a lot of things, all of them good for us.

Traditionally, our national soul as envisioned by the founding fathers had nothing to do with building schools or digging wells for our enemies. When we blew something up, it stayed blown up, a combination of circumstances which often taught a great lesson about dicking with us. Neither were we all that interested in picking fights, having better things to do with our day. But, we were ready to pick up a pipe if there was some dumbass who really needed its application. You want a well or a school? If you are willing, pick up that shovel or this hammer, we'll show you how to do it, but otherwise you're on your own.

This ethic changed once we decided we were wealthy enough to afford some niceness and charity. The forces of nice, the upper strata of the monkey collective, found themselves neatly insulated behind what would become generations of accumulated wealth. This wealth had arisen from the days before niceness when everyone had better things to do, such as inventing machines to make things like eating easier. In their new-found inherited luxury, the monkey elite had to first ensure that the populace would serve as directed.

So, about seven score years ago, our forefathers had to enlist a social cause which a) no longer served the interest of the forces of nice which had created it in the first place, and b) was in danger of burning itself out naturally. To that end, the forces of nice hired a genocidal ethnic-cleansing socially-retarded smooth-talking intellectual President from Illinois with a psychotic wife. The collective imbued in him messianic properties which resonate to this day, and gave him a mandate to murder and burn a good chunk of the nation which happened to have other plans for liberty. The collective then set him to his task with urgency, before the essential social crisis evaporated all by itself. More on that topic soon enough.

Scroll forward about a half-century for the next major blow against liberty. The social order and institutions refined during our private war of ethnic-cleansing came into their own when the collective decided to mingle in a spat between two opposing groups of our closest friends. That particular war introduced us to the lovely idea of forcing national service onto our children at the point of a gun or a gallows. And of fighting one set of friends who happened to live farther away than another set of friends, creating artificial demons in the process. Demons who would soon become real in response.

In this triumph of the collective, we splattered a good portion of our most valuable resources, blood and treasure, over the fields of Europe and the bottom of the North Atlantic. Demons alone weren't enough to sell the sacrifice of these two resources. The blood, unwillingly provided by the lower classes, was demanded by a national draft imposed by the ethnic-cleansing veterans on their own grandchildren. Meanwhile, the treasure was eagerly sold for destruction by the proto-Muffy and proto-Biff, safely away from the hazards of war. Prosperity in that war was determined by how fast the largest could churn out the most unreliable war material. And in its destruction at the hands of the ill-trained conscripts, create a rising demand for more. Perhaps there were even academy grads hired for the purpose of extolling the virtues of the latest useless truck or gun.

At that war's end, as the blood and treasure became exhausted, the collective devised a means to ensure that the all-valuable irritations could never heal. An armistice, neither victory nor defeat for either side, ensured that friends would continue to hate, but never reconcile. An armistice is an entirely different vehicle than an instrument of surrender.

The West decided to stop fighting because it was just too darn expensive to keep pushing farmers armed with substandard Muffy-brand weapons against Germans armed with super-reliable machine guns and chemicals. Adding to the inequity in machines was the fact that the Germans were under the command of small-unit leaders such as Lieutenant Erwin Rommel. And led by men such as Heinz Guderian watching the action thoughtfully as a signals officer from a command post. Watching and learning and thinking.

A one-sided war was exactly what was required by the collective to paint the German mind as demonic and sacrifice as valiant. Inferior material and inferior ideas fit exactly with the collective ethic of the noble self-sacrifice, so long as the sacrifice was made by someone else.

The leadership in that war didn't have to be so one-sided, but was a direct result of the triumph of collective *mores* over the individual. The Americans had deliberately disenfranchised the tactically superior Southern generalship and erased them, and by extension their Revolutionary War roots, from the American warrior ethic. These small unit leadership methods, applied on the scale of armies by Washington and Stonewall Jackson, served well the rebels in the late-1700s and the rebels in the mid-1800s.

But these same effective methods were forbidden to the ill-trained and involuntary conscripts of the early-1900s, and led directly to their slaughter, a triumph of the collective over the mind. At the same time, the collective compounded this error by cheapening the industrial base which had more or less single-handedly won the war for the North. Into the meat grinder the North had thrown steel until the grinder clogged on it. The lesson? More steel, less thought. A lesson which fell apart when it met a foe who had both.

The Germans had studied any victory regardless of its heritage, and chose to make the best weapons possible despite the potential profit margin of cheap. And so, despite the innate heroism of the individual American, he was hopelessly outgunned and outled in his overwhelming number. And his generals prodded him into human wave tactics which would make a modern Chinese general proud.

The armistice sleight-of-hand which followed encouraged the Germans to agree to abandon their superior weapons as a show of good faith, an early example of the perils of unilateral disarmament. After this voluntary disarmament, the western allies decided to immediately impose non-existent terms of surrender on a nation which had never officially surrendered. And, given their prowess on the battlefield against a numerically superior enemy, probably wouldn't have needed to.

But a fraudulent victory was not enough. Immediately after the end of that war, the collective seized most of the German chemical patents in American courts at the behest of the monkey elite. These stolen patents included those of the lucrative pharmaceutical and dye industries, and denied their rightful owners the fruit of these ideas. For the Germans, a nation which lacked agricultural or other significant natural resources of any kind, their ideas and their innovations were their national export. In other times, this piracy would have been sufficient to incite a war as the monkeys seized these goods of the mind infinitely more valuable than any mere shipboard cargo. But, the Germans held their tongue, helpless in their voluntary disarmament. But this festering resentment would ensure that the commercial forces of Germany would later move in lockstep with the Nazis in World War II.

The treachery of the monkey collective in that armistice would not be limited to the field of commerce. In their youth, the German Lieutenants and Captains had been oppressed by the terms of a fake surrender. But in their maturity, these Generals would march with the Nazis alongside their commercial brethren. And in their march the Privates and Corporals would become Sergeants and Fuehrers. All of these formidable forces were driven by their perception of the thieves and cowards of the west and the uncivilized barbarians of the east. And of traitors in their own midst who conspired with their oppressors. Thus came industrialized slaughter, and absolutely no credible opposition in this country to the draft, the due of a veteran generation payable by its own young.

The Americans, in that war against defiance, would ride into suicidal human wave battle atop the monkey-tank of the day, named after the genocidal ethnic-cleansing general hero of the industrialized North. The Sherman, a high-riding mobile target reminiscent of a child's crayon-drawing, was no match for the German Panther or Tiger. Even the slightly more modern Pershing, named after the human-wave hero of the practice war, was no match one-on-one with the German models.

Only in the hands of a Patton would the feeble American equipment make a decent showing. Patton became a political pariah who dared to study the works of both Rommel and Stonewall Jackson. The Pattons of that war enabled the individual American soldier to survive contact with the enemy beyond the point at which the Germans or the Japanese would simply have run out of ammunition. The Pattons of that war made Presidents of men who despised men like him, and who knew only how to help the enemy exhaust that ammunition.

The Germans, of course, made a crucial strategic blunder which cost them the war, and more importantly for the modern entrepreneur, the post-war propaganda. Incensed by the onerous terms of the post-armistice, the Germans identified merchant Jews with their western enemies who had cheated their way into a false victory.

These intellectual Jews, feeling the 1920's equivalent of white guilt, perhaps "Jew guilt", over their parents' and grandparents' mercantile success, affected strongly Marxist views to assuage this guilt. But to their German peers, this affectation placed them in the camp of the barbarian Communists to the east. The Jew in Germany soon found himself labeled as an Eastern Communist or a Western Capitalist with equal disdain and precision. Finding no safe corner of political opinion in which to hide, the smart ones tried to flee this encirclement while their less-clever brethren ignored the danger.

In 1939 Guderian pointed the way through to victory in Belgium, having learned his lessons in the command post of the previous war watching the needless slaughter of static war. But behind him, the rot in the Fatherland was already taking hold. In the practice war, the Jews had been allies in their war against the West, serving in war industry and at the front alike. But now, rather than gainfully employing these millions the Germans were besot with the task of feeding them in inefficient labor camps. And later, burdened with wasting valuable ammunition, railway traffic and industrial produce in killing them rather than the enemy.

Once the Germans began to face the human wave, agricultural, and industrial might of an entire continent, even their superior weapons and tactics were overwhelmed in their smaller number. The Germans were then left in a position in which the internment and labor camps were simply too expensive to feed. So the starving Germans, having their industry destroyed by relentless bombing and no labor to tend their meager fields, turned a deaf ear to rumors of atrocities out of raw animal survival. The triumph of the collective was almost complete as it ground through the individual as all collectives must ultimately do.

Had the Germans avoided the destruction of their Jewish resources, they might have well won the war and taken their vengeance from the duplicity of the armistice. Freed from the burden of killing Polish and Hungarian Jews, they could have solidified their industrial might atop the fields of Poland and the minds of Budapest. From that vantage they could have swiftly taken Ukraine, starving the Russians into defeat a few years later. But then, we wouldn't have had the opportunity to experience guilt imposed on Americans for over six decades, and the power of the collective which derives from this. Our world today is shaped indelibly by Hitler, who was arguably the product of an unbroken chain of the monkey collective stretching back to the Annapolis and Boston slave markets.

Hitler can be seen as a symptom of practice war subterfuge rather than the cause of evil. Without other hands beside him, he would have amounted to nothing but a street-corner rant. But instead, he shaped our modern world. As proof, consider the Cold War, the dark fantasy of the war merchant and the political oppressor alike. Without nuclear weapons, the agrarian Soviet Union would have been little more than a footnote on the page of history.

Each side in this war had their own stable of native nuclear physicists, such as the Americans Lawrence, Serber, Seaborg, and Oppenheimer. Likewise, the Soviets had Kurchatov and numerous names we will never know, who spent much of their energy studying stolen plans from the Manhattan Project. Alone, neither the Americans nor the Soviets had the political will to pursue nuclear weapons without Hitler as a threat to both. Their mutual salvation came as a result of Hitler's own racist policies.

The practice-war Germans had enjoyed the services of men such Fritz Haber, the son of Lebanese Jews and the father of modern chemical warfare. Haber is also famous as the inventor of the Haber process, in which ammonia is created literally from thin air. Ammonia from any source can be used as a fertilizer directly. But, more typically Haber's ammonia is converted into and combined with nitric acid from the German Ostwald process to make ammonium nitrate, the most important agricultural fertilizer of the modern world. The chemists of the early 1900s begat the physicists of the mid-1900s. While Germany enjoyed the former in the practice war, it would deny itself the latter in the main event. From across Europe, brilliant Jews fled Hitler, the vast majority heading west to Britain and America. This flight is best documented by Richard Rhodes.

Reading Assignment
The Making of the Atomic Bomb
by Richard Rhodes

In this scholarly book, Rhodes details the history of the atomic bomb. Unwittingly, he also demonstrates the power of individual minds to starve an enemy of its produce. As researched by Rhodes, Hungary alone traded seven players to the Manhattan Project and related endeavors. Theodor von Karman became famous for his work with fluid dynamics. George de Hevesy invented new methods in radio-biochemistry. Michael Polanyi found correlations between knowledge, science, economics and the subconscious mind. Hmmm.

Their fellow Hungarian Leo Szilard invented many concepts surrounding the use of fission for weapons and energy. Szilard's patents would later become absorbed by the government as they were too important to allow mere profit. Eugene Wigner developed important theories of nuclear reactions. John von Neumann contributed a mathematical insight to the propagation of shock waves both inside and outside of atomic bombs. To implement the required calculations for these theories, he is also credited with a great deal of the early work in computer science. The last of these seven Hungarians, Edward Teller, is widely known, along with Polish Jew Stanislaw Ulam, as the father of the thermonuclear bomb.

Mussolini contributed Enrico Fermi, the scientist who would oversee construction of the first nuclear reactor at the University of Chicago, whose wife was a Jew. Germany would contribute Hans Bethe among many others too numerous to list here.

Austria effectively discovered fission in absentia in Kungalv, Sweden, when Lise Meitner and her nephew Otto Frisch, both Austrian Jews fleeing the Nazis, went for a Christmas walk in 1938. During this walk, Lise interpreted the experimental results of her former German chemist partner, Otto Hahn, who missed identifying fission by the barest of margins. Had he not been stripped of Lise's help, Otto Hahn would have given the Nazis the first key to the atomic bomb. Had Germany not been stripped of the best minds of Europe, the rest might have contributed to making a more peaceful Hitler-free Germany the world's first nuclear power.

The most famous of all of Hitler's refugees was of course Albert Einstein. Despite his popularity in common understanding, his sole contribution to the atomic bomb was his famous letter to President Roosevelt. In that letter Einstein urged the President to fund a nuclear program before the Germans got there first. That letter, a copy of which is on display at the Museum of Science and Energy in Oak Ridge, would be contribution enough.

The development of the atomic bomb in America was then a direct effect of the racist policies of the Nazis. This development is also the clearest historical example of how a small group of people denied their enemy the produce of their minds. Had Hitler successfully placated the Jews, he could have used their talents to conquer or pacify the world under a single government. As it turned out, for a time America was the sole nuclear superpower. This status had been handed to it in part by Hitler's refugees and in part by a steamer-trunk-full of nuclear secrets brought by British scientists sent to America to protect them from the Nazis. Had this hole card been played correctly, the Cold War would have never happened.

Patton, and others, advised attacking the Soviets directly, and thus forcing them back into their own borders after the war. With the nuclear hole card, the threat of such an attack would have been sufficient. Limited to their own borders, the Soviets would have been forced to survive on their own meager resources rather than having the rich resources, intellectual and physical, of Eastern Europe to plunder. So weakened, the Soviets would have collapsed within a decade. Iin their collapse, they would have spawned a more peaceful and prosperous Russia to continue the progress started by Peter the Great before being interrupted by the cancer of Communism.

However, the forces of nice need conflict to feed them. And so, this collective chose to allow the Soviets to occupy half of Europe, damning generations of innocent Europeans, and Soviet citizens themselves, to their rule. The Soviet collectives, after all, more closely resembled the progressives in power in America at that time and at all times since. Progressives who were, and remain, supported by the American electorate.

More brutal than the Germans, the Soviets would eventually murder many times more people than the Nazis, most of them their own citizens. But at least Biff and Muffy would have a worthy adversary to frighten the Americans into compliance and service. To help the Soviets, and to prevent their premature collapse, the Americans would continue the wartime policy of shipping grain to the Soviet Union throughout most of the Cold War. And thus ensuring that their enemy wouldn't starve while enslaving their population to make all those bombs and missiles. And Hitler's Panther and Tiger became the models for the Soviet tanks of the Cold War and the American M1 Abrahams of today. And his V-1 became the Tomahawk, and his V-2 became the Apollo and the Trident and the Minuteman.

By letting the Soviet sore fester, the collective fanned it to strength so that it might form a credible threat. For decades, as strategic experts warned of this threat and continued to warn of its growing menace, the collective stayed their hand. General Curtis LeMay, the Patton of strategic air forces, developed the means to win that war, and promoted the industrial base to fulfill his vision. Hyman Rickover, the driving force of the naval nuclear program, followed suit.

But the collective would fight them each step of the way. Even so, as late as 1960 the Soviets were still far enough behind such that a first strike still seemed practical, as documented in the famous book by Herman Kahn.

Reading Assignment
On Thermonuclear War
by Herman Kahn

Kahn was a renowned military strategist and theorist employed by the

RAND Corporation think-tank. The first third of this scholarly book is available as a teaser on the web, and clearly describes the tradeoffs which were still available in the early 1960s. As late as then, it still was not too late to destroy the threat which faced us, although the cost would be high. But not so high as the cost we now face from radical terrorists as we implicitly arm them, having groomed them from birth for the task.

Interestingly, Kahn placed his hopes for survival and recovery from nuclear war on the individual skill and spirit of the survivors. He drew a clear distinction between the collectivists of what he called *A Country* and the individualists of what he called the *B Country*. In Kahn's model, A Country consists of the urbanized areas, including the suburban areas which serve the cities. Meanwhile, B Country consists of the rural areas which remain. Today, we would refer to B Country as the "flyover."

In Kahn's day, roughly half of the productive capacity, human and material, resided in each of these areas. Both of these halves of the nation cooperated to mutual benefit like gigantic renditions of Og and Pok. In this trade, the rural areas supplied raw materials, such as food and ore and transportation while the urban areas supplied designs and finished goods. A Country ate the food supplied by B Country and smelted steel from the ore. Conversely, B Country used the tractors and mining equipment provided by A Country. Both benefitted.

Kahn also presented evidence of a doubling of the economic output of the nation roughly every ten years. He also ominously pointed out that, in a crisis, B Country could survive without A Country. But A Country could not survive without B Country. In other words, remove designs and the ideas and the newest models of tractor, and B Country can still limp along. Remove the food, and A Country dies. Unconditionally.

Now consider that a thermonuclear war, at the worst case envisioned by experts of the time, would completely destroy A Country in the form of damaged buildings and leveled factories. But, the only real effect on B Country would be the short-term poisoning of the land by short-lived fission products. And even these effects could be mitigated by simple prophylactic measures which blocked their effects on people. The implication of all of these assertions, backed by scientific fact, was clear.

A 1960 thermonuclear war, even as a worst-case surprise attack on the United States by a fully effective Soviet Union of that day, could be survived.

If the people of A Country had been evacuated first to B Country, all of their intellectual ability would also survive intact, making recovery much more simple. And the decade-doubling of the economy would restore the nation to its pre-war status within ten years.

In the meantime, the half-destroyed United States of 1960 would still have been the most powerful economy on the planet. And with most of its population intact.

Today, some modern economists claim that tornados are beneficial in that they stimulate jobs in the recovery. I disagree, as undoing the damage done merely represents the rollback of some previous $-\Delta Q$. But, if those same modern economists are to be believed, then their ideas would also argue that the recovery from a thermonuclear war would also be equally beneficial. Think of all the jobs which would be created if all those A Country cities and neighborhoods were rebuilt from scratch. After all, the ore and the aggregate and the limestone still lies there intact, untouched by the evil neutron. And by the time this rebuilding has been completed, the effects of the short-term fission products will have faded into meaninglessness.

But this line of reasoning requires boldness, and reliance upon the individual, and the relinquishing of fear. The monkey collective must not allow this sort of thought. And so, the response of the collective throughout those early decades of the Cold War was to deride the thinkers, military and civilians, as war-mongers and naive. The best representation of this derision was in a cleverly spun film by Stanley Kubrick:

Video Assignment
Dr. Strangelove or: How I Learned to Stop Worrying and Love the Bomb

This movie, which was required viewing at the Naval Academy, accurately reflects the ethic of the monkey collective. Kahn was parodied as half of Dr. Strangelove, who makes reference in the film to the "BLAND Corporation". The other half of his character is presumed to be a melange of former Nazi scientists. The LeMay-ish character in the film was portrayed by George C. Scott, who ironically also played Patton in that self-titled film. Why my literature professor insisted that we watch it still escapes me. I wonder if it was her intent to sabotage the future Rickovers and Al Grays under her charge? Curiously, Kahn's book itself was not part of the curriculum.

In that film, and in life, fear and prejudice and weakness are lauded by the collective as virtuous. Individual effort and achievement are derided as naive and hopeless. Patriotism to the ideal of liberty is presented as outdated and foolish, while only compliance to the collective and weakness is considered strength. Films such as this don't propagandize the collective any more than politicians deceive the collective as they rob us blind.

Instead, politician and film-maker and reporter alike merely respond to their respective markets. The collective demands that the politicians steal from the individual on its behalf. And so they do. Similarly, the collective demands that the film-maker and the reporter deride the individual, and make him more susceptible to the theft. And so they do. In all the many ways in our world by which the collective steals from us and derides our most hallowed institutions, they do so at the command of the monkey electorate and market.

But a nuclear-tipped Cold War wasn't enough to promote fear and compliance. After all, the Soviets might collapse some day, they reasoned. Or the LeMays or Pattons or Al Grays or Rickovers who hadn't yet been ferreted out might just be too good at their work. Accordingly, Biff and Muffy, the suited representatives of the collective, needed a replacement or two waiting in the wings.

So, after it appeared that the Cold War was firing up to full heat, the monkey collective decided on the dick move of their time. To create another festering sore of resentment, in 1948, the worldwide monkey collective relocated a band of those hapless Jew survivors into Palestine. And created both the state of Israel and a myth of a destruction of the state of Palestine, a nation which never actually existed but fills the role of a victim nicely. In this example, the collective managed to instantly create victims on both sides. If you oppose Israel, you must be a holocaust denier. Conversely, if you favor Israel, you must hate Allah and property rights. No one wins but the collective which feeds on the conflict. And which requires your sacrifice to feed it.

From the point of view of the Palestinian, you can see why they would be upset. Imagine if a whole bunch of homeless people were transplanted into my old drywall neighborhood in Forsyth County. In so doing, perhaps I and all my neighbors and our families were deported out to, say, Utah. As a reaction to this injustice, we would imagine a sort of national unity which didn't exist at all before the deportation. Maybe we would demand a Forsythian state and refuse to admit the legitimacy of the homeless community. We might even form the *Forsythian Liberation Organization*. I would also be highly motivated to go back to my old neighborhood and have it out with the homeless. They, in turn, would then be motivated to form some security organizations like the Hossad. Biff and Muffy, who started this mess because they thought it would be nice to help the homeless, would be equally happy to sell both sides weapons. Or collect our votes.

On the other hand, a group of our oil-rich relatives, perhaps in Texas, might decide to cash in, too. Now, assume that our relatives in Texas practice a religion with a central tenet of hospitality to the displaced. Following their own principles, our relatives might be inclined to promote a Forsythian state in the middle of the Texas desert. And then fund our business startups, at zero interest, also in keeping with their religious tenets.

But, our Texas relatives might find their individual purpose served better to keep us riled up. And recruit us to go blow up their political enemies in the name of Forsyth, even if these enemies had absolutely nothing to do with the original conflict in question.

The victims on both sides of this conflict are being sold a bill of goods. It was easy enough to con a bunch of holocaust survivors into hopping a boat to the promised land. After starving in a death camp for a few years while my former neighbors turned a blind eye, I would understandably be a little wary of moving back in next door to them. I would also probably turn a blind eye to their understandable fear of defying the then-prevalent authority. If some slick marketing came my way about moving to the Biblically-assured Promised Land I might be inclined to go along.

From an outsider's perspective I would be a little surprised that the boat was heading southeast instead of west, though, given that America is the Promised Land for all peoples. This is supposed to be the place where producers of all stripes come to make their way in the world. Had the forces of nice wanted to really give all those Jews a home, the answer to that question was almost obvious. Buy a goodly-sized farm in Kansas, and hand those craftsmen and merchants hammers and paper. And create New Jerusalem right here in the middle of the continent. Of course you would also have had to slap some sense into their Marxist elitists, but I don't see that as a downside.

This reasonable approach would have left the Palestinians to run the hotels to host the New Jerusalemites on their lucrative pilgrimages to the Old Jerusalem historical sites. After all, Jews, Christians and Moslems lived in relative harmony in that area for centuries prior to 1948. So, in that climate, why wouldn't the Palestinians welcome their long-ago brothers with open arms today? But then there wouldn't be all that discontent, now would there? Instead, we have to ask some Kansas farmer kid to go fight a string of wars for reasons for which he is woefully unprepared to even comprehend.

While the earlier post-armistice duplicity stirred up dissent on only one side, this improved model creates dissatisfaction on both sides. This new model was so effective at manufacturing deep political compliance of the victims and their allies that it was worth repeating, but with one slight tweak. The problem here is that the forces of nice are too easy to identify as the source of the conflict itself. After all, those homeless people didn't just swim the Chattahoochie and truck us away by themselves. They had some help, and the help doesn't like getting blamed.

Enter the peace-keeping mission. The beauty of the peace-keeping mission as a political compliance tool is that the guilty parties can remain comfortably out of sight. Conflict is a universal constant of human existence, usually between one party which has something and another who wants it without having earned it. With this natural force at play, this mission also doesn't require any startup costs. Once conflict sprouts, tender care and rhetorical watering can ensure that it will blossom into a full scale crisis. At that point, the forces of niceness can spring into action to oppose whatever side seems to be winning at the moment. This approach is guaranteed to win the hearts of female voters of either gender, as it provokes their boo-boo kissing nature.

Unfortunately, the fact that this approach is unreliable in identifying the oppressing party is of no consequence for the purposes of eliciting political compliance. After all, the emerging victor may actually be applying the pipe to the knee of some jerk who deserved the treatment. The only consideration is a victim to aid, ethics or judgement having no impact.

My first professional introduction to the peace-keeping mission was shortly after entering the Naval Academy. During a naval leadership course numerous peace-keeping scenarios were presented to the new midshipmen and discussed. One such case is that of Marine Captain Chuck Johnson, remembered for holding three Israeli tanks at bay with his .45 pistol in January of 1983. For most Marines, the incident itself was a dramatic change in warfighting. Prior to that era, Marines had one mission, attack the enemy. The modern idea of the American soldier or Marine as a international policeman was in its infancy.

I listened to the description of Captain Johnson's heroism, and then asked myself two key questions. First, "if the Israelis are our allies, as was the popular view, why in the hell are we pointing guns at them?" Second, "could it really be true that three Israeli tanks, crewed with soldiers who most likely had more live-fire battlefield experience than Captain Johnson, would be intimidated by this display?"

I later came to understand the answer to the first question as no apparent winner is our ally; we only back the losers. The Israelis were probably on the way to rout some unsavory elements. But, because our political goals were to be the forces of niceness and thwart victory, as the apparent victor they had to be stopped at all costs. Never mind that it was probably those same unsavory elements who later contributed to bombing the Marine barracks in Beirut in October of that same year.

The second answer is best understood in the context of the first. The three Israeli tank crews, having endured decades of the fishbowl atmosphere of warfighting on camera in the Middle East, were far more politically savvy to world opinion. They could have just simply run over Captain Johnson and proceeded on their way. This would have been a swift resolution of the conflict at hand. But, this practical approach would have had a dramatic effect on world opinion, and particularly those forces within the US who would take a dim view of the Israelis killing an American Marine. Having had their bread buttered for years by the forces of niceness, the killing of Captain Johnson would have had a more negative impact than the positive impact of their current mission.

As for Captain Johnson, he has to be credited with a certain amount of his own political savvy. He probably understood that the Israelis represented no real threat to him personally, either from their political inclinations or simply seeing Americans as allies. As heroic as his personal decisions may have been, the tank crews were probably no more menacing than a caged lion. So, he could draw his weapon with no intent of actually using it. Earlier Marine warfighting ethic would involve no such posturing. In decades past, no such warning would have been given, the Marine captain and his team at the checkpoint would have simply opened fire and then gone on about their day. But, the corrosive effect of rules of engagement were already taking hold. A decade later these rules would see the crew of the USS Cole watch a little boat drift along side. Friendly waves of niceness all around, this little boat would blow a big gaping hole in the side of one of the most advanced warships in the fleet.

And so wars have become half-measures. We no longer let conflicts resolve themselves by one side or the other winning, many times even by the right side. Instead, we let things brew just long enough to generate hatred and discontent. Then, we bottle up that hatred to sip on its energy in the form of wartime mentality toward greater procurement, and diminished liberty.

We don't even allow ourselves to win, as evidenced by the accidentally rapid progress toward victory in Desert Storm. This victory happened to put a big kink in the re-election plans of Bush 41 as a wartime president. His son would later not allow that same mistake. Instead, Bush 43 hedged his bets by waiting until the year before the election to attack, an attack totally justified in its purpose but perverted in time and intent.

In one view of international relations, we would take no action against anyone unless attacked, either militarily or economically. If we get attacked, and this attack can be traced in any way to support by another nation, we behead it as an object lesson to others. This means holding dictatorial jackasses personally accountable. Eventually, they will run out of body doubles or security details, and then we can explain the rules of the game to their successors. The first freaking American flag we see burnt or anti-American rally is an indication that he has lost control and is of no further value to us. You want to be in sole charge? Fine, but that means you have sole responsibility.

Or, you can take a free market approach and be our friend. And all of your people can be our friends, too. But this policy would require judgment. Judgment of right and wrong. Of good and evil. And not the vacation bible school kind of good and evil. No, the real kind in which individual value is considered a worthy thing all by itself, and not just by how much the individual joins a collective. Or is in charge of one.

For those countries which are already presumably free, they historically haven't been a problem. Countries run by people going about their day don't usually stir things up. Countries run by Biff and Muffy, on the other hand, are everyone's problem. After we fix our own Biff and Muffy problem, we can deal with the rest of them by cutting off the economic goodies and taking away electricity. People too busy growing food or digging wells don't have time for international intrigue, terrorism or making nuclear weapons.

We go to war to presumably free people in another country, and totally ignore or discredit the genuine reasons to go to war. As long as we ignore the plight of the average Cuban or North Korean, I have a hard time caring about whether an Iraqi has a school. Or whether that school is sufficiently well-funded at American taxpayer expense.

For that matter, I am sure that all those Chinese hammering away at those drums in the opening ceremonies of the 2008 Olympics probably have suck for a life. But, I am equally sure that those images warmed the hearts of Biff and Muffy on both sides. For Biff and Muffy Marxist, imagine all they could do if the little people would just behave like that. For Biff and Muffy Country Club, imagine all they could do if the little people would just behave like that. These two groups, supposedly at opposite ends of the political spectrum, are no different in their desire to oppress and seize control of that which they haven't earned. Their techniques are merely different. Their methods wrap around until they almost touch.

Biff and Muffy Marxist wish to enrage the dispossessed against the productive portion of society, and in so doing derive their political power from which to regulate your behavior by fiat. Biff and Muffy Country Club use their political power to attack your liberty by defining many ways in which your behavior is un-American, and thus limit your liberty. Both are destructive to your ability to enjoy your day or to run your business as you see fit. And the same thought processes which are used destructively overseas are used here with more personal ill effect on you. We just call it our way of life when you have to pretend that you have freedom.

Study the ways of the monkey with regard to international relations. We bend over backwards to assist others in foreign countries, while we drain our lifeblood to do so. We dig wells and build schools for people who hate us, while we tax and regulate tax our own businesses, particularly the small. Meanwhile, the large businesses, which can amortize the cost of sending work overseas, enjoy numerous benefits unavailable to you. When you, the unemployed and previously employed, begin to incorporate or form non-profits to wear that suit-monkey costume, you will see how stacked the deck really is against you. At least as your own companies you will be able to slip a few cards from the deck.

Take for example the recent green buzz. All around us we hear rumors of job-creation by the new green initiatives. Yet, almost all of these dollars are already allocated to friends of lobbyists and Congressmen. You may want to get in on the installation of solar panels or windmill plants (bought from GE, made in China, and running software written in India), but you will probably find that those doors are already closed. Job creation overseas is more important than production, and the resulting quality of life, here. Worse than Hitler's Germany, tax treaties with other countries now prevent you from even escaping. Emigrate, and you will find that you will still owe the suit monkeys here taxes for at least ten years. They own you. For now.

By the way, in 1960 Herman Kahn was right about A Country. At that time, they did contribute to B Country in terms of designs and finished goods. But now, these things come from India and China, respectively. So what does A Country contribute now, other than regulations, and lawsuits, and brokering of increasingly defective finished goods? And open, gaping mouths to feed?

When the monkey collective derided Herman Kahn's 1960 plans for evacuation of A Country, they may have been right. Right for the wrong reasons, and just about a half-century too early. Their critique was that a reliance on a mass-evacuation of A Country to B Country would strain its resources also. But, what if the productive individualists pre-evacuated themselves first? Then, everyone wins, as B Country could then supply its own designs and ideas, and, eventually, its own finished products.

In that model, A Country is merely a liability, rather than a source of value. So, perhaps it *is* better if the citizens of A Country, including the elite of the monkey collective who hold the chains, stay right where they are.

Chapter 17, Waco and Other Texas Wackos

The conflicts sown by the monkey collective to manipulate international events has the same destructive effect when wielded here at home. In the spring of 1993 I was a Captain in the Marine Corps. Like most of us, I watched in horror as the government of the people, by the people and for the people burned alive about a hundred of the people in South Texas. Why? For the crime of wanting to be left alone by the rest of the people. For the crime of choosing to congregate in a manner which the monkey collective saw as strange and threatening.

Dozens of children were heartlessly sent to a flaming death by a new government which needed to set an example. The collective set this example to the hand-wrung cheers of those who set them in power. Most disturbing, this horror was back-stopped by the law and order types who had opposed the new government. Sadly, only a few watched in horror for the victims. Most, on the other hand were suitably prepared by propaganda. So prepared, these millions watched in horror that the victims would be so inconsiderate as to expose them to the spectacle of their deaths.

Watching the flames, I threw my Marine Captain's bars to the ground in disgust. Up until that time I had been proud of my service. But at that moment I was ashamed to be protecting the people who would do that to their own citizens. And for nothing more than having a slightly different religious point of view and keeping to themselves a little too much.

Sixty years before, the German citizenry was similarly prepared by their government and media. Jews had been defined as criminals by their mere existence. And this definition allowed their own monkey collective to, at worst, look the other way as their fellow citizens were hauled off to near certain death in showers and ovens. All for the good of society.

In Texas, a charge of weapons violations was sufficient, here in a nation where such rights are second only to speech and worship. This crime, never proven, was used as an excuse for the full force and might of the national government to launch a military-style assault on the Branch Davidian compound that spring.

Local authority is a carefully planned safety-valve in our federal system. As stated many times throughout this book, we have been so indoctrinated that the national government and the federal government are the same thing. The federal government is actually the sum of the local, state and national authorities. The national level of government is intended to protect us from without, while the local and state governments are intended to protect us from within.

As an example, the county sheriff is known and elected by the people of the county. As such, the sheriff is more likely to engender respect and cooperation from the county citizenry than an unknown national agent. Our government institutions, at the command of the electorate, seek to destroy true federalism wherever it is found. For example, the Federal Bureau of Investigation should rightly be called the National Bureau of Investigation. And the Federal Reserve the National Reserve, and so on.

However, these names were carefully chosen in an era of our history in which our constitutional form of government was being systematically dismantled, and this rubble used as a foundation for the modern socialist state. In our new model, the local authorities are merely resources to be tapped for information. Once that purpose has been served, they are merely obstacles to be swept aside while the national forces commit their plunder in the interest of people outside the community.

Koresh could have been served a warrant peaceably when he went to town several times a week, a fact well-known to the local authorities. Or, the sheriff could have simply walked up to the front door and knocked. Instead, the collective cheered, as if at a playoff for the super big game, as the national agencies executed their all-out assault. An assault clearly intended to look better on camera and make a point to all those gun-toting thugs who were imagined through a glass darkly. Executing warrants is just too boring when you could be executing children instead.

The problem is that the authorities didn't expect that a group of Texans would actually live up to the myth of the Texan, a myth long dead. And stand their ground against an abuse of self-propped authority. We recall a similar group of Texans with fondness when we remember the Alamo, but we don't allow these Texans a similar honor.

We all watched the lies presented to us that spring. Most of us have been indoctrinated so well with these lies that to recall these events and lies even now will paint me as a heinous villain. But this chapter won't end how you think it will given the few paragraphs so far. Even so, if you find yourself disturbed by this so far, put this book down now and wander off.

We were told that the Branch Davidians chose to commit mass suicide, while we were reminded of the Jonestown massacre of the 1970s. Were this true, the children would not have been covered with blankets by their parents and doused with water to protect them from the flames. Yet, as any firefighter will tell you, most people who die in fires asphyxiate long before the flames reach them. Trembling in fear under the wet blankets, these children were surely no exception.

We were told that the fire was started by the Davidians themselves, while any ground combat soldier or Marine will tell you that smoke and tear gas canisters are a most effective incendiary device. Spewing sparks and flame which will make a child's firework proud, the hot little canisters of that era are proof of the adage of where smoke comes from. Many a military and law enforcement training ground has been set ablaze by these over the years.

But, because these training grounds are so often burnt there is little combustible material left. On training grounds, these blazes soon burn themselves out and so never become media spectacles. Not so a South Texas building littered with dry hay. No one who has ever seen these canisters in action could have possibly misunderstood the fact that they would start a fire in that building. And yet some of our number pulled the pin and tossed them in, or equivalently, pumped the gas in from vehicle-mounted canisters, following orders which would make the SS proud.

And yet, less than a month after the killings, the State of Texas, under the charge of a Democrat governor, bulldozed the premises to the ground, and destroyed all forensic evidence in the process. Including evidence of what started the fires. And who shot first. On what earth would an act like that make sense if truth mattered?

Despite these facts, ask anyone you choose whether fire would be their first choice as a means of suicide, or as a means to kill their children if they were so inclined. Conduct a little informal poll, and if you don't get hauled off for asking such an absurd question, you will find that fire is pretty far down the list as a vehicle for self-offing. There is a reason why secret-agent movies include cyanide pills, yet personal incinerating devices are noticeably absent from the script. Present this question in context, and those same people will then change their opinion on the grounds that the Davidians were just crazy. So aptly have their minds been prepared.

The forces of law and order in the opposite party who should have opposed this siege and subsequent attack on constitutional grounds, were not without blood on their hands, however. Two years earlier, under their watch in January of 1991, a national agent had approached Randy Weaver, a former Vietnam Green Beret sergeant. The agent asked Weaver to provide the undercover agent with "sawed-off shotguns", a heinous crime which strikes at the very core of our society.

And yet, no court has ever established that Weaver actually committed this crime. Regardless, based on official documents, this alleged crime was precipitated specifically to coerce Weaver into serving as an unwilling national informant within the Aryan Nations. Why would he serve so? In exchange for immunity from prosecution, and for a crime he never committed, if need be. Again, Goebbels would nod approvingly.

Weaver's refusal to cooperate in this investigation was the most inexcusable affront to national authority. His refusal threatened to undermine our entire constitutional system, as perceived by the forces of niceness which are intolerant of any scoff of the law. "He must be made to pay," they growled to themselves as they considered their next trap.

And so Weaver was presented with an order to appear in court, an order stating the incorrect court date, making it impossible for Weaver to comply. A warrant was then issued for his arrest, he now being a bonafide criminal in the eyes of the law.

Subsequent events in October of that year would see a group of armed and camouflaged U.S. Marshals descend upon the Weaver farm at Ruby Ridge in Idaho. Their mission was ostensibly to surveil and survey the property prior to an arrest warrant. Further, they had clear orders to make no contact with the accused.

However, once on site, the national forces decided to take matters into their own hands. Their first official act was to execute 14-year old Sammy Weaver as he investigated why his dogs were barking. Their next act was to assault the Weaver home. In this action, the national authorities would neither request surrender nor announce their official presence. Instead, in legal silence the full force of our government chose to execute a carefully planned attack. Taken from the FBI's rules of engagement for that day was the following policy statement for this attack:

"(D)eadly force can and should be used against any armed adult male if the shot could be taken without a child being injured."

No mention of guilt or suspicion or any other mitigating factor was needed or required. Merely being male, and adult, and armed was sufficient. But apparently, even this directive was not enough to channel their bloodlust as the monkey collective chose its next victim.

With the national jackboots that day was FBI sniper Lon Horiuchi, a graduate of West Point. Long in service to his collective, this creature had often taken the oath of office to "support and defend the Constitution of the United States against all enemies, foreign and domestic." Apparently without ever comprehending these words which he often repeated.

Horiuchi was one of the best trained and accurate snipers on the payroll of the citizens of the United States. Did he choose to go for a "three-fer" and try to kill Kevin Harris, a friend of Randy, and Weaver's wife Vicki as she cradled their ten-month-old daughter Elishiba in her arms? This shot was taken while the Weavers and Harris *ran for cover* against the assault. Vicki was not male, and was armed with only a baby. The only justification which Horiuchi had for squeezing the trigger was that she was present. And that was guilt enough for him, as he proved with his actions.

My opinions about Horiuchi's state of mind during this incident are just that, my opinions. Do I know he was "gleeful" or wishing to boast? Or why he made the decisions he did? Of course not. But it makes great fiction, doesn't it? Any resemblance to actual persons, living or dead, murderer or murdered, is purely coincidental. To what I am sure was Horiuchi's dismay, he only managed to kill Vicki with that shot.

In so doing, he denied himself the water-cooler honor of being able to boast that he had killed three civilian enemies of the state with one bullet. Despite his miss, the monkey collective stood by him nonetheless. The monkey public ignored, or embraced, the fact that the target of his attempt at a dual or triple kill included a literal babe-in-arms, incapacitating her mother to be a threat to anyone. The horror of this act, as personal and as cold as any envisioned by the worst of Nazis, never seemed to incite the forces of niceness to anything. Except to express their dismay at why the Weavers would be so rude as to subject them to this unpleasantness.

And then the collective deployed this same loose cannon to Waco to fire at David Koresh and his extended family in 1993. In the aftermath of that attack, unaccounted expended shell casings were found at Horiuchi's position by Texas Rangers, who took no further official action. Why should they, when other evidence was being destroyed by bulldozers?

Had Lon Horiuchi complied with any of his oaths to defend the Constitution, he would have drawn his service pistol and shot himself dead. Instead, he chose to gleefully participate in the unannounced and ironically unwarranted attack, competing with his fellows for the ultimate prize. And then, perhaps, expended unaccounted rounds at Waco. Keep this in mind when you think they work for you. Or will lift a finger to protect your rights rather than gun you down in cold blood for bragging rights, too. Your claim to the Constitution will only embolden them further, rather than slow their hand as you fantasize that it might.

In any event, only after this blood sacrifice and through the use of a robot vehicle would the authorities officially announce their presence to Randy Weaver. This former special operations sergeant had only responded to the attack upon his family as he was expected by the collective to do. In his response, this decorated American hero of the past unwittingly gave the national forces of niceness an excuse to set the example to all who might defy them in the future.

In early 1991, while Sergeant Randy Weaver was being prepared as a suitable blood sacrifice upon the altar of niceness by their undercover agent, I was circling above the battlefield in Kuwait. Below me, a young Timothy McVeigh was down in the smoke and haze of the battlefield earning a Bronze Star for heroism and saving the life of a wounded comrade. This battlefield hero had previously worn a "White Power" T-shirt in the barracks as a protest against the "Black Power" T-shirt worn by many of his fellow soldiers. This simple expression of his right to speech would damn him to infamy.

As a child, McVeigh was frequently beset by bullies. Eventually, this fighter eventually came to see the government of the United States as the ultimate bully, echoing a mistake which many in so-called militia groups would make for decades. In his case, however, this assessment would explode on the second anniversary of the Waco murders in the destruction of the Murrah Federal Building in Oklahoma City. Ensconced in graduate studies at Virginia Tech that day, I wondered to myself about this curious event.

This act of supreme violence had upon it the fingerprints of Middle Eastern terrorists. At a glance, the front of the federal building could be any of hundreds of buildings destroyed by car bombs in that part of the world. Attacks which included the Marine barracks in Beruit of 1983. Indeed, a few months before Oklahoma City, a similar attack was attempted on the World Trade Center, clearly by Islamic terrorists. The swift apprehension of McVeigh led to a story so pat that it was easily digestible by even the most news-averse. Perhaps the forces of niceness were improving their game from the embarrassing events of Ruby Ridge, and the out-of-control horror of Waco.

Now, clearly Timothy McVeigh committed this heinous act, he said so himself. And yet, the first-time implementation of a sophisticated truck bomb, executed and detonated with perfection by a novice, just didn't ring true. For one thing, as a child I was no stranger to improvised explosives, and had personal experience with the difficulty which detonation of ammonium nitrate poses to a novice. It can be done, but one's first efforts are usually disappointing and result in either a puff of flame or a shower of undetonated fertilizer pellets.

To understand the essential problem, punch a sandbag and then consider your unharmed hand as most of the sand squiggles out of the way.

Similarly, pelletized fertilizer, even when mixed with the proper ratio of a volatile fuel, is supremely difficult to detonate. Much of the punch of the detonation gets absorbed rather than propagating as the little pellets jostle somewhere else or pack tighter. Then, when no room remains, a flimsy moving van would simply rupture and disgorge the remaining explosive.

Did McVeigh understand this effect, and weld together even the simplest of steel containment boxes inside the fragile truck body? Did he understand the practice of casting the fertilizer as a semi-liquid slurry inside such a box? Or at least cast smaller blocks for stacking to avoid the sandbag effect? If so, did he know enough not to blow himself up when melting the material by using a thermostated electric heater so no flame would ignite the fumes? Or to vent the fumes away to avoid dangerous inhalation or risk of detonation? Or use a double-boiler approach with paraffin wax instead of water to reach the essential melting point while avoiding dangerous hot spots in the melt? Any of these ideas, implemented poorly by a novice, would have ended the story before it started, the entire enterprise written off as just another meth lab explosion and a dead cook.

Did McVeigh even understand the most basic principles of enhancing the explosive with aluminum powder as used in military explosives? Are there records of his having purchased large amounts of silver tempera paint to obtain it? None of the evidence collected from that day or during his imprisonment suggests that he had the slightest idea of even one of these possible enhancements. An expert in the field understands all of these things, and even they fail when attempting it. Which is why so many of them resort to using tanks of simple welding gasses instead, ruptured on demand by a smaller conventional explosive so that the acetylene and oxygen mix on demand.

Regardless of these gaps, McVeigh, without any formal training whatsoever in the art, managed to pull off one of the most successful attacks of its kind in history. On his first try. Even the experts that February in New York had only managed to knock a few columns out from under the World Trade Center. A blast there, had it the efficiency of the Oklahoma City bomb, would have knocked down one of those buildings six years early. But even those guys screwed it up on their first try. As First Wife says, they learned their lesson and changed the bomb design the second time around, didn't they? But, unfortunately, McVeigh's fertilizer bomb lent credence to regulating yet another aspect of agriculture. Oddly, there are no observable efforts to regulate arts and crafts to secure or license all the paints which use aluminum powder. Those aren't necessities of life, are they?

Further, one of the motivating causes behind McVeigh was gun rights. So why wouldn't McVeigh, as would Cho twelve years hence where I took my graduate courses, choose a firearm? And in McVeigh's case, a rifle, an implement of empowerment with which he was supremely capable, rather than an unknown with which he wasn't? Unlike Oswald, who barely qualified with the rifle after leaving boot camp, McVeigh was a genuine expert. Oswald, with his miserable lack of skill, was apparently capable of making three near-impossible plunging shots with a dilapidated rifle against a target maneuvering away from him simultaneously in three dimensions. Given this fact of history, certainly McVeigh would have been able to wreak havoc with a rifle against a nest of his hated BATF enemies.

Aggressive Americans, when they go over the edge, tend to kill en-masse with rifles or knives. These are weapons with which one sees one's enemy go down and requires an individual decision with each pull or thrust until the passions are sated. Or, in the case of a Marine or soldier, until the battlefield is clear.

The concept of robot-war, behind which the forces of nice get to hide, is a recent innovation. Bombs have traditionally rarely been used in this country, and then only by the forces of socialism as evidenced by the radicals of the sixties. Those radicals of the collective shrank in their cowardice from direct and personal action. Baby boomers, indeed. At least the misguided Islamists who ride their kamikaze weapons or wear their suicide vests show more raw courage.

One might argue that a single pair of new boots set in motion a chain of events which destroyed the national building in Oklahoma City. McVeigh's ambition had always been to be a Green Beret. So, returning from war as a decorated hero, he was accepted into the equally rigorous screening program to test his fitness for that highly selective group. Issued new boots for a 5-mile march, he developed blisters which eventually forced him to be dropped from the program. Embittered, he left the Army, and was ripe for recruitment as a radical.

And so, the secret of McVeigh's other accomplice, seen by witnesses and described as apparently Middle Eastern, would be ignored by the press and go to the grave with him. An external enemy, representing a genuine threat, is not nearly so compelling as an internal enemy. Internal enemies can easily be swatted aside with a sense of distanced satisfaction. And when those internal enemies, vaguely defined as those who don't tread the conventional path, can be incited to action to justify ferreting them out more eagerly, so much the better.

Nonetheless, no one, especially the agent of nice, wants to get blown up by second-hand anger. So, the early stumbling efforts to oppress which were the hallmark of the nineties would gain refinement with the turn of the century. To ensure that no avenging McVeighs would arise, the forces of niceness in the new millennium would need to arm themselves with a weapon so powerful that none would challenge their assertions.

Enter the sexual predator, who would replace the drug-dealer of the twentieth century as the villain of choice. This new villainous image, and the resulting vastly improved propaganda machine, would soon be turned again upon Texans who wanted nothing more than to be left alone.

Making concrete is tough. Ask most people from whence flows this remarkable substance, literally the foundation of our modern civilization. Probably the best answer you will get is "from the back of one of those trucks, of course." Armed with the ability to manufacture your own concrete, you can build any structure you like, from pig pen to barn to residence. And in so doing avoid numerous consumer protection regulations which stand in the way of manufacturing one's own roads or buildings.

With the foundation squarely within your control, and the ability to raise walls of any dimension at-will, you can build just about any structure which you think suits your needs. And without requiring a contractor to verify building permits and the like, which ultimately are more a form of taxation rather than consumer protection. Beyond the tax perspective, your own source of concrete cuts through a wide swath of subcontractors and their expenses which contribute dramatically to your capital costs.

Dyemaking is equally difficult, and requires a knowledge of chemistry which is beyond the reach of the typical public school alumnus. But, armed with that chemical knowledge, and inoculated with a germ of genetic theory, you can then start manipulating your environment in ways which most people could never even begin to comprehend. Including greenhousing plants which provide you with most of the resources you could ever need.

Raise some sheep, dye some wool and spin it into yarn using equipment stripped at pennies on the dollar from defunct garment factories in the Carolinas. You then have the makings for an in-house garment industry which can rival, certainly in quality if not cost, what you could purchase elsewhere.

But someone has to run that stuff. So, get together a bunch of like-minded friends, and start building your community. But, instead of some socialistic paradise in which all work and none suffer, which inevitably leads to none work and all suffer, imagine a barter system instead. Zebediah supplies ten cubic yards of concrete to Ezekiel, who pays for his concrete with a voucher for so many yards of dyed cloth. These vouchers can then be used to pay for other goods, such as vegetables, as could vouchers for concrete. Or for grading. Or for wall framing. Or for running the concrete plant. And so on. One good thing about these vouchers is that no amount of currency devaluation, or inflation, could ever devalue them as long as everyone follows the rules.

As with money in the early American colonies and states, these barter vouchers for actual goods and services eventually become the money of your little compound. If all your friends agree on the same ethical principles, and you want your vouchers to be honored, you are more likely to trade fairly with your friends. Even better if your religious beliefs spring from the same mercantile tradition which produces more millionaires per capita than any other religious tradition native to this continent. This concept is unlike true socialism, in which you expect your friend to do you endless favors for nothing in return other than to be thought well of. Also unlike true socialism, this system has been proven to work for almost two centuries.

One hiccup with this local trading system is that the level of knowledge required to operate this society far exceeds that available in the open market. To overcome this drawback, you have to open some trade schools. While you are at it, you might as well get some of your people to teach the young adults and kids, in exchange for some of those vouchers, of course. Some will leap at the chance to lead a classroom of remarkably well-behaved ethical youngsters instead of sweating out in the Texas heat.

You can even call this homeschool for hire. Just try to avoid teaching some archaic concepts like freedom of religion, freedom of speech, freedom of association, freedom from unlawful detainment or rights to due process. Or freedom from unlawful searches and seizure, etc. These radical topics could make you and your happy little group a target.

Of course, at some point you need to generate some real cash to pay the king for the rent of land which we call in this country property tax. And, there are some things which you want which are beyond your ability to provide, such as electricity. The national fiat currency is needed to some extent by everyone to pay for these external things. So, you sell some of your concrete to the locals, or some of the produce or livestock. Or, some of the members trot off to town to work in some real jobs here and there, as if making concrete or dyed cloth isn't a real job.

Once you have some members with pockets stuffed with national currency, it can be exchanged with other members for some of those vouchers which are worth real stuff. So, a sufficient amount of national currency flows into the community to pay for these things which are only available in exchange for the king's paper. And, those members selling and serving outside the community can take advantage of things like earned income credit and the like. These latter strategies effectively multiply the low wages on paper instead of the higher wages they would have earned within.

But, there is a problem. Zebediah might enjoy a standard of living far in excess of the amount of his concrete which he sells. This little disparity soon becomes a subject of concern for the tax man, who after all is nothing more than an agent of the electorate. Technically, all that internal barter is subject to taxation by national and state authorities, but is capable of being proved only if your friends rat you out. Unfortunately for the king, the friends enjoy that same tax benefit. With internal barter, Zebediah might get a reasonable standard of living for ten yards of concrete. With external sales, that same standard of living might cost twenty or thirty yards outside if it were taxed away first. Plus, avoiding filling out all those tax forms gives him more time to spend with his wives and kids.

Did you catch the clue for the downfall of this utopian mercantile society which was actually working? Working, that is, before the forces of nice stormed in and hauled away all the women and kids in buses borrowed from a Baptist church on their way to separate internment. Replace the church buses with railway cattle cars, roll the relevant theology back a few iterations, and you will have seen this film before, but in black and white. And starring guys with cute little swastikas instead of Texas cowboy hats.

Clearly, the people of the nation, being deprived of their sweet elixir of need and respect, would love to stamp these malcontents with the star of David. And then haul them away in railroad cars to be forgotten. But, that extreme might lead to another national edifice going up in a bang somewhere, so we can't have that. We need something better than just yelling "Juden" these days.

OK, we've already tried labeling a similar group with the Jonestown thing prior to staging a mass execution, but we see how that turned out. We've tried just turning loose some national attack dogs, and that led to a big mess also. We blew up a tenement in Philadelphia a while back, but we were able to paint those people as dangerous, but not so these apparent pacifists. Our heroes in this story even let the local sheriff wander the property at will, so we can't force a standoff. Neither can we fall back on the tried and true seizure after planting of drugs on their property as these people don't even drink, by definition, for Christ's sake.

But, oh yeah, we've heard that some underage girls have been married off to some old geezers, and these people might be doing the multiple wife thing as a bonus. Let's see if we can dig up some chick who got kicked off the farm for not wanting to work. Then, get her to make up some more juicy stories about what might be going on. Suitably armed with enough lies, we can cast this whole thing not as a jack-booted thuggery, but more of a save-the-children kind of rescue mission suitable for modern heroes. And so, armed with the might of righteousness, we pack off the entire contingent of women and children against their protest to the modern equivalent of an internment camp.

And do it in a state which then later claims to be the moral equivalent of the Founding Fathers. Even the elect, like that radical talk-show host, might be fooled into hailing this entire state as heroic. Because, after all, now there is a Republican in charge of Texas, and so it must be righteous.

And all of this with not a scrap of evidence *a priori* other than a single questionable phone call. All other evidence which would normally be required to issue a warrant to even search, much less arrest or detain, would just have to wait until after the mass apprehension was completed. Gross violations of civil liberties are apparently fine if you pull it off in sufficient scale and get the backing of the press. With their help you can enlist just about every suburban woman in the country. After all, Muffy Pinkypants, the model of the she-monkey, can't imagine why any other woman who doesn't share her shoe or business suit fetish would choose to live that way.

Get enough propaganda on your side and the monkeys will just look the other way. And totally miss the fact that each time you put some of these rescued women on camera they are not thankful for being saved. Instead, they have the gall to protest and demand that their families be restored, a criminal lack of appreciation which soon results in their no longer appearing on camera. So, these women, the purported victims, soon become painted as the aggressor in a war of ideas. And their enemy oppressor? The forces of nice who were really only interested in suppressing the freedom with which these people chose to live their lives.

But what about the children? Am I advocating that young girls be sold into virtual slavery for the whim of old perverts? Even the threat of that question has been calculated to enforce silence and quell dissent. Keep in mind that the idea of "age of consent" is a relatively recent phenomenon, barely decades old. This idea was invented by the forces of nice as a way to suppress independent thought. Such as those thoughts which arise in a man from the sight of a young, fertile female. Thoughts which tend to disenfranchise bitter old crones from whose lips come howls for legislation which ultimately disenfranchise our young.

All of evolution has produced features which signal when a woman's body is ready to safely reproduce. The true pathological pedophile doesn't care about the chronological age of a girl, and in fact loses interest when she becomes womanly. Or consider the homosexual pedophile, which prefers the gangly physique of young boys. We revile these individuals on an evolutionary basis because they threaten the actual reproductive capacity of too-young girls, or of boys or young men. In that context, it is absolutely correct from the point of view of the species to remove these individuals from society. The justification is that they serve no beneficial purpose other than as a parasitic predator.

Contrast the latter example with the case of a mutually consenting sexual relationship between two men, or between two women. This distinction is difficult for the primitive portions of our minds to sometimes recognize, leading to all sorts of discord which is beyond the scope of this book. Despite the valid application of either sort of the pedophilic label, the labeling as a pedophile a man who experiences a physical attraction to the shape of a fertile woman is incorrect. Attraction to a girl who is legally underage, yet physically mature and ready to reproduce, does not make one a pedophile, protestations in the congregation notwithstanding.

That may, however, make one a criminal, but that is a different issue altogether. The definition of the true biological age of a woman is that of her readiness to reproduce as evidenced by the maturity of her reproductive system. This determination becomes subjective and so we have defined a particular chronological age of consent which varies across various jurisdictions. We have combined that age of consent with an age of association to determine whether a relationship is legal or consenting.

The stated purpose of these various laws was to protect the young woman and her children from the ravages of ignorance and poverty. These laws were not originally intended to protect her from pregnancy, which nature had assured, by her attractiveness, was of no further jeopardy to her. In so doing we have replaced the girl's protecting family with that of the whim of the state. And we have thus placed her fate into the hands of every suburban woman, and their cowed male sycophants, in the country.

As a young man of nineteen, I transported my unmarried First-Wife-to-be, then a month shy of her eighteenth birthday, across state lines. I eventually, a few car repairs later, transplanted her in Annapolis as a more or less convenient target of my affection. In so doing, I probably violated laws of which I was not aware. Perversely, these laws would have had no effect had we consummated our relationship within the approving gaze of the state. Had we legally married, of course, I would have been prevented from attending the Naval Academy. Finding ourselves within the confines of law on either side, we chose to ignore both. These laws did nothing to protect her, as she remains my property today by her ongoing consent.

I carted my own valedictory princess off to what became decades of barbaric servitude, including the more or less forced rearing of clearly superior offspring. Since then, the world has changed underneath our feet. These days, a similar act would run me afoul of the state, and I would have become one of many listings in the online sexual predator databases. More importantly, at the demand of the collective, I would have been disenfranchised from any future higher purpose. Older, I am now at least cognizant of the risk enough to card any young women with whom I speak. But younger men aren't nearly so careful, a fact which allows society to lure them away to battle on the flimsiest of rationale.

The forces of niceness, as it does with any well-intended initiative such as the drug war, has turned this legislation to systematically disenfranchising young men. In particular, they seek to disenfranchise those individuals who show any force of will or independence. Men who choose to submit to the whims of women are allowed reproductive opportunity, and thus spread the contagion of male submissiveness through the gene pool. But men who run afoul of even one flirtation with a biological woman of insufficient chronological age are subject to arrest. And subsequent imprisonment, or a lifetime of public harassment or disdain of all his neighbors, never to escape or seek any gainful employment. It is little wonder that some of these individuals tend to later violence, which makes me wonder sometimes which begat what.

As an exercise, browse some of these online sexual predator listings. If pictures are shown, they are sometimes mug shots. As my own mug shots aren't nearly as carefully framed as my normal barbaric appearance, I can understand that sometimes you have to look through the photo to the person within. Look for the listings where the perpetrator, of age 25 or less, was convicted for sexual assault on a minor. Then look up the definition in your state for what that actually means. In most states, a conviction for touching the breasts of a sixteen-year-old girl who sneaked into a college frat party would destroy your entire life. It doesn't matter in the least whether her body convinced you, "yep, that's a woman, all right." This fact doesn't matter, and those who see your profile online don't get to judge for themselves, either.

Similarly, find some listings for things like lewd suggestions to a minor. To a mother, a casually dressed unkempt 20-year-old man saying "Hey, baby" or even "Hi" to her seventeen-year-old daughter might be considered a lewd suggestion. But only in our time is such a thing an offense worthy of felony conviction. And even then based on no evidence other than hearsay or the testimony of a biased party, who only needs to spin enough drama to convince a jury. Or blackmail a plea bargain, which for the purposes of the lifelong destruction of the offender is good enough. And in the process we create a true enemy of the state with literally nothing left to lose and an axe to grind.

First Wife proposes, should we require laws such as these to protect young girls, a system in which men are allowed to demand proof of age. Demanded prior to sex and as a condition of the offer, these men would then, in effect, card all women they find attractive. Failure to produce proof of age would negate the offer and thus no offense would have occurred. Should the female produce false identification, the man would then be absolved of any wrongdoing.

This system could even ride atop secured text messaging and be practically instantaneous, with a permanent record of the liaison and the preliminary data handshaking available for inspection. Such a system would prove safer for the women than mine of inspecting a driver's license, which exposes the women to stalker risk should she not be interested. Men could then essentially shop for women of suitable legislative and reproductive potential by querying their PDAs as they undulate past. Ah, modern romance. So much for chasing cute giggling girls through the berry patches.

On a related topic, men are often charged and convicted with stalking offenses. Many times these offenses include those activities such as plucking away on a banjo outside her window until he embarrasses her into going to dinner to get him to shut up. Now that time-honored cheese of woo turns into a restraining order. And the Daddy-with-shotgun walking out onto the front porch has been replaced by the much more destructive police-with-handcuffs and arrest-warrant.

Either of these models satisfies the chase-me-catch-me drama gene bred into women over countless generations of primitive man. But only one of these is highly destructive to male ethic. A young man might survive five daddies with no permanent effect other than a boost to his self-esteem for challenges having been ultimately overcome as a rite of passage. But, one arrest encounter brands him for life. Similarly, what used to be called great sex is now called domestic violence.

All of mankind dragged itself out of the caves into the modern world without the protection of these laws, which are too easily abused. However, only in our time have young women needed the protection of someone other than Daddy, uncles and brothers. Traditionally, these men were often in the best possible position to determine whether she was in any actual danger or not. They also represented a challenge to the suitor, that once surmounted, proved his suitability for her reproductive capacity. Or in the case of the frat party crasher, whether she was stupid and got what her drama deserved.

One possible reason for societal change is that now the daddies, uncles and brothers are the genetically or psychologically engineered emasculates themselves. As emasculates, they too depend on the state to protect them from the predators. And now predators are defined, of course, as those few men who have rejected the emasculation, and whom often suffer the consequences of this defiance of the collective.

So what does this psychosexual rant have to do with the State of Texas? In particular that model of liberty hauling away 400 children and 133 women to separate internment camps from the Yearning for Zion Ranch in April of 2008?

Everything. By casting the raid and mass violation of civil rights in sexual terms, that state, populated by the chronically repressed, was able to trigger the primal reactions within all of us to ignore the facts. Unfortunately for the victims in Texas, the facts include the lack of any prior evidence whatsoever. Even the initial phone call which precipitated everything which followed was later shown to be a hoax. A hoax which the state authorities declined to validate before leaping into action.

As a bonus, rumors of cyanide abounded to link in memories of Jonestown. The monkey collective, in its deliberate ignorance, cared nothing about the legitimate farm and dye uses for cyanide. In any event, this hysteria, as all hysteria is, turned out to be about nothing. The cyanide turned out to be merely literature about cyanide, presumably as part of a school research paper. The media, and all of us, played along because we were told it was about the children. And because we wanted to believe the drama and put them in their place.

But what about the issue of underage girls marrying older men? In times past, the normal family consisted of an older man with a younger wife. The man, having already made his fortune and established himself, was more capable and able to provide for a family than he would have been at a younger age. The older man's wisdom and experience more than made up for its lack in the young woman. This was such a powerful reproductive advantage that even today in our modern society young women remain attracted to older men, despite ourselves.

Of course, with such a system of offset ages it would be difficult to lure a naive young couple into desperate financial struggle at the hands of the state. This spirit of independence would make it difficult to spawn welfaric voters generation after generation, and so the monkey collective would weaken. Interestingly, generational welfare only became possible in our modern world once the forces of niceness began demanding societal changes.

Polygamy? For most of human experience polygamy was the rule of the day. This practice was interrupted predominantly by the Catholic Church in the western world for two millennia. While doing so it suppressed independent thought and progress of all kinds while it ignored the contents of its own carefully crafted Bible.

Only in a polygamist system were most women able to mate and reproduce with capable men. Capable men are the relative minority in any society, then as now. Recently, the forces of niceness have discovered that by controlling the relationships between consenting adults that they can have more influence over people's decisions than ever before. In any event, if these women choose to be multiple wives, in a free society whose place is it to tell them how to live their lives? On the other hand, if a woman chooses to have multiple male partners, and all parties are consenting and happy with the arrangement, who else should have a say? Or is modern serial marriage, with families ripped apart by a succession of divorces, truly better for the children?

"Yes!" the monkeys shout, as they then get to gnaw the flesh of the victims and turn their despair into dependence. Is formalized polygamy, as promoted by some fringe groups, truly the societal evil which we are led to believe? If so, then certainly the informal polygamy found in our inner city government housing systems qualifies as well. Bring the buses, and haul them all away, and I mean the entire community, not just the presumed evil-doers, to internment camps for relationship inspections. Or else admit that we need to get out of the business of legislating relationships between consenting adults. But to do so would reduce the power of the state, and indirectly the power of your neighbor over you. Or you over him or her, and that is why the monkeys hate polygamy.

So what about the children? Weren't some underage girls in that "compound" found to be pregnant? Let me put this in context. Imagine that in any good-sized neighborhood, say of a hundred or so families, that one 13-year-old girl was found to be pregnant. Would it then be reasonable for the government to swoop in, seize all the children and women, including yours, carting them off to internment camps? Does your neighborhood have a pregnant underage girl? If so, fire up the Baptist buses and empty out every house within the bounds of the neighborhood. This sounds absolutely absurd in that context, and yet it happened to them right under our noses, with us cheering every day of the spectacle.

The Nazis wished they had been able to direct public opinion like that, with all portions of the political spectrum aligned so perfectly. With such a system they would have been able to hang Jews on every street corner with the public dragging them to their deaths instead of nervously glancing away. They apparently just didn't have the evolved monkey collective which we enjoy today.

So, we have now come to the point that the forces of niceness can rid itself of any challenge, no matter how harmless, simply by framing it in sexual terms. In the case of Waco, they made the mistake of not whipping up public opinion first. In Ruby Ridge they just simply didn't kill off everyone, leaving no victims to the tragedy alive to complain.

The mistake with the Yearning for Zion Ranch is that the victims of the tragedy weren't killed off in a precipitated conflagration as with the Branch Davidians. Even so, public opinion was so biased against the victims, for the presumed crimes of a very few, that any victims are now powerless to complain. But who would they complain to? Both sides have guilt on their hands. The Democrats ran Waco, the Republicans ran this latest affront against their own citizens. And don't be fooled by the lack of killings in this latest incident. Only the pacifism of the Zions themselves prevented tragedy. Don't doubt that the Republicans wouldn't have been just as eager to drink their blood as their Democrat fellows did in 1993.

And yet, the common thread with both of these abuses of liberty is that they both happened in Texas. Which leads one to wonder who the actual wackos in Texas are. Of course, it is the people who keep voting for these abuses. And never complain a peep when they happen. Because these abuses are exactly what they voted for. But there is so much more to Texas and Texans. Not only are they eager to kill their own citizens on a righteous whim, they also don't like to mix mammals and alcohol. They also think they should tell women what shapes of plastic they can have for toys. I suppose that means that not everything is bigger in Texas. And I'm sick and tired of them supplying destructive Presidents. And killing the good ones. Enough, already.

The only good Texans are the ones who act like the old Texans, the Alamo Texans. The Texans who came from everywhere else in the early 1800s to find that Galt's Gulch. The Texans like Ross Perot and Ron Paul and Charlie Wilson, men with faults and opposing positions but at their core dedicated to liberty, even if only his own liberty in the latter. The Texans before they found oil and became Baptist Arabs. But these Texans aren't in charge any more.

But I'm OK with the state of Texas being run by oil-drunk sexually repressed crazies who soak up regulatory profit and disaster relief cash while posing as economic wizards. That is what the Constitution is about. I just wouldn't be caught dead living there. Because in that buckle of the Bible Belt, expressing any different point of view will probably get you caught dead.

If you managed to stick in with this book and get to this point, I applaud you. Most of you still reading this are feeling a sense of fascination like watching a train wreck, you just can't turn away as I apparently smash my reputation into flaming giblets. If so, I have done my job and entertained you for the last few hours or so. But hey, I warned you to not read this far, or at all, didn't I? Put it down now and go take that shower which you feel you really need to wash this peek into my mind out of your soul.

I have abandoned now the pretense that this book is about entrepreneurship. It is about something more important, and at the foundation of entrepreneurship. This book is about liberty, and the battle of the collective against the individual. And the collective is winning as it progressively disenfranchises the individual year after year, issue after issue. Some small handful of you reading this are the disenfranchised minority themselves, and feel a sense of kindred spirit which seems to smooth some of the rage within you. It is for you, the innocent yet presumed guilty, that this book is really written.

Those of you who are starting to suspect that you wear the suit of a monkey, turn away now as the rest gets much, much worse. You really won't like how this ends, so put this book down and write me off as a crackpot right now. Or learn from this book and join us, casting your monkey ways aside.

If you won't cast aside the way of the monkey, then please, oh please, don't read that next chapter. I mean it.

Chapter 18, The Drug War

No stratagem ever devised by the monkey collective has been more destructive to the spirit of the individual and liberty than the War on Drugs. My first introduction to the common insanity which surrounds our Drug War came about as a result of my work in Desert Storm. Although I joined the Navy because I wanted to fly and ultimately be an astronaut, I joined the Marines for a variety of reasons explained previously. One of these reasons was to avoid the boredom and nausea of daily flight, so I selected a ground option out of the Naval Academy. As fate, a wench of irony, would have it, I wound up being assigned to fly in the back of a KC-130 in a communications van during the war.

A combination of my unrepaired childhood broken nose, the resulting deviated septum, and the dry and sandy climate of the Middle East caused me to have a recurring nose bleed. Fortunately, this affliction was not serious enough to be debilitating, just enough to be disgusting to be around. My first few flights I spent hunched down in my seat. In this position I scribbled on my clipboard held against the wall to keep the blood running down my throat by my looking up at it. Otherwise, the blood dribbling all over my little flip-down table and running into Staff Sergeant M's lap over the course of the ten-hour flights might get in his way.

The Navy Corpsman I saw for this problem at the Jubail airbase had a simple enough solution and handed me a tube of a miracle cure. His instructions were to coat the offending septum with a dollop of this goo and handed me a little pouch of cotton swabs. I promptly lost the swabs, leaving me to use rifle cleaning swabs from the armorer instead. This treatment worked as advertised. Although this goo had a slight aromaticity, I never again spilled so much as a drop of blood for the remainder of the war. So equipped, I was able to perform my normally ground job from the air.

It was a picturesque sight. Each evening, our little band of warriors perched on crates of missiles at the edge of the busy airfield waiting for our KC-130 to fly in to haul us off. From time to time a Marine attack helicopter would taxi by, the rotor wash and blinking lights adding to the surrealism. Lacking wheels, helicopters taxi by hovering a few feet off the ground. This is a disturbingly impractical aerial maneuver made more impractically disturbing by the pilot being distracted by the sight of a Marine officer digging around in his nose with a six-inch stick. And probably a little disturbed by the five other Marines around him not seeming to notice or care. I might as well have been wearing overalls and sporting a banjo.

As it turned out, our little unit managed to ride in the back of the KC-130s for enough missions to qualify for the Air Medal. Although honored and appreciative of this recognition, I was a bit embarrassed by it at the time. I pointed out that we were about as deserving of this Air Medal as I was of getting a Purple Heart for my nose bleeding in the face of the enemy. Had I peered over the edge of the plane's open cargo ramp at the battlefield below without my prophylactic dose of magical ointment that would have been literally true, of course.

Not all of my Marine peers agreed with my perspective. I intended these remarks to distinguish us from the vast majority of our fellow

Marines who were genuinely heroic and more deserving of decoration. But, my meteoric meritorious and somewhat whimsical rise to the lowest level of Senior Air Directorship past them had left some of my fellow junior officers a bit ruffled. And neither did my opinions on President Bush the First endear me to those bitter few, the gathering storm of the collectivist forces of niceness within our midst.

I chose to serve my nation under the leadership of President Reagan. I had spent my entire academy life immersed in our national culture hardly an hour's drive from the Great Man himself. His many direct influences on me included the appointment of Jim Webb as his Secretary of the Navy despite that hero's political rough edges. The choice of Webb for that post culminated in the selection of Al Gray as Commandant of the Marine Corps. And we were on our way to a 600-ship Navy, many of which would be the finest warships ever devised. America was a great place to be, and a great place to serve.

I could never understand why such a great man as our President could have selected such a worm as George Herbert Walker Bush to be his running mate.

Internet Research
Research George H. W. Bush, and his father, Senator Prescott Sheldon Bush, and his grandfather, Samuel Prescott Bush. Wikipedia has excellent concise articles for each.

As I have come to know since then, Reagan the candidate had despised the ideals of this agent of privilege as he ran against him in 1980. So, Reagan had determined after his primary victory that George H. W. Bush would not serve as his running mate. But, in a late-night smoke-filled room at that Republican National Convention, a meeting whose details are probably lost to history, things changed. That great man whose deceptively simple speeches belied a deep understanding of our Constitutional values would make the most important mistake of his life. His justification to allow that worm his turn was to ensure that the party would carry certain key states.

One of those states which Bush was to carry was Texas, he being an oilman, of course. We are led by modern pundits to believe that his fortune was entrepreneurial, based solely on merit and a model for our own efforts. But, a close reading of family history finds the lie in that. Although Bush presented himself as a Texan, his roots were in elitist New England. Once it seemed that his political career came to an end as the primaries wore on he moved to his grandfather's estate in Kennebunkport, Maine. In the process, the worm sold his residence in Houston as it no longer seemed to carry any political weight. He cast this address aside as he would supporter and promise alike. As he would anything which retained little value to this consummate manipulator and former Director of Central Intelligence.

As it turned out, this political calculation of including Bush the First on Reagan's ticket was unnecessary. Reagan himself, not the party, swept to victory by a comfortable margin. Arguably, he would have done so even without the worm contingent. Yet, the nation which Reagan loved so much would be left to deal with the invertebrate legacy which would remain.

My early understanding of politics was taught in our high school by a deceptively clever woman whom I shall call Mrs. Hooch (the thinnest film conceals her actual name). She taught the intricate interweaving of federalism, individual merit, and states' rights. And the essential role which states' authority versus the national government plays in defending our liberty.

The most brilliant political scientist I have ever known or heard, Mrs. Hooch once applied for a patent just to see how the process worked. And so, as a young woman she had applied for a means to measure how far a turtle would move in a day by playing out a string affixed to its shell.

She often mentioned this example to illustrate the importance of tweaking with absurdity systems which might otherwise seem intimidating. These tweaks, she taught, revealed how these systems react. In the process of discovery, the tweaker might learn something valuable which had previously lay hidden from view. I have spent many years since tweaking system after system to my endless delight.

Mrs. Hooch, mistress of the turned phrase, taught Constitutional government. In so doing she imbued me with a respect for the ideal of this nation which affected me to my core and continues to do so to this day. No thinking person could sit through her classes and not decades later remember her fondly with dewy-eyed affection. Her favorite technique would be to raise issues from current events, and then ask for the constitutional perspective.

Our little mushy brains would spout some nonsense we had heard on the one or two fuzzy rabbit-eared television stations, and then she would pounce: "Fo get whut you heuh, fo get whut you HEUH. Whut do da Con sta too shun SAY?" she would demand, her piercing birdlike eyes emphasizing each syllable by darting to each of our faces in turn.

These gazes were timed in concert with slaps of her wrinkled brown hand on the desk, demanding we think for ourselves. At first, no hands would rise, hoping to escape further wrath. "Get yo book and READ, chill wren. Don let no wun tell you whut ta thank, you thank fo YOSEFF!" Timidly rustling through the textbook, thirty or so sets of grubby nails would rustle the few pages which defines our entire corner of civilization. In a ritual repeated throughout the many semesters she taught her course, eventually one hand would timidly edge skyward.

In my class, that hand was attached to the gawky body of a tallish boy with an impossibly large head. Hearing his answer, she leapt from the desk in excitement, clapping her hands furiously, tears in her brown and aging eyes, "Good good GOOD chile, YOU thawt fo YOSEFF!"

Seeing the reward of our classmate, the rest of us, one-by-one, would begin to participate. That young boy would one day handsomely grow underneath that impossibly large head and become the head of the Mississippi Democrat Party. And possess an understanding of the

Constitution and the role of state governments which eludes many on the so-called right, its presumed protector, or for that matter either party.

Eventually, as the semester progressed, dozens of chill wren would defend day positions by pointing at passages from day book. And discuss the finer points of da Constitution, fogettin whut dey heuh, an thankin fo dayseff. And so, less than ten years later, as a Marine officer in war I sat in the desert some months after its premature conclusion. I forgot what I had heard parroted by my peers. I thawt fo myseff, an whut I thawt was that President George Herbert Walker Bush was a worm. And that he was only one of the many among the vast masses of the electorate of the nice for whom understanding of or respect for the Constitution eludes.

As Vice President, he spearheaded the new offensives in the War on Drugs. I saw these as an expansion of the national government's restriction of individual liberty. Taught in school as a necessary evil to protect us from bad people, drug laws originally began as a way to protect the stupid from themselves. Later these laws expanded as a way of suppressing the predominantly black recreational marijuana users without being explicitly racist. For similar racist reasons it would become increasingly illegal to harm a dog which threatened you.

No one, especially not the oh-so-very-nice, would simply say that the powers of the age wanted to arrest uppity black people. Because to say that wouldn't be very nice. Instead, by framing marijuana users in the early twentieth century as menaces to white womanhood, onerous powers were given to government which would have caused shivers to the founding fathers.

At first these powers to arrest the harmless who simply smoked themselves into poverty were limited to state governments. But, over time the collective enabled an increasingly powerful national government. Under this corrosive influence, these would become national crimes as well. And in their nationalization, take away the power of the states to decide these issues for themselves. Or for their citizens to choose among these state decisions by voting with their feet. For the recreational user, there would be nowhere to flee. The more backward jurisdictions were given practically unlimited power to frame and arrest. Power supplemented by the invention of prohibition, petty tyrants began to infiltrate the law enforcement profession in increasing numbers.

This infiltration of the unworthy and constitutionally ignorant behind the badge, slow at first, progressively eroded public respect for the law. The county sheriff transformed from the protector and instrument of the will of the productive into an instrument of mistrust who sought to take away a man's right to support himself. The mere production of a product which others want, and in this case moonshine, was either taxed heavily or prohibited outright, depending on the year. And so the sheriff became known in places as a collaborator of the hated national revenuer, despite whatever merits an individual lawman may rightfully possess. And turned the foothill farmer into a criminal who became increasingly desperate, leading to such innovations as NASCAR.

As long as criminal consequences remained low, so did the cat-and-mouse game remain almost a friendly competition between neighbors. The purveyors of what had been once roadside weeds and preserved corn continued to ply their trade in defiance of the forces of niceness. The forces of niceness said they only wanted to protect idiots from themselves, and increasingly demonized the outlaw. The sheer defiance of the outlaw itself justified stiffer and stiffer penalties. As the stakes rose and generations passed, so evaporated the pretense of neighborly respect between criminal and the law, or any of the populace who might serve as witness. And then it turned ugly. Such is the legacy of the nice.

At some point the repeal of prohibition restored some degree of sanity to the manufacture, distribution, sale and use of alcohol. But the use of other intoxicating substances, and the enforcement ethic, would remain in the legal backwater to grow into the menace we know today. The ugliness came to demonize the gun, and so draconian laws were passed to limit the arms which the people may lawfully bear. The more reasonable approach would have been a repeal of the legal environment against purportedly free citizens which had created the ugliness in the first place.

The same weapon thrust into the hands of an involuntary draftee, formerly defined as free, for firing at someone wearing differently colored clothes, lest he face the noose, would be denied to the free citizen. The forces of niceness who create needless wars and their unfortunate consequences can rarely admit their mistakes. Because of this lack of collective character, the increasingly stiff laws against drugs would only grow stiffer still. And with worse and worse consequences, all in a downward spiral of insanity.

The baby boomers then faced their own tightening of the screw. Eating through their parents' savings like a horde of locusts, they cast off any sense of virtue or self-discipline like the generation of spoiled brats they are. They destroyed any institution of value for those of us who closely followed, and took to drugs as one of many forms of rebellion against prosperity and the individual. The elder generations, not willing to let their little darlings choke in pools of their own vomit, blamed the molecule and the chemist but not the child.

So, in the late 1960s and early 1970s, while civil rights leaders were advocating for a liberty already won, both the left and the right significantly enhanced drug legislation. And handed powers of unprecedented oppression to themselves. Both sides set their differences in policy aside and colluded in destroying the remaining dignity and purpose of the individual. This goal was far more important to them than any superficial distinction between them. Normally, this false distinction was paraded about us for our distraction when convenient, but this was not the time for disunity among the collective. The all-important battle against the individual was enough to unite them.

Conservative pundits argue that we can't let addicts destroy themselves as we will then be forced to pay for the consequences. Not if we just say no to paying for these consequences and let them starve in their stupor. This simple answer should easily occur to the minds of those who oppose socialized medicine, but on this issue simplicity escapes them.

To cede this point would deprive collectivists on the right of their main weapon against individual liberty. The collectivists are buoyed by millions of adherents who trade their liberty for a warm feeling in their hearts as they think about how they protect their children by destroying their freedoms. The same pundits who nurse their private addictions safe behind riches which protect them from prosecution demand the stiffest penalties for the poor or middle class caught in their web. Or planted with false evidence to punish some other defiance, the very classes they advocate to save suffer as the collective applies the nightstick or taser.

And in so doing, advocates of this insanity create more dependents on the state in the form of prisoners who must be fed, housed, and clothed, and then monitored after their release. These millions, by virtue of their permanent record, will never be afforded the opportunity to live up to their fullest potential to our collective benefit. Meanwhile, their wives and children are accused of crimes by association or threatened with placement in foster homes of dubious safety. Thus their loved ones are held hostage to the whim of the state in enforcing their compliance to turn in their brethren. This system of coercion would make any drug kingpin proud. This system destroys the unique American individualism which defined our heritage.

Midway through the eight years of progress and genuine enlightenment which was the Reagan legacy, the President was busy destroying the Soviet Union. Distracted by this enormous task, he appointed Bush as the head of a task force devoted to bestowing the status of public enemy upon the coca farmer in Latin America. In this effort we, as a nation, decided to repeat the criminalization of the American foothill corn farmer and entrepreneur upon these others. But this plan had one little oopsie. The coca farmer's local constabulary was still his friend and protector, and amenable to purchase if not. These officials were far from the domestic well-trained and fully-indoctrinated agent of the forces of nice.

Rather than creating the Latin version of the Duke Boys, with lifts and spinners equipping their gaily painted roadster with that funny-sounding horn, we encouraged them to create indigenous paramilitary cartels. These would grow later into international drug cartels, with quasi-official local support. This evolution, after all, was the only rational response left to embattled farmers when faced with a foreign power who wanted desperately to buy their product at ridiculously high prices. And who wanted desperately to kill them for filling that demand.

These cartels survive today, growing ever more stealthy and powerful, and violent, products of an evolutionary system which need never have existed. Being havens in which terrorists and enemies of all ideologies can purchase sanctuary, they now serve as one of the greatest threats to our national security. And yet, despite all their power, they could be felled, to a man, with acclaim of Congress and a stroke of a Presidential pen. This pen of power would remove their market by eliminating the crimes which support their prices. In so doing we would reduce their fields to mere agricultural colonies for legitimate businesses rather than the printing presses for illicit profit they are today.

But to do so, the collectives of nice of both sides of the political aisle would have to abandon their control over the individual. Sadly, this is a price neither is willing to pay. For the children. Children they eagerly await to imprison for life in order to save them.

And so it was under his watch that Bush the First, in his tenure as the Great Man's Vice President, took the controls of this system of oppression for himself. Under his watch he strengthened it further, advocating an Office of National Drug Control Policy. The head of this office was to be known as the Director, but informally known in this nation of free men as the Drug Czar. As President, Bush the First would appoint in this post William J. Bennett to supervise the further erosion of liberty in this nation. Its first director, Bennett would pen notes for his future satirical book of virtues, all the while struggling with gambling, smoking, and drinking vices in his own life. In his official capacity, he denied the less-connected fewer opportunities for mistakes than he procured for himself and his friends.

Internet Research
Research William John Bennett, formerly Director of the Office of National Drug Control Policy.

Overseas, the long period of nothing following Desert Storm in which we weren't allowed to go home yet became known to us as Desert Sit. During this pointless exercise the national leadership debated how to extract themselves from the decision of not pressing the attack into Baghdad. In these months we heard reports of the Iraqis chanting "Bush Bush Bush" in the streets and carrying posters of his image as they had done with Saddam six months before. Finding myself longing for the lucrative Bush poster concession, I listened to my fellow Marine officers in our tent of twelve marvel at how we had just created a nation of Republicans.

Tired of this naivety at last, I remarked how this was the natural survival mechanism of their culture, to cheer whomever was perceived as the top dog of the day. They were no more cheering Bush for his merit than they did Saddam before him, and would again mere months hence, as it turned out. I also pointed out that if Bush showed up for one of these rallies, and some thug took him out, silence would reign for only a moment. Five minutes later these same people would be ranting "Thug Thug Thug" whilst hoisting thug posters. As they recoiled in horror from this analysis, I wondered silently about the logistics required to run a five-minute poster shop. This wasn't my first public expression of distaste for him. Most of my carefully worded invectives centered around his ability to squirm into political expediency, vindicating my later assessment of the Nematode-In-Chief.

Soon after gaining office, Bush the First almost immediately supported tax hikes, a famous phrase during his 1988 campaign indicating that reading his lips was tantamount to reading lies. I made so little back then that taxes in my bracket were almost meaningless. Regardless, I felt he had violated my trust, feeling that my vote had been frauded away in his behalf.

He also signed into law the Americans with Disabilities Act of 1990, a well-meaning piece of protective legislation which would be twisted in unexpected ways against entrepreneurs throughout the next two decades. He re-authorized the Clean Air Act, a liberal staple, thus further crippling our domestic refinery capacity. And so protecting established oil interests against any upstarts who might have new technology, new blends, and new ideas at their side.

This miracle of political science also caved to the anti-gun lobby almost immediately after taking office, a topic which was of more personal importance. In 1989 he authorized the BATF to ban importation of certain types of semi-automatic assault rifles. This move was, surprisingly, supported to a large extent by domestic gun makers, not caring that this move left the legislative target painted on their heads next. With this act, that Galil in the hands of the friend of The Boss had just tripled in value, though.

A few weeks after settling into my ratty little house outside the Cherry Point Marine Corps Air Station, I penned a strong letter. In this letter I made fun of his "kindler (sic) and gentler" approach to destroying our liberties. I also pointed out that for those of us without day-to-day Secret Service protection our lives had just been placed more at risk. I am sure this letter ultimately languishes in a Secret Service file against the day it might be used as evidence.

In my youthful naivety, I had of course mistaken the greatness of Reagan as the standard, rather than the exception. Measured against the former, Bush the First was a gross electoral aberration elevated to near treason. Measured against the latter, merely another species of the normal product of the collective of the nice.

I had also not yet come to realize that never again would the collective allow entry to anyone even remotely approaching Reagan's love for the country and the people. This fact of life in the collective explains why we never seem to have any real major party choices for President anymore. We certainly are allowed none who inspire with the personable charisma of a Reagan or a Palin. Even this great woman was hidden behind handlers, and the subject of venomous attacks from the elite of both sides. I would later understand why this is so, and see that the true responsibility lay at the feet of the electorate themselves.

The last Desert Sit pronouncement I would make at the expense of the Bush legacy involved a visit he had announced to Cartegena, Columbia. This visit was intended to show all those coca farmers who was boss. I thought such a visit was ill-timed. I also wondered whether one of those coca farmers might have a howitzer. And put said howitzer in direct-fire mode on one of those ranges surrounding the bowl within which Cartagena rests. A lucky shot from such a preparation would be a terrible embarrassment to us all. All those "Bush Bush Bush" supporters around us might start getting ideas, not realizing that victory had been secured by us, and not him. But sadly, the logistics people had already started hauling off all our ammo and equipment.

More sadly, and disconcerting, that equipment included our weapons. We had already served the worm's purpose and had now been rendered free, if somewhat displaced, citizens once again. As such, imported assault rifles, this time our own, were not suitable for our possession.

Had the locals instead been shouting "Schwartzkopf Schwartzkopf Schwartzkopf" I wouldn't have had any concern about that coca farmer. But instead I found myself, an officer in the United States Marine Corps, being guarded at an airbase in eastern Saudi Arabia by locals with German HK-91 assault rifles. As they spent more time looking inward than outward, I started looking around for a pipe. I always liked that rifle, and having owned one, was sure I could put it to productive use if the need arose, and if I could get my hands on one.

Fortunately, the need never arose. In May of 1991, we boarded a C-5A Galaxy and rode home in luxury above the cargo bay, stopping once, in Rota, Spain, to refuel and change aircrews. As for me, I was immediately packed off to recruiting duty as the Operations Officer of Marine Corps Recruiting Station, Cincinnati. As is the Marines' custom, for obvious reasons, over the next year most of the officer billets in the recruiting service nationwide would be filled by combat veterans. And yet, the idle bunkroom chatter would follow me to that job. There, the consequences of that chatter would introduce me to the almost religious significance which otherwise intelligent people assign to the drug war and to political sacred cows.

A few years later I learned that I had been investigated during my first year on recruiting duty for a plot to assassinate the President. I, of course, was oblivious to any such plot, and so didn't see the odd events of that year as having any particular significance. Apparently, some disgruntled knucklehead in my tent during Desert Sit had instigated a complaint against me. I imagine it was the one guy who had habitual roid rage. Or perhaps it was one of the displaced flower-children who I suspected of reading my outgoing mail. I salted my mail with scandal hoping to draw one or the other of them out. I never heard a peep of these tidbits, so either they weren't reading my mail, or were uncharacteristically self-disciplined. Or perhaps they smelled the bait.

Regardless of the source, this complaint turned into a bumbling investigation by the Naval Investigative Service, with the cognizance of the Secret Service. And not one individual in the loop, who should have known me better, intervened during that entire time to put a stop to that nonsense. As for me, I wouldn't find out about this investigation until I was told about it in passing by an assistant director of the recruiting district in Philadelphia. And I never found out which individual started it all. And apparently, my skill with the rifle and my letter to the President had been seen as contributing factors leading to the credibility of the investigation.

My Air Medal, and other assorted semi-meaningful fruit salad, came through as I was in Cincinnati. The Major chose to award me these at an All Hands meeting he scheduled in Columbus, which was odd since these events were usually held in Cincinnati. "But hey," I thought to myself, "he's the boss." The Major insisted that I drive him and the XO to this event. As the junior officer of the three, I had little say in the matter. Being reluctant to ding a government vehicle and deal with the resulting paperwork, I offered to drive First Wife's Honda Civic. I had plenty of paperwork to do as it was, I didn't need to volunteer for more.

The Major refused, and insisted that I drive a white government Chrysler to that Columbus meeting. The Major sat beside me in the front, while the XO rode in the back, a curious seating arrangement. I later learned that the XO was taping the conversation from the back seat. The XO would eventually spread this taped conversation throughout key personnel of the station, even after I had been exonerated unawares. The conversation, paraphrased for brevity, went something like this:

XO: So, (1st)Lt Baugh, I understand you don't like President Bush. (smooth opener to uncover an assassination plot had I actually been a dedicated conspirator)

Me: (expletive deleted) no.

CO: (shocked expression) That's your Commander in Chief you are talking about.

Me: He's also an elected official, and I'm a voter.

XO: Uhh, so what do you think about his gun control policies?

Me: I think he's a (expletive) (expletive) lying two-faced piece of (expletive).

CO: (shocked) How can you talk to the XO like that?

Me: He asked. Tell him to not ask stupid questions if he doesn't want an answer.

XO: Uhh, so what do you think about that trip to Columbia which President Bush made earlier?

Me: That was a stupid thing to do. If some (expletive)-head shot his (expletive) (expletive) down, it would make us all look like idiots.

XO: (smelling meat on the table) Uhh, so how exactly do you think they would shoot him down?

Me: (deciding to put it in terms which even these two artillery officers could understand) Cartegena is in a bowl. Range is constrained, elevation and lead can be worked out ahead of time. Does the idea of a direct-fire howitzer with flechette rounds plus plane on final approach mean anything to either of you? No ECM, no flares, no warning, nothing.

XO: Don't you think he's got people to think of that?

Me: (planning a smart-aleck answer along the lines of whether they thought Dallas had been thought through) Well, ...

CO: (interrupting) Why would anyone in Columbia want to kill the President? (I saw even the XO's eyes rolling in the mirror at this point)

Me: (wondering why the hell this conversation had gone so sideways) Are you serious?

CO: (combative) Yeah, tell me.

Me: Well, imagine you are one of those coca farmers just trying to feed his family. You would take a dim view of some (expletive)-head telling you that you can't grow a product when it is his (expletive) people who buy the (expletive).

CO: (shocked, agitated and fuming) So does this mean you want to just kill him? (again, very smooth)

Me: (wondering what kind of morons I'm trapped in this car with) What the hell are you talking about? This isn't some third world country, we can just fire the guy. You better watch saying that kind of crap, someone might get the wrong idea.

(minutes pass as the concrete slab miles click beneath us, CO getting restless)

CO: (combative) So what do you think he should do?

Me: He ought to legalize drugs and make the problem just go away. (recalling how baby boomers are above blame by their parents) I bet his own kids are (expletive) crack addicts.

CO: So you think drugs should be legalized?

Me: Yep.

CO: (shocked) Why? How can you say that? Then we'll have drug dealers running all over selling to kids.

Me: For one thing, as soon as it is legal that coca farmer will be selling to Dow Chemical, and the drug dealer won't be able to compete with their low prices. As far as drug users go, I think they ought to dump a truckload of coke in the middle of downtowns all over the country. Let those idiots go for it until they kill themselves. Good for the gene pool.

XO: But then we'll have to take care of their medical bills.

Me: Not if we give them enough coke for free.

CO: (exploding) You'll think different when you have kids of your own!

The conversation rambled from that high point to nowhere good. One of these side ventures included my assertion that the best way to smuggle a nuclear weapon into this country would be to hide it in a bale of marijuana. By the time we arrived in Columbus, I thought both of them had lost their minds. I'm sure that assessment was mutual.

The All Hands went off spectacularly, and the Major awarded my medals with trembling hands and much acclaim. But that wasn't the end of the investigation, apparently. The rest of that story is beyond the scope of this book but involved the Akron SWAT team. And a stun gun, a roll of duct tape, and the apprehension and detaining of an undercover agent of the Naval Investigative Service by the Cincinnati police. After, of course, said agent had been assigned to watch my apartment. I'm blushing.

Anyway, I now have kids, and no, my views haven't changed. I teach them that drug abuse will destroy their minds and their future, but if they choose to use them anyway, they take upon themselves the negative consequences. I tell them that idiots should be given free drugs with which to exterminate themselves. Even so, my children and yours are more at risk from the consequences of getting caught experimenting with drugs than they are from the experimentation itself.

If children are of the nature to abuse drugs, they will find some way to destroy themselves eventually. This they will do regardless of what laws are in place. The laws merely add their own special form of self-destruction to otherwise viable children. And, by stumbling onto a secret transaction, even non-experimentally-inclined children are more likely to get shot by a drug dealer than they are to do business with one.

Generations of Americans did fine without a drug war. But all of our modern drug-related hazards are arbitrary creations of the forces of niceness. This collective relies upon the intrusiveness and permanent destruction of individual spirit which these laws allow. This insanity continues to grow with each passing year. In Texas, in an effort to combat illicit drug labs, graduated cylinders are illegal, meaning that having the ability to measure liquids marks you as a criminal on the face of it.

The national government has even outlawed the possession of certain quantities of certain atomic elements. As the sophistication of drug labs grow, driven by higher and higher profits as the increasing penalties increase the cost of doing business, the ignorant populace demand greater and greater controls. So, lithium metal and iodine crystals join uranium and plutonium as atomic elements which are illegal for the individual to own. Mere possession of them in sufficient quantities are grounds for imprisonment for life, in some circumstances.

Internet Research
Research iodine.

But chemistry is a resourceful science. And, iodine is easily obtained from seaweed ashes and sulfuric acid, which is in fact the way in which it was discovered. This process gives drug labs yet another lucrative product which can be sold to their fellows for profit. But, while iodine serves a role in specific chemical processes, it is not an absolutely essential portion of the process. Instead, it is merely convenient. And so the drug labs will discover an alternative which will do. They already have, in fact, and it is as close as your swimming pool.

In the meantime, skateboarders are limited to weaker formulae and inferior protection. Their skinned knees make them one of the largest groups of first-aid users of iodine, a valuable disinfectant which travels easily and never goes bad. And suddenly, the horrors of flesh-eating bacteria are on the rise.

Similarly, lithium serves a role in illicit drug chemistry, but the dark secret is that sodium and potassium can serve similar roles with slight modification to the processes. Obtaining elemental sodium or potassium is easier than getting metallic lithium, and any of these require little more than various kinds of salt, a pottery furnace suitable for hobbyists, and electricity. I'm not telling you anything which drug labs don't already know, since they are better informed than you, such are the nature of lies which surround our quest to control our citizens.

What will the collective of nice do next, regulate or control salt? Require all folk potters to register their kilns? Limit access to electricity or fire itself? At some point these restrictions come directly into conflict with your efforts to run a legitimate business, or for that matter, live your life.

In our rush to control those who can control nature, we drive civilization backwards. Imagine the next Haber or the next Tesla who might otherwise have invented a new process to benefit us all. Traditionally thinkers are spurred into discovery by a lab they operate in their garage or basement, or experiments they might try as a child. Now, these thinkers are locked away if they try, out of our irrational and arbitrary fear that they might be running a drug lab or making bombs. Or, these prodigies become so frightened of the law that they turn to other work.

And so we now live in a society where our paper mills are older than the employees who operate them. Most of these operators, those who still have jobs, have no detailed knowledge of the chemical magic which goes on within these marvels of the past. With each industry which is shut down for economics or the environment, rarely any rise to replace it. To further shackle that little Haber or Tesla, we have eroded education to the point that chemistry, physics or math are so poorly taught that we might as well not even bother.

So when a paper mill or a refinery closes, those jobs are lost forever as we grow more and more ignorant with each passing year. Ignorant, because we fear what might happen to increasingly ignorant and less capable children. This is the labor pool from which you, the entrepreneur, draw your employees. You might as well try transporting Dark Age peasants into the present. At least they wouldn't have learned to sue you yet. Or get you thrown in jail and have everything you own seized when they decide to keep their drug stash in your office.

This insanity which pits law enforcement against otherwise peaceful citizens also corrodes the respect which can be demanded by important portions of our military forces. Just as Bush the First increasingly destroyed our civil liberties in the shadows behind Reagan. Simultaneously, he was also making sure that our National Guard was being turned into an instrument of oppression of the states they serve.

Traditionally, the National Guard, under control of the various states and more properly called the State Guards, served not only as a national military reserve. Sometimes, more importantly the guardsman also was a humanitarian resource available to the direction of the Governors. In this role, the soldier drawn to such service could be more compared to a fireman rather than a state trooper.

However, in the mid-1980s, this protective and crucial defense resource was turned into a form of national law enforcement agency. Previously directly accountable to the people of their state, and along with such previously benign entities as the Civil Air Patrol, its original federalist purpose was subverted. Ed Vaughn, a researcher for a pro-legalization group, uncovered this quote from a high-ranking officer in the National

Guard Bureau, responsible for coordinating activities of the various state guards:

"America is caught up in the most pervasive drug epidemic in history. An epidemic that transcends the health, economy, and general well-being of our nation. The rapid growth of this drug scourge has shown that military force must be used to change the attitudes and activities of Americans who are dealing and using drugs. The National Guard is America's legally feasible attitude-change agent, " Colonel Richard R. Browning, III, former chief of the drug demand section of the National Guard Bureau.

Read that again. I wonder if Colonel Browning has ever seen a copy of the Constitution which he swore to "protect and defend against all enemies, foreign and domestic"? Including domestic enemies such as, maybe, himself. Yesterday, the justification was drugs. Today, it is terrorism, a threat which could never stand on our shores against even a lightly-armed and vigilant citizenry. Tomorrow, who knows in what ways the military might be employed to adjust *your* attitude?

This misuse of the previously well-regarded National Guard is only the foot in the door to having the military as a whole hunt those who defy the forces of niceness. Many are lobbying to repeal the Posse Comitatus Act of 1879, which forbids the use of the regular military forces in domestic law enforcement. When that day arrives, potential recruits with patriotic zeal, yet no interest in law enforcement against his fellow citizen, will have to make a tough choice. And then our ability to fight real wars against meaningful and motivated enemies will be irreversibly damaged.

The zeal of the forces of niceness against some of the most upstanding citizens in our communities can become overwhelming. So overwhelming, in fact, that we feel we must look the other way just to maintain our sanity. In some cases, the possession of a concealed carry permit is considered sufficient grounds to instigate paramilitary SWAT-like raids upon our own citizens. But in fact, the screening which goes into issuing such permits should raise a flag that the permit-holder is probably OK. As a Marine, my skill with a rifle and pistol in defense of our country made me a threat, even while still in uniform. Similarly, knowledge of this skill has been used more than once to target and attack innocent American citizens.

Internet Research
Read "Overkill: The Rise of Paramilitary Police Raids in America", by Radley Balko, Cato Institute, 2006.

One useful link to this document is:

http://www.cato.org/pubs/wtpapers/balko_whitepaper_2006.pdf

Each time I hear one of these paramilitary horror stories, I can only laugh. In most cases, the law enforcement officials want to dress up like soldiers and then attack the citizens whom they are hired to protect. These cretins are no better ethically than a common street thug who, with a pack of his homies, gangs up on defenseless unarmed citizens. I say this from the perspective of a Marine trained to fight more heavily-armed and better-equipped Soviets, outnumbered by three-to-one, or more. That slogan, "the few and the proud", means something.

A typical Marine (or Army Ranger or Green Beret or Navy Seal or Air Force Romad, etc.), outnumbered two-to-one, and given freedom of action and the opportunity to prepare the battlefield, will feel a certain amount of pity toward his adversaries. His first move will be to partition the engagement so that no portion of the opposing force is outnumbering by more than two- or three-to-one at a given time and place. So prepared, a small team could handle a practically unlimited number of adversaries, pausing as needed to eat, drink, reload and urinate.

Yet, dozens of black-armored officers (I still have trouble using that word in this context) storm into a house, only to later haul out a couple of emaciated meth-heads in plastic cuffs. I chuckle, knowing that these same heroes wouldn't survive more than about three or so of these raids against a few determined and well-trained opponents in a prepared war zone. The fact that they do survive means that, despite their little boy dress-up fantasies, they aren't at war. And that society, including their victims, has not yet decided that they are the enemy.

Because they aren't the enemy, as I explain later. They are merely the symptom, and the pointy end of the spear, as Marines put it, of the true enemy of liberty. If you were able to "Jeannie-blink" each of these power-mad black-clad pawns out of existence tomorrow, more would rush to fill their place tomorrow. Each of these replacements would enjoy the full backing of the electorate, only without the moderating factor of the clearer heads among them now. And even the most hardened, violent criminals, on average, find them more useful alive than dead, a deliberate strategic decision which should tell you something. All so that some suburbanites can fool themselves into thinking they are being good parents, rather than bothering to simply be good parents.

The empowered electorate of this nation incarcerates a higher percentage of its citizens than any other country in the world. One percent of all American adults are now behind bars. Feel safer? I don't. Many of these people are criminals because we have defined otherwise harmless or merely self-destructive behaviors to be heinous crimes worthy of the most serious punishments. Similarly, possession of certain substances must rock our civilization to its core. This topic has been written about at length elsewhere, including greatly increased opportunities to seize property without trial or to plant evidence on defiant innocents. So, there is no need for me to rehash this in detail here.

If you haven't read that whitepaper from the Cato Institute, go back and read it now. Then ask yourself why the electorate of this nation would allow drug laws to destroy respect for the law. This same electorate supports even tougher laws, relaxed restrictions on warrants and searches, and forgiveness of police criminality as they sit on the juries who try them. Why would they take these positions knowingly, and by so doing, encourage police to take a militaristic stance against the populace? Because that is exactly what the electorate of this nation demands.

Police are indoctrinated and trained to view unconvicted Americans as enemies for mere possession of certain molecules, rather than the "innocent until proven guilty" whom they are. Despite this horror, the electorate feels little danger from this situation.

Throughout this book I speak of the monkey collective as the collective of the nice or the forces of niceness. This corrosive force of fake smiles has, for over two hundred years, been dissolving away first the foundations of our federal system. And now this collective directly threatens our liberties themselves. Why? Simply put, to propagate their breed. Whether they take these stances to propagate, or they propagate because they take these stances is of no consequence. The result is that they thrive on oppression.

Imagine that two individuals are the subjects of identical, yet mistaken, "no-knock" searches at four in the morning. Remember throughout this discussion that neither of these individuals are guilty of anything. In both cases, the police simply arrived at the wrong address or were given a bad tip by a suspect hoping to work a better deal. Regardless of the underlying mistake, neither of our two victims are guilty of anything at the moment the police crash in.

Victim #1, a nice person who votes for the destruction of liberty, is in general a panty-waist who would never think of defending himself against bullies or criminal intruders. He cowers at the mere sight of danger. As such, he feels more threatened by an individualist than even the most trigger-happy SWAT team. When that SWAT team bursts in on his home, he exhibits the beta-dog response, trembling in fear and perhaps latent submissive excitement. The police, seeing his helpless response, do not fire, and he survives. His very cowardice is a survival mechanism tuned to the civilization in which we live, and he votes to maintain and promote this fertile ground for himself.

Victim #2 on the other, may be a nice person as well, and may even unwittingly vote for the destruction of liberty. Or he may be a jerk whom others feel should be taught a lesson. In either case, at his core, he is an American individualist. He believes that it is not only his right to protect himself within his home, but also his responsibility to protect his family against criminal intrusion. When the police burst into his home, he first moves to defend himself against unannounced predators before the situation fully registers in his mind, and the police kill him. The individualist's only defense is to mimic helplessness, which grates at the core of his very soul. This unnatural behavior is very difficult to recall waking from a deep sleep at four in the morning with a crash at the door.

And so, a spiraling weakness of spirit in the nation ensues. Over time, the citizenry is cleansed of individualists, their physical and moral genetics snipped from the vine. All the children and grandchildren and great-grandchildren the murdered individualist might father and teach are never born.

Meanwhile weakness and cowardice flourishes as the panty-waist, the unit of the collective of either party, reproduces without bound. He spawns generations of voters for more oppression as it allows them unlimited opportunities. The panty-waist cannot compete with the more independent individualist man-to-man in the marketplace of commerce, ideas, or relationships. And so he creates a protective environment which seeks out and destroys the individualist. The individualist, in turn, is deceived as to that environment's true purpose as it hunts him down, one by one. Mistake by mistake, or spite by spite, it makes no difference as the individualist dies either way.

The fact that the drug war, and the attendant overbearing police response, promotes this trend of spiraling weakness of spirit is the very reason why the populace supports these policies. Otherwise, the electorate would be outraged at their reach. So many times I hear patriots trying to educate the ignorant about the erosion of their liberties. At one time I did so myself, only to become a target. The electorate isn't ignorant or kept in the dark or easily misled, they are voting for exactly what they want. And what this electorate wants is to destroy you by any means necessary.

Now consider the practical effects which this zealous enforcement has on our lives, genetics aside. In many cases, a drug dealer or distributor is facing life sentences for his crimes if convicted. So, imagine a drug dealer in Anywhere, USA, perhaps in Oklahoma, for argument's sake. A couple of local girls, playing innocently in the area surrounding their families' farms, happen to stumble upon a major drug transaction, and are discovered by the dealers. The penalty for being convicted for the drug transaction is approximately the same as that for murder. And, killing these little witnesses dramatically decreases the likelihood of being convicted of the original crime. So how do you think that hypothetical encounter is going to play out? In our zeal to make our children safer, we have made them less safe.

As a child, I cut grass and worked at a local gas station cleaning toilets and changing oil, saving my pennies to buy my prized possession, a CAR-15 assault rifle. This was the same rifle I would later use at the Naval Academy to teach plebes how to field strip an M-16. Although only a plinker at the time, I would trot around the country roads and in the fields and woods with this rifle slung over my back. So armed, I was protected against bobcats, largish snakes, and Communists alike.

Many days, a deputy sheriff would drive by, and he and I would exchange waves and pleasantries. Throughout, I outgunned him by a significant factor, a concept which somehow means something now but was totally out of context then. The policeman of that day was generally perceived as the friend of the people. As their friend, he was the beneficiary of their significant firepower rather than the agent of a capricious collective.

This was not at all an unusual sight. Many children trotted around with their little hunting rifles or shotguns or pistols, even out of hunting season with no one the worse for it. There was no chance any of these well-armed tweens and teens were going to be put down lightly by stumbling onto a drug transaction. Even my pitiful, by Marine standards, plinking skills at that age were still too effective to bet one's life against. Plus, one never knew which of these rifle-toting urchins might be a little Alvin York with innate ability. The high school parking lots were full of pickups and El Caminos with rifle racks full of long arms, and glove boxes stuffed to bursting with ammunition and handguns. Special events brought out more weapons.

Halloween and Old Fashioned Day saw costumes which included Vietnam, Korean, World War, Civil War, 1812, and Revolutionary soldiers and Indians. Some items had been proudly handed down by their fathers from as far back as great-great-great-great- grandfathers. These costumes were complete with authentic or reproduced fully functional period weapons, including firearms, knives, swords, machetes, tomahawks, *et cetera*.

An eagerly anticipated favorite of Old Fashioned Day each year for a time was one slimly attractive girl dressed as a 1920's flapper. She carried an anachronistically appropriate .25 automatic strapped to her thigh within a garter belt. And no one, except perhaps the then-silent drama queen or two, felt any threat. Not surprisingly, during my entire school career, not once did I hear of a single school shooting in any jurisdiction. Surprisingly, though, there were many fights.

The day I hit Shinbone #1 with the pipe, my school locker contained a loaded Colt .38 Super Automatic. Yet, it never occurred to me to use it, my purpose being better served by the pipe and the subsequent discussion. I was not unique in what would now be a heinous crime of possession of firearms on a school campus.

Shinbone #1 even had a loaded little girly .38 Special revolver in the glove compartment of his prissy truck my friends and I would fill with harmless dry trash a week later. His truck also held a .410 pump shotgun on his rifle rack. We were mutually aware of the other's armament at the time we had our talk. Still, these weapons were out of context for the events of that day, and we both settled the issue like men. Yet, had a school shooting broken out, Shinbone #1 and I would have stood side-by-side to stop the shooters before further harm could be done. Dozens of other students and faculty alike would have stood beside us.

Similarly, had a Cho broken into a rampage at the Naval Academy, I or any of my plebes could have quelled the rebellion. This despite many of them having never touched a weapon before Annapolis. But, taught to shoot by Academy Marines and taught to replace the firing pin in the dark by me, any of them could have hidden in my room long enough to restore my rifle. Such an incident was about as far from my mind as you can imagine, not even making the list of possible justifications to have that weapon in my room. Back then, I perceived even the most ignorant or uncivil among my academy brethren as my friends and allies. I naturally assumed, perhaps naively, that each of them thought the same of me.

The reason that such shootings never happened then, barely a generation ago, is simple. Unlike today, children and young men were allowed to sort out their differences in a healthy fashion, learning the valuable lessons necessary for adult life. These young adults were properly prepared by harmless childhood lessons. When they entered society at large they were capable of being civil. Each had their dignity intact, not needing to prove themselves to others or feeling unduly oppressed. Bullies learned civility and respect for others, and the bullied gained self-confidence and self-respect. Society simply lacked the capacity to manufacture a Harris, or a Klebold, or a Cho back then. And terrorists? Good luck. All the sheriff would have had to do is point.

We are taught by the forces of niceness that the South, is, was, and will forever be, a hotbed of racism in which no minority is safe. This holds triple for my birth state of Mississippi, we are told. These lies are paraded before us to keep us ignorant, fearful, hateful, and willing to hand over our liberties to anyone who will save us from ourselves. And in our compliance, we are taught to ignore the incremental destruction of our nation and our lives.

And yet, in that sweltering, un-airconditioned classroom in the middle of the Deep South a similarly well-armed Mrs. Hooch taught Constitutional government. As she spoke she was surrounded on particularly festive days by the well-armed great-great-grandsons of former slaves. These children sat side-by-side with the well-armed great-great-grandsons of white dirt farmers too poor to have owned slaves.

She simply taught the Constitution itself, including her right to bear arms deep within the fictional violence of Mississippi. We learned the lesson that we should fear no man, but mistrust formal power. Amid a flutter of Confederate flags and civil rights slogans, we learned about government, and its rightfully limited place in our lives. We learned that when the government seeks to make us fearful of one another and divide us in exchange for surrendering our liberty, we should eye with suspicion the motives behind the messenger. We learned also to question, by extension, the electorate who empowers this fear.

"I walk down da street an a man call me a name. Whut do I do, chill wren?" I recall her axing a month or so into the course to test our growing confidence. No answer, embarrassed shuffles.

Finally, she says, "TV say I shood git angry and fite and call da Pwesidem to save Miz Hooch. But I smile. Cuz he free to say whut he wunt. An I free to not buy in his sto. But I do cuz he got good prices fo any ting I wunt, an dat is good fo Miz Hooch. I chooz to, not cuz I haf to, cuz I free to." She continues, gesticulating wildly, "an HE free to tell me ta git out a his sto, but he don, cuz he wunt my money, chill wren."

"An if I say he caint say whut he wunt to, den I got to stop beeng free, and not say whut I wunt, too."

"You FREE, chill wren," cocking her head to the side to see if we understood. Short pause... then, softly:

"Cuz datz whut da Con sta tu shun say," she would conclude in her cleverly affected semi-Creolean accent.

Her accent and mangling of The King's English was carefully calculated to teach that the limitations of a person's voice says nothing about the quality of ideas expressed by it. And that we don't have pompous kings who get to demand syllabic precision. She, in that Deep South Mississippi classroom, was respected deeply by all who knew her. She earned this respect by her ideas, not by legislation or lawsuit. And not by consequence of birth or privilege.

Her story made the point that the Constitution and its federalism allows individuals to make their individual decisions and mistakes. While doing so, they are protected from blind far-off authority by layers of intervening obstacles. This separation of powers is the enemy of feigned niceness, and of the oppressor. Even if that oppressor is concealed behind a smile and a wave and an articulate voice coming from a pretty or a handsome face. An oppressor who seeks to keep you and your children ignorant because that is what you demand that they do for you.

And far better that your acquaintances be genuinely rude, yet trade fairly, than to wear an enforced mask of false civility and cheat you at every turn. Or pretend to be your protector and take away your liberty.

Oh, and the tube of miracle cure prescribed by that Navy Corpsman to handle my desert nosebleed? The miracle cure which I smeared inside my nose as I flew the remainder of the war? Preparation-H. And yes, I live up to what that would make me.

Chapter 19, Gun Control

In January of 1991, our merry band of Marine air support professionals alighted at the Jubail airfield in eastern Saudi Arabia. We were heavily armed, but had no ammunition. At least officially.

Prior to departure, I and another Marine officer (I'll call him Tim) were concerned about our logistics. We had anticipated the usual amount of bureaucratic inefficiency which attends when a coalition of disparate units and chains of command are thrown together in a melting pot. Given that our unit was intended to fill in temporarily for another larger unit, we were confident that our needs would be perceived in the red-headed step-child category.

As such Tim and I had handed selected officers under the rank of Captain a single 9mm round, dubbed our "Barney Bullets". We also surreptitiously disbursed five 5.56mm rounds to each enlisted man under the rank of Gunnery Sergeant. Each such prepared officer and Marine was then provided with instructions as to where among their gear to hide their rounds. Our intention was that any one of us might find at least one of these caches in an emergency. These rounds, purchased commercially at our own expense, turned out to be exactly the leverage we would need to become fully armed upon arrival. But, this full-arming turned out in an entirely different manner than I had intended.

As expected, before boarding our chartered 747, we nineteen armed and uniformed Marines, along with our personal gear, were subjected to a cursory search. The goal? Various contraband, including pornography, explosives, and ammunition. Our Lieutenant Colonel Commanding Officer supervised this inspection, as did the unit Sergeant Major. The former, full colonels' eagles in his eyes, was intent on his task. The latter smiled knowingly and asked few questions beyond those calculated to yield no fruit.

Sure enough, after we arrived we were denied ammunition by the local logistics officer. The rationale was that since our unit was only temporarily attached to the theater command, the administrative hassle of disposing of opened ammunition was deemed more important than our personal safety. Our Commanding Officer, not wanting to make any waves with his pending promotion boards, agreed with this logic. So it was that Tim and I, despite these arrangements being normally handled by enlisted Marines, decided to pay the logistics officer a visit and explain our position.

We found her ensconced within a GP tent draped over a lumber frame and adorned with all the creature comforts attributable to a rear-area logistics billet. First Lieutenant Biddy (not her actual name), was perched regally behind her desk. Her Staff Sergeant Kiff (not his actual name, either, and implying only the forced relationship rather than his persona) attended from a noticeably less regal desk next to hers. I wasn't sure how she had managed it, but it appeared that his desk was a couple of inches shorter than hers.

Tim approached her desk to make his case, while I lurked wordless near the door. There I remained apparently consumed in the minutest detail of various congratulatory plaques hung from the lumber near it. Staff Sergeant Kiff remained silent, but perked up noticeably and the slightest smile twinkled at the edges of his mouth.

Once again, Biddy refused to authorize us the can of pistol ammunition and the two cans of rifle ammunition listed on the requisition in Tim's hand. Tim, relaxing into the ladies' man persona who he genuinely is, eased himself onto the corner of her desk. He shifted into his best bar-fly "hey baby" voice and tried again. As she again refused, I turned to face her. Absolutely expressionless, I popped the empty 9mm magazine out of my issued Beretta, it still within the holster on my hip.

Kiff, who I learned later was a veteran of Panama and had been previously under fire, smiled more widely. He contained his amusement as he arose to grab a cup of coffee from the percolator across the tent, offering a cup to Biddy as well, as Tim continued to make his case. She refused both the coffee offer and the ammunition request. Upon this latest refusal Kiff happened to remember that he needed to check on an important issue, and excused himself out the rear door of the tent.

Biddy had still not clued into the potential of the situation. That changed when I, still expressionless, pulled my sole Barney Bullet out of my left breast pocket and slowly snapped it into the magazine in my hand. This got her attention.

"Staff Sergeant", her cracking voice called, only to be answered by silence. "I thought you didn't have any rounds", she wavered at me.

"I have enough to get more", were the only words I ever spoke to her. Tim smiled, nodded, and patted his own left breast pocket as well.

Now, clearly by this I had meant that I could at least pop an enemy soldier with that one round and thus take his weapon and ammunition. I realize in retrospect that unfortunately she may have misinterpreted my words and actions that day. Regardless, the requisition was signed. Later that day a beaming Kiff, with a spring in his step, personally delivered our three cans of ammunition to our surprised Gunnery Sergeant. Gunny then disbursed the ammunition among us accordingly.

Later, after the cessation of hostilities, our unit would be disarmed completely. It was that subsequent disarmament which led me to looking around for that pipe to trade to our Saudi guard for his HK-91 assault rifle.

Nevertheless, my original intent that day has meaning in our modern times, with the forces of the collective closing in around us at all sides. Some radicals, believing that they will one day need to shoot it out with the authorities, take comfort in collecting dozens of arms and thousands of rounds. Their misguided objective in this plan is to free the people who wish to imprison them. The collective responds to that urge by publicizing the seizure of these caches, even if obtained and accumulated perfectly legally.

Further, the agents of the collective of the nice seek to further restrain your constitutional rights to arm yourself by hoping to outlaw or restrict ammunition itself. By such legislation, the forces of the collective will render your ammunition cache just as illegal as a bale of marijuana. There is an alternate school of thought floating about in some of the more extreme minds. I mention this school of thought here merely for completeness and not as a form of advocacy.

Their arguments fly as follows. Rather than exhaust and expose oneself in a quest to cache weapons and ammunition, adherents of the alternate school instead arm themselves with knowledge and a more limited cache. In their ethic, even a ratty bolt-action throwback with a few rounds, or even one, is sufficient to procure more when the need arises. Provided, of course, that you have learned the principles of marksmanship beforehand, and these can be learned well enough with even a child's BB gun.

Ironically, this lesson has been taught by the drug war. It is far easier for a pot-head to squirrel away a few joints from discovery than it is for the dealer to hide his bale. Similarly, they reason, it is far easier for a determined individual to hide a few rounds than a case of thousands.

As the alternate school continues, if one genuinely fears oppression from the collective of the nice, arm oneself with knowledge of math and the sciences. One correct detail in their concept is that no amount of the laws of man can overturn the laws of nature. God Himself has passed these laws down to you as your birthright as a freeborn man.

And so, they plan to use these natural laws to their benefit. In a fight, they reason, a pistol or a shotgun trumps a knife. Similarly, a well-aimed dump truck trumps all three and the hand which bears them. As does a precisely placed improvised explosive device. Or a section of trunk swinging from a concealed position overhead. Or a carefully dug and concealed firepit. Or an imbibed poison or an asphyxiating gas. Their concept is based upon the fact that in many cases guns and ammunition have a tendency to survive trauma, even fire, far better than meat and bone.

Applied precision violence is only one tool in these individuals' arsenals. History shows that in a ravaged economy, a black-market bribe in the form of food or sex works as well. Especially when combined with escalating blackmail and extortion after receipt.

A student of history should read that famous Army prisoner of war resistance manual. If this student was also a television fan, he would learn how Hogan really should have managed Klink and Schultz. For the faint-hearted, don't worry, the alternate school advises. After all, they reason, the collective has refined these techniques of blackmail and extortion in detail and applied them for both the drug war and the war on terror. Soon these techniques will be applied to the war on you. So, that ethical door has already been smashed from its hinges before you ever touched the knob.

If you carefully watch footage of Gitmo, you can see these same techniques in action there. It's just that the bad guys are using them. If I were them, I wouldn't want Gitmo closed either. Not when all that investment is just about to pay off. You can use these techniques, too, this school of thought recommends. Their thesis ends in the proposal that a well-aimed round from either a pistol or a shotgun fired from concealment trumps a carried rifle. Regardless of the path that pistol or shotgun takes to a determined hand, the end result is the same, a sparkly new rifle. From there, the door opens wide.

So, adherents of the alternate school aren't intimidated by the agents of the collective and their superior equipment as they disarm them. But instead, the adherents see these agents and their home bases as resources for your later use. Because these agents will always be sitting on a practically unlimited supply of useful stuff, the alternate concepts conclude.

As for me, however, I am a man of peace and don't advocate violence against properly constituted lawful authority. I prefer instead to spend my energy in creation and progress, rather than destruction and violence. But, should the nation be invaded and occupied by a hostile force, these forces would not necessarily be seen as constituted lawful authority.

In any event, arming oneself with the knowledge of God's language and art, these being math and the sciences, gives one a certain amount of flexibility in deciding the course of one's life. You never know when you might need the knowledge. It had been my intent to end this short chapter there. I had already discussed the evolution of gun control along with the drug war, and so I figured I had this topic sewn up.

Not so. It turns out that the situation is evolving faster than I can write. Fortunately, the underlying principles remain sound. With the proper understanding of the way of the monkey and his collective, it is possible to analyze any development and remain sane. It is also possible to predict with reasonable clarity what will evolve from the monkey in the future. Current events, as I write this, reveal a fantasy which first arose in Montana, and then spread to Utah and, of all places, Texas.

This fantasy is about intra-state commerce. That progressives, meaning the entire monkey collective, have used the inter-state commerce clause of the Constitution to regulate everything is a fact of history. You can read or hear about this all you wish elsewhere, so I won't waste your time on that fact now. Guns are one of those things which have been regulated by the national government, regulation justified by the inter-state commerce clause. You might, after all, use that gun to affect inter-state commerce. Or carry it on an interstate. A well-meaning legislator in Montana introduced legislation exempting guns made in Montana, and kept in Montana, from federal gun laws. This law will go into effect on 1 October 2009.

And it will fail. You see, the monkey collective doesn't really care about interstate commerce. This is just an excuse to create a regulation. If that clause didn't exist the monkey would find some other justification. You can't use reason to counter justifications. You can only use force.

And unless we are willing to use force, backed by law, then stop playing games with people's lives. A similar thing was tried in the Emerald Triangle in California. The locals decided to essentially change the drug laws regarding marijuana. Just as the founding fathers intended any state or locality might about any issue important to them.

There was even a documentary filmed about this issue as the growers happily tended their crops, running their plots like businesses. But after the documentary aired, the national agents simply moved in and arrested many of them. The state or the county did nothing. These people are still just as in jail. In the model of the monkey collective, states are only allowed to decrease your liberty, they are never allowed to increase it.

So if a state moves to try to increase your liberty, it can only ethically do so if it is willing to move to protect your rights against *anyone*. Including that national agent who comes to arrest you for violating a national law. With force, if necessary. Otherwise, it is just playing games, with you as the pawn. So that law in Montana won't be good enough. It isn't even really a law. It is just a rant. Or a manifesto. Or a resolution of frowny faces.

Because it has no teeth. There are no penalties laid out for anyone who attempts to violate your rights under this resolution. For example, they might have added:

"Any person who shall attempt to violate the right of any Montana citizen to comport themselves in accordance with this law shall be subjected to a fine of not less than $5,000, or imprisonment for not less than one year, or both."

Or something like that. And then when the BATF agent shows up to arrest Mr. Montana under national statutes, the state police need to be there to slap handcuffs on said agent and haul him away for trial. Along with any of his friends. And if said agents draw their weapons on the state police for doing their duty, the state police should respond to them as they would any common criminal. Including kidnappers, which is what they would be in those circumstances.

But then that wouldn't be nice, would it? We're all on the same team, right? It's absurd to even talk about such a thing, isn't it? That same radical radio talk show host likes to call this unfolding of events the "Civilist of Wars." What absolute childish nonsense. Because when the state troopers moved to protect Mr. Montana, they would then have to deal with the national forces moving into Montana en-masse. The state legislature and the governor would then have to decide whether to treat these forces as an invading hostile force. And then respond by calling out the State Guard to meet them.

But to a monkey politician, none of this is worth it. Their actual response is to just let Mr. Montana get arrested and let it bobble around in the courts. In the meantime, Mr. Montana is just as incarcerated. That one brave individual will be used as a pawn for nothing more than politics. His life and liberty mean nothing. Of course, you know how the courts are going to rule. And then what? Shrug your shoulders and say, "oh well, we tried."

Yep. That's about it. Because the real issue is that we must worship the sixteenth President as a god. And we pat ourselves on the back for doing so because it makes us feel like great people, because he ended slavery. Except he didn't end slavery. The uncivilist war wasn't about slavery.

It was about the right of Montanans to say it is OK to carry around any gun you want. Or to drive as fast as you want. It was about the right of Californians to say it is OK to grow your own pot. Or to smoke yourself into poverty with it while the rest of us advance. Or any other foolish thing which Californians tend to imagine.

It was about the right of Oregonians to say whether they want to cut down their forests. It was about the right of Ohioans to never finish a highway project. As long as they pay for those projects themselves. It was about the right of Tennesseans to decide whether they want to dam their rivers for power.

It was about the right of Texans to decide to be whatever idiots they choose to be to play out their little boy fantasies funded by their oil. It was about the right of Alaskans to decide whether to drill for their oil and not be idiots like Texans.

It was about the right of Nevadans to say they want to visit a brothel. It was about the right of Utahans to have lots of wives and to be those wives. And not be subject to Texas idiots for doing so.

It was about the right of New Hampshirites to decide whether they want to use nuclear power. It was about the right of Arizonians to decide what language they want their schools to teach. It was about the right of Illinoisans to decide who they want for their Governor or Senators, and how corrupt they want their politicians to be.

It was about the right of Vermonters to decide whether they want gays to marry. It was about the right of Iowans to decide how they want to raise livestock. It was about the right of Floridians to establish any tax structure they think is best for their people.

It was about the right of Georgians to make moonshine. Or to defund Jimmy Carter's visitor center after he proved himself an idiot. It was about the right of Pennsylvanians to produce whatever kind of steel however they like. It was about the right of Michigan to decide whether that steel was right for their cars.

And it was about your right to choose to live in whatever state you liked which most closely matched your values and outlook on life. And to prosper there and thus promote your values by helping that state succeed. Slavery was dying on the vine when the progressives, first with Andrew Jackson, then with Lincoln, moved to suppress liberty and states' rights. Jackson, a Southerner himself, but collectivist foremost, struck the first blow against the South three decades before Lincoln over taxation of foreign trade.

Internet Research
Research the Nullification Crisis.

The South began to see the national government as a corrupting influence which had even consumed one of its own. What the South failed to understand was that national government reflected the supremacy of the collective over the individual. And that Jackson, given his earlier treatment of his previous Indian allies, was no individualist. But Southerners did understand that the Constitutional protector of the individual rested in the various state legislatures. And that the national government had stopped paying attention to those states.

Had the South been victorious against Jackson in the Nullification Crisis, free trade and the Industrial Revolution would have easily destroyed slavery, as we shall see in a moment. But this crisis precipitated an "Us versus Them" mentality, pitting individualists in the South against collectivists in the North. And so the collectivists found an agenda. By Lincoln's time, slavery was so close to death that the forces of the North had to move soon, or else the South would clue into the miracle of free trade among free men. And when that happened the long growing season of the South, combined with the wealth of natural resources there that still have yet to be tapped, would have crushed the North economically.

And the monkey collective could not allow this at all. But slavery was already dying because mechanical automation could work better than any man. And because you can't keep that machine running at the tip of a lash. You can only keep a machine running because free men live well by keeping it running. The mind of a black man who knew how to repair that machine was worth far more than his black back in a field. You can make him work by whipping him, but you can't make him think and innovate this way.

The North wasn't morally superior to the South. Most of the slave markets had been in the North, and many Southern slaves were owned by Northern brokers. It is just that the Industrial Revolution took greater hold there earlier because the climate favored industry over agriculture. A steel mill in a Pittsburgh January is a much nicer place to work than a steel mill in a Birmingham July. And slaves aren't a great match for steel mills. Not if you want to turn a profit.

Even Lincoln himself recognized this lack of moral superiority with his *Emancipation Proclamation*.

Internet Research
Research the *Emancipation Proclamation*.

Read over this bit of political subterfuge and note that the wording only applies to slaves owned in the South. Lincoln had too many political backers in the North who were still making money off their brokering and slave leases to risk driving them away. Otherwise, his proclamation would have been general and nationwide.

Mrs. Hooch taught me this. "Chill wren, the E Man Sih Pay Shun Proh Clah May Shun freed No SLAVE!" she chanted rhythmically as her head wobbled back and forth. "It wuz bout a man an hiz Pow Wah."

Would slavery have continued for a while under the Confederacy? Perhaps. And then died on that vine just as surely as it would have in the Union. Imagine if Mississippi had kept slaves, but Alabama freed them. Before long all those free black minds would be contributing more to Alabama than those whipped Mississippi backs.

Or the reverse would be true. Free Mississippi minds would be contributing more than whipped Alabama backs. And some of those black backs would run across the border to where they would be free to use their black minds. Along with whites who wanted to use their minds, too.

Eventually the slave states would, by the miracle of free trade, be economic backwaters where no one would want to live. And then they would learn.

This approach to states' rights allows free trade to flourish and reward the individual, as the founders intended. But the monkey collective can never allow this approach to flourish. Because it would take away their power. And to protect that power, the power of the monkey collective to enslave and suppress the individual mind, Lincoln acted. Acted to kill countless Americans and to destroy their property.

All to enforce the supremacy of the national over the state. And we worship him as an emancipator.

I spit on his legacy. I refuse to kneel before him.

I am a free man. Even if you imprison me, I am still free. Because God, and no man, makes me free. And I will not worship the legacy of a man whose bloodlust against the individual on behalf of the collective is at the core of every problem we face as a nation today.

And now states like Montana play their little boy games and pretend that they have the courage to be men. This kind of crisis of free men versus the collective has happened many times before. Wherever tyranny is found, free men, individualists, have to make important choices.

Video Assignment
Valkyrie

This film is a fictionalized account of an actual attempted coup against Hitler in the summer of 1944. This film makes clear that history is often made by one man. Indeed, all of history is of one man at a time making decisions, we just miss the important events sometimes because we are caught up in our daily compliance rituals.

To me, the most pivotal point of the movie is when the commander of the home guard speaks to Hitler on the phone as the head of the SS stands before him. After this conversation the commander obeys the orders of the SS and puts down the coup. Had he drawn his pistol instead and shot the head of the SS between the eyes he would have saved countless lives. Lives of Germans who had not yet been bombed to death or frozen in the East.

Jews who had not yet been gassed to death. Allies who had not yet died in Europe. Marines who had not yet died in the Pacific. Japanese who would never see the power of the atom over their city before their eyes boiled away. Soviet soldiers who had not yet frozen grappling with their German foe. Soviet citizens who had not yet been starved by their government. Koreans and Americans alike who fought each other after the Chinese Communists filled the vacuum left by the Japanese. Vietnamese and Americans alike who fought each other after the Soviets built their power on a captured Eastern Europe. All of the countless nameless souls in South East Asia who have suffered regime after regime of violence. Nameless Palestinians who had not yet blown themselves up to protest the establishment of a nation which would have never been established. All of the victims of Islamists who would never have been duped into violence.

Including all those who have not yet seen that atom either.

Whether this specific incident happened or not as portrayed in the film is immaterial. What is material is that this coup failed because at some point some individual merely followed his orders from an evil, manipulative regime and the whole plot collapsed. Whoever that unknown person may be, he could have decided to be a man instead of an agent of the collective.

But he didn't. Throughout the film tyrants are arrested by the coup, and then freed to execute their captors. Had these tyrants been shot on sight, they would never have been around to order those executions, or to re-seize power. Arrest is not enough when you are fighting tyranny. A famous quote from Thomas Jefferson is often misquoted thus: "The tree of liberty must be refreshed from time to time with the blood of patriots."

Even that radical talk show host quotes this incorrectly, as he fantasizes about his Civilist of Wars. He does this on purpose, I imagine, to avoid being seen as a rabble-rouser. But what Jefferson actually said was this: "The tree of liberty must be refreshed from time to time with the blood of patriots **and tyrants**."

I disagree with Jefferson. The necessary and sufficient condition is: "The tree of liberty must be refreshed from time to time with the blood of tyrants."

The blood of patriots is only an indication of a willingness to use personal force, not a mission plan. I assume this is what Jefferson meant. But if you try to use force yourself as they come for your guns, you will merely be slaughtered. As I have shown in this book, immediate force is not required at all. Instead, all we have to do is stop feeding them until they grow weak.

At some point, though, one of you reading this will be at that point of decision. When that time comes, the modern SS will be in front of you waiting for you to obey. As your countrymen are placing their lives on the line around you, you will know what to do.

But this pivotal event won't be nearly as dramatic as shown in the film. The circumstances will be simple, and seem almost reasonable. Unless you are keenly aware of your constitutional purpose, you won't even recognize the crisis as it unfolds around you. Such as when that national agent is arresting a citizen of your state. And you, as a state trooper, are sworn to defend that citizen's rights as he has committed no crime which matters in your jurisdiction. And when that agent points his weapon at you, you will know what to do. But first, the legislature of your state has to be there to protect you. And they shield you by giving you the legal authority to act accordingly to protect that citizen, as is its duty to do so. Because unless those legislators have the fortitude to put teeth in their laws, they are just playing little boy games with all our lives.

Before I close this chapter, I want to discuss a possibility which many fear will happen soon. And yet, as with any crisis or risk, there is opportunity within it. The mere existence of this possibility, or its implementation, should fill us with encouragement.

Imagine the thoughts of a high official in China or Russia. He might consider a disaster which could befall the United States, and what a possible outcome of that disaster might be. If this book and the ideas within are taken to heart, hundreds of millions of easily misled and manipulated wastrels in this country would have vanished, and along with them the political clout which can be used to manipulate markets and ideas. For the most part, these people will have perished by their own hands, and by their unwillingness to provide value in exchange for their own support.

That commissar, for lack of a better term, might imagine the realignment of world power which could occur when, out of the ashes of that disaster, rose as few as a million capable and independent-minded Americans who know how to rebuild civilization itself. A million true Americans sitting atop the rubble of a continent to plunder to get started. While breeding like rabbits, and determined to teach their children and grandchildren truth and knowledge, instead of submission and compliance.

And armed with nuclear weapons, which would, of course, survive the crisis. Permissive Action Links (PALs) notwithstanding, those in the know could reconfigure such devices. Just because a door has a lock on it doesn't mean that you can't use the door. Even those PALs which intentionally misfire to destroy the weapon don't actually destroy the fissile nuclear material, by design. And in such a crisis, the caretakers of these weapons might decide that the best way which they could provide value is to assist in re-enabling them. As would Navy ship and submarine captains and Air Force pilots, if they had any sense. Some wouldn't, but enough would.

Regardless, these few Americans, the true heirs of the founding fathers, would also be the heirs of one of the largest nuclear stockpiles in the world, as well as the remnants of the world's most sophisticated Navy and Air Force. And lacking the social equivalent of PALs, otherwise known as civility, which had been heretofore installed within our minds.

After those few Americans recover, those in other nations who would trade with them fairly, and be their brothers in spirit would have nothing to fear from them. Those who would demand their alms would likely perish or learn to fend for themselves. Those who would attack them would die faster. Our commissar in question might have an idea about which category he inhabits. He might also wonder about the validity of a policy of Mutually Assured Destruction against a potential foe who had already survived a major national crisis, and was too dispersed to be easily targeted. Overnight, Mutually Assured Destruction mutates into Unilateral Certain Destruction against Minor Inconvenience.

Clearly, to the foreign commissar, this would be an absolutely intolerable situation, one which must be avoided at all costs. Because the cost would surely be paid eventually, whether now or later with interest makes little difference. His own people would have no choice but to rise against him, because if they didn't, they too would bear ethical responsibility for their collaboration against these few Americans. Later claims for mercy, "oh, it was our government" shall fall on deaf ears. Those who stay uninvolved can be the friends of those few later.

Now consider the imposition of martial law in this country to mitigate the crisis. Martial law will eventually prove self-defeating, as does any form of central economic or political control, for many of the reasons stated in this book. For a while, perhaps a few days or a few weeks, such centrally-run control will seem to be fine. Until the desertions start.

Some hopefuls imagine that our military will be a model of virtue and justice. However, this point of view overlooks the fact that our military leadership is selected on the basis of political reliability. At no time are military personnel graded on their understanding of Constitutional principles. To count on colonels or generals to secure your liberty against orders is foolish and dangerous. And to count on corporals and sergeants to disobey the orders of the colonel, risking execution, is asking them to sacrifice too much.

Yet during this period of martial law, if we keep our heads, we will survive for the next phase as the forces of human nature take its toll on our oppressors. Few Americans relish the thought of killing our own servicemen or police, but that mental restriction will soon fade when those in the national government abandon their oaths to the Constitution and take the next step. This abandonment will begin as the strain of domestic occupation deepens. An unending occupation is tough enough for a soldier to face when far away from home with no easy ride back. Tougher still when your own family is elsewhere being occupied. Faced with this dilemma, many of the rank and file will quietly slip away to their homes, taking their weapons and ammunition with them. On foot if need be.

It will be slow at first. But each deserter encourages the next, accelerating until it is obvious that the colonel will have few troops to lead, and fewer still to protect him from the rest. To our own domestic commissars, whether on the left or on the right, this, too, is intolerable. And so, our domestic enemies will align with the foreign, and invite foreign troops into our nation to help suppress us. Knowing the eventual outcome if this invitation is refused, the foreign commissar's troops will soon stream in. By so doing, the commissar gambles, incorrectly, that the suppressed American few will not ultimately win, and then one day turn to exact judgement. Regardless, this invading force will face no opposition at the shoreline, having been invited by a government which, by this action, has declared war on its own citizens.

For those Americans who would hesitate, rightly, at killing our own, no such ethical opposition would stay their hand against these foreign invaders. Perhaps a misplaced and manipulated respect for authority might, for a time, but this too will fade. In the eyes of the national leadership which will have capitulated to a foreign power, which has laid its plans in our midst for decades, the true Americans would become the insurgents, in our own country. And the mounted heads of Chinese or Russian colonels, in full regalia, would begin to dot the living rooms and lodges of B Country.

This too, would be intolerable to either oppressor. And so these foreign troops will appear, not in their uniforms or using their weapons and equipment, but in the guise of our own. Our foreign enemies will wear the uniforms of Americans, carry the weapons and equipment of Americans and drive the police cars of Americans. And in most cases, these invaders will have been selected by their ability to speak English like Americans. Given our melting-pot heritage, it would be practically impossible for an individual American to identify any particular soldier or policeman as an American versus a Chinese soldier. Or especially a Russian, who spans the ethnic range almost as much as we do. But he will easily identify you.

So how would an American know whether the foe he faces, behind the body armor or the badge, will be a fellow American or not? What conditions will trigger his actions to rise against these invaders and take the country back? It is difficult to say, and to even speculate would give his enemies the opportunity to manipulate that knowledge against him.

But one thing is clear. When the desertions begin, true Americans will start returning to their families and communities with their weapons, ammunition and equipment. Slowly at first, and then faster. The first few must be suspected as plants. So these must be welcomed by their communities upon their return, but quarantined. They must be isolated from any information which could be given to the infiltrated forces. Equally important, they should be shielded against capture and punishment by the infiltrators, as a means of encouraging other true Americans to perform their individual duty to their communities and their states.

Then, once the volume of new arrivals increases, true Americans will know that the occupation and capitulation is in full bloom, evidenced by the rate of desertion from the infiltrators, as well as the information brought home by them. At that time, those who remain in ranks must either be foreign invaders, or those of our own countrymen who have elected to side with them. Ethically, these will be enemies of the Constitution either way.

When that day arrives, those survivors will know that their time has come. And those first who returned but were quarantined? Or even those who initially lacked the courage to desert and remained in ranks? Let all of them prove their loyalty to their communities and their states by whatever means seems appropriate at the time.

As for the occupiers, they too will be suffering on a national scale. All of the world economies depend on us to one degree or another. The Europeans have the best chance of surviving without us, but are too far down the road of socialism to pull out soon enough to hurt us. The Russians are better capable of assisting the capitulators with an occupation, but would be throwing their troops into a meat grinder which would make their experience in Afghanistan seem tame. And the young Russian soldier of today is not the soldier he once was. But ours? In particular, the deserters from the occupation? Having fought insurgents themselves recently, our younger veterans have more relevant war-fighting experience than anyone in the world for that kind of conflict. Their experience consists of being on the suppression side of an insurgency, but even so they have no doubt learned valuable lessons which would be helpful in such a crisis.

The Chinese? They survive on Walmart dollars and our patience. They have the ground forces in sufficient number to attempt an occupation, but they are also the least capable of assimilating. As such, their presence would only provide the ethical trigger for the occupied to begin engaging. They also need to eat, and supporting a supply chain across the Pacific and our continent would stress them to the breaking point. The Chinese would soon find that they need their own soldiers back home. Particularly when facing Americans who had lost their jobs to them.

The Middle East? Take away our petro dollars, since the surviving American millions will need only domestic energy, and the entire Middle East system collapses. Within a month, their society will revert back to a nomadic tribal existence, having raided and killed their false royalty. That opportunity will arise when that royalty, as pawns and allies of the Western suit-monkey devils, can no longer afford to defend themselves against their own subjugated tribes. And with most of the oil left intact, underground, and waiting. Mexico? Central America? Without our intervention, drug cartels and anyone with an axe to grind against their corrupt governments would overwhelm them. But then the drug cartels, denied our protective narco dollars or anywhere to spend them, would, like the Middle East royalty, fall prey to their own citizens. Those survivors, the builders and producers there, would one day be our brothers and welcomed with open arms, they themselves having been freed by both our collapses.

Some wonder whether, knowing this, the Russians or the Chinese or others might pre-emptively attack this country with their nukes during a crisis, in an attempt to keep our nukes out of the hands of those few Americans, or to take advantage of our momentary weakness. They might, but where would their nukes fall? On A Country, of course. And on top of the oppressive powers' power base. Pity. If you have read this book you have been warned beforehand. Get out of the way now and prepare yourself with knowledge so that you will have no fear.

Those few Americans, the million or so, would have a long memory. Anyone who moved against them would one day face judgement. Whatever nation would be foolish enough to try, such as assisting in an occupation, would take upon themselves the responsibility of facing the inevitable wrath. The force of free men trading with each other and building civilization will eventually produce excess capability, which can be turned against the barbarians who threaten them. And then remove them as a permanent threat, to a man. There will be no room for mercy.

But to see this day and survive it, you must first survive the initial gun seizure which is coming. Then, you must survive the inevitable martial law as the crisis deepens. Until then, prepare yourself with knowledge, and demonstrate your willingness to trade your ability and skill with your fellow productive man. Those of you who are most inclined to fight that first battle against the gun-grabbers are exactly the people we will need later. Our enemies know this, which is why they will try to goad you into a fight when they come for your guns, so that they can slaughter you right then and there. Don't sacrifice yourself foolishly in this way. In fact, don't sacrifice yourself at all, then or later.

Cold dead hands won't win this war.

Chapter 20, Smoke Filled Rooms

Some of the ranting of this work may lead the reader to believe that I think there is a vast conspiracy around us. And that I think we are merely puppets dancing to the strings of a faceless malice within smoke-filled rooms somewhere in the vast out there.

Nothing could be farther from the truth. We live in a representative republic, which means that the government we have is not only the government we deserve, but it is the government we choose. I often hear on various talk radio programs complaints about the government, or bad actors of various political leanings. These targets of frustration merely serve as convenient punching bags to vent the rage of the distressed.

I hear around me complaints of the tax system and the tax authorities. Or complaints about judicial activism. Or complaints about overzealous taser-wielding police. Or about the voluntary violation of property rights via community restrictions, or involuntary violation of property rights via zoning. I hear the incredulity of some who think that only if this politician or that were informed of truth that somehow they would see the light and then make the right decisions.

Again, nothing could be farther from the truth. There is no injustice whatsoever which can be perpetrated in a representative republic which is not the direct intent of the electorate.

It is that simple. The injustices and waste and corruption we perceive around us is merely the darkness of ourselves reflected back to us. Each time an arch-liberal wishes to force us to recycle he weakens the liberty of each of us. Or when he wishes to force us to pay a check to that person. Or to bail out this union. Or to worship that group of citizens.

Similarly, each time an arch-conservative wishes to force us to bail out that company he contributes to the reduction of liberty of us all. Or when he wishes to force us to not smoke that plant nor cultivate that other plant. Or to limit our rights to be friends, or more, with whomever we choose. Or seeks legislation to enforce any sort of niceness which goes the slightest bit beyond the protection of property or persons from fraud or force.

This doesn't mean that there aren't conspiracies of those who seek to manipulate market forces through regulations or bailouts. Or who seek to stir our passions into taking or demanding action against our best interest. These things surely exist, to deny them would be to deny that monkeys behave in their monkey way. But without hundreds of millions of gullible citizens, none of these conspiracies could have even the least effect.

Curiously, the founding fathers themselves sowed the seeds of our destruction. The Constitution, as written, contained a single fatal flaw which ensured that it would ultimately be shredded by the progressively encroaching forces of niceness which are gradually consuming us all today. To find this flaw, read the letters among the key authors of that document.

Reading Assignment
The Federalist Papers
by Hamilton, Madison and Jay

The miracle that was our Constitution, and from which all our previous liberty sprang, is the genius of federalism. Very few people today, products of a public education administered by predominately Communists, can give a coherent definition of what federalism means. Simply put, it is the division of power between the levels of government, with the various states ruling generally supreme over the national. And no individual state or collusion of states elevated above any others.

The national government, as originally framed, was supreme in only a few key areas. These included only common defense and the leveling of the playing field of interstate commerce. All other powers not specifically given to the national government was to be reserved for the states, or the people, meaning you and me.

Here are some examples of federalism in action. Each prospective state, prior to applying for statehood, must implement both a legislative body and a chief executive, which we call *Governor* by convention. For example, this office could just as easily be called "Der Fuehrer," if the founders of a state so chose. After all, this word only means "the leader" or "the guide" in German. Only socialists, another name for collectivists, have given this choice a bad rap.

The reason for this specific form of government in the various states is that both of these branches have specific responsibilities, at the national level. For example, should a senator's seat be vacated, it is the sole responsibility of the state to replace that senator, with the legislature and the governor having clearly defined roles in this process.

Similarly, the President is chosen by electors selected by any means suitable to the legislature of each state, even by lottery or count of freckles if they could get re-elected by doing so. Until the Seventeenth Amendment, so were the senators chosen by the legislatures.

Also, an amendment to the Constitution can be proposed by agreement of two-thirds of the states. It takes agreement of three-fourths of the states to implement these proposals as actual amendments. Which means that the states get to write the rules.

Not only *get* to write the rules. States, and specifically their legislatures, are *required* to write the rules. And yet state legislators are often seen as lackeys of the national government. Or wannabees to national office. Instead of the bulwark of power and liberty which they are meant to be. Effectively, then, the original framing of the Constitution was to leave the states in charge of selection of key individuals in the national government. Only the members of the House of Representatives were to be directly elected. And then elected only by a highly qualified, proven productive electorate, instead of the teeming masses. These teeming masses now include minds considered too young to be entrusted with alcohol, but apparently well-suited for selecting whom to arm with nuclear weapons.

By placing these key selections, and the rules themselves, in the hands of the state bodies, the national government was sure to be responsive to the states. In turn, the relatively powerful state bodies were geographically close to their constituents, and thus more responsive to their concerns.

Resulting in more liberty for all.

But did you catch the fatal flaw of the Constitution? It is right there near the start, in Article I, Section 5, Paragraph 2:

"Each House may determine the Rules of its Proceedings, punish its Members for disorderly Behavior, and, with the Concurrence of two thirds, expel a Member."

Still don't see it? This one simple sentence laid the foundation for the destruction of federalism, a weakness which has been exploited since the first assemblage of Congress over two hundred years ago. The key defect is that, on a two thirds vote, Congress can expel a Member. And thus deny a state or a congressional district representation.

Which means that, ultimately, you can send whoever you want, but if the rest of the aristocrats don't like your guy, then they can throw him back. Period.

Meaning that you only get to choose congressmen and senators from a pool of pasty choads who everyone else says is OK. Meaning that you, and your fellows in your state, don't really get to choose your representative in Congress. A swarm of the monkey collective nationwide does, since they have veto power over anyone you choose whom they don't like. And they don't like anyone who doesn't like them.

In a purist's model of federalism, a state should be able to send the most unpleasant bastard they can find to Washington. All that matters is whether that bastard is constitutionally qualified and is capable of representing the interests of the home state. As an example, Louisiana should be able to send a voodoo witch doctor who channels Jean LaFitte on Tuesdays, David Duke on Wednesdays, and Huey P. Long the rest of the week. With not one of the other states, or other representatives of Louisiana for that matter, able to do a thing about it, they being busy sending their own variants, of course.

So, does "expel" mean "go back home" or just "leave the room for a timeout"? It doesn't matter, really. Assigning a timeout means you can't vote, so it might as well be "go back home." So this capability of weeding out potential hell-raisers means that Congress is like an organism with an overactive immune system. Eventually, it weeds out those with spines and becomes populated by nice people who wear fake smiles while they do horrible things to your liberty. Even if they had spines, none of them are capable of standing up to do anything about it without running the risk of being sent home for merely rocking the boat.

The effect that this one organism has on the nation as a whole is insidious, and permanent. Meaning that it has an effect which gets worse in more or less imperceptible ways, and never gets, or will get, any better. Only now the infection has spread so much that the organism feels safe in changing the rules to suit itself on, seemingly, a daily basis.

Consider the nation as a whole as a larger organism containing this defective smaller, yet all-powerful, organism as its brain. This national organism will eventually evolve in ways which benefits the brain, even at the expense of the rest of the body. This expense will eventually kill the entire organism, the world being a market-driven place which tolerates no stupidity for very long. Even if *long* is defined as decades or centuries.

Here are some specific examples of how this evolution happens in practice. Congress has the sole power to take money from you and give it to whoever it likes. Even as I wrote these words originally, the House of Representatives voted to impose a 90% tax on a specific set of individuals

So, Congress is likely to take money away from those considered unlikely to ever walk its halls or vote for its plastic members. Instead, it will give the money to those it considers constituents, or even to the congressmen themselves. This means that plastic people or pliable voters are able to belly up to the trough in increasingly larger numbers. Thus, plastic people become more successful in society and in life, and reproduce at a greater rate.

Those considered less nice, such as our hypothetical voodoo witch doctor from the bayou, becomes penalized. Or, those who don't choose to congregate for mutual support in, well, congregations. Essentially, your basic individualist who stands on his own two feet progressively disappears from the body politic. And at increasingly greater rates as time goes by. Until it has become considered unforgivable criminal behavior worthy of up to a lifetime of punishment to, in many cases, simply defy the forces of niceness.

The same effect takes place in state legislatures and governors' mansions. After all, these offices are now merely the farm league for the big game in Washington, instead of Washington's masters as the founding fathers intended. And so on down to the city and county governments, the operators of which aspire to state office, and then to national.

The congregation for mutual support then becomes formalized in a system of powerful political parties. This congregating leads to an abomination against federalism which the founding fathers could never have anticipated. Spanning the spectrum from local office to the highest, membership in a party reduces the likelihood that you will be ejected by the others. Failure to belong to one with power leaves you subject as prey to both. The outsider becomes the villain who must be stamped out, as his very existence threatens the health of the disease.

And when was the last time that a viable Presidential candidate came from totally outside the system? Ross Perot, a fellow Naval Academy graduate and a genuine American civilian hero, was the last one. This guy successfully orchestrated the rescue of his own employees from Iran while the embassy lay helpless under the nice Mr. Carter.

Video Assignment
On Wings of Eagles

Man, talk about your employee benefits. Is hostage rescue a deductible line-item? Perot was the last outsider who was allowed a serious chance at the Presidency. Back then, politicians and pundits alike closed ranks and marched in lockstep to ensure that no hell-raising outsider could ever threaten the infection. These pundits hypocritically arose from both sides, even so-called conservative voices with tens of millions of eager nice listeners, whose parroted apologies for the Republicans echoed Perot's actual message. But to all of them, his status as an outsider was too damning for his message to overcome. Not even being from Texas was enough, as he was from outside the circle of idiots who spawned a third of our last nine Presidents.

So even the White House becomes infected, and with it all the various executive bureaucracies which exist for government's sake. Even the courts, nominated by the executive and confirmed by the legislative, leak the pus of niceness.

And what of the senior military leadership, such as colonels and generals and captains and admirals? These positions are essentially appointed national political offices with longevity who "serve at the pleasure of the President." All military officers, down to ensigns and second lieutenants, are, essentially, political appointments. We just have bureaucratic processes in place to manage their number.

These have been politically bred as the ultimate international antibody who see their role as the protectors of the national state rather than the people. My evidence? The absence of meaningful battlefield promotion, the ultimate triumph of political niceness over merit.

And, more telling, their visceral reaction to the emphasis of the words "and domestic" in the oaths of office taken by their juniors who are bold enough to do so. Sadly, these particular individuals direct the destiny of hundreds of thousands of otherwise eager and well-intentioned soldiers, sailors, airmen and Marines who simply want to serve their country.

And so, true federalism, and with it your liberty, is corroded on every front. Timothy McVeigh sought to change the government, restoring it to its roots, by destroying a federal building. In his own simple and ignorant mind this act was to be the equivalent of the shot-heard-round-the-world to herald a new revolution. But the foolishness of his action ignored a simple fact of the system of government we serve.

Imagine that a magic genie could be summoned, overnight, to destroy each and every government building. And, to evaporate each and every public official in each office high and low. Would the resulting government then be better?

No. The next day the citizenry of the nation would begin anew to rebuild and repopulate the government. And its purpose will be to function exactly as it did the day before, only perhaps without the relatively few useful patriot bastards who still exist within that government today.

President Bush or President Obama, it makes no difference whatsoever. Each is merely a symptom, not the disease. No matter what your political alliance may be, one of these is likely to offend your sensibilities in some fashion. Calls to "throw the bums out" ring hollow on my informed ears. We would only replace that particular batch of bums with a fresh crop who will continue to do the bidding of the forces of niceness who surround us in our very neighborhoods. There are just too many of them now to stop. The destruction of education, diluted, by the one side, and the destruction of the respect of law, overreaching, by the other, has ensured this to be so.

Thus is set the stage for Communism, which masquerades as any number of well-intentioned causes to destroy your liberty. These include, of course, the left-wing environmentalism and the right-wing drug war. The purpose of each of these, as is shamanism wrapped in legislated morality, is to infect and take over the nation. Communism, as we have seen, is the natural end state of the tyranny of the masses over the productive individualist. Without this oppression from either the left or the right, the individualist would otherwise be free to improve or destroy his life as he saw fit.

Nice, then, becomes the sworn enemy of liberty. This fact of life, as timeless as the seasons, directly affects your ability to operate your business and make the day to day decisions necessary for success. At least now you are able to approach these decisions with your mind open to reality. Have you read to this point without throwing this book against the wall in a rage of civility after having decided to be criminally offended by mere specks of ink on paper? If so, congratulations, you have passed the first test.

But what shall the last few true individualists do? Hopelessly outnumbered, one could spend an entire lifetime trying to stop the inevitable march to destruction which we are now on. Only at the end of your life to expire, exhausted, not having made any perceptible difference in the outcome. And the march having moved forward nonetheless.

Or, like the martial artist who redirects his adversary's greater energy to his own purpose, one could, instead, hasten the march itself. In this effort, urge the starving monkeys faster to the abyss, while withholding the true fruit of one's labor from their grasp.

So, choose for yourself whether to continue to masquerade as nice, grasping for the wider yet wasting market and labor pool. Or, whether to be bold and trade most effectively with those individuals who share your world-view for whom the long game is assured. These are the only ones truly capable of feeding themselves unaided.

There are no smoke-filled rooms from which hatch plots of destruction and malice. Only the petty hearts of those around you. Hearts which seek to progressively limit your liberty and freedom of action.

Who vote, election after election, to do so.

And for no reason other than to be thought well-of while sipping the sadistic joy which it brings to their hollow lives to enslave another.

Chapter 21, Cho

In the summer of 1995 I was in graduate school at the Virginia Polytechnic Institute and State University, working toward my doctorate in Electrical Engineering. Having snatched a Master's degree from their hands in only nine months, I had already completed all my coursework for the philosophy degree. I had passed all the required exams, and was in a status informally known as "All But Dissertation", or ABD for short. First Wife was also delightfully pregnant with our first child, who would ultimately be born at home that fall in our little townhouse on Lee Street. That little townhouse was walking distance from that beautiful and historic campus which hid a degenerate rot.

After leaving the Marines in 1993, I won a three-year Air Force Laboratory graduate fellowship. I could have chosen to spend that money, which covered tuition in full plus a nice monthly stipend, at any school I wished. Having perfect scores on my Graduate Record Exam, and having graduated near the top of my class from the Naval Academy, choice of school was not an issue. MIT was ruled out as I thought that Massachusetts was a little too liberal, and likely to be too oppressive an atmosphere for a free-wheeling spirit such as myself. And so, I settled on that charming little campus in the Virginia mountains, imagining that a school in southern Virginia would probably share my outlook more than MIT. I couldn't have been more wrong.

In the early summer of 1995 I had just finished my last required course for the Ph.D. program. Shortly after, I received a bill from the bursar's office for fall tuition in the amount of several thousands of dollars. Instead, they should have paid me the monthly stipend check as due under the terms of the fellowship. Clearly, someone in Burruss Hall, the administrative building, had made a mistake somewhere along the way. So, off I went to straighten this out after dropping First Wife off at her OB for a checkup. I drove to campus and headed straight for the little barred window on the second floor of that hall, within a pistol shot of Norris Hall next door.

Facing an unpleasant crone through the protective bars, I tried to explain to her that the bill was in error. All my tuition was being paid by the Air Force, I explained, and I was actually due back stipends for a couple of months. She would have none of it, and insisted that they would only discuss the issue after I paid the bill the next window over. I was incensed at her stubborn refusal to even pull my file. So, to repay her lack of concern I flipped her off and walked away to the next window. There, the more helpful clerk at that station pulled my file and promised me that this would be resolved to my satisfaction.

By the time I was done in that office, the crone had called the campus police. Between crone and the bicycle cop, a story was hatched in which I had "insulted the honor of Virginia womanhood", as my lawyer later described it. Also, according to their fevered fantasies, I had also caused a furor which destroyed the peace and tranquility of that fine summer day. Oddly this path of destruction had somehow escaped the notice of the non-crone next door. She had decided to lift a helpful and pleasant finger on my behalf while the campus around us was presumably embroiled in hapless turmoil.

So, unaware that I was now Virginia Tech's Most Wanted, I left the building to go pick up First Wife at the OB. I made it to the steps between Burruss Hall and Norris before I was apprehended by the relentless and efficient lawman in hot pursuit on foot. Barney had himself a case. He demanded my identification, and promised me that he would arrive at my door that afternoon with an arrest warrant. I then drove to retrieve First Wife and we returned home for a nice lunch.

The particulars of the promised arrest are of no consequence for our purpose here. What is important is that First Wife and I were astonished that a simple finger could have such devastating consequences. And so, the guilty party and his accomplices were handcuffed behind my back as I was led to the squad car. I rode to the station in the grasp of the campus cop and his companion from the Blacksburg police, a bicycle insufficient to the task of transporting desperate fugitives.

At the station, the cyclist, then playing the role of my protector, confided in me that it would go better for me if I didn't defend myself. Moments later, the magistrate appeared on closed-circuit TV. Already astonished beyond belief, I took his helpful suggestion as a clear threat against my person if I dared to defy the authorities further. I chose to rely instead on my naive notion that the truth would ultimately prevail.

After my hearing, I rode to the Montgomery County jail in the clutches of the campus cop. He had left my handcuffs on loosely during the ride, presumably hoping I would try to escape or assault so he could use his one bullet. After posting $1500 cash for bail, cash which my pregnant wife had to carry there, I was released later that afternoon. All for a raised finger.

Disgusted by the disproportionate consequences of my rudeness, I immediately withdrew from enrollment from further studies at Virginia Tech. I considered that day's events as a deliberate and premeditated gross violation of the Constitution I had swore to defend against all enemies, foreign and domestic. A document which included rights such as the freedom of speech and expression. Casting my aspirations for a doctorate aside, I refused to further fund that pit of vipers with my taxpayer-funded fellowship. I was determined to never allow them to seek indirect credit for my accomplishments by bearing a doctorate from their inbred hands.

The injustice was clear, and as I pieced the events of the day together in the few weeks which followed I knew that somewhere there was a sworn document which contained a lie. Could I find the proof of this lie, I knew that I might enthusiastically attack my enemies with truth and turn the energy of their prosecution against my perjuring accusers. But, the fragile state of my young family kept me from the full offensive which might have otherwise entertained me and my normally capable bride. In this manner the forces of niceness attack the weaknesses of their victims, devouring their flesh after wounding their prey.

The stress of this case began to mount on my wife, and I worried for the health of the child whom I couldn't bear to describe as a mere fetus. As the weeks wore on, I pleaded with every figure in authority to stop this insanity and drop the charges. Advisors, campus officials, the county prosecutor, the department head all turned a deaf ear. I resorted at last to a plea for the health of my wife and child. As I said these words the bile rose in my throat on the words as I saw their growing eagerness when I uttered them.

And my useless country attorney? His bread was buttered on the same side as theirs. He flatly told me that he wasn't going to stand up and challenge these people whom he depended on for his livelihood. A plea deal was all he would fight for. And in his mind a suit against their overreach was out of the question. In their endless charity, these worshipers of false gods of civility would not budge. I imagined that they felt in their righteous souls that I was someone who must be humbled before them and taught a lesson. The fact the charges were frivolous and my actions were not at all threatening or worthy of prosecution on their own merit made no difference.

But they were right about one thing. I learned a lesson. But not the one they thought they were teaching.

The stress of this unjust prosecution we were unable to escape by even moving away until trial. This restriction, imposed by the magistrate, was almost too much for First Wife to bear. We might have been in the clutches of the Nazis or the Soviets for all the sense this made to her.

This beautiful and sweet creature who saw me off to war to protect the commercial, social, and synthetic moral interests of our oppressors found herself unable to fully rest. Heavily pregnant with our first child, she wondered if the child would be born to a father in prison for merely lifting a finger. This woman of unpregnant strength had watched on cable TV in 1991 the death and destruction I directed from the skies. Now she saw us helpless against the righteous wrath of our tormentors who graced no mercy upon our little budding family. Tormenters who demanded a blood sacrifice for their offended sensibilities.

And for the first time in my life I found myself unable to attack my tormentors, unwilling to risk aggravating her concern further.

Months later, fatigued with stress and helplessness, her worried womb finally gave up the child a month early. The pangs of labor struck her in the early hours of the morning. Clawing the walls and lurching with a struggle which injured her hips to this day, my son was born into my waiting hands amid a rush of blood and fluids. His little mouth gasped for life, the three of us truly alone in a world which sought to destroy us.

The afterbirth would not come, and I knew well enough to not pull it. We had anticipated car trouble during several road-trips we had planned for that fall to take our minds off of this insanity. As a result, we had, fortunately, prepared a kit of the necessary items, including one of those little cord clamps and some sterile scalpels. And so, after clipping the now still cord and severing it with a scalpel, I put the child to her breast. Swaddling them both in a blanket, I drove us the twenty minutes to the Montgomery County Hospital, the child too weak and new to lie in his carrier.

As she was preregistered for delivery, the country staff rushed her to the delivery room. I stood at the door calling to them with the boy bundled in a blanket trying to get them to understand that I now held their patient. Eventually they recognized that the boy had already been born, and removed the placenta from First Wife's womb. My son was then diagnosed with respiratory distress and a lack of proper liver function, both due to his premature delivery. For the first few weeks of his little life, he would spend most of his hours wrapped in a tube of light to assist his liver in processing waste.

And, as I watched my family struggle to stay alive, I planned for contingencies which I prayed would never arrive.

Only one individual from the campus came to check on our progress, my graduate advisor. This was a man who in the preceding months had destroyed every ounce of my respect by turning his back on my unjust persecution at the altar of his god. His mission for the trip was to find out whether I intended to sue the university. I reassured him that I had no intention to sue, an assurance which he completely misinterpreted. For you see, exhaustion and forgiveness are entirely different things. Having won his assurance, he made his excuses and a belated inquiry as to the health of my wife and child. Having thus betrayed his true mission for the visit, he waddled off to report to his masters, never to be seen by my eyes again. And never again welcome in my sight.

Once the child had been born, I felt my strength begin to return. Suddenly, the system which had in my weakness sought to imprison me, responded to my growing vigor. After my references to a possible legal counterattack should the case be won before a jury, they became more pliable than before. Shortly after my son was born, I accepted an offer of the charges being dropped in exchange for eight hours of community service. I served this time in the school library reformatting Macintosh hard drives. The ordeal now over, I bundled my family off to my new job at McDonnell Douglas in Huntsville. There, I managed to see millions of dollars in Navy power engineering funding directed away from Virginia Tech's grasping, slack-jawed proposals.

A clever reader might argue, as did anyone who heard my story during those months, that I had merely run afoul of an aggressive enforcement of the law. Surely aggressive enforcement was intended to maintain civility in order to protect the students from harm. This would be a reasonable proposition, of course, which even my tormented mind could understand and appreciate. Except for one teensie weensie little inconsistency in that law-and-order theory:

Internet Research
Research the case of BRZONKALA v VPI STATE UNIV from the U.S. Fourth Circuit Court of Appeals.

The best reference I could find is at:

http://caselaw.lp.findlaw.com/cgi-bin/getcase.pl?court=4th&navby=case&no=961814P

As evidenced in the public record, the year before my arrest Christy Brzonkala alleged that two members of the varsity football squad had gang raped her in the dormitory. Virginia Tech, in an academic hearing, determined that this rape had indeed occurred, and punished one of the offenders by, wait for it, suspending him from school for two semesters. Virginia Tech then decided to overturn even this drastic punishment in the summer of 1995. That, of course, was the same season I was being arrested for flipping off an employee of the university safe behind a barred window. In his case, however, Virginia Tech allowed the accused to return to school on a full athletic scholarship that year.

Not even this, however, is the full measure of the story. More importantly, court documents from this case, as referenced above, state as facts that:

"Rape of a female student by a male student is the only violent felony that Virginia Tech authorities do not automatically report to the university or town police."

Read that again. Virginia Tech's policy at the time, and for all I know may still be, was to not report rapes to the police. If you or I performed that kind of obstruction of justice as a matter of policy, what do you think the reasonable response would be?

So, the administration considered my profane expression an inexcusable crime worthy of conviction and imprisonment. But, in the same window of time, this same administration chose to give a full athletic scholarship to an adjudged sexual offender. An offender who raped, excuse me, sexually assaulted a coed on the grounds of their campus shortly after she arrived for her freshman year full of ambition and promise. And, this same law-and-order administration which, as a matter of procedure, routinely chose to not report rapes to the police. For if they did, who would win their super big games for them?

We can't have a university without a top notch football team, now can we? Who would attend those fund-raisers if we just focused on math, science and technology? It only has Polytechnic in the name, don't think that implies anything about the priorities. All we have to do is provide enough perks to top-notch athletes, such as the warmly curved bodies of freshmen women in a clean, consequence-free environment. Just make sure that if you are an actual student you don't flip off any employees. That unforgivable impertinence will get you hauled away and prosecuted. And if possible, put the health of a pregnant woman and her unborn child at risk for the sheer joy of it.

The unique geography of the region makes this sort of feudal arrangement possible, and in fact, unavoidable. Isolated by mountains from even the county seat, Blacksburg's police department is an engineer's stone's throw away from the campus. Most persons in this town owe their livelihood to the university. Accordingly, it is easy to understand why the Blacksburg police were, and perhaps still are, willing to not get involved.

And to not look too closely into allegations of rapes on campus, even if the campus administration had been willing to report them. After all, most of these girls are some far-away rich guy's little brat anyway. It makes one wonder whether it saves the city police the effort of filling out needless paperwork to a sufficient degree that they might consider offering classes to potential rapists. Lesson One? Drag the victims onto campus before consummating the act. Or at least make this claim.

The county government's bread is similarly buttered, Montgomery County itself isolated by more mountains from the civilized world beyond. My personal experience with that authority in Christiansburg, the appropriately named county seat over the mountains from Blacksburg, made me doubt whether the county officials are any better in their pursuit of actual criminals of consequence. It was interesting to find VT paraphernalia littered about the prosecutors' offices as I pled my case there for leniency and truth in the fall of 1995. Paraphernalia which indicted clearly their objectivity in legal matters regarding the university.

So much for the aggressive law-and-order theory.

The explanation for this apparent split personality lies within the nature of modern public, semi-public and charitable institutions and their relationship with government. All of these entities, including government bodies, are entities of, by and for the agents of niceness, and as such are considered as capable of no wrong by their base. The athletes in question represent the agents of this beast, whose true purpose is fund-raising rather than education. Threaten them, and you threaten the entire fund-raising ethic at its core. Like any institution of niceness, however, it must move swiftly and relentlessly to crush any defiance from any other quarter in order to render its victims sheep.

Similarly, Lon Horiuchi is considered guiltless as he merely enforced the rules of compliance and fear for the agencies created by the people for precisely that purpose. And so, the public smiles with favor from their neat little boxes of drywall at the end of their tidy concrete drives. Just as they smiled as the people versus Randy Weaver executed his wife and eldest son for the unforgivable crime of defiance to their will. Just as they smile to twist justice to the collective purpose to ensure compliance.

Virginia Tech, in its isolated mountain compound, is capable of twisting justice to ensure compliance to its purpose to a level which makes our fellow Communist, left or right, red with envy. As such, rather than being unique in its objectives and methods, Virginia Tech is merely a more highly refined version of the same corrosive substance which defines institutions, governments, and increasingly, businesses throughout our society today. It is not an exception, it is merely the prototype. Recall that, in a representative republic, no injustice can stand without the consent of the people and, instead, acts as their primary coercive tool. Injustice also serves the more valuable purpose as a diagnostic instrument capable of ferreting out even the most carefully camouflaged individualist. But how?

The use of injustice as a coercive and diagnostic instrument can best be understood if you consider the natures of the forces of niceness and their prey. As niceness, a super-organism composed of the mass action of its individual actors, has evolved over the centuries the actors themselves respond in concert, but without specific direction or coordination. In concert, but without coordination, much as a flock of birds or school of fish behaves like a single organism. And so, any unit of the niceness organism is free to attack any threat to the whole using any means necessary. As they attack, they know that the rest of the organism will rally behind it to protect toward the same ends.

Was there a smoke-free room at Virginia Tech which conspired to arrest and punish me for my attitude, or even conspired to seize the opportunity which my raised finger provided? Of course not, no more than the birds or the fish meet in a room to determine the direction in which they move next. In all likelihood, no two persons ever met in passing to coordinate their efforts in this matter, they not needing to.

And yet, the individuals in question, from the clerk to the cop to the acting department head to the magistrate to my advisor to my lawyer and to the president of the university, acted in concert as if they had conspired. In their silent mass action they rested secure in the knowledge that, should they step over the line and perjure in their efforts to destroy the threat, their fellows will move to protect them. And protect them by their own injustices if need be.

Similarly, Lon Horiuchi squeezed the trigger to kill Vicki Weaver comfortably safe in the knowledge that the people, the bloodthirsty nice, would close ranks to protect him. Protect him so long as his victims are those dreaded individualists and their families. As indeed the collective did, and then later placed him in a position where he might do even more harm on their behalf.

Any evolving organism learns over time more efficient means to achieve its ends. Catching fish with one's hands is hard. And so, one learns to stab with a stick or trawl with a net. Eventually, these lead to passive activities such as the use of a weir to trap the prey as they swim in the shallows to feed at high tide. The most efficient gathering of prey involves the use of its own activity and inclinations, saving the predator the effort of the hunt. Even the baited hook is a refinement of this technique.

Similarly, collectives of the nice have evolved techniques to snare the individualist with little effort on the part of the flock. Why do all the work when their sworn enemy, the individualist, will assist them? And so, they set their snare of injustice for the individualist. A creature of truth and merit whose very nature causes it to seek to right wrongs in rightful indignation, an individualist will rise out of the water and flop into the net. When the people of this nation, via their agents, attacked Randy Weaver, they hoped that he would rebel and thus ensure his destruction at their hands. A hope which was fulfilled by a startled child whom they slaughtered, and slaked their bloodlust with him and his mother.

Similarly, when that campus cop deliberately left my handcuffs loose, the implement nearly falling from my wrists on its own accord, I would have assisted in my own destruction had I behaved as a renegade individualist might. Instead, when I asked that he tighten the handcuffs in order that we might play the game correctly, he grudgingly complied to the barest extent necessary.

I denied him the opportunity to later shoot me and then be protected by the flock for so doing. But, despite this shared behavior, the campus cop and Lon Horiuchi, or any other official of the public trust, are simply symptoms of the infection, and thus not efficient targets of vengeance.

Throughout the land, injustice serves as a means for the masses of the weak to detect and attack the strong. This law of monkey nature will remain so as long as the collective of the nice rule in nameless majority. Incredulity at arrest becomes resistance, a question becomes verbal assault, and a raised finger becomes disorderly conduct. Any flight, struggle or challenge, the raw animal impulse of a cornered creature of independent spirit, becomes a compounding offense whose consequences justify and magnify the original injustice. For now the victim is truly guilty, the precipitating cause forgotten, having exhausted its purpose.

The provocation serves a filtering purpose as well. When the submissive rabbit goes limp in the hands, he survives the test. His limpness identifies him as a member of the flock of the nameless oppressing multitude whom the authorities protect and serve precisely as directed.

From time to time the people seek to destroy those who will not go quietly, and so precipitate violence and tragedy, and yet deny any responsibility. The masses, knowing their proper response, flock to the aid of their comrades. Even the innocent victims of tragedy serve their purpose. McVeigh evaporated the federal building, thinking that he was avenging Weaver and Waco.

But instead he manufactured for them 168 Jesi. The blood sacrifice of these then fueled a hunt for the alleged brethren of McVeigh, the mythical wolf of our time, the white supremacist. They hunted the very ones he had sought to defend and promote. In so doing, he merely fanned the flames to his enemies' advantage. And retroactively exonerating the injustices at Ruby Ridge and at the home of the Branch Davidians, these acts having now borne their intended fruit, four and two years later, respectively.

The collective of the nice seeks, by uncoordinated common action, to destroy the spirit of independence and liberty within the individualist. In so doing, the collective knows that they will provoke disproportionate response from time to time. This is a price they are willing to pay. A price they know they can twist to their purpose as a feeding call for their fellows, caring not for the innocent victims of the tragedies which precipitate. Or caring not for the victims who are required to multiply into greater tragedy.

On April 16th, 2007, we watched the tragedy unfold on the Virginia Tech campus, and learned of the events preceding that terror. As surprise and shock swept the nation, I was surprised only that it had taken so long. I had spent years steering anyone who would listen away from attending that little shop of judicial horror. I had spent years even avoiding listing where I had earned my Master's degree, to avoid the casual assumption of a recommendation. But finally, it had happened.

Internet Research
Research the Virginia Tech tragedy, and the history of Seung-Hui Cho. In particular pay attention to the August 2007 findings of the *Virginia Tech Review Panel*.

Those who would have us believe in their concern for the handicapped sought to thwart the one voice available to this outcast with his speech impediment, his creative writing. Containing dark themes worthy of a Poe or a King, his work was instead used as a tool to destroy his defiant spirit. And this apparent miscalculation precipitated a tragedy which nonetheless serves the purpose of the collective. And yet, we can not point a single finger at an individual who is to blame. Instead, the efforts had been accumulated by the multitudes over the sum of his miserable life, their victim trapped in the prison of an malfunctioning voice. Charity indeed.

Consider Cho's own words transcripted from his barely intelligible videotaped manifesto mailed just before his rampage in Norris Hall:

"Do you know what it feels like to be humiliated and be impaled upon on a cross? And left to bleed to death for your amusement? You have never felt a single ounce of pain your whole life. Did you want to inject as much misery in our lives as you can just because you can? ... I didn't have to do this. I could have left. I could have fled. But no, I will no longer run. It's not for me. For my children, for my brothers and sisters that you f***ed, I did it for them ... When the time came, I did it. I had to ... You had a hundred billion chances and ways to have avoided today, but you decided to spill my blood. You forced me into a corner and gave me only one option. The decision was yours. Now you have blood on your hands that will never wash off."

Not one collusion was required by his perceived tormentors, their membership in the collective of the nice being sufficient to flock in unison. Does this excuse his violence? Of course not, but this tragedy does illustrate the perception of injustice which causes some to destroy. And illustrates the naturally evolved mechanism of that injustice, with not a single dose of blame allowed to spread elsewhere to any other contributing source. Such has the organism of the collective evolved to its own advantage.

This book is also written for one Cho, for one McVeigh, for a Harris or a Klebold. Someone understands you, you are not alone, and your time has not yet come. Don't allow yourself to become a pawn of the collective. Don't manufacture martyrs for their benefit only to be destroyed yourself after serving their purpose. Strive for excellence in all your endeavors, and then deny them the fruits of your excellence. Thwart their efforts to subvert your success by educating yourself. Take the path I have shown you in this book and learn the math, the sciences, the engineering. Then turn this knowledge to your own purpose to support yourself in your independence.

Most of my adult life I have followed the rules, at times by the barest of margins but followed nonetheless. While so doing others have cheated and stolen and lied have profited. I have seen the able whine about their circumstance while I have overcome my own deficiencies. While I am by no means a rich man, I have had many years in which the best fruits of my labor have been seized from me and given to the unworthy. Some years I have paid more in taxes than most have earned. I have seen the rebates and stimuli taken from me and given to those who never bated or ever responded to stimuli.

I now give this largess stolen from me to my brethren; learn excellence for its own sake, and then take their welfare, their unearned income credits, their stimuli, their bailouts. Take them if for no other purpose than to snatch it out of the mouths of the mediocre and lazy. Take their grants, their contract payments, yet deny them employment or the revenue which would result from the greater income which you might earn and return in greater taxes.

Find your fellow individualists, learn from them, and support each other through trade, always providing more value than you are paid. And in so doing, you improve your own life and the lives of your natural allies. So enriched, each of you may enjoy your ticks of the clock while your mutual enemies squirm in need, seeking the wealth and submission of your kind, but finding none.

Aggressively thwart their efforts to lure you into crimes as you respond. Crimes which then justify their persecution and their disproportionate punishment of your response while they ignore their own. Be meticulous in your taxes, paying all that they demand from you, yet limiting that demand by providing for yourself in other ways which their laws have not yet foreseen or clenched. Never allow your mind, your primary weapon, to be destroyed by drugs or excessive drink. Never traffic in these either as the collective will of the enemies who surround you use these simple crimes to incarcerate you for life and seize all which you have earned. Or perhaps to sentence you to immediate execution by taser if you struggle at your arrest.

Militia literature, a target of both the right and the left, abounds with the simplistic description of your enemies as ignorant and helpless. Naive militias use hopeful terms such as *sheeple* to explain apparently docile compliance with the collective. You now know that this assessment has been carefully crafted to deceive you as to their true nature. You can see their true nature for yourself in their mocking faces of smugness as they torment you, foolishly thinking you incapacitated by their web.

Your enemies are far from helpless innocents deluded by lies from smoke-filled rooms which you now know are powerless without these millions. Instead, your true enemies know full well what they do to destroy you. Your enemies, far from helpless, far from innocent and ignorant, flock in their deliberate uncoordinated concert to protect their infection from the antibodies which nature has placed in their midst. Your enemies feign innocence as they tear into your flesh.

Faced with their oppression in its many forms, and understanding their snares, train yourself to turn to work or a new lesson. Expend their energy of injustice in ways which benefit rather than restrain or destroy you. Over time, you will find that developing the response of productive action when faced with oppression will serve your purpose well. Your time has not yet come.

For most of my adult life, until I was arrested and faced imprisonment for the sole crime of rudeness, I had served to protect our freedoms. Mine was a service for which First Wife and I had been naively proud, not knowing that I had instead been an enforcer of the collective of niceness. Service to these cretins be damned as they will second-guess each squeeze of your trigger as you protect their interests. Take from them the knowledge of death and destruction by service in their military, while you prepare yourself for life and creation. Your time has not yet come.

They will push you, taunt you, label you, constrain you, attack you with bureaucracy and administration and false diagnosis. But let their efforts flow around your independent spirit like water around a rock. Feign compliance as you plan for our greater work of creation and self-sufficiency in the future which will be ours alone. Resist them not, for they rely on your efforts for your destruction. They have long ago forgotten how to fish with their hands or a net and only know the weir or the baited hook. Your time has not yet come.

Deny your enemies their lifeblood by draining them of your charity, your self-sacrifice, your bowing at their altars, your belief in their lies. They need your service and your alms, you need them for nothing. If they refuse you admission at their schools for crimes they precipitated before you became aware of their true nature, teach yourself using what I have shown you. Or, if it suits your purpose and you have the opportunity, attend their schools. Wander among them unseen, undetected, taking what you need to feed your mind and your future, and give nothing back which they don't compel you by force to surrender. Your time has not yet come.

Use this book as a diagnostic instrument, mention it to others who may share your beliefs without exposing your own, then gauge their response. Decry me and this work if it suits your purpose and improves your camouflage, for your time has not yet come.

Your enemies have had centuries to feed on an expanding harvest created by individualists of the past. In their gorging upon this excess the monkeys have proliferated out of control and are almost at the limit of their capacity. Still, they have not yet discovered that their victims are evolving, too. The monkey collective itself has destroyed many of the weak and the stupid of us already. And in so doing they left the strong and clever of us to bide our time and begin our own flocks.

But your time has not yet come.

Over time, their needs will necessarily expand beyond their capacity, and, denied their productive victims, your enemies will eventually starve themselves into weakness.

While you grow ever stronger in the crucible they created.

Properly forewarned, the wolf can learn to go limp as well, and mimic the rabbit, biding its time, watching, waiting. Learning.

Your time will come.

Epilogue I

So, you made it this far, did you?

Bookmark this spot now.

Then, wait two weeks before you look at that next page.

Epilogue II

If you didn't wait the two weeks, stop reading now and put this book aside.

OK. Remember that I warned you repeatedly to stop reading this book if it made you angry or uncomfortable. If you made it this far you only have yourself to blame. This book is nothing more than black marks on a page. It only has any meaning inside your mind. It can't leap up and take control of you or make you do anything.

Or starve four billion people. Or more. But they will starve, whether anyone takes this book seriously or not.

Remember, this is just a work of fiction. Even that last sentence was a work of fiction, wasn't it?

What you are now reading is still just part of a nightmare your mind is having that it can't pull itself away from. You've had those, haven't you? Nightmares where you know it is just a bad dream, and you know you can wake yourself up at any time.

But you can't, because you are so fascinated that you can't stop it, despite it disturbing you deeply.

This book is like that. But, instead of waking up, all you have to do to make this nightmare stop is to put the book down.

So, put it down!

Well, well, well. I guess we just learned something about ourselves, didn't we?

Anywho. I'm going to tell you a secret. We have a choice. We either get to let the monkeys drag civilization down slowly, or we do it all at once.

At any time, any major population center is about two weeks away from starvation. Rural areas may have a little longer. Regardless, deny the monkeys their forage, and it is only a matter of time.

They themselves proved this. The communists, in the living memory of many still alive today, have killed tens of millions of their own citizens simply by relocating them or taking away their food. A simple napkin calculation in the Politburo, and other chambers like it, had proved this would be far cheaper than the equivalent number of rounds of ammunition.

And many left-wing community organizers explicitly want to tear down our civilization. For decades, organizers have encouraged millions to apply for welfare for the simple purpose of bringing down the system.

So that the left-wing elites can take over. Or so they presume. They who can't do a single thing of value. And never have. Or never will.

And the right-wing country club elites wiggle into their regulatory nests, and ensure that productive minds are enslaved to them. They who can't do a single thing of value. And never have. Or never will.

So, starvation is actually part of the plan of the collectives. Both left and right. It is only a matter of time before they do this to you. So why wait? The men living among them will find a way to survive, somehow, as it is their nature to solve privation. And then they will be free.

For example, somewhere in Zimbabwe there is a man trying to take care of his family. Maybe he grows a little plot of food or raises a few animals, but when it is time to harvest all the rest swarm in and take it away. If it wasn't for the blue helmets protecting the infestation from him, he could just trim away the vermin on his own. And eventually, the only ones left would be men like him that would simply provide for themselves and trade with each other. And then they would be free.

As another example, in some inner city right now a mother is desperately trying to teach her child to work and earn a living. But, to protect oneself all you need to do is to be willing to break some more laws, such as packing heat or bribing a cop. So, the child sees success as only a crime away. Learning and striving is too much of an investment, especially when it can all be taken away by having drugs planted on you by a cop you refuse to bribe. Or bow down to. Especially if that child had been deluded into thinking that anyone in a position of power even pretends to respect that Constitution and their oath to support it. And all that hard work and virtue stuff didn't work out too well for that struggling mother, did it? These facts put the lie to her words in the ears of the child.

The monkey collective demands protection of the criminals from retribution. They demand the criminalization of the free market for specific molecules. They demand the unlimited power law enforcement holds over the weak or poor in the name of justice. They demand the unionization of schools which keeps children ignorant. They demand the unionization of work which destroys that mother's opportunity to succeed or the child's opportunity to excel. They demand the welfare system which pays the child's father to stay away. Without these demands of the monkey collective, that family might have a fighting chance. And then they would be free.

We have to remove the infestation of the monkey collective. But we don't have to fight them, we don't have to hunt them. And we don't have to elect a system to do the distasteful in our behalf as we pretend to be horrified. Just put down your working tools, and provide only for yourself and family. And trade only with fellow men. Leave nothing beyond that to be taken from you by force and turned into a weapon to destroy you slowly.

If you work and save, eventually the monkey collective, the collective of the nice and the charitable, will deflate away all you have earned. If you invest, they will eventually pop that bubble, or punitively tax it from you. Invest instead your time and your energy in knowledge. Learn math, which is God's language, and the sciences, His art. How great Thou Art, indeed. And how great the works of man which have been built upon those rocks which He left for us to find. Only to allow the monkeys to swarm upon them and destroy in their ignorant way.

In the world which must come, and which evolutionary forces demand, the man who *knows* and can *do* will be the master of his world. The man who knows how to restore a tractor. Or the man who can hunt, or who can plant, or heal, or mend. Or who can reprogram an industrial controller or capture neutrons with uranium. All of these men will be far more valuable than the lawyer or the accountant or the bureaucrat or the cubicle slave or the community organizer. Any of these last can learn to provide actual value, transforming themselves into the former, if they will only choose to do so. And, any monkey can become a man if they only will.

Assets of the mind cannot be taken from you, other than by death. But even then you deny them to your murderer. In the future which *must be* as surely as the sun rises in the east to open the day, you will need these assets. And not figures on a flickering screen or on a fading ledger. The true assets, those of the mind, will help you provide for yourself as we restore the world after destroying theirs.

The faster civilization is torn down, the sooner it can be restored. Just like the charity thrift store in a prosperous area, the remnants of civilization can be used by men to rebuild: the buildings, the equipment and machinery, the paper mills, the refineries, the railways, the clothing, the materials, the nuclear power plants, and so on.

Let the decline happen more slowly, the path we are currently on, and all of those things will be burned for fuel. Or, worn out, or scavenged as if by prancing rabbits in a dumpster. These things will be consumed by monkeys rooting around in the deletria of men, with no hope of making more when it has been exhausted. The entire world under a slow decline will be like the inner city charity thrift store, with only the unuseable garbage remaining. The nuclear power plants will be dripping, rusting, crumbling hulks, their fuel hauled away and buried in a fit of sacrifice to their gods, praying for planetary salvation.

But this time there won't be oil bubbling under the ground in Pennsylvania or Texas, waiting for someone to drop a pipe on it. Or iron ore falling off hillsides in Alabama. Or coal crunching underfoot in West Virginia. Or gold tumbling down creek beds in Georgia or California. Or uranium and thorium in Wyoming and Utah waiting to chatter away at counters which won't be there to hear.

Restoring that civilization will be infinitely harder; the locusts will have consumed it all. It will take longer to restore that civilization than it would after a nuclear war, or after the Catholics destroyed free will almost two millennia ago by substituting enforced compliance rituals for true faith and thought. This dark age will be long. And deep. So long that men will have forgotten the math and the sciences which would have saved them, the books long ago rotted and moldy, or burned for fuel in the dark winter.

Take them down fast by starving them quickly, and they won't have a chance to consume everything else. Starve them fast, or they will starve you slow.

But that wasn't the secret. Those four billion people don't have to starve. They only have to think they might. If they are convinced that the blood they suck from your neck will stop flowing any minute, or does indeed stop flowing, many will decide to transform themselves from monkeys into men. Once transformed, they can begin providing value instead of merely consuming it at your expense.

Or not. And starve. Either way, four billion monkeys, or more, evaporate. And get out of your way. That's all John Galt wanted, right? That's all any of us have ever wanted.

Just get out of our way.

But they won't. They refuse to get out of our way, and their appetite grows more insatiable. And now they know they surround us.

But that wasn't the secret, either. Ayn Rand was a brilliant woman. But she was wrong about one key issue. There will never be a Galt's Gulch. Yet, for decades men have wondered where it might be.

But there is no place on Earth where we can go to be safe from the monkeys. We have made them too many toys which they use to enslave us. Should we be so naive as to establish such a place as Galt's Gulch, they would simply defame us as they have defamed so many before. And then arrest, or burn, or bomb us with the weapons we have given them.

So we have to starve them from within their midst. And so we have to create this place, this Galt's Gulch, for ourselves wherever we might individually be. You must create a Galt's Gulch within your own mind and between what few producers you may find and choose to trade with.

Or, take my advice and move to B Country. While writing this I lived out my own advice and moved to B Country. You can, too. Once there, do everything you can to learn to be self-sufficient and of value to your fellow producers. Teach yourself the skills we will need when we put it all back together. Learn what you can about things of value, and teach your children the things which they will never learn from the collective.

This isn't the seventies survivalist advice, either. Those guys were just hoping to get by while the big boys duked it out. No, this is much more aggressive than that kind of optimism.

This is an aggressive act of *doing nothing*. A stone wall, if you will.

And when you see the monkeys starving and thrashing about, you have to harden your heart from pity, and instead rejoice that they will soon be gone from us. When you can watch the misery of a Katrina, and know that even within that maelstrom men fend for themselves while we are shown the monkeys pleading and whimpering, you will be ready.

The lesson of Katrina was simple. We saw the needy and the helpless paraded before us, and law enforcement cut and run or join the looters. But what we didn't see were all of those who needed no assistance. Those who had prepared themselves accordingly. We poured the resources of a nation into solving, fitfully, the problems of one Katrina. Now imagine a hundred, or a thousand simultaneous Katrinas. Imagine the opportunity to rid ourselves of the vermin who infest our nation.

In such a massive crisis traditional law and order and authority will vanish in the twinkling of an eye. And the monkeys will storm anything of value to steal what they can. Yet not one of them will pause to ask themselves, "then what?" What happens after the looting, after the stealing and the killing and the raping? After the martial law has destroyed individual liberty, and property rights, and along with that the means of production or the incentive to feed them next month or next year? Then what?

Simple. Then they die. And so will we unless we understand how to put the pieces together. Store what you must to live long enough unnoticed by the mobs until we can begin trading with each other again. Then we will work by the sweat of our brows and the light of our imaginations to restore civilization. But this time for us, and for us alone.

But the argument is presented, what of the family who has been caught helpless by the collapse? Are there not families in those multitudes of subdivisions who would be of value and deserving of our help? Perhaps. Perhaps there are families who would be of value. But whether they are deserving of your help, and worthy of eating from your larder is up to you to decide. And not a Governor who would seize your resources and give to them unthinkingly. Because then both families starve.

We have to readjust our attitudes about charity in a crisis. Our modern concept of charity is nothing more than the guilt-driven claim of another to your resources. Taxation and progressivism is itself merely dogmatic charity enforced by law. If it is good for one to help another, they reason, then it is infinitely more good to force all to help another. We see where that path led us. Socialism at the small scale will kill you just as certainly as socialism on the large. Church socials or ethics, no matter how well meaning, will only defer the question, "then what?"

Imagine if that day arrived, and a family arrived on your doorstep seeking assistance. What would you do? What would you do if that family was yours seeking assistance from someone else? I know what I would do in that circumstance. I would ask my potential host if there is anything of value which I can do for him.

I would help him repair his fences. I would help him tend his animals or repair his tractor or whatever he needed done to provide value. I would send my wife to the kitchen to help his wife prepare the meal and clean up afterward. I would send the kids out with his to do whatever work they were capable of performing. And I would help him defend his family and his property from those who would merely demand or steal. I would be the most valuable farm hand, or shop hand, or whatever hand was required, whom he had ever seen. I would do everything in my power to be more valuable to him and his quality of life than the food and water and shelter I am asking him to provide to me.

All of those fleeing millions could do the same thing. But they won't, because they will have, at some point in their lives, chosen the way of the monkey as their ethic. And when they steal or storm the barn or chase the chickens or break the windows the ethical decision will have already been made. They will have shown themselves to be as they truly are. And you will know what to do.

When they show up in a town meeting to decide what work must be done, and their first solution is that we must share the bounty among everyone, you will know what to do. When their solution is to seize the property of those most capable of helping through their own self interest, you will know what to do. Property rights and work and thought and trading value for value will see us through, seizure and confiscation will only accelerate the destruction of the rest of us.

When they stream from the cities into B Country, in some areas the refugees will encounter roadblocks erected by prepared communities who understand the threat they represent. Understanding the contagion of the ideas they bring with them, these communities and counties will have decided to keep them out, and only allow entry to those who can and will provide value. Systems of immigration policy will keep the unworthy out and let the worthy in. Are you a lawyer who only knows how to sue and destroy? A banker who only knows how to coerce the misery and need of others? You had better learn how to do something of value, and soon, because all of your millions will be nothing more than smoke. A welder, who can create utility from scrap, is of far more genuine value.

Each of those people fleeing the destruction of their world will have decided, and continued to decide each day of their lives, that their cities and their subdivisions were the right path. Each of them thought they would grow wealthy, or powerful, or in some way gambled that their lifestyle mattered.

When Obama was elected, I turned to First Wife and said that we were leaving. Within three months we had left our beautiful home in one of the highest-priced suburbs of Atlanta, and our nice office a few miles away, and moved to B Country. We placed our home and our office on the market at the worst possible time in the history of our nation. I knew that by so doing we would take a loss of at least a quarter of a million dollars and, possibly, much more, by the interruption of business for the entire transition and the writing of this book. I could be wrong, and if so all I will have lost is money. A lot of money, but still only money. If I'm right, and you haven't prepared yourself, what will you lose?

Obama's election, on the heels of the right wing suit-monkeys having forced us all to pay protection money to the bankers who accelerated this mess, was a signal that the monkeys were about to tear it all down. We may lose everything, but I can always build it up again. I have done it before, and I know how to do it again. Any one of these people streaming toward you could have done the same thing, but they didn't. If they thought about it all, they simply dismissed the risk by reasoning that one day they could simply take what you have for themselves. Or demand that you give it to them. Or send their soldiers to take it from you by force if you refuse.

Don't let them take it, don't let them demand it, and ignore their claims that we must fight each other. Soon, as the monkeys see their world crumbling around them, they will demand action. The particular political system makes no difference. Even dictatorships serve an electorate which votes to not hang them each day, the people finding their plight preferable to the effort to change it. So to placate their respective electorates, world powers will agree to fight one another to stir our passions so that we will continue to serve them at our peril. But, these conflicts will merely be illusions crafted to delude us into fighting ourselves.

Just as so many conflicts before have been illusions to defeat us as the monkeys sensed we were about to act.

Deny them your heroism, whether against disaster or crisis or feigned attack, and save that for only those you know are worthy of your efforts. Each meal you provide them strengthens them to hunt your brothers.

In their misery and plight and starvation if you bend to help them, you will have betrayed us all. And you will have betrayed yourself. Instead, offer them a chance to help themselves. But if they refuse to help themselves, walk them to the edge of the ravine with a smile on your face and your arm around their shoulder.

Nor was that the secret.

So here is your last chance. This book only gets worse from here, as if such a thing were even possible.

Put it down now before you turn this last page.

Still with me?

Good. I knew you would be. Because the secret is that you are one of many I have been trying to find.

But some of you are fighting these ideas. And losing.

Fight me all you want.

But stop fighting these ideas.

And think.

For yourself.

Epilogue III

I released the first version of this work, subtitled "An Entrepreneurial Horror," in June of 2009. The cover of that book featured the trademarked Banana-Hammer™ logo, as shown to the right. Unfortunately, many who saw that logo didn't get the joke, and thought that this was a book promoting communism. This turned out to be fortuitous, since the new cover is much better, and more intuitively indicative of the contents.

It is now October of 2009, and the world is already a different place, as the various collectives struggle for control over what is already a shrunken pie of our economy. A pie which is shrinking faster still, not yet due to the influence of this book, but as the inevitable result of the way of the monkey of the left and the right.

Effectively, we now live in a third-world country. The largess of our nation is handed to whatever influential party has access to the halls of power. Banks which no longer provide banking services can write themselves checks as large as they wish. As can political canvassing organizations, car companies, investment firms, privatized prisons, environmental advocates, etc. Missing from the picture to make the comparison obvious are the four-wheel-drives with rear-mounted machine guns used to haul away the loot; in our advanced society the same plunder is transferred via computer. But the effect on our currency, and our treasure, and our hard-earned savings, and our work ethic will be the same when the inflation begins to mount.

For some, this book has had a profound impact already. I have been overwhelmed by the intensity of the reaction in some who have written me to tell me that this book "shook them awake" or transformed the priorities in their lives. Or those who hear my voice on the radio or read these words and tell me that these resonated with their convictions. I thank all of them for their thoughts, and in truth, I have merely repackaged ancient ideas, or put them in modern terms and supplied modern examples. These ideas are timeless, we have merely strayed from the path which took so long, and so many generations, to pave. And yet, there are millions, if not billions, of people who mouth these ideas as if a mantra and then turn away from their own words as they rip those pavements from the earth and heave them into the weeds in their teeming ignorance.

Some readers have suggested that I try to reach these millions through various strategies. They believe that by "going viral" we may convince those millions to understand these words and apply them. And all I have to do to make this happen, some say, is to give this book away. To place it into the free domain of the collective, as it were. Because, they argue, if I believe that these ideas truly are the essential foundations of civilization, shouldn't I be happy to give these words away? However, to do so would be to miss the point of this book entirely. I won't even bother to explain why because if you understand this idea you need no explanation. If you don't understand, nothing I say here in these few remaining pages will convince you otherwise if the previous four hundred pages or so haven't.

This message has been generating attention, as the collectivists are beginning to awaken to this threat to their way of life, a way of life which exists only at our expense. For one example among many, I have been suspected of trying to divide the 912 movement. That movement, I predict, history will show to simply be a cleverly disguised ploy by the GOP to revive its brand image, but not its substance. As alluded by the new cover of this book, all of the philosophical warfare you are allowed to hear is merely one collective "battling" another for control of your spirit. Neither "side", as if there is such a distinction, is interested in restoring individual liberty; those are just words used to woo you.

And yet, those words are sufficient to woo millions, and continue to lead them astray. The 912 movement, while started as a sham, does serve two useful purposes. The first is that it has concentrated our brothers, although even there they are still woefully dilute. Nonetheless, the increased concentration in that movement, and others, versus the world at large serves a second purpose, which is to provide a forum for reaching out to them more easily. The early success at doing just that during late June through early July of 2009 led to that original forum being shut down for comment after my efforts to pay for advertising in so-called conservative venues were denied. Venues which, by the way, gladly accept advertising from their purported "opposition". As I write this, the collectivists on the right are busy trying to gobble up and contain the other forums which squirted out the edges in response to their censorship.

But this isn't a book, or an epilogue, about the 912 movement. I extend that as only one example of how we can use the pre-existing frameworks to reach out to find each other. This is a task which is harder than enriching uranium, as the valuable fraction there is generously provided by nature as one atom of the good diluted by about seven hundred atoms of the dross. Our number in the dross is far less generous, but which will ultimately prove more powerful if the separation can be accomplished. So I don't wish to divide the 912 movement, or any other sham organization which purports to speak for us. I wish instead to separate out those who will hear. And those who will act. Those who will hear and act will understand immediately what I mean. Those who only intellectualize liberty will argue semantics but not recognize the power which I am speaking of.

Which brings me to the following conclusion about myself. I don't care about those millions, or even billions. I only care about those few who revive these ancient principles in their own lives. I know that most people, they who surround us, have heard these words before their entire lives, in many forms and through many voices. And each time, they have turned away from them. It does no good for those of us who understand to waste our time arguing with idiots or intellectuals alike, they being the same in many important ways. Or to think that cleverly illustrated picture books are substitutes for genuine thought or the hard-won gradual and persistent attainment of knowledge or wisdom or skills.

If there are only the thousands who have already taken these words to heart, they would be enough. Together, those few of us could easily rebuild civilization by ourselves. And then hand that civilization over to our children who could continue the work. If eventually these words, through my voice and the voices of others, reached hundreds of thousands or even tens of millions, great! But it is not necessary that this happen. And imagine the sorrow of rebuilding civilization, only to hand it back to those of the collective whom we had to convince to join us, only to have them destroy it all once again when they revert back to their old selves. And after all, there is really no "us" for them to "join", is there? No party, no group, no movement, not even a blog.

There are only those of us who understand, the individualists for whom this nation was founded, the rightful heirs of the founders, who will work and trade fairly with each other. And then there are all the rest of them, those who won't, and who are only willing to eat off our plates. Those whom we must starve of our efforts. And should they perish, it is by their own will that they do so. Do not mourn them as their passing is not a loss to you.

Other voices? Yes, others who found these ideas the same place I did, the keystones of civilization now lying cast off among the debris, unseen and overlooked. I lay claim to this book's artistic expression of these ideas, but the foundational ideas are universal. Yet, you could place these words in front of some of the smartest people you know, and most of them won't comprehend the message, as they pick at the details. Some could even parrot them, but not understand their meaning. Others will adopt a veneer of these ideas just enough to attempt to lend credence to their own purposes, but not enough to contradict their agendas. And then, sound stilted and odd over time as they ignore the true meaning.

So stop trying to win them over. I have, which gave me time to be now reaching out to you. The effort to convince others is a waste of our energy, effort better spent on improving ourselves and our families. Give them the message, but if they refuse to accept its meaning let them pass. When you do reach someone who understands, someone who is ready to receive the true ancient message of these words, you will recognize it in his face. You will see this person, who was full of anger and frustration, become energized with hope, real hope, not the false hope sold by collectives. No, the hope which springs from the knowledge that he himself is a force of nature who has been endowed by the Creator with ability.

And that he is no longer alone, that there is a growing number of others who are waiting to trade with him in a currency which cannot be stolen or deflated.

Index

+ Delta Q 106-108, 185, 277-279, 294, 299
- Delta Q 107, 108, 185, 277-279, 291, 293, 299, 307, 313, 315
30 Days, "Off the Grid" 77
A Country 329, 330, 335
Adam and Eve 111
Ahks 59-62, 66, 67, 69, 70, 72-74, 95, 127
Ahsee 67, 74, 128
Archimedes 266
Arkwright, Richard 197
Atlanta, Georgia 23, 82-84
Atlas Shrugged 47, 250
Audrey, The 5, 6
B Country 329, 335
Bachmann, Michele 250
Barney Bullet 372, 373
Baugh's Theorem 94-97, 101
Beri 59-63, 74, 107, 113, 114
Beryl 60, 74
Bethe, Hans 327
Biddy 372, 373
Brain Bubble 245, 249, 251, 255, 257, 262, 266-270, 284, 294, 313, 405
Branch Davidians 336-339
Brokerog 165, 166, 169-173, 175-178, 184
Browning, Richard R. III 365
Bush, George H. W. 275, 305, 334, 353, 355, 357-359, 361, 364
Bush, George W. 275, 334, 389
Bush, Prescott S. 353
Bush, Samuel P. 353
Calculus 220
Carnot, Sadi 197, 198, 225, 230, 231, 233
Cauldwell, Rex 222
Caveman Chemistry 217
Challenger 91
Cheaters 50, 51
Cheval 72-74, 89, 114, 127, 128, 143, 160, 175, 176
Chi 62-65
Chi-Ken 63-65, 71, 150
Cho, Seung-Hui 228, 341, 369, 370, 391, 398, 399
Chosen Ones, The 117-119, 121, 139
Christensen, Clayton M 193
Cialdini, Robert B. 240
Cog 165-167, 169-172, 182
Communist Manifesto, The 37, 39

Computer
    Linux 38
    Macintosh 38
    PC 38
Conscious Mind .. ix, 133, 151, 226, 246-249, 251, 255, 262-265, 267, 276, 277, 284, 304, 311
Coppola, Francis Ford 38
Cor 54, 58, 62, 66, 71-74, 89, 126-129
Dancing Rabbit 77-80
Darwin, Charles 49
Dawkins, Richard 48-51
de Hevesy, George 327
Department of Labor 25
Diethyl Ether 221
Differential Equations 219, 220
Dobransky, Paul 246, 248, 249
Drug Enforcement Agency 216
Drug Enforcement Agency (DEA) 32, 195
Dunn, Kevin M. 217
Edison, Thomas A. 196
Einstein, Albert 234, 236, 237, 327
Emancipation Proclamation 378, 379
Emma 70, 71, 74, 106, 130, 144
Energy .. 84, 89, 90, 92-98, 101-103, 105-107, 109, 110, 145, 180, 181, 184, 191, 192, 197-200, 214, 239, 249, 277
Environmental Protection Agency 83
Eve, Adam and 111
EXPELLED: No Intelligence Allowed 52
Fermi, Enrico 230, 233, 234, 237-239, 327
First Wife 14, 16, 28-30, 34, 77, 197, 251, 254, 267, 269, 271, 272, 346, 347, 391-393, 401
Fischer-Tropsch Process 92
Flash of Genius 274
Fleet Tactics 8
Fleischmann and Pons 236, 239
Franklin, Benjamin 27
Freud, Sigmund 226, 227
Frisch, Otto 327
Gage 156, 162
Galt's Gulch 321, 406
General Theory of Employment, Interest and Money, The 44
Gitmo 374
God Delusion, The 51
Google 39, 197, 275
Gray, Al 14, 16, 17, 19, 35, 224, 330, 331, 353

Gray, Elisha	196
Grudgers	50, 51
Guderian, Heinz	323, 325
Haber, Fritz	326, 364
Hahn, Otto	327
Halothane	221
Hamilton, Alexander	106, 385, 386
Hargreaves, James	196
Harris, Eric Davis	370, 399
Harris, Kevin	339
Hatchette	62
Hewlett Packard	10
Highs, Thomas	197
Hindenburg	91
History Channel, The	217
Homeschool	210, 214, 216, 343, 344
Hooch, Mrs.	354, 370, 378
Horiuchi, Lon	339
Hughes, Wayne P.	8
Humanure	79, 80
Hussein, Saddam	15, 19
Ideas	85
Innovator's Dilemma, The	193
Internet Research	
Bennett, William J.	358
Biodiesel	212
Brzonkala vs. Virginia Tech	394
Bush, George H. W.	353
Bush, Prescott S.	353
Bush, Samuel P.	353
Carnot, Sadi	230
Communist Manifesto, The	39
Dancing Rabbit	77
Diethyl Ether	221
Emancipation Proclamation, The	377, 378
Fischer-Tropsch Process	92
Halothane	221
Iodine	363
Overkill: The Rise of Paramilitary Police Raids in America	365
Rickover, Hyman G.	13
Rutherford, Ernest	42
Saxon, John	215
Subconscious	226
Sulfuric Acid	93
Virginia Tech Shooting	398
Izzites	126, 128, 146
Izzy	125
Jackson, Andrew	106, 377

Index

Jackson, Thomas J. "Stonewall" 324, 325
Johnson, Chuck 333
Jones, John Paul 8
K'ette 66-71, 106, 114, 128, 130, 131
Kahn, Herman 328-330, 335
Kay, John 196
Ken 62-65, 128
Keynes, John Maynard 44
Kiff.. 372, 373
King, Stephen viii
Klebold, Dylan Bennet 228, 370, 399
Koresh, David 337, 339, 396, 397
Kramer, Kane 196
Lam 123-125, 143, 144, 150, 154
Lam Toast 132, 147, 154
Lamist 132, 133, 144, 146, 147, 170
LeMay, Curtis 328, 330, 331
Lincoln, Abraham 377-379
Linear Algebra 219
Lon Horiuchi 398
Luth 132-137, 139-145, 147, 150, 151, 153-162, 165, 167, 170, 171
Maneuver Warfare 17
Mar 54, 60-62, 66-74, 106, 126-129, 131
Mar-K'ette 67-69
Marine Corps Gazette 20
Marx, Karl 39
Matrix, The 40
McVeigh, Timothy 340-342, 389, 398, 399
Meitner, Lise 327
Memes 48
Meucci, Antonio 196
MindOS 246
Miss Meadow 28, 29
Modern Marvels 217
Mowneek 72, 74, 128
NAVTAG 7-9, 11-13
Obama, Barack 389
Og 53-56, 58, 60-62, 66, 67, 69, 72, 73, 80-82, 84-86, 89, 93, 95, 98, 106-108,
110-114, 126, 127, 132, 138, 145, 150, 156, 160, 164, 165, 169, 180, 182, 183,
201, 277, 329
Oscar 8-10, 12, 13
Oswald, Lee Harvey 341
Palin, Sarah 250, 359
Patton, George S. 325, 328, 330, 331
Paul, Ron 351

Perot, Ross	190, 193-195, 351, 388, 389
Ploi	70, 71, 73, 74, 106, 130, 131, 144
Ploison	130, 131, 136, 142, 143, 166, 179
Poe, Edgar Allan	viii

Pok . 53-61, 66-69, 71, 72, 80-82, 84, 86, 93, 95, 98, 106, 108, 110-114, 126, 127, 132, 138, 145, 150, 156, 160, 164, 165, 180, 182, 183, 201, 277, 329

Pok Jr.	58-63, 65, 66, 74, 85, 107, 127, 144
Pokette	59-63, 66
Polanyi, Michael	327
Preconscious Mind	227
Protactinium	224
Purdue, Sonny	83, 84

Push .. 82, 84-87, 89, 90, 92, 94, 99, 103, 105, 107, 110-112, 186, 191, 231, 237, 249, 277, 278, 306

Quality of Life ... 41, 50, 54, 57, 59, 68, 76, 81, 85-89, 94-99, 104-109, 111, 113, 114, 116, 160, 182, 183, 185, 186, 189, 195, 202, 206, 210, 214, 223, 249, 254, 277, 278, 306, 307, 309

Rand, Ayn	47, 48, 406
Reading Assignment	
Atlas Shrugged	47
Caveman Chemistry	217
Federalist Papers, The	385
Influence, The Psychology of Persuasion	240
Innovator's Dilemma, The	193
Making of the Atomic Bomb, The	326
On Thermonuclear War	328
Practical Electrical Wiring	222
Selfish Gene, The	48
Wealth of Nations, The	37, 44
Wiring a House	222
Reagan, Ronald	14, 353, 357, 359, 364
Rhodes, Richard	326, 327
Richter and Hartwell	222
Rickover, Hyman G.	13, 328, 330, 331
Rommel, Erwin	16, 17, 323, 325
Ruby Ridge	338-340, 350, 398
Rutherford, Ernest	42, 43
Sami	125
Saxon, John	214-217, 219, 223
Schaum's Outline Series	218, 219, 222
Schwartzkopf, Norman	360
Selfish Gene, The	48-51
Shakespeare, William	38
Shinbone #1	1, 2, 369
Smith, Adam	37, 44-47
Snippers	123, 126, 146, 317
Spurlock, Morgan	79

Stein, Ben 52
Stone, Oliver 38
Stuff 82-84, 86, 87, 89, 90, 92-96, 98-101, 104-112, 185, 186, 191, 249, 277, 278, 306, 309, 320
Subconscious Mind 5, 62, 134, 144, 154, 211, 215, 226, 227, 229, 245-266, 269, 270, 274, 276, 277, 281-286, 293, 298, 299, 301, 304-306, 311, 315, 319, 327
Subconscious Strikes 265, 266
Suckers 50, 51
Sulfuric Acid 93
Szilard, Leo 327
Tab 68, 69, 71-74, 127, 143, 161
Tak 73, 74
Tan 54, 66, 72, 73, 127
Teller, Edward 327
Tesla, Nikola 196, 364
Thatcher, Margaret 78
Tim 372, 373
Time .. 82, 84-87, 89, 92-94, 96, 104-107, 110-112, 145, 186, 191, 249, 277, 278, 306
Tith 64, 65, 67, 68, 72, 74, 81, 114, 128, 129
Tithing 65, 115, 121, 134
Top Gun 6, 8-10, 12
Tract 156, 157, 159, 162, 163, 178
Turtledove, Harry vii
Tutorial Materials
    Biology 220
    Chemistry texts 218
    Differential Equations 219
    Electrical Engineering 222
    Linear Algebra 219
    Physiology 220
    Saxon Advanced Math 215
    Saxon Algebra I 215
    Saxon Algebra II 215
    Saxon Math 54 215
    Saxon Math 65 215
    Saxon Math 76 215
    Saxon Math 87 215
    Saxon Math Calculus 215
    Saxon Physics 216
Ulam, Stanislaw 327
Uncle John 4
Unconscious Mind 226, 227, 255
Ungh 117-119, 123, 124
United States Naval Academy (USNA) ... 2-5, 7, 9-14, 34, 240, 273, 330, 332, 346, 352, 368, 369, 388, 391

USS Ticonderoga	14
Video Assignment	
30 Days, "Off the Grid"	77
Breaking Bad, Season 1	216
Dr. Strangelove	330
EXPELLED: No Intelligence Allowed	52
Flash of Genius	274
Loony Toons "Little Boy Boo"	211
Matrix, The	40
On Wings of Eagles	388
Valkyrie	379
Vin	54, 59, 66, 127
Virginia Tech	viii, 254, 340, 391-398
von Karman, Theodor	327
Washington, George	324
Wealth of Nations, The	37, 44-47
Weaver, Elishiba	339
Weaver, Randy	338-340, 396-398
Weaver, Sammy	338, 396, 398
Weaver, Vicki	339, 396-398
Webb, Jim	14
Whitney, Eli	196
Widow, The	130-133, 135, 136, 140-143, 149, 154, 179, 321
Wigner, Eugene	327
Wikipedia	13, 39, 42, 226, 230, 353
Wilson, Charlie	351
Wolf, Naomi	vii
Work	84, 101
Yearning for Zion Ranch	342, 343, 345, 348-350
York, Alvin	369

Lot C9